Personal consumption expenditures as a percent of disposable personal income	Gross national product (GNP)			Disposable personal income			
	Current prices (per capita dollars)	1972 prices (billions of dollars)	Annual real rate of growth	Current prices (per capita dollars)	1972 prices (billions of dollars)	Annual real rate of growth	Year
92.7	846	314.6	6.6	683	229.8	—	1929
93.8	734	283.2	−10.0	605	201.1	−8.0	1930
99.8	465	222.7	−14.2	390	166.5	−15.0	1932
98.0	515	238.4	8.5	414	174.2	5.3	1934
93.3	644	298.2	13.5	518	214.7	12.1	1936
97.6	653	298.2	−5.4	504	207.8	−5.9	1938
94.3	757	343.3	7.6	570	244.3	17.6	1940
87.7	946	398.5	16.3	690	278.1	13.8	1941
76.1	1173	460.3	15.3	863	317.3	14.1	1942
74.8	1405	530.6	15.1	972	332.2	4.7	1943
74.4	1521	568.6	7.1	1051	343.9	3.5	1944
80.2	1518	560.0	−1.5	1065	338.6	−1.5	1945
90.6	1482	476.9	−14.7	1122	332.4	−1.8	1946
96.1	1616	468.3	−1.7	1168	318.8	−4.1	1947
93.2	1767	487.7	4.1	1278	335.5	5.2	1948
95.2	1729	490.7	0.5	1254	336.1	0.2	1949
93.4	1879	533.5	8.7	1355	361.9	7.7	1950
92.1	2131	576.5	8.3	1457	371.6	2.7	1951
91.8	2203	598.5	3.7	1506	382.1	2.8	1952
91.6	2285	621.8	3.8	1571	397.5	4.0	1953
92.2	2247	613.7	−1.2	1574	402.1	1.2	1954
92.8	2407	654.8	6.7	1654	425.9	5.9	1955
91.3	2491	668.8	2.1	1731	444.9	4.5	1956
91.4	2574	680.9	1.8	1792	453.9	2.0	1957
91.5	2567	679.5	−0.4	1821	459.0	1.1	1958
92.5	2736	720.4	6.0	1898	477.4	4.0	1959
92.3	2800	737.2	2.2	1947	489.7	2.6	1960
91.6	2849	756.6	2.6	1991	503.8	2.9	1961
91.8	3023	800.3	5.8	2073	524.9	4.2	1962
92.3	3143	832.5	4.0	2144	542.3	3.3	1963
90.9	3313	876.4	5.3	2296	580.8	7.1	1964
90.5	3541	929.3	6.0	2448	616.3	6.1	1965
90.5	3830	984.6	6.0	2613	646.8	5.0	1966
89.5	4008	1011.4	2.7	2757	673.5	4.1	1967
90.5	4327	1058.1	4.6	2956	701.3	4.1	1968
91.1	4615	1087.6	2.8	3152	722.5	3.0	1969
89.4	4795	1085.6	−0.2	3390	751.6	4.0	1970
89.4	5135	1122.4	3.4	3620	779.2	3.7	1971
91.0	5609	1185.9	5.7	3860	810.3	4.0	1972
88.8	6210	1255.0	5.8	4315	865.3	6.8	1973
89.0	6668	1248.0	−0.6	4667	858.4	−0.8	1974
89.1	7157	1233.9	−1.1	5075	875.8	2.0	1975
90.8	7900	1300.4	5.4	5477	907.4	3.6	1976
91.9	8701	1371.7	5.5	5954	939.8	3.6	1977
92.2	9641	1476.9	4.8	6571	981.5	4.4	1978
92.0	10942	1483.7	3.2	7293	1011.5	3.1	1979
91.8	11787	1480.7	0.2	8002	1018.4	0.7	1980
92.2	12888	1510.3	1.0	8768	1040.2	2.1	1981

ECONOMICS

PRIVATE AND PUBLIC CHOICE

JAMES D. GWARTNEY
Florida State University

with the assistance of
A. H. STUDENMUND
Occidental College

RICHARD STROUP
Montana State University

THIRD EDITION

ACADEMIC PRESS
A Subsidiary of Harcourt Brace Jovanovich, Publishers
New York   London   Paris   San Francisco
San Diego   São Paulo   Sydney   Tokyo   Toronto

This book was designed by Edward A. Butler.
Cover art by Andy Lackow.

Academic Press, Inc.
757 Third Avenue, New York, New York 10017

United Kingdom Edition published by
Academic Press, Inc. (London) Ltd.
24/28 Oval Road, London NW1 7DX

ISBN: 0-12-311045-9
Library of Congress Catalog Card Number: 81-71896

Printed in the United States of America

CONTENTS

MYTHS OF ECONOMICS

OUTSTANDING ECONOMISTS

PERSPECTIVES IN ECONOMICS AND BOXED FEATURES

PREFACE

We believe that this is an exciting time to study and teach economics. Both economic events and advancements in economic theory are changing the introductory economics course. In some cases, recent theoretical contributions have supplemented our previous knowledge. In other instances, they have enlightened it; and in still others, they have corrected it. Since the real world is the experimental laboratory of the economist, events often contribute to our understanding of issues. The bitter experience of the 1970s illustrates that economic problem solving is a far more complex and demanding task than was envisioned even a decade ago. A modern principles course must explain why this is so and what lessons we should learn from the recent economic instability that has plagued western economies.

Our goal is to provide readers with a theoretical framework that will help them more fully understand the economic forces of our economy. We believe that this can be accomplished most effectively by integrating recent economic advancements into our more traditional models. We reject the idea that a principles course should merely teach students *what* economists think. We believe that it should equip them with economic tools and teach them *how* economists think. We seek to develop a logical and consistent economic framework that is based on the foundations of economics. Of course, there are areas where controversy abounds. In those instances, we seek to explain the nature of the controversy and the reasons for its presence.

We do not believe that recent theoretical developments can be merely tacked onto the traditional analysis. This is particularly important in macroeconomics. At a more advanced level, macroeconomics has already undergone dramatic changes. While many of the factors contributing to that change are *discussed* in principles texts, to date, they have not been *integrated* into our standard macro models. This is precisely what makes this book different from others on the market. While we have maintained the traditional Keynesian expenditure–output equilibrium, recent developments have been *incorporated* into the model. Recent theoretical and empirical work on search theory, constraints on aggregate supply, adaptive and rational expectations, public choice theory, tax avoidance, and the relative price effects between various aggregate markets are all integrated into the traditional macro model.

THE THIRD EDITION

The emphasis on the economic way of thinking and core theory–application mixture is maintained in this edition. Without reducing the readability of the text, we sought to be more concise. This edition is a little shorter than the previous one; it contains two fewer chapters. Approximately one-third of the material is new; much of the remainder has been revised.

Chapter 5 on government expenditures and taxation is more comprehensive than in the previous edition. While the usual facts and figures are given, the analysis portion of the chapter is expanded. The impact of tax rates on economic activity is analyzed in more detail. The new feature on taxes and the underground economy should make the chapter more interesting to students.

The macroeconomics section has been altered in several areas. Chapter 8 focuses entirely on aggregate demand. Chapter 9 discusses the concept of aggregate equilibrium and the workings of a simple Keynesian model. Chapter 10 addresses fiscal policy. We believe this material is clearly presented and logically organized. Chapter 11 is entirely new; building on the prior material on the production possibilities of an economy, this chapter introduces a supply constraint into the Keynesian model. The determinants of aggregate supply are discussed. Expanding on the material of Chapter 5, the impact of taxes on aggregate supply is considered. Chapter 12 incorporates the recent institutional changes in the banking industry and analyzes their impact on the conduct of monetary policy. A new feature on the Deregulation and Monetary Control Act is included.

Additional dimensions of macroeconomics are incorporated into a standard model in the next four chapters. Chapter 13 incorporates money into a Keynesian model with an aggregate supply constraint. Chapter 14 discusses the views of the monetarists. The material in Chapter 15, which focuses on the implications of both adaptive and rational expectations, is virtually all new. Inflation, unemployment, and the Phillips curve are discussed as the concept of "smart" (if not rational) decision-makers is built into our macro model. The section concludes with a chapter considering the importance of the economy's microstructure in the framework of macroeconomics. Recent policy issues are also analyzed in Chapter 16.

The microeconomics section has also been revised significantly. Chapter 18 contains additional material on production and more clearly illustrates the linkage between production theory and the firm's cost curves. Two chapters comparing and contrasting competition and monopoly follow immediately. Survey data indicates that this is the format followed by most instructors. The intermediate cases of monopolistic competition and oligopoly are combined into a single chapter. The industrial structure section concludes with a new chapter on regulation and deregulation. The growth of social regulation, as well as recent moves toward deregulation in several industries, is discussed. The implications of public choice analysis are incorporated into our discussion of regulation.

The factor market section has been condensed. Chapter 25 on capital markets does contain a new feature on the capitalization of expected income from agricultural price support programs into the value of land with acreage allotments that should help enliven what is often rather dull material. The market failure–public choice section has been condensed into just two chapters. The chapter on international finance incorporates recent economic events and contains a new feature on the pros and cons of the gold standard. We think this material will be of interest to students while helping to clarify an issue where confusion often abounds.

Our objective in this revision has been to strengthen and expand the analysis set forth in earlier editions. We have aimed to maximize the pedagogical usefulness of *Economics: Private and Public Choice* by elucidating concepts in greater depth without sacrificing the breadth and clarity that distinguished the prior editions.

DISTINGUISHING FEATURES OF OUR APPROACH

Most of all, we believe that economics is a way of thinking. We seek to emphasize those points that will challenge students to think like economists. The following points are of specific interest in this regard:

1. *Economic Principles Are Presented in a Highly Readable Fashion.* Difficult language and terminology can often hinder successful learning, particularly of economic concepts. Feedback from both students and instructors has indicated that readability was one of the strengths of the prior editions. In writing this edition, we have built upon this strength, so as to minimize the obstacles faced by beginning students of economics.

Without sacrificing accuracy, we have sought to employ simple language. Simplicity, however, has not been substituted for depth. Rather, our aim is to highlight the power and accessibility of economic concepts. Where complex ideas are essential to our analysis, they are developed fully. We believe that the economics required for the 1980s can be challenging and applicable to the real world, and comprehensible to the student as well.

2. *Economic Reasoning and Its Applications Are Emphasized.* Although models, theories, and exercises are important, they are only tools with which to develop the economic way of thinking. Abstractions and mechanics are not stressed so as to obscure major concepts. We consistently emphasize the basics and their real-world applications.

3. *Microeconomic Reasoning Is a Fundamental Component of Macroeconomic Analysis.* The central principle of economics is that incentives matter. The microstructure of an economy does have macroeconomic ramifications. Microincentives influence such macrofactors as the rate of unemployment, the level of saving and investment, and aggregate output. In this text, the importance of the micro-incentive structure that is the foundation of our macroeconomic markets is highlighted.

4. *Economic Tools Are Applied to Both the Market and the Political Process.* Most textbooks tell students how an *ideal* market economy would operate, how real-world markets differ from the hypothetical ideal, and how ideal public policy can correct the shortcomings of the market. In addition to discussing these three basic issues, we analyze what real-world public policy is *likely to do.* This central focus emphasizes both the power and the relevance of modern economics. Built on the pioneering work of Kenneth Arrow, Duncan Black, James Buchanan, Gordon Tullock, and others, the economic analysis of public, as well as private, choice fills a void many other textbooks fail even to acknowledge.

Students are often puzzled by the gulf between the ideal theoretical "solutions" of economists and the events of the real world. The economics of public choice bridges this gulf. Using the tools of economics, we can do far more than describe how the government can promote more efficient use of resources. We can illustrate why good politics sometimes conflicts with economic efficiency.

5. *The Role of the Human Decision-Maker Is Stressed.* To the student, it often appears that economists exclude human beings from the economic process. In most economics textbooks, business decision-makers are depicted as having perfect knowledge of demand and cost. Like computers, they always arrive at the maximum-profit solution. Government planners, knowing precisely the deficiency in aggregate demand and the size of the multiplier, simply increase government spending by the right amount to restore full employment. The employer, knowing the marginal productivity of each resource, utilizes each in exactly the proper proportion. Decision-making is treated as a mechanical exercise, removed from the real world. Throughout this book, we attempt to stress the importance of information, uncertainty, trial-and-error decision-making, adaptive expectations, and other factors that influence real-world choices. Economics is more than a set of guidelines. If students are to be convinced of its applicability, we must delineate the dynamic factors that influence and motivate human beings.

DISTINGUISHING FEATURES OF OUR PRESENTATION

We have employed several features of organization and design in order to make this presentation more interesting to students.

1. *Myths of Economics.* In a series of boxed articles, nine commonly held fallacies of economic reasoning are dispelled. Following a statement of each myth is a concise explanation of why it is incorrect. Each myth falls in a chapter containing closely related material.

2. *Perspectives of Economics.* These features provide additional detail on a specific topic or issue. They permit us to provide additional breadth on a topic or focus on the application of an economic principle without disrupting the normal flow of the text.

3. *Outstanding Economists.* Designed to foster the student's lasting interest in economics, these articles present brief profiles of eighteen economists who either have made major contributions to the field or are currently influencing economic thought. Although contemporary economists (for example, Martin Feldstein, John Kenneth Galbraith, Milton Friedman, Lester Thurow, and Friedrich Hayek) are emphasized, such giants of economic history as Adam Smith, David

Ricardo, Karl Marx, Alfred Marshall, John Maynard Keynes, and Joseph Schumpeter are also included. This series should serve both to enhance the student's appreciation of economic history and to signify the contributions of many prominent present-day economists.

4. *Key Terms.* The terminology of economics is often confusing to introductory students. Key terms are introduced in the text in boldface type; simultaneously, each term is defined in the margin opposite the first reference to the term.

5. *Chapter Learning Objectives.* A statement of learning objectives, composed of the major concepts discussed, follows the text of each chapter. Students are encouraged to study the learning objectives before and after reading each chapter.

6. *Discussion Questions.* Intended to test the student's grasp of the economic way of thinking, a set of discussion questions concludes each chapter. These questions, and the discussions they provoke, provide students with the opportunity for self-testing and the review of important material.

SUPPLEMENTARY MATERIALS

The textbook is accompanied by a **Coursebook.** More than just a study guide, the **Coursebook** contains numerous true–false, multiple-choice, and discussion questions; problems for more detailed analysis and projects are also suggested. Almost every chapter contains a short article designed to supplement the classroom teaching of the important concepts presented in the text. In this series of readings, contrasting positions are often presented; discussion questions follow each article, challenging students to demonstrate their understanding of the material and to distinguish a sound argument from economic nonsense. As in the textbook, the emphasis is on helping the student to develop the economic way of thinking.

An **Instructor's Testbank** is also available. Over 2300 multiple-choice test questions, many of which have been pretested extensively, are included in the testbank. Each question carries a specific reference to the section of the textbook where the material tested by the item is covered. The testbank is also available on computer tape.

An **Instructor's Manual** is available upon request. It is divided into two parts. The first part contains teaching tips, sources of supplementary materials, and other information likely to be of assistance to instructors. The second part is a detailed outline of each chapter in lecture note form.

ACKNOWLEDGMENTS

A project of this type is truly a team effort. We sought to mold this edition into the shape desired by our users, both actual and potential. The comments of reviewers were extremely helpful. Their efforts made it possible for us to make what we consider to be a substantial improvement in the content and organization of the text.

Our debt to two people, Woody Studenmund and J. R. Clark, is especially great. Professor Studenmund (Occidental College) made many helpful suggestions, particularly in the areas of macroeconomics and international finance. Along with his colleague, Robert L. Moore, Studenmund also helped us improve the organization of the micro core material. Even when we failed to accept his advice his commitment to the improvement of the manuscript did not wane. His positive attitude was an inspiration to us.

Professor J. R. Clark (Fairleigh Dickinson University) provided us with a careful review of the entire manuscript. In some instances, he supplied a draft statement illustrating how a specific point could be made more clearly. When weariness set in, he offered encouragement. The manuscript bears his imprint.

Others made important contributions in specific areas. In addition to his reorganizational suggestions, Professor Robert L. Moore provided material on bonds that was revised and included in Chapter 13. Professor James Cobbe (Florida State University) enhanced the discussion of the development chapter. Professor James Devine (Occidental College) made a significant contribution to the biographical sketch on Marx.

Several reviewers struggled through most of the manuscript and provided us with direction at each stage of this project: These include:

Barry L. Boyer
Fort Steilacoom Community College

Ronald G. Brandolini
Valencia Community College

Elba K. Brown
University of Texas of El Paso

Douglas W. Copeland
Kansas State University

Robert B. Harris
Indiana–Purdue University at Indianapolis

C. Blair Housley
West Georgia College

William W. Howard
Phoenix College

Dwight R. Lee
Virginia Polytechnic Institute and State University

Sam F. Parigi
Lamar University

Allen R. Sanderson
Princeton University

Stanley Sofas
Santa Barbara City College

Robert W. Thomas
Iowa State University

C. Richard Torrisi
University of Hartford

In addition, others reviewed specific chapters and provided us with valuable comments as the manuscript developed. In several cases, highly significant changes were made in response to their suggestions. We are grateful to the following for their assistance:

Richard K. Anderson
Texas A & M University

James Bassler
San Diego State University and National University at San Diego

John Cooper
Lewis and Clark College

David Denslow
University of Florida

Roger Garrison
Auburn University

Fred Gottheil
University of Illinois, Champaigne-Urbana

Roy B. Helfgott
New Jersey Institute of Technology

Loren Lee
Lewis and Clark College

Herman I. Liebling
Florida International University

Thomas J. Meeks
Virginia State University

John Neal
Lake-Sumter Community College

Dale O'Bannon
Lewis and Clark College

James A. Overdahl
Iowa State University

Willard W. Radell, Jr.
Indiana University of Pennsylvania

John Vahaly
University of Louisville

Janice Weaver
University of North Alabama

Robert Welch
Midwestern State University

We have also benefited from review comments and discussions with Terry Anderson, John Baden, Gail L. Cramer, Marshall Colberg, William Laird, Tom McCaleb, and Charles Rockwood on the coverage of various topics in the text. Harvey Arnold and John Bethune assisted us with the preparation of supplementary material.

We owe a special debt to our editor, Susan Elliott Loring. While we did not particularly look forward to her telephone calls as various deadlines approached, we do recognize that she did a superlative job of coordinating this project. In general, she was able to keep the project on schedule with diplomatic skills rather than with lashes of the editorial whip. For that, we are grateful.

Georgia Lee Hadler (Project Editor) and Martha Wiseman (Copy Editor) did an extraordinary job of clarifying our ideas, correcting our grammatical errors, and improving the flow of the manuscript. Both deserve not only a thank you but also an "A" in Econ 200. We are also most appreciative for the time and talent that Sheridan Hughes (Director of Production) and Edward A. Butler (Director of Design) provided to the project. As is true for the prior editions, Linda Zingale did a superlative job of typing the manuscript. Her special efforts to help us meet the various deadlines are particularly appreciated. Last but certainly not least we appreciate the contribution of Amy Gwartney. She did whatever needed to be done in order to assure the success of the project.

PART ONE

THE ECONOMIC WAY OF
THINKING—AN INTRODUCTION

THE ECONOMIC APPROACH

The ideas of economists and political philosophers, both when they are right and when they are wrong, are more powerful than is commonly understood. Indeed, the world is ruled by little else. Practical men, who believe themselves to be quite exempt from any intellectual influences, are usually slaves of some defunct economist.[1]
John Maynard Keynes

As Professor Keynes's own example has since proved, ideas have consequences and influence events in the real world. In turn, ideas are influenced by real-world experience. Economic ideas are no exception. The events and patterns of the last 15 years—soaring inflation, rising unemployment, and a decline in the after-tax income of many Americans—have exerted a dramatic impact upon the economics profession. They have also generated additional interest in the subject matter of economics. People are seeking to comprehend more fully the continually unfolding economic events.

We believe that this book will help you understand the recent economic turmoil—the ideas that undergirded it, the policies that contributed to it, and the possible directions that can now be taken to escape its grasp. This is not to imply that economists have the answer to the problems of a troubled world. Economics is not an answer but, rather, a way of thinking. In fact, economics is more likely to provide an appreciation of the limitations of "grand design" proposals than it is to offer utopian solutions. Nonetheless, we believe that "economic thinking" is a powerful tool capable of illuminating a broad range of real-world events. Our goal is to communicate the basics of economics and to illustrate their power.

WHAT IS ECONOMICS ABOUT?

Economics is about people and the choices they make. The unit of analysis in economics is the individual. Of course, individuals group together to form collective organizations such as corporations, labor unions, and governments. However, the choices of individuals still underlie and direct these organizations.

---

[1]John Maynard Keynes (1883–1946) was an English economist whose writings during the 1920s and 1930s exerted an enormous impact on both economic theory and policy. Keynes established the terminology and the economic framework that are still widely used today when economists study problems of unemployment and inflation.

EXHIBIT 1 A general listing of desired economic goods and limited resources

Economic Goods	Limited Resources
Food (bread, milk, meat, eggs, vegetables, coffee, etc.)	Land (various degrees of fertility)
Clothing (shirts, pants, blouses, shoes, socks, coats, sweaters, etc.)	Natural resources (rivers, trees, minerals, oceans, etc.)
Household goods (tables, chairs, rugs, beds, dressers, television sets, etc.)	Machines and other man-made physical resources
Space exploration	Nonhuman animal resources (cattle, horses, buffalo, etc.)
Education	Technology (physical and scientific "recipes" of history)
National defense	Human resources (the knowledge, skill,
Recreation	and talent of individual human
Time	beings)
Entertainment	
Clean air	
Pleasant environment (trees, lakes, rivers, open spaces, etc.)	
Pleasant working conditions	
More productive resources	
Leisure	

Our history is a record of our struggle to transform available, but limited, resources into things that we would like to have—economic goods.

Thus, even when we study collective organizations, we will focus on the ways in which their operation is affected by the choices of individuals.

Economic theory is developed from fundamental postulates about how individual human beings behave, struggle with the problem of scarcity, and respond to change. The reality of life on our planet is that productive resources—resources used to produce goods—are limited. Therefore, goods and services are also limited. In contrast, the desires of human beings are virtually unlimited. These facts confront us with the two basic ingredients of an economic topic—scarcity and choice. **Scarcity** is the term used by economists to indicate that man's desire for a "thing" exceeds the amount of it that is freely available from Nature. Nature has always dealt grudgingly with man; the Garden of Eden has continually eluded man's grasp.

A good that is scarce is an **economic good.** The first column of Exhibit 1 contains a partial listing of scarce or economic goods. The list includes food, clothing, and many of the items that all of us commonly recognize as material goods. But it also includes some items that may surprise you. Is leisure a good? Would you like to have more leisure time than is currently available to you? Most of us would. Therefore, leisure is a scarce good. What about clean air? A few years ago many economics texts classified clean air as a free good, made available by nature in such abundant supply that everybody could have all of it they wanted. This is no longer true. Our utilization of air for the purpose of waste disposal has created a scarcity of clean air. Many of the residents of Los Angeles, New York, Chicago, and other large cities would like to have more clean air.

Few of us usually think of such environmental conditions as economic goods. However, if you are someone who would like more open spaces, green areas, or dogwood trees, you will recognize that these things are scarce. They, too, are economic goods.

Scarcity: Fundamental concept of economics which indicates that less of a good is freely available than consumers would like.

Economic Good: A good that is scarce. The desire for economic goods exceeds the amount that is freely available from Nature.

Time is also an economic good. Most of us would like to have more time to watch TV, take a walk in the woods, do our schoolwork, or sleep; but we each have only 24 hours in a day. The scarcity of time imposes a definite limitation on our ability to do many of the things we would like to do.

Choice: The act of selecting among alternatives.

Since scarcity of productive resources, time, and income limit the alternatives available to us, we must make choices. **Choice** is the act of selecting among restricted alternatives. A great deal of economics is about how people choose when the alternatives open to them are restricted. The choices of the family shopper are restricted by the household budget. The choices of the business decision-maker are restricted by competition from other firms, the cost of productive resources, and technology. The spending choices of the political decision-maker are restricted by the taxable income of the citizenry and voter opposition to taxes.

The selection of one alternative generally necessitates the foregoing of others. If you choose to spend $10 going to a football game, you will have $10 less to spend on other things. Similarly, if you choose to spend an evening watching a movie, you must forego spending the evening playing Ping-Pong (or participating in some other activity). You cannot eat your cake and have it, too.

Each day, we all make hundreds of economic choices, although we are not normally aware of doing so. The choices of when to get up in the morning, what to eat for breakfast, how to travel to work, what television program to watch—all of these decisions are economic. They are economic because they involve the utilization of scarce resources (for example, time and income). We all are constantly involved in making choices that relate to economics.

Our Losing Struggle with Scarcity

Resource: An input used to produce economic goods. Land, labor skills, natural resources, and capital are examples.

Scarcity restricts us. How can we overcome it? **Resources,** including our own skills, can be used to produce economic goods. Human effort and ingenuity can be combined with machines, land, natural resources, and other productive factors (see the second column of Exhibit 1) to increase the availability of economic goods. These are our "tools" in our struggle with scarcity. It is important to note that most economic goods are not like manna from heaven. Human energy is nearly always an ingredient in the production of economic goods.

The lessons of history confirm that our desire for economic goods far outstrips our resources to produce them. Are we destined to lead hopeless lives of misery and drudgery because we are involved in a losing battle with scarcity? Some might answer this question in the affirmative, pointing out that a substantial proportion of the world's population go to bed hungry each night. The annual income of a typical worker in such countries as Pakistan and India is less than $200. And the population in these and other areas is increasing almost as rapidly as their output of material goods.

Yet the grip of scarcity has been loosened in most of North America, Western Europe, Japan, and the Soviet Union. Most Americans, Japanese, and Europeans have an adequate calorie intake and sufficient housing and clothing. Many own luxuries such as automatic dishwashers, home video games, and electric carving knives. Over the last century, the average number of hours worked per week has fallen from 60 to about 40 in most Western nations. From a material viewpoint, life is certainly more pleasant for those people than it was for their forefathers 250 years ago. However, despite this progress, scarcity is still a fact of life, even in relatively affluent countries. Most of us have substantially fewer goods and resources and less time than we would like to have.

Scarcity and Poverty Are Not the Same Thing

It should be noted that scarcity and poverty are not the same thing. Poverty implies some basic level of need, either in absolute or relative terms. Absence of poverty means that the basic level has been attained. In contrast, the absence of scarcity means that we have not merely attained some basic level but have acquired as much of all goods as we desire. Poverty is at least partially subjective, but there is an objective test to determine whether a good is scarce. If people are willing to pay—give up something—for a good, that good is scarce. Although the battle against poverty may ultimately be won, the outcome of the battle against scarcity is already painfully obvious. Our productive capabilities and material desires are such that goods and services will always be scarce.

THE ECONOMIC WAY OF THINKING

It [economics] is a method rather than a doctrine, an apparatus of the mind, a technique of thinking which helps its possessor to draw correct conclusions. [J. M. Keynes]

Reflecting on a television appearance with the economist Paul Samuelson and other social scientists (noneconomists), Milton Friedman stated that he was amazed to find that economists, although differing in their ideological viewpoints, usually find themselves to be allies in discussions with other social scientists.[2] One does not have to spend much time around economists to recognize that there is "an economic way of thinking." Admittedly, economists, like others, differ widely in their ideological views. A news commentator once remarked that "any half-dozen economists will normally come up with about six different policy prescriptions." Yet in spite of their philosophical differences, there is a common ground to the approach of economists.

Economic Theory: A set of definitions, postulates, and principles assembled in a manner that makes clear the "cause and effect" relationships of economic data.

That common ground is **economic theory,** developed from basic postulates of human behavior. Theory has a reputation for being abstract and difficult, but this need not be the case. Economic theory, somewhat like a road map or a guidebook, establishes reference points, indicating what to look for and what can be considered significant in economic issues. It helps us understand the interrelationships among complex and often seemingly unrelated events in the real world. A better understanding of cause and effect relationships will enhance our ability to predict accurately the probable and possible consequences of alternative policy choices. Economics has sometimes been called the "science of common sense." This is as it should be. After all, common sense is nothing more than a set of beliefs based on sound theories that have been tested over a long period of time and found to be accurate.

Seven Guideposts to Economic Thinking

The economic way of thinking involves the incorporation of certain guidelines—some would say the building blocks of basic economic theory—into one's thought process. Once these guidelines are incorporated, we believe that economics can be a relatively easy subject to master.

Students who have difficulty with economics almost always do so because they fail to develop the economic way of thinking. Their thought process is not

---

[2]The philosophical views of Professor Friedman and Professor Samuelson differ considerably. They are often on opposite sides of economic policy issues.

consistently directed by a few simple economic concepts or guideposts. Students who do well in economics learn to utilize these basic concepts and allow their thought process to be governed by them. We will outline and discuss seven principles that are fundamental characteristics of economic thinking and essential to the understanding of the economic approach.

1. Scarce Goods Have a Cost—There Are No Free Lunches. The benefits of scarce goods can be obtained only if someone is willing to exert personal effort or give up something. Using the terms of economics, scarce goods cost someone something. The cost of many scarce goods is obvious. A new car costs $9000. The purchaser must give up $9000 of purchasing power over other goods in order to own the car. Similarly, the cost to the purchaser of a delightful meal, new clothes, or a Las Vegas weekend is obvious. But what about a good such as public elementary education? Even though the education is usually free to students, it is not free to the community. Buildings, books, and teachers' salaries must be paid for from tax revenues. The taxpayer incurs the cost. If these scarce resources were not used to produce elementary education, they could be used to produce more recreation, entertainment, housing, and other goods. Providing for public education means that some of these other scarce goods must be foregone. Similarly, provision of free medical service, recreation areas, tennis courts, and parking lots involves the use of scarce resources. Again, something must be given up if we are to produce these goods. Taxpayers usually bear the cost of "free" medical services and tennis courts. Consumers often bear the cost of "free" parking lots in the form of higher prices in areas where this service is provided. By now the central point should be obvious. Economic thinking recognizes that the provision of a scarce good, any scarce good, involves a cost. We must give up other things if we are to have more of a scarce good. Economic goods are not free.

2. Decision-Makers Choose Purposefully. Therefore, They Will Economize. Since resources are scarce, it is all the more important that decisions be made in a purposeful manner. Decision-makers do not deliberately make choices in a manner that wastes and squanders valuable resources. Recognizing the restrictions imposed by their limited resources (income, time, talent, etc.), they seek to choose wisely; they try to select the options that best advance their own personal objectives. In turn, the objectives or preferences of individuals are revealed by the choices they make.

Economizing Behavior:
Choosing with the objective of gaining a specific benefit at the least possible cost. A corollary of economizing behavior implies that when choosing among items of equal cost, individuals will choose the option that yields the greatest benefit.

Economizing behavior results directly from purposeful decision-making. Economizing individuals will seek to accomplish an objective at the least possible cost. When choosing among things that yield equal benefit, an economizer will select the cheapest option. For example, if a hamburger, a fish dinner, and a New York sirloin steak are expected to yield identical benefits, economizing behavior implies that the cheapest of the three alternatives, probably the hamburger, will be chosen. Correspondingly, when choosing among alternatives of equal cost, economizing decision-makers will select the option that yields the greatest benefit (that is, utility or satisfaction). Purposeful decision-makers will not deliberately pay more for something than is necessary.

Purposeful choosing implies that decision-makers have some knowledge on which to base their evaluation of potential alternatives. Economists refer to this evaluation as utility. **Utility** is the subjective benefit or satisfaction that an individual expects from the choice of a specific alternative.

Utility: The benefit or satisfaction expected from a choice or course of action.

3. Incentives Matter—Human Choice Is Influenced in a Predictable Way by Changes in Economic Incentives.   This guidepost to clear economic thinking might be called the basic postulate of all economics. As the personal benefits from choosing an option increase, other things constant, a person will be more likely to choose that option. In contrast, as the costs associated with the choice of an item increase, the person will be less likely to choose that option. Applying this basic economic postulate to a group of individuals suggests that as an option is made more attractive, more people will choose it. In contrast, as the cost of a selection to the members of a group increases, fewer of them will make this selection.

This basic economic concept provides a powerful tool with which to analyze various types of human behavior. According to this postulate, what would happen to the birthrate if the U.S. government (a) removed the income tax deduction for dependents, (b) imposed a $1500 "birth tax" on parents, and (c) made birth-control pills available, free of charge, to all? The birthrate would fall—that's what. What would happen if the government imposed a $5000 tax on smokestacks, required automobile owners to pay a substantial license fee that was directly related to the exhaust level of the car, and gave a 10 percent tax reduction to all corporations that did not utilize the air for waste disposal purposes? Answer: There would be a decline in air pollution. In both of these hypothetical examples, the policy would increase the cost and/or reduce the benefits of a specific activity. Economics suggests that the level of the activities would be reduced in both cases because of the "predictable" impact that changes in personal benefits and costs have on human actions.

Our analysis suggests that an instructor could influence the degree of cheating on an examination simply by changing the student payoffs. There would be little cheating on a closely monitored, individualized, essay examination. Why? Because it would be difficult (that is, costly) to cheat on such an exam. Suppose, however, that an instructor gave an objective "take-home" exam, basing the students' course grades entirely on the results. Many students would cheat because the benefits of doing so would be great and the risk (cost) minimal. The economic way of thinking never loses sight of the fact that changes in incentives exert a powerful and predictable influence on human decisions.

4. Economic Thinking Is Marginal Thinking.   Fundamental to economic reasoning and economizing behavior are the effects stemming from decisions to change the status quo. Economists refer to such decisions as **marginal.** Marginal choices always involve the effects of net additions or subtractions *from the current conditions.* In fact, the word "additional" is often used as a substitute for marginal. For example, we might ask, "What is the marginal (or additional) cost of producing one more automobile?" Or, "What is the marginal (or additional) benefit derived from one more glass of water?"

Marginal decisions need not always involve small changes. For example, the decision to build a new plant is a marginal decision. It is marginal because it involves a change at the border. *Given the current situation,* what marginal benefits (additional sales revenues, for example) can be expected from the plant, and what will be the marginal cost of constructing the facility?

It is important to distinguish between "average" and "marginal." Even though a manufacturer's current average cost of producing automobiles may be $10,000, for example, the marginal cost of producing an additional automobile

Marginal: Term used to describe the effects of a change, given the current situation. For example, the marginal cost is the cost of producing an additional unit of a product, given the producer's current facility and production rate.

(or an additional 1000 automobiles) might be much lower, say, $5000. Costs associated with research, testing, design, molds, heavy equipment, and similar factors of production must be incurred whether the manufacturer is going to produce 1000 units, 10,000 units, or 100,000 units. Such costs will clearly contribute to the average cost of an automobile. However, given that it is necessary to undertake these activities in order to produce the manufacturer's current output level, they may *add little* to the cost of producing *additional* units. Thus, the manufacturer's marginal cost may be substantially less than the average cost. When determining whether to *expand* or *reduce* the production of a good, the choice should be based on marginal costs, not the current average cost.

We often confront decisions involving a possible change, *given the current situation*. The marginal benefits and marginal costs associated with the choice will determine the wisdom of our decisions. Thus, what happens at the margin is an important part of economic analysis.

5. Information, Like Other Resources, Is Scarce. Therefore, Even Purposeful Decision-Makers Will Not Have Perfect Knowledge about the Future When They Make Choices. Rational decision-makers recognize that it is costly to obtain information and make complex calculations. Although additional information and techniques that improve one's decision-making capabilities are valuable, often the potential benefit is less than its expected cost. Therefore, sensible consumers will conserve on these limited resources, just as they conserve on other scarce resources.

6. Remember the Secondary Effects—Economic Actions Often Generate Secondary Effects in Addition to Their Immediate Effects. Frédéric Bastiat, a nineteenth-century French economist, stated that the difference between a good and a bad economist is that the bad economist considers only the immediate, visible effects, whereas the good economist is also aware of the **secondary effects,** effects that are indirectly related to the initial policy and whose influence is often seen or felt only with the passage of time.

Secondary Effects: Economic consequences of an initial economic change, even though they are not immediately identifiable. Secondary effects will be felt only with the passage of time.

Secondary effects are important in areas outside of economics. The immediate effect of an aspirin is a bitter taste in one's mouth. The indirect effect, which is not immediately observable, is relief from a headache. The immediate effect of drinking six quarts of beer might be a warm, jolly feeling. The indirect effect, for many, would be a pounding headache the next morning. In economics, too, the secondary effects of an action may be quite different from the initial impact. According to the economic way of thinking, the significant questions are: In addition to the initial result of this policy, what other factors will change or have changed? How will future actions be influenced by the changes in economic incentives that have resulted from policy A?

An economic system is much like an ecological system. An ecological action sometimes generates indirect and perhaps unintended secondary effects. For example, the heavy use of DDT on a field in order to kill a specific population of insects may have an undesirable effect on other creatures. Economic actions can generate similar results. For example, price controls on natural gas have the desired effect of reducing heating expenditures for some consumers, but they also reduce the incentive of producers to bring more natural gas to the market. Other consumers will therefore be forced to rely more heavily on more expensive energy sources, pushing the prices of these energy sources upward. Thus, the controls also generate an unintended result: an increase in the energy costs of some consumers. Straight economic thinking demands that we recognize the secondary effects, which will often be observed only with the passage of time.

7. The Test of a Theory Is Its Ability to Predict. Economic Thinking Is **Scientific Thinking.** The proof of the pudding is in the eating. The usefulness of an economic theory is revealed by its ability to predict the future consequences of economic action. Economists develop economic theory from the analysis of how incentives will affect decision-makers. The theory is then tested against the events of the real world. Through testing, we either confirm the theory or recognize the need for amending or rejecting it. If the events of the real world are consistent with a theory, we say that it has predictive value. In contrast, theories that are inconsistent with real-world data must be rejected.

Scientific Thinking: Development of theory from basic postulates and the testing of the implications of that theory as to their consistency with events in the real world. Good theories are consistent with and help explain real-world events. Theories that are inconsistent with the real world are invalid and must be rejected.

If it is impossible to test the theoretical relationships of a discipline, the discipline does not qualify as a science. Since economics deals with human beings, who can think and respond in a variety of ways, can economic theories really be tested? The answer to this question is yes, if, *on average,* human beings will respond in a predictable way to a change in economic conditions. The economist believes that this is the case. Note that this does not necessarily imply that *all* individuals will respond in a specified manner. Economics usually does not seek to predict the behavior of a specific individual; it focuses, rather, on the general behavior of a large number of individuals.

How can one test economic theory when, for the most part, controlled experiments are not feasible? Although this does impose limitations, economics is no different from astronomy in this respect. Astronomers also must deal with the world as it is. They cannot change the course of the stars or planets to see what impact the changes would have on the gravitational pull of the earth.

MYTHS OF ECONOMICS

"Economic analysis assumes that people act only out of selfish motives. It rejects the humanitarian side of humankind."

Probably because economics focuses on the efforts of individuals to satisfy material desires, many casual observers of the subject argue that its relevance hinges on the selfish nature of humankind. Some have even charged that economists, and the study of economics, encourage people to be materialistic rather than humanitarian.

This point of view stems from a fundamental misunderstanding of personal decision-making. Obviously, people act for a variety of reasons, some selfish and some humanitarian. The economist merely assumes that

actions will be influenced by costs and benefits, as viewed by the decision-maker. As an activity becomes more costly, it is less likely that a decision-maker will choose it. As the activity becomes more attractive, it is more likely that it will be chosen.

The choices of both the humanitarian and the egocentric individual will be influenced by changes in personal costs and benefits. For example, both will be more likely to try to save the life of a small child in a three-foot swimming pool than in the rapid currents approaching Niagara Falls. Both will be more likely to give a needy person their hand-me-downs rather than their best clothes. Why? Because in both cases, the latter alternative is more costly than the former.

Observation would suggest

that the right to control one's destiny is an "economic" good for most persons. Most of us would prefer to make our own choices rather than have someone else decide for us. But is this always greedy and selfish? If so, why do people often make choices in a way that is charitable toward others? After all, many persons freely choose to give a portion of their wealth to the sick, the needy, the less fortunate, religious organizations, and charitable institutions. Economics does not imply that these choices are irrational. It does imply that if you make it more (less) costly to act charitably, fewer (more) persons will do so.

Economics deals with people as they are—not as we would like to remake them. Should people act more charitably? Perhaps so. But this is not the subject matter of economics.

So it is with economists. They cannot arbitrarily institute changes in the price of cars or unskilled labor services just to observe the effect on quantity purchased or level of employment. However, this does not mean that economic theory cannot be tested. Economic conditions (for example, prices, production costs, technology, transportation cost, etc.), like the location of the planets, do change from time to time. As actual conditions change, economic theory can be tested by analyzing its consistency with the real world. The real world is the laboratory of the economist, just as the universe is the laboratory of the astronomer.

In some cases, observations of the real world may be consistent with two (or more) economic theories. Given the current state of our knowledge, we will sometimes be unable to distinguish between competitive theories. Much of the work of economists remains to be done, but in many areas substantial empirical work has been completed. Throughout this book we will refer to this evidence in an effort to provide information with which we can judge the validity of various economic theories. We must not lose sight of the scientific method of thinking, because it is a requisite for sound economic thinking.

POSITIVE AND NORMATIVE ECONOMICS

Positive Economics: The scientific study of "what is" among economic relationships.

Economics as a social science is concerned with predicting or determining the impact of changes in economic variables on the actions of human beings. Scientific economics, commonly referred to as **positive economics,** attempts to determine "what is." Positive economic statements postulate a relationship that is potentially verifiable. For example: "If the price of butter were higher, people would buy less." "As the money supply increases, the price level will go up." We can statistically investigate (and estimate) the relationship between butter prices and sales, or the supply of money and the general price level. We can analyze the facts to determine the correctness of a statement about positive economics.

Normative Economics: Judgments about "what ought to be" in economic matters. Normative economic views cannot be proved false because they are based on value judgments.

Because it utilizes ethical judgments as well as knowledge of positive economics, **normative economics** involves the advocacy of specific policy alternatives. Normative economic statements are about "what ought to be," given the philosophical views of the advocate. Value judgments may be the source of disagreement about normative economic matters. Two persons may differ on a policy matter because one is a socialist and the other a libertarian, one a liberal and the other a conservative, or one a traditionalist and the other a radical. They may agree as to the expected outcome of altering an economic variable (that is, the positive economics of an issue) but disagree as to whether that outcome is "good" or "bad."

In contrast with positive economic statements, normative economic statements cannot be tested and proved false (or confirmed to be correct). The government *should* increase defense expenditures. Business firms *should not* maximize profits. Unions *should not* increase wages more rapidly than the cost of living. These normative statements cannot be scientifically tested, since their validity rests on value judgments.

Positive economics does not tell us which policy is best. The purpose of positive economics is to increase our knowledge of all policy alternatives, thereby eliminating a potential source of disagreement about policy matters. The knowledge that we gain from positive economics also serves to reduce a potential source of disappointment with policy. Those who do not understand how the economy operates may advocate policies that are actually inconsistent with their philosophical views. Sometimes what one thinks will happen if a policy is instituted may be a very unlikely result in the real world.

Our normative economic views can sometimes influence our attitude toward positive economic analysis. When we agree with the objectives of a policy, it is easy to overlook its potential liabilities. However, desired objectives are not the same as workable solutions. The effects of policy alternatives often differ dramatically from the objectives of their proponents. Sound positive economics will help each of us evaluate more accurately whether or not a policy alternative will, in fact, accomplish the desired objective.

The task of the professional economist is to expand our knowledge of how the real world operates. If we do not fully understand the implications, including the secondary effects, of alternative policies, we will not be able to choose intelligently among them. It is not always easy to isolate the impact of a change in an economic variable or policy. Let us consider some of the potential pitfalls that retard the growth of economic knowledge.

Violation of the *Ceteris Paribus* Condition

Economists often preface their statements with the words *ceteris paribus,* meaning "other things constant." "Other things constant, an increase in the price of housing will cause buyers to reduce their purchases." Unfortunately for the economic researcher, we live in a dynamic world. Other things seldom remain constant. For example, as the price of housing rises, the income of consumers may simultaneously be increasing. Both of these factors, higher housing prices and an expansion in consumer income, will have an impact on housing purchases. In fact, we would generally expect them to exert opposite effects—higher prices retarding housing purchases but the rise in consumer income stimulating the demand for housing. Thus, the task of sorting out the specific effects of interrelated variables becomes more complex when several changes take place at the same time.

Economic theory acts as a guide, suggesting the probable linkage among economic variables. However, the relationships suggested by economic theory must be tested as to their consistency with events in the real world.

Statistical procedures can often be utilized to help economists identify correctly and measure more accurately relationships among economic variables. In fact, the major portion of the day-to-day work of many professional economists consists of statistical research designed to improve our knowledge of positive economics. Without accurate knowledge of positive economics, policymakers will be unable to establish a consistent link between their programs and economic goals.

Association Is Not Causation

In economics, causation is usually very important. The incorrect identification of causation is a potential source of error. Statistical association does not establish causation. Perhaps an extreme example will illustrate the point. Suppose that each November a medicine man performs a voodoo dance to arouse the cold-weather gods of winter and that soon after he performs his dance, the weather in fact begins to turn cold. The medicine man's dance is *associated* with the arrival of winter, but does it *cause* the arrival of winter? Most of us would answer in the negative, even though the two are linked statistically.

Unfortunately, cause and effect relationships in economics are not always self-evident. For example, it is sometimes difficult to determine whether a rise in income has caused consumption to increase or, conversely, whether an increase in consumption has caused income to rise. Similarly, economists sometimes argue whether rising money wages are a cause or an effect of inflation. Economic theory, if rooted to the basic postulates, can often help to determine the source of causation, but sometimes competitive theories may suggest alternative directions of causation. Thus, we must guard against drawing unwarranted conclusions when the direction of causation is unclear.

The Fallacy Of Composition

Fallacy of Composition: Erroneous view that what is true for the individual (or the part) will also be true for the group (or the whole).

What is true for the individual (or subcomponent) may not be true for the group (or the whole). If you stand up for an exciting play during a football game, you will be able to see better. But what happens if everybody stands up at the same time? What benefits the individual does not benefit the group as a whole. When everybody stands up, the view of individual spectators fails to improve; in fact, it probably becomes even worse.

Persons who argue that what is true for the part is also true for the whole may err because of the **fallacy of composition.** Consider an example from economics. If you have an extra $10,000 in your bank account, you will be better off. But what if everyone suddenly has an additional $10,000? This increase in the supply of money will result in higher prices, as persons with more money bid against each other for the existing supply of goods. Without an increase in the availability (or production) of scarce economic goods, the additional money will not make everyone better off. What is true for the individual is misleading and fallacious when applied to the entire economy.

Potential error associated with the fallacy of composition highlights the importance of considering both a micro- and a macroview in the study of economics. Since individual human decision-makers are the moving force behind all economic action, the foundations of economics are clearly rooted in a microview. Analysis that focuses on a single consumer, producer, product, or productive resource is referred to as **microeconomics.** As Professor Abba Lerner puts it, "Microeconomics consists of looking at the economy through a microscope, as it were, to see how the millions of cells in the body economic—the individuals or households as consumers, and the individuals or firms as producers—play their part in the working of the whole organism."[3]

Microeconomics: The branch of economics that focuses on how human behavior affects the conduct of affairs within narrowly defined units, such as individual household or business firms.

Macroeconomics: The branch of economics that focuses on how human behavior affects outcomes in highly aggregated markets, such as the markets for labor or consumer products.

However, as we have seen, what is true for a small unit may not be true in the aggregate. **Macroeconomics** focuses on how the aggregation of individual microunits affects our analysis. Macroeconomics, like microeconomics, is concerned with incentives, prices, and output. But in macroeconomics the markets are highly aggregated. In our study of macroeconomics, the 80 million households in this country will be lumped together when we consider the importance of consumption spending, saving, and employment. Similarly, the nation's 15 million firms will be lumped together into something we call

---

[3]Abba P. Lerner, "Microeconomy Theory," in *Perspectives in Economics,* ed. A. A. Brown, E. Neuberger, and M. Palmatier (New York: McGraw-Hill, 1968), p. 29.

"the business sector." In short, macroeconomics examines the forest rather than the individual trees. As we move the microcomponents to a macroview of the whole, it is important that we bear in mind the potential pitfalls of the fallacy of composition.

WHAT DO ECONOMISTS DO?

The primary functions of economists are to teach, conduct research, and formulate policies. Approximately one-half of all professional economists are affiliated with an academic institution. Many of these academicians are involved in both teaching and scientific research.

The job of the research economist is to increase our understanding of economic matters. The tools of statistics and mathematics help the researcher to carry out this task. Government agencies and private business firms generate a vast array of economic statistics on such matters as income, employment, prices, and expenditure patterns. A two-way street exists between statistical data and economic theory. Statistics can be utilized to test the consistency of economic theory and measure the responsiveness of economic variables to changes in policy. At the same time, economic theory helps to explain *which* economic variables are likely to be related and *why* they are linked. Statistics do not tell their own story. We must utilize economic theory to interpret properly and understand more fully the actual statistical relationships among economic variables.

Economics is a social science. The fields of political science, sociology, psychology, and economics often overlap. Because of the abundance of economic data and the ample opportunity for scientific research in the real world, economics has sometimes been called the "queen of the social sciences." Reflecting the scientific nature of economics, the Swedish Academy of Science in 1969 instituted the Nobel Prize in economics. The men and women of genius in economics now take their place alongside those in physics, chemistry, physiology and medicine, and literature.

A knowledge of economics is essential for wise policy-making. Policymakers who do not understand the consequences of their actions will be unlikely to reach their goals. Their actions may even be in conflict with their targeted objectives. Recognizing the link between economic analysis and policy, Congress in 1946 established the Council of Economic Advisers. The purpose of the council is to provide the president with analyses of and recommendations on the economic activities of the federal government, particularly the attainment of maximum employment. The chairmanship of the Council of Economic Advisers is a cabinet-level position.

Final Word

The primary purpose of this book is to encourage you to develop the economic way of thinking so that you can differentiate sound reasoning from economic nonsense. Once you have developed the economic way of thinking, economics will be relatively easy. And utilizing the economic way of thinking can be fun. Moreover, it will help you to become a better citizen. It will give you a different and fascinating perspective about what motivates people, why they act the way they do, and why their actions sometimes are in conflict with the best interest of the community or nation. It will also give you some valuable insight into

OUTSTANDING ECONOMIST
Adam Smith (1723–1790) and the Historical Roots of Economics

Economic principles are as old as recorded history. However, in comparison with other disciplines, the study of economics as a science is a recent development. English, French, and German scholars wrote essays and pamphlets on the subject during the first half of the eighteenth century, but the foundation of economics as a systematic area of study was not laid until 1776, when Adam Smith published his monumental work, *An Inquiry into the Nature and Causes of the Wealth of Nations.*

One can build a strong case that *The Wealth of Nations* was the most influential book that had been written since the Bible. The political and intellectual leaders of Smith's time thought that national wealth consisted of money held in the form of gold and silver. Thus, governments established all sorts of constraints on the freedom of individual economic activity. Political institutions encouraged citizens to sell their produce abroad in exchange for gold and silver. Simultaneously, people were discouraged, and in some cases restrained, from purchasing foreign-made goods. In addition, governmental infringements on the economic freedom of individuals promoted monopolies, protected guild associations from potential competitors, and in general discouraged production and limited exchange. Economic action motivated by private gain was generally thought to be antisocial.

Smith's book was nothing less than a revolutionary attack on the existing orthodoxy. He declared that the wealth of a nation did not lie with gold and silver but rather was determined by the goods and services available to the people, regardless of whether the products were produced at home or abroad. Smith had no confidence in appeals to altruism or attempts to upgrade the moral behavior of humankind. He believed that the public interest was best served by governments which established an environment that encouraged the free exchange of goods and services.

The harmony of individual self-interest, voluntary exchange, and economic progress was the central theme of *The Wealth of Nations*. Smith believed that individual self-interest would be harnessed and directed by the "invisible hand" of competitive market prices if kings and politicians would remove legal restrictions that retarded productive activity and exchange. Smith perceived individual self-interest not as a curse but as a powerful vehicle for economic progress. If left to pursue their own interests, individuals would apply their talents to the activities they performed best. For example, skilled hunters would employ their talents in the provision of game and exchange their product for other goods. Similarly, skilled tradesmen would specialize in their craft and trade the fruits of their labor for other requirements of life. Smith believed that if freed from government regulation, buyers and sellers would find it in their own interest to work, produce, and exchange goods and services in a manner that promoted the public interest. Production and the wealth of a nation would be increased in the process.

As Keynes noted 160 years later, the world is ruled by ideas. Even though Smith's thinking conflicted with the social environment of his time, his idea that self-interest, economic freedom, and national wealth were all in harmony eventually turned the world upside down. The English historian Henry Thomas Buckle declared that *The Wealth of Nations* represented "the most valuable contribution ever made by a single man towards establishing the principles on which government should be based." It has been said that with this single book Smith laid down the principles by which the next several generations would be governed. Smith's idea greatly influenced those who mapped out the structure of government in the United States. By the end of the eighteenth century, institutional reform had lifted the hand of government from several areas of economic activity in England and throughout Europe. Today the nineteenth century is sometimes referred to as the "era of economic freedom." Adam Smith, more than any other individual, deserves the credit for establishing the intellectual climate that eventually led to the economic freedom, industrialization, and prosperity of the Western world during the nineteenth century.

By the time of Smith's death in 1790, five editions of *The Wealth of Nations* had been published, and it had been translated into several foreign languages. The study of the relationship between production, exchange, and wealth began to occupy the time of an increasing number of intellectuals. Economics was soon to become a new and widely accepted field of study in major universities throughout the world.

how people's actions can be rechanneled for the benefit of the community at large.

Economics is a relatively young science. Current-day economists owe an enormous debt to their predecessors. The Outstanding Economist feature analyzes the contribution of Adam Smith, the father of economics.

CHAPTER LEARNING OBJECTIVES

1   Scarcity and choice are the two essential ingredients of an economic topic. Goods are scarce because desire for them far outstrips their availability from Nature. Since scarcity prevents us from having as much of everything as we would like, we must choose from among the alternatives available to us. Any choice involving the use of scarce resources requires an economic decision.

2   Scarcity and poverty are not the same thing. Absence of poverty implies that some basic level of need has been met. Absence of scarcity would mean that all of our desires for goods have been met. We may someday be able to eliminate poverty, but scarcity will always be with us.

3   Economics is a method of approach, a way of thinking. The economic way of thinking emphasizes the following:

(a) Among economic goods, there are no free lunches. Someone must give something up if we are to have more scarce goods.

(b) Individuals make decisions purposefully, always seeking to choose the option they expect to be most consistent with their personal goals. Purposeful decision-making leads to economizing behavior.

(c) Incentives matter. People will be more likely to choose an option as the benefits expected from that option increase. In contrast, higher costs will make an alternative less attractive, reducing the likelihood that it will be chosen.

(d) Marginal costs and marginal benefits (utility) are fundamental to economizing behavior. Economic reasoning focuses on the impact of marginal changes.

(e) Since information is scarce, uncertainty will be present when decisions are made.

(f) In addition to their initial impact, economic events often alter personal incentives in a manner that leads to important secondary effects that may be felt only with the passage of time.

(g) The test of an economic theory is its ability to predict and to explain events of the real world.

4   Economic science is positive. It attempts to explain the actual consequences of economic actions and alternative policies. Positive economics alone does not state that one policy is superior to another. Normative economics is advocative; using value judgments, it makes suggestions about "what ought to be."

5   Testing economic theory is not an easy task. When several economic variables change simultaneously, it is often difficult to determine the relative importance of each. The direction of economic causation is sometimes difficult to ascertain. Economists consult economic theory as a guide and use statistical techniques as tools in attempting to improve our knowledge of positive economics.

6   Microeconomics focuses on narrowly defined units, such as individual consumers or business firms. Macroeconomics is concerned with highly aggregated units, such as the markets for labor or goods and services. When shifting focus from micro- to macrounits, one must be careful not to commit the fallacy of composition. Both micro- and macroeconomics utilize the same postulates and tools. The level of aggregation is the distinction between the two.

7   The origin of economics as a systematic method of analysis dates back to the publication of *The Wealth of Nations* by Adam Smith in 1776. Even though legal restraints on

economic activity abounded at the time, Smith argued that production and wealth would increase if individuals were left free to work, produce, and exchange goods and services. Smith believed that individuals pursuing their own interests would be led by the "invisible hand" of market incentives (prices) to employ their productive talents in a manner "most advantageous to the society." Smith's central message is that when markets are free—when there are no legal restraints limiting the entry of producer-sellers—individual self-interest and the public interest are brought into harmony.

THE ECONOMIC WAY OF THINKING — DISCUSSION QUESTIONS

1 Indicate how each of the following changes would influence the incentive of a decision-maker to undertake the action described.

(a) A reduction in the temperature from 80° to 50° on one's decision to go swimming

(b) A change in the meeting time of the introductory economics course from 11:00 A.M. to 7:30 A.M. on one's decision to attend the lectures

(c) A reduction in the number of exam questions that relate to the text on the student's decision to read the text

(d) An increase in the price of beef on one's decision to have steak every night this week

(e) An increase in the rental price of apartments on one's decision to build additional housing units

2 What does it mean to economize? Do you attempt to economize? Why or why not?

3 Write a couple of paragraphs, explaining in your own words the meaning and essential ingredients of the economic way of thinking.

4 **What's Wrong with This Economic Experiment?**

A researcher hypothesizes that the medical attention received by U.S. citizens is inadequate because many people cannot afford medical care. The researcher interviews 100 randomly selected individuals and asks them, "Would you use physician services or hospital and nursing-home medical facilities more if they were not so expensive?" Ninety-six of the 100 answer in the affirmative. The researcher concludes that there is a critical need to allocate more resources to the provision of free medical care for all citizens.

5 "Reasonable rental housing could be brought within the economic means of all if the government would prevent landlords from charging more than $200 per month rent for a quality three-bedroom house." Use the economic way of thinking to evaluate this view.

6 SENATOR DOGOODER: I favor an increase in the minimum wage because it would help the unskilled worker.

SENATOR DONOTHING: I oppose an increase in the minimum wage because it would cause the unemployment rate among the young and unskilled to rise.

Is the disagreement between Senator Dogooder and Senator Donothing positive or normative? Explain.

The goods people sell usually are made by processes using a high proportion of the skills they are gifted in, whereas the goods people buy usually are made by processes they are comparatively ungifted in.[1]
Robert A. Mundell

2

SOME TOOLS OF THE ECONOMIST

In the last chapter you were introduced to the economic approach. In this chapter, we discuss a few important tools that will help you to develop the economic way of thinking.

What Shall We Give Up?

Scarcity calls the tune in economics. We cannot have as much of everything as we would like. Most of us would like to have more time for leisure, recreation, vacations, hobbies, education, and skill development. We would also like to have more wealth, a larger savings account, and more consumption goods. However, all of these things either are scarce or require the use of scarce resources. They are in conflict with one another. How can I have more leisure time and simultaneously accumulate more wealth? How can I increase my current consumption and simultaneously increase my savings account? The answer is, I can't. The choice of one requires me to give up something of the other.

OPPORTUNITY COST IS THE HIGHEST VALUED OPPORTUNITY LOST

An unpleasant fact of economics is that the choice to do one thing is, at the same time, a choice *not* to do something else. Your choice to spend time reading this book is a choice *not* to play tennis, go out on a date, listen to a math lecture, or attend a party. These things must be given up because of your decision to read. The highest valued alternative that must be sacrificed because one chooses an option is the **opportunity cost** of the choice.

Note that the cost of an event is *not* the drudgery and undesirable aspects

Opportunity Cost: The highest valued benefit that must be sacrificed (foregone) as the result of choosing an alternative.

---

[1]Robert A. Mundell, *Man and Economics: The Science of Choice* (New York: McGraw-Hill, 1968), p. 19.

that may be associated with the event. The distinction between (a) the undesirable attributes of an option and (b) the highest valued opportunity foregone in order to realize the option is a fundamental distinction because only the latter is considered a cost by the economist.[2]

Cost is subjective; it exists in the mind of the decision-maker. It is based on expectation—the expectation of how one would evaluate the alternative given up. Cost can never be directly measured by someone other than the decision-maker because only the decision-maker can place a value on what is foregone.[3]

Cost, however, often has a monetary component that enables us to approximate its value. For example, the cost of attending a movie is equal to the highest valued opportunity that is given up because of (a) the time necessary to attend and (b) the purchasing power (that is, money) necessary to obtain a ticket. The monetary component is, of course, objective and can be measured. When there is good reason to expect that nonmonetary considerations are relatively unimportant, the monetary component will approximate the total cost of an option.

Opportunity Cost and the Real World

Is real-world decision-making influenced by opportunity cost? Remember, the basic economic postulate states that the likelihood that an option will be chosen varies inversely with its cost to the decision-maker. So economic theory does imply that differences (or changes) in opportunity cost will influence how decisions are made.

Let us consider several examples that demonstrate the real-world application of the opportunity cost concept. Poor people are more likely to travel long distances by bus, whereas the wealthy are more likely to travel by airplane. Why? A simple answer would be that the bus is cheaper; therefore, the poor will be more likely to purchase the cheaper good. But is the bus cheaper for a relatively well-off individual whose opportunity cost of travel time is high? Suppose that a round-trip airline ticket from Kansas City to Denver costs $150, whereas a bus ticket costs only $110. However, the bus requires ten hours of travel time, and the airplane only two hours. Which would be cheaper? It depends on one's opportunity cost of time. If one's opportunity cost is evaluated at less than $5 per hour, the bus is cheaper, but if one's time is valued at more than $5 per hour, the airplane is clearly the cheaper option. Since the opportunity cost of the travel time will usually be greater for the wealthy than for the poor, the airplane is more likely to be cheaper for high-income recipients.

The concept of opportunity cost helps us to understand labor allocation and wage differences. Workers whose skills make them valuable elsewhere must be paid wages sufficient to compensate them for the foregoing of their highest valued employment alternatives. Thus, a filling station owner is unlikely to hire a physician as an attendant because the physician would have to be paid a wage at least equal to his or her opportunity cost—perhaps $100 per hour or more for delivering babies or removing infected tonsils. Similarly, it would be necessary for an employer to pay a skilled carpenter a higher wage than an unskilled

---

[2]For an excellent in-depth discussion of this subject, see A. A. Alchian, "Cost," in *International Encyclopedia of the Social Sciences* (New York: Macmillan, 1969), 3: 404–415.

[3]See James M. Buchanan, *Cost and Choice* (Chicago: Markham, 1969), for an analysis of the relationship between cost and choice.

worker because of the carpenter's opportunity cost; the wage opportunities foregone with another employer would be greater for the more skilled worker. Skills and abilities, inasmuch as they make one more valuable to alternative employers, will also increase one's earnings capability.

Elderly retirees watch considerably more television than high-income lawyers, accountants, and other professionals. Why? Is it because the elderly can better afford the money cost of a TV? Clearly, this is not the case. This phenomenon is straightforward when one considers the differences in the opportunity cost of time between the retirees and the professionals. In terms of earnings foregone, watching television costs the professional a lot more than it costs the elderly. The professional watches less TV because it is an expensive good in terms of time.

Why do students watch less television and spend less time at the movies or beach during final exam week? Doing these things is more costly, that's why. Using valuable study time to go to the beach would most likely mean foregoing a passing grade in history, although a student's grade in economics might be unaffected if he or she kept up during the semester and developed the economic way of thinking.

By now you should have the idea. Choosing one thing means giving up others that might have been chosen. Opportunity cost is the highest valued option sacrificed as the result of choosing an alternative.

THE PRODUCTION POSSIBILITIES CURVE

The resources of every individual are limited. Purposeful decision-making and economizing behavior imply that individuals seek to get the most out of their limited resources. They do not deliberately waste resources.

The nature of the economizing problem can be brought into clearer focus by the use of a production possibilities diagram. **A production possibilities curve** reveals the maximum amount of any two products that can be produced from a fixed quantity of resources.

Production Possibilities Curve: A curve that outlines all possible combinations of total output that could be produced, assuming (a) the utilization of a fixed amount of productive resources, (b) full and efficient use of those resources, and (c) a specific state of technical knowledge.

Exhibit 1 illustrates the production possibilities curve for Susan, an intelligent economics major. It indicates the combinations of grades possible for two alternative amounts of study time—six and eight hours. If she uses her six hours of study time efficiently, she can choose any grade combination along the six-hour production possibilities curve. However, when her study time is limited to six hours per week, Susan is able to raise her grade in one of the subjects only by accepting a lower grade in the other. If she wants to improve her overall performance (raise at least one grade without lowering the other), she will have to apply more time to academic endeavors. For example, she might increase her weekly study time from six to eight hours. Of course, this would require her to give up something else—leisure.

Can the production possibilities concept be applied to the entire economy? The answer is yes. You cannot have both guns and butter, as the old saying goes. An increase in military expenditures will require the use of resources that otherwise could be applied to the production of nonmilitary goods. If scarce resources are being used efficiently, more of one thing will require the sacrifice of others. Exhibit 2 illustrates the concept of the production possibilities curve for an economy producing only two goods: food and clothing.

What restricts the ability of an economy to produce more of everything?

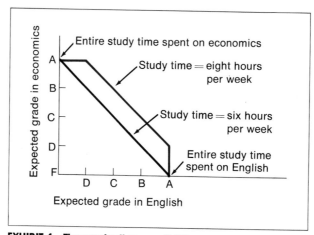

EXHIBIT 1   The production possibilities curve for grades in English and economics

The production possibilities, in terms of grades, for Susan are illustrated for two alternative quantities of total study time. If she studied 6 hours per week, concentrating entirely on economics, she would expect an A, but would flunk English because she spent all of her time studying economics. On the other hand, studying 6 hours per week, she could attain (a) a D in English and a B in economics, (b) a C in both, (c) a B in English and a D in economics, or (d) an F in economics but an A in English. The black line represents her production possibilities curve for 6 hours of studying.

A higher grade in one subject costs a grade reduction in the other. Could she make higher grades in both? Yes, if she were willing to apply more resources, thereby giving up some leisure. The colored line indicates her production possibilities curve if she studied 8 hours per week.

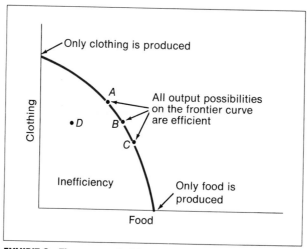

EXHIBIT 2   The concept of the production possibilities curve for an economy

When an economy is using its limited resources efficiently, it is at the edge of its production possibilities frontier (for example, points *A, B,* and *C*). Thus, production of more clothing requires the economy to give up some other goods—food in this simple example. *With time,* a technological discovery or expansion of the economy's resource base could make it possible to produce more of both, shifting the production possibilities curve outward. Or the citizens of the economy might decide to give up some leisure for more of both goods. These factors aside, however, limited resources will constrain the production possibilities of an economy.

The same thing that kept Susan from making a higher grade in *both* English and economics—lack of resources. There will be various maximum combinations of goods that an economy will be able to produce when:

1. it uses some fixed quantity of resources,
2. the resources are not wasted or used inefficiently, and
3. the level of technology is constant.

When these three conditions are met, the economy will be at the perimeter of its production possibilities frontier (points such as *A, B,* and *C,* Exhibit 2). The production of more of one good, clothing, for example, will necessitate less production of other goods (for example, food).

When the resources of an economy are used wastefully and inefficiently, the economy is operating at a point inside the production possibilities curve— point *D,* for example. Why might this happen? It happens because the economy is not properly solving the economizing problem. A major purpose of economics is to ensure that we are getting the most out of the resources available, that we move to the perimeter of the production possibilities curve. We will return to this problem again and again.

Shifting the Production Possibilities Curve Outward

Could an economy ever have more of all goods? Could the production possibilities curve be shifted outward? The answer is yes, under certain circumstances. There are three major methods.

1. An Increase in the Economy's Resource Base Would Expand Our Ability to Produce Goods and Services. If we had more and better resources, we could produce a greater amount of all goods. Many resources are man-made. If we were willing to give up some current consumption, we could invest a greater amount of today's resources into the production of long-lasting physical structures, machines, education, and the development of human skills. This **capital formation** would provide us with better tools and skills in the future and thereby increase our ability to produce goods and services. Exhibit 3 illustrates the link between capital formation and the *future* production possibilities of an economy. Initially, the two economies illustrated confront an identical production possibilities curve (*RS*). However, since Economy A (Exhibit 3a) allocates more of its resources to investment than Economy B, with the passage of time A's production possibilities curve shifts outward by a greater amount. The growth rate of A—the rate of expansion of the economy's ability to produce goods—is enhanced because the economy allocates a larger share of its output to investment. Of course, it is costly to shift the production possibilities curve of an economy outward. As more of today's resources are used to produce "tools" that will make us more productive tomorrow, fewer will be available for producing current consumer goods. More investment in machines and human skills will necessitate less current consumption.

Capital Formation: The production of buildings, machinery, tools, and other equipment that will enhance the ability of future economic participants to produce. The term can also be applied to efforts to upgrade the knowledge and skill of workers and thereby increase their ability to produce in the future.

2. Advancements in Technology and Human Knowledge Would Expand the Economy's Production Possibilities. **Technology** defines the relationship between resource inputs and the output of goods and services. Technological improvements make it possible for a given base of resources to generate a greater output.[4]

Technology: The body of skills and technical knowledge available at any given time. The level of technology establishes the relationship between inputs and the output they can generate.

---

[4]Without modern technical knowledge it would be impossible to produce the vast array of goods and services responsible for our standard of living. Thomas Sowell makes this point clear when he notes:

The cavemen had the same natural resources at their disposal as we have today, and the difference between their standard of living and ours is a difference between the knowledge they could bring to bear on those resources and the knowledge used today.

See Thomas Sowell, *Knowledge and Decisions* (New York: Basic Books, 1980), p. 47.

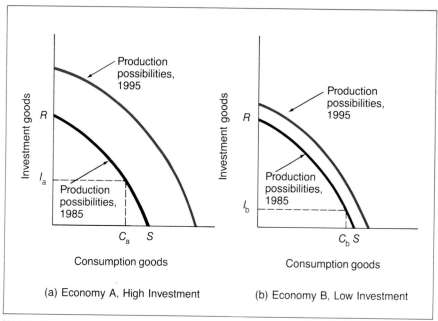

EXHIBIT 3 Investment and production possibilities in the future

Here we illustrate two economies that initially confront identical production possibilities curves (*RS*). The economy illustrated on the left allocates a larger share of its output to investment (*I*$_a$, compared to *I*$_b$ for the economy on the right). As a result, the production possibilities of the high-investment economy will shift outward by a larger amount than will be true for the low-investment economy.

For example, the discovery of drought-resistant hybrid seeds has led to vast expansions in the output of corn per acre (and per worker-hour of labor). Thus, a technological improvement also shifts the production possibilities curve outward. If we were to devote more resources now to research and development, we would speed up the rate of technological change. Of course, this would mean giving up current consumption, capital formation, or leisure.

3. By Working Harder and Giving Up Current Leisure, We Could Increase Our Production of Goods and Services.   Strictly speaking, this is not an expansion in the production frontier because leisure is also a good. We are giving up some of that good to have more of other things.

The work effort of individuals not only reflects their personal preferences but is also a function of public policy. For example, high tax rates may induce individuals to reduce their work time. The basic economic postulate implies that as high tax rates reduce the *personal* payoff from working (and earning taxable income), individuals will shift more of their time to other areas, including the consumption of leisure, and the production possibilities curve for material goods will shift inward.

It is apparent that the production possibilities curve for material goods is not fixed. It is influenced by both individual preferences and public policy. We will discuss this topic more thoroughly as we proceed.

Division of Labor and Production Possibilities

Division of Labor: A method that breaks down the production of a commodity into a series of specific tasks, each performed by a different worker.

In a modern economy, individuals do not produce all, or even most, of the items that we consume. Instead, we sell our labor services (usually agreeing to perform specified productive functions) and utilize the derived income to purchase desired goods. We are induced to follow this course because **division of labor** and exchange allow us to produce far more goods and services through cooperative effort than would be possible if each household sought to produce its own food, clothing, shelter, transportation, and other desired goods.

Observing the operation of a pin manufacturer more than 200 years ago, Adam Smith noted that specialization and division of labor permitted people to attain a far greater output than would have been possible if each worker alone had performed all of the functions necessary to produce a pin. When each worker specialized in a productive function, ten workers were able to produce 48,000 pins per day, or 4800 pins *per worker*. In the absence of specialization and division of labor, Smith doubted an individual worker would have been able to produce as many as 20 pins per day.[5]

The division of labor permits us to break production tasks into a series of related operations. Each worker performs a single task that may be only one of hundreds of tasks necessary for the production of a commodity. There are several reasons why the division of labor often leads to enormous gains in overall output per worker. First, specialization permits individuals to take advantage of their existing abilities and skills. (Put another way, specialization permits an economy to take advantage of the fact that individuals have different skills.) Productive assignments can be undertaken by those individuals who are able to accomplish them most efficiently. Second, when individual workers specialize in just one task (or one narrow area), they become increasingly proficient, acquiring knowledge and experience in the specific task with the passage of time. The most important source of gain from the division of labor, however, is probably the facilitation of alternative production techniques, particularly those that rely upon the intensive use of machinery and high-level technology. The division of labor allows us to adopt complex, large-scale production techniques unthinkable for an individual household. As our knowledge of technology and the potential of machinery expand, capital-intensive production procedures and the division of labor permit us to attain living standards undreamed of just a few decades ago.

TRADE TIPS AND COMPARATIVE ADVANTAGE

Economizing means getting the most out of the resources available. How can this be accomplished? How can we move the perimeter of the economy's production possibilities curve? In answering these questions, we must understand several important principles.

First, let us consider the economizing problem of Woodward and Mason, individuals in the construction business. Exhibit 4 presents certain facts about the abilities of Woodward and Mason. Woodward is highly skilled, fast, and reliable. During a month, Woodward can build either four frame houses or two

---

[5]See Adam Smith, *An Inquiry into the Nature and Causes of the Wealth of Nations* (1776; Cannan's ed., Chicago: University of Chicago Press, 1976), pp. 7–16, for additional detail on the importance of the division of labor.

EXHIBIT 4 Comparative advantage and producing a much-needed vacation

The monthly production possibilities of Woodward and Mason are:

Frame Houses per Month		Brick Houses per Month	
Woodward	Mason	Woodward	Mason
4	1	2	1

Initially, they worked all year, each of them producing both frame and brick houses. Annually, Woodward was able to produce 16 of each, and Mason only 6 of each. Thus, their beginning total output was 22 frame and 22 brick units.

After both specialized in their areas of greatest comparative advantage, Mason produced only brick houses. During the first 11 months, Mason produced 11 brick houses. Woodward worked 5½ months producing 22 frame houses and another 5½ months producing 11 brick houses. As the chart shows, after specialization, Woodward and Mason were able to match last year's joint output in just 11 months. The law of comparative advantage made it possible for them to maintain their previous output level and still take a much-needed vacation.

	Annual Output before Specialization		11-Month Output after Specialization	
	Frame Houses	Brick Houses	Frame Houses	Brick Houses
Woodward	16	16	22	11
Mason	6	6	0	11
Total	22	22	22	22

brick houses. By way of comparison with Woodward, Mason is less skilled. It takes Mason an entire month to build either a frame or a brick house. Thus, Mason is slower than Woodward at building both kinds of houses.

Last year, both builders worked the entire 12 months. Woodward spent 8 months producing 16 brick houses and the other 4 months producing 16 frame houses. Mason was able to produce only 6 frame and 6 brick houses during the year. Their joint output was 22 frame and 22 brick houses.

Since Woodward has an *absolute advantage* (Woodward can build both frame and brick houses more rapidly than Mason) in the production of houses, few observers would believe that Woodward and Mason could gain from specialization and trade of products. However, they would indeed gain. Suppose Mason specialized in the production of brick houses. In 11 months Mason could produce 11 brick houses. Simultaneously, suppose that Woodward spent 5½ months producing each type of house. Woodward could produce 22 frame houses (4 per month) in those 5½ months, and 11 brick houses (2 per month) in another 5½ months. After they specialize, it would be possible for Mason and Woodward to produce 22 frame houses (11 each) and 22 brick houses (all by Woodward) with just 11 months of work. If 5 of Mason's 11 brick houses were traded to Woodward for 6 frame houses, then Mason would be able to attain last year's individual output rate (6 frame and 6 brick). Similarly, upon receipt of the 5 frame houses from Mason in exchange for 6 brick ones, Woodward would also be left with last year's output rate (16 frame and 16 brick). Thus, with specialization and exchange, Woodward and Mason could both attain last year's production rate with just 11 months of work. They could take a vacation the last month of the year.

Despite the fact that Woodward was better than Mason at producing both frame and brick houses, the two were able to gain from the trade and specialization.[6] Was it magic? What is happening here? Our old friend, opportunity cost, will help us unravel this seemingly paradoxical result. In what sense is Woodward better at producing brick houses than Mason? True, in a month, Woodward can produce twice as many brick houses as Mason, but what is Woodward's opportunity cost of producing a brick house? Two frame ones, right? In the same time required to produce a single brick house, Woodward can produce two frame houses.

Consider Mason's opportunity cost of producing a brick house. It is only one frame house. So who is the cheaper producer of brick houses? Mason is, because Mason's opportunity cost of producing a brick house is one frame house, compared to Woodward's opportunity cost of two frame houses.

The reason that Woodward and Mason could both gain is that their exchange allowed each of them to specialize in the production of the product that, *comparatively* speaking, they could produce cheapest. Mason was the cheaper producer of brick houses. Woodward was the cheaper producer of the frame ones. They were able to economize—get more out of their resources—by trading and specializing in the thing that each did comparatively better.

This simple example demonstrates a basic truth known as the law of comparative advantage, which lies at the heart of economizing behavior for any economy. Initially developed in the early 1800s by the great English economist David Ricardo, the **law of comparative advantage** states that the total output of a group, an entire economy, or a group of nations will be greatest when the output of each good is produced by the person (or firm) with the lowest opportunity cost.

If a product, any product, is produced by one producer when it could have been produced by another with a lower opportunity cost, the economy gives up more than is necessary. It is not economizing. Economizing, or maximum economic efficiency, requires that output always be generated by the producer who has the lowest opportunity cost.

Perhaps one additional example will help to drive home the implications of the law of comparative advantage. Consider the situation of an attorney who can type 120 words per minute. The attorney is trying to decide whether or not to hire a secretary, who only types 60 words per minute, to complete some legal documents. If the lawyer does the typing job, it will take four hours; if a secretary is hired, the typing job will take eight hours. Thus, the lawyer has an absolute advantage in typing compared to the prospective employee. However, the attorney's time is worth $50 per hour when working as a lawyer, whereas the typist's time is worth $5 per hour as a typist. Although a fast typist, the attorney is also a high opportunity cost producer of typing service. If the lawyer types the documents, the job will cost $200, which is the opportunity cost of four hours of lost time as a lawyer. Alternatively, if the typist is hired, the cost of having the documents typed is only $40 (eight hours of typing service at $5 per hour). Thus, the lawyer's comparative advantage lies in practicing law. The attorney

Law of Comparative Advantage: A principle which states that individuals, firms, regions, or nations can gain by specializing in the production of goods that they produce cheaply (that is, at a low opportunity cost) and exchanging those goods for other desired goods for which they are high opportunity cost producers.

---

[6]Throughout this section we will assume that individuals are equally content to produce either product. Dropping this assumption would add to the complexity of the analysis, but it would not change the basic principle.

will gain by hiring the typist and spending the additional time specializing in the area of comparative advantage.

DIVISION OF LABOR, SPECIALIZATION, AND EXCHANGE IN ACCORDANCE WITH THE LAW OF COMPARATIVE ADVANTAGE

It is difficult to exaggerate the gains derived from specialization, division of labor, and exchange in accordance with the law of comparative advantage. These factors are the primary source of our modern standard of living. Can you imagine the difficulty involved in producing one's own housing, clothing, and food, to say nothing of radios, television sets, automatic dishwashers, automobiles, and telephone services? Yet most families in the United States, Western Europe, Japan, and Australia enjoy these conveniences. They are able to do so largely because their economies are organized in such a way that individuals can cooperate, specialize, trade, and therefore reap the benefits of the enormous increases in output—both in quantity and diversity—thus produced. An economy that fails to realize potential gains stemming from the division of labor and specialization in accordance with the law of comparative advantage is operating inside of its production possibilities curve, at a point such as D of Exhibit 2. This is the case for most so-called less developed economies. For various reasons, production in these economies is primarily centered in the individual household. Therefore, the output level per worker of these economies falls well below the level that could be attained if labor were applied in a more efficient manner.

Comparative Advantage and Regional Specialization

We have emphasized that parties can gain from exchange even if one of them is more skilled in the production of both items traded. This principle holds true for trade between regions and nations as well as between individuals. Parties will find it particularly advantageous to trade those goods that they can produce most efficiently for commodities that would be extremely costly to produce on a personal or local level.

Why are oranges not grown in Kansas? Why don't more southern California orange growers raise wheat? Comparative advantage explains a great deal about the regional specialization that we often take for granted. Relative to California, Kansas is far more efficient in the production of wheat than it is in the growing of oranges. Similarly, the endowments of southern California give it a comparative advantage in the production of oranges rather than wheat. Thus, California oranges tend to be exchanged for Kansas wheat.

Since the endowments of land, labor skills, and capital differ among regions, so, too, does the opportunity cost of producing different products. In the open spaces of the Great Plains, fertile land is cheap. Consequently this region tends to specialize in feed grains, beef, and dairy products. Florida, with its mild winter climate and sunny beaches, specializes in citrus crops and tourism. In the East and upper Midwest, the transportation network is highly developed, and raw materials are readily accessible. Manufacturing and trade dominate these regions. Residents of each region tend to specialize in those things that they do best.

Comparative Advantage and Trade between Nations

The principle of comparative advantage applies to trade between nations as well. Whenever differing natural endowments, labor skills, or other factors result in differences in the opportunity cost of producing goods, a nation can gain by specializing in the production of products for which it is best equipped (that is, the low opportunity cost producer) and exporting these goods in exchange for those products that the country is least able to produce. Countries with an abundance of rich farmland, such as Canada, Australia, Argentina, and even the United States, export feed grains, beef, and other agricultural products. Switzerland, a country with a labor force that has passed precision skills down from generation to generation, exports watches and scientific instruments. When highly skilled diamond cutters immigrated to Israel, this small nation without a single diamond mine utilized this comparative advantage to become the world's largest exporter of cut diamonds.

The list is seemingly endless. Japan, with few material resources but a highly efficient labor force, imports many raw materials and exports radios, small appliances, cameras, and small manufactured goods. India and Korea, countries with an abundance of labor relative to land, export products such as textiles, which require large amounts of labor. All of these countries gain by selling products they can produce at a low opportunity cost and buying products for which their production opportunity cost would be high.

When one begins to think about it, the law of comparative advantage is almost common sense. Stated in layman's terms, it merely means that if we want to accomplish a task with the least effort, each of us should specialize in that component of the task that we do best.

The principle of comparative advantage is universal. It is just as valid in socialist countries as it is for capitalists. If socialist planners are interested in getting the most out of available resources, they, too, should apply the principle of comparative advantage.

Dependence, Specialization, and Exchange

Specialization and mutual interdependence are directly related. If the United States specializes in the production of agricultural products and Middle East countries specialize in the production of oil, the two countries become mutually interdependent. Similarly, if Texas specializes in production of cotton and Michigan in production of wheat, mutual interdependence results. In some cases this dependence can have serious consequences for one or both of the parties. The potential costs of mutual interdependence (for example, vulnerability to economic pressure applied by a trading partner who supplies an important economic good) and its potential benefits (for example, economic interaction that may well increase international understanding and reduce the likelihood of war) should be weighed along with the mutual consumption gains when one is evaluating the merits of specialization.

Specialization and Work Alienation

Specialization clearly makes it possible to produce more goods. But it also may result in many workers performing simple, boring, and monotonous functions. Our friend Woodward may get tired of building just frame houses, and Mason's life may lose a certain zest because he does nothing but produce brick ones. On a more practical level, specialization often results in assembly-line production techniques. Workers may become quite skilled because they perform identical tasks over and over again, but they may also become bored if the work is personally unrewarding. Thus, strictly speaking, some of the gains associated with the expansion of physical output may result in worker dissatisfaction.

You may be thinking that economists consider nothing but material goods and ignore the importance of human beings. It may seem that they do not care if a worker hates a job because it is repetitive, unchallenging, and boring. Our initial approach to the topic of specialization is vulnerable to this charge. We stressed only physical production because it makes the principle simpler to communicate. However, specialization could be considered strictly from the viewpoint of utility, in which both output and job satisfaction are taken into account. After all, job satisfaction is an economic good.

An individual's opportunity cost of producing a good (or performing a service) includes the sacrifice of both physical production of other goods and any reduction (or improvement) in the desirability of working conditions. This approach does consider both material goods for one's satisfaction and the job satisfaction that is important to any human being. It does not, however, alter the basic principle. Individuals could still gain by producing and selling those things for which they have a comparatively low opportunity cost, including the job satisfaction component, while buying other things for which their opportunity cost is high. They would tend to specialize in the provision of those things they *both* do well and enjoy most. Persons with a strong aversion to monotonous work would be less likely to choose such work even though they might be skilled at it. Those with a smaller comparative advantage, measured strictly in terms of physical goods, might have a lower opportunity cost because they find the work more rewarding.

The introduction of working conditions and job preferences does not invalidate the basic concept. It is still true that maximum economic efficiency, in the utility sense, requires that each productive activity be performed by those persons with the lowest opportunity cost, including costs associated with their personal evaluation of other jobs.

Personal Motivation and Gaining from Specialization and Exchange

What motivates people to act? How does the purposeful decision-maker choose? Economic thinking implies that people will choose an option only if they expect the benefits (utility) of the choice to exceed its opportunity cost. Purposeful decision-makers will be motivated by the pursuit of personal gain. They will never knowingly choose an alternative for which they expect the opportunity cost to exceed the expected benefits. To do so would be to make a choice with the full awareness that it meant the sacrifice of another, preferred course of action. That simply would not make sense. To say that people are motivated by personal gain does not, of course, mean that they are inconsiderate of others. Other people's feelings will often affect the personal benefit received by a decision-maker.

When an individual's interests, aptitudes, abilities, and skills make it possible to gain by exchanging low opportunity cost goods for those things that he or she produces at a high opportunity cost, pursuit of the potential gain will motivate the individual to trade precisely in this manner. If free exchange is allowed, it will not be necessary for people to be assigned the "right" job or to be told that, comparatively speaking, they should trade A for B because they are good at producing A but not so good at producing B. In a market setting, individuals will voluntarily specialize because they will gain by doing so. Thus, when people simply follow their own interests, the goods (or resources) they sell will be produced primarily by means of skills with which they are heavily endowed. Similarly, decision-makers seeking personal gain will tend to buy those things that require skills they do not possess and let others do the productive activities they find unrewarding (relative to the payment for those services).

THREE ECONOMIZING DECISIONS FACING ALL NATIONS: WHAT, HOW, AND FOR WHOM?

We have outlined several basic concepts that are important if one is to understand the economizing problem. In this section we outline three general economizing questions that every economy, regardless of its structure, must answer.

1. What Will Be Produced? All of the goods that we desire cannot be produced. What goods should we produce and in what quantities? Should we produce more food and less clothing, more consumer durables and less clean air, more national defense and less leisure? Or should we use up some of our productive resources, producing more goods today even though it will mean fewer goods in the future? If our economy is operating efficiently (that is, on its production possibilities curve), the choice to produce more of one commodity will reduce our ability to produce others. Sometimes the impact may be more indirect. Production of some goods will not only require productive resources but may, as a by-product, reduce the actual amount of other goods available. For example, production of warmer houses and more automobile travel may, as a by-product, increase air pollution, and thus reduce the availability of clean air (another desired good). Use of natural resources (water, minerals, trees, etc.) to produce some goods may simultaneously reduce the quality of our environment. Every economy must answer these and similar questions about what should be produced.

2. How Will Goods Be Produced? Usually, different combinations of productive resources can be utilized to produce a good. Education could be produced with less labor by the use of more television lectures, recording devices, and books. Wheat could be raised with less land and more fertilizer. Chairs could be constructed with more labor and fewer machines. What combinations of the alternative productive resources will be used to produce the goods of an economy?

The decision to produce does not accomplish the task. Resources must be organized and people motivated. How can the resources of an economy be transformed into the final output of goods and services? Economies may differ as to the into the final output of goods and services? Economies may differ as to the combination of economic incentives, threats of force, and types of competitive behavior that are permissible, but all still face the problem of how their limited resources can be utilized to produce goods.

3. For Whom Will Goods Be Produced? Who will actually consume the products available? This economic question is often referred to as the distribution problem. Property rights for resources, including labor skills, might be established and resource owners permitted to sell their services to the highest bidder. Goods would then be allocated to those who could meet the bids. Prices and private ownership would be the determining factors of distribution. Alternatively, goods might be split on a strict per capita basis, with each person getting an equal share of the pie. Or they might be divided according to the relative political influences of citizens, with larger shares going to persons who are more persuasive and skillful than others at organizing and obtaining political power. They could be distributed according to need, with a dictator or an all-powerful, democratically elected legislature deciding the various "needs" of the citizens.

The Three Decisions Are Interrelated

One thing is obvious. These three questions are highly interrelated. How goods are distributed will exert considerable influence on the "voluntary" availability of productive resources, including human resources. The choice of what to produce will influence how and what resources are used. In reality, these three basic economic questions must be resolved simultaneously, but this does not alter the fact that all economies, whatever their other differences, must somehow answer them.

TWO METHODS OF MAKING DECISIONS—THE MARKET AND GOVERNMENT PLANNING

Market Mechanism: A method of organization that allows unregulated prices and the decentralized decisions of private-property owners to resolve the basic economic problems of consumption, production, and distribution.

Collective Decision-Making: The method of organization that relies on public sector decision-making (that is, voting, political bargaining, lobbying, etc.). It can be used to resolve the basic economic problems of an economy.

In general, there are two methods of organizing economic activity—a **market mechanism** and **collective decision-making.** There is, of course, some overlap between these two classifications and some variation within them. The rules and guidelines for a market economy will be established at the outset by the public decision-making process. The accepted forms of competition may vary among market economies. There may be some differences in how the rights and responsibilities of property owners are defined. Once the rules of the game are established, however, a market economy will rely on the unregulated pricing mechanism to direct the decisions of consumers, producers, and owners of productive resources. The government will not prevent a seller from using price reductions and quality improvements as a method of competing with other sellers. Nor will the government prevent a buyer from using price as a method of bidding a product or productive resource away from another potential buyer. Legal restraints (for example, government licensing) will not be utilized to limit potential buyers or sellers from producing, selling, or buying in the marketplace. The free interplay and bargaining between buyers and sellers will establish the conditions of trade and answer the three basic economic questions. The government's role is secondary—only that of the referee and rule-maker.

As an alternative to market organization, economic decisions can be made by collective decision-making—by elected representatives, direct referendum, or some other governmental mechanism (for example, military force). Central planning and political factors replace market forces. The decision to expand or contract the output of education, medical services, automobiles, electricity, steel, consumer durables, and thousands of other commodities is made by government officials and planning boards. This is not to say that the preferences of individuals are of no importance. If the government officials and central

MYTHS OF ECONOMICS

"In exchange, when someone gains, someone else must lose. Trading is a zero-sum game."

People tend to think of making, building, and creating things as productive activities. Agriculture and manufacturing are like this. They create something genuinely new, something that was not there before. Trade, however, is only the exchange of one thing for another. Nothing is created. Therefore, it must be a zero-sum game in which one person's gain is necesarily a loss to another. So goes a popular myth.

Voluntary exchange is productive for three reasons. First, it channels goods and services to those who value them most. People have fallen into the habit of thinking of material things as wealth, but material things are not wealth until they are in the hands of someone who values them. A highly technical mathematics book is not wealth to a longshoreman with a sixth-grade education. It becomes wealth only after it is in the hands of a mathematician. A master painting may be wealth to the art connoisseur but of little value to a cowboy. Wealth is created by the act of channeling goods to persons who value them highly.

When a good is exchanged for money, it is being channeled toward the person who values it most. When you pay $300 per month for the use of an apartment, rented from the owner for that amount, a good is channeled toward the party who values it most. You value the apartment more than the $300 or you would not have agreed to the transaction. Thus, you gain. No one values it more highly or they would bid more than $300 for it. The apartment owner places greater value on the $300 than on the use of the apartment, otherwise he or she would not rent to you. The owner, too, gains. The trade makes both you and your landlord better off.

Second, exchange can be advantageous to trading partners because it permits each to specialize in areas in which they have a comparative advantage. For example, exchange permits a skilled carpenter to concentrate on building house frames while contracting for electrical and plumbing services from others who have comparative advantages in those areas. Similarly, trade permits a country such as Canada to specialize in the production of wheat, while Brazil specializes in coffee. Such specialization enlarges joint output and permits both countries to gain from the exchange of Canadian wheat for Brazilian coffee.

Third, voluntary exchange makes it possible for individuals to produce more goods through cooperative effort. In the absence of exchange, productive activity would be limited to the individual household. Self-provision and small-scale production would be the rule. Voluntary exchange permits us to realize gains derived from the division of labor and the adoption of large-scale production methods. Production can be broken down into a series of specific operations. This procedure often leads to a more efficient application of both labor and machinery. Without voluntary exchanges, these gains would be lost.

The motivating force behind exchange is the pursuit of personal gain. Unless *both* parties expect to gain from an exchange, it will not take place. Mutual gain forms the foundation for voluntary exchange. Trade is a positive-sum game.

planners are influenced by the democratic process, they have to consider how their actions will influence their election prospects. If they do not, like the firm that produces a product that consumers do not want, their tenure of service is likely to be a short one.

In most economies, including that of the United States, a large number of decisions are made through both the decentralized pricing system and public sector decision-making. Both exert considerable influence on how we solve fundamental economic problems. Although the two arrangements are different, in each case the choices of individuals acting as decision-makers are important. Economics is about how people make decisions; the tools of economics can be applied to both market and public sector action. Constraints on the individual and incentives to pursue various types of activities will differ according to whether decisions are made in the public sector or in the marketplace. But people are people. Changes in personal costs and benefits will still influence their choices. In turn, the acts of political participants—voters, lobbyists, and politicians—will influence public policy and its economic consequences.

David Ricardo (1772–1823) and the Early Followers of Smith

Following the pioneering work of Adam Smith, other economists developed economic principles and applied them to the social problems of their day. The contributions of three Englishmen, David Ricardo, Thomas Malthus, and John Stuart Mill, were particularly important.

By 1800, the Industrial Revolution had begun to transform the Western world. Most economists of that time believed that gains from specialization, expansion in trade among nations, and industrialization would significantly improve people's living standards. Thomas Malthus was an exception.

Malthus did not see how humankind could escape the "population trap." If wages temporarily rose above the subsistence level, fewer people would die of starvation and families would have more children. Thus, economic progress would trigger a population explosion, leading merely to an increase in the number of people seeking to consume the exist-ing supply of food. An expansion in the production of goods would increasingly necessitate the use of land that was less fertile. Thus, Malthus perceived that food production would, at best, increase arithmetically (1,2,3, 4,5, and so on), whereas the population, if unchecked by starvation, would expand geometrically (1,2,4,8, 16, and so on).

Because Malthus used economic analysis to arrive at his gloomy prediction, economics soon earned the title "the dismal science," a label that persists to this day. Although the view of Malthus may have some applicability to less developed countries, the experience of the industrial world during the last 200 years is clearly in conflict with the heart of Malthusian analysis. Malthus failed to perceive the explosion of production that could be generated by technological improvements and capital formation.

David Ricardo is generally recognized as the greatest of the early post-Smith economists. The work of Ricardo lacked the social insight and breadth of knowledge that characterized Smith's writings, but his approach was more systematic. The rigorous logic of his presentation was a major reason for the enormous influence that he had on the direction of economics.

A successful stockbroker prior to his becoming an economist, Ricardo literally invented economic model building. His major work, *The Principles of Political Economy and Taxation* (1817), was published just six years before his untimely death.

Ricardo is best known for his rigorous proof of the law of comparative advantage. Using a simple numerical example, he demonstrated that it would benefit England to specialize in cloth even if Portugal could produce both cloth and wine more cheaply, provided that England was the *relative* low-cost producer of cloth. Ricardo went on to illustrate that if Portugal specialized in wine, for which it possessed an even greater cost advantage than for cloth, it, too, would be better off. Thus, both countries would gain if they specialized in the production of those products for which they were the *relative* low-cost producers. Ricardo's ideas comprised the heart of the nineteenth-century free-trade doctrine.

John Stuart Mill was the leading economist of the post-Ricardo era. Mill's father was James Mill, an economist and intimate friend of Ricardo. At the age of 13, John Stuart was introduced to the writings of Smith, Ricardo, and Malthus. Mill's major contribution as an economist was his ability to organize and synthesize the analyses of earlier writers. His *Principles of Political Economy* (1848) was a masterful summation of economic analysis as it had developed from Smith through Malthus and Ricardo. The two-volume work served as the standard economics text at English universities for several decades.

Much has changed since the days of these early economists. Economics is now more systematic, more mathematical, and, some would say, more rigorous. Nonetheless, it is still based on the postulate that incentives matter (Smith's self-interest). Economic gain stemming from the division of labor and specialization in production is no less important now than it was when Smith articulated the idea 200 years ago. The law of comparative advantage is as significant today as it was when Ricardo developed it in 1817. Modern economics owes an enormous debt to these pioneers in the field.

LOOKING AHEAD   The following chapter presents an overview of the market sector. Chapter 4 focuses on how the public sector, the democratic collective decision-making process, functions. It is not enough merely to study how the pricing system works.

If we are to understand fully the forces that exert a powerful influence on the allocation of economic resources in a country such as the United States, we must apply the tools of economics to both market and public sector choices.

We think that this approach is important, fruitful, and exciting. How does the market sector really work? What does economics say about what activities should be handled by government? What types of economic policies are politically attractive to democratically elected officials? Is sound economic policy sometimes in conflict with good politics? We will tackle all these questions.

CHAPTER LEARNING OBJECTIVES

1 Because of scarcity, when an individual chooses to do, to make, or to buy something, the individual must simultaneously give up something else that might otherwise have been chosen. The highest valued activity sacrificed is the opportunity cost of the choice.

2 A production possibilities curve reveals the maximum combination of any two products that can be produced with a fixed quantity of resources, assuming that the level of technology is constant. When an individual or an economy is operating at maximum efficiency, the combination of output chosen will be on the production possibilities curve. In such cases, greater production of one good will necessitate a reduction in the output of other goods.

3 The production possibilities curve of an economy can be shifted outward by (a) current investment that expands the future resource base of the economy, (b) technological advancement, and (c) the foregoing of leisure and an increase in work effort. The last factor indicates that the production possibilities constraint is not strictly fixed, even during the current time period. It is partly a matter of preferences.

4 Production can often be expanded through division of labor and cooperative effort among individuals. With division of labor, production of a commodity can be broken down into a series of specific tasks. Specialization and division of labor often lead to an expansion in output per worker because they (a) permit productive tasks to be undertaken by the individuals who can accomplish those tasks most efficiently, (b) lead to improvement in worker efficiency as specific tasks are performed numerous times, and (c) facilitate the efficient application of machinery and advanced technology to the production process.

5 Joint output of individuals, regions, or nations will be maximized when goods are exchanged between parties in accordance with the law of comparative advantage. This law states that parties will specialize in the production of goods for which they are low opportunity cost producers and exchange these for goods for which they are high opportunity cost producers. Pursuit of personal gain will motivate people to specialize in those things that they do best (that is, for which they are low opportunity cost producers) and sell their products or services for goods for which they are high opportunity cost producers.

6 Exchange is productive. Voluntary exchange (a) channels goods into the hands of people who value them most, (b) permits individuals to specialize in the areas of their greatest comparative advantage, and (c) creates the opportunity for greater productive efficiency and increased output through specialization, division of labor, and large-scale production techniques. Trade is a positive-sum game that improves the economic well-being of each voluntary participant.

7 Every economy must answer three basic questions: (a) What will be produced? (b) How will goods be produced? (c) How will the goods be distributed? These three questions are highly interrelated.

8 There are two basic methods of making economic decisions: the market mechanism and public sector decision-making. The decisions of individuals will influence the result in both cases. The tools of economics are general. They are applicable to choices that influence both market and public sector decisions.

THE ECONOMIC WAY OF THINKING—DISCUSSION QUESTIONS

1 "The principle of comparative advantage gives individuals an incentive to specialize in those things that they do best." Explain in your own words why this is true.

2 Economists often argue that wage rates reflect productivity. Yet the wages of house-painters have increased nearly as rapidly as the national average, even though these workers use approximately the same methods that were applied 50 years ago. Can you explain why the wages of painters have risen substantially even though their productivity has changed little?

3 It takes one hour to travel from New York City to Washington, D.C., by air but five hours by bus. If the airfare is $55 and the bus fare $35, which would be cheaper for someone whose opportunity cost of travel time is $3 per hour? for someone whose opportunity cost is $5 per hour? $7 per hour?

4 Explain why the percentage of college-educated women employed outside of the home exceeds the percentage of women with eight years of schooling who are engaged in outside employment.

5 Explain why parking lots in downtown areas of large cities often have several decks, whereas many of equal size in suburban areas usually cover only the ground level.

6 Is exchange productive? If so, what does it produce? Who gains when goods are voluntarily exchanged?

someone whose opportunity cost of travel time is $3 per hour? for someone whose opportunity cost is $5 per hour? $7 per hour?

7 (a) Do you think that your work effort is influenced by whether or not there is a close link between personal output and personal compensation (reward)? Explain.

(b) Suppose that the grades in your class were going to be determined by a random draw at the end of the course. How would this influence your study habits?

(c) How would your study habits be influenced if everyone in the class were going to be given an A grade? if grades were based entirely on examinations composed of the multiple-choice questions in the *Coursebook?*

(d) Do you think that the total output of goods in the United States is affected by the close link between productive contribution and individual reward? Why or why not?

3

SUPPLY, DEMAND, AND THE MARKET PROCESS

I am convinced that if it [the market system] were the result of deliberate human design, and if the people guided by the price changes understood that their decisions have significance far beyond their immediate aim, this mechanism would have been acclaimed as one of the greatest triumphs of the human mind.[1]
Nobel laureate Friedrich Hayek

Consider the awesome task of coordinating the economic activity of the United States, a nation with 80,000,000 household-consumer units. The labor force is composed of approximately 105,000,000 workers, each possessing various skills and job preferences. There are more than 15,000,000 business firms, which currently produce a vast array of products ranging from hairpins to jumbo jets.

How can the actions of these economic participants be coordinated in a sensible manner? How do producers know how much of each good to produce? What keeps them from producing too many ballpoint pens and too few bicycles with reflector lights? Who directs each labor force participant to the job that best fits his or her skills and preferences? How can we be sure that the business firms will choose the correct production methods? In this chapter we analyze how a market-directed pricing system answers these questions.

In a market economy, no individual or planning board tells the participants what to do. Markets are free, some would say competitive, in the sense that there are no legal restrictions limiting the entry of either buyers or sellers. The economic role of government is limited to defining property rights, enforcing contracts, protecting people from fraud, and similar activities that establish the rules of the game. Although centralized planning is absent, it does not follow that the participants are without direction. As we shall see, the decentralized decision-making of market participants provides direction and leads to economic order.

In the real world, even economies that are strongly market oriented, such as ours in the United States, use a combination of market and public sector answers to the basic economic questions. In all economies, there is a mixture of market sector and government allocation. Nevertheless, it is still quite useful to understand how the free-market pricing system functions, how it motivates people, and how it allocates goods and resources.

---

[1]Friedrich Hayek, "The Use of Knowledge in Society," *American Economic Review* 35, (September, 1945), pp. 519–530.

SCARCITY NECESSITATES RATIONING

Rationing: An allocation of a limited supply of a good or resource to users who would like to have more of it. Various criteria, including charging a price, can be utilized to allocate the limited supply. When price performs the rationing function, the good or resource is allocated to those willing to give up the most "other things" in order to obtain ownership rights.

When a good (or resource) is scarce, some criterion must be set up for deciding who will receive the good (or resource) and who will do without it. Scarcity makes **rationing** a necessity.

There are several possible criteria that could be used for rationing a limited amount of a good among citizens who would like to have more of it. If the criterion were First come, first served, goods would be allocated to those who were fastest at getting in line or to those who were most willing to wait in line. If beauty were used, goods would be allocated to those who were thought to be most beautiful. The political process might be utilized, and goods would be allocated on the basis of ability to manipulate the political process to personal advantage. One thing is certain: Scarcity requires that some method be established to decide who gets the limited amount of available goods and resources.

Competition Is the Result of Rationing

Competition is not unique to a market system. Rather, it is a natural outgrowth of scarcity and the desire of human beings to improve their conditions. Competition exists in both capitalist and socialist societies. It exists both when goods are allocated by price and when they are allocated by other means—collective decision-making, for example.

Certainly the rationing criterion will influence the competitive techniques utilized. When the rationing criterion is price, individuals will engage in income-generating activities that enhance their ability to pay the price. The market system encourages individuals to provide services to others in exchange for income. In turn, the income will permit them to procure more of the scarce goods.

A different rationing criterion will encourage other types of behavior. When the appearance of sincerity, broad knowledge, fairness, good judgment, and a positive TV image are important, as they are in the rationing of political positions, people will dedicate resources to the projection of these qualities. However, competition cannot be eliminated by changing the way in which it manifests itself or the form in which it is displayed. No society has been able to eliminate competition, because no society has been able to eliminate the necessity of rationing. When people who want more scarce goods seek to meet the criteria established to ration those goods, competition occurs.

The market is one method of rationing and allocating scarce goods and resources. Let us investigate how it works.

CONSUMER CHOICE AND THE LAW OF DEMAND

The income of consumers is almost always substantially less than their wants. The authors have desires for backyard tennis courts, European vacations, and summer homes in the mountains, but we have not purchased any of them. Why? Because given the restriction of limited income, our desire for other goods is even more urgent. Our incomes would allow us to purchase backyard tennis courts only if we spent less on food, trips to the beach, housing, books, clothes, and other forms of recreation. We have a choice and have chosen to forego the courts instead of the other goods.

How do consumers decide which things to buy and which things to forego? Sensibly, they want to get the most satisfaction from the spending of their money. Economizing behavior suggests that rational consumers will spend their limited incomes on the things from which they expect the most satisfaction. Given personal tastes, they will choose the best alternatives that their limited incomes will permit. Prices influence consumer decisions. An increase in the price of a good will increase a consumer's opportunity cost of consuming it. More of other things must be given up if the consumer chooses the higher-priced commodity.

According to the basic postulate of economics, an increase in the cost of an alternative will reduce the likelihood that it will be chosen. This basic postulate implies that higher prices will discourage consumption. Lower prices will reduce the cost of choosing a good, stimulating consumption of it. This inverse relationship between the price of a good and the amount of it that consumers choose to buy is called the **law of demand.**

Law of Demand: A principle which states that there is an inverse relationship between the price of a good and the amount of it buyers are willing to purchase.

The availability of substitutes—goods that perform similar functions—helps to explain the logic of the law of demand. No single good is absolutely essential. Margarine can be substituted for butter. Wood, aluminum, bricks, and glass can be substituted for steel. Insulation, car pools, slower driving, bicycling, and small cars are substitute products that allow households to reduce their gasoline consumption. As the price (and therefore the consumers' opportunity cost) of a good increases, people have a greater incentive to turn to substitute products and economize on their use of the more expensive good. Prices really do matter.

Exhibit 1 is a graphic presentation of the law of demand. In constructing a demand curve, economists measure price on the vertical or y axis and amount demanded on the horizontal or x axis. The demand curve will slope

EXHIBIT 1 The law of demand

As the price of beef rose during 1977–1979, consumers substituted chicken, fish, and other food products for beef. The consumption level of beef (and other products) is inversely related to its price.

The numerical data used in this example are from *Statistical Abstract of the United States—1980* (Washington D.C.: U.S. Government Printing Office), pp. 131, 705.

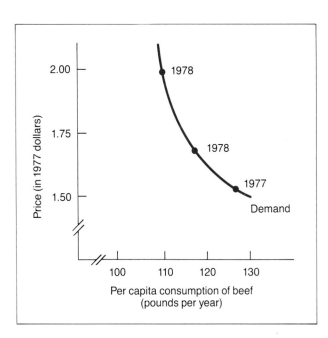

downward to the right, indicating that the amount demanded of a good, beef in this example, will increase as price declines. During 1977–1979, there was a sharp increase in the price of beef. Consumers responded, no doubt unhappily, by using less of it. In 1977, when the average price of beef was $1.48 per pound, the per capita annual beef consumption was 125.9 pounds. As the beef price rose to $1.69 per pound in 1978, annual consumption declined to 120.1 pounds. By 1979, the average price of beef had risen to $1.88 per pound; the annual consumption of beef declined still more, to 107.6 pounds, as consumers substituted chicken, fish, and other products for the more expensive beef.[2]

Some commodities may be much more responsive to a change in price than others. Consider a good for which there are several good substitutes—a Florida vacation, for example. If the price of a Florida vacation increases, perhaps because of higher gasoline prices, consumers will substitute more movies, local camping trips, baseball games, TV programs, and other recreational activities for the vacation. As illustrated by Exhibit 2, since good substitutes are available, an increase in the price of Florida vacations will cause a sharp reduction in quantity demanded. Economists say that demand for Florida vacations is *elastic*,[3] the term used to indicate that quantity demanded is quite responsive to a change in price.

Other goods may be much less responsive to a change in price. Suppose the price of physician services were to rise 15 percent, as indicated by Exhibit 2. What impact would this price increase have on the quantity demanded? The higher prices would cause some people to prescribe their own medications for colds, flu, and minor illnesses. Others might turn to painkillers, magic potions, and faith healers for even major medical problems. Most consumers, however, would consider these to be poor substitutes for the services of a physician. Thus, higher medical prices would cause a relatively small reduction in the quantity

EXHIBIT 2 Responsiveness of demand to a price change

A 15 percent increase in the price of Florida vacations (D_1) caused the quantity demanded to decline from Q_0 to Q_1, a 50 percent reduction. In contrast, a 15 percent increase in the price of physician services (D_2) resulted in only a 5 percent reduction in quantity demanded (from Q_0 to Q_2). Economists would say that the demand for Florida vacations is elastic, but the demand for physician services is inelastic.

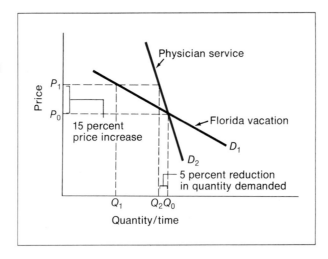

---

[2]The per capita annual consumption of both poultry and fish products rose during 1977–1979.

[3]The mathematical formula for price elasticity of demand is (a) percent change in quantity demanded divided by (b) percent change in price. If the absolute value of this expression exceeds 1, demand is elastic. If it is less than 1, demand is inelastic. For those in a microeconomics course, this is explained in more detail in the chapter on demand and consumer choice.

demanded. The demand for medical service is thus *inelastic,* the term used to indicate that the amount demanded is *relatively* unresponsive to a change in price.

However, despite differences in the degree of responsiveness, the fundamental law of demand holds for all goods. A price increase will induce consumers to turn to substitutes, leading to a reduction in the amount purchased. A price reduction will make a commodity relatively cheaper, inducing consumers to purchase more of it as they substitute it for other goods.

The demand schedule is not something that can be observed directly by decision-makers of a business firm or planning agency. Nonetheless, when prices are used to ration goods, consumer reactions to each price communicate information about the preferences of consumers—how they value alternative commodities. The height of the unseen demand curve indicates the maximum price that consumers are willing to pay for *an additional unit* of the product. If consumers value *additional units* of a product highly, they will be willing to pay a large amount (a high price) for it. Alternatively, if their valuation of *additional units* of the good is low, they will be willing to pay only a small amount for it.

PRODUCER CHOICE AND THE LAW OF SUPPLY

How does the market process determine the amount of each good that will be produced? We cannot answer this question unless we understand the factors that influence the choices of those who supply goods. Producers of goods and services, often utilizing the business firm,

1. organize productive inputs, such as labor, land, natural resources, and intermediate goods,
2. transform and combine these factors of production into goods desired by households, and
3. sell the final products to consumers for a price.

Profit: An excess of sales revenue relative to the cost of production. The cost component includes the opportunity cost of all resources, *including those owned by the firm.* Therefore, profit accrues only when the value of the good produced is greater than the sum of the values of the individual resources utilized.

Production involves the conversion of resources to commodities and services. Producers will have to pay the owners of scarce resources a price that is at least equal to what the resources could earn elsewhere. Stated another way, each resource employed will have to be bid away from all alternative uses; it (or its owner) will have to be paid its opportunity cost. The sum of the amount paid by the producer to each of the productive resources, including the cost of production coordination and management, will equal the product's opportunity cost.

All economic participants have a strong incentive to undertake activities that generate profit. **Profit** is a residual "income reward" granted to decision-makers who carry out a productive activity that increases the value of the resources. If an activity is to be profitable, the revenue derived from the sale of the product must exceed the cost of employing the resources that have been converted to make the product. Profitability indicates that consumers value the product more than any other which could be produced from the resources. Sometimes decision-makers use resources unwisely. They convert resources to a product that consumers value less than the opportunity cost of the resources utilized. **Losses** result, since the sales revenue derived from the project is insufficient to pay for the employment cost of the resources.

Loss: Deficit of sales revenue relative to the cost of production, once all the resources utilized have received their opportunity cost. Losses are a penalty imposed on those who misuse resources. Losses occur only when the value of the good produced is less than the sum of the values of the individual resources utilized.

Entrepreneur: A profit-seeking decision-maker who decides which projects to undertake and how they should be undertaken. If successful, an entrepreneur's actions will increase the value of resources.

Persons who undertake production organization, those who decide what to produce and how to produce it, are called **entrepreneurs.**[4] The business of the entrepreneur is to figure out which projects will, in fact, be profitable. Since the profitability of a project will be affected by the price consumers are willing to pay for a product, the price of resources required to produce it, and the cost of alternative production processes, successful entrepreneurs must be either knowledgeable in each of these areas or obtain the advice of others who have such knowledge.

Prosperous entrepreneurs must convert and rearrange resources in a manner that will increase their value. An individual who purchases 100 acres of raw land, puts in streets and a sewage disposal system, divides the plot into 1-acre lots, and sells them for 50 percent more than the opportunity cost of all resources used is clearly an entrepreneur. This entrepreneur "profits" because the value of the resources has been increased. Sometimes entrepreneurial activity is less complex. For example, a 15-year-old who purchases a power mower and sells lawn service to the neighbors is also an entrepreneur, seeking to profit by increasing the value of resources. In a market economy, profit is the reward to the entrepreneur who undertakes the project. It is also a signal to other entrepreneurs to enter a highly productive market, competing for the original entrepreneur's profit.

How will producer-entrepreneurs respond to a change in product price? Other things constant, a higher price will increase the producer's incentive to supply the good. New entrepreneurs, seeking personal gain, will enter the market and begin supplying the product. Established producers will expand the scale of their operation, leading to an additional expansion in output. Higher prices will induce producers to supply a greater amount. The direct relationship between the price of a product and the amount of it that will be supplied is termed the **law of supply.**

Law of Supply: A principle which states that there will be a direct relationship between the price of a good and the amount of it offered for sale.

Exhibit 3 presents a graphic picture of this law. The supply curve summarizes information about production conditions. Unless the profit-seeking producer receives a price that is at least equal to the opportunity cost of the resources employed, the producer will not *continue* to supply the good. The height of the supply curve indicates both (a) the minimum price necessary to induce producers to supply a specific quantity and (b) the valuation of the resources utilized in the production of the marginal unit of the good. This minimum supply price will be high (low) if the opportunity cost of supplying the marginal unit is high (low).

MARKETS AND THE COORDINATION OF SUPPLY AND DEMAND

Consumer-buyers and producer-sellers make decisions independent of each other, but markets coordinate their choices and direct their actions. To the

---

[4]This French-origin word literally means "one who undertakes." The entrepreneur is the person who is ultimately responsible. Of course, this responsibility may be shared with others (partners or stockholders, for example) or partially delegated to technical experts. Nonetheless, the success or failure of the entrepreneur is dependent on the outcome of the choices that he or she makes.

Market: An abstract concept which encompasses the trading arrangements of buyers and sellers that underlie the forces of supply and demand.

Equilibrium: A state of balance between conflicting forces, such as supply and demand.

Short-Run Market Equilibrium

Short Run: A time period of insufficient length to permit decision-makers to adjust fully to a change in market conditions. For example, in the short run, producers will have time to increase output by utilizing more labor and raw materials, but they will not have time to expand the size of their plants or install additional heavy equipment.

economist a market is not a physical location. A **market** is an abstract concept that encompasses the forces generated by the buying and selling decisions of economic participants. A market may be quite narrow (for example, the market for razor blades). Alternatively, it is sometimes useful to aggregate diverse goods into a single market, such as the market for "consumer goods." There is also a broad range of sophistication among markets. The New York Stock Exchange is a highly computerized market in which buyers and sellers who never formally meet exchange corporate ownership shares worth millions of dollars each weekday. In contrast, the neighborhood market for lawn-mowing services may be highly informal, since it brings together buyers and sellers primarily by word of mouth.

Equilibrium is a state in which conflicting forces are in perfect balance. When there is a balance—an equilibrium—the tendency for change is absent. Before a market equilibrium can be attained, the decisions of consumers and producers must be brought into harmony with one another.

The great English economist Alfred Marshall pioneered the development of supply and demand analysis. From the beginning, Marshall recognized that time plays a role in the market process. Marshall introduced the concept of the **short-run,** a time period of such short duration that decision-makers do not have time to *adjust fully* to a change in market conditions. During the short run, producers are able to alter the amount of a good supplied only by utilizing more (or less) labor and raw materials with their *existing* plant and heavy equipment. In the short run, there is insufficient time to build a new plant or obtain new "made-to-order" heavy equipment for the producer's current facility.

As Exhibit 1 illustrates, the amount of a good demanded by consumers will be inversely related to its price. On the other hand, a higher price will

EXHIBIT 3   The supply curve

As the price of a product increases, *other things constant,* producers will increase the amount of product supplied.

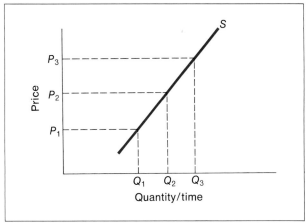

induce producers to utilize their existing facilities more intensively in the short run. As Exhibit 3 depicts, the amount of a good supplied will be directly related to its market price.

The market price of a commodity will tend to bring these two conflicting forces, supply and demand, into balance. This means that unless the quantity supplied by producers is already precisely equal to the quantity demanded by consumers, there will be a tendency for the market price to change until a balance is reached.

Exhibit 4 illustrates both supply and demand curves in the short run for a hypothetical commodity—smoos. At a high price, $12 for example, smoo producers will plan to supply 600 units per month, whereas consumers will choose to purchase only 450. An excess supply of 150 units will result. The inventories of smoo producers will rise. Rather than continue to accumulate undesired inventories, some smoo producers will cut their price. This reduction in price will make smoo production less attractive to producers. Some of the marginal producers will go out of business, and other firms will reduce their current output. Simultaneously, the lower price will induce consumers to purchase more smoos. Eventually, after the smoo price has declined to $10, the quantity supplied by producers and the quantity demanded by consumers will be brought into balance at 550 units per month. At this price ($10), the production plans of producers will be in harmony with the purchasing plans of consumers.

What will happen if the price of smoos is low—$8 for example? The amount demanded by consumers (650 units) will exceed the amount supplied by producers (500 units). An excess demand of 150 units will be present. Some consumers who would like to purchase smoos at $8 per unit will be unable to do so because of the inadequate supply. Rather than do without the good, some will be willing to pay a higher price. Recognizing this fact, producers will raise their price. As the price increases to $10, producers will expand their output and consumers will cut down on their consumption. At the $10 price, short-run equilibrium will be restored.

Long-Run Market Equilibrium

Long Run: A time period of sufficient length to enable decision-makers to adjust fully to a market change. For example, in the long run, producers will have time to alter their utilization of all productive factors, including the heavy equipment and physical structure of their plants.

In the **long run,** decision-makers will have time to adjust fully to a change in market conditions. With the passage of time, producers will be able to alter their output; not only will they use their current plant more intensively, but given sufficient time, they will be able to change the size of their production facility. The long run is a time period of sufficient duration to permit producers to expand the size of their capital stock (the physical structure and heavy equipment of their plant).

A balance between amount supplied and amount demanded is the only prerequisite for market equilibrium in the short run. However, if the current market price is going to persist in the future, an additional condition must be present: The opportunity cost of producing the product must also be equal to the market price.

If the market price of a good is greater than the opportunity cost of producing it, suppliers will gain from an expansion in production. Profit-seeking entrepreneurs will be attracted to the industry, and output (supply) will increase until a lower market price eliminates profits.[5] In contrast, if the market price is

EXHIBIT 4   Supply and demand

The table below indicates the supply and demand conditions for smoos. These conditions are also illustrated by the graph on the right. When the price exceeds $10, an excess supply is present, which places downward pressure on price. In contrast, when the price is less than $10, an excess demand results, an excess demand results, which causes the price to rise. Thus, the market price will tend toward $10, at which point supply and demand will be in balance.

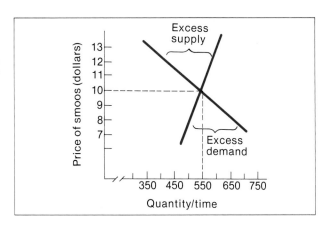

Price of Smoos (Dollars)	Quantity Supplied (Per Month)	Quantity Demanded (Per Month)	Condition in the Market	Direction of Pressure on Price
13	625	400	Excess supply	Downward
12	600	450	Excess supply	Downward
11	575	500	Excess supply	Downward
10	550	550	Balance	Equilibrium
9	525	600	Excess demand	Upward
8	500	650	Excess demand	Upward
7	475	700	Excess demand	Upward

less than the opportunity cost of a good's production, suppliers will lose money if they continue to produce the good. The losses will drive producers from the market. Supply will decline, pushing prices upward until the losses are eliminated.

SHIFTS IN DEMAND AND CHANGES IN QUANTITY DEMANDED

A demand curve isolates the impact that price has on the amount of a product purchased. Of course, factors other than price—for example, consumer income, tastes, prices of related goods, and expectations as to the future price of a product—also influence the decisions of consumers. If any one of these factors change, the entire demand curve shifts. Economists refer to such shifts in the demand curve as a *change in demand*.

[5]Bear in mind that economists utilize the opportunity cost concept for *all* factors of production, including those owned by the producers. Therefore, the owners are receiving a return equal to the opportunity cost of their investment capital even when profits are zero. Thus, zero profits mean that the capitalist owners are being paid precisely their opportunity cost, precisely what they could earn if their resources were employed in the highest valued alternative that must be foregone as the result of current use. Far from indicating that a firm is about to go out of business, zero economic profits imply that each factor of production, including the capital owned by the firm and the managerial skills of the owner-entrepreneur, is earning the market rate of return.

Let us take a closer look at some of the factors that would cause the demand for a product to change. Expansion in income makes it possible for consumers to purchase more goods. They usually respond by increasing their spending on a wide cross section of products. Changes in prices of closely related products also influence the choices of consumers. If the price of butter were to fall, many consumers would substitute it for margarine. The demand for margarine would decline (shift to the left) as a result. Our expectations about the future price of a product also influence our current decisions. For example, if you think that the price of automobiles is going to rise by 20 percent next month, this will increase your incentive to buy now, before the price rises. In contrast, if you think that the price of a product is going to decline, you will demand less *now,* as you attempt to extend your purchasing decision into the future, when prices are expected to be lower.

Failure to distinguish between a change in *demand* and a change in *quantity demanded* is one of the most common mistakes of introductory economics students.[6] A change in demand is a shift in the entire demand curve. A change in quantity demanded is a movement along the same demand curve.

Exhibit 5 clearly demonstrates the difference between the two. The demand curve D_1 indicates the initial demand (the entire curve) for doorknobs. At a price of $3, consumers would purchase Q_1. If the price declined to $1, there would be an increase in quantity demanded from Q_1 to Q_3. Arrow *A* indicates the change in *quantity demanded*—a movement along demand curve D_1. Now suppose that there were a 20 percent increase in income, causing a housing boom. The *demand* for doorknobs would increase from D_1 to D_2. As indicated by the *B* arrows, the entire demand curve would shift. At the higher income level, consumers would be willing to purchase more doorknobs at $3, at $2, at $1, and at other prices than was previously true. The increase in income leads to an increase in *demand*—a shift in the entire curve.

EXHIBIT 5 The difference between a change in demand and a change in quantity demanded

Arrow *A* indicates a change in *quantity demanded,* a movement along the demand curve D_1 in response to a change in the price of doorknobs. The *B* arrows illustrate a change in *demand,* a shift of the entire curve.

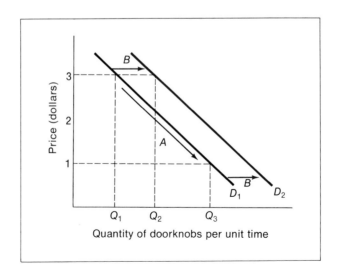

---

[6]Questions designed to test the ability of students to make this distinction are favorites of many economics instructors. A word to the wise should be sufficient.

How does the market react to change in demand? What happens to price and the amount supplied of a good if demand increases? Exhibit 6 will help to answer these questions while yielding insight into real-world past events. In the mid-1970s, there was a sharp rise in the price of gasoline. Many car owners attempted to economize on their use of the more expensive fuel by substituting smaller cars for their gas-guzzling, heavier models. There was an increase in *demand* for compact cars. The demand curve for such cars shifted to the right (from D_1 to D_2). At the original equilibrium price, $5000, there was an excess demand for compact cars. The excess demand caused the price of compact cars to rise. Market forces eventually brought about a new balance between supply and demand, establishing a new equilibrium price ($7000, for example) at a higher sales level. The pricing system responded to the increase in demand by granting (a) producers a stronger incentive to supply more compact cars and (b) consumers an incentive to search for other, cheaper substitute methods of conserving gasoline than purchasing compact cars.

SHIFTS IN SUPPLY

The decisions of producers lie behind the supply curve. Other things constant, the supply curve summarizes the willingness of producers to offer a product at alternative prices. However, price is not the only factor that producers consider. Costs are also important. Production requires the use of valuable resources—labor, machines, land, building, and raw materials. Use of these resources is costly to suppliers.

Remember that entrepreneurs will supply only those products for which they expect benefits (primarily sales revenues) to exceed their production cost. Factors that reduce the producer's opportunity cost of production—lower resource prices or a technological improvement, for example—would increase the incentive to supply a larger output. Cost reductions would cause supply to increase (shift to the right). In contrast, higher input prices and changes that

EXHIBIT 6   A shift in demand

As conditions change over time, the entire demand curve for a product may shift. Facing higher gasoline prices, many consumers decided to purchase compact cars in the mid-1970s. The *demand* for compact cars increased, causing both an increase in price and greater sales.

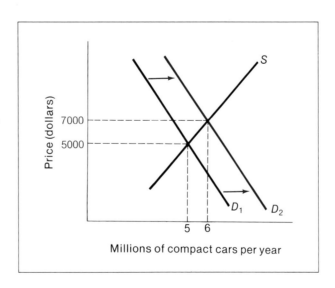

OUTSTANDING ECONOMIST
Alfred Marshall (1842—1924)

Early economists such as Adam Smith and David Ricardo thought that the price of a good was determined by its cost of production. Later, other economists, known as the "marginalists," emphasized the importance of demand and consumer preferences. They argued that goods commanded a high price, not because the goods were costly to produce, but because consumers valued *additional* units very highly. Alfred Marshall put these two ideas together in 1890 when he introduced the concept of supply and demand.

Marshall noted that "the greater the amount to be sold, the smaller must be the price at which it is offered in order that it may find

purchasers." Similarly, he argued that the supply of a commodity reflects the cost of the resources required to produce the good. In turn, the price of the commodity is determined by the balancing of these two forces—supply and demand.

In a famous analogy, Marshall likened the importance of supply and demand to the blades of a pair of scissors. When discussing which was most important, he wrote:

We might reasonably dispute whether it is the upper or the under blade of a pair of scissors that cuts a piece of paper, as whether value is governed by utility [consumer demand] or cost of production [supply].[7]

Although it is true that the blades of supply and demand operate jointly to determine price, Marshall recognized that the passage of time affects the relative importance of the supply and demand sides of the market in its response to change. In the short run, both supply and demand are highly significant, interacting to determine price. In contrast, in the long run, the supply side of a market is more important. As Marshall pointed out nearly a century ago, "the longer the time period, the more important will be the influence of cost of production" on price.

Alfred Marshall's father wanted him to enter the ministry, but young Marshall turned down a theological scholarship at Oxford in order

---

[7]Alfred Marshall, *Principles of Economics*, 8th ed. (London: Macmillan, 1920), p. 348.

to study mathematics at Cambridge. He completed his master's degree at Cambridge and stayed on to teach mathematics for nine years.

Marshall's serious study of economics began in 1867, about the time he began teaching mathematics. After reading John Stuart Mill's *Principles,* Marshall translated the economics of Mill into mathematical equations. By 1875, Marshall's economic doctrines were well developed, and in 1885, he was appointed to the Chair of Political Economy at Cambridge, a position he occupied for almost a quarter of a century.

In his *Principles of Economics* (1890), Marshall introduced many of the concepts and tools that form the core of modern microeconomics. He pioneered the development of partial equilibrium analysis, a procedure that permits one to focus on the *primary* effects of a specific change, separating them from secondary effects that are believed to be relatively small (and therefore unimportant). Elasticity, the short run, the long run, equilibrium—all of these concepts were initially developed by Marshall. More than any other English economist, Marshall turned economics into a science. His work laid the foundation for the empirical, hypothesis-testing methodology of modern economics. Marshall's influence was so great during the first 25 years of the twentieth century that this period is sometimes referred to as the "Age of Marshall." Clearly, his legacy is still accepted and honored today.

increase the producer's opportunity cost would cause supply to decline (shift to the left).

As with demand, it is important to note the difference between (a) a change in quantity supplied and (b) a change in supply. A change in quantity supplied is a movement along the same supply curve in response to a change in price. A change in supply indicates a shift in the entire supply curve.

How does the market react to a change in supply? Exhibit 7 illustrates the impact of a technological improvement that reduced the cost of producing electronic desk calculators in the 1970s. The reduction in cost made it more

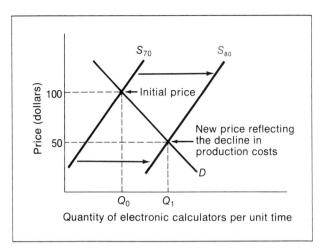

attractive for entrepreneurs to produce these calculators. Several new firms began production. Old firms also expanded their production, contributing to the expansion of supply. At the old $100 price, consumers would not buy the larger supply of electronic calculators. A reduction in price was necessary to bring the wishes of producers and consumers back into balance. By 1980 the price of electronic calculators had fallen to $50.

Sometimes the removal or erection of market restrictions will cause the supply curve to shift. During the 1973 Middle East crisis, Arab oil-producing countries used political action to stop the flow of crude oil to Western nations. Temporarily, the United States was completely cut off from this source of petroleum. The reduction in supply led to a shortage of gasoline *at the original* price.

A market economy eliminates a shortage by allowing the price to rise. The smaller supply is rationed to those willing to pay higher prices (see Exhibit 8). The rise in the price of gasoline induces consumers to use less of it. Sunday leisure trips become more expensive. Unnecessary travel is curtailed. A new, higher equilibrium price, P_2, results, and the quantity demanded (a movement along the demand curve) is reduced at the now higher price. At this new, higher equilibrium price, the consumption decisions of consumers have again been brought into harmony with the quantity supplied by producers.

TIME AND THE ADJUSTMENT PROCESS

The signals that the pricing system sends to consumers and producers will change with market conditions. But the market adjustment process will not be completed instantaneously. Sometimes various signals are sent out only with the passage of time.

The response of consumers to a change in market conditions will generally be more pronounced with the passage of time. Consider the response of consumers to the higher gasoline prices during the 1970s. Initially consumers cut out some unnecessary trips and leisure driving. Some drove more slowly in order

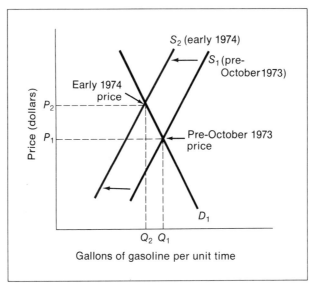

EXHIBIT 8   A decrease in supply

During the October 1973 Middle East conflict the Arab countries reduced the supply of crude oil to the United States and other nations. This action reduced the supply of gasoline. In a market economy such action would cause the price of gasoline to rise, and the smaller supply would be rationed to buyers willing to pay the higher prices.

to get better gasoline mileage. As Exhibit 9 illustrates, these adjustments led to some reduction in gasoline consumption. However, as the high gasoline prices persisted, new car purchases began to shift toward smaller cars that used less gas. Since people usually waited for their current gas-guzzler to wear out before they bought a new, smaller car, it took several years before the full impact of this adjustment was felt. Once people had shifted to higher-mileage automobiles, there was a significantly larger reduction in gasoline consumption than had been initially observed. The adjustment process for gasoline is a typical one. The demand response to a price change will usually be less in the short run than over a longer period of time.

Similarly, the adjustments of producers to changing market conditions will take time. Suppose that there is an increase in demand for radios. How will this change be reflected in the market? Initially, retailers will note that radios move off their shelves more rapidly. Their inventories will decline. During the first few weeks, however, individual radio retailers will be unsure whether the increase in demand is a random, temporary phenomenon or a permanent change. Therefore, they will most likely increase their wholesale orders while leaving the retail price constant. Since all retailers will now be placing larger orders, the sales of manufacturers will increase, and their inventories will decline. A few alert entrepreneurs may anticipate the expansion in demand and develop their production plans accordingly. With the passage of time, other producers, initially oblivious to the increase in demand, will take note of the strong demand for radios. Some will raise their prices. Others will increase their output. Most

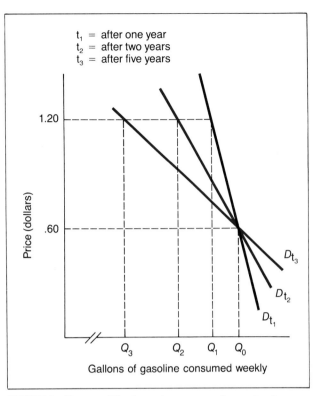

S_{78}

EXHIBIT 9   Time and the buyer's response to a price increase

Usually, the shorter the time period, the less responsive is consumption to a change in price. The gasoline price increases of the 1970s illustrate the point. Initially, gasoline consumption did not decline very much (from Q_0 to Q_1 during the first year) as the price of gasoline rose. However, with the passage of time, consumers adjusted more fully and the consumption of gasoline fell by a larger amount (to Q_3).

manufacturers perceiving the strong demand will do both. Retailers will soon pass the higher prices on to consumers.

Once the increase in demand is widely perceived by suppliers, the price of radios will rise sharply. Profits will exist in the industry. The astute entrepreneurs who anticipated the increase in demand will have expanded their production capacity. They will be rewarded with substantial profits. Other radio suppliers will hastily attempt to expand their production in order to increase their profits. However, instituting a rapid increase in production will be costly for producers who failed to anticipate (and plan for) the higher level of demand. Such firms will have to resort to overtime payments, air shipments of raw materials, and/or the employment of inexperienced workers in order to increase their output rapidly. With the passage of time, output can be expanded in a more orderly fashion and at a lower cost.

Although producers will expand their output at different rates, the profitable opportunities will induce additional supply, which will eventually moderate the price of radios. However, all of these responses will take time, even though economists sometimes talk as if the process were instantaneous.

Price Ceiling: A legally established maximum price that sellers may charge.

Buyers often believe that prices are too high, and sellers generally perceive prices as too low. Unhappy with the prices established by market forces, individuals sometimes attempt to have prices set by legislative action. Fixing prices seems like a simple, straightforward solution. Simple, straightforward solutions, however, often have unanticipated repercussions. Do not forget the secondary effects.

Price ceilings are often popular during a period of inflation, a situation in which prices of most products are continually rising. Many people mistakenly believe that the rising prices are the cause of the inflation rather than just one of its effects. Exhibit 10a illustrates the impact of fixing a price of a product below its equilibrium level. Of course, the price ceiling does result in a lower price than would result from market forces, at least in the short run. However, that is not the end of the story. At the below-equilibrium price, producers will be unwilling to supply as much as consumers would like to purchase. A shortage ($Q_c - Q_p$, Exhibit 10a) of the goods will result. A **shortage** is a situation in which the quantity demanded by consumers exceeds the quantity supplied by producers *at the existing price*. Unfortunately, fixing the price will not eliminate the rationing problem. Nonprice factors will now become more important in the rationing process. Producers will be more discriminating in their sales to eager buyers. Sellers will be partial to friends, buyers who do them favors, even buyers who are willing to make illegal black-market payments.

Shortage: A condition in which the amount of a good offered by sellers is less than the amount demanded by buyers at the existing price. An increase in price would eliminate the shortage.

In addition, the below-equilibrium price reduces the incentive of sellers to expand the future supply of the good. Fewer resources will flow from suppliers into the production of this good. Higher profits will be available elsewhere. With the passage of time, the shortage conditions will worsen as suppliers direct resources away from production of this commodity and into other areas.

What other secondary effects can we expect? In the real world, there are two ways that sellers can raise prices. First, they can raise their money price, holding quality constant. Or, second, they can hold the money price constant while reducing the quality of the good. Confronting a price ceiling, sellers will rely on the latter method of raising prices. Rather than do without the good, some buyers will accept the lower-quality product. It is not easy to repeal the laws of supply and demand (see Myths of Economics, below).

It is important to note that a shortage is not the same as scarcity. Scarcity is inescapable. Scarcity exists whenever people want more of a good than Nature has provided. This means, of course, that almost everything is scarce. Shortages, on the other hand, are avoidable if prices are permitted to rise. A higher, unfixed price (P_0 rather than P_1 in Exhibit 10a) would (a) stimulate additional production, (b) discourage consumption, and (c) ration the available supply to those willing to give up the most in exchange, that is, to pay the highest prices. These forces, an expansion in output and a reduction in consumption, would eliminate the shortage.

Price Floor: A legally established minimum price that buyers must pay for a good or resource.

Surplus: A condition in which the amount of a good that sellers are willing to offer is greater than the amount that buyers will purchase at the existing price. A decline in price would eliminate the surplus.

Exhibit 10b illustrates the case of a **price floor,** which fixes the price of a good or resource above its equilibrium level. At the higher price, sellers will want to bring a larger amount to the market, while buyers will choose to buy less of the good. A **surplus** ($Q_p - Q_c$) will result. Agricultural price supports and minimum wage legislation are examples of price floors. Predictably, nonprice factors will

EXHIBIT 10 The impact of price ceilings and price floors

Frame (a) illustrates the impact of a price ceiling. When price is fixed below the equilibrium level, shortages will develop. Frame (b) illustrates the effects of a price floor. If price is fixed above its equilibrium level, then a surplus will result. When ceilings and floors prevent prices from bringing about a market equilibrium, nonprice factors will play a more important role in the rationing process.

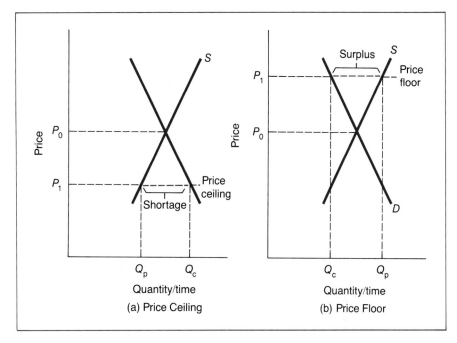

(a) Price Ceiling

(b) Price Floor

again play a larger role in the rationing process than would be true without a price floor. Buyers can now be more selective, since sellers want to sell more than buyers, in aggregate, desire to purchase. Buyers can be expected to seek out sellers willing to offer them favors (discounts on other products, easier credit, or better service, for example). Some sellers may be unable to market their product or service.[8] Unsold merchandise and underutilized resources will result.

Note that a surplus does not mean the good is no longer scarce. People still want more of the good than is freely available from Nature, even though they desire less, *at the current price,* than sellers desire to bring to the market. A decline in price would eliminate the surplus but not the scarcity of the item.

HOW THE MARKET ANSWERS THE THREE BASIC ECONOMIC QUESTIONS

How does the market's pricing mechanism resolve the three basic economic questions—*what* goods will be produced, *how* will they be produced, and *for whom* will they be produced?

In a market economy, what will be produced is determined by the consumer's evaluation of a good (demand) relative to its opportunity cost (supply). If consumers value a good (in terms of money) more than its opportunity cost, they will choose to purchase it. Simultaneously, profit-seeking producers will

---

[8]Our theory indicates that minimum wage legislation (a price floor for unskilled labor) will generate an excess supply of inexperienced, low-skilled workers. The extremely high unemployment rate of teenagers—a group with little work experience—supports this view.

supply a good as long as consumers are willing to pay a price that is sufficient to cover the opportunity cost of producing the good. The result: There is an incentive to produce those goods, and only those goods, to which consumers attach a value at least as high as the production costs of the goods.

How goods will be produced is determined by the economizing behavior of suppliers. Suppliers have a strong incentive to use production methods that minimize costs, because lower costs will mean larger profits. Thus, producers can be expected to organize production efficiently—to utilize a division of labor, to discover and adapt new technologies, and to choose labor–capital combinations that will result in lower production costs.

What assurances are there that producers will not waste resources or exploit consumers by charging high prices? Competition provides the answer. Inefficient producers will have higher costs. They will find it difficult to meet the price competition of sellers who use resources wisely. Similarly, in a market with many sellers, competition among firms will, on the whole, keep prices from straying much above production costs. When prices are above the opportunity costs of a good, profits for the producers will result. As we have discussed, the profits will attract additional suppliers into the market, driving the price downward.

To whom will the goods be distributed? Goods will be allocated to consumers willing and able to pay the market price. Of course, some consumers will be more able to pay the market price—they have larger incomes (more "dollar votes") than others. The unequal distribution of income among consumers is directly related to what is produced and how. The income of individuals will reflect the extent of their provision of resources to others. Those who supply large amounts of highly valued resources—resources for which market participants are willing to pay a high price—will have high incomes. In contrast, those who supply few resources or resources that are *not* valued highly by others will have low incomes.

As long as the preferences and productive abilities of individuals differ, a market solution will lead to an unequal distribution of income. Many people are critical of the pricing system because of its method of distribution. But unequal income distribution is not unique to a market economy. Other systems also use unequal income shares to provide the incentive for individuals to undertake activities. Since efforts to alter the distribution of income will also affect supply conditions, this issue is highly complex. As we proceed, we will investigate it in more detail.

THE COMMUNICATING, COORDINATING, AND MOTIVATING FUNCTIONS OF THE MARKET

The mechanics of supply and demand are important because they help us to understand forces present in the real world. However, sometimes we economists have a tendency to focus on the mechanics without fully explaining their importance. Economic activity is conducted by human decision-makers. Knowledge, coordination, and motivation are critical to the operation of every economy. If people do not know where their services are valued highly, what

MYTHS OF ECONOMICS

"Rent controls are an effective method of ensuring adequate housing at a price the poor can afford."

When rents (a price for a good) are set below the equilibrium level, the amount of rental housing demanded by consumers will exceed the amount that landlords will make available. *Initially,* if the mandated price is not set too much below equilibrium, the impact of rent controls may be barely noticeable. However, with the passage of time, their effects will grow. Inevitably controls will lead to the following results.

1. The Future Supply of Rental Houses Will Decline. The below-equilibrium price will discourage entrepreneurs from constructing new rental housing units. Private investment will flow elsewhere, since the controls have depressed the rate of return in the rental housing market. The current owners of such housing may be forced to accept the lower price. However, potential future suppliers of rental housing have other alternatives. Many of them will opt to use their knowledge and resources in other areas.

2. Shortages and Black Markets Will Develop. Since the quantity of housing supplied will fail to keep pace with the quantity demanded, some persons who value rental housing highly will be unable to find it. Frustrated by the shortage, they will seek methods by which they may induce landlords to rent to them. Some will agree to prepay their rent, including a substantial damage deposit. Others will resort to tie-in agreements (for example, they might agree also to rent or buy the landlord's furniture at an exorbitant price) in their efforts to evade the controls. Still others will make under-the-table payments in order to secure the cheap housing.

3. The Quality of Rental Housing Will Deteriorate. Economic thinking suggests that there are two ways to raise prices. The nominal price can be increased, quality being held constant. Alternatively, quality can be reduced, the same nominal price being maintained. When landlords are prohibited from adopting the former, they will utilize the latter. They will paint rental units less often. Normal maintenance and repair service will deteriorate. Tenant parking lots will be eliminated (or rented). Cleaning and maintenance of the general surroundings will be neglected. Eventually, the quality of the rental housing will reflect the controlled price. Cheap housing will be of cheap quality.

4. Nonprice Methods of Rationing Will Increase in Importance. Since price no longer plays its normal role, other forms of competition will develop. Prohibited from price rationing, landlords will rely more heavily on nonmonetary discriminating devices. They will favor friends, persons of influence, and those with life-styles similar to their own. In contrast, applicants with many children, unconventional life-styles, or perhaps dark skin will find fewer landlords who cater to their personal requirements. Since the cost to landlords of discriminating against those with characteristics they do not like has been reduced, such discrimination will become more prevalent in the rationing process.

5. Inefficient Use of Housing Space Will Result. The tenant in a rent-controlled apartment will think twice before moving. Why? Even though the tenant might want a larger or smaller space, or even though the tenant might want to move closer to work, he or she will be less likely to move because it is much more difficult to find a vacancy if rent control ordinances are in effect. As a result, turnover will drop somewhat, and people will end up living in apartments not quite suited to their needs.

Are conditions in the real world consistent with economic theory? More than any other major city in the United States, New York City has experimented with rent controls. The result has been an unusually large number of furniture and housing "package rentals" as both landlords and renters seek to avoid the impact of the controls. Complaints about the failure of landlords to undertake repairs, maintain rental units properly, and provide complimentary services such as garbage pickup and rat control efforts are far more common in New York City than in any other place in the United States. Economic theory helps to explain why this is the case.

During the inflation-plagued 1970s, the popularity of rent controls increased. Washington, D.C., San Francisco, Los Angeles, and several other cities experimented with various types of control schemes. Studies indicate that a three-pronged pattern emerged after the imposition of rent controls. First, investment in new construction came to a standstill after the controls were imposed. Even in cases where newly constructed buildings were exempted from the controls, construction was adversely affected; landlords feared the imposition of the controls once a new apartment dwelling was in place. Second, the rent controls induced many landlords to convert their apartment buildings to condominium complexes. For example, in Washington, D.C., a city that effectively instituted rent controls in 1974, the number of condominiums jumped from 1000 in 1976 to approximately 10,000 in 1979. San Francisco, New York, and other large cities with controls experienced a similar "boom" in conversion to the condominium market. Finally, vacancy rates declined as the rent control communities began to feel the effects of the developing housing shortage.

Although rent controls may appear to be a simple solution, the truth of the matter is that a decline in the supply of rental housing, poor maintenance, and shortages are the inevitable results. Controls may initially lead to lower housing prices for some, but in the long run the potential for the deterioration of the quality of urban life is almost unlimited. In the words of socialist economist Assar Lindbeck of Sweden: "In many cases rent control appears to be the most efficient technique presently known to destroy a city—except for bombing."[9] Though this may overstate the case somewhat, economic analysis suggests that the point is well-taken.

---

[9]Assar Lindbeck, *The Political Economy of the New Left, 1970* (New York: Harper and Row, 1972), p. 39.

goods are desired by consumers, or which production methods are efficient, they cannot be expected to economize resources. Similarly, unless actions are coordinated, an economy will come to a standstill. In addition, as many leaders of centrally planned economies have discovered, people must be motivated to act before production plans can be realized. An efficiently operating economy must communicate, coordinate, and motivate the actions of decision-makers. In this section, we will take a closer look at how the pricing system performs these functions.

Communicating Information to Decision-Makers

Communication of information is one of the most important functions of a market price. We cannot *directly* observe the preferences of consumers. How highly do consumers value tricycles relative to attic fans, television sets relative to trampolines, or automobiles relative to swimming pools? Product prices communicate up-to-date information about the consumer's valuation of additional units of these and numerous other commodities. Similarly, we cannot turn to an engineering equation in order to calculate the opportunity cost of alternative commodities. But resource prices tell the business decision-maker the relative importance others place on production factors (skill categories of labor, natural resources, and machinery, for example). With this information, in addition to knowledge of the relationship between potential input combinations and the output of a product, producers can make reliable estimates of their opportunity costs.

Without the information provided by market prices, it would be impossible for decision-makers to determine how intensively a good was desired relative to its opportunity costs—that is, relative to other things that might be produced with the resources required to produce the good. Markets collect and register bits and pieces of information reflecting the choices of consumers, producers, and resource suppliers. This vast body of information, which is almost always well beyond the comprehension of any single individual, is tabulated into a summary statistic—*the market price.* This summary statistic provides market participants with information on the relative scarcity of products.

When weather conditions, consumer preferences, technology, political revolution, or natural disaster alter the relative scarcity of a product or resource, market prices communicate this information to decision-makers. Direct knowledge of why conditions were altered is not necessary in order to make the appropriate adjustment. A change in the market price provides sufficient information to determine whether an item has become more or less scarce.[10]

Coordinating the Actions of Market Participants

Market prices coordinate the choices of buyers and sellers, bringing their decisions into line with each other. If suppliers are bringing more of a product to market than is demanded by consumers at the market price, that price will fall. As the price declines, producers will cut back their output (some may even go out of business), and simultaneously the price reduction will induce consumers to utilize more of the good. The excess supply will eventually be eliminated, and balance will be restored in the market.

Alternatively, if producers are currently supplying less than consumers are purchasing, there will be an excess demand in the market. Rather than do without, some consumers will bid up the price. As the price rises, consumers will be encouraged to economize on their use of the good, and suppliers will be encouraged to produce more of it. Again, price will serve to balance the scales of supply and demand.

Prices also direct entrepreneurs to undertake the production projects that are demanded most intensely (relative to their cost) by consumers. Entrepreneurial activity is guided by the signal lights of profits and losses. If consumers really want more of a good—for example, luxury apartments—the intensity of their demand will lead to a market price that exceeds the opportunity cost of constructing the apartments. A profitable opportunity will be created. Entrepreneurs will soon discover this opportunity for gain, undertake construction, and thereby expand the availability of the apartments. In contrast, if consumers want less of a good—for example, books by Watergate criminals—the opportunity cost of supplying such books will exceed the sales revenue from their production. Entrepreneurs who undertake such unprofitable projects will be penalized.

An understanding of the importance of the entrepreneur also sheds light on the market adjustment process. Since entrepreneurs, like the rest of us, have imperfect knowledge, they will not be able instantaneously to identify profitable opportunities and the disequilibrium conditions that accompany them. However, with the passage of time, information about a profitable opportunity will become more widely disseminated. More and more producers will move to

---

[10]The market adjustment to the destruction of the anchovy crop off the coast of Peru in 1972 provides an excellent example of the role of price as a communication signal. The normal anchovy run off the coast of Peru did not materialize in 1972. Anchovies are a major source of protein for animal feed. Soybeans are a good substitute for anchovies. It was not necessary for American farmers to know any of these things in order to make the correct response. As soybeans were used more intensively in feed grains, the price of soybeans increased during 1972–1974. Responding to the summary statistic (higher soybean prices), farmers increased their production of soybeans, which moderated the adverse effects of the anchovy destruction.

supply the good, which is intensely desired by consumers relative to its cost. Of course, as entrepreneurs expand supply, they will eventually eliminate the profit.

The move toward equilibrium will typically be a groping process. With time, successful entrepreneurial activity will be more clearly identified. Successful methods will be copied by other producers. Learning-by-doing and trial-and-error will help producers sort out attractive projects from "losers." The process, however, will never quite be complete. By the time entrepreneurs discover one intensely desired product (or a new, more efficient production technique), change will have occurred elsewhere, creating other unrealized profitable opportunities. The wheels of dynamic change never stop.

Motivating the Economic Players

One of the major advantages of the pricing system is its ability to motivate people. Prices establish a reward–penalty system that induces the participants to work, cooperate with others, invest for the future, supply goods that are intensely desired by others, economize on the use of scarce resources, and utilize efficient production methods. Pursuit of personal gain is a powerful motivator.

This reward–penalty system will direct the actions of entrepreneurs. They will seek to supply goods that are intensely desired relative to their opportunity cost, because such projects are profitable. In contrast, they will try to avoid using resources to produce things that are valued less than their opportunity cost because such projects will result in losses. No government agency needs to tell decision-makers what to produce or what not to produce. No central authority forces the milkman to deliver milk, the construction firm to produce houses, the farmer to produce wheat, or the baker to produce bread. Producers choose to engage in these and millions of other productive activities because they consider them to be in their self-interest.

Similarly, no one has to tell resource suppliers to acquire, develop, and supply productive inputs. Why are many young people willing to undertake the necessary work, stress, late hours of study, and financial cost to acquire a medical or law degree, a doctoral degree in economics or physics, or a master's degree in business administration? Why do others seek to master a skill requiring an apprentice program? Why do individuals save to buy a business, capital equipment, or other assets? Although many factors undoubtedly influence one's decision to acquire skills and capital assets, the expectation of financial reward is an important stimulus. Without this stimulus, the motivation to work, create, develop skills, and supply capital assets to those productive activities most desired by others would be weakened. Market forces supply this essential ingredient so automatically that most people do not even realize it. Responding to the reward–penalty system of the market, the actions of even self-interested people will be channelled into the areas of production that are most highly desired relative to their opportunity cost.

More than 200 years ago, the father of economics, Adam Smith, first articulated the revolutionary idea that competitive markets bring personal self-interest and general welfare into harmony with each other. Smith noted that the butcher, for example, supplies meat to customers, not out of benevolence, but rather out of self-interest. Emphasizing his point, Smith stated:

Every individual is continually exerting himself to find out the most advantageous employment for whatever capital he can command. It is his own advantage, indeed, and not that of the

*society which he has in view. But the study of his own advantage naturally, or rather neces-
sarily, leads him to prefer that employment which is most advantageous to society. . . . He
intends only his own gain, and he is in this, as in many other cases, led by an invisible
hand to promote an end which was no part of his intention. By pursuing his own
interest he frequently promotes that of the society more effectually than when he really
intends to promote it.*[11]

Market prices coordinate the decentralized individual planning of economic participants and bring their plans (self-interest) into harmony with the general welfare. This was the message of Adam Smith in 1776. It was an idea whose time had come.

Qualifications

In this chapter, we have focused on the operation of a market economy. The efficiency of market organization is dependent on (a) competitive markets and (b) well-defined private-property rights. Competition, the great regulator, is capable of protecting both buyer and seller. The presence of independent alternative suppliers protects the consumer against a seller who seeks to charge prices substantially above the cost of production. The existence of alternative resource suppliers protects the producer against a supplier who might otherwise be tempted to withhold a vital resource unless granted exorbitant compensation. The existence of alternative employment opportunities protects the employee from the power of any single employer. Competition can equalize the bargaining power between buyers and sellers.

Although property rights are often associated with selfishness, they might be viewed more properly as an arrangement that (a) forces resource users to bear fully the cost of their action and (b) prohibits persons from engaging in destructive forms of competition. When property rights are securely defined, suppliers will be required to pay resource owners the opportunity cost of each resource employed. They will not be permitted to seize and utilize scarce resources without compensating the owner, that is, without bidding the resources away from alternative users.

Similarly, securely defined property rights will eliminate the use of violence as a competitive weapon. A producer you do not buy from (or work for) will not be permitted to burn your house down. Nor will a competitive resource supplier whose prices you undercut be permitted to slash your automobile tires or hammer your head against concrete.

Lack of competition and poorly defined property rights will alter the operation of a market economy. As we proceed, we will investigate each of these problems in detail.

**CHAPTER LEARNING
OBJECTIVES**

1 Because people want more of scarce goods than Nature has made freely available, a rationing mechanism is necessary. Competition is the natural outgrowth of the necessity for rationing scarce goods. A change in the rationing mechanism utilized will alter the form of competition, but it will not eliminate competitive tactics.

---

[11]Adam Smith, *An Inquiry into the Nature and Causes of the Wealth of Nations* (New York: Modern Library, 1937), p. 423.

2   The law of demand holds that there is an inverse relationship between price and amount of a good purchased. A rise in price will cause consumers to purchase less because they now have a greater incentive to use substitutes. On the other hand, a reduction in price will induce consumers to buy more, since they will substitute the cheaper good for other commodities.

3   The law of supply states that there is a direct relationship between the price of a product and the amount supplied. Other things constant, an increase in the price of a product will induce the established firms to expand their output and new firms to enter the market. The quantity supplied will expand.

4   Market prices will bring the conflicting forces of supply and demand into balance. If the quantity supplied to the market by producers exceeds the quantity demanded by consumers, price will decline until the excess supply is eliminated. On the other hand, if the quantity demanded by consumers exceeds the quantity supplied by producers, price will rise until the excess demand is eliminated.

5   When a market is in long-run equilibrium, supply and demand will be in balance and the producer's opportunity cost will equal the market price. If the opportunity cost of supplying the good is less than the market price, profits will accrue. The profits will attract additional suppliers, cause lower prices, and push the market toward an equilibrium. On the other hand, if the opportunity cost of producing a good exceeds the market price, suppliers will experience losses. The losses will induce producers to leave the market, causing price to rise until equilibrium is restored.

6   Changes in consumer income, prices of closely related goods, preferences, and expectation as to future prices will cause the entire demand curve to shift. An increase (decrease) in demand will cause prices to rise (fall) and quantity supplied to increase (decline).

7   Changes in input prices, technology, and other factors that influence the producer's cost of production will cause the entire supply curve to shift. An increase (decrease) in supply will cause prices to fall (increase) and quantity demanded to expand (decline).

8   The constraint of time temporarily limits the ability of consumers to adjust to changes in prices. With the passage of time, a price increase will usually elicit a larger reduction in quantity demanded. Similarly, the market supply curve shows more responsiveness to a change in price in the long run than during the short-term time period.

9   When a price is fixed below the market equilibrium, buyers will want to purchase more than sellers are willing to supply. A shortage will result. Nonprice factors such as waiting lines, quality deterioration, and illegal transactions will play a more important role in the rationing process.

10   When a price is fixed above the market equilibrium level, sellers will want to supply a larger amount than buyers are willing to purchase at the current price. A surplus will result.

11   The pricing system answers the three basic allocation questions in the following manner.

(a) *What goods will be produced?* Additional units of goods will be produced only if consumers value them more highly than the opportunity cost of the resources necessary to produce them.

(b) *How will goods be produced?* The methods that result in the lowest opportunity cost will be chosen. Since lower costs mean larger profits, markets reward producers who discover and utilize efficient (low-cost) production methods.

(c) *To whom will the goods be distributed?* Goods will be distributed to individuals according to the quantity and price of the productive resources supplied in the marketplace. A great number of goods will be allocated to persons who are able to sell a large quantity of highly valued productive resources; few goods will be allocated to persons who supply only a small quantity of low-valued resources.

12 Market prices communicate information, coordinate the actions of buyers and sellers, and provide the incentive structure that motivates decision-makers to act. The information provided by prices instructs entrepreneurs as to (a) how to use scarce resources and (b) which products are intensely desired (relative to their opportunity cost) by consumers. Market prices establish a reward–penalty system, which induces individuals to cooperate with each other and motivates them to work efficiently, invest for the future, supply intensely desired goods, economize on the use of scarce resources, and utilize efficient production methods. Even though decentralized individual planning is a characteristic of the market system, there is a harmony between personal self-interest and the general welfare, as Adam Smith noted long ago. The efficiency of the system is dependent on (a) competitive market conditions and (b) securely defined private-property rights.

THE ECONOMIC WAY OF THINKING — DISCUSSION QUESTIONS

1 What is the purpose of prices? Do prices do anything other than ration goods to those with the most dollar votes? Explain. What factors determine the price of a good?

2 How many of the following "goods" do you think conform to the general law of supply: (a) gasoline, (b) cheating on exams, (c) political favors from legislators, (d) the services of heart specialists, (e) children, (f) legal divorces, (g) the services of a minister? Explain your answer in each case.

3 Which of the following do you think would lead to an increase in the current demand for beef: (a) higher pork prices, (b) higher incomes, (c) higher feed grain prices, (d) a banner-year corn crop, (e) an increase in the price of beef?

4 (a) "The motivating force behind a market economy is individual self-interest."
(b) "Cooperation among individuals is the keystone of a market system. Without cooperation there would be no exchange and economic welfare would suffer drastically."
Are these statements true or false? Explain your answer.

5 "We cannot allow the price of gasoline to go any higher because it is as essential to the poor as to the rich. We cannot allow the rich to bid gasoline away from the poor. I would prefer to ration ten gallons of gas to each driver—both rich and poor." (Overheard during the gasoline shortage of the 1970s.)
(a) Do you agree with this opinion? Why?
(b) Do you think gasoline is more essential than food? Should the rich be allowed to bid food away from the poor? Should food be rationed, equal portions being granted to both rich and poor? Why or why not?
(c) Were your answers to both (a) and (b) consistent? Explain.

6 **What's Wrong with This Way of Thinking?**

"Economists argue that lower prices will necessarily result in less supply. However, there are exceptions to this rule. For example, in 1970 ten-digit electronic calculators sold for $100. By 1980 the price of the same type of calculator had declined to less than $30. Yet business firms produced and sold five times as many calculators in 1980 as in 1970. Lower prices did *not* result in less production and a decline in the number of calculators supplied."

7 A severe frost hit Brazil in July 1975, damaging the coffee crop. The 1976 harvest was 9.5 million bags, down from the 1975 harvest of 23 million bags. Since Brazil is the

world's leading coffee producer, there was a substantial reduction in the world supply of coffee in 1976. Use supply and demand analysis to describe:

(a) what happened to the price of coffee in 1976;

(b) the U.S. per capita consumption of coffee in 1976 compared to that in 1975;

(c) the price of tea in 1976;

(d) the revenues of coffee producers in 1976 (be careful).

Coffee is allocated by the market. Did the sharp reduction in supply create a shortage? Why or why not?

Industrious students should obtain real-world data to back up their analysis. Information on coffee prices and consumption for the United States is available in the *Statistical Abstract of the United States* (annual).

4

SUPPLY AND DEMAND FOR THE PUBLIC SECTOR

The economic role of government is pivotal. The government sets the rules of the game. It establishes and defines property rights, which are necessary for the smooth operation of markets. As we shall soon see, public policy is an important determinant of economic stability. The government sometimes uses subsidies to encourage the production of some goods while applying special taxes to reduce the availability of others. In a few cases—education, the mail service, and local electric power, for example—the government becomes directly involved in the production process.

Because of government's broad economic role, it is vital that we understand how it works and the circumstances under which it contributes to the efficient allocation of resources. What functions does government perform best? Why does it sometimes fail to perform as we would like? What activities might best be left to the market? Recent work in economics, particularly in the area of public choice, is relevant if we are seeking intelligent answers to these age-old questions.

In this chapter, we focus on the shortcomings of the market and the potential of government policy as an alternate means for resolving economic problems. Issues involving market and public sector organization will be discussed repeatedly throughout this book. Political economy—how the public sector works in comparison with the market—is an integral and exciting aspect of economic analysis.

IDEAL ECONOMIC EFFICIENCY

We need a criterion by which to judge market and public sector action. Economists use the standard of **economic efficiency.** The central idea is straightforward. It simply means that *for any given level of effort* (cost), we want to obtain the largest possible benefit. A corollary is that we want to obtain any specific level of benefits *with the least possible effort.* Economic efficiency is simply getting the most out of the available resources.

But what does this mean when applied to the entire economy? Individuals are the final decision-makers of an economy. Individuals will bear the costs and reap the benefits of economic activity. When applied to the entire economy, two conditions are necessary for ideal economic efficiency to exist:

Rule 1. *Undertaking an economic action will be efficient if it produces more benefits than costs for the individuals of the economy.* Such actions result in gain—improvement in the well-being of at least some individuals without creating welfare losses to others. Failure to undertake such activities means that potential gain has been foregone.

Rule 2. *Undertaking an economic action will be inefficient if it produces more costs to the individuals than benefits.* When an action results in greater total costs than benefits, somebody must be harmed. The benefits that accrue to those who gain are insufficient to compensate for the losses imposed on others. Therefore, when all persons are considered, the net impact of such an action is counterproductive.

When either rule 1 or rule 2 is violated, economic inefficiency results. The concept of economic efficiency applies to all possible income distributions, although a change in income distribution may alter the precise combination of goods and services that is most efficient. Positive economics does not tell us *how* income should be distributed. Of course, we all have ideas on the subject. Most of us would like to see more income distributed our way. But for each kind of income distribution, there will be an ideal resource allocation that will be most efficient.

A closer look at supply and demand when competitive pressures are present will help you to understand the concept of efficiency. The supply curve reflects the producer's opportunity costs. Each point along the supply curve indicates the *minimum* price for which the units of a good could be produced without a loss to the seller. Each point along the demand curve indicates the consumer's valuation of the good—the *maximum* amount that the consumer of each unit is willing to pay for the unit. Any time the consumer's valuation exceeds the producer's opportunity cost—the producer's minimum supply price—production and sale of the good can generate mutual gain.

When only the buyer and seller are affected by production and exchange, competitive markets directed by the forces of supply and demand are efficient. Exhibit 1 illustrates why this is true. Suppliers of a good, bicycles in this example, will produce additional units as long as the market price exceeds the production cost. Similarly, consumers will gain from the purchase of additional units as long as their benefits, revealed by the height of the demand curve, exceed the market price. Market forces will result in an equilibrium output level of *Q*: All units for which the benefits to consumers exceed the costs to suppliers will be produced. Rule 1 is met; all potential gains from exchange (the shaded area) between

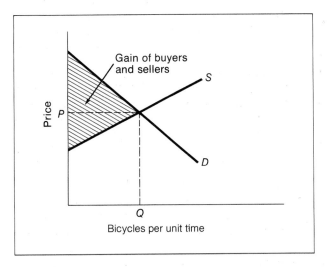

consumers and producers are fully realized. Production beyond Q, however, will prove inefficient. If more than Q bicycles are produced, rule 2 is violated; consumers value the additional units *less* than their cost. With competitive markets, suppliers will find it unprofitable to produce units beyond Q because costs will exceed revenues.

Thus, both consumers and producers will be guided by the pricing system to output level Q, just the right amount. The market works beautifully. Individuals, pursuing their own interest, are guided as if by an invisible hand to promote the general welfare. This was the message of Adam Smith, more than 200 years ago.

WHY MIGHT THE INVISIBLE HAND FAIL?

Is the invisible hand still working today? Why might it fail? There are four important factors than can limit the ability of the invisible hand to perform its magic.

Lack of Competition

Competition is vital to the proper operation of the pricing mechanism. It is competition that drives the prices for consumer goods down to the level of their cost. Similarly, competition in factor markets prevents both (a) sellers from charging exorbitant prices to producers and (b) buyers from taking advantage of the owners of productive resources. The existence of competitors reduces the power of both buyers and sellers to rig the market in their own favor.

Modern mass production techniques often make it possible for a large-scale producer to gain a cost advantage over smaller competitors. In several industries—automobiles, steel, aircraft, and aluminum, for example—a few large firms produce the entire output. Because an enormous amount of capital investment is required to enter these industries, existing large-scale producers may be partially insulated from the competitive pressure of new rivals.

Since competition is the enemy of high prices, sellers have a strong incentive to escape from its pressures by colluding rather than competing.

Competition is something that is good for the other guy. Individually, each of us would prefer to be loosened from its grip. Students do not like stiff competitors at exam time, when seeking entry to graduate school, or in their social or romantic lives. Similarly, sellers prefer few real competitors.

Exhibit 2 illustrates how sellers can gain from collusive action. If a group of sellers could eliminate the competition from new entrants to the market, they would be able to raise their prices. The total revenue of sellers is simply the market price multiplied by the quantity sold. The sellers' revenues would be greater if only the restricted output Q_2 were sold rather than the competitive output Q_1. The artificially high price P_2 is in excess of the competitive opportunity cost of supplying the good. The price of the good does not reflect its actual level of scarcity.

It is in the interests of consumers and the community that output be expanded to Q_1, the output consistent with economic efficiency. But it is in the interests of the sellers to make the good artificially scarce and raise its price. If the sellers can use collusion, government action, or other means of restricting supply, they can gain. However, the restricted output level would violate rule 2. Inefficiency would result. There is a conflict between the interests of the sellers and what is best for the entire community.

When there are only a few firms in the industry and competition from new entrants can be restrained, the sellers may be able to rig the market in their favor. Through collusion, either tacit or overt, suppliers may be able to escape competitive pressures. What can the government do to preserve competition? Congress has enacted a series of antitrust laws, most notably the Sherman Antitrust Act and the Clayton Act, making it illegal for firms to collude or attempt to monopolize a product. It established the Federal Trade Commission, which prohibits "certain methods of competition in commerce," such as false advertising, improper grading of materials, and deceptive business practices.

For the most part, economists favor the principle of government action to ensure and promote competitive markets, but there is considerable debate about the effectiveness of past public policy in this area. Few economists are satisfied with the government's role as a promoter of competition.

EXHIBIT 2   Rigging the market

If a group of sellers can restrict the entry of competitors and connive to reduce their own output, they can sometimes obtain more total revenue by selling fewer units. Note that the total sales revenue P_2Q_2 for the restricted supply exceeds the sales revenue P_1Q_1 for the competitive supply.

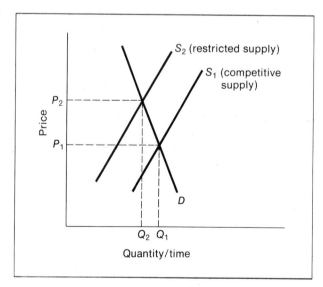

Two general criticisms are voiced. Many suggest that the government should pursue a more vigorous antitrust policy. They believe that antitrust action should be taken to expand the number of rivals in several industries—automobiles and steel, for example—that are currently dominated by a few firms. On the other hand, other critics argue that antitrust policy and business regulation, both past and present, have often, paradoxically, restricted competition. Consumers have been "protected" against *low* prices and producers from new rivals. These critics argue that government regulatory policy has been part of the problem rather than part of the solution. They believe this results from an inherent flaw in the political process—the disproportionate power of special interests.

Externalities—What Have You Been Doing to Your Neighbor?

Externalities: The side effects of an action that influence the well-being of nonconsenting parties. The nonconsenting parties may be either helped (by external benefits) or harmed (by external costs).

Production and consumption of some goods will result in spillover effects that the market will fail to register. These spillover effects, called **externalities,** are present when the actions of one individual or group affect the welfare of others without their consent.

Examples of externalities abound. If you live in an apartment house and the noisy stereo of your next-door neighbors keeps you from studying economics, your neighbors are creating an externality. Their actions are imposing an unwanted cost on you. Driving your car during rush hour increases the level of congestion, thereby imposing a cost on other motorists. If an examination is graded on the curve, cheating creates an externality inasmuch as it raises the class average.

Not all externalities result in the imposition of a cost. Sometimes human actions generate *benefits* for nonparticipating parties. The homeowner who keeps a house in good condition and maintains a neat lawn improves the beauty of the entire community, thereby benefiting community members. A flood-control project that benefits the upstream residents will also generate gain for those who live downstream. Scientific theories benefit their authors, but the knowledge gained also contributes to the welfare of others.

Why do externalities create problems for the market mechanism? Exhibit 3 can help us answer this question. With competitive markets in equilibrium, the cost of a good (including a normal profit for the producer) will be paid by consumers. Unless consumer benefits exceed the opportunity cost of production, the goods will not be produced. But what happens when externalities are present?

Suppose that a firm discharges smoke into the air or sewage into a river. Valuable resources, clean air and pure water, are utilized, but neither the firm nor the consumers of its products will pay for these costs. As Exhibit 3a shows, the supply curve will understate the opportunity cost of production when these external costs are present. Since the producer will consider only the private cost and ignore the cost imposed on secondary parties, supply curve S_1 will result. If all costs were considered, supply would be S_2. The actual supply curve S_1 will not reflect the opportunity cost of producing the good. The producer will be misled into thinking that the opportunity cost is low enough to merit an increase in supply. Output will be expanded beyond Q_2 (to Q_1), even though the community's valuation of the additional units is less than their cost. The second efficiency condition, rule 2, is violated. Inefficiency in the form of excessive air and water pollution results. In the *total* picture, the harm the pollution does outweighs the benefits to some of the people involved.

As Exhibit 3b shows, external benefits can also create problems. When they are present, the market demand curve D_1 will not fully reflect the total

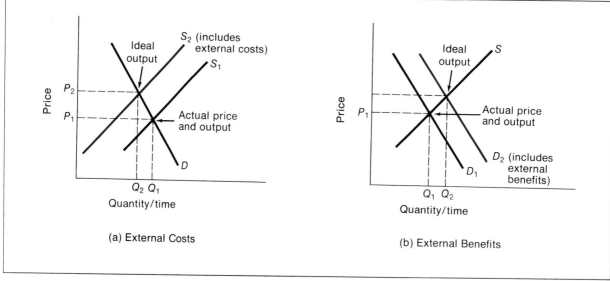

EXHIBIT 3 Externalities and problems for the market

When external costs are present (a), the output level of a product will exceed the desired amount. In contrast, market output of goods that generate external benefits (b) will be less than the ideal level.

benefits, which include those that accrue to secondary parties. Output Q_1 will result. Could the community gain from a greater output of the product? Yes. The demand curve D_2 reflects both the direct benefits of consumers and the secondary benefits bestowed on secondary parties. Expansion of output beyond Q_1 to Q_2 would result in net gain to the community. However, since neither consumers nor producers can capture the secondary benefits, consumption level Q_1 will result. The potential net gain from the greater output level Q_2 will be lost. Rule 1 of our hypothetical efficiency criterion is violated.

Competitive markets will fail to give consumers and producers the right signals when externalities are present. The market will tend to underallocate resources to the production of goods with external benefits and overallocate resources to the production of goods that impose external costs on nonconsenting parties.

Public Goods—More Problems for the Market

Public Goods: Jointly consumed goods. When consumed by one person, they are also made available to others. National defense, poetry, and scientific theories are all public goods.

Some goods cannot be provided though the marketplace because there is no way of excluding nonpaying customers. Goods that must be consumed jointly by all are called **public goods.** National defense, the judicial and legal system, and the monetary system are examples of public goods. The national defense that protects you also protects others. There is no feasible way in which national defense could be provided to some citizens but not to others. Similarly, the actions of a central monetary authority are a public good. The monetary system that influences the prices of things you buy also influences the prices and incomes of others.

Why are public goods troublesome for the market? Typically, in the marketplace, there is a direct link between consumption and payment. If you do not pay, you do not consume. Similarly, the payments of consumers provide the incentive to supply products. Public goods, however, are consumed jointly. If a public good is made available to one person, it is simultaneously made available to others. Since people cannot be excluded, their incentive to reveal their true valuation of the good is destroyed. Why would you voluntarily pay your "fair share" for national defense, the courts, or police protection if these goods were provided in the market? If others contribute a large amount, the public good will be provided pretty much regardless of what you do. If others do not pay, your actions will not make much difference anyway. Thus, each person has an incentive to opt out, to refuse to help pay voluntarily for the public good.

When everybody opts out, what happens? Not very much of the public good is produced. This is precisely why the market cannot handle public goods very well. Resources will be underallocated to the production of public goods because most people, following their self-interest, will refuse to pay for them. Due to the nature of public goods, there is often a conflict between self-interest and the public interest of economic efficiency.

Economic Instability

If markets are to function well, a stable monetary exchange system must be provided. Many market exchanges involve a time dimension. Houses, cars, consumer durables, land, buildings, equipment, and many other items are paid for over a period of months or even years. If the purchasing power of the monetary unit, the dollar in the United States, gyrated wildly, few would want to make long-term transactions, because of the uncertainty. The smooth functioning of the market would be retarded.

The government's spending and monetary policies exert a powerful influence on economic stability. If properly conducted, they can contribute to economic stability, full and efficient utilization of resources, and stable prices. However, improper stabilization policy can cause massive unemployment, rapidly rising prices, or perhaps both.

Economists are not in complete agreement on the extent to which public policy can stabilize the economy and promote full employment. They often debate the impact of various policy tools. All agree, however, that a stable economic environment is vital to a market economy. Those pursuing a course in macroeconomics will find both the potential and the limitations of government action as a stabilizing force in the economy discussed further in Part Two.

THE ECONOMICS OF COLLECTIVE ACTION

The pricing system will fail to meet our ideal efficiency standards if (a) markets are not competitive, (b) externalities are present, (c) public goods necessitate joint consumption, or (d) the aggregate economy is characterized by instability and the resultant uncertainty. If public sector action can correct these deficiencies, net gains for the community are possible. Public policy does not have to be a zero-sum game.

It is important to understand that sometimes public sector action can be expected to improve the efficiency of the market. However, it is also important to recognize that collective action is merely an alternative form of economic organization. Like the market, it is determined by human behavior and the decisions of individuals.

If we are going to make meaningful comparisons between market allocation and collective action, we need to develop a sound theory that will help us understand both forms of economic organization. **Public choice analysis** has significantly advanced our understanding of the collective decision-making process in recent years. Something of a cross between economics and political science, public choice theory applies the principles and methodology of economics to collective choices.

In addition to their market choices, individual voters, politicians, lobbyists, and bureaucrats make "public choices" that affect many others besides themselves. In a democratic setting, individual preferences will influence the outcome of collective decisions, just as they influence outcomes in the market. The government is *not* a supra-individual that will always make decisions in the "public interest," however that nebulous term might be defined. It is merely an institution through which individuals make collective decisions and carry out activities collectively.

Public choice theory postulates that individual behavior in the political arena will be motivated by considerations similar to those that influence market behavior. If self-interest is a powerful motivator in the marketplace, there is every reason to believe it will also be a motivating factor when choices are made collectively. If market choices are influenced by changes in projected *personal* costs relative to benefits, there is every reason to expect that such changes will also influence political choices. Public choice theory, in other words, postulates that the number of saints and sinners in the two sectors will be comparable.

In analyzing the behavior of people in the marketplace, economists develop a logically consistent theory of behavior that can be tested against reality. Through theory and empirical testing we seek to explain various economic actions of decision-makers and, in general, how the market operates.

In the public sphere our purpose should be the same: to explain how the collective decision-making process really operates. This means developing a logically consistent theory linking individual behavior to collective action, analyzing the implications of that theory, and testing these implications against the events of the real world.

Since the theory of collective decision-making is not as well developed as our theory of market behavior, our conclusions will, of course, be less definitive. However, in the last 25 years, social scientists have made great strides in our understanding of resource allocation by the public sector.[1] Currently, this subject is often dealt with at a more advanced academic level. However, even on an introductory level, economic tools can be utilized to shed light on how the public sector handles economic activities.

Differences and Similarities between Market and Collective Action[2]

There are some basic characteristics that influence outcomes in both the market and the public sectors. As we have noted, there is reason to believe that the motivational factors present in both sectors are similar. However, there are basic structural differences. Voluntary exchange coordinated by prices is the

---

[1]The contributions of Kenneth Arrow, James Buchanan, Duncan Black, Anthony Downs, Mancur Olson, and Gordon Tullock have been particularly important.

[2]The "Public Choice" section of this book analyzes the topics of alternative forms of economic organization—market versus collective action—in more detail.

dominant characteristic of a market economy (although, of course, when externalities are present, involuntary exchange may also result). In a democratic setting, the dominant characteristic of collective action is majority rule, effective either directly or through legislative procedures. Let us take a look at both the differences and similarities between the two sectors.

1. Competitive Behavior Is Present in Both the Market and Public Sectors. Although the market sector is sometimes referred to as "the competitive sector," it is clear that competitive behavior is present in both sectors. Politicians compete with each other for elective office. Bureau chiefs and agency heads compete for additional taxpayer dollars. Public sector employees, like their counterparts in the private sector, compete for promotions, higher incomes, and additional power. Lobbyists compete to secure funds, favorable rulings, and legislation for the interest groups they represent. The nature of the competition and the criteria for success do differ between the two sectors. Nonetheless, both sectors must confront the reality of scarcity, and therefore the necessity of a rationing mechanism. Competitive behavior is an outgrowth of the need to ration scarce goods and resources.

2. Public Sector Organization Can Break the Individual Consumption–Payment Link. In the market, a consumer who wants to obtain a commodity must be willing to pay the price. For each person there is a one-to-one correspondence between consuming the commodity and paying the purchase price. In this respect, there is a fundamental difference between market and collective action. The government usually does not establish a one-to-one relationship between the tax bill of an individual consumer and the amount of political goods that that individual consumes.

Your tax bill will be the same whether you like or dislike the national defense, agriculture, or antipoverty policies of the government. You will be taxed for subsidies to higher education, sugarbeet growers, airlines, cultural centers, and many other **political goods**[3] regardless of whether you consume or use them. In some cases you may even be made worse off by a government program, but this fact will not alter the amount of your payment (taxes) for political goods. In other cases, you may receive very large benefits (either monetary or subjective) from a governmental action without any significant impact on your tax bill. The direct link between individual consumption of the good and individual payment for the good is not required in the public sector.

Political Good: Any good (or policy) supplied by the political process.

3. Scarcity Imposes the Aggregate Consumption–Payment Link in Both Sectors. Although the government can break the link between payment for the good and the right to consume the good for an *individual,* the reality of the *aggregate consumption–aggregate payment link* will remain. Provision of scarce goods requires the foregoing of alternatives. Someone must cover the cost of providing scarce goods regardless of the sector utilized to produce (or distribute) them. There are no free lunches in either the private or the public sector. Free goods provided in the public sector are "free" only to individuals. They are most

---

[3]"Political good" is a broad term used to designate any action supplied through the public sector. Note that political goods may be either private goods or public goods.

certainly not free from the viewpoint of society. Taxpayers must pay for goods that the government might choose to distribute free to individual consumers.

An increase in the amount of goods provided by the public sector will mean an increase in the total costs of government. More political goods will mean more taxes. Given scarcity, the link between aggregate consumption and aggregate costs of production cannot be broken by public sector action.

4. The Element of Compulsion Is Present in the Public Sector. As we have already discussed, voluntary exchange is the dominant characteristic of market organization. Except when externalities are present, involuntary exchange is absent. In the marketplace, a minority need not yield to the majority. For example, the views of the majority, even an overwhelming majority, do not prevent minority consumers from purchasing desired goods.

Governments possess an exclusive right to the use of coercion. Large corporations like Exxon and General Motors are economically powerful, but they cannot require you to buy their products. In contrast, if the majority (either directly or through the legislative process) decides on a particular policy, the minority must accept the policy and help pay for its costs, even if that minority strongly disagrees. If representative legislative policy allocates $10 billion for the development of a superweapon system, the dissenting minority is required to pay taxes that will help finance the project. Other dissenting minorities will be compelled to pay taxes for the support of welfare programs, farm subsidies, foreign aid, or hundreds of other projects on which reasonable people will surely differ. When issues are decided in the public sector, dissidents must, at least temporarily, yield to the current dominant view.

The right to compel is sometimes necessary to promote social cooperation. For example, legislation compelling individuals to stop when the traffic light turns red or to drive on the right side of the road clearly enhances the safety of us all. Thus, sometimes it will be possible to increase social cooperativeness and even expand the available options by public sector actions or policies that place some limitation on our choices.

5. When Collective Decisions Are Made Legislatively, Voters Must Choose among Candidates Who Represent a Bundle of Positions on Issues. The legislative voter cannot choose the views of Representative Free Lunch on poverty and business welfare and simultaneously choose the views of challenger Ms. Austerity on national defense and tariffs. Inability to separate a candidate's views on one issue from his or her views on another greatly reduces the voter's power to register preferences on specific issues. Since the average representative is asked to vote on approximately 2000 different issues during a two-year term, the size of the problem is obvious.

To the average individual, choosing a representative is a bit like choosing an agent who will both control a substantial portion of one's income and regulate one's activities. The specific agent preferred by an individual voter may or may not be elected. The voter's agent will be only one voice within the legislative body that will make many decisions that affect the voter's welfare. Simultaneously, the agent has the responsibility to represent hundreds of thousands of other persons on each legislative issue. There is no way that the agent can articulate the positions of both group A and group B on a specific issue. Similarly, it will be impossible for the voter to select one agent to represent views on issue X and another agent to represent views on issue Y. As a result of the "bundle-purchase" nature of the political process, the likelihood that a collective decision will reflect the precise views of an individual voter is low.

6. Income and Power Are Distributed Differently in the Two Sectors. In the marketplace, individuals who supply more highly valued resources have larger incomes. The number of dollar votes available to an individual reflect her or his abilities, ambitions, skills, perceptiveness, inheritance, and good fortune, among other things. An unequal distribution of consumer power results.

In the public sector, ballots call the tune when decisions are made democratically. One citizen, one vote is the rule. However, this does not mean that political goods and services—those resources that make up political power or political income—are allocated equally to all citizens by the collective decision-making process. Some individuals are much more astute than others at using the political process to obtain personal advantage. The political process rewards those who are most capable of delivering votes—not only their own individual votes but those of others as well. Persuasive skills (i.e., lobbying, public speaking, public relations), organizational abilities, finances, and knowledge are vital to success in the political arena. Persons who have more of these resources can expect to benefit more handsomely, in terms of both money and power, from the political process than individuals who lack them.

The Supply of and Demand for Public Sector Action

In the marketplace, consumers demand goods with their dollar votes. Producers supply goods. The actions of both are influenced by personal self-interest. In a democratic political system, voters and legislators are counterparts to consumers and producers. Voters demand political goods with their political resources—votes, lobbying, contributions, and organizational abilities. Vote-conscious legislators are suppliers of political goods.

How does a voter decide which political supplier to support? Many things influence the voter's decision, but personal self-interest surely must be high on the list. Will the policies of Senator Snodgrass or those of the challenger, Ms. Good Deal, help *me* most? Where do they stand on the major issues? What are their views on those issues that may seem unimportant to others but are of vital importance to *me?* Are they likely to raise or lower *my* taxes? All of these factors influence the voter's personal benefits and costs from public sector action. Economic theory suggests that they influence choices among the candidates.

Other things constant, voters will support those candidates whom they expect to provide them with the most benefits, net of costs. The greater the expected gains from a candidate's election, the more voters will do to ensure the candidate's success. A voter, like the consumer in the marketplace, will ask the supplier, "What can you do for me and how much will it cost?"

The goal of the political supplier is to put together a majority coalition—to win the election. Vote-seeking politicians, like profit-conscious business decision-makers, will have a strong incentive to cater to the views of their constituents. The easiest way to win votes, both politically and financially, is to give the constituents, or at least appear to give them, what they want. A politician who pays no heed to the views of his or her constituents is as rare as a business-person selling castor oil at a football game.

There are two major reasons that voters are likely to turn to public sector economic organization: (1) to reduce waste and inefficiency stemming from non-competitive markets, externalities, public goods, and economic instability and (2) to redistribute income. Public sector action that corrects, or appears to correct, the shortcomings of the market will be attractive. If properly conducted, it will generate more benefits to the community than costs. Much real-world public policy is motivated by a desire to correct the shortcomings of the market. Anti-trust action is designed to promote competition. Government provision of national defense, crime prevention, a legal system, and flood-control projects is related to the public-good nature of these activities. Similarly, externalities account for public sector action in such areas as pollution control, education, pure research, and no-fault insurance. Clearly, the tax, spending, and monetary policies of the government are utilized to influence the level of economic activity in most Western nations.

Demand for public sector action may also stem from a desire to change the income distribution. There is no reason to presume that the unhampered market will lead to the most desirable distribution of income. In fact, the ideal distribution of income is largely a matter of personal preference. There is nothing in positive economics that tells us that one distribution of income is better than another. Some persons may desire to see more income allocated to low-income citizens. The most common scientific argument for redistribution to the poor is based on the "public-good" nature of adequate income for all. Alleviation of poverty may help not only the poor but also those who are well-off. Middle- and upper-income recipients, for example, may benefit if the less fortunate members of the community enjoy better food, clothing, housing, and health care. If the rich would gain, why will they not voluntarily give to the poor? For the same reason that individuals will do little to provide national defense volun-tarily. The antipoverty efforts of any single individual will exert little impact on the total amount of poverty in the community. Because individual action is so insignificant, each person has an incentive to opt out. When everybody opts out, the market provides less than the desired amount of antipoverty action.

Others may desire public sector redistribution for less altruistic reasons—they may seek to enhance their own personal incomes. Sometimes redistribution will take the form of direct income transfers. In other cases, the redistribution strategy may be indirect; it may simply increase the demand for one's service. Regardless of the mechanism, higher taxes will generally accompany income redistribution.

Substantial income redistribution may adversely affect the efficiency of resource allocation and the incentive to produce. There are three major reasons why large-scale redistribution is likely to reduce the size of the economic pie. First, such redistribution weakens the link between productive activity and reward. When taxes take a larger share of one's income, the benefits derived from hard work and productive service are reduced. The basic economic postulate suggests that when the benefits allocated to producers are lowered (and benefits of nonproducers are raised), less productive effort will be supplied. Second, as public policy redistributes a larger share of income, individuals will allocate

Rent Seeking: Actions by individuals and interest groups designed to restructure public policy in a manner that will either directly or indirectly redistribute more income to themselves.

more resources to **rent seeking.**[4] Rent seeking is a term used by economists to classify actions designed to change public policy—tax structure, composition of spending, or regulation—in a manner that will redistribute income to oneself. Resources allocated to rent seeking (perhaps "favor seeking" would be more descriptive) will be unavailable to increase the size of the economic pie. Third, higher taxes to finance income redistribution and an expansion in rent-seeking activities will generate a response. Taxpayers will be encouraged to take steps to protect their income. More accountants, lawyers, and tax shelter experts will be retained as people seek to limit the amount of their income that is redistributed to others. Like the resources allocated to rent seeking, resources allocated to protecting one's wealth from public policy will also be wasted. They will not be available for productive activity. Therefore, given the incentive structure generated by large-scale redistributional policies, there is good reason to expect that such policies will reduce the size of the economic pie.

CONFLICTS BETWEEN GOOD ECONOMICS AND GOOD POLITICS

What reason is there for believing that political action will result in economic inefficiency? Current economic and political research is continually yielding knowledge that will help us to answer this question more definitively. We deal with it in more detail in a later chapter, but three important characteristics of the political process are introduced here.

1. The Rationally Ignorant Voter. Less than one-half of the American electorate can correctly identify the names of their congressmen and women, much less state where their representatives stand on various issues. Why are so many people ignorant of the simplest facts regarding the political process? The explanation does not lie with a lack of intelligence of the average American. The phenomenon is explained by the incentives confronting the voter. Most citizens recognize that their vote is unlikely to determine the outcome of an election. Since their vote is highly unlikely to resolve the issue at hand, citizens have little incentive to seek costly information in order to cast an intelligent vote. Economists refer to this lack of incentive as the **rational ignorance effect.**

Rational Ignorance Effect: Voter ignorance that is present because individuals perceive their votes as unlikely to be decisive. Voters rationally have little incentive to inform themselves so as to cast an intelligent vote.

The rationally ignorant voter is merely exercising good judgment as to how her or his time and effort will yield the most benefits. There is a parallel between the voter's failure to acquire political knowledge and the farmer's inattention to the factors that determine the weather. Weather is probably the most important factor determining the income of an individual farmer, yet it makes no sense for the farmer to invest time and resources attempting to understand and alter the weather. An improved knowledge of the weather system will probably not enable the farmer to avoid its adverse effects. So it is with the average voter. The average voter stands to gain little from acquiring more information about a wide range of issues that are decided in the political arena.

---

[4]See James M. Buchanan, Robert D. Tollison, and Gordon Tullock, *Toward a Theory of the Rent-Seeking Society* (College Station: Texas A & M University Press, 1981), for additional detail on rent seeking.

Since the resolution of these issues, like the weather, is out of their hands, voters have little incentive to become more informed.

Thus, most voters simply rely on information that is supplied to them freely by candidates and the mass media. Conversations with friends and information acquired at work, from newspapers, from TV news, and from political advertising are especially important because the voter has so little incentive to incur any personal information-gathering cost. Few voters are able to describe accurately the consequences of, for example, raising tariffs on automobiles or abolishing the farm price support program. This should not surprise us. In using their time and efforts in ways other than studying these policy issues, they are merely responding to economic incentives.[5]

Special Interest Issue: An issue that generates substantial *individual* benefits to a small minority while imposing a small *individual* cost on other voters. In total, the net cost to the majority might either exceed or fall short of the net benefits to the special interest group.

2. The Problem of Special Interest. A **special interest issue** is one that generates substantial personal benefits for a small number of constituents while imposing a small individual cost on a large number of other voters. A few gain a great deal *individually,* whereas a large number lose a little *as individuals.*

Special interest issues are very attractive to vote-conscious politicians (that is, to those most eager and most likely to win elections). Voters who have a small cost imposed on them by a policy favoring a special interest will not care enough about the issue to examine it, particularly if it is complex enough that the imposition of the cost is difficult to identify. Because of the cost of information, most of those harmed will not even be aware of the legislator's views on such an issue. Most voters will simply ignore special interest issues. The special interests, however, will be vitally concerned. They will let the candidate (or legislator) know how important an issue is to them. They will help politicians, both financially and otherwise, who favor their position, and will oppose those who do not.

What would you do if you wanted to win an election? Support the special interest groups. Milk them for financial resources. Use those resources to "educate" the uninformed majority of voters about how you support policies that are in their interest. You would have an incentive to follow this path even if the total community benefits from the support of the special interest were less than the cost. The policy might cause economic inefficiency, but it could still be a political winner.

Why stand up for a large majority? Even though the total cost may be very large, each person bears only a small cost. Most voters are uninformed on the issue. They do not care much about it. They would do little to help you get elected even if you supported their best interests on this issue. Astute politicians will support the special interest group if they plan to be around for very long.

The political process tends to be biased in favor of special interest groups. There is thus sometimes a conflict between good politics and ideal public policy. Throughout, as we consider public policy alternatives, we will remind you to consider how public policy is likely to operate when special interest influence is strong.

3. Political Gains from Shortsighted Policies. The complexity of many issues makes it difficult for voters to identify the future benefits and costs. Will a tax

---

[5]Anthony Downs, in *An Economic Theory of Democracy* (New York: Harper, 1958), and Gordon Tullock, in *Toward a Mathematics of Politics* (Ann Arbor: University of Michigan Press, 1967), among others, have emphasized this point.

cut reduce the long-run rate of unemployment? Are wage–price controls an efficient means of dealing with inflation? Can pro-union legislation raise the real wages of workers? These questions are complex. Few voters will analyze the short-run and long-run implications of policy in these areas. Thus, voters will have a tendency to rely on current conditions. To the voter, the best indicator of the success of a policy is, How are things now?

OUTSTANDING ECONOMIST
James Buchanan (1919–   )

Twenty-five years ago, most economists were content to concentrate on the workings of the marketplace, its shortcomings, and what government action might do to correct these deficiencies. Both political scientists and economists envisioned the public sector as a type of supra-individual, a creature making decisions in the public interest. James Buchanan set out to change all of this. He, perhaps more than anyone else, is responsible for what some have called the "public choice revolution."

Buchanan perceives government to be an outgrowth of individual behavior. Individual human beings are the ultimate choice-makers, shaping and molding group action as well as private affairs. By means of the tools of economics, theories are developed to explain how the political process works. Real-world data are used to test the theories. Buchanan's approach is that of scientific politics.

Noting that approximately 40 percent of every dollar earned in the United States in channeled through the public sector, Buchanan argues:

It just doesn't make any sense to concentrate, as traditional economic theory does, on the 60 percent of your income and product that's related to the private sector and to provide no explanation of why the remainder is used in the way it is. So the extension of the highly sophisticated tools of analysis that economics has developed over the past 200 years to the realm of political choices was a natural and logical one. [6]

In their widely acclaimed book, *The Calculus of Consent,* [7] Buchanan and Gordon Tullock develop a theory of constitutions and analyze

political behavior under alternative decision rules (for example, simple majority, legislative procedure, etc.). With the individual always used as the foundation of the analysis, they develop theories concerning special interests, logrolling, and the types of activities that are most likely to be provided through the public sector. Empirical work testing many of the implications of the book continues today. In a more recent book, *The Limits of Liberty,* [8] which Buchanan considers complementary to the earlier book with Tullock, Buchanan applies his individualistic perspective to explain the emergence of property rights, law, and government itself, with a view toward unraveling some of the problems of the 1970s.

A past president of the Southern Economic Association, Buchanan has also written widely on externalities, public goods, and public finance. His doctoral degree is from the University of Chicago, and he is a member of the Mont Pelerin Society. He taught at Florida State, Virginia, UCLA, and Virginia Polytechnic Institute before accepting his present position as Distinguished Professor of Economics and general director of the Center for the Study of Public Choice at George Mason University.

---

[6]Quoted in Judith Scott-Epley, "From Constitutions to Car Inspections: Looking for a Better Way," *Virginia Tech Magazine* (September/October 1981), p. 230.

[7]J.M. Buchanan and G. Tullock, *The Calculus of Consent* (Ann Arbor: University of Michigan Press, 1962).

[8]J.M. Buchanan, *The Limits of Liberty* (Chicago: University of Chicago Press, 1975).

Political entrepreneurs seeking to win an election have a strong incentive to support policies that generate current benefits in exchange for future costs, particularly if the future costs will be difficult to identify on election day. Therefore, public sector action will be biased in favor of legislation that offers immediate (and easily identifiable) current benefits in exchange for future costs that are complex and difficult to identify. Simultaneously, there is a bias against legislation that involves immediate and easily identifiable costs (for example, higher taxes) while yielding future benefits that are complex and difficult to identify. Economists refer to this bias inherent in the collective decision-making process as the **shortsightedness effect.**

Shortsightedness Effect: Mis-allocation of resources that results because public sector action is biased (a) in favor of proposals yielding clearly defined current benefits in exchange for difficult-to-identify future costs and (b) against proposals with clearly identifiable current costs yielding less concrete and less obvious future benefits.

The nature of democratic institutions restricts the planning horizon of elected officials. Positive results must be observable by the next election, or the incumbent is likely to be replaced by someone who promises more rapid results. Policies that will *eventually* pay off in the future (after the next election) will have little attractiveness to vote-seeking politicians if those policies do not exert a beneficial impact by election day. As we shall subsequently see, the short-sighted nature of the political process reduces the likelihood that governments will be able to promote economic stability and a noninflationary environment.

What if shortsighted policies lead to serious problems after an election? This can be sticky for politicians; but is it not better to be an *officeholder* explaining why things are in a mess than a *defeated candidate* trying to convince people who will not listen why you were right all the time? The political entrepreneur has a strong incentive to win the next election and worry about what is right later.

LOOKING AHEAD

In the following chapter, we will take a look at the government's actual spending and tax policies. In subsequent chapters, the significance of economic organization and issues of political economy will be highlighted. The tools of economics are used with a dual objective. We will attempt to point out what government *ideally should do,* but we will also focus on what we can *expect government to do.* Not surprisingly, these two are not always identical. Political economy—the use of economic tools to explain how both the market and the public sectors actually work—is a fascinating subject. It helps us to understand the "why" behind many of today's current events. Who said economics is the dismal science?

CHAPTER LEARNING OBJECTIVES

1   Two conditions must be met to achieve economic efficiency: (a) All activities that produce more benefits than costs for the individuals within an economy must be undertaken, and (b) activities that generate more costs to the individuals than benefits must not be undertaken. If only the buyer and seller are affected, production and exchange in competitive markets are consistent with the ideal-efficiency criteria.

2   Lack of competition may make it possible for a group of sellers to gain by restricting output and raising prices. There is a conflict between (a) the self-interest of sellers that leads them to collude, restrict output, and raise product prices above their production costs and (b) economic efficiency. Public sector action—promoting competition or regulating private firms—may be able to improve economic efficiency in industries in which competitive pressures are lacking.

3   The market will tend to underallocate resources to the production of goods with

external benefits and overallocate resources to those products that generate external costs.

4 Public goods are troublesome for the market to handle because nonpaying customers cannot easily be excluded. Since the amount of a public good that each individual receives is largely unaffected by whether he or she helps pay for it, most individuals will contribute little. Thus, the market will tend to undersupply public goods.

5 The public sector can improve the operation of markets by providing a stable economic environment.

6 The public sector is an alternative means of organizing economic activity. Public sector decision-making will reflect the choices of individuals acting as voters, politicians, financial contributors, lobbyists, and bureaucrats. Public choice analysis applies the principles and methodology of economics to group decision-making in an effort to help us understand collective organizations.

7 Successful political candidates will seek to offer programs that voters favor. Voters, in turn, will be attracted to candidates who reflect the voters' own views and interests. In a democratic setting, there are two major reasons why voters will turn to collective organization: (a) to reduce waste and inefficiency stemming from noncompetitive markets, externalities, public goods, and economic instability and (b) to alter the income distribution.

8 Public sector action may sometimes improve the market's efficiency and lead to an increase in the community's welfare, all individuals considered. However, the political process is likely to conflict with ideal economic efficiency criteria when (a) voters have little knowledge of an issue, (b) special interests are strong, and/or (c) political figures can gain from following shortsighted policies.

THE ECONOMIC WAY OF THINKING—DISCUSSION QUESTIONS

1 Explain in your own words what is meant by external costs and external benefits. Why may market allocations be less than ideal when externalities are present?

2 If producers are to be provided with an incentive to produce a good, why is it important for them to be able to prevent nonpaying customers from receiving the good?

3 Do you think that real-world politicians adopt political positions in order to help their election prospects? Can you name a current political figure who consistently puts "principles above politics"? If so, check with three of your classmates and see if they agree.

4 Do you think that special interest groups exert much influence on local government? Why or why not? As a test, check the composition of the local zoning board in your community. How many real estate agents, contractors, developers, and landlords are on the board? Are there any citizens without real estate interests on the board?

5 "Economics is a positive science. Government by its very nature is influenced by philosophical considerations. Therefore, the tools of economics cannot tell us much about how the public sector works." Do you agree or disagree? Why?

6 Which of the following are public goods: (a) an antimissile system surrounding Washington, D.C., (b) a fire department, (c) tennis courts, (d) Yellowstone National Park, (e) elementary schools?

7 "Political organization cannot reform human beings. We should not expect it to. The public sector is an alternative to the market. Political organization will influence the direction of human action primarily by modifying the incentive structure. For some types of activity, public sector organization is likely to improve on the market, and for others, the market is likely to be superior." Do you agree or disagree? Why?

In this world nothing is certain but death and taxes.
Benjamin Franklin (1789)

5

GOVERNMENT SPENDING AND TAXATION

Whether the setting is the halls of Congress, the classroom, or a social gathering, a discussion of the economic role of government generally means controversy. In this chapter we will focus on the facts of government. How big is it? What services does it provide? How much does it cost? We will also illustrate how the functions of government have changed in recent decades. In addition, we will analyze the impact of taxes on resource allocation. Some of today's liveliest controversies surround these issues.

The role of government in the economy is not limited to its tax and spending activities. Public policy also defines property rights, enforces contracts, regulates business activities, and often imposes price floors (or ceilings) for various products. In recent years, government regulatory activities have expanded substantially. In fact, some economists now argue that government expenditures are not an adequate measure of the economic significance of the public sector, since they fail to register fully the importance of regulatory actions. Nonetheless, taxation and government expenditures are the most direct means by which the government influences the economy. Analysis of the government's taxation and spending policies will reveal a great deal about the size and economic character of government.

WHAT DO FEDERAL, STATE, AND LOCAL GOVERNMENTS BUY?

There are three levels of government in the United States, the federal, the state, and the local levels, the major responsibilities of which differ considerably. A breakdown of expenditures and taxes will highlight some of these differences.

The federal government spends the most of the three, approximately three-fifths of total government expenditures. Exhibit 1 shows the broad categories of federal expenditures for the fiscal year 1981. The federal government is solely responsible for national defense. A little less than 30 percent of all

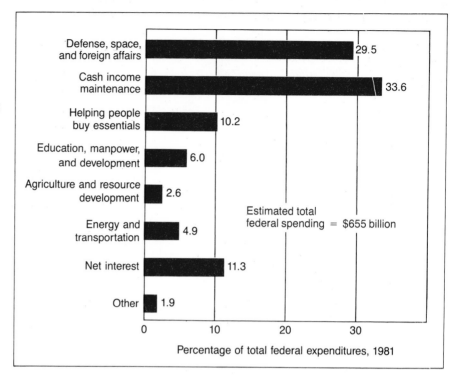

federal expenditures went for defense and related areas (space, veterans' benefits, and foreign affairs) in 1981. The largest item in the federal budget was cash income maintenance—social security, unemployment payments, and public assistance to the poor and disabled. These income transfers comprised approximately one-third of the total federal budget. Programs to help people buy essentials (medical care, housing, food, etc.) made up 10.2 percent of all federal spending in 1981. This category differs from cash income maintenance in that persons must purchase specific goods in order to qualify for the assistance. Expenditures on education, manpower development, agriculture, energy, and transportation also constitute major items in the federal budget from year to year. Interest payments on the national debt for 1981 constituted more than 11 percent of total federal outlays.

Exhibit 2 is a graphic presentation of state and local government expenditures. In the United States, public education has traditionally been the responsibility of state and local governments. Thirty-one percent of state and local government expenditures were allocated to education during the fiscal year 1979. State governments supplement federal allocations in the areas of social welfare, public welfare, and health. These social welfare expenditures composed 18 percent of the total spending of state governments during 1979. Highways, utilities, insurance trusts, law enforcement, and fire protection are other major areas of expenditure for state and local governments.

Government Purchases and Transfer Payments

It is important to distinguish between (a) government purchases of goods and services and (b) transfer payments. Government purchases include items such as

EXHIBIT 2 What state and local governments buy

Education, public welfare, and general administrative expenditures comprise the major budget items of state and local governments.

U.S. Department of Commerce.

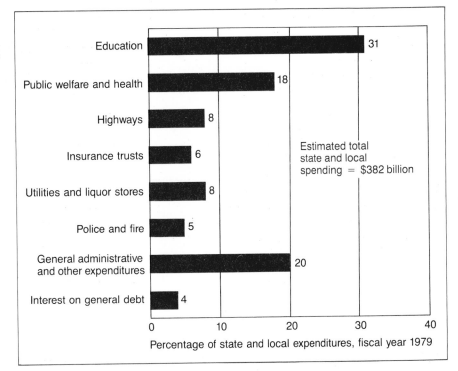

EXHIBIT 2 What state and local governments buy

Education, public welfare, and general administrative expenditures comprise the major budget items of state and local governments.

U.S. Department of Commerce.

paper, typewriters, automobiles, office space, and electricity that are necessary to conduct ordinary business activity. In addition, public sector activity also requires the purchase of unique goods such as nuclear reactors, jet planes, superhighways, and liquid-fuel-powered rockets. Governments also purchase the labor services of teachers, clerks, lawyers, accountants, and public relations experts. Resources utilized to produce goods purchased by the government will, of course, be unavailable to produce goods for private purchase.

Transfer payments involve the redistribution of income from some individuals to others.[1] Simply put, income is taxed away from Peter in order to provide additional income to Sarah. No product is produced in the process. Transfer payments, unlike government purchases, do not *directly* reduce the resources available to the private sector. However, they do alter the incentive structure of the economy and almost certainly exert an *indirect* impact upon the size of the economic pie. The taxes necessary to finance transfer payments will reduce the personal payoff from saving, investing, and working. If receipt of transfer payments is inversely related to income level, they will also reduce the *recipient's* incentive to earn taxable income. As we proceed, we will investigate the linkage between aggregate output and the incentive structure in more detail.

[1]The public administration costs associated with income transfer programs do involve the direct use of resources, and therefore they are counted as government purchases. Only the redistribution portion is counted as a transfer payment.

HOW BIG IS GOVERNMENT?

Exhibit 3 presents four alternative measures of governmental size. In 1980, the purchases of federal, state, and local governments amounted to $534.8 billion, or 20.4 percent of total U.S. output. Thus, government purchases consumed a little more than one-fifth of our resources. Government employment offers a second gauge by which we can measure the size of government. In 1980, approximately one out of every six workers (16.4 percent) was employed by a governmental unit.

As we have already pointed out, government purchases fail to tell the whole story. Governments not only employ people and provide goods and services; they also tax the income of some and transfer it to others. Once transfer payments are included, total government expenditures in 1980 amounted to $869.0 billion, or 33.1 percent of the gross national product (GNP).[2] The total tax bill was slightly less, amounting to 31.8 percent of GNP. Therefore, in 1980 approximately one-third of the national output was channeled through the public sector.

On a per capita basis, government expenditures were equal to $3915 in 1980. If government expenditures in 1980 had been divided equally among the 78 million households in the United States, each household would have received $11,140.

The Growth of Government

The public sector in the United States has not always been so large. As Exhibit 4 illustrates, total government expenditures amounted to only 10 percent of GNP in 1929. During the 1930s, government expenditures increased rapidly. By 1940, the public sector generated 18.5 percent of GNP. Government expenditures soared during World War II, but they dropped back substantially at the conclusion of the war. Relative to GNP, government expenditures were only slightly higher in 1950 than in 1940. Since 1950, government expenditures have increased substantially relative to the size of our economy. Only 21.3 percent of

EXHIBIT 3   Four measures of the size of government (federal, state and local), 1980

1 Government purchases of goods and services	a) Billions of dollars	534.8
	b) Percentage of GNP	20.4
2 Government employment[a]	a) Millions of employees	16.0
	b) Percentage of total work force	16.4
3 Total government expenditures including transfer payments	a) Billions of dollars	869.0
	b) Percentage of GNP	33.1
4 Total taxes	a) Billions of dollars	834.2
	b) Percentage of GNP	31.8

[a]Data are for October of 1979.

Facts and Figures on Government Finance—1981 and *The Economic Report of the President, 1981* (Washington, D.C.: U.S. Government Printing Office, 1981). Intergovernmental transfer payments (i.e., federal grants to states and local governments) are not counted twice.

---

[2]The gross national product (GNP) is discussed in detail in Chapter 6. For a definition of GNP, see p. 107.

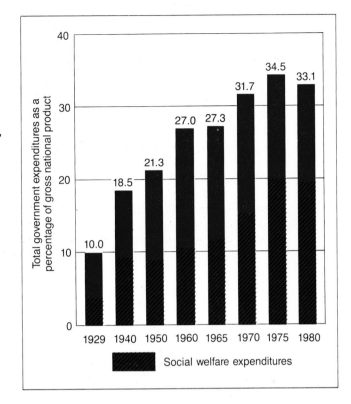

our total output was channeled through government in 1950, compared to the 33.1 percent figure for 1980.

The decline in the purchasing power of the dollar has contributed to the growth of government spending measured in dollar terms. However, as we have shown, government expenditures have expanded not just in dollar terms but also in proportion to total output.

The Changing Composition of Government

Traditionally, the federal government has been responsible for national defense in the United States. Since defense is a classic example of a public good, it is not surprising that this good is supplied through the public rather than through the private sector. Police and fire protection, road maintenance, and education have traditionally been financed and distributed by state and local governments. Each of these goods generates external "spillover effects" and exhibits public-good characteristics. The police and fire departments available to help protect my life and property are also available for your protection. At least until congestion becomes a problem, my use of the roadways does not reduce their availability to you. Education contributes to the feasibility of a modern democratic society, thereby generating a benefit to persons other than the highly educated. Given the characteristics of police and fire protection, roads, and education, it is not surprising that for many years these items have been supplied by and through the public sector.

However, these traditional public sector functions are not responsible for the growth of government in recent years. The relative size of the public sector has increased because the government has expanded its social welfare and income redistribution activities. As Exhibit 4 illustrates, the social welfare expenditures of the government expanded slowly, as a share of GNP, during the 20 years following World War II and then virtually exploded during the 1965–1975 period. As the Great Society programs enacted during the administration of Lyndon Johnson grew to maturity, the government's role in providing (or subsidizing) medical care, housing, food, and school lunches expanded. Expenditures for training and development, designed to upgrade the quality of the work force and improve the employment opportunities of disadvantaged groups, were enlarged. But perhaps most significantly, the government emerged as a major redistributor of income from one group to another—from the working population to retirees, from the employed to the unemployed, from the taxpayer to disadvantaged groups, such as female-headed households with dependent children. In 1965 income transfers were 5.9 percent of the GNP. By the mid-1970s, the government was redistributing more than 10 percent of total output away from current producers to income transfer recipients. As the government undertook these additional social welfare responsibilities, expenditures in these areas grew far more rapidly than the income of taxpayers. Even after adjustment for inflation, during the 1965–1980 period social welfare expenditures jumped 178 percent, compared to an "inflation-adjusted" expansion in national output of only 57 percent. As a result, the size of social welfare expenditures, *as a share of the GNP,* grew from 11.2 percent in 1965 to approximately 20 percent during the latter half of the 1970s (see Exhibit 4).

As the social welfare role of government has expanded, the proportion

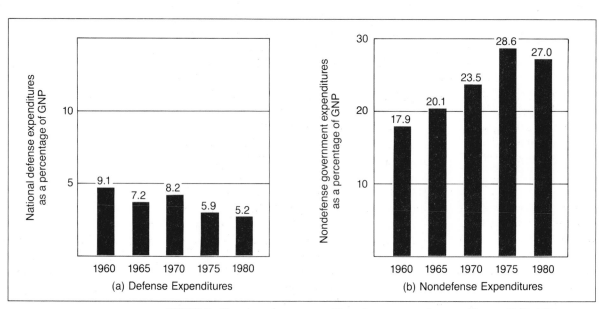

EXHIBIT 5   The changing composition of government expenditures, 1960–1980

During the last two decades, defense expenditures have declined as a percentage of the GNP, and nondefense government expenditures have risen rapidly. President Reagan pledged to reverse these trends when he took office in 1981.

Facts and Figures on Government Finance—1981 and *Statistical Abstract of the United States—1980,* p. 366.

of national output allocated to national defense has declined. As Exhibit 5 illustrates, national defense expenditures consumed 9.1 percent of the GNP in 1960. The figure declined during the first half of the 1960s and rose during the latter half of the decade as the war in Vietnam escalated. However, by 1980 national defense expenditures had declined to 5.2 percent of the GNP. In contrast, nondefense expenditures rose from 17.9 percent of the GNP in 1960 to 28.6 percent in 1975, before falling back to 27.0 in 1980. The desirability of these trends was hotly debated during the presidential campaign of 1980. President Reagan, when he took office, pledged to enlarge the defense sector and curtail the growth rate, if not the absolute size, of the government's social welfare expenditures.

TAXES TO PAY FOR A GROWING GOVERNMENT

When the government spends money and utilizes resources, costs are incurred. The money to cover the costs of government is collected in the form of taxes.[3] As Exhibit 6 shows, most tax revenue comes from five sources: (a) personal income taxes, (b) payroll taxes, (c) sales taxes, (d) property taxes, and (e) corporate income taxes. Let us take a closer look at each of these major sources of tax revenue.

Personal Income Taxes

Approximately 37 percent of the total tax dollars is raised via the personal income tax. This tax is particularly important at the federal level, where it accounts for 46 percent of the total budget receipts (Exhibit 6). Since World War II, the income tax has also become an important source of revenue at the state level, where it now accounts for almost one-fourth of the tax receipts of states. Only six states (Florida, Nevada, South Dakota, Texas, Washington, and Wyoming) now fail to levy a state income tax.

A distinctive characteristic of the federal income tax is its progressive structure. A **progressive tax** takes a larger percentage from high-income recipients. For example, utilizing the rate structure applicable to income in 1982, the tax liability of a married couple with $5000 of taxable income is $192. The **average tax rate** (ATR) can be expressed as follows:

Progressive Tax: A tax that requires those with higher taxable incomes to pay a larger percentage of their incomes to the government than do those with lower taxable incomes.

Average Tax Rate: One's tax liability divided by one's taxable income.

$$ATR = \frac{\text{tax liability}}{\text{taxable income}}$$

The couple's average tax rate on $5000 of income is 3.84 percent ($192/$5000). Since the federal income tax structure is progressive, the average tax rate will increase with taxable income. For example, the tax liability (1982) of a couple with a taxable income of $10,000 is $930, resulting in an average tax rate of 9.3 percent, considerably higher than the ATR for $5000 of taxable income.

---

[3]The costs of government may also be felt in other ways. When government spending is financed by money creation, the costs of government will take the form of inflation. If government is financed by borrowing during normal times, the costs of government will be felt in the form of rising interest rates as government borrowing bids up the price of financial capital in the loanable funds market. Each of these issues will be dealt with in subsequent chapters.

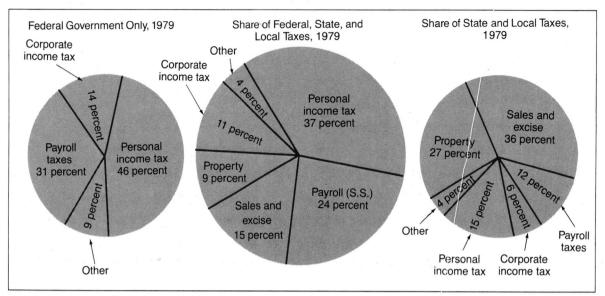

EXHIBIT 6   Paying for government

Personal income, payroll, and corporate income taxes are the major sources of tax revenues for the federal government. Sales and property taxes are the major sources of state and local revenues.

U.S. Office of Management and Budget and U.S. Department of Commerce.

Marginal Tax Rate: Additional tax liability divided by additional income. Thus, if $100 of additional earnings increased one's tax liability by $30, the marginal tax rate would be 30 percent.

The economic way of thinking stresses that what happens at the margin is of crucial importance in personal decision-making. The **marginal tax rate** (MTR) can be expressed as follows:

$$\text{MTR} = \frac{\text{change in tax liability}}{\text{change in income}}$$

The marginal tax rate reveals both how much of one's additional income can be retained and how much must be turned over to the tax collector. For example, when the marginal tax rate is 25 percent, $25 of every $100 of *additional* earnings must be paid to the taxing authority. The individual is permitted to keep $75 of his or her additional income.

The marginal tax rate, like the average tax rate, will increase with income when the tax structure is progressive. Prior to 1981, the marginal tax rates on taxable income ranged from 14 percent in the lowest income bracket to 70 percent in the highest income bracket. However, a 50 percent *marginal* tax rate ceiling was imposed by tax legislation passed in 1981. Under current tax legislation, marginal tax rates range from 11 percent to a maximum of 50 percent (for joint returns with a taxable income of more than $109,400 in 1983).

Payroll Taxes

Although income from all sources is covered by the income tax, only earnings derived from labor are subject to the payroll tax. Interest, dividends, rents, and other income derived from capital are not subject to payroll taxes. Payroll taxes on the earnings of employees and self-employed workers are utilized to finance social security (including Medicare) and unemployment compensation benefits. Payroll taxes constitute the second largest and the most rapidly expanding

source of tax revenue. As of 1979, 24 percent of all tax revenues originated from payroll taxes. In 1979, payroll taxes comprised 31 percent of all *federal* revenues, compared to only 16 percent in 1960.

Payroll taxes are often criticized because of their regressive structure. Actually, the payroll tax encompasses both proportional and regressive features. **A proportional tax** is one that takes the same percentage of income, regardless of income level. Until the maximum taxable income ceiling is reached, the payroll tax is proportional. For example, in 1984, each employee pays a tax rate of 6.70 percent on earnings for all earnings up to $39,600. Beyond that taxable income ceiling, no additional payroll tax is levied. Thus, a worker earning $10,000 incurs a payroll tax of $670, whereas one earning $20,000 is taxed earnings brackets than from low-income recipients. Since the social security twice that amount, or $1340. Until the taxable income ceiling is met, all workers pay according to exactly the same tax rate.

A regressive tax takes a smaller *percentage* of income from those in higher payroll tax does not apply beyond the maximum income ceiling, it is regressive for incomes beyond that point. For example, a person with an income twice the taxable ceiling will pay exactly the same amount of payroll taxes (and only one-half the average tax rate) as another individual whose earnings are equal to the taxable ceiling. All persons with earnings above the taxable ceiling will pay a lower average tax rate than persons with earnings below the ceiling. Thus, since the payroll tax does not apply to earnings above the ceiling, its basic structure can be considered regressive.

Proportional Tax: A tax for which individuals pay the same percentage of their income (or other tax base) in taxes, regardless of their income level.

Regressive Tax: A tax that takes a smaller percentage of one's income as one's income level increases. Thus, the proportion of income allocated to the tax would be greater for the poor than the rich.

Sales and Excise Taxes

Taxes levied on the consumption expenditures for a wide range of goods and services are called sales taxes. A tax levied on specific commodities such as gasoline, cigarettes, or alcoholic beverages is called an excise tax. There is little difference between the two, except that one is a general tax whereas the other is quite specific.

The sales tax provides the backbone for tax revenues at the state level. In 1980, 49 percent of all state tax revenues originated from this source. Even though the federal government does not levy a general sales tax, this tax still constitutes 15 percent of total tax revenue of government at all levels (Exhibit 6).

Property Taxes

Despite their unpopularity, property taxes still constitute the bulk of local tax revenues. In 1979, 77 percent of all local tax revenue was generated from this source. Property taxes are often criticized because they are cumbersome. The assessor must set a value on taxable property. This generally involves a certain amount of judgment and arbitrariness. During a period of rising prices, property that has been recently exchanged is likely to command a higher valuation than similar property without an easily identifiable indicator of current value. High administration costs and problems associated with providing equal treatment for similarly situated taxpayers reduce the attractiveness of property taxes. Despite their declining importance, property taxes still constitute 9 percent of all public sector revenues, an amount only slightly less than that generated by the corporate income tax.

Corporate Income Tax

The corporate income tax is levied on the accounting profits of the firm. Its structure is relatively simple. In 1983, the first $25,000 of corporate profit is taxed at a rate of 15 percent. Corporate profit between $25,000 and $50,000 is taxed at 18 percent. Corporate earnings in the range from $50,000 to $75,000 are taxed at a rate of 30 percent; the rate rises to 40 percent for the range from $75,000 to $100,000. All corporate earnings above $100,000 are taxed at a flat rate of 46 percent. Corporate incomes in the United States have been taxed since 1909. The tax currently generates approximately 14 percent of all federal tax receipts and 11 percent of the total tax revenues for all levels of government (see Exhibit 6). In addition to the federal tax, a number of states and some local governments also levy a corporate profit tax.

Inadvertently, the corporate income tax encourages debt financing rather than equity ownership. This results because no adjustment is made for factors of production owned by the firm and the equity capital invested by the owners. A corporation that utilizes debt financing will incur an interest cost, which will reduce its accounting profits and tax liability. In contrast, if the same firm utilizes equity financing (e.g., raises financial capital by issuing additional stock), the interest cost will not appear on the firm's accounting statement. Therefore, even though there is an opportunity cost of capital, regardless of whether it is raised by equity financing or debt, only the latter will reduce the firm's tax liability.

THE ISSUES OF EFFICIENCY AND EQUITY

There are two major factors to consider when choosing among taxation alternatives. First, taxes should be consistent with the concept of economic efficiency. Taxes should not encourage people to use scarce resources wastefully. A tax system is inconsistent with economic efficiency if it encourages individuals (a) to buy goods costing more than their value to consumers and/or (b) to channel time into tax-avoidance activities.

Second, a tax system should be equitable; that is, it should be consistent with widely accepted principles of fairness. Economists often speak of "horizontal" and "vertical" equity. Horizontal equity means equal treatment of equals. If two parties earn equal incomes, for example, horizontal equity implies that the two should be taxed equally. The corollary concept of vertical equity requires that persons who are situated differently should be taxed differently. It

Ability-to-Pay Principle: The equity concept that persons with larger incomes (or more consumption, or more wealth) should be taxed at a higher rate because their ability to pay is presumably greater. The concept is subjective and fails to reveal how much higher the rate of taxation should be as income increases.

encompasses what economists refer to as the **ability-to-pay principle,** the seemingly straightforward idea that taxes should be levied according to the ability of the taxpayer to pay. However, deciding exactly what this means is at least partially subjective. Most people find it reasonable that the rich should pay more taxes than the poor. Many find it reasonable that the rich should pay a *higher proportion* of their income (or wealth or consumption) in taxes than should the poor. Of course, progressive taxation incorporates this concept. But how much higher a rate should those with higher incomes pay? At this point the consensus breaks down. There is little agreement among either laymen or professional economists about the proper degree of tax progressivity.

A tax system must take equity into account if it is to succeed. The cost of enforcing a system widely presumed to be unreasonable or unfair is certain to be extremely high. However, equity must be balanced with efficiency. A tax system that ignores economic efficiency will also be extremely costly to an economy.

THE BURDEN OF TAXATION

There are two components to the burden of taxation: (a) the loss of private sector purchasing power as revenues are transferred to the government and (b) an excess burden incurred when prices are distorted and resources are channeled into tax avoidance, leading to economic inefficiency. When the government uses tax revenues (purchasing power) to buy missiles, education, highways, and similar goods, costs are incurred. Resources that would otherwise be available to produce private sector goods are channeled into the production of public sector goods. This cost—we might think of it as the direct cost of government—can only be diminished by a reduction in the size of the public sector.

Excess Burden of Taxation: A burden of taxation over and above the burden associated with the transfer of revenues to the government. An excess burden usually reflects losses that occur when beneficial activities are foregone because they are taxed.

Deadweight Loss: A net loss associated with the forgoing of an economic action. The loss does *not* lead to an offsetting gain for other participants. Thus, it reflects economic inefficiency.

Neutral Tax: A tax that does not (a) distort consumer buying patterns or producer production methods or (b) induce individuals to engage in tax-avoidance activities. There will be no excess burden if a tax is neutral.

However, the **excess burden of taxation** reflects costs and losses beyond the actual level of tax revenues collected. It is determined by the method in which tax revenues are gathered—by what is taxed and what is not, causing individuals to give up taxed but otherwise beneficial activities for untaxed activities. For example, if two individuals decide to forego a mutually advantageous exchange because the tax makes the transaction unprofitable, they incur a burden from the taxation even though they do not pay a tax, since the transaction did not take place. Similarly, if an individual decides to allocate more time to leisure or household production and less to market work—because the latter is taxed and the former is not—a burden over and above tax revenues collected from the individual is imposed: Income from market work is lost to the individual, and whatever benefits for others that resulted from the work are foregone. Excess burdens reflect economic inefficiency, *relative to our hypothetical ideal.* They impose a **deadweight loss** on an economy, because they reflect a cost imposed on some individuals without any offsetting benefit to others.

An ideal tax system would not alter the incentive of individuals to allocate their time and income into those areas that yield them the most satisfaction. A tax of this kind is called a **neutral tax.** A neutral tax would *not* encourage individuals to spend more of their income on business travel, housing, medical service, or professional association publications and less of their income on food because the former are tax-deductible and the latter is not. Similarly, a neutral tax would *not* encourage an individual to allocate more time and money to invest-

Head Tax: A lump-sum tax levied on all individuals regardless of their income, consumption, wealth, or other indicators of economic well-being.

ments that reduce the tax burden (depreciable assets, municipal bonds, tax-free retirement plans, etc.) and to devote less time and money to savings and work activities that generate taxable income.

However, there is a problem with the concept of a neutral tax. About the only tax that would meet the hypothetical ideal of neutrality is a **head tax,** a tax imposing an equal lump-sum tax on all individuals. A head tax would impose the same dollar tax liability on the poor as on the rich (or the same liability on those who consume few goods as on those who consume many goods). Since a head tax conflicts with the concept of vertical equity—the view that persons who are situated differently should be taxed differently—it fails to pass our test of fairness.

Thus, we generally tax things like income, consumption, and property. However, taxes imposed on productive economic activity can be an important source of economic inefficiency. As a general rule, taxes will reduce the level of the activity being taxed. An excess burden is generally unavoidable.

Exhibit 7 illustrates this point and clarifies the distinction between the tax burden associated with the transfer of purchasing power and the excess burden of taxation. Here we show the impact of a 40-cent tax imposed on each pack of cigarettes. Prior to the imposition of the tax, 35 billion packs of cigarettes were produced and sold to consumers at a market price of 80 cents per pack. The cigarette tax increases the cost of supplying and marketing cigarettes by 40 cents per pack. Thus, the supply curve of cigarettes shifts *vertically* by the amount of the tax. However, consumers would not purchase as many cigarettes as before if the full burden of the tax were passed on to them in the form of a 40-cent increase in the per pack price of cigarettes. Thus, when the supply curve shifts vertically, the market price of cigarettes rises by less than the amount of the tax. Since the amount of cigarettes demanded is thus responsive to the higher price, some of the burden of the cigarette tax will fall on the cigarette producers.

EXHIBIT 7   The impact of a tax on economic activity

Here we illustrate the impact of a 40-cent tax (per pack) on cigarettes. Since the tax increases the cost of supplying cigarettes for consumption, the supply curve is shifted vertically by the amount of the tax. However, at the higher price consumers reduce their consumption. The equilibrium price increases from 80 cents to $1.00 per pack. Consumers pay 20 cents more per pack and sellers receive 20 cents less as the result of the 40-cent tax. In addition, consumers and producers lose the mutual gains from exchange (triangle ABC) that would be realized if the tax did not reduce the volume of trade between cigarette producers and consumers.

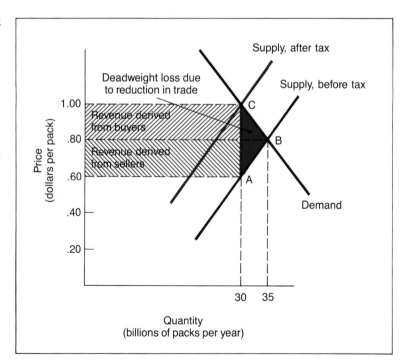

In our hypothetical example, a new equilibrium price of cigarettes will occur at a price of $1.00 per pack and an annual output rate of 30 billion packs of cigarettes. The tax will raise $12 billion (40 cents times 30 billion packs) of revenue. The burden of the tax will fall equally on producers and consumers (20 cents per pack each). This burden—the first component of the tax burden—consists of the loss of 20 cents per pack to both the sellers and the buyers. But note that the production and consumption of cigarettes have been reduced by 5 billion packs. The mutual advantageous gains that would have accrued to producers and consumers (the triangle ABC) are lost. This loss is the second component of the burden of the tax. (Remember that trade is a positive-sum game, so a reduction in the volume of trade will result in economic loss.) This loss, associated with the unrealized exchanges, is an excess burden, a deadweight loss, since it is *not* accompanied by an offsetting gain in the form of additional tax revenue for the government.

In our example, the burden of the tax was divided equally between sellers and buyers. This will not always be true. If the demand curve were steeper (and the supply curve flatter), the price of the taxed good would rise by a larger amount, imposing more of the burden on buyers. In contrast, if the demand curve were flatter (and the supply curve steeper), the market price would rise by a smaller amount, and a larger share of the tax burden would fall on sellers.

Tax Incidence: The manner in which the burden of the tax is distributed among economic units (consumers, employees, employers, etc.). The tax burden does not always fall on those who pay the tax.

The burden of taxes is not always borne by the person who writes a check to the Internal Revenue Service. Economists use the term **tax incidence** when discussing the question of how the burden of a tax is distributed among parties. Since the distribution of the tax burden is dependent upon the slope of the supply and demand curves for the activity being taxed, this is not an easy question to answer.

Tax Rates, Income, and Work

As Exhibit 6 illustrates, over 60 percent of the tax revenue of the United States is derived from the taxation of personal income and work (the payroll tax). The impact of these taxes on economic efficiency and total output is one of today's most controversial economic topics. In the past, most economists believed that tax rates on income, such as those used in the United States, exerted little adverse influence upon the incentive of individuals to engage in productive activities. While admitting that the U.S. tax system was imperfect, economists adhered to the view that since it was difficult to alter work activities and thereby avoid the income tax, most individuals would not tend to do so. Since marginal tax rates have increased substantially in recent years, a reevaluation of the traditional view is underway. Today, some economists believe that high marginal tax rates on income-generating activities are an important source of economic inefficiency. Some have even argued that the high marginal rates generate an excess burden of taxation running into the hundreds of billions of dollars.[4]

Exhibit 8 outlines the economic context of the current debate. Here we consider a labor market where workers earn an equilibrium wage of $5.40 per hour in the absence of the taxation of income. Forty hours of work per week are supplied by workers in this market at the $5.40 hourly wage. Now, consider the impact of a flat 20 percent tax rate on income (or payroll). Just as the cigarette tax made it more costly to supply that product, so, too, will the income

---

[4]For example, see Lawrence Summers, "Taxation and Capital Accumulation in a Life Cycle Growth Model," *American Economic Review* (forthcoming).

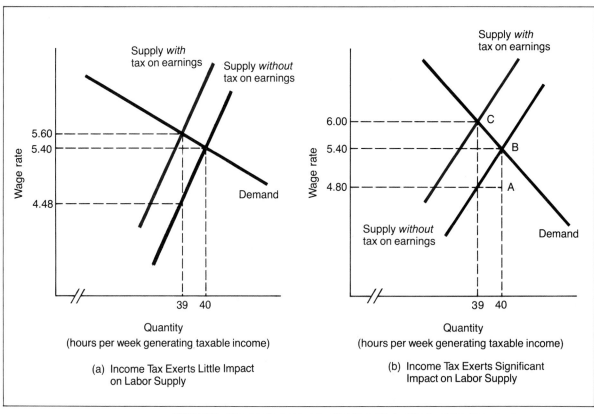

EXHIBIT 8 The controversy over the incentive effects of the income tax

Here we illustrate two alternative outcomes associated with the imposition of a 20 percent tax on income. According to the traditional view (a), when the aggregate labor supply curve is vertical, or almost vertical, the tax will result in only a small reduction in work effort (from 40 to 39 hours per week). In contrast, according to a more recent view (b), if the labor supply curve is flatter, the tax will lead to a larger reduction (from 40 to 36 hours per week) in time spent generating taxable income.

tax make it more costly to supply labor. Thus, the supply curve of labor will decline (shift vertically) by the amount of the tax. According to the traditional view, illustrated by Exhibit 8a, the income tax will exert relatively little impact on hours worked, since the aggregate supply curve of labor is vertical (or almost vertical). The equilibrium wage, including the tax, will be only slightly higher ($5.60 per hour), and the after-tax wage rate of workers will decline substantially (to $4.48). Since the labor supply curve is almost vertical, the burden of the income tax will fall primarily on workers. Furthermore, this will be true regardless of whether the tax is paid directly by the individuals (as in the case of the personal income tax) or whether the check to the IRS is made out by their employer (as in the case of the payroll tax).

The essential element of the traditional view is that since workers lack good alternatives to the earning of taxable income, they will be unable, or virtually unable, to shift from current work to other income-generating activities in order to avoid the burden of the tax. The challengers of the traditional position reject this view. They point out that output is influenced by more than just hours worked. They argue that (a) leisure, (b) household production, (c) jobs with nonmonetary benefits, (d) tax avoidance, and (e) tax evasion are alternatives to simply paying the tax.

According to this view, as high marginal tax rates reduce the personal payoff derived from *taxable* work activities, individuals will shift to these untaxed alternatives. Some will consume more leisure—for example, they will increase their vacation time and absenteeism and reduce overtime hours. Others will allocate more time to untaxable household activities, such as fixing their cars, painting their houses, and producing additional home-prepared meals, rather than working and purchasing new cars, new houses, and meals at restaurants. Still others will take jobs with lower pay but higher nonmonetary benefits and allocate more time to real estate investments with attractive tax benefits. Business ventures designed to show an accounting loss in order to shelter their taxable income will also flourish. All of these alternatives are perfectly legal. However, some individuals may even use illegal means in order to evade the payment of taxes. Participation in the **underground economy** is one device that many believe is widely used to avoid or reduce taxes (see "The Underground Economy," page 101).

If this view is correct—if there are fairly good, feasible alternatives to the payment of high tax rates—one result will be a flatter labor supply curve, as illustrated by Exhibit 8b. As it becomes more costly to supply labor that generates taxable income, people will shift to other alternatives. High marginal tax rates will cause a decline in the work time allocated to activities that generate taxable income and an increase in inefficient tax-avoidance activities. Waste and sizable deadweight losses will be incurred. The triangle ABC (Exhibit 8b), which indicates *only* the inefficiency stemming from lost hours of work actually understates society's excess burden.

Underground Economy: Unreported barter and cash transactions that take place outside of recorded market channels. Some are otherwise legal activities undertaken in order to evade taxes. Others involve illegal activities such as trafficking in drugs, prostitution, extortion, and similar crimes.

Tax Rates, Tax Revenues, and the Laffer Curve

Tax Rate: The per unit or percentage rate at which an economic activity is taxed.

Tax Base: The level of the activity that is taxed. For example, if an excise tax is levied on each gallon of gasoline, the tax base is the number of gallons of gasoline sold. Since higher tax rates generally make the taxed activity less attractive, the size of the tax base is inversely related to the rate at which the activity is taxed.

Laffer Curve: A curve illustrating the relationship between tax rates and tax revenues. The curve reflects the fact that tax revenues are low for *both* high and low tax rates.

It is important to distinguish between a change in **tax rates** and a change in *tax revenues*. The quantity or level of an activity that is taxed—the **tax base**—is *inversely* related to the rate at which the activity is taxed. An increase in a tax rate will lead to a *less than proportional* increase in tax revenues. Higher tax rates will make it more costly to engage in the activity, inducing individuals to shift to substitutes. If there are attractive substitutes, the decline in the activity due to the tax may be substantial. Perhaps a real-world example will help clarify this point. In 1981 the District of Columbia increased the tax rate on gasoline from 10 cents to 13 cents per gallon, a 30 percent increase. But one can be reasonably assured that the 30 percent tax rate increase will *not* lead to a 30 percent increase in tax revenues. The higher tax rate will discourage motorists from purchasing gasoline in the District of Columbia. There is a pretty good alternative to the purchase of the more highly taxed (and therefore higher-priced) gasoline—the purchase of gasoline in Virginia and Maryland, where the tax rates, and therefore prices, are slightly lower. Thus, the quantity of gasoline sold in Washington, D.C., will be lower than would have been the case in the absence of the tax. The revenue gains associated with the higher rate of taxation will be at least partially eroded.

Arthur Laffer, an economist from the University of Southern California, has popularized the idea that sometimes an increase in tax rates can even lead to a *decline* in tax revenues. As the result of Laffer's efforts, the curve illustrating the relationship between tax rates and tax revenues is now called the **Laffer curve.** Exhibit 9 illustrates the concept of the Laffer curve for the taxation of income-generating activity. Obviously, tax revenues would be zero if the tax rate were zero. What is not so obvious is that tax revenues would also be zero (or at

EXHIBIT 9 **The Laffer curve**

Since taxation affects the quantity of an activity that is taxed, a change in tax rates will not lead to a proportional change in tax revenues. As the Laffer curve indicates, beyond some point (*B*), an increase in tax rates may actually cause tax revenues to fall. Since large tax rate increases will lead to only a small expansion in tax revenue as *B* is approached, there is no presumption that point *B* is an ideal rate of taxation.

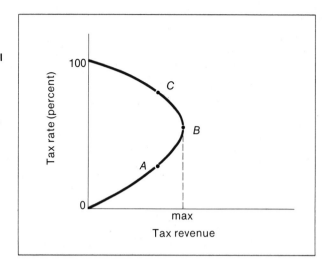

least very close to zero) if the tax rate were 100 percent. Confronting a 100 percent tax rate, most individuals would go fishing or find something else to do rather than engage in productive activity which is taxed, since the 100 percent tax rate would completely remove the material reward derived from earning taxable income. Production in the taxed sector would come to a halt, and without production, tax revenues would plummet to zero.

As tax rates are reduced from 100 percent, the incentive to work and earn taxable income *increases,* income expands, and tax revenues rise. Similarly, as tax rates increase from zero, tax revenues expand. Clearly, at some rate greater than zero but less than 100 percent, tax revenues will be maximized (point *B,* Exhibit 9). This is not to imply that the tax rate that maximizes revenue is ideal. In fact, as the maximum revenue point (*B*) is approached, relatively large tax rate increases will be necessary in order to expand tax revenues. In this range, the excess burden of taxation will be substantial. Unfortunately, no one knows how high marginal tax rates on income can be increased before we begin approaching the maximum revenue point. We do not even know if, at the margins of income levels, we may have imposed tax rates in the counter-productive range, where higher tax rates lead to a decline in tax revenues. As we noted previously, the maximum tax rate on personal income was lowered from 70 percent to 50 percent, effective in 1982. Some economists, including Arthur Laffer, have argued that this aspect of the recently enacted tax-reduction package will actually lead to an increase in the tax revenue derived from high-income taxpayers. As the 1982 tax return data become available, research on this topic should improve our understanding of the linkage between tax rates and tax revenues, particularly for high marginal rates.

Rising Tax Rates on Income, 1965–1980

As we have indicated, government expenditures—particularly social welfare and income transfer expenditures—increased rapidly from the mid-1960s through the 1970s. Not surprisingly, the average and marginal tax rates on income followed suit. Several factors contributed to these rising tax rates. First, inflation pushed taxpayers into higher marginal tax brackets. Even though the purchasing power of the average family income increased very little between 1965 and 1980, *money incomes* more than doubled. Since the U.S tax structure is progressive, a rising money income led to higher marginal (and average) tax rates for the typical income recipient, even though the purchasing power of the average income was virtually unchanged.

Second, payroll taxes to finance social security and Medicare benefits rose substantially. In 1965, the social security payroll tax was 3.625 percent (this percentage is levied on both the employee and the employer) of the employee's first $4800 of earnings. Thus, the maximum tax (employee's share) was $174. By 1982, this payroll tax had risen to 6.70 percent levied against the first $31,800 of earnings, for a maximum tax of $2131. Therefore, during the 1965–1982 period, the maximum social security payroll tax rose 1125 percent! By 1982, a majority of U.S. households were paying more payroll taxes than income taxes.

Exhibit 10 illustrates how the rising tax rates affected a typical working couple with two children (residing in California). One spouse is assumed to have earned the average weekly manufacturing wage, while the other earned one-half that wage during the year. Adjusted for the increase in prices during the period, the combined earnings of the couple increased only slightly during the 1965–1980 period. Nonetheless, the couple's tax liability (federal income and payroll tax, plus the California state income tax) increased steadily. By 1980, the average tax rate for the couple had risen to 20.9 percent, compared to only 13.7 percent in 1965. The couple's marginal tax rate jumped to 35.13 percent in 1980, up from 23.6 percent in 1965.

The case illustrated by Exhibit 10 was not at all atypical for households with working members for this time period. Clearly, tax rates on income, both average and marginal, rose substantially during the 1965–1980 period. In 1981, Congress passed legislation reducing federal income *tax rates* by approximately 23 percent over a four-year period. The legislation also called for the indexing of the income tax beginning in 1985 (see feature on indexing, page 100).

Although a 23 percent rate reduction would appear to be substantial, it should be noted that inflation will continue to push taxpayers into higher tax brackets until 1985. Analysis of the rate reductions indicates that if the inflation rate is in the 10 percent range, *higher tax rates* stemming from the impact of inflation will just about offset the rate reductions enacted in 1981 for all taxpayers with incomes of less than $50,000.[5] Thus, although the Reagan administration's tax package may keep taxes from rising, for most people they will not reverse the trend observable in Exhibit 10.

WHO PAYS THE TAX BILL?

How is the burden of taxation distributed among income groupings in the United States? This is not an easy question to answer. However, economists have tackled the problem, making estimates based on various assumptions of tax incidence. Studies in this area support three broad conclusions.

1. The federal income tax is primarily paid by the top half of income recip-

---

[5]See Stephen A. Meyer and Robert J. Rossana, "Did the Tax Cut Really Cut Taxes?" Federal Reserve Bank of Philadelphia *Business Review* (November/December 1981), 3–12. Also see revised data in January/February 1982 issue of the same journal.

EXHIBIT 10 The marginal tax rate on income for a typical working couple residing in California, 1965–1980

Year	Working Couple with Two Children		
	Combined Weekly Earnings[a] (Measured in 1980 Dollars)	Average Tax Rate (Percent)[b]	Marginal Tax Rate (Percent)[b]
1965	424	13.7	23.6
1970	424	16.7	26.8
1975	440	19.0	31.85
1980	436	20.9	35.13

[a]One person earning the average weekly manufacturing wage with a working spouse earning one-half the average weekly manufacturing wage.

[b]Includes federal income tax, California income tax, and federal social security tax. All calculations assume the couple uses the standard deduction method of calculating their tax liability.

ients. In 1978, taxpayers with incomes of $15,000 or more (48.7 percent of the total) contributed 86 percent of the federal personal income tax revenue.[6] Only 14 percent of the federal income tax revenue was drawn from the bottom half of income recipients. (See Exhibit 11, columns 1 and 2.)

2. When all taxes (federal, state, and local) are considered, the average tax rate for both those with very low incomes (less than $5000) and those with high incomes (more than $50,000) is higher than for middle-income recipients. Excluding these two extremes, the average tax rate, at all levels of government, for units with incomes *between* $5000 and $50,000 is remarkably proportional (see Exhibit 11).[7]

3. Two-thirds of the taxpayers in 1978 had taxable incomes between $10,000 and $50,000. Taxes paid by this group of middle-income recipients accounted for almost 73 percent of *all* tax revenues. This group contributed approximately 70 percent of the federal income tax revenues in 1978. The bulk of the income and therefore the tax revenues came from this group rather than from persons in higher income brackets. In 1978, only 2.6 percent of the tax returns came from persons making $50,000 or more. This small group of high-income recipients generated more than 25 percent of the federal income tax revenue and approximately 15 percent of the total tax revenue for all levels of government.

THE TAXES PAID IN OTHER COUNTRIES

How do the tax burden and the accompanying size of the public sector in the United States compare with those in other countries? Exhibit 12 helps to answer

[6]There is little reason to expect that the 1981–1984 tax cut will significantly shift the tax burden away from high-income recipients. See James Gwartney and Richard Stroup, "Tax Reductions, Incentive Effects, and the Distribution of the Tax Burden," Federal Reserve Bank of Atlanta *Economic Review* (March 1982), for evidence on this point.

[7]Studies conducted by the Tax Foundation, Inc. (Washington, D.C.), and M. B. McElray, as reported in "Capital Gains and the Concept of Measurement of Purchasing Power," in *Business and Economics Statistical Section Proceedings* (American Statistical Association, 1970), are highly consistent with the findings of Exhibit 11.

EXHIBIT 11   Who pays the tax bill?

On average, the federal income tax is progressive (column 3), but when all taxes (state, local, and federal) are considered, both low- and high-income recipients have a slightly higher tax rate than those in middle-income tax brackets (column 5).

Adjusted Gross Income Class (Dollars)	Federal Income Tax Only, 1978			All Taxes	
	Share of Taxable Returns (Percent) (1)	Share of Income Tax (Percent) (2)	Average Tax Rate (Percent) (3)	Share of All Taxes (Percent) (4)	Overall Average Tax Rate (Percent) (5)
Under 5000	7.4	0.3	3.0	1.8	35
5000–9999	23.8	4.7	7.2	10.1	32
10,000–14,999	20.1	9.2	9.9	13.3	30
15,000–24,999	28.8	26.0	12.6	29.8	30
25,000–49,999	17.3	34.5	16.8	29.6	30
50,000–99,999	2.1	12.8	25.2	8.1	33
Over $100,000	0.5	12.6	37.4	7.3	45
Total	100.0	100.0	14.4	100.0	32

The federal income tax data are from the *Statistical Abstract of the United States—1980,* Tables 450 and 452. The data for all taxes are projections based on Roger A. Herriot and Herman P. Miller, "The Taxes We Pay," *Conference Board Record* (May 1971), p. 36, and Joseph A. Pechman and Benjamin A. Okner, *Who Bears the Tax Burden?* (Washington, D.C.: Brookings Institution, 1974), pp. 1–10.

EXHIBIT 12   The size of government—an international comparison

Facts and Figures on Government Finance—1981.

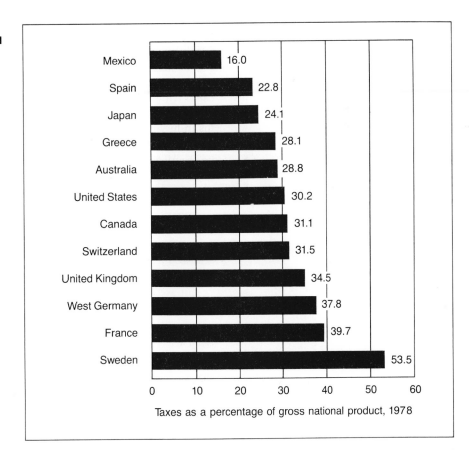

Taxes as a percentage of gross national product, 1978

that question. Taxes are usually higher in Western European countries (for example, West Germany, the United Kingdom, Sweden, and France) than in the United States. These higher tax rates reflect greater public sector involvement in the provision of housing, health care, retirement insurance, and aid to the poor. The size of the public sector, as measured by the share of income going to taxes, is smaller in Mexico, Japan, Greece, and Spain than in the United States. The figure for Japan partially reflects the lack of defense expenditures in that country.

LOOKING AHEAD

Government expenditures and tax rates are important determinants of an economy's output and employment. As we proceed, we will investigate this topic in detail. However, we need to develop a better understanding of how aggregate output is measured. This is the topic of the following chapter.

INDEXING TAX RATES

Under tax legislation passed in 1981, personal income tax brackets (and the personal exemption allowance) will be adjusted for the effects of inflation beginning in 1985. Adjusting money-income figures for the effects of inflation is called indexing. Several nations, including Canada, Brazil, France, and Israel, have instituted indexing plans.

How will the U.S. plan work? The inflation rate during the 12 months ending in September of each year will be calculated. This rate will then be used as the basis for adjusting the tax rate brackets for the upcoming year. The accompanying table illustrates the concept of indexing for an economy that experienced a 10 percent rate of inflation during the previous year. Column 1 presents the marginal tax rates faced by persons whose incomes fall into the tax brackets of column 2. Suppose that during a period of 10 percent inflation the money income of an individual rose from $5000 to $5500, exactly the rate of inflation during the period. Without indexing, this individual would be pushed into a higher marginal tax bracket (15

percent rather than 10 percent), with an increased tax liability of $575— 10 percent of the first $5000 plus 15 percent of the additional $500 of income. The average tax rate of the individual would increase from 10 percent to 10.5 percent ($575 divided by $5500).

Indexing keeps inflation from pushing individuals *with incomes of constant purchasing power* into higher tax brackets. With indexing, as column 3 illustrates, tax brackets are widened to compensate for the inflation-induced component of a rising *money* income. This will keep an individual's tax rate constant, unless income increases more rapidly than the inflation rate. For example, with indexing, the tax liability of the

individual whose income increases from $5000 to $5500 will be $550. The individual's average tax rate remains constant at 10 percent. The individual's marginal tax rate is also unchanged.

Indexing protects individuals from tax rate increases that would otherwise be automatically imposed by inflation. Any changes deemed necessary in the tax rates must be voted by Congress. This aspect of indexing is unlikely to be popular with vote-maximizing political entrepreneurs. Therefore, it would not be surprising to see pressure build to delay or repeal the indexing feature of the 1981 tax legislation as we approach the date that it is to be placed in effect.

Marginal Tax Rate (Percent) (1)	Preindexing Income Tax Bracket (Dollars) (2)	Income Tax Brackets after Indexing for 10 Percent Inflation (Dollars) (3)
10	0– 5,000	0– 5,500
15	5,001–10,000	5,501–11,000
20	10,001–15,000	11,001–16,500
25	15,001–20,000	16,501–22,000

THE UNDERGROUND ECONOMY

Earning unreported (and therefore untaxed) income is a substitute for earning reported, taxable income. As rising marginal tax rates reduce the *personal* payoff derived from earning taxable income, the incentive to turn to substitute activities that generate unreported (and therefore undetected) income is enhanced. Economists refer to these unreported economic activities as the underground economy.

There are two major components of the underground economy: (a) production and distribution of illegal goods and services and (b) the nonreporting of transactions involving legal goods and services. Drug trafficking, smuggling, prostitution, and other criminal activities are examples of the first component. Income from such activities is generally unreported in order to avoid detection by law enforcement authorities.

Persons engaging in the "legal activities" sector of the underground economy usually do so in order to evade taxes. Of course, such tax evasion is illegal, even though the activities themselves are not. However, the likelihood of detection by the authorities is very small for certain types of activities. Since cash transactions are difficult to trace, they provide the lifeblood of the underground economy. In general, the risk involved in the underreporting or nonreporting of income is less for persons engaged in business activities involving a large number of cash transactions. Small business proprietors who fail to ring up all cash sales, taxicab drivers who accept unreported fees or tips, craft workers who sell their services for cash that is only partially reported to the IRS—all these individuals are a part of the underground economy.

Sometimes employees will be hired "off the books" in order to evade taxes or regulations. The employer evades the payroll taxes, while employees pocket "tax-free" cash wage payments without endangering their eligibility for welfare, unemployment compensation for previous jobs, or social security benefits gained from other work.

There is substantial indirect evidence that the underground economy is growing. There has been a dramatic increase in the demand for large denomination currency, which particularly indicates that more major transactions are conducted with cash. The following table illustrates the increase in the holdings of cash relative to checking account money during the 1970s.

Year	Currency Held by the Public as a Percentage of the Total Money Supply
1952	21.4
1956	20.6
1960	20.1
1964	21.0
1968	21.4
1972	22.3
1976	25.7
1978	26.8
1980	28.0

Note that the holdings of currency relative to checking account money increased from 21.4 percent in 1968 to 28.0 percent in 1980. The increased use of currency is particularly surprising given the expansion in the use of credit cards during the 1970s. Barter clubs (barter transactions are also difficult to detect) are springing up rapidly, particularly in the West. Flea markets, which seldom charge taxes or record transactions, are a thriving business activity.

For obvious reasons, it is not easy to measure accurately the size of the underground economy. Most economists who have studied the issue believe that in the United States it is approximately 10 percent as large as reported income. Some estimates place it as high as 15 percent of measured income. In 1976, the IRS utilized special audit procedures in an effort to measure the size of the underground economy. Their results indicated that unreported economic activity during that year totaled between $100 billion and $135 billion, approximately 10 percent of the measured personal income. Peter Gutmann of Baruch College believes the underground economy is nearly 15 percent of national income and that it is growing almost twice as rapidly as measured income. He believes the underground economy is undermining the compliance incentive presumed to be built into the income tax system.[8]

The underground economy is not a problem unique to the United States. In fact, available evidence indicates it is even more widespread in Western Europe, where tax rates are higher. In 1978, the Organization for Economic Cooperation and Development estimated that between 3 and 5 percent of the total labor force in Western Europe worked "off the books" and thereby evaded taxes. In Italy, Great Britain, and Sweden, the estimated size of the underground economy ranges from 10 to 30 percent of the national income. Apparently, the underground economy has become a sizable sector of Western economies.

---

[8]See Peter M. Gutmann, "The Subterranean Economy," *Taxing and Spending* (April 1979). Also see Edgar Feige, "How Big Is the Irregular Economy?" *Challenge* (November/December 1979), 5–13, and Charles Haulk, "Thoughts on the Underground Economy," Federal Reserve Bank of Atlanta *Economic Review* (March/April 1980), 23–27, for additional detail on the subject.

1 Government purchases of goods and services constitute approximately 21 percent of the national output. Slightly less than one out of every six Americans works for the local, state, or federal government. Taking into account transfer payments, total government expenditures amounted to 33.1 percent of the gross national product in 1980.

2 Government expenditures grew very rapidly during the 1965–1975 period. As a share of total output, government expenditures rose from 27.3 percent in 1965 to 34.5 percent in 1975, before falling back to 33.1 percent in 1980. The vast expansion in expenditures for income transfer programs, medical care, education, human resource development, and other social welfare programs accounted for the growth in the relative size of government.

3 During the last two decades, government expenditures in traditional areas such as national defense, highways, and police and fire protection have grown less rapidly than total output. In contrast, income transfer programs have grown far more rapidly than national income. A reevaluation of these trends—particularly the decline in defense spending and growth of social welfare spending—seemed to be underway as the Reagan administration took office in 1981.

4 Personal income taxes, payroll taxes, and corporate income taxes are the major sources of federal tax revenues. Sales taxes provide the major tax base for state government, whereas local governments still rely primarily on property taxes for their revenue.

5 Payroll taxes constitute the most rapidly expanding source of tax revenues. In 1979, payroll taxes contributed 24 percent of the total tax revenue and 31 percent of the tax revenue at the federal level. The social security payroll tax is a regressive tax because it is not levied on income beyond a designated maximum.

6 As the marginal tax rates increase, the proportion of income available for private expenditures declines. Since it determines the amount of earnings that one is permitted to keep for private expenditures, the marginal tax rate exerts a major impact on the incentive of individuals to earn taxable income.

7 Both efficiency and equity should be considered when choosing among taxation alternatives. A tax system that induces inefficient behavior will be very costly to a society. Similarly, it will be costly to induce compliance with a tax system that is perceived as unreasonable or unfair.

8 Ideally, we would all prefer a neutral tax system—one that did not distort prices or induce individuals to channel scarce resources into tax-avoidance activities. However, a tax on productive activity will always alter some prices. Our goal should be to adopt an equitable system that will minimize the inefficiency effects.

9 The impact of taxes on the incentive to work is a topic of current debate among economists. The traditional view is that since there are few good substitutes for the earning of taxable income, the aggregate labor supply curve is vertical, or almost vertical. Thus, taxes on income do not significantly reduce the quantity of labor supplied. Challengers to this view argue that leisure, household production, tax shelters, and the underground economy are fairly good substitutes for the earning of taxable income. Therefore, they believe that high marginal tax rates will significantly reduce productive work effort and encourage tax avoidance, with economic inefficiency as the result.

10 It is important to distinguish between a change in tax rates and a change in tax revenues. The size of the tax base will generally be inversely related to the rate of taxation. Therefore, an increase in tax rates will lead to a less than proportional increase in tax revenues, particularly if there are good substitutes for those things that are taxed.

11 At very high rates of taxation, it is possible that an *increase* in tax rates will cause a *reduction* in tax revenues, because such a large number of people will shift away from the activity that is being taxed. The Laffer curve illustrates this possibility.

12 Studies of the U.S. tax system indicate that (a) approximately 86 percent of the federal income tax revenue is derived from the upper half of income recipients; (b) *in general,* the average (and marginal) tax rates are highest for those with very low incomes and those with very high incomes; and (c) the bulk of taxes (more than 70 percent) is paid by persons with incomes between $10,000 and $50,000, because these people receive the bulk of income.

13 The public sector as a share of the total economy is smaller in the United States and Canada than in most industrial Western European economies but larger than in Japan.

THE ECONOMIC WAY OF THINKING—DISCUSSION QUESTIONS

1 The major categories of government spending are (a) national defense, (b) education, and (c) income transfers and antipoverty expenditures. Why do you think that the public sector has become involved in these activities? Why not leave them to the market?

2 Do you think that the tax burden in the United States is too large or too small? Explain. What policies, if any, would you advocate to change the tax burden and its distribution? Be specific and defend your position.

3 The progressive personal income tax is the major source of tax revenue in the United States. What do you think are the advantages of this tax? What are its disadvantages? What changes, if any, would you make in the nature of this tax? Why?

4 "Transfer payments exert no influence on our economy because they merely transfer income from one group of individuals to another." Evaluate.

5 Do you think that the indexing of the U.S. tax structure is a good idea? Why or why not? Can you think of any reason why Congress did not immediately index tax rates in 1981 when the legislation was passed rather than delaying the institution of indexing until 1985? Will indexing make it easier or harder for Congress to increase tax revenues without voting for a tax increase? Explain. Do you think Congress may want to repeal or delay indexing prior to 1985? Why or why not?

6 Do you know of anyone participating in the underground economy? Do you think that as many people would participate in the underground economy if marginal tax rates were lower? Why or why not?

7 Do you believe that the U.S. tax structure is equitable? Do you think it is efficient? How might it be improved? Discuss.

PART TWO

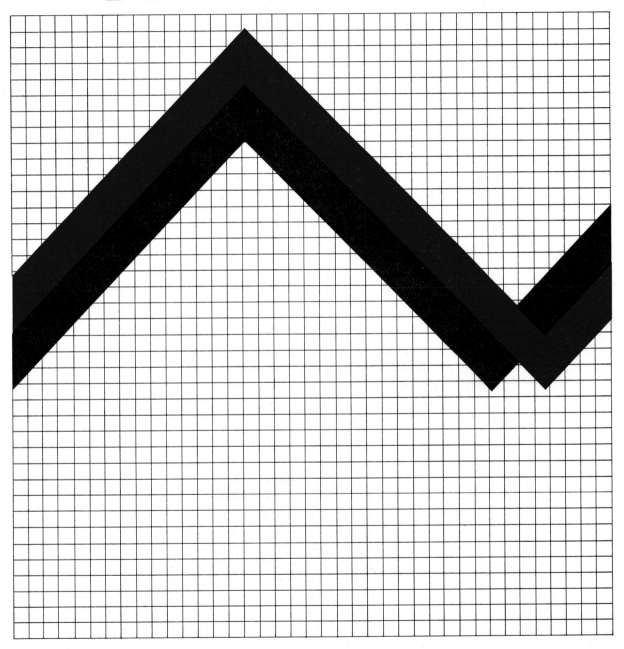

MACROECONOMICS

The Gross National Product is one of the great inventions of the twentieth century, probably almost as significant as the automobile and not quite so significant as TV. The effect of physical inventions is obvious, but social inventions like the GNP change the world almost as much.[1]
Professor Kenneth Boulding

TAKING THE NATION'S ECONOMIC PULSE

Ours is a society that is infatuated with measurement. We seek to measure everything from the figure of Miss America to the speed of Goose Gossage's fastball. Therefore, the fact that we have devised methods for measuring something as important as the performance of our economy is not surprising. However, it is surprising that we waited so long. In the early 1930s, the Department of Commerce for the first time systematically developed and published data on the performance of the economy. Before that, there were no generally accepted methods or procedures for taking "the pulse of our economy." economy."

As the opening quote from Professor Boulding indicates, the development of an economic measuring rod was an extremely important "invention." Without such an invention, it would be difficult to apply any public policy. In this chapter, we will explain how the flow of an economy's output is measured. In addition, we will analyze both the strengths and weaknesses of the measurement tools that have been developed.

THE CONCEPT OF THE GNP

The gross national product (GNP) is the most widely used measure of economic performance. Newspaper writers and television commentators report the latest GNP statistics as proudly as they announce the latest baseball scores. GNP is almost a household expression. What does it indicate? Why is it important?

The **gross national product** is a measure of the market value of goods and services that were produced during a specific time period. GNP is a "flow"

Gross National Product: The total market value of all "final product" goods and services produced during a specific period, usually a year.

---

[1]Kenneth Boulding, "Fun and Games with the Gross National Product—The Role of Misleading Indicators in Social Policy," in *The Environmental Crisis,* ed. Harold W. Helfrich, Jr. (New Haven, Connecticut: Yale University Press, 1970), p. 157.

concept. It is typically measured in terms of an annual rate. By analogy, a water gauge is a device designed to measure the amount of water that flows through a pipe each hour. Similarly, GNP is a device designed to measure the market value of production that "flows" through the economy's factories and shops each year.

What Counts toward GNP?

Since GNP seeks to measure only *current production*, it cannot be arrived at merely by summing the totals on all of the nation's cash registers. Many transactions have to be excluded. What does GNP include and what does it exclude?

1. Only Final Goods Are Counted. A "final good" is a good in the hands of its ultimate user. Goods go through many stages of production. But GNP counts only the dollar market value of all final goods and services produced during a year.

Exhibit 1 will help to clarify this important point. Before the final good, bread, is in the hands of the consumer, it will go through several stages of production. The farmer produces a pound of wheat and sells it to the miller for 20 cents. The miller grinds the wheat into flour and sells it to the baker for 35 cents. The miller's actions have *added 15 cents* to the value of the wheat. The baker combines the flour with other ingredients, makes a loaf of bread, and sells it to the grocer for 60 cents. The baker has *added 25 cents* to the value of the bread. The grocer stocks the bread on the grocery shelves and provides a convenient location for consumers to shop. The grocer sells the loaf of bread for 69 cents, *adding 9 cents* to the value of the final product. Only the market value of the final product—69 cents for the loaf of bread—is counted by GNP. The market value of the final product is the amount *added* to the value of the good at each stage of production—the 20 cents added by the farmer, the 15 cents by the miller, the 25 cents by the baker, and the 9 cents by the grocer.

EXHIBIT 1   GNP and stages of production

Most goods go through several stages of production. This chart illustrates both the market value of a loaf of bread as it passes through the various stages of production (column 1) and the amount *added* to the value of the bread by each intermediate producer (column 2). GNP counts only the market value of the final product. Of course, the amount added by each intermediate producer (column 2) sums to the market value of the final product.

Stages of Production	Market Value of the Product (Dollars) (1)	Amount Added to the Value of the Product (Dollars) (2)
Stage 1: farmer's wheat	0.20	0.20
Stage 2: miller's flour	0.35	0.15
Stage 3: baker's bread (wholesale)	0.60	0.25
Stage 4: grocer's bread (retail)	0.69	0.09
Amount added to GNP		0.69

If the market value of the product at each intermediate stage of production (for example, the sum of column 1) were added to GNP, double counting would result. GNP would overstate the value of the final products available to consumers. To avoid this problem, GNP includes only the value of final goods and services.

2. Only Goods Produced during the Period Count. Keep in mind that GNP is a measure of current production. Therefore, exchanges of goods or assets produced during a preceding period do not contribute to current GNP.

The purchase of a used car *produced last year* will not enhance current GNP, nor will the sale of a "used" home, constructed five years ago. Production of these goods was counted at the time they were produced. Current sales and purchases of such items merely involve the exchange of existing goods. They do not involve current production of additional goods. Therefore, they are not counted.

Since GNP counts long-lasting goods like automobiles and houses when they are produced, it is not always an accurate gauge of what is currently being consumed. During an economic slowdown, few new durable assets will be produced. However, the consumption of durable goods that were produced and counted during an earlier period will continue. During good times, there will be a rapid expansion in the production of durable assets, but their consumption will be extended over a longer time period. Because of this cycle, GNP tends to understate consumption during a recession and overstate it during an economic boom.

Pure financial transactions are not counted toward GNP, since they do not involve current production. Purchases or sales of stocks, bonds, and U.S. securities do not count. They represent exchange of current assets, not production of additional goods. Similarly, private gifts are excluded, as are government transfer payments like welfare and social security payments. They do not enhance current production, and it would be therefore inappropriate to add them to GNP.

Dollars as the Common Denominator of GNP

In grammar school, each of us was instructed about the difficulties of adding apples and oranges. Yet this is precisely the nature of the aggregate measurement problem. Literally millions of different commodities and services are produced each year. How can the production of houses, movies, legal services, education, automobiles, dresses, heart transplants, astrological services, and many other items be added together?

These vastly different commodities and services have only one thing in common. Someone pays for each of them in terms of dollars. Dollars act as a common denominator; units of each different good are weighted according to their dollar selling price. Production of an automobile adds 80 times as much to GNP as production of a briefcase, because the new automobile sold for $8000, compared to $100 for the new briefcase. A heart transplant adds 50 times as much to GNP as an appendectomy, because the heart transplant sold for $10,000 and the appendectomy for only $200. A fifth of whiskey adds more to GNP than a week's supply of household water because the purchaser paid more for the whiskey than for the water. The total spending on all final goods produced during the year is then summed, *in dollar terms,* to obtain the annual GNP.

TWO WAYS OF MEASURING GNP

There are two ways of looking at and measuring GNP. The GNP of an economy can be reached by totaling *either* the spending on goods and services purchased or the costs of producing and supplying those goods and services. That is, GNP can be calculated by adding up the total expenditures on the final goods and services supplied to purchasers. Or, alternatively, GNP can be determined by adding up the total cost of supplying the goods and services, including the residual income of the producer-entrepreneurs. *Either* sum will equal GNP. This is true because, in simple terms, the money spent on the final goods and services by purchasers can be seen as providing the wherewithal to produce and supply those goods and services.

There is a circular flow of consumption expenditures and resource costs illustrated for a very simple economy in Exhibit 2. There are only two sectors—households and businesses—in the economy of Exhibit 2. The dollar flow of expenditures and receipts is demonstrated within the circular flow diagram. The flow of real products and resources is indicated by the arrows outside the circular flow loops. Goods and services produced in the business sector are sold to consumers in the household sector. Households supply the factors of production and receive income payments in exchange for their services. In turn, all the income of households is expended on the purchase of goods and services.

The bottom loop of Exhibit 2 illustrates the dollar flow of factor cost payments (wages, rents, interest, and profits) from the business sector to the household sector in exchange for productive resources (labor, land, capital equipment, and entrepreneurship). These factor payments constitute the income of households. The price of the productive resources is determined by the forces of supply and demand operating in resource markets. Businesses utilize the services of the productive resources to produce goods and services.

The top loop of Exhibit 2 illustrates the dollar flow of consumer expenditures from households to businesses in exchange for goods and services. Business firms derive their revenues from the sale of products (food, clothing, medical services, etc.) that they supply to households. The prices of these goods and services are determined in product markets.

Of course, modern economies are much more complicated than our simple two-sector circular flow model. In addition to the personal consumption expenditures of the household sector, there are governmental purchases of goods and services (for example, highways, education, warplanes, and police protection). Rather than purchase all productive inputs from households, businesses may undertake investment expenditures (business spending on machinery, production facilities, and other capital assets) out of their retained earnings, thus enhancing their future productive capabilities. In addition, foreigners may both purchase domestic goods and services and sell foreign-made products to the domestic market.

Nonetheless, the general principle still holds. Gross national product can be determined by either (a) summing the total expenditures on the "final product" goods and services produced during a period or (b) summing the total cost incurred as a result of producing the goods and services supplied during the period. Exhibit 3 summarizes the components of GNP for both the expenditure approach and the resource cost–income approach.

EXHIBIT 2 Circular flow—a two-sector model

This simplified two-sector model illustrates the two ways of looking at gross national product. The dollar flow of household consumption expenditures for the final goods and services supplied by the business sector must equal the dollar flow of factor compensation payments (wages, rents, interest, and profits) to the productive inputs (labor, land, capital, equipment, and entrepreneurship) supplied by the household sector. Both the household expenditures (top loop) and the factor compensation payments (bottom loop) will sum to GNP.

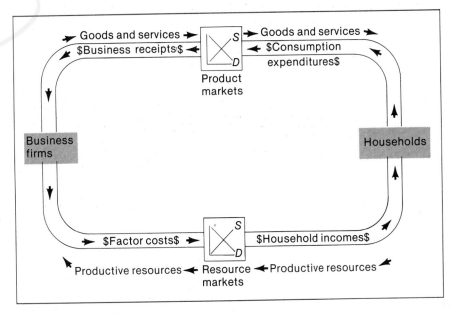

It is important to note that the residual income of the producer-entrepreneur is included in the total cost of supplying goods and services, the second form of GNP measurement. Since the business revenues derived from the sale of goods and services will either be paid to resource suppliers or accrue to capitalist entrepreneurs in the form of profits, the two methods of calculating GNP will yield identical outcomes. Note that profits are considered a cost of production. Since profits are a residual rather than a contractual payment, some might object to this classification. This view is incorrect. Even though profits are a residual payment, business decision-makers would be unwilling to

EXHIBIT 3 The two ways of measuring GNP

Even though modern economies are far more complicated than the two-sector circular flow model of Exhibit 2, there are still two methods of calculating GNP. It can be calculated either by summing the expenditures of the "final product" goods and services of each sector (left, below) or by summing the costs associated with the production of these goods and services (right, below).

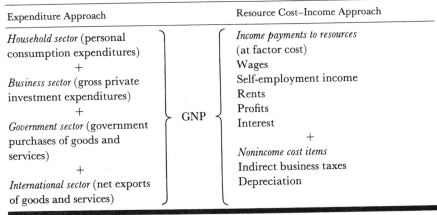

Expenditure Approach		Resource Cost–Income Approach
Household sector (personal consumption expenditures)		*Income payments to resources* (at factor cost)
+		Wages
Business sector (gross private investment expenditures)		Self-employment income
		Rents
+	GNP	Profits
Government sector (government purchases of goods and services)		Interest
		+
+		*Nonincome cost items*
International sector (net exports of goods and services)		Indirect business taxes
		Depreciation

supply the capital assets utilized in the production process and undertake the risk of loss if they did not expect their chances of receiving profitable rewards to be good. Profits might be regarded as the payment to the entrepreneur for undertaking production. Wage payments induce workers to supply labor services. Similarly, the expectation of profit induces business decision-makers to supply capital equipment and undertake the entrepreneurial risk involved in the production process. The latter is just as much a cost of production as the former.

In a sense, the expenditure approach to GNP measurement focuses on the buyer's valuation of the goods produced during the year. Purchasers buy particular goods because they value them more than the alternatives that are available. They expect a product to yield a benefit greater than its purchase price; otherwise, they would not purchase it. GNP, the sum of all of these expenditures on final products, will thus understate purchasers' valuation of the goods.

In contrast, the resource cost—income approach stresses the sacrifices incurred by the production of the goods and services. The production of goods involves human toil, wear and tear on machines, foregoing current consumption, risk, managerial responsibilities, and other of life's unpleasantries. In a market economy, resource owners voluntarily supply productive services in exchange for income. From the standpoint of resource owners, these income payments (wages, self-employment income, rents, profits, and interest) must exceed the value of the alternatives foregone (consumption of leisure, for example) when time, effort, and resources are devoted to production. Otherwise, the resource owners would be unwilling to supply their services. Thus, when GNP is calculated by adding up all the income payments to resource suppliers, it clearly overstates the disutility incurred in the production of final goods and services.

From an accounting viewpoint, the total payments to the factors of production, *including the producer's profit or loss,* must be equal to the sales price generated by the good. This is true for each good or service produced, and it is also true for the aggregate economy, as must be obvious from the previous discussion. This is a fundamental accounting identity.

$$\begin{matrix} \text{Dollar flow of expenditures on} \\ \text{final goods} \end{matrix} = \textbf{GNP} = \begin{matrix} \text{dollar flow of the producer's costs} \\ \text{on final goods} \end{matrix}$$

Thus, GNP obtained by adding up the dollar value of final goods and services purchased will equal GNP obtained by adding up the total of all "cost" items, including the producer's profits, associated with the production of final goods.

THE EXPENDITURE APPROACH

As Exhibit 3 indicates, when the expenditure approach is used to calculate GNP, four basic components of final products purchased must be considered. The left side of Exhibit 4 presents the value of these four components of GNP for 1981.

1. Consumption Purchases. Personal consumption purchases are the largest component of GNP; in 1981 they amounted to $1858 billion. Most consumption expenditures are for nondurable goods or services. Food, clothing, recreation, medical and legal services, education, and fuel are included in this category.

EXHIBIT 4 Two ways of measuring GNP—1981 data (billions of dollars)

The left side shows the flow of expenditures and the right side the flow of resource costs. Both procedures yield GNP.

Expenditure Approach			Resource Cost–Income Approach	
Personal consumption		1858	Employee compensation	1772
Durable goods	232		Proprietors' income	135
Nondurable goods	743			
Services	883		Rents	34
			Corporate profits	192
Gross private investment		450		
Fixed investment	434		Interest income	215
Inventories	16			
			Indirect business taxes	
Government purchases		591	(includes transfers)	255
Federal	230			
State and local	361		Depreciation (capital consumption)	322
Net exports		26		
Gross national product		2925	Gross national product	2925

U.S. Department of Commerce. These data are also available in the *Federal Reserve Bulletin,* which is published monthly.

These items are used up or consumed in a relatively short time. Durable goods such as appliances and automobiles, comprise approximately one-eighth of all consumer purchases. These products are enjoyed over a longer period even though they are fully counted at the time they are purchased.

2. Investment Purchases. Investment or capital goods provide a "flow" of *future* consumption or production service. Unlike food or medical services, they are not immediately "used." A house is an investment good because it will provide a stream of services long into the future. Business plants and equipment are investment goods because they, too, will provide productive services in the future. Changes in business inventories are also classed as investment goods, since they will provide future consumer benefits.

Many goods possess both consumer and investment good characteristics. There is not always a clear distinction between the two. National accounting procedures have rather arbitrarily classified business purchases of final goods as investment and considered household purchases, except housing, as consumption.

In 1981, total investment expenditures were $450 billion, including a $16 billion expansion in inventory stock. The inventory component of investment fluctuates substantially. When business conditions are improving, inventories often decline. On the other hand, during a recession, inventories sometimes increase rapidly because firms are unable to sell all of their current production. Later, we will take a closer look at the role of inventory fluctuations, since many economists believe that these changes play an important role in the determination of economic instability.

3. Government Purchases. In 1981, federal, state, and local government purchases were $591 billion, or 20 percent of total GNP. The purchases of state and local governments exceeded those of the federal government by a wide margin. The government component includes both investment and consumption services. Education, police protection, missiles, buildings, and generation of electric power, as well as medical, legal, and accounting services, are included in the government component. Since transfer payments are excluded, the size of the public sector greatly exceeds the amount counted as actually spent by the government on goods and services.

4. Net Exports. Exports are domestic goods and services purchased by foreigners. Imports are foreign goods and services purchased domestically. We want GNP to measure only the nation's production. Therefore, measuring GNP in terms of total purchases requires that we (a) add the dollar value of domestic goods purchased by foreigners and (b) subtract the dollar value of foreign goods purchased by Americans. For national accounting purposes we can then combine these two factors into a single entry, *net exports,* where

$$\text{Net exports} = \text{total exports} - \text{total imports}$$

If the dollar value of the goods and services that we sell to foreigners exceeds the dollar value of our purchases from them, the net export component will be an addition to GNP. In contrast, if we are buying more goods and services from foreigners than we are selling to them, net exports will be negative. In 1981, net exports were positive. We exported $26 billion more goods and services to foreigners than we imported from them.

THE RESOURCE COST–INCOME APPROACH

Exhibit 4 illustrates how, rather than adding up the flow of expenditures on final goods and services, we could add up the flow of costs incurred in their production in order to reach GNP. Labor services play a very important role in the production process. Thus, it is not surprising that employee compensation, $1772 billion in 1981, is the largest cost incurred in the production of goods and services.

Self-employed proprietors undertake the risks of owning their own businesses and simultaneously provide their own labor services to the firm. Their earnings in 1981 contributed $135 billion to GNP, 4.6 percent of the total. Together, employees and self-employed proprietors accounted for approximately two-thirds of GNP.

Machines, buildings, land, and other physical assets also contribute to the production process. Rents, corporate profits, and interest are payments to persons who provided either physical resources or the financial resources with which to purchase physical assets. Rents are a return to resource owners who permit another to utilize their assets during a time period. Corporate profits are compensation earned by stockholders, who both bear the risk of the business undertaking and provide the financial resources with which the firm purchases resources. Interest is a payment to parties who extend loans to producers.

Not all cost components of GNP result in an income payment to a resource supplier. There are two major indirect costs.

1. Indirect Business Taxes. These taxes are imposed on the sale of many goods, and they are passed on to the consumer. The sales tax is a clear example. When you make a $1 purchase in a state with a 5 percent sales tax, the purchase actually costs you $1.05. The $1 goes to the seller to pay wage, rent, interest, and managerial costs. The 5 cents goes to the government. Indirect business taxes boost the market price of goods when GNP is calculated by the expenditure approach. Similarly, when looked at from the factor cost viewpoint, taxes are an indirect cost of supplying the goods to the purchasers.

2. Depreciation. Utilizing machines to produce goods causes them to wear out. Depreciation of capital goods is a cost of producing current goods, but it is not a direct cost because it reflects what is *lost* to the producer when machines and facilities wear out. Depreciation does not involve a direct payment to a resource owner. It is an estimate, based on the expected life of the asset, of the decline in the value of the asset during the year. In 1981, depreciation (sometimes called capital consumption allowance) amounted to $322 billion, approximately 11 percent of GNP.

Depreciation and Net National Product

Net National Product: Gross national product minus a depreciation allowance for the wearing out of machines and buildings during the period.

The inclusion of depreciation costs in GNP points out that it is indeed a "gross" rather than "net" measure of economic production. Since GNP fails to allow for the fact that the wearing out of capital goods does not mean the production of new final goods or real additions to capital stock during the year, GNP overstates the net output of an economy.

The **net national product** (NNP) is a concept designed to correct this deficiency. NNP is the total market value of the consumption and government goods and services produced plus any *net* additions to the nation's capital stock. In accounting terms, net national product is simply GNP minus depreciation.

Since NNP counts only the net additions to the nation's capital stock, it is less than GNP. Net investment—the additions to capital stock—is always equal to gross investment minus depreciation. NNP counts only net investment.

The Relative Size of GNP Components

Of course, the relative importance of the components of GNP changes from time to time. Exhibit 5 shows the average proportion of GNP accounted for by each of the components during 1978–1980. When the expenditure approach is utilized, personal consumption expenditure is by far the largest and most stable component of GNP. Consumption accounted for 61 percent of GNP during 1978–1980, compared to 17 percent for investment and 20 percent for government expenditures. When GNP is measured by the resource cost–income approach, compensation to employees is the dominant component (61 percent of GNP). During 1978–1980, rents, corporate profits, and interest combined to account for 15 percent of GNP.

GROSS NATIONAL PRODUCT OR GROSS NATIONAL COST?

As we have indicated, both the cost and the expenditure approaches lead to the same estimate of GNP. They are simply two ways of calculating the same thing. Considering the two approaches together helps to keep the GNP in per-

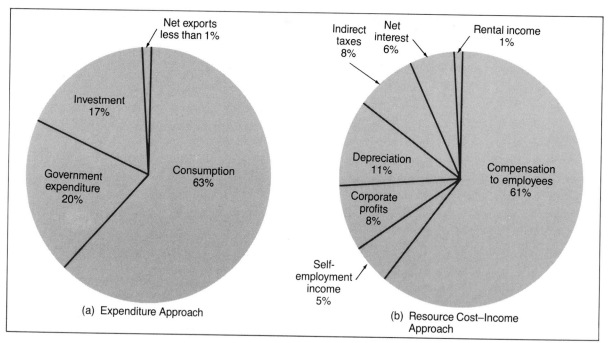

EXHIBIT 5   Major components of GNP in the United States, 1978–1980

The relative sizes of the major components of GNP usually fluctuate within a fairly narrow range. The average proportion of each component during 1978–1980 is demonstrated here for both (a) the expenditure and (b) the resource cost–income approaches.

Economic Report of the President, 1982.

spective. From the purchaser's viewpoint, it is indeed a gross national product. "Good things," as seen through the eyes of a purchaser, were produced, and either households, investors, foreigners, or the government paid for them. However, production also involves costs. Owners of labor services, capital goods, and managerial skills made the sacrifices necessary to bring the final products into existence. Viewed from the producer's position, GNP might better be termed a gross national cost because resource owners had to forego things in order to produce goods and services.

As we will emphasize below, GNP is not a measure of how much "better off" we are. There are both positive and negative sides to it. Perhaps it might best be thought of as an index of current productive activity—activity that results in the goods and services that we desire, at the expense of work, waiting, risk, and depreciation, which we do not desire.

PROBLEMS WITH GNP AS A MEASURING ROD

GNP is not a perfect device for measuring current production and income. Some items are excluded, even though they would be properly classed as "current production." Sometimes production results in harmful "side effects," which are not fully accounted for. In this section, we will focus on some of the limitations and shortcomings of GNP as a measure of economic performance.

Watch Out for Price Changes

GNP Deflator: A price index that reveals the cost of purchasing the items included in GNP during the period relative to the cost of purchasing these same items during a base year (currently, 1972). Since the base year is assigned a value of 100, as the GNP deflator takes on values greater than 100, it indicates that prices have risen.

Money GNP: GNP valued at the current prices of the period.

Real GNP: GNP in current dollars deflated for changes in the prices of the items included in GNP. Mathematically, real GNP_2 is equal to money GNP_2 multiplied by (GNP Deflator$_1$/GNP Deflator$_2$). Thus, if prices have risen between periods 1 and 2, the ratio of the GNP deflator in period 1 to the deflator in period 2 will be less than 1. Therefore, this ratio will deflate the money GNP for the rising prices.

Were more goods and services produced in 1978 than 1981? How many more? We often like to compare GNP during two different years in order to answer such questions. But price changes make such comparisons more complex. GNP will increase if either (a) more goods and services are produced or (b) prices rise. Often both (a) and (b) will contribute to an increase in GNP. Since we are usually interested in comparing only the output or actual production during two different time intervals, GNP must be adjusted for the change in prices.

How can we determine how much the prices of items included in GNP have risen during a specific period? We answer this question by constructing a price index called the **GNP deflator.** The Department of Commerce estimates how much of each item included in GNP has been produced during a year. This bundle of goods will include automobiles, houses, office buildings, medical services, bread, milk, entertainment, and all other goods included in the GNP, *in the quantities that they are actually produced during the current year.* The Department then calculates the ratio of the value of this bundle of goods *at current prices* divided by the value of the bundle *at the prices that were present during the designated earlier base year.* When prices are rising (falling), this ratio will be greater (less) than 1. The base year chosen (currently 1972 for the GNP deflator) is assigned 100. The GNP deflator is equal to the calculated ratio multiplied by 100. When the GNP deflator exceeds 100, this indicates that, *on average,* prices are higher than they were during the base period.

We can use the GNP deflator to measure GNP in dollars of constant purchasing power. If prices are rising, we simply deflate the **money GNP** during the latter period to account for the effects of inflation. When GNP is stated in terms of constant dollars, economists call it **real GNP.**

Exhibit 6 illustrates how real GNP is measured and why it is important to adjust for price changes. Money GNP increased 146.6 percent between 1972 and 1981. Does this mean that output expanded by 146.6 percent during the period from 1972 to 1981? Indeed not. The GNP deflator in 1981 was 193.7, compared to 100.0 in 1972. Prices rose by 93.7 percent during the period. In determining the real GNP for 1981 in terms of 1972 dollars, we deflate the 1981 money GNP for the rise in prices:

$$\text{Real GNP}_{81} = \text{money GNP}_{81} \times \frac{\text{GNP deflator}_{72}}{\text{GNP deflator}_{81}}$$

Because prices were rising, the latter ratio is less than 1. In terms of 1972 dollars, the real GNP in 1981 was $1510 billion, only 27.3 percent more than

EXHIBIT 6   Changes in prices and the real GNP

Between 1972 and 1981, GNP increased by 146.6 percent. But when the 1981 GNP was deflated to account for price increases, real GNP increased by only 27.3 percent.

	GNP (Billions of Dollars)	Price Index (GNP Deflator)	Real GNP (1972 Dollars)
1972	1186	100.0	1186
1981	2925	193.7	1510
Percent increase	146.6	93.7	27.3

U.S. Department of Commerce.

in 1972. Thus, although money GNP expanded by 146.4 percent, real GNP increased by only 27.3 percent.

A change in money GNP tells us nothing about what happened to the rate of real production unless we also know what happened to prices. Money income could have doubled while production actually declined, if prices more than doubled. Money income could have remained constant while real GNP increased, if prices fell during the time period. Data on both money GNP and price changes are essential for a meaningful comparison of real income between two time periods.

Sins of Omission—Exclusion of Nonmarket Production

The GNP fails to count household production because such production does not involve a market transaction. Thus, the household services of 100 million people are excluded. If you mow the yard, repair your car, paint your house, pick up relatives from school, or perform similar household productive activities, your labor services add nothing to GNP, since no market transaction is involved. Such nonmarket productive activities are sizable—10 or 15 percent of total GNP, perhaps more. Their exclusion results in some oddities of national income accounting.

For example, if a writer and the writer's assistant marry, and, if after the marriage the spouse-assistant works for love rather than money, GNP will decline because the services of the spouse-assistant will now be excluded: There is no longer a market transaction. If a parent hires a baby-sitter in order to enter the labor force, these actions have a double-barreled impact on GNP. It will rise as a result of (a) the amount the baby-sitter is paid plus (b) the parent's on-the-job earnings.

The omission of many nonmarket productive activities makes comparisons over time and among countries at various stages of market development less meaningful. For example, more women are currently involved in *market* work than was true 30 years ago. There is widespread use of appliances today to perform functions previously performed by women at home providing unpaid household labor. This fact, along with increasing market specialization, indicates that excluded household activities are less important today than 30 years ago. This means the current GNP, even in real dollars, is overstated relative to the earlier period, since a larger share of total production was previously excluded.

Similarly, GNP comparisons overstate the output of developed countries by way of comparison with underdeveloped ones. A larger share of the total production of underdeveloped countries originates in the household sector. For example, Mexican families are more likely than their U.S. counterparts to make their own clothing, raise and prepare their own food, provide their own child-rearing services, and even build their own homes. These productive labor services, originating in the household sector, are excluded from GNP. Therefore, GNP in Mexico understates output there by more than GNP in the United States understates U.S. output.

More Omissions—The Underground Economy

In the preceding chapter, we indicated that many transactions go unreported because they involve either illegal activities or tax evasion (which is illegal, although the activities generating the income may not be). Many of these "underground" activities produce goods and services that are valued by purchasers. Nonetheless, since the activities are unreported, they do not contribute to GNP. Estimates of the size of the underground economy in the United States range from 10 to 15 percent of total output. Most observers, as we have noted, believe that these unrecorded transactions have grown much more rapidly than measured output in recent years. If this is true, it implies that the published GNP figures are actually understating the growth rate of output, since an expanding proportion of total output is being excluded.

Production of Economic "Bads"

Production and consumption of some economic goods also have harmful side effects, which detract from the total consumption level of the population. GNP counts only work that was paid for or goods that were purchased. It does not count goods that were used up, destroyed, or diminished in value *if there was not a market transaction.* Junk piles, garbage, cancer created by cigarette smoking, deterioration of minds and bodies because of the consumption of harmful drugs, alcohol, and air and water pollution—all of these "disproducts" associated with current consumption are excluded because they do not go through the market. These and other undesirable items are clear deductions from our total available goods and resources. Their total might be called the gross national disproduct.

In order to balance the productive accounts properly, the unaccounted-for disproduct should be subtracted from the total product. Net national product does make an allowance for the reduction in capital stock associated with this year's production. But what of the reduction in other assets and goods associated with current production? Both GNP and NNP exclude many of these items. Current depletion of natural resources, like the depreciation of capital stock, reduces our ability to produce future goods. But this is not considered in our national product accounts. Neither is the reduction in the quality of air that we breathe nor the purity of our river waters.

Paradoxically, many of these "economic bads" engender a higher GNP in the future. Cigarette smoking results in more cancer, thereby increasing GNP in the medical service sector! Crime results in more police protection, household locks, legal services, and detention centers. Air pollution results in increased purchases of air purifiers, house paints, and window washers. Water pollution results in a greater cost of producing pure water. In each case, the expenditures intended to counteract the negative side effects of production actually enlarge GNP.

When production generates harmful side effects, these side effects reduce either the availability of a current good (for example, clean air, good health, noncongested environment) or our ability to produce future goods (for example, depletion of natural resources). GNP does not account for these negative side effects. Thus, it tends to overstate our "real output" of desired goods.

Exclusion of Leisure and Human Costs

Simon Kuznets, the "inventor" of GNP, indicated that the failure to include human cost fully was one of the grave omissions of national income accounting (see Outstanding Economist, page 121). GNP excludes leisure, a good that is valuable to each of us. One country might attain a $6000 per capita GNP with an average work week of 30 hours. Another might attain the same per capita GNP with a 50-hour work week. In terms of total output, the first country has the greater production because it "produced" more leisure, or sacrificed less human cost. Yet GNP does not reflect this fact.

The average number of hours worked per week in the United States has declined steadily. The average nonagricultural production worker spent only 35 hours on the job in 1980, compared to more than 40 hours in 1947, a 12 percent reduction in weekly hours worked. Clearly, this reduction in the length of the work week increased the standard of living of Americans, even though it did not enhance GNP.

GNP also fails to take into account the human costs—the physical and mental strain—that are associated with many jobs. On average, jobs today are less physically strenuous and less exhausting but are perhaps more monotonous than they were 30 years ago. These shortcomings—failure to consider leisure and the human costs of employment—reduce the significance of longitudinal GNP comparisons.

The Problem of New and Changing Goods

GNP comparisons over time are made even more complex because new goods are always being introduced and the quality of existing goods changes. How meaningful is a comparison between per capita income (or production) in 1900 and that in 1980? In 1900, there were no jet planes, television sets, commercial radios, automatic dishwashers or clothes dryers, automobiles, rock and roll stereo records, electric typewriters, or air conditioners. On the other hand, there were plenty of open spaces, trees, noncongested (but rough) horse and coach roads, pure-water rivers, hiking trails, cheap lands, areas with low crime rates, and wild blackberry bushes.

The bundles of goods available during the two years are vastly different. It does not make sense to talk about what it would have cost in 1900 to consume the typical bundle of goods consumed in 1980. A billionaire could not have purchased the typical 1980 middle-income bundle of goods in 1900—many of the goods did not exist. Nor does it make sense to talk about the current cost of consuming the typical 1900 bundle of goods. Yet, as we have already indicated, comparisons of money GNP are meaningless without the ability to adjust for price changes for equivalent goods—the cost of purchasing the typical bundle. When the *available* bundle of goods differs widely between two points in time or two countries, comparative GNP statistics lose much of their relevance.

As Exhibit 7 shows, the per capita real GNP in 1930 was approximately one-third the 1980 level. Does this mean that, on average, Americans produced nearly three times as many goods in 1980 as in 1930? The answer is no. Many goods were available in 1930 that were not available in 1980, and vice versa. It would be impossible for us to have produced 2.95 times the *1930 output* in 1980. Our productive capacity has increased remarkably. However, as to whether the 1980 productive capacity is two, three, or four times the 1930 level, GNP cannot give a definitive answer.

The introduction of new goods and the changes in quality of current commodities present a problem even when one is comparing GNP between two periods that are separated by only 10 or 15 years. There have been tremendous changes in the convenience packaging and preparation of foods since the mid-1960s. Heart transplants are an "invention" of the last decade. The quality of medical and dental surgery has changed significantly. Cable television has expanded the viewing alternatives open to millions of Americans during the last decade. All of these changes reduce the meaningfulness of GNP comparisons over time.

The closer together the time periods under consideration, the more meaningful will be the comparisons of real GNP. However, ours is a dynamic world. Differences in the availability and quality of goods add to the shortcomings of

EXHIBIT 7 Per capita real GNP, 1930–1980

In 1980, per capita real GNP was 88 percent greater than in 1950, 2.56 times the 1940 level, and 2.95 times the 1930 value. How meaningful are these numbers?

Year	Per Capita Real GNP (in 1972 Dollars)
1930	2256
1940	2595
1950	3535
1960	4079
1970	5248
1980	6645

Derived from U.S. Department of Commerce data.

LOOKING AHEAD

GNP and the related income concepts provide us with a measure of economic performance. In the following chapter, we will take a closer look at the movements of prices and real output in the United States and other countries. As we proceed, we will investigate the factors that underlie these movements. Models that rely heavily on the interrelationships among household consumption, business investment, and government expenditures will be central to our analysis. As we compare the implications of our analysis with the real world, measurement of GNP and related indicators of income will help us sort out sound theories from economic nonsense.

CHAPTER LEARNING OBJECTIVES

1 Gross national product is a measure of the market value of the final goods and services produced during a specific time period.

2 Dollars act as a common denominator for GNP. Production of each final product is weighted according to its selling price. Alternatively, GNP can be calculated by adding up the dollar factor cost of producing the final goods. The two methods sum to an identical result.

3 When the expenditure approach is utilized, there are four major components of GNP: (a) consumption, (b) investment, (c) government, and (d) net exports.

4 The major components of GNP as calculated by the resource cost–income approach are (a) wages and salaries, (b) self-employment income, (c) rents, (d) interest, (e) corporate profits, and (f) nonincome expenses, primarily depreciation and indirect business taxes.

5 GNP may increase because of an increase in either output or prices. A price index—the GNP deflator—is used to measure the impact of price changes on total output. Real GNP can be determined by adjusting money GNP to account for price changes between periods.

6 GNP is an imperfect measure of current production. It excludes household production and the underground (unreported) economy. It fails to account for the negative side effects of current production, such as air and water pollution, adverse impacts on health, depletion of natural resources, and other factors that do not flow through markets. It adjusts imperfectly for quality changes. GNP comparisons are less meaningful when the typical bundle of available goods and services differs widely between two time periods (or between two nations).

7 Despite all its limitations, GNP is of tremendous importance because it is an accurate tool enabling us to identify short-term economic fluctuations. Without such a reliable indicator, economic theory would be unable to determine the cause of economic slowdowns and economic policy would be helpless against them.

8 Economists frequently refer to four other income measures that are related to GNP: net national product, national income, personal income, and disposable income. All of these measures of income tend to move together.

9 Economists are currently seeking to develop alternative measuring rods of economic well-being. A recently devised measuring device, the measure of economic welfare (MEW), includes many nonmarket economic goods consumed during the period, subtracts the estimated cost of economic bads, and excludes expenditures on regrettable necessities, such as police protection and national defense. The growth rate of MEW has been less rapid than that of GNP during the post-World War II period.

10 The circular flow model illustrates that the aggregate supply of goods and services to households, businesses, governments, and foreigners and the aggregate income of resource suppliers are merely alternative methods of viewing the same thing. Thus,

actual aggregate output and actual aggregate income will always be equal. The only way in which we can increase aggregate income is by increasing the aggregate supply of goods desired by economic participants.

1 Why does a pound of beef add more to GNP than a pound of wheat? Does it reflect demand or costs? Comment.

2 Explain why the rate of growth in GNP in current dollars can sometimes be a misleading statistic.

3 What is real GNP? How is it determined? Calculate the change in real GNP between 1970 and 1980.

4 Indicate which of the following activities are counted as part of this year's GNP:
    (a) The services of a homemaker
    (b) Frank Murry's purchase of a 1981 Chevrolet
    (c) Frank Murry's rental payments on a 1981 Chevrolet
    (d) The purchase of 100 shares of AT&T stock
    (e) Interest on a bond issued by AT&T
    (f) Family lawn services provided by a 16-year-old
    (g) Family lawn services purchased from the neighbor's 16-year-old, who has a lawn-mowing business
    (h) A multibillion dollar discovery of natural gas in Oklahoma
    (i) Deterioration of the water quality of Lake Michigan

5 Why might the GNP be a misleading index of changes in output between 1900 and 1980 in the United States? of differences in output between the United States and Mexico?

6 "GNP counts the product of steel but not the disproduct of air pollution. It counts the product of automobiles but not the disproduct of 'blight' due to junkyards. It counts the product of cigarettes but not the disproduct of a shorter life expectancy due to cancer. Until we can come up with a more reliable index, we cannot tell whether economic welfare is progressing or regressing." Explain why you either agree or disagree with this view.

7 **What's Wrong with This Way of Thinking?**

"An agricultural program that pays farmers to reduce their planted acreage and cut back on the production of farm products can increase everyone's income. The reduction in the supply of farm products will cause their prices to rise, which will result in an increase in the income of farmers. The higher level of farm income will cause farmers to increase their purchases of manufacturing products, which will expand the income of city dwellers. The farm subsidies will increase the income not only of farmers but also of the nation as a whole."

7

UNEMPLOYMENT, ECONOMIC INSTABILITY, AND INFLATION

A stable environment is crucial to the efficient operation of an economy. The stability issue can be broken down into three specific economic goals: (a) growth of real output, (b) full employment, and (c) price stability. Obviously, these three goals are interrelated. Without full employment, the potential output of an economy will not be fully realized. Similarly, fluctuation in prices will generate uncertainty and retard economic growth. In this chapter, we will look at the stability of real output, employment, and prices. We will analyze the historical record and discuss some of the measurement problems in this area. The concept of full employment will be introduced and its meaning discussed. We will also analyze some of the side effects of price instability, particularly the inflation problem that has plagued many Western economies in recent years.

The government's spending and monetary policies exert an important impact upon the stability of an economy. In the United States, the Employment Act of 1946 pledges that the federal government will pursue policies designed to "promote maximum employment, production, and purchasing power." In 1978 Congress amended the 1946 legislation and for the first time established numeric targets for employment rates and price stability. In the Full Employment and Balanced Growth Act of 1978, better known as the Humphrey–Hawkins Act, the federal government established the goals of (a) 4 percent unemployment by 1983 and (b) zero percent inflation by 1988 (with an intermediate target of 3 percent inflation by 1983). However, setting a goal and achieving it are two separate things. As we proceed, we will investigate the impact of public policy on economic stability in detail. Let us begin with an examination of the growth and employment record for the United States during the last 50 years.

SWINGS IN THE ECONOMIC PENDULUM

During the last 50 years, real GNP has grown at a rate of approximately 3.5 percent annually. However, the rate of growth has not been steady. One of the major objectives of macroeconomics is to determine the cause of fluctuations in aggregate markets and thereby suggest policy alternatives that would reduce economic instability.

Exhibit 1 illustrates the fluctuation in real GNP during the last 50 years. The annual growth of aggregate real output exceeded 8 percent for several short periods. In several other years, output as measured by real GNP actually declined. In 1938, it fell by nearly 5 percent. From 1929 to 1939, a period of time referred to as the Great Depression, economic growth came to a complete standstill. Between 1929 and 1933, real GNP actually declined by more than 25 percent! The 1929 level of real GNP was not reached again until 1939. Since the 1930s, growth has been more stable. However, economic booms and serious declines in the rate of output continue to occur. World War II was characterized by a rapid expansion of GNP, which was followed by a decline after the war. The real GNP did not reach its 1944 level again until 1951, although the output of *consumer* goods did increase significantly in the years immediately after the war as the conversion was made to a peacetime economy. The years 1954, 1958, 1960, 1970, 1974, and 1979–1981 were characterized by downswings in economic activity. Upswings in real GNP came in 1950, 1955, most of the 1960s, 1972–1973, and 1976–1977.

Not only have movements in the aggregate product market been uneven, but so have conditions in the aggregate labor market. A key measure of labor market conditions, the **rate of unemployment,** has fluctuated widely during the last several decades. In the midst of the Great Depression, one out of every four persons in the labor force was looking for a job but was unable to find one. With the expansion of the wartime economy from 1940 to 1945, unemployment fell

Rate of Unemployment: The percent of persons in the civilian labor force who are not employed. Mathematically, it is equal to:

$$\frac{\text{Number of persons unemployed}}{\text{number in civilian labor force}} \times 100$$

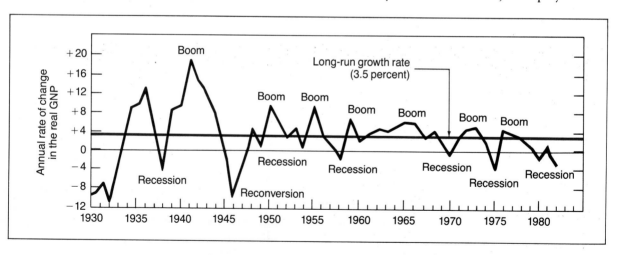

EXHIBIT 1 Instability in the growth of real GNP

Note that although fluctuations are present, the periods of positive growth outweigh the periods of declining real income. The long-run real GNP in the United States has grown approximately 3.5 percent annually.

sharply. In 1940, 15 percent of the civilian labor force was unemployed. During the period from 1943 to 1945, the rate fell to less than 2 percent (see Exhibit 2). Since World War II, the rate of unemployment has been more stable, but significant unevenness nevertheless continues. The rate of unemployment reached 6 percent in 1949 but fell to 3 percent by 1952. It jumped from 4.3 percent in 1957 to 6.8 percent in 1959. During most of the 1960s, the rate declined steadily until it reached a low of nearly 3 percent in 1968, but it again climbed to nearly 6 percent in the early 1970s. During the recession of 1974–1975 the unemployment rate jumped to over 9 percent. Since that time, it has been abnormally high by historical standards, generally falling between 6 percent and 8 percent. Thus, conditions in the aggregate labor market, like those in the aggregate product market, have been characterized by instability.

The historical data show that periods of economic expansion and low rates of unemployment have traditionally been followed by economic slowdown and contraction. During the slowdown, real GNP grows at a slower rate, if at all. During the expansion phase, real GNP grows rapidly. Economists refer to these fluctuations in economic conditions as business cycles. As the term implies, a **business cycle** is a period of up-and-down motion in aggregate measures of current economic output and income. Exhibit 3 illustrates a hypothetical business cycle. When most businesses are operating at capacity level, the real GNP is growing rapidly, and the rate of unemployment is low, **boom** conditions exist. Boom conditions result in a high level of economic activity. As aggregate business conditions slow, the economy begins the contraction phase of a business cycle. During the *contraction,* the sales of most businesses fall, real GNP grows at a slow rate or perhaps declines, and unemployment in the aggregate labor market rises. When economic activity is low and unemployment is high, these conditions are referred to as a **recession** or, if they are quite serious, a **depression.** As we have already seen, depression conditions dominated the 1930s. We experienced recessions in 1949, 1954, 1958, 1960–1961, 1970, 1974–1975, 1980 and again in 1981. After the recession reaches bottom and economic conditions begin to improve, the economy enters an expansionary stage. During the *expansion* phase, business sales rise, GNP grows rapidly, and the rate of unemployment declines.

A Hypothetical Business Cycle

Business Cycle: Fluctuations in the general level of economic activity as measured by such variables as the rate of unemployment and changes in real GNP.

Boom: The high point of the business cycle as indicated by a low rate of unemployment and rapid growth in real GNP.

Recession: The low point of the business cycle, characterized by a high rate of unemployment and a slow rate of growth, or even a decline, in real GNP. In an effort to be more precise, some economists have defined a recession as two consecutive quarters in which there is a decline in real GNP.

Depression: A prolonged and very severe recession.

EXHIBIT 2 Unemployment and instability in the aggregate labor market

Shaded areas represent periods of business recession as defined by the National Bureau of Economic Research. The normal rate of unemployment is from Robert J. Gordon, *Macroeconomics* (Boston: Little, Brown, 1978).

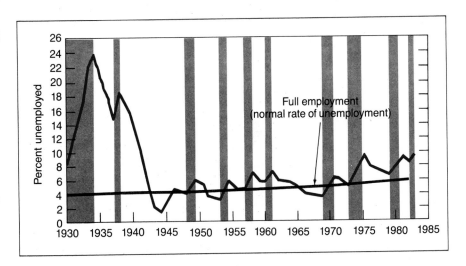

EXHIBIT 3 The business cycle

In the past, ups and downs have often characterized aggregate business activity. Despite these fluctuations, an upward trend in real GNP is usually observed.

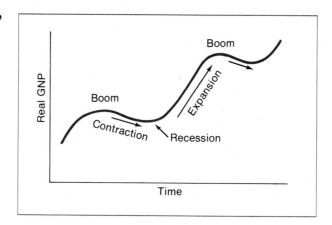

The expansion blossoms into another boom. The boom, however, eventually peters out and turns to a contraction, beginning the cycle anew.

Our hypothetical cycle indicates steady and smooth movement from boom to recession and back again to boom. In the real world, cycles are not nearly as regular or predictable. As demonstrated in Exhibits 1 and 2, past periods of expansion and contraction have been irregular, and they have not exhibited the smooth continuity of our hypothetical cycle. Certain phases of the cycle have sometimes been quite long. The 1930s were characterized by prolonged depression. During the 1950s, the expansionary phases were short, and an extended boom was never really attained. In contrast, expansion and prolonged boom characterized the 1960s. Nevertheless, the phases of expansion, boom, contraction, and recession are still present.

Despite these cyclical patterns, the trend in real GNP in the United States and most other industrial nations has clearly been upward. During the last 50 years the long-run rate of growth in real GNP has been approximately 3.5 percent (see Exhibit 1). In some years growth has been greater, and in others less, than the long-run trend, but years of positive growth clearly outweigh the periods of falling real GNP.

EMPLOYMENT FLUCTUATIONS IN A DYNAMIC ECONOMY

The unemployment rate is a closely observed indicator of economic health. Nonetheless, it is often difficult to determine exactly what the rate is telling us. The unemployment rate reflects a complex set of individual choices and collective institutional arrangements that sometimes change with the passage of time. The messages or lessons to be drawn from any one given rate of unemployment may be very different for different time periods.

At the most basic level, it is important to note that *not working* and unemployment are not the same thing. Persons may not be currently working in the marketplace for a variety of reasons. Some may have retired. Others may be attending school in order to acquire the knowledge and skills that will enhance their future livelihood. Still others may be out of the labor force as a result of illness or disability. As we shall see, the definition of unemployed, for the purpose of computing the rate of unemployment, is more specific than simply "not working."

As Exhibit 4 illustrates, the members of the noninstitutional adult population can be grouped into three broad categories: (a) persons not in the labor force, (b) persons in the armed forces, and (c) persons either working or seeking work in the civilian labor force. In 1981, there were 60.1 million people at the age of 16 or over who were neither employed nor looking for market work. This is not to say that these people were idle. Most were attending school, working in their households, vacationing, and/or recovering from illness. Nonetheless, their activities were outside the market labor force.

The **rate of labor force participation** is the number of adult persons in the labor force as a percentage of the total noninstitutional population 16 years of age and over. In 1981, the rate of labor force participation was 64.4 percent, indicating that more than three out of every five adults were in the labor force.

Labor force participants fall into two subgroups: the employed and the

EXHIBIT 4   Population, employment, and unemployment, 1981

Noninstitutional Population (Age 16 and Over)	Number of Persons[a]
Not in labor force	60.1
Armed forces	2.1
Civilian labor force	106.5
Employed	99.0
Unemployed	7.5
New entrant to the labor force	0.9
Reentrant to the labor force	2.0
Quit last job	0.9
Laid off (waiting to return)	1.2
Lost last job	2.7
Total	168.7
Rate of labor force participation (percent)	64.4
Civilian rate of employment (as a percentage of the total noninstitutional population)	58.7
Rate of unemployment (as a percentage of the civilian labor force)	7.0

[a]Data are for July 1981, measured in millions, except those expressed as percentages.

U.S. Department of Labor, *Monthly Labor Review* (December 1981).

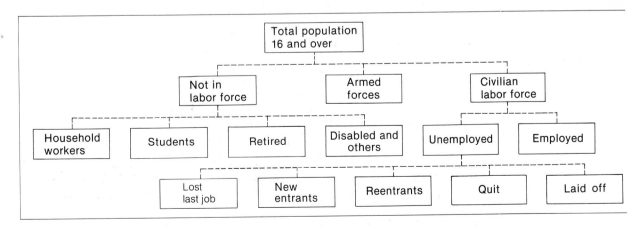

The above diagram illustrates the alternative participation status categories for the adult population.

unemployed. The Bureau of Labor Statistics, which assembles the official labor force data for the United States, classifies a person who is not working as **unemployed** if he or she is either (a) actively seeking employment or (b) waiting to begin or return to a job.[1] Workers are constantly flowing into and out of the unemployment category. At any given time, some industries are expanding and therefore hiring additional workers. In contrast, others are contracting and laying off workers. In addition, workers, many of whom are switching from schooling or household work, are constantly entering or reentering the work force and experiencing periods of unemployment. Between the time they begin actively seeking work and the time they begin a job, they will be counted among the unemployed. In 1981 (July) 7.5 million persons were unemployed. Of these, 900,000 were entering the work force for the first time. Another 2.0 million were reentering the job market. In addition, 1.2 million others were on layoff, waiting to return to their previous positions. Another 900,000 had quit their previous positions. Of the 7.5 million unemployed workers, only 2.7 million had been terminated from their previous positions. These data make it clear that even the unemployed are not a homogeneous employment category.

As long as workers are mobile—as long as they can voluntarily quit a position or switch from one job to another—some unemployment will be present. Job switching, although it is usually accompanied by a period of unemployment, often leads to a better matching of employee job skills and preferences with the requirements of the economy. Job moves of this type actually *improve* the efficiency of the economy and lead to a higher real income for the economy's participants (see Myths of Economics, page 134). However, unemployment can also be a sign of economic inefficiency. Unemployment may reflect demand conditions for labor, policy changes, and/or the inability or lack of incentive on the part of potential workers and potential employers to arrive at mutually advantageous agreements. To clarify matters, economists divide unemployment into three categories: frictional, structural, and cyclical. Let us take a closer look at each of these three classifications.

Unemployed: The term used to describe a person, not currently employed, who is either (a) actively seeking employment or (b) waiting to begin or return to a job.

Frictional Unemployment

Frictional Unemployment: Unemployment due to constant changes in the economy that prevent *qualified* unemployed workers from being immediately matched up with existing job openings. It results from lack of complete information on the part of both job seekers and employers and from the amount of unemployed time spent by job seekers in job searches (pursuit of costly information).

Unemployment that is caused by the constant change in the labor market is called **frictional unemployment**. Frictional unemployment occurs because (a) employers are not fully aware of all available workers and their job qualifications and (b) available workers are not fully aware of the jobs being offered by employers.

The basic cause of frictional unemployment is imperfect information. The number of job vacancies may match up with the number of persons seeking employment. The qualifications of the job seekers may even meet those sought by firms seeking employees. However, frictional unemployment will still occur because it is costly—it takes time—for qualified job seekers to identify firms demanding their services, and vice versa.

Employers looking for a new worker seldom hire the first applicant who walks into their employment office. They want to find the "best available"

---

[1] More precisely, persons are counted among those actively seeking employment if they have looked for a job at any time during the preceding four weeks. Persons who are available for work but are not working because they are on layoff or are waiting to start a new job within the next 30 days are also counted among the unemployed.

worker to fill their opening. It is costly to hire workers who perform poorly. Sometimes it is even costly to terminate their employment. So employers search — they expend time and resources trying to screen applicants and choose only those who have the desired qualifications.

Similarly, persons seeking employment usually do not take the first job available. They, too, search among potential alternatives, seeking the best job available as they perceive it. They undergo search cost (submit to job interviews, use employment agencies, and so on) in an effort to find out about opportunities. As job seekers find out about more and more potential job alternatives, the benefits of *additional* job search diminish. Eventually, the unemployed worker decides that the benefit of additional job search is not worth the cost and chooses the "best" of the current alternatives. All of this takes time, and during that time the job seeker is contributing to the frictional unemployment of the economy.

Policies that influence the costs and benefits of searching will influence the level of frictional unemployment. If the job seeker's search cost is reduced, he or she will spend more time searching. For example, higher unemployment benefits make it less costly to continue looking for a more preferred job. Thus, an increase in unemployment benefits would cause employees to expand their search time, thereby increasing the rate of frictional unemployment. In contrast, an improvement in the flow of information about jobs might reduce the benefits derived from additional search time. Other things constant, improved methods of disseminating job information among unemployed workers would allow workers to shop among job alternatives more quickly and effectively. Thus, most economists believe that a national job information data bank would reduce search time and lower frictional unemployment.

Structural Unemployment

Structural Unemployment: Unemployment due to structural changes in the economy that eliminate some jobs while generating job openings for which the unemployed workers are *not* well qualified.

Structural unemployment occurs because of changes in the basic characteristics of the economy that prevent the "matching up" of available jobs with available workers. Employment openings continue to exist because the unemployed workers do not possess the necessary qualifications to fill them.

There are many causes of structural unemployment. Dynamic changes in demand may change the skill requirements of some jobs. Some skills may become obsolete, whereas others may be in short supply relative to demand. An influx of younger, less experienced workers who fail to meet the requirements of available jobs could cause structural unemployment. Dramatic shifts in defense and other government expenditures often promote excess demand and job vacancies in one area while generating excess supply and unemployment in another. Institutional factors, such as minimum wage legislation, might reduce the incentive of business firms to offer on-the-job training, which would have improved the matchup between job openings and available employees.

Structural unemployment may also be affected by the age–sex composition of the work force. An influx of youthful workers will tend to increase structural unemployment. Quite reasonably, youthful workers will change jobs more often and are more likely to shift from the labor force to schooling and back to the labor force than older workers. Thus, their unemployment rate will exceed that of their older counterparts. In turn, when they are a larger proportion of the total labor force, they will push the overall unemployment rate upward.

Similarly, an increase in dual-earner families will tend to increase the unemployment rate. When both husband and wife work, it will be easier for either to (a) switch jobs, (b) engage in more lengthy job searches, and (c) move back and forth between schooling (or household work or child rearing) and the labor force. In addition, a job switch for one earner may also necessitate a job switch for the spouse.

Cyclical Unemployment

Cyclical Unemployment: Unemployment due to recessionary business conditions and inadequate aggregate demand for labor.

Cyclical unemployment results when the sales of most businesses decline, GNP contracts, and there is a decline in demand for labor *in the aggregate*. Previously, we saw that when there is a decline in demand in some industries and expansion in others, some frictional unemployment arises, since workers and employers have imperfect information about job openings and potential employees. As Exhibit 5 illustrates, lack of information also helps to explain why a decline in the aggregate demand for labor results in unemployment. When the demand for labor declines, some workers are laid off (or fail to be hired) at the existing wage rate. Initially, workers are not sure whether they are being laid off because of a *specific* shift in demand away from their previous employer or a *general* decline in aggregate demand. Not realizing how drastically their job prospects

---

MYTHS OF ECONOMICS

"Unemployed resources would not exist if the economy were operating efficiently."

Nobody likes unemployment. Certainly, extended unemployment can be a very painful experience. However, not all unemployment reflects waste and inefficiency. The time a person spends unemployed and in search of a job can sometimes yield a high return to both the individual and society. Since information is scarce, a person will not be aware of available opportunities as soon as he or she begins looking for a job. Information about available alternatives is acquired by shopping. One would certainly expect individuals to spend a significant amount of time shopping in order to seek out their most preferred job opportunity. Often, this shopping is easiest (cheapest) if the job seeker is unemployed. Thus, job seekers usually do not take just any available job. They search, all the while acquiring valuable information, because they believe that the searching will lead to a more preferred job opportunity.

Similarly, employers shop when they are seeking labor services. They, too, acquire information about available workers that will help them select employees who are best suited to their needs. The shopping of job seekers and employers results in some unemployment, but it also communicates information that leads to an efficient matchup between the characteristics of job seekers (including their preferences) and job requirements.

Parallel "unemployment" exists in the rental housing market. Dynamic factors are also present in this market. New housing structures are brought into the market; older structures depreciate and wear out. Families move from one community to another. Within the same community, renters move among housing accommodations as they seek the housing quality, price, and location that best fit their preferences. As in the employment market, information is imperfect. Thus, renters shop among the available accommodations, seeking the most for their housing expenditures. Similarly, landlords search among renters, seeking to rent their accommodations to those who value them most highly. "Frictional unemployment" of houses is inevitable, but does it indicate inefficiency? No. It results from people's attempt to acquire information that will eventually promote an efficient matchup between housing units and renters.

Of course, some unemployment, particularly cyclical unemployment, is indicative of inefficiency. However, the unemployment due to the shopping of job seekers and employers makes available more information, a scarce resource, and will eventually result in a more efficient matchup of applicants with job openings (and, thus, greater economic efficiency) than would be possible otherwise.

EXHIBIT 5 Unemployment and a decline in aggregate demand

A decline in aggregate demand—the shift from D_1 to D_2—will reduce the level of employment from Q_1 to Q_2, unless the wage rate falls from W_1 to W_2. Because they expect to find jobs at W_1, workers will not initially accept the lower wage rate. Cyclical unemployment of $Q_1–Q_2$ will result.

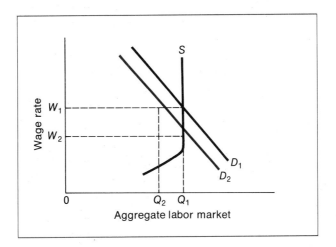

have deteriorated, they continue unsuccessfully to search for jobs at the old wage rate W_1. Unemployment rises.

If the unemployment were merely frictional, workers would soon be able to find jobs at or near their previous wage rate. However, since the unemployment is caused by a decline in aggregate demand, the search of many workers for jobs at the old wage will be fruitless. Their duration of unemployment will be longer than expected. With time, the unemployed workers will have to lower their expectations and be willing to take some cut in wages. However, by the time that employees have lowered their expectations, aggregate demand may have declined even more, and the high level of cyclical unemployment may continue or even worsen.

After aggregate demand stops declining, there will be a gradual reduction in cyclical unemployment as worker expectations about job prospects become more realistic. The greater the reduction in aggregate demand, the greater will be the reduction in wages necessary to eliminate the cyclical unemployment, and the longer it may take for workers to adjust their wage expectations to the reduced rate.

Substantial reductions in aggregate demand will lead to sharp increases in the rate of unemployment and to long periods of unemployment above the "normal rate." As we proceed, we will investigate potential sources of cyclical unemployment and consider policy alternatives to reduce it.

What Is Full Employment?

Under the Employment Act of 1946, the federal government committed itself to a policy of "maximum," or full, employment. Almost every elected official in recent years has supported the policy objective of full employment. What does full employment mean? The concept is somewhat ambiguous. By now, it should be obvious that some unemployment results because unemployed workers take time to shop among job alternatives and employers take time to shop among available workers. Much of this shopping is efficient, since it leads to a better match between the skills of employees and the skills necessary to carry out productive tasks.

Clearly, when most people speak of "full employment," they do not mean zero unemployment. Some amount of unemployment merely reflects the operation of a dynamic labor market. How much is that amount?

Economists define **full employment** as the level of employment that results when the rate of unemployment is normal, considering both frictional and structural factors. Currently, most economists believe that full employment exists when between 94 and 95 percent of the labor force is employed.

Even the economist's concept of full employment is not entirely clear-cut. It incorporates the idea that at a given time there is some **normal rate of unemployment** in a dynamic exchange economy. This normal rate of unemployment results from both frictional and structural factors. It is a rate that is sustainable into the future. However, it is not immutably fixed. Changes in the composition of the labor force as well as in political institutions will affect the normal rate of unemployment. As we previously discussed, when youthful workers and women become a larger proportion of the work force, structural unemployment will rise. This will increase the normal rate of unemployment.

This is precisely what has been happening in recent years. In 1958, youthful workers, ages 16 to 24, constituted only 15.6 percent of the labor force. As the postwar "baby boom" generation entered the labor market, youthful workers as a share of the labor force rose dramatically. By 1980 one out of every four workers was in the 16- to 24-age grouping. In contrast, prime-age workers (over age 25) declined from 84.4 percent of the U.S. work force in 1958 to only 75.3 percent in 1980.

The representation of females in the work force has been growing for years. In 1930, 78 percent of all labor force participants were males. Most were household heads with the sole responsibility for providing the money income for their families. In contrast, less than 15 percent of all wives living with their husbands participated in the work force. By 1980, this situation had changed dramatically. More than one-half of all wives were in the work force. Women constituted 42 percent of the labor force, up from 22 percent in 1930.

The increase in the representation of youthful workers and women caused the normal rate of unemployment to rise during the 1970s. If the age–sex composition of the labor force in 1980 had been the same as for the late 1950s, studies indicate that the rate of unemployment in 1980 would have been between .8 and 1.2 percent lower.

Public policies also affect the normal rate of unemployment. Policies that (a) encourage workers to reject job offers and continue to search for employment, (b) prohibit employers from offering wage rates that would induce them to employ (and train) low-skill workers, and (c) reduce the employer's opportunity cost of using layoffs to adjust rates of production will increase the normal rate of unemployment. The full employment rate—the actual rate of employment that it will be possible to attain and sustain in the future during normal times— is very much a function of public policy.

Without detracting from the importance of full employment, we must not forget that employment is a means to an end. We use employment to produce desired goods and services. Full employment is an empty concept if it means employment at unproductive jobs. The meaningful goal of full employment is *productive employment*—employment that will generate at the lowest possible cost goods and services desired by consumers.

Full Employment: The level of employment that results from the efficient use of the civilian labor force after allowance is made for the normal rate of unemployment due to dynamic changes and the structural conditions of the economy. For the United States, full employment is thought to exist when between 94 and 95 percent of the labor force is employed.

Normal Rate of Unemployment: The long-run average rate of unemployment due to the frictional and structural conditions of labor markets. This rate is affected by both dynamic change and public policy. Cyclical unemployment is *not* a part of of normal unemployment.

The Rate of Unemployment or the Rate of Employment— Some Statistical Problems

The definition of "unemployed" is not without ambiguity. Remember that persons are counted as unemployed only if they are (a) available for and seeking work or (b) awaiting recall from a layoff. These criteria can lead to some paradoxical outcomes. For example, a person who quits looking for work because his or her job-seeking efforts have been discouraging is not counted as unemployed. On the other hand, a welder vacationing in Florida, receiving unemployment compensation while awaiting recall to a $30,000-per-year job in the automobile industry, is considered to be among the ranks of the unemployed.

One can argue that the statistical definition of "unemployment" results in both (a) persons being excluded even though they would prefer to be working (or working more) and (b) others being included who are not seriously seeking employment. Workers whose employment prospects are so bleak that they no longer consider it worthwhile to search for employment are *not* counted as unemployed because they are no longer *actively* seeking employment. During a serious recession, these discouraged workers may comprise a sizable proportion of the work force. Persons who return to school only because they cannot find work are not numbered among the unemployed. Similarly, part-time workers who desire full-time employment are classified as employed rather than un-employed if they work as much as a single hour per week. Persons in the latter category are certainly underemployed, if not unemployed.

On the other hand, some persons may be classified as unemployed who are not seriously seeking market employment. An individual who rejects available employment because it is less attractive than the current combination of household employment, continued search for a job, unemployment benefits, food stamps, and other government welfare programs is numbered among the unemployed. Required work registration in order to maintain eligibility for food stamps and assistance from Aid to Families with Dependent Children (AFDC) also adds to the ambiguity of the unemployment statistics. Some persons may register for employment (and therefore be numbered among the unemployed) with the primary objective of maintaining their food stamp and/or AFDC benefits.[2] Persons engaged in criminal activities (for example, drug pushers, gamblers, and prostitutes) or working "off books" in the underground economy may be counted among the unemployed, if they are not otherwise gainfully employed. Although estimates are difficult to project, some researchers believe that as many as a million persons classified as unemployed participate in the underground economy.

As the result of these ambiguities some economists argue that the **rate of employment** is a more objective and meaningful indicator of job availability than is the rate of unemployment. The civilian rate of employment is the number of persons employed (over the age of 16) in the civilian labor force as a percentage of the number of persons (over the age of 16) in the noninstitutional population. Both of these variables (the civilian level of employment and the noninstitutional adult population) can be readily measured. In addition, they are relatively unambiguous. Their measurement does not require a subjective judg-

Rate of Employment: The number of persons 16 years of age and over who are employed as a percentage of the total noninstitutional population 16 years of age and over. One can calculate either (a) a civilian rate of employment, in which only civilian employees are included in the numerator, or (b) a total rate of employment, in which both civilian and military employees are included in the numerator.

---

[2]See Kenneth W. Clarkson and Roger E. Meiners, "Government Statistics as a Guide to Economic Policy: Food Stamps and the Spurious Increase in the Unemployment Rates," *Policy Review* (Summer 1977), pp. 25–51, for a clear statement of this view.

ment as to whether a person is actually "available for work" or "actively seeking employment."

The rate of employment is relatively free of the defects that may distort the unemployment figures. For example, when a large number of discouraged job seekers stop looking for work, the rate of unemployment drops. In contrast, the rate of employment does not follow such a misleading course.

Does it make any difference which of the two one follows? Exhibit 6 presents data on the rates of both employment and unemployment for various years from 1950 to 1981. During the recessions that occurred in the years covered, the unemployment rate generally rose and the employment rate fell. However, the implications of the two rates as to the severity of each recession are quite different. Consider the data for 1975. The rate of unemployment for 1975 was 8.5 percent, the highest rate for any single year during the post-World War II era. This would certainly suggest that the 1975 recession was quite severe. In contrast, the rate of employment in 1975 was 55.3 percent (down from 57.0 percent in 1974), a figure that compares quite favorably with civilian rates of employment during a prosperous year—1965, for example. In fact, the civilian employment rate was higher in 1975 than 1965 (55.3 percent as compared to 55.0 percent), even though the unemployment rate in 1975 was more than twice the rate of the earlier year (8.5 percent as compared to 4.2 percent.)

Which of the two figures should the wise observer follow? The answer is both. Our economy has been undergoing several structural changes that affect both the rate of unemployment and the rate of employment. The increased incidence of working wives, the influx of a higher percentage of youthful workers into the work force, and changes in eligibility requirements for various

EXHIBIT 6   The rates of employment and unemployment

| Year | Noninstitutional Population (Age 16 and Over) | | | |
	Total (Millions)	Number Employed in Civilian Labor Force (Millions)	Civilian Rate of Employment (Percent)	Rate of Unemployment (Percent)
1950	106.6	58.9	55.3	5.3
1955	112.7	62.2	55.2	4.4
1960	119.8	65.8	54.9	5.5
1965	129.2	71.1	55.0	4.2
1970	140.2	78.6	56.1	4.9
1971	143.0	79.4	55.5	5.9
1972	146.6	82.2	56.1	5.6
1973	149.4	85.1	57.0	4.9
1974	152.3	86.8	57.0	5.6
1975	155.3	85.8	55.2	8.5
1976	158.3	88.8	56.1	7.7
1977	161.2	92.0	57.1	7.1
1978	164.0	96.0	58.5	6.1
1979	167.0	98.8	59.2	5.8
1980	169.8	99.3	58.5	7.1
1981	172.0	100.4	58.3	7.6
1982 (Apr.)	174.0	99.3	57.1	9.4

U.S. Department of Labor, *Monthly Labor Review* (various issues).

income transfer programs—all of these factors contribute to the diversity of the unemployed population. Clearly, "the unemployed" is not a homogeneous category.

Actual and Potential GNP

Potential Output: The level of output that can be attained and sustained into the future, given the size of the labor force, expected productivity of labor, and normal rate of unemployment consistent with the efficient operation of the labor market. For periods of time, the actual output may differ from the economy's potential.

Supply-Constrained Economy: An economy for which the ability to produce output will be constrained by (a) the scarcity of resources and (b) the economy's institutional arrangements. Given these two factors, there will be a maximum output rate that the economy will be able to sustain into the future.

If an economy is going to realize its potential, full employment is essential. When the actual rate of unemployment exceeds the normal level, the actual output of the economy will fall below its potential. Some resources that could be productively employed will be underutilized.

The Council of Economic Advisers defines the **potential output** as:

. . . the amount of output that could be expected at full employment. . . . It does not represent the absolute maximum level of production that could be generated by wartime or other abnormal levels of aggregate demand, but rather that which could be expected from high utilization rates obtainable under more normal circumstances.

The concept of potential output encompasses two important ideas: (a) full utilization of resources, including labor, and (b) a **supply-constrained economy.** Potential output might properly be thought of as the maximum sustainable output level consistent with the economy's resource base, given its institutional arrangements.

Estimates of the potential output level involve three major elements—the size of the labor force, the quality (productivity) of labor, and the normal rate of unemployment. Since these factors cannot be estimated with certainty, there is not uniform agreement among economists as to the potential rate of output for the U.S economy. Relying upon the projections of potential output developed by the Council of Economic Advisers, Exhibit 7 illustrates the record of the U.S. economy since 1954. During the 1950s, the rate of unemployment was above the "normal rate." Excess capacity was present because the level of aggregate demand was insufficient to maintain full employment. The gap between potential and actual GNP was particularly large during the recessions of 1954, 1958, and 1961. During the 1960s, the gap narrowed as the economy approached and *temporarily* exceeded its capacity. Actual output again failed to approach its potential during the recessions of 1970, 1974–1975, and 1979–1981.

EXHIBIT 7 Actual and potential GNP

The graph indicates the gap between the actual and potential GNP for the period from 1954 to 1981. The presence of a gap between potential and actual GNP indicates that the resources of the economy are not being fully utilized.

President's Council of Economic Advisers

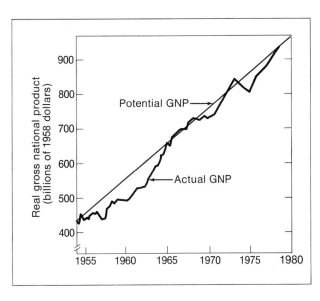

MEASURING THE INFLATION RATE

Inflation: A rise in the general level of prices of goods and services. The purchasing power of the monetary unit, such as the dollar, declines when inflation is present.

Inflation is an overall rise in the the level of prices, such that it costs more to purchase the typical bundle of goods and services chosen by consumers. Of course, even when the general level of prices is stable, some prices will be rising and others will be falling. However, during a period of inflation the impact of the rising prices will outweigh that of falling prices. Because of the higher prices (on average), a dollar will purchase less than it did previously. Therefore, inflation might also be defined as a decline in the value (the purchasing power) of the monetary unit.

We have explained how the GNP deflator is used to adjust money GNP for rising prices during a period. However, suppose we want to measure the impact of inflation on household income. The **consumer price index** is the most common means of measuring the inflation rate for items purchased by the typical household unit. The CPI, calculated monthly by the Bureau of Labor Statistics, is an estimate of how much it costs to buy the typical market basket purchased by urban middle-income families in comparison to the cost in an earlier year.[3] This representative market basket includes eggs, bread, housing, entertainment, medical services, and other goods, in the amounts that they are purchased by most middle-income families. As prices rise, the cost of purchasing this representative market basket will go up, reflecting the higher prices.

Consumer Price Index: An indicator of the general level of prices. It attempts to compare the cost of purchasing the market basket bought by a typical consumer during a specific period with the cost of purchasing the same market basket during an earlier period.

A base year is chosen, and the CPI for that year is arbitrarily assigned a value of 100. For example, the base year is currently 1972–1973. Thus, the current cost of purchasing the typical market basket is compared to its cost during the base year. If it now costs $1000 to purchase the same market basket that could have been purchased for $500 in the base year, the price index is 200. A price index of 200 indicates that prices are now 100 percent higher than during the base year.

The annual inflation rate for consumer goods and services is the percentage change in the consumer price index from one year to the next. Mathematically, the inflation rate (i) can be written as:

$$i = \frac{\text{This year's CPI} - \text{last year's CPI}}{\text{last year's CPI}} \times 100$$

Thus, if the CPI in year 2 was 220, compared to 200 during year 1, the inflation rate would equal 10 percent ([220 − 200]/200] × 100). Since the CPI is calculated monthly, we often compare its value during a specific month with the value during the same month one year earlier in order to calculate the inflation rate during the most recent 12 months.

How rapidly have prices risen in the United States? Exhibit 8 illustrates

---

[3]Actually, the Bureau of Labor Statistics now publishes two indexes of consumer prices—one for "all urban households" and the other for "urban wage earners and clerical workers." The two differ slightly because the typical bundles of goods purchased by the two groups are not identical.

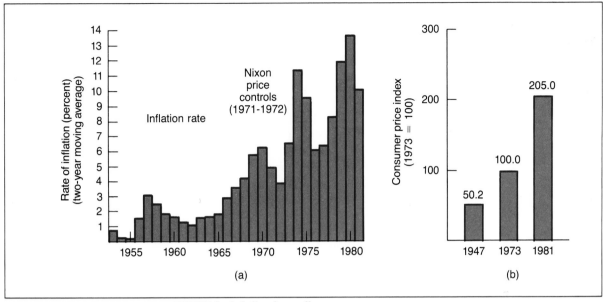

EXHIBIT 8   Inflation in our times

During the period from 1952 to 1965, the annual rate of inflation never exceeded 3 percent. Since 1966, the annual rate of inflation has never fallen below 3 percent, even for a single year. During 1952–1965, the average annual rate of inflation was 1.4 percent; during 1967–1981, it was 7.8 percent. As graph (b) illustrates, it took 26 years for consumer prices to double (1947–1973) after World War II, but then they doubled again in only 8 years (1973–1981).

the record for the last 30 years. During the 1950s and into the mid-1960s, the annual rate of inflation was usually less than 2 percent. Since the mid-1960s, there has been a sharp increase in the rate of inflation. During the 1967–1973 period, the average annual inflation rate rose nearly 5 percent. Since 1973, inflation in the United States has been accelerating upward. The inflation rate averaged 9.3 percent for the 1974–1981 period. Exhibit 8b illustrates the impact of sustained inflation. It took 26 years (1947–1973) for the price level to double after World War II. In contrast, as the inflation rate accelerated upward, in only 8 years (1973–1981) the price level had doubled again.

The rate of inflation among countries varies widely. As Exhibit 9 shows, inflation has been a way of life for some time in such South American countries as Chile, Argentina, Brazil, and Peru. Annual rates of inflation of 50 percent or more were experienced by these countries during most of the 1970s. The inflation rate in most Western industrial nations is much lower, generally ranging between 5 percent and 15 percent. However, as was true for the United States, these rates are considerably higher than the inflation rates for the same countries during most of the 1950s and 1960s. During the earlier period, the annual rate of inflation for countries such as France, West Germany, Italy, and Australia, as well as for the United States, was generally less than 5 percent. It is clear that the last 15 years, at least when gauged by the post-World War II standard, have been a period of substantial inflation for Western economies.

EXHIBIT 9 Worldwide inflation

Country	Compound Annual Rate of Change in Consumer Prices	
	1970–1975	1975–1980
Chile	266	82
Argentina	72	211
Brazil	21	51
Colombia	18	25
Ecuador	14	12
Peru	13	51
France	9	10
West Germany	6	4
Italy	12	16
Japan	13	7
Switzerland	8	2
United Kingdom	13	14
Australia	10	11
Canada	7	9
United States	7	9

International Monetary Fund, *International Financial Statistics* (monthly).

THE EFFECTS OF INFLATION

Inflation reduces the purchasing power of money income received in the future (for example, payments from pensions, life insurance policies, and receipts from outstanding loans). If decision-makers do not consider inflation when they agree to a contract, debtors will gain at the expense of lenders. Does this mean that inflation helps poor people? Not necessarily. We must remember that people need reasonably good credit before they can borrow money. This limits the ability of persons in the lowest income brackets to acquire debt. Most studies in this area suggest that unanticipated inflation results in a moderate redistribution from recipients of both low (less than $5000) and high (more than $50,000) incomes to those in the middle-income groupings.

A more important redistributional effect of unanticipated inflation is the transfer of wealth between age groupings. Persons under 35 years of age are more likely to be debtors. Inflation helps them pay back their housing mortgages, car loans, and other outstanding debts. In contrast, those over 50 years of age are more likely to have savings, paid-up life insurance policies, bonds, and other forms of fixed future income. Inflation eats away at the purchasing power of these savings. Thus, it tends to redistribute income from the old to the young.

However, the biggest gainer from unanticipated inflation is the federal government. Households are net lenders, and the government is the largest debtor. Therefore, unanticipated inflation tends to transfer wealth from households to the government.[4]

---

[4]See G. L. Bach, "Inflation: Who Gains and Who Loses?" *Challenge* (July/August 1974), pp. 48–55, for evidence supporting this view.

DOES THE CPI OVERSTATE THE INFLATION RATE?

Many economists believe that the consumer price index (CPI) is seriously flawed. They believe that it has often overstated the rate of inflation. The wages of approximately 25 percent of the labor force and the expenditures of more than half of the federal budget are tied to the CPI. Therefore, this is a serious matter. There are two major reasons why economists believe that the CPI is flawed.

1. Failure to Account for Consumer Substitution Away from Goods That Rise in Price. The CPI assumes that consumers purchase the market basket consumed during an earlier base period, currently 1972–1973. However, as the prices of various products rise at different rates, consumers will shift their purchases away from products that have become more expensive toward goods that have become relatively cheaper. Thus, the more expensive products tend to comprise a smaller proportion of the typical market basket.

However, the CPI makes no allowance for this shift. For example, when the price of gasoline rose sharply during the 1970s, people drove less and shifted to smaller, higher mileage automobiles. The proportion of personal consumption expenditures allocated to gasoline fell from 3.5 percent in 1972 to 2.8 percent in 1980. Despite this decline in gasoline consumption, the CPI continues to weight gasoline as if consumers were still purchasing the base-year amount.

Consumers reduce the burden of inflation by purchasing less of goods that rise in price most rapidly. Failure of the CPI to consider this fact results in an overstatement of the inflation rate.

2. The Overstatement of Housing Costs. The most serious shortcoming of the CPI is probably its treatment of home ownership costs. The home ownership component accounts for nearly 25 percent of the market basket on which the index is based. The CPI treats the price of a house and the mortgage interest payments of the house as separate transactions. The price of housing is counted *once* when it is purchased and *again* as the interest rate component on the mortgage.

Mortgage interest costs are not included for households that did not buy a house during the survey year. However, for those who did buy a house, *all* mortgage interest due for the first half of the term of the mortgage (usually a period of 10 to 15 years) is included. This procedure makes it seem as if all homeowners refinanced their mortgages each month. Thus, when interest rates rise, as they did during the 1970s, the CPI tells us how much home ownership costs rose, assuming that everyone bought a new home during the period. However, this is not the case. Most homeowners have home mortgages of fixed interest rates. Thus, their home ownership costs do not rise, as the CPI implies they do.

With billions of dollars of both wage payments and government expenditures hanging upon the CPI, it is imperative that these flaws be corrected.

Anticipated Inflation: An increase in the general level of prices that is expected by economic decision-makers. Past experience and current conditions are the major determinants of an individual's expectations with regard to future price changes.

An analysis of the debtor–creditor impact of inflation is incomplete without the recognition that after a period of inflation, individuals eventually begin to incorporate the expectation of future inflation into their decision-making. **Anticipated inflation** is a change in the level of prices that is expected by decision-makers. Once both borrowers and lenders anticipate inflation, they will adjust their behavior to account for it. For example, lenders will demand and borrowers will grant a higher interest rate on loans because both parties expect the value of the dollar to depreciate. Suppose that a borrower and a lender would agree to a 5 percent interest rate if they anticipated stable prices during the course of the loan. However, if both expected prices to rise 10 percent annually, they would agree instead to a 15 percent interest rate. The higher interest rate would compensate the lender for the expected decline in the purchasing power of the dollar during the course of the loan.

When inflation is fully anticipated, debtors do not systematically benefit at the expense of lenders. Debtors gain at the expense of creditors only if the actual rate of inflation exceeds the rate expected at the time the terms of the transaction are agreed upon.

Once the inflation is widely anticipated, generalizations about wealth transfers among groups will no longer hold true. Persons will adopt a variety of

Escalator Clause: A contractual agreement that periodically and automatically adjusts the wage rates of a collective-bargaining agreement upward by an amount determined by the rate of inflation.

economic arrangements designed to protect their wealth and income against erosion by inflation. For example, collective-bargaining agreements will incorporate **escalator clauses** or contain a premium for the expected rate of inflation. Home mortgage interest rates will rise to incorporate the inflation factor. Similarly, life insurance premiums will decline per $1000 of future retirement or death benefits, since the money interest rate of the insurance company's current assets will rise as a result of inflation.

Contrary to the satirical statement at the beginning of the chapter, inflation will affect the prices of the things we sell as well as the prices of the goods we buy. Both wages and prices will rise during a period of inflation. Before we become too upset about inflation "robbing us of the purchasing power of our paychecks," we should recognize that inflation influences the size of those paychecks. The weekly earnings of employees would not have risen at an annual rate of 7 percent during the 1970s if the rate of inflation had not increased rapidly during the period (the CPI rose at an annual rate of 8 percent). Given the rate of output during the period, it would clearly be wrong to argue that Americans could have consumed 8 percent more goods and services during 1970–1980 had it not been for inflation.

The Dangers of Inflation

Merely because money income initially tends to rise with prices, it does not follow that there is no need to be concerned about inflation, particularly high rates of inflation. Three negative aspects of inflation are particularly important.

1. Price Changes Can Frustrate the Intent of a Long-Term Contract. Since the rate of inflation varies, it cannot be predicted with certainty. Most market exchanges, including long-term contracts, are made in *money* terms. If unanticipated inflation takes place, it can change the result of long-term contracts, such as mortgages, life insurance policies, pensions, bonds, and other arrangements that involve a debtor-lender relationship.

2. Rapid Price Changes Cause Uncertainty. If one is not sure whether prices are going to increase, decrease, or remain the same, any contract that has a time dimension becomes hazardous because of uncertainty. The builder does not know whether to tack on a charge of 2, 5, or 10 percent to a contract, even though inflation is bound to increase building costs by some amount during the time necessary for construction. Union workers do not know whether to accept a contract calling for a 5 percent wage increase for the next two years. Inflation could partially or completely negate the increase. If price changes are unpredictable (for example, if prices rise 10 percent one year, then level off for a year or two, and then increase again by 10 or 15 percent), no one knows what to expect. Long-term money exchanges must take into account the uncertainty created by inflation.

Unfortunately, studies indicate that higher rates of inflation are associated with greater *variability* in the inflation rate. It becomes increasingly difficult to forecast just how much prices (and costs) will rise during the next month (or over the next several months). Therefore, the risks undertaken when entering into long-term contracts are enlarged. Given this additional uncertainty, many decision-makers will forego exchanges involving long-term contracts. Thus, mutually advantageous gains will be lost. The efficiency of markets is reduced.

'Ten More Years and Our Bank Loot Won't Be Worth Digging Up.'

Some observers believe that the "randomness" associated with high, variable rates of inflation undermines the legitimacy of an economic system. The links between productive effort and reward are weakened as the economic system takes on the characteristics of a "poker game," as Kenneth Boulding once stated.[5] The economic "winners" are those lucky enough to reap an inflationary windfall, rather than those who supply goods and productive resources efficiently to others. Such uncertainty, and the windfalls that accompany it, clearly reduce the ability of markets (a) to communicate information about *relative* scarcities and (b) to provide decision-makers with the incentive to deal efficiently with the basic economic problem (how scarce resources can be transformed into desired goods).

3. Real Resources Are Used Up As Decision-Makers Seek to Protect Themselves from Inflation. Since the failure to anticipate accurately the rate of inflation can have a substantial effect on one's wealth, individuals will divert scarce resources from the production of desired goods and services to the acquisition of information on the future rate of inflation. Inflation forecasting and financial consulting will become booming industries during inflationary times. Productive members of the labor force will use their talent both (a) to determine what the future movements of wages and prices are likely to be and (b) to

---

[5]Kenneth Boulding, *Beyond Economics: Essays on Society, Religion, and Ethics* (Ann Arbor: University of Michigan Press, 1968), p. 206. Also see Robert Higgs, "Inflation and the Destruction of the Free Market Economy," *The Intercollegiate Review* (Spring 1979), for an excellent discussion on the side effects of inflation.

adjust their decision-making to protect their wealth and future income against the expected changes. This process of seeking information and adjusting one's decision-making is costly. For example, firms will be unable to establish list prices for any length of time. Catalogues will continually have to be updated and reissued. Business planning will be unnecessarily frustrated by the need for continuous reassessment of factor and product prices. The use of valuable resources in each of these activities will reduce the consumption alternatives available to the citizens of the economy.

Stagflation

Stagflation: A period during which an economy is experiencing both substantial inflation and a slow growth in output.

As recently as a decade ago, most economists thought that inflation was generally associated with prosperity and rapid economic growth. During the 1970s, however, the United States experienced two inflationary recessions. Economists have coined the term **stagflation** to describe the phenomenon of rapid inflation *and* sluggish economic growth. One of the challenges of the 1980s is to develop a solution to the problem of stagflation—to develop economic policies that will reduce the rate of inflation, lead to a more efficient utilization of resources, and increase the future production possibilities available to economic participants. Again and again, we will return to this issue as we probe more deeply into macroeconomics.

What causes inflation? We must acquire some additional tools before we can analyze this question in detail, but we can outline a couple of theories. First, economists emphasize the link between aggregate demand and supply. If aggregate demand rises more rapidly than supply, prices will rise. Second, nearly all economists believe that a rapid expansion in a nation's stock of money causes inflation. The old saying is that prices will rise because "there is too much money chasing too few goods." The hyperinflation experienced by South American countries has been the result mainly of monetary expansion. Later, we will analyze several other popular inflation theories—the monopoly power of business and labor, for example. However, we must do more groundwork in order to understand these issues fully.

LOOKING AHEAD

In this chapter we have looked at the historical record for real income, employment, and prices. Measurement problems and the side effects of economic instability were discussed. In the following chapter we will discuss the historical roots of macroeconomics and introduce an important macroeconomic concept—aggregate demand. As we proceed, our ultimate goal is to develop an economic way of thinking, or models as some would say, that will help us understand unemployment, inflation, and economic instability.

CHAPTER LEARNING OBJECTIVES

1 Aggregate labor and product markets have been characterized by instability. GNP has increased much more rapidly during some periods than during others. The unemployment rate has varied considerably during the last 50 years, reaching a high of 25 percent in 1935 and attaining a low of less than 2 percent during World War II. Since World War II, the rate has been more stable, but fluctuations continue to occur.

2　Boom, contraction, recession, and expansion are terms used by economists to describe the economic performance of aggregate markets. During an expansion, the unemployment rate declines and output increases rapidly. Boom is the term used to describe the peak level of output of a business cycle. Contraction is characterized by increasing unemployment, declining business conditions, and a low rate of growth. When economic activity is at a low level, this condition is referred to as a recession, or depression if it is quite serious.

3　Even an efficient exchange economy will experience some unemployment. Frictional unemployment results because of imperfect information about available job openings and qualified applicants. Structural unemployment stems from changes in the composition of the work force or the presence of factors that prevent the "matching up" of available applicants with available jobs. Currently, frictional and structural unemployment in the United States are thought to involve between 5 and 6 percent of the labor force.

4　Cyclical unemployment results because aggregate demand for labor is insufficient to maintain full employment. A primary concern of macroeconomics is how cyclical unemployment can be minimized.

5　Full employment is the level of employment that is consistent with a normal rate of unemployment, reflecting dynamic change and the structure of the economy. The normal rate of unemployment that is consistent with full employment is not immutable. Both public policies and changes in the composition of the labor force affect the normal rate of unemployment.

6　Employment is a means to an end. The meaningful goal of full employment is full, productive employment—employment that produces desired goods and services.

7　The statistical definition of "unemployed" is ambiguous. Some persons are not counted as unemployed because they are currently too discouraged to "actively seek employment." Others are counted even though they may be "employed" in the underground economy or only casually seeking employment (perhaps because of the incentive structure that they confront). Because of these ambiguities, some observers believe that the rate of employment (the percentage of the noninstitutional population, age 16 and over, that is employed) may be a more objective and accurate indicator of current employment opportunities.

8　The concept of potential output encompasses two important ideas: (a) full utilization of resources and (b) a supply constraint that limits our ability to produce desired goods and services. When the resources of the economy are not fully and efficiently utilized, output will fall below its potential rate.

9　Inflation is a general rise in the level of prices. Alternatively, we might say that it is a decline in the purchasing power of the monetary unit—the dollar in the case of the United States. The inflation rate has accelerated upward in the United States since the mid-1960s.

10　It is important to distinguish between anticipated and unanticipated inflation. Once decision-makers come to anticipate inflation, they will adjust their current decisions, making an allowance for the expected impact of inflation on the purchasing power of future income.

11　Inflation will have a harmful effect on an economy because it often (a) changes the intended terms of trade of long-term contracts, (b) increases the uncertainty of exchanges involving time, and (c) consumes valuable resources as individuals use their skills and talents to protect themselves from inflation. High and highly variable rates of inflation will be particularly harmful.

1 Explain why even an efficiently functioning economic system will have some unemployed resources.

2 What is full employment? How does public policy affect the percentage of the labor force that will be employed at full employment? What other factors influence the level of full employment? Give an example of a public policy that decreases (increases) the number of persons who will be employed at full employment.

3 How does the rate of employment differ from the rate of unemployment? Which is the better indicator of employment opportunity? Why?

4 "My money wage rose by 6 percent last year, but inflation completely erased these gains. How can I get ahead when inflation continues to wipe out my increases in earnings?" Evaluate. Do you agree with the view implicit in this question?

5 What are the most harmful effects of inflation? Explain why it matters whether inflation is accurately anticipated.

6 **What's Wrong with This Way of Thinking?**

"The value of today's dollar is only one-fourth of what it was in 1940. Five years from now it will be worth only 20 cents. We cannot maintain our standard of living when the value of our currency is declining so rapidly."

7 "As the inflation proceeds and the real value of the currency fluctuates widely from month to month, all permanent relations between debtors and creditors, which form the ultimate foundation of capitalism, become so utterly disordered as to be almost meaningless; and the process of wealth-getting degenerates into a gamble and a lottery." Do you agree with this well-known economist's view? Why or why not? How high do you think the inflation rate would have to climb before these effects would become pronounced? Do you see any evidence in support of this view in the United States?

THE COMPONENTS OF AGGREGATE DEMAND

I believe myself to be writing a book on economic theory which will largely revolutionize—not, I suppose, at once but in the course of the next ten years—the way the world thinks about economic problems.[1]
John Maynard Keynes

Although economics dates back to the writings of Adam Smith in 1776, the development of macroeconomics is relatively new. Modern macroeconomic analysis became prominent when John Maynard Keynes (pronounced "canes") published his *General Theory* in 1936.[2] Professor Keynes, an Englishman, has influenced macroeconomic analysis more than any other economist. He developed several of the basic concepts and much of the terminology that form the core of macroeconomics today.

The objectives of this chapter are threefold. First, we will acquaint the reader with the economic views that Keynes challenged and the circumstances in the world economy that led to the Keynesian revolution. Second, we will outline Keynes's challenge, pointing out how Keynes departed from the prevailing orthodoxy and why the Keynesian view eventually attained widespread acceptance. Third, we will introduce the concept of aggregate demand, which occupies a position of central importance in the Keynesian model. The major components of aggregate demand will be analyzed in detail.

Macroeconomics should enhance our understanding of the factors that determine output, employment, and the level of prices. Although our modern analysis still owes much to the writings of Keynes and his early followers, our knowledge of macroeconomics continues to expand. As we proceed, we will incorporate recent advances in macroeconomics. In subsequent chapters we will (a) develop more fully the supply side of macroeconomics, (b) integrate the banking system and monetary economics into our macroeconomic model, and (c) analyze the impact of inflation (and the expectation of inflation) on the levels of output and employment.

---

[1] Letter from John Maynard Keynes to George Bernard Shaw, New Year's Day, 1935.

[2] John Maynard Keynes, *The General Theory of Employment, Interest, and Money* (London: Macmillan, 1936).

Prior to the Great Depression of the 1930s, most economists felt that a market economy would automatically provide for the full employment of resources. Of course, there would sometimes be *temporary* periods of high unemployment, reflecting the disruptive impact of such things as droughts, technological change, wars, and political conditions. But pre-Keynesian economists—we often refer to them as **classical economists**—believed that the pricing system would soon adjust to disruptive forces and guide the economy back to full employment.

Three important assumptions formed the basis of classical economic thinking.

Classical Economists: Economists prior and up to the time of Keynes, who focused their analysis on economic efficiency and production. They believed that economic forces would automatically guide the economy to full employment.

1. Say's Law—Supply Creates Its Own Demand. A nineteenth-century French economist, J. B. Say, maintained that a general overproduction of goods relative to total demand was impossible because supply (production) would always create its own demand. According to Say's law, total demand would always be sufficient to purchase the output because the act of producing the good would generate an amount of demand (income) exactly equal to the value of the goods produced.

Say's Law: The view that production creates its own demand. Thus, there cannot be a general oversupply because the total value of goods and services produced (income) will be always available for purchasing them.

Say's law is based on a view that people do not work just for the sake of working but in order to obtain the income that will in turn purchase desired goods and services. The purchasing power necessary to buy (demand) desired products is generated by production. A farmer's supply of wheat generates income to meet the farmer's demand for shoes, clothes, automobiles, and other desired goods. Similarly, the supply of shoes generates the purchasing power with which shoemakers (and their employees) demand the farmer's wheat and other goods *they* desire. Classicists understood that it was possible to produce too much of some goods and not enough of others. But at such times, they reasoned, the prices of goods in excess supply would fall, and the prices of products in excess demand would rise. The pricing system would correct such imbalances as might temporarily exist. However, a *general* overproduction of goods, relative to aggregate demand, was an impossibility, according to classical economists.

2. Flexible Interest Rates Would Assure That Funds Saved Would Be Channeled into Investment. Of course, classical economists were aware that not all income derived from production is immediately spent on goods and services. Sometimes individuals save a portion of their income instead of spending it on current consumption. However, classical economists did not believe that this posed any problem in the long run, because **interest rate** flexibility would assure that each dollar saved would eventually be channeled back into the spending stream as business investment, based on a supply and demand concept. If households were temporarily saving more than business decision-makers were investing, the excess supply of saving would cause the interest rate to decline. As the interest rate fell, businesses would find it profitable to undertake additional investment, and savers would find it less profitable to save. Eventually, equilibrium would be restored at the lower interest rate. On the other hand, if the quantity of investment undertaken by the business sector were temporarily greater than the saving of households, an excess demand for funds would be present, causing the interest rate to rise. The higher interest rate would make

Interest Rate: The price paid for the use of money or loanable funds for a period of time. It is stated as a percentage of the amount borrowed. For example, an interest rate of 10 percent means that the borrower pays 10 cents annually for each dollar borrowed.

saving more attractive and discourage investors from borrowing. Again, equilibrium would soon be restored.

3. Flexible Wages and Prices Would Assure Movement toward the Full Employment of Resources.
The third major argument used to bolster the classical position was flexibility of wages and prices. The classical economists believed that even if the interest rate did not efficiently eliminate any excess saving relative to investment, price flexibility would soon restore full employment of resources. If consumption and investment expenditures were insufficient to buy back the products produced, prices would decline. At the lower level of prices, households would be able to purchase the total amount of goods produced at the **full-employment rate of output.**

But could goods be produced profitably at lower prices? Classicists believed so, if resource prices also declined. A general reduction in demand for products would lead to a decreased demand for resources, including labor. As Exhibit 1 illustrates, the reduction in demand for labor might well lead to *temporary* unemployment. For a time, a wage rate such as W_b might be present, even though recessionary market conditions would dictate a larger decline in wage rates (to W_e). During this phase, the unemployment rate would be abnormally high. However, competition from the unemployed would leave workers no choice but to accept lower wage rates. Wage rates would decline (points b, c, and d), and eventually equilibrium (and full employment) would be restored at W_e. At the new, lower equilibrium wage rate, businesses would hire all workers desiring employment, causing unemployment to fall to the level consistent with an efficient, dynamic labor market.

For the classical economists, wage flexibility was an automatic mechanism; they recognized the cyclical nature of economic activity but believed that market forces would always ensure economic recovery and a return to full employment. Recessions would always be temporary.

Full-Employment Rate of Output: The rate of output associated with the full employment of both labor and capital resources. It is sustainable into the future, not just a temporary high rate. It is determined by both the availability of resources and the incentive structure emanating from the nation's economic institutions.

EXHIBIT 1 A decline in demand for labor—the classical view

Pre-Keynesian economists believed that prolonged unemployment was impossible: If the demand for labor decreased (from D_1 to D_2), falling wages would eventually restore equilibrium in the labor market. Abnormally high rates of unemployment might occur *temporarily,* if wage rates such as W_b (and disequilibrium points like c and d) were present, but eventually wages would always fall again to the equilibrium rate (W_e).

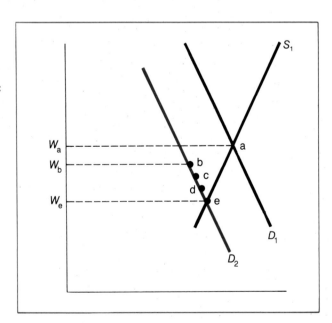

The prolonged depression of the 1930s shook the faith of both laymen and economists in the classical theory. Wage rates fell, but the economy continued to stagnate. Almost 25 percent of the labor force was unemployed; many plants closed down or operated at 50 percent capacity. Businesses went bankrupt. Potential gains from market exchange and specialization were lost as trade slowed. And these depressing economic conditions continued for a decade. Falling wages were *not* leading to economic recovery.

It was against this background of massive unemployment and idle industrial capacity that John Maynard Keynes's model was developed—a model that explained why a market system might not automatically rebound from a depression and reestablish the full employment of resources. Keynes's writing led to a revolution in economic thinking about questions of unemployment and the operation of highly aggregated markets. Quite properly, he has been called the father of macroeconomics.

Keynes raised two major objections to the classical view that a market economy would automatically return to full employment after a downturn.

1. Contrary to Say's Law, A Market Economy Does Not Guarantee That Aggregate (Total) Demand Is Sufficient to Purchase the Full-Employment Level of Output. Keynes argued that Say's analysis was incorrect: Saving constitutes a *leakage* from the income–expenditure stream. If this saving leakage exceeds the investment of business firms, then the total spending of consumers and investors will be insufficient to buy back the goods produced. In response to the weak demand, firms will not continue to produce goods that they are unable to sell. Stagnation and depression will be the result.

Keynes rejected the view that the interest rate would assure a balance between saving and investment. He stressed that people save and invest for various reasons; no single factor like the interest rate automatically links and controls these activities. Households are the major source of saving; people save for future retirement, a home, a car, a college education, and many other things. The decision to save is far more dependent on income than on the interest rate. Investment spending, Keynes argued, is determined primarily by technological advances, expected future business conditions, innovations, and profitability rather than by the interest rate. If the business outlook is poor, little investment will be undertaken even at low interest rates: No business decision-makers want to invest and expand if their products will not be purchased because of insufficient consumer demand. During a business contraction, there are few new investment opportunities that are profitable. Business decision-makers will reduce their capital expenditures, and this reduction in investment will cause the recession to worsen. Thus, according to the Keynesian view, there is no reason to believe that the interest rate will bring the plans of savers into balance with the plans of investors at full employment.

2. Flexible Wages and Prices Will Not Assure Full Employment. Keynes also attacked the classical idea that declining wages and prices would eventually guide the economy back to full employment. He emphasized that wages and prices tend to be inflexible in movement downward: In many industries they are not immediately or automatically responsive to a decline in demand. For an economy dominated by large businesses and trade unions, unemployment could continue for a long time before wages and prices declined enough to restore full employment.

However, Keynes argued that even if wages and prices *were* flexible, it was doubtful that they could restore full employment. He charged that classical economists were guilty of the fallacy of composition.[3] Just because a reduction in the price of a single good (or resource) causes an increase in the amount of that good demanded, it does not follow that a decline in the price of all goods and resources will cause more of all goods to be demanded. What is true for a narrowly defined market may not be true for all markets in aggregate. After all, as wages decline, income also declines. Workers with less purchasing power (income) will reduce their demand for the goods and services of producers. The fall in consumer demand (generated by the lower wages) will reduce the incentive of producers to expand their output or invest in additional capital equipment. Keynes argued that falling wages, far from improving matters, reduce both consumer income and aggregate demand, causing the recession (or depression) to continue.

The message of Keynes was that declining income and prolonged unemployment would result when consumption spending and investment spending were deficient. Neither the interest rate nor falling wages (and prices) could ensure that the flow of consumer and investment expenditures would be sufficient to enable business firms to produce the full-employment level of output. In contrast to the classical economists, Keynes argued that prolonged periods of unemployment were possible. The Great Depression was proof enough for many that Keynes's message should be heeded.

THE CONCEPT OF AGGREGATE DEMAND

Aggregate Demand: Total current spending for goods and services. It has four components: (a) consumption, (b) investment, (c) government, and (d) net exports.

If a market system does not have an automatic mechanism assuring full employment, as Keynes charged, what *does* determine the level of output and employment? The Keynesian answer is aggregate demand. In the Keynesian framework, **aggregate demand** is comprised of the total spending on goods and services. For a purely private domestic economy, the sum of the consumption and investment expenditures constitutes aggregate demand. When government and foreign trade are integrated into the analysis, aggregate demand has four components: (a) consumption, (b) investment, (c) government purchases, and (d) net exports (exports minus imports).

The concept of planned aggregate demand is a key element of Keynesian economic theory. Keynes argued that producers would supply only the quantity of goods sufficient to meet the planned demand of consumers, investors, government, and foreigners. Therefore, subject to the constraint imposed by the scarcity of resources, planned aggregate demand (the total expected spending on consumption, investment, government, and net exports) would determine the level of output and employment. If producers expect demand to be strong enough for purchasers to buy their products, they will produce the goods. On the other hand, if they perceive that demand is so weak that there will be no

---

[3]See Chapter 1, pp. 13–14.

market for their output, business decision-makers will *not* produce the goods, even if this means idle machines and workers. Therefore, in the Keynesian framework, (a) aggregate demand (total spending) and (b) total output and employment will vary directly. Aggregate demand *determines* the level of output and employment. Let us examine the major components of aggregate demand.

THE DETERMINANTS OF CONSUMPTION

It is important that we understand the concepts of consumption and saving. When we receive a paycheck, what do we usually do with it? Literally, there are only two possibilities. We can either spend it or save it. Household expenditures on current goods and services are called **consumption.** Consumption goods are products that are used up in a very short period of time. Food, clothing, recreational activities, entertainment, and medical services are all examples of consumption expenditures.

Consumption: Household spending on consumer goods and services during the current period. Consumption is a "flow" concept.

Saving: Disposable income that is not spent on consumption. Saving is a "flow" concept.

Dissaving: Consumption expenditures that are in excess of disposable income and that are made possible by either borrowing or drawing on past savings.

Sometimes we set aside part of our paycheck. That portion of disposable income that is not used to purchase consumption goods is called saving. **Saving** is the difference between one's current disposable income and the amount spent on current goods and services. It is income not consumed. Sometimes our current spending on goods exceeds our disposable income. When that is the case, we are dissaving. **Dissaving** is negative saving.

Note that both consumption and saving are flow concepts. One's consumption might be $1000 per month, or $12,000 per year. Similarly, saving (without an s) is the amount saved during a specific time period.

Since current disposable income must be either spent or saved,

$$\text{Disposable income} = \text{consumption} + \text{saving}$$

Alternatively, we can rewrite this relationship as

$$\text{Consumption} = \text{disposable income} - \text{saving}$$

or

$$\text{Saving} = \text{disposable income} - \text{consumption}$$

What determines how much of our income is spent on consumption? Keynes's theory of consumption was straightforward. In *The General Theory of Employment, Interest, and Money,* Keynes asserted:

The fundamental psychological law . . . is that men are disposed, as a rule and on the average, to increase their consumption as their income increases, but not by as much as the increase in their income.[4]

According to Keynes, if we want to know how much a household will consume, one factor stands out above all others. The primary determinant of consumer spending is disposable income. There is a strong, positive relationship between the amount spent on consumption and the disposable income of households. This relationship between consumption spending and disposable income is

---

[4]John Maynard Keynes, *The General Theory of Employment, Interest, and Money* (London: Macmillan, 1964), p. 96.

OUTSTANDING ECONOMIST
John Maynard Keynes
(1883–1946)

Keynes wrote to playwright George Bernard Shaw, in 1935 (see the opening quote for this chapter), that the book he was working on would "revolutionize" economics. His words were prophetic. *The General Theory of Employment, Interest, and Money* was published in 1936. It would not be an exaggeration to rank this book alongside Smith's *Wealth of Nations* and Marx's *Das Kapital* as one of the most influential economic treatises ever written.

Keynes was the son of John Neville Keynes, an eminent economist in his own right. The younger Keynes was educated at Cambridge, where he became a student and admirer of Alfred Marshall, the great English economist. Although he was schooled in Marshallian economics, with its emphasis on equilibrium and automatic market adjustments, he was unable to reconcile the worldwide depression of the 1930s with the ease of the market adjustment implied by the Marshallian view.

In his *General Theory,* Keynes rejected the notion that free-market prices and wages automatically adjust and push the economy to full employment. He asserted that insufficient consumer spending can cause an economy to stagnate permanently at less than full employment. Businesses will not produce unless there is a demand for their products. Thus, if an economy is experiencing depression and economic stagnation, additional spending is needed to stimulate demand. Under such circumstances, a tax reduction or a direct increase in government expenditures is required in order to stimulate aggregate demand, production, and employment. Stagnation and excessive unemployment need not be tolerated. Public policy can prevent their occurrence. This was the message of Keynes in the midst of the Great Depression.

As Keynes anticipated, his ideas, like those of other great scholars and philosophers, were not immediately accepted. His writings were often disorganized and confusing. Many critics thought that his ideas were an attack on the puritan ethic or on the virtue of saving. Others thought that his views were a threat to the market economy. Personally, Keynes believed that his ideas strengthened the case for the private sector by proposing a cure for its most serious shortcoming, the recession. He praised the virtue of profits. "The engine which drives enterprise," Keynes wrote, "is not thrift but profit." He was unimpressed with Marxian ideas, which he found to be "illogical and so dull."

The Keynesian view offered an explanation for the prolonged unemployment of the 1930s. In spite of the criticism, the message soon caught on, particularly among the new generation of economists. By the 1950s, the Keynesian analysis was dominant in academic circles throughout the Western world. By the 1960s, the Keynesian view formed the foundation for the macroeconomic policy of the United States and most other Western nations. As the 1960s drew to a close, even a Republican president who had always been committed to "the balanced-budget concept" pronounced that he, too, was a Keynesian.

Keynes's personal life was full and varied. He earned millions of dollars speculating in the stock market, much of it on behalf of Cambridge University. He was prominent in British social circles and was connected with the Bloomsbury group of artists and intellectuals. He married Lydia Lopokova, a ballerina in Diaghilev's Russian ballet. He enjoyed art, drama, opera, bridge, and debate with professional economists and prime ministers. In 1942, King George VI made him a lord.

The economic events of the 1970s have tempered the optimism of macroeconomists and policy planners. The complexity of economic stabilization policy is now more vividly recognized. In some respects, the economics profession is currently undergoing a reevaluation of Keynesian analysis. Nonetheless, the imprint of Keynes is sure to endure. Keynes revolutionized our way of thinking about aggregate demand, output, and employment. He established the framework for modern-day macroeconomics. Time may alter the specifics of Keynesian theory, but the general aggregative approach and Keynesian framework will continue to form the core of macroeconomics in the foreseeable future.

Consumption Function: A fundamental relationship between disposable income and consumption. As disposable income increases, current consumption expenditures will rise, but by a smaller amount than the increase in income.

called the **consumption function.** It occupies a central position in the Keynesian model of income determination.

Exhibit 2 illustrates the disposable income–consumption link for U.S. families in 1980. Empirical studies linking consumption and disposable income for households, covering short-term periods such as a year, yield a consumption function similar to that of Exhibit 2. There are four essential features of the household consumption function.

1. There is a break-even level of disposable income, at which the average family consumes all of its income. For the consumption function of Exhibit 2, the break-even income level is $15,000.

2. For families with an income less than the break-even point, consumption spending is greater than disposable income. On average, these families are dissaving. They do so by either borrowing or drawing from their past savings.

3. Families with income in excess of the break-even point will consume only part of their income. The remainder is saved.

4. As income increases, the consumption spending of households increases also, although not at as rapid a rate as saving. Therefore, high-income families spend a *smaller percentage* of their disposable income on consumption. More income is allocated to saving than for a low-income family. The household consumption function suggests that as income rises, individuals will increase both their current consumption and saving. Families will use some, but not all, of the additional income for current consumption. By the same token, if income should fall, the consumption function implies that families will not absorb the entire reduction just by contracting their current consumption. Saving will also be reduced, cushioning the hardship of decline in consumption.

EXHIBIT 2   The estimated consumption function in the short run

The percentage of income saved in the short run increases with income level.

U.S. Department of Agriculture. The 1973 data were inflated to account for the change in the value of the dollar during the period.

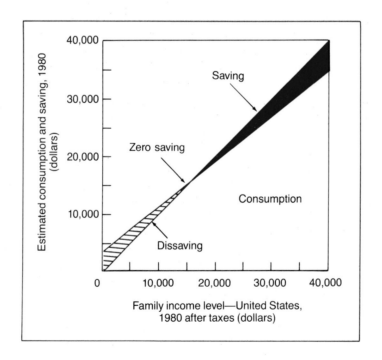

How Large Is Your Propensity to Consume?

Average Propensity to Consume: Current consumption spending divided by current disposable income.

Keynes used the expression "propensity to consume" to describe the relationship between a household's current consumption and disposable income. The propensity to consume can be either an average or a marginal concept. The **average propensity to consume** (APC) of your household is your current consumption spending divided by your disposable income:

$$APC = \frac{\text{current consumption}}{\text{current disposable income}}$$

For example, if you had a disposable income of $20,000 and spent $19,000 on current consumption items, you would have an APC of 0.95.

As income increases, in the short run, your average propensity to consume usually declines. This results because, on a short-term basis, you usually spend a smaller than average portion of your *additional*, or marginal, income on consumption. A greater share of the *additional* income is allocated to saving. The **marginal propensity to consume** (MPC) of a household is the fraction of additional disposable income that is allocated to consumption:

Marginal Propensity to Consume: *Additional* current consumption divided by *additional* current disposable income.

$$MPC = \frac{\text{additional consumption}}{\text{additional disposable income}}$$

If your income increases by $100 and you therefore increase your current consumption expenditures by $80, your marginal propensity to consume is 0.8. Eight-tenths of the extra $100 is spent on current consumption. The remainder is allocated to saving.

Economists used to believe that MPC declined with income. However, recent research in this area indicates that MPC is (a) less than APC and (b) constant or virtually constant. We will assume here that MPC is constant, and less than APC, partially because of these recent statistical studies and partially because this will simplify our exposition without negating the basic analysis.

Exhibit 3 uses the family income–consumption estimates of Exhibit 2 to illustrate how both APC and MPC are calculated. In 1980, households with an income of $5000 spent $7000 on current consumption. Their average pro-

EXHIBIT 3   Short-run consumption and saving propensities

This table uses the estimated family income and consumption data for 1980 (see Exhibit 2) to illustrate how APC, MPC, and MPS are calculated.

Family Income (Dollars) (1)	Current Consumption (Dollars) (2)	Additional Consumption, Δ(2) (Dollars) (3)	APC (2) ÷ (1) (4)	APS (1) − (2) ÷ (1) (5)	MPC (3) ÷ Δ(1) (6)	MPS 1 − MPC (7)
5,000	7,000	—	1.40	−0.40	—	—
10,000	11,000	4,000	1.10	−0.10	0.80	0.20
15,000	15,000	4,000	1.00	0	0.80	0.20
20,000	19.000	4,000	0.95	0.05	0.80	0.20
25,000	23,000	4,000	0.92	0.08	0.80	0.20
30,000	27,000	4,000	0.90	0.10	0.80	0.20
35,000	31,000	4,000	0.89	0.11	0.80	0.20
40,000	35,000	4,000	0.88	0.12	0.80	0.20

pensity to consume—current consumption divided by income—was 1.40. When income rose to $10,000, consumption increased to $11,000. APC declined to 1.1 as income rose to $10,000. As income rose from $5000 to $10,000, consumption increased from $7000 to $11,000. Thus, consumption expanded by $4000 due to the $5000 of additional income. MPC is equal to 0.8. As income continues to rise, consumption increases, though not as rapidly as income (since MPC is less than 1). APC declines with income, because the marginal propensity to consume (0.8) is less than the average propensity.

Remember, saving is merely income that is not spent on current consumption. The average propensity to save (APS) is:

$$\text{APS} = \frac{\text{saving}}{\text{income}}$$

The marginal propensity to save (MPS) is the fraction of additional disposable income that is allocated to saving:

$$\text{MPS} = \frac{\text{additional saving}}{\text{additional disposable income}}$$

Exhibit 3 also illustrates APS (column 5) and MPS (column 7) for U.S. households in 1980. Note that as income increased, the proportion of income allocated to saving (APS) rose.

Since disposable income must be either spent on consumption or saved, APC plus APS must equal 1, and MPC plus MPS must also equal 1.

The Consumption Function for the Entire Economy

Exhibits 2 and 3 presented consumption data for households. Exhibit 4 reveals the consumption function data for an entire economy in the short run, based on the assumption that the aggregate consumption function possesses the same general characteristics as the household function in the short run. (Later we will see how applicable the data are over time—in the long run.) Again, both saving and consumption increase with disposable income. However, consumption spending does not increase as rapidly as income. This can be seen by observing the height of the consumption line relative to the thin 45-degree reference line. Because the 45-degree line bisects the 90-degree angle formed by the vertical and horizontal axes of the graph, the vertical height of the 45-degree line will equal the horizontal distance from the origin to the vertical line. Therefore, disposable income can be measured either along the horizontal axis or by the vertical distance to the 45-degree line. Clearly, as disposable income increases, the consumption line (C) falls short of the 45-degree line by larger and larger amounts. The vertical distance between the 45-degree line and the consumption function (AB for example) equals saving at each income level. Consumption and disposable income are just equal to $1.7 trillion (Exhibit 4a). Of course, saving would be zero at that income level (Exhibit 4b). As income rises, consumption increases less rapidly. For example, as income increases from $1.7 trillion to $1.9 trillion, consumption expands to $1.8 trillion. A $200 billion increase in disposable income leads to a $100 billion expansion in consumption.

EXHIBIT 4   The consumption and saving schedules

Graph (a) pictures the positive relationship between consumption spending and disposable income. The 45-degree line outlines all points for which consumption and disposable income are equal. The vertical distance between the 45-degree line and the consumption function C indicates the level of saving (or dissaving). Graph (b) shows the saving function alone. Note that the amount of saving at an income level (graph b) will always equal the difference between the 45-degree line and the consumption function (graph a) for the corresponding level of income.

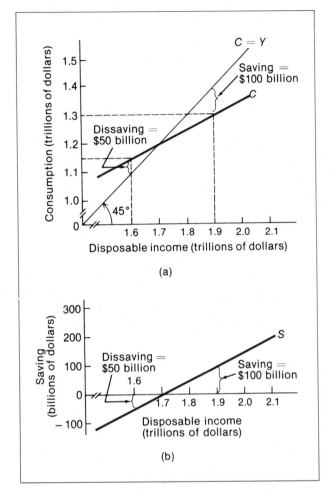

Thus, for this hypothetical aggregate consumption function, MPC = 0.50.[5] When disposable income is $1.9 trillion, households will save $100 billion. The saving schedule is derived by finding the difference between the 45-degree line and the consumption function C. When disposable income is less than $1.7 trillion, consumption spending will exceed income (Exhibit 4a). Thus, households will be dissaving (Exhibit 4b). Positive saving will take place when disposable income exceeds $1.7 trillion.

In the absence of changes in government policy, most economists believe that the consumption and saving schedules in both the long and short runs are

---

[5]The mathematically inclined student will note that the MPC is simply the slope of the consumption schedule. The slope of any line is the vertical change divided by the horizontal change as a result of a movement from one point to another along the line. The slope of the consumption schedule between any two points is the additional consumption (vertical change) divided by the additional income (horizontal change). Thus, the slope of the line is $\Delta C / \Delta Y$. This is also the definition of MPC.

quite stable. This stability reflects the important influence of income as a determinant of both consumption and saving. We will see that the schedules vary, however, between the long and short runs.

Consumption in the Long Run

Thus far, we have focused on the relationship between consumption and income during a single year. The household data indicate that (a) there is a strong positive link between income and consumption, and (b) consumption declines as a *proportion* of income when income expands. Relying on data similar to those presented in Exhibit 3, the early Keynesian economists believed that with the passage of time consumption would decline as a percentage of income as income rose. They feared that inadequate consumption would become a major source of economic stagnation, generated by a shortfall in aggregate demand. As Exhibits 5 and 6 illustrate, the historical record has not borne out this fear. As disposable income has risen over time, consumption expenditures have not only risen but have risen proportionally.

Exhibit 5 presents a "scatter diagram" of the consumption–disposable income relation for each year from 1950 to 1981. There was no tendency for consumption to decline *as a percent of disposable income* as real income rose over time. In fact, the scatter points of Exhibit 5 approximate a straight line with a slope of .91. This indicates that out of each dollar of disposable income, roughly 91 cents went for consumption expenditures in the years covered.

Exhibit 6 is a bar-graph illustration of the stability of consumption in the long run. Between 1946 and 1980, *real* per capita disposable income doubled. Nominal income increased by a much larger amount. Nonetheless, consumption expenditures, *as a percent of disposable income,* fluctuated within a narrow band around 91 percent. These long-run data indicate that there was no tendency for APC to decline as income rose. Thus, *in the long run,* APC and MPC must be approximately equal to each other. If they were not equal, as income expanded over time, APC would either rise (if MPC was greater than APC) or fall (if MPC was less than APC, as is true for short-run data). Thus, while the short-run data imply that MPC is less than APC, the long-run data fail to confirm this relationship.

Consumption, Permanent Income, and the Life Cycle of Income

How can one account for the observed differences in the short-run and long-run consumption–income links? Economists have developed two closely related theories to explain this phenomenon.

Permanent Income Hypothesis: The hypothesis that consumption depends on some measure of long-run expected (permanent) income rather than current income.

1. The Permanent Income Hypothesis. Nobel Prize-winning economist Milton Friedman has offered an explanation—the **permanent income hypothesis.**[6] According to this hypothesis, the consumption of households is determined largely by their long-term expected or permanent income. Since consumption is a function primarily of long-range expected income, it will not fluctuate very much in response to a temporary expansion in income or a transitory reduction in income. If current income rises above the permanent income of a

---

[6]See Milton Friedman, *A Theory of the Consumption Function* (Princeton, New Jersey: Princeton University Press, 1957).

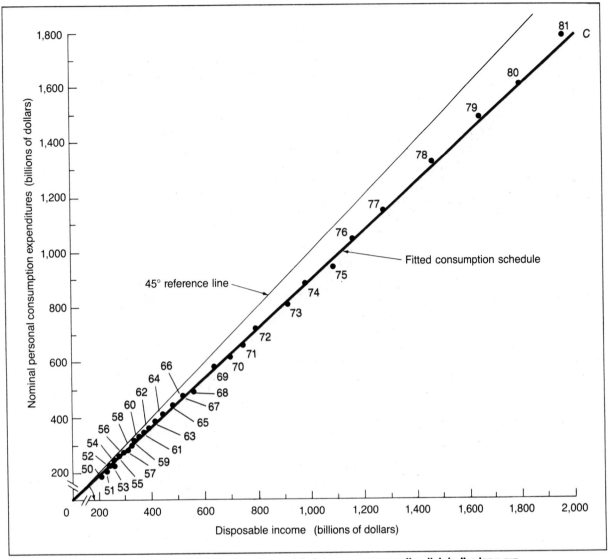

EXHIBIT 5 The disposable income—consumption link in the long run

The points on this diagram show the amount of disposable income spent on current consumption during each year from 1950 to 1981. In contrast with the household data for a specific year (Exhibits 2 and 3), the historical data do *not* indicate that consumption expenditures decline as a *percentage of income* as income rises. Over time, Americans have consistently allocated between 90 and 93 percent of their disposable income to consumption.

household, much of the additional income will be allocated to saving. Current consumption will increase only moderately. Similarly, if current income declines sharply (falling below the level of permanent income), individuals will reduce their saving (or perhaps dissave) in order to maintain a consumption level that is consistent with their long-term permanent income.

Perhaps some examples will clarify the central idea of the permanent income hypothesis. Consider the case of a construction worker whose income has increased 25 percent in recent weeks because of working overtime. The permanent

EXHIBIT 6 The stability of personal consumption

Here we use a bar graph to illustrate the stability of consumption as a percent of disposable income in the long run. Even though real disposable income per capita doubled between 1946 and 1980, consumption as a percent of disposable income fluctuated between 90 and 93 percent.

Economic Report of the President, 1980, Table B-21

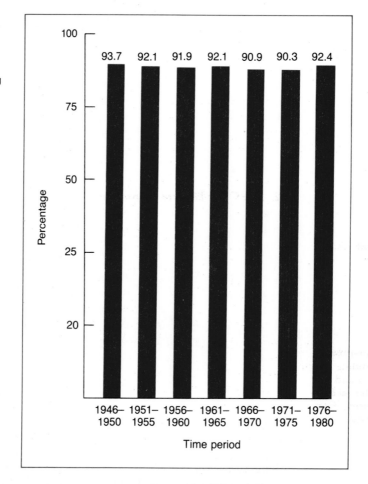

income hypothesis suggests that the worker, recognizing that such a high level of income is only temporary, will save a large fraction of the overtime earnings for "a rainy day." In contrast, an engineer who is temporarily unemployed as a result of a cutback in defense spending is likely to cushion the temporary reduction in income by borrowing or dipping into past savings (dissaving). Therefore, the consumption of the unemployed engineer will not decline as rapidly as the engineer's income.

How does the permanent income hypothesis explain the discrepancy between the short-run, cross-sectional income–consumption data and the long-run, historical income–consumption data? At any given time, households experiencing an income above their long-run permanent level will be over-represented among high-income recipients. Since their current income is above their permanent income, they will spend a smaller fraction of their uncharacteristically high current income. Their *current* APC and MPC will be below their long-run rates. In contrast, households currently experiencing an income below their long-run permanent level will be overrepresented among low-income recipients. Since their consumption patterns reflect their permanent income, they will spend a larger fraction of their unusually low current income. Their APC and MPC will be above their long-run rates.

Thus, the permanent income hypothesis explains both (a) the decline in MPC and APC as illustrated by Exhibits 2 and 3 and (b) the proportional relationship between consumption and income illustrated by Exhibits 5 and 6. The cross-sectional data of Exhibits 2 and 3 reflect a short-run phenomenon—the fact that the proportion of income allocated to saving will be larger (smaller) when one's current income is above (below) one's long-term, permanent income. On the other hand, the data illustrated by Exhibits 5 and 6 reflect long-run factors. Just as the permanent income hypothesis implies, the historical data show that in the long run, consumption is approximately proportional to income.

2. Life Cycle Income Hypothesis. Franco Modigliani of MIT has developed a theory that is also based upon the view that individuals' consumption will be determined primarily by long-run factors—particularly their expected lifetime income.[7] According to Modigliani's **life cycle hypothesis,** individuals will attempt to stabilize their consumption expenditures by way of comparison with the usual shape of their lifetime incomes. The young devote much of their energy to the acquisition of educational and vocational skills rather than to activities that generate current income. Major expenditures associated with the establishment of a family are likely to be incurred. During this period, individuals will choose to consume a large amount of their relatively low income. APC may well exceed 1. By middle age, once skills and experience have been acquired, incomes will rise. During this phase, consumption will be low (and personal saving high) relative to income. With retirement, income will decline and consumption will again be large (APC will probably exceed 1) relative to income. Thus, the following general pattern emerges: Young people dissave, middle-aged persons repay their debts and save for retirement, and the elderly again dissave as they draw from their previously accumulated assets. In the long run—over an entire life cycle—consumption can be seen as stable, or proportional to overall life income; and the fluctuations of consumption from one phase of the life cycle to another—in the short run—vary appropriately according to immediate rises and declines in income. Thus, the life cycle hypothesis is consistent with both the observed short-run and long-run consumption function data. In addition, according to this theory, the high saving/consumption ratio for those with large incomes, as observed in the short-run data, merely reflects the overrepresentation of middle-aged (prime working years) individuals among this group. Similarly, the low saving/consumption ratio in the lower income groupings is a reflection of the disproportional percentage of youthful workers and the elderly among low-income recipients.

Life Cycle Hypothesis: The theory that consumption spending during each period of one's life will reflect the income and pattern of financial obligations expected over one's entire lifetime. Typically, it implies that, *as a proportion of income,* consumption spending will be high for the young and the elderly and low for middle-aged persons (during their prime working years).

Other Factors Affecting Consumption

Keynes considered income to be the primary determinant of consumption; but other factors also exert an influence. As we proceed, we shall find four factors besides income to be of significance.

1. Expectation of Inflation. When consumers believe that prices are going to

---

[7]See F. Modigliani and A. Ando, "The Life Cycle Hypothesis of Saving: Aggregate Implications and Tests," *American Economic Review* (March 1963), pp. 55–84.

rise in the future, they have an incentive to spend more on current consumption. "Buy now before prices go higher" becomes the order of the day. The expectation of an acceleration in the rate of inflation will stimulate current spending on goods and services.

2. Expectations about Future Business Conditions. If people expect their incomes to rise in the future, they will be likely to spend a larger portion of their current incomes. In contrast, pessimism about future prospects will probably cause households to reduce their current spending. For example, as unemployment rose in the mid-1970s, many employed workers became pessimistic about future employment prospects and reduced their spending.

3. Taxes. The disposable income of consumers is directly affected by levels of personal taxation. An increase in tax rates will reduce the disposable income of consumers, inducing them to cut back on consumption. On the other hand, a reduction in taxes will enlarge the disposable income of consumers, providing an indirect stimulus for current consumption.

4. The Interest Rate. Although Keynes rejected the view that the interest rate exerted significant impact on consumption, recent work has shown that spending on consumer durables, such as major appliances and automobiles, is quite sensitive to the interest rate. Since these items are often financed by borrowing, higher interest rates increase the monthly payments necessary for their purchase and thereby discourage people from buying them.

INVESTMENT AND AGGREGATE DEMAND

Spending on investment goods will increase aggregate demand during the current period. Production of investment goods, like production of consumption goods, requires labor, natural resources, and other factors of production. Additional investment means more employment of both people and machines. Like consumption and saving, investment is a flow concept. Macroeconomists define **investment** as the flow of expenditures on durable assets that either increase our ability to produce products *in the future* or yield consumer benefits *in the future*. Current expenditures on assets such as new plant facilities, machines, transport equipment, tools, and additions to inventories are counted as investment, since they enhance our ability to supply goods and services in the future. Household expenditures on long-lasting goods such as housing are also included in investment. In contrast with consumption goods, investment goods are durable. Their useful life expectancy is measured in years.

There are two major subcategories of investment—fixed investment and inventories. **Fixed investment** consists of those durable assets (sometimes called capital goods) that are designed to enhance our productive capacity in the future. **Inventory investment** consists of the *additions* to raw materials and final products not yet sold. At any given time, firms generally hold a stock of raw materials and finished goods. With the passage of time, they often add to or subtract from these inventories. The change in these inventory holdings during a period forms the inventory component of investment.

It is important to distinguish between investment expenditures and

Investment: The flow of expenditures on durable assets (fixed investment) plus the addition to inventories (inventory investment) during a period. These expenditures enhance our ability to provide consumer benefits in the future.

Fixed Investment: Expenditures on new durable assets, such as buildings and equipment, that increase our ability to produce goods and services in the future.

Inventory Investment: Changes in the stock of unsold goods and raw materials held during a period.

financial transactions, such as the purchase of stocks or bonds. Even though the latter are often referred to as "investments" by noneconomists, they do not involve the purchase of long-lasting productive assets. If you spend $1000 on 100 shares of corporate stock, you are merely purchasing ownership rights that previously belonged to someone else. The transaction involves only the *transfer* of an asset. It does not create additional productive equipment that will increase our economy's ability to produce goods and services in the future. Similarly, the purchase of a bond is merely a method of extending a loan to the party issuing the bond. Since neither stock nor bond purchases add to the availability of long-lasting productive assets, they are not included in investment.

The Determinants of Investment

Net investment is the addition to the nation's capital goods and business inventories during a period. Additions to capital stock will increase the capacity of the nation to produce goods in the future. Capital goods are not an "end" in themselves but rather a means to produce an end. Machines are produced today so that our output of consumer goods can be increased in the future.

What determines the level of investment? Three factors are particularly important.

1. Current Sales Relative to the Productive Capabilities of the Existing Capital Stock. If current sales go up, a firm can usually squeeze a little more output from its existing plant and equipment. It makes sense for firms to maintain some excess capacity. Then they will be able to meet a temporary expansion in demand. However, when current sales continue at the higher level for an extended period, pressure will eventually be placed on the firm's existing plant capacity. At some point, it will be profitable to invest, to expand the firm's stock of capital. Clearly, the relationship between the firm's current sales and existing capital stock is crucial. If current sales are well below productive capacity, there is little incentive to invest, but as current sales approach the capacity limit of the firm's existing plant and equipment, the incentive to invest increases.

2. Expectations concerning Future Sales. Investment decisions, like other choices, must be made taking into account some uncertainty. They will be based on one's future expectations, as well as current business conditions. Business-people invest in buildings and machines because they expect to be able to sell, at a profit, the products produced. If business expectations are bleak or if businesspeople expect the demand for their products to decline, their incentive to invest is sharply reduced. Expectation about future business conditions will exert a powerful influence on investment. Optimism leads to expansion in investment, but business pessimism causes firms to delay or call off their investment plans.

3. The Interest Rate. The interest rate contributes to the opportunity cost of all investment projects. If the firm must borrow, the interest rate will contribute directly to the cost of an investment project. If the firm uses its own funds, it foregoes interest that could have been earned by loaning the funds to someone else, rather than investing them. A higher interest rate increases the opportunity cost of an investment project, reducing the incentive to undertake it. Lower interest rates have the opposite effect. Although investment may be less sensitive to the interest rate than to changes in consumption demand, the interest rate will nonetheless exert an impact, at least during normal times.

The relationship between the interest rate and investment allows us to anticipate the effect of an important policy tool—control over the money supply. In Chapter 13, we will illustrate how monetary policy can alter the interest rate, at least in the short run, and thereby stimulate additional investment. During normal times, Keynesians expect investment to be responsive to a change in the interest rate, but they are less confident that this will be true under depressed economic conditions. When an economy is in a recession and future business prospects are bleak, even a sharp decline in the interest rate may not have much impact on investment. Thus, under depressed conditions, falling interest rates may not be able to eliminate an excess supply of saving.

GOVERNMENT EXPENDITURES AND AGGREGATE DEMAND

Government spending on goods and services comprises the third major component of aggregate demand. Governments purchase a wide variety of goods. Some government purchases (highways, flood-control projects, aircraft, and office buildings, for example) are similar to investment in that they are long-lasting and yield a stream of benefits over time. Other government purchases are basically consumption goods and are used up during the current time period. School lunch programs, police and fire protection, and meals for the elderly are examples of government purchases of this variety.

Both investment and consumption types of government expenditures require labor and the use of other scarce resources. They add to aggregate demand—the total spending figure. However, government transfer payments, such as social security, welfare payments, and agriculture subsidy programs, do not directly contribute to demand. They merely "redistribute" demand from taxpayer donors to government beneficiaries.

The level of government spending is a policy variable, subject to alteration by the political process. Of course, economic conditions will exert varying degrees of influence upon both the level and composition of government expenditures chosen. Nonetheless, policy-makers have substantial discretionary power to alter the rate of government spending to suit their political needs, in ways that reflect their political (not necessarily purely economic) priorities. As we proceed, we will investigate in detail the significance of changes in government expenditures—how they affect aggregate demand, output, and employment.

NET EXPORTS AS A COMPONENT OF DEMAND

Net exports, the purchases of domestic goods by foreigners minus the goods imported from foreigners, are the fourth and final component of aggregate demand. Net exports usually comprise only 1 or 2 percent of gross national product in the United States. However, since these are net figures—that is, they are exports minus imports—they substantially understate the importance of the international trade sector and its potential impact on aggregate demand. In 1980, gross exports of goods and services constituted nearly 13 percent of our GNP, and imports summed to 12 percent of GNP. The international sector appears to be growing as a share of total U.S. output.

However, trade between nations involves the exchange of different currencies. This specialized area of study will be dealt with in a subsequent chapter. For now, we will assume that net exports are determined by forces outside the scope of the macroeconomic model we are building. In a later chapter on international trade, we will consider their potential as a source of economic disturbance.

LOOKING AHEAD

Having filled in the historical background of the Keynesian revolution and introduced the concept of aggregate demand and its determinants, we are now prepared to develop a simple Keynesian macroeconomic model. Throughout the next eight chapters we will add features that will enhance our understanding of how macroeconomic markets work and the proper role of public policy in this important area. A building block approach will be utilized. As one topic is covered, new points will be introduced that were previously either ignored or oversimplified. As we proceed, then, the complexity of our model will increase. Despite the complexity, we believe our model will serve as a consistent, logical framework that will permit you to understand the great economic issues of our day—business instability, inflation, full employment, and economic growth.

CHAPTER LEARNING OBJECTIVES

1 Classical economists thought that flexible wages (and prices) and the interest rate would eliminate the possibility of prolonged unemployment resulting from overproduction. Although temporary unemployment was possible, the classicists believed that a capitalist market economy would automatically generate full employment.

2 Keynes attacked the classical view that a market economy would generate full employment. He charged that there were two flaws in the classical argument:

(a) Saving and investment are to be considered separate activities, carried out by different people for different reasons. When conditions are depressed, investment is likely to be far more responsive to business expectations, technological changes, and innovations than to the interest rate. Similarly, income, rather than the interest rate, will be the primary determinant of saving. Therefore, the interest rate will not ensure that saving will equal investment at the full-employment output level.

(b) Wages and prices in the real world tend to be inflexible in movement downward. Therefore, falling wages cannot restore full employment. Even if wages were flexible, falling wages would not restore full employment because declining wage rates would also reduce income, consumption, and aggregate demand.

3 Aggregate demand is comprised of the total spending on goods and services during a given time period. Planned aggregate demand occupies a central position in the Keynesian analysis because, according to Keynes, regardless of the availability of underemployed and underutilized resources, producers will not supply goods and services unless they expect demand to be strong enough to assure sufficient sales.

4 Aggregate demand has four spending components: (a) consumption, (b) investment, (c) government, and (d) net exports.

5 The primary determinant of consumption is disposable income. As disposable income increases, consumption expenditures will rise, although in the short run they will generally rise less rapidly than income.

6 Historical data indicate that, in the long run, consumption expenditures comprise an approximately constant percentage of income. Thus, even though the short-run, cross-sectional data indicate that the average propensity to consume declines with

increasing income, this has not been the case in the long run. The permanent income and the life cycle hypotheses explain the apparent discrepancies between the short-run and the long-run consumption–income relationships.

7 The major determinants of investment are (a) current sales relative to the capacity of the existing productive facilities, (b) expectations about future sales, and (c) the interest rate. Keynes believed that during a period of depressed economic conditions, investment would be largely unresponsive to changes in the interest rate.

8 Government spending is a component of aggregate demand. It is also a policy variable, subject to alteration by the political process.

THE ECONOMIC WAY OF THINKING—DISCUSSION QUESTIONS

1 The classical economists believed that market forces would always move the aggregate labor market toward full employment. Outline their views and explain why you either agree or disagree with them.

2 Professor Keynes did not believe that the unhampered market mechanism would necessarily provide for the full employment of resources. Outline the views of Keynes and indicate why you either agree or disagree.

3 What is the difference between APC and MPC? What are the major determinants of MPC and MPS?

4 Annual data on household expenditures illustrate that high-income recipients save more of their income than persons with lower incomes. However, as income grows over time, saving does *not* increase as a share of income. Provide an explanation for these seemingly contradictory findings.

5 How will each of the following factors influence the consumption schedule?
  (a) The expectation that consumer prices will rise more rapidly in the future
  (b) Pessimism about future employment conditions
  (c) A reduction in income taxes
  (d) An increase in the interest rate
  (e) A decline in stock prices
  (f) A redistribution of income from older workers (age 45 and over) to younger workers (under 35)
  (g) A redistribution of income from the wealthy to the poor

PRICE, OUTPUT, AND UNDEREMPLOYMENT EQUILIBRIUM—THE KEYNESIAN MODEL

In the last chapter, we introduced the major components of aggregate demand and discussed their determinants. In this chapter, we will utilize those components to develop a simple Keynesian model of income determination. The important Keynesian concept of the multiplier will also be introduced and applied to help us understand the Keynesian view of the business cycle.

It is difficult to exaggerate the importance of the situation in the 1930s to the thinking of Keynes and his followers. The simple model that he developed and that we outline in this chapter was, after all, an attempt to explain the chronic unemployment of that period. Thus, the model has its greatest applicability when unutilized resources are available—conditions similar to those of the Great Depression.

THE KEYNESIAN CONCEPT OF MACROEQUILIBRIUM

In the previous chapter we examined the decisions of consumers, business investors, and the government, noting that the sum of these expenditures yields the total (aggregate) demand for goods and services for an economy that is not engaged in international trade. We now turn to the ways in which aggregate demand determines the equilibrium level of income and employment within

---

[1]Paul A. Samuelson, "Lord Keynes and the General Theory," *Econometrics* (July 1946), p. 151.

Equilibrium (Macro):
Condition that exists when planned aggregate demand is equal to total income (aggregate supply). At this level of income, the planned injections into the income stream will just equal the planned leakages from the income stream. Since there is a balance of forces, the equilibrium income level will be sustained, even if it does not coincide with full employment.

the framework of the Keynesian model. When an economy is in **equilibrium,** there is a balance of forces such that the existing level of output will be maintained into the future. There is no tendency for output to either expand or decline.

There are two closely related methods of approaching aggregate equilibrium: (a) the aggregate demand–aggregate supply approach and (b) the leakage–injection approach. We will focus first on the aggregate demand–aggregate supply approach.

We will make several assumptions here in order to simplify the analysis. First, a closed economy will be assumed. The impact of the foreign sector will be analyzed in later chapters. Second, at the outset we will focus on the operation of a purely private economy. The impact of government expenditures and taxes will be introduced as we proceed. Third, the analysis of monetary factors and their importance within the Keynesian model will be deferred until Chapters 12 and 13. Fourth, we will assume that the price level remains constant until full employment is reached. Without inflation, changes in total income will lead to changes in both *real* income and employment as long as the economy has not yet approached its capacity. For the short run, the assumption of stable prices may approximate real-world conditions, particularly if substantial unemployed resources are present. Fifth, we will assume that there is a specific full-employment rate of income, reflecting the structural and institutional condition of the economy.[2] Once the full-employment income level is reached, additional demand will lead only to higher prices. *Money* income may increase, but *real* income cannot be expanded beyond the economy's full-employment income level.

In this chapter we will focus on an economy that is operating at less than full employment. The economy's full-employment output constraint will be integrated more fully into our model in Chapter 11. Our major purpose is to develop a macroeconomic model capable of explaining the movements of supply and demand in highly aggregated markets. As we proceed, the simplifying assumptions of our model will be relaxed.

The Equilibrium Condition — Planned Expenditures Must Equal Total Output

Aggregate Supply: The total value of current output produced. In the Keynesian model, the aggregate supply of goods and services is always equal to income for all possible levels of income.

Economists refer to the total expenditures on goods and services as aggregate demand. For a purely private economy, the sum of the consumption and investment expenditures constitutes aggregate demand. **Aggregate supply** is composed of the total output of all goods and services produced during a given period. The business sector utilizes labor, land, machines, and other resources to produce output. The payments to the factor suppliers (which constitute income to the resource owners) are equal to the value of the goods and services produced during the period. Aggregate income and aggregate supply (output) are merely opposite sides of the same set of transactions. They are always equal.

---

[2]As discussed in Chapter 7, full employment implies the "normal rate of unemployment." Structural and institutional factors that cause the "normal rate of unemployment" to change will also alter the full-employment rate of output. See pp. 135–136 for additional detail on the meaning of full employment.

Planned Aggregate Demand:
The total planned consumption and investment expenditures (when all sectors are considered, the expenditures of governments and foreigners would also be included) on goods and services during the period.

When an economy is in equilibrium, **planned aggregate demand** must be just equal to the value of the total output produced (aggregate supply). In equation form, the equilibrium condition for a purely private economy is

$$\underbrace{\text{Total output (or total income)}}_{\substack{\text{aggregate}\\\text{supply}}} = \underbrace{\text{planned consumption} + \text{planned investment}}_{\substack{\text{planned aggregate}\\\text{demand}}}$$

Put another way, within the Keynesian model, an economy is in equilibrium when the flow of income generated from the goods and services produced gives rise to a level of spending that is just sufficient to purchase the existing level of output.

Equilibrium and Disequilibrium—Circular Flow Approach

Loanable Funds Market: A general term used to describe the market arrangements that coordinate the borrowing and lending decisions of business firms and households. Commercial banks, savings and loan associations, the stock and bond markets, and life insurance companies are important financial institutions in this market.

The circular flow diagram that we initially introduced in Chapter 6 (Exhibit 2) can be usefully applied to illustrate the concept of Keynesian macroequilibrium. Saving and investment were not included in our earlier circular flow diagram. Exhibit 1 modifies the earlier analysis to include saving and investment. (We will continue to exclude the government and foreign trade sectors for the moment.) In order to simplify the analysis, we will assume that all saving originates in the household sector. In reality, some of the profit of business firms may be retained as business saving. However, since the bulk of the nation's saving is derived from the household sector, our simplifying assumption is largely consistent with the real world.

Most saving takes place in the household sector, but business firms are the major source of investment expenditures. Investors and savers are different sets of people. Their actions are directed through the **loanable funds market.** The loanable funds market is composed of a variety of financial institutions, including commercial banks, savings and loan associations, and others, which

EXHIBIT 1 The circular flow with saving and investment

When saving and investment are included, there are two pathways by which funds can travel from households to product markets: (a) directly through household consumption expenditures or (b) indirectly through the loanable funds market (saving), the extension of loans to businesses for investment expenditures. In equilibrium, the flow of consumption and investment expenditures (top loop) will equal the flow of income to resource owners (bottom loop).

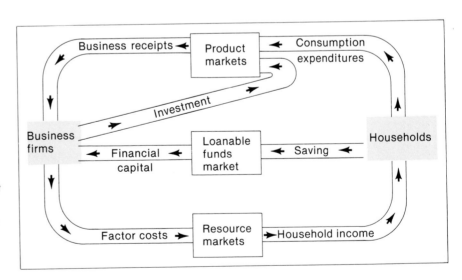

reflect the borrowing and saving decisions of business firms and individuals. As Exhibit 1 illustrates, households supply funds to the loanable funds market. Business firms desiring funds for investment purposes demand funds from the loanable funds market.

With the addition of saving and investment to the circular flow diagram, there are now two ways in which funds can flow from households to product markets. Households will spend some of their income on consumer goods. However, the portion of household income that is saved will flow into the loanable funds market. Firms will utilize these funds to finance new investments. In turn, these investment expenditures will combine with household expenditures to create the total flow of expenditures (demand) into product markets.

If the planned expenditures of consumers and investors (top loop of Exhibit 1) are just equal to the value of the goods and services produced during the period (bottom loop), there is no tendency for output to change. The spending plans of consumers and investors mesh precisely with the production plans of business decision-makers. The economy is in equilibrium.

What would happen if the planned expenditures of consumers and investors (aggregate demand) were less than the value of the products that the businesses produced during the period (aggregate supply)? The business firms would be unable to sell all of the output produced during the period. Their inventories would rise, and they would reduce production during the subsequent period. When planned aggregate demand is less than planned output, disequilibrium is present. Future output will decline.

Suppose, on the other hand, that the spending of consumers and investors exceeds the value of the output produced during the period. This implies that the business firms are selling more goods and services than they are producing. Their inventories are declining. The rapid sales and declining inventories will induce producers to expand output during the next period. Therefore, when planned aggregate demand exceeds current output, the level of output will expand.

Equilibrium and Disequilibrium— Tabular Presentation

Perhaps the equilibrium levels of output, income, and employment are easier to grasp when the major components are presented in tabular form. Exhibit 2 presents data for hypothetical consumption, saving, and investment schedules for a purely private economy. Investment is assumed to be determined by such factors as business expectations and technological change. Thus, it is not dependent on the level of income. The consumption function, however, as we have seen, is positively related to income. Net national product is used as the measure of income, so that household income received will also be equal to disposable income. Thus, net investment, rather than gross investment, is also used.

Aggregate equilibrium for the economy is present when output is $3000 billion. At that output level, consumers plan to spend $2800 billion for current goods and services, setting aside $200 billion in saving. Business decision-makers also plan to invest $200 billion. The total planned level of spending $(C + I)$, $3000 billion, is just equal to income at that output level. The plans of producers, investors, and consumers are perfectly balanced and consistent with one another. The equilibrium rate of output, $3000 billion, will be sustained in the future.

However, the plans of business and household decision-makers will come into conflict at income levels other than equilibrium. What will happen if the

EXHIBIT 2 Equilibrium level of income, output, and employment

Possible Levels of Employment (Millions of Persons) (1)	Aggregate Supply (Output and Income) (NNP = DI) (Billions of Dollars) (2)	Planned Consumption (Billions of Dollars) (3)	Planned Saving (Billions of Dollars) (4)	Planned Investment (Billions of Dollars) (5)	Unplanned Inventory Changes (Billions of Dollars) (6)	Planned Aggregate Demand, C + I (Billions of Dollars) (7)	Tendency of Employment, Output, and Income (8)
80	2900	2750	150	200	−50	2950	Increase
90	2950	2775	175	200	−25	2975	Increase
100	3000	2800	200	200	0	3000	Equilibrium
110	3050	2825	225	200	+25	3025	Decrease
120	3100	2850	250	200	+50	3050	Decrease

output of the economy temporarily expands to $3050 billion? Employment will increase from 100 to 110 million. At the higher income level, households will plan to save $225 billion, spending $2825 billion on consumption. Business firms will plan to invest $200 billion. Aggregate demand will be $3025 billion, $25 billion less than aggregate supply. The spending of consumers and investors will be insufficient to purchase the total output produced. Unwanted and unplanned business inventories will accumulate; business decision-makers will be unable to sell as much as they had planned. The actual investment of the business sector will be $225 billion, $200 billion in planned investment and a $25 billion unplanned inventory investment.[3] Because of insufficient consumer demand, the investment plans of business decision-makers will have gone astray.

The story does not end here, however. How will business decision-makers respond to their excess inventories? They will cut back production and planned investment for the next time period. Output and income will decline toward the equilibrium level. Employment will decline, and unemployment will rise. Given the consumption–saving plans of households, the economy will be unable to maintain the $3050 billion income level and the employment level associated with it.

What will happen if income falls temporarily below equilibrium? Suppose the income level of the economy pictured by Exhibit 2 is $2950 billion. At that income level, the planned consumption and investment spending will generate an aggregate demand of $2975 billion (column 7). Business firms will be selling more than they are currently producing. Their inventories will decline below normal levels. Businesspeople will respond to this happy state of affairs by expanding output. Production will increase, providing jobs for previously unemployed workers. Income will rise toward the equilibrium level of $3000 billion.

In summary, an economy is able to sustain only the equilibrium level of income. When aggregate income exceeds the equilibrium level, planned aggregate demand will be insufficient to purchase all of the goods and services produced. Unwanted inventories will accumulate, causing business decision-makers to cut back production and employment. Future income will fall. In

---

[3]The reader should note the distinction between *planned* investment and *actual* investment. *Actual* investment must always equal *actual* saving. Investment necessitates saving—that is, a reduction in consumption. But *planned* investment will not equal *planned* saving when businesspeople find that their inventories are rising or falling in an *un*planned manner.

contrast, when aggregate income is less than the equilibrium level, planned aggregate demand will exceed the current level of production. Inventories will diminish, stimulating business decision-makers to expand output and employment. Future income will rise. The economy will always tend to move toward equilibrium, that level of output for which planned aggregate demand is just equal to income.

Equilibrium and Disequilibrium—Graphic Presentation

The Keynesian analysis can also readily be presented graphically. Exhibit 3 is comprised of a graph for which planned aggregate demand, consumption plus investment, is measured on the y axis and total income (NNP) on the x axis. The 45-degree line extends from the origin and maps out all points that are equidistant from the x and y axes. Therefore, all points on the 45-degree line represent output levels for which aggregate demand and total income are equal.

As long as an economy is operating at less than its full-employment output level, the 45-degree line can also be thought of as an aggregate supply schedule.[4] Remember that aggregate supply (output) and aggregate income must be equal. The market value of all final goods and services must equal the income payments received by those who produced them. The aggregate supply schedule outlines the willingness of producers to offer alternative levels of output.

Business decision-makers will produce (supply) a level of output only if they expect consumers and investors to spend enough to purchase that output level. The 45-degree line outlines all levels of output (income) for which total spending will be sufficient to purchase the output level, thereby inducing businesses to supply it. Aggregate demand will equal aggregate supply for all points on the 45-degree line. Thus, the 45-degree line maps out all possible equilibrium levels of output. Note that there are many possible equilibrium levels of total income, output, and employment, not just one.

Exhibit 4 graphically depicts the consumption and aggregate demand schedule for the data of Exhibit 2. Consumption is positively related to income. As income rises, planned consumption increases, although by a smaller amount than income. Thus, the consumption function will be flatter than the 45-degree line. Since investment is determined independent of income, when planned investment ($200 billion) is added (vertically) to the consumption schedule, the result yields aggregate demand.

The equilibrium level of total income (NNP) will be at the point where planned aggregate demand is just equal to aggregate supply (total income). Consequently, the equilibrium level of income will be at $3000 billion, where the aggregate demand function ($C + I$) crosses the 45-degree line. Under the conditions that we have outlined, no other level of income could be sustained.

Using the graphic analysis, let us consider why total income will move toward the $3000 billion equilibrium level. When total income exceeds $3000 billion—for example, $3050 billion—the aggregate demand function lies below the 45-degree line. Remember that the $C + I$ line indicates how much people want to spend at each income level. When the $C + I$ line is below the 45-degree line, total spending is less than total income (output). Thus, unwanted

---

[4]The shape of the aggregate supply schedule, once full employment is reached, will be discussed in the following chapter.

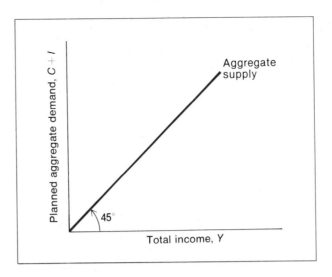

inventories will accumulate, leading businesses to reduce their future production. Employment will decline. Income will fall back from $3050 billion to the equilibrium level of $3000 billion.

In contrast, if total income is temporarily below equilibrium, there is a tendency for income to rise. Suppose that income is temporarily at $2950 billion. At that income level, the $C + I$ function lies above the 45-degree line. Aggregate demand exceeds aggregate supply (income). Businesses are selling more than they are currently producing. Their inventories are falling. They will react to this state of affairs by hiring more workers and expanding production. Income will rise to the $3000 billion equilibrium level. Only at the equilibrium level, the point at which the $C + I$ function crosses the 45-degree line, will the plans of consumers and investors sustain the existing income level into the future.

EXHIBIT 4 Graphic presentation of equilibrium

Here the data of Exhibit 2 are presented graphically. Given the level of aggregate demand, equilibrium income will be $3000 billion, where the planned demand of consumers and investors is just equal to aggregate supply. At a lower level of income, $2950 billion, for example, excess demand would cause income to rise. At a higher level, such as $3050 billion, aggregate demand would be insufficient to maintain the output level.

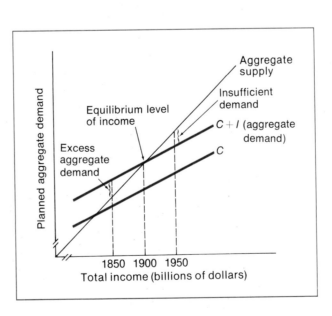

Adding Government Demand

Thus far we have focused on a purely private economy. As we discussed in the preceding chapter, government expenditures also contribute to total spending on goods and services, thereby forming the third major component of aggregate demand. Government tax revenues *reduce* the amount of income available for consumption spending. Therefore, taxes, like saving, are a withdrawal from the national income stream.

For a mixed economy, like that of the United States, total aggregate demand is the sum of consumption (C), investment (I), and government spending on goods and services.[5] It is often referred to as $C + I + G$. Adding government expenditures does not alter the basic idea of macroequilibrium. In equilibrium, aggregate income (supply), often referred to as Y, must still equal aggregate demand. Exhibit 5 illustrates the equilibrium level of income for a mixed private—government economy. Planned aggregate demand is equal to aggregate supply at income level Y_e. At that level, the total spending of consumers, business investors, and the government is just equal to the income payments to factor suppliers.

If national income were temporarily greater than Y_e, it would tend to fall because of insufficient demand. On the other hand, if income were temporarily less than Y_e, the aggregate demand would exceed income, causing businesses to expand production during the next period. The plans of business decision-makers, consumers, and government could all be realized simultaneously only at income level Y_e, given the current demand. Thus, there would be a tendency for income to converge on Y_e.

What if full employment required a higher income level, such as Y_f? If this were the case, the economy would experience unemployment. Aggregate demand would be insufficient to maintain income level Y_f. **Within the Keynesian analysis, aggregate equilibrium need not coincide with full employment. In fact, for a purely private economy, Keynesians argue that there is no reason even to expect that full employment will be present when the economy is in equilibrium. Therefore, from the Keynesian perspective, prolonged periods of unemployment are not surprising.**

What happens if aggregate demand is so strong that the economy is unable to supply the equilibrium level of income even when all resources are fully employed? Full employment acts as a supply-side constraint, preventing the attainment of output rates beyond the full-employment rate. Excess aggregate demand at full employment merely results in rising prices—inflation. National income measured in current prices will rise because of the inflation, but real output will be constrained to the full-employment capacity of the economy.

How can aggregate demand be controlled so that it will generate the income level consistent with full employment, but not so high a level as to cause inflation? This is a vitally important macroeconomic question. Introduction of the government sector into the model introduces several policy alternatives that might be used to regulate aggregate demand. To some extent, the level of government spending is a policy variable. The government might spend more (or less) on such things as highways, defense, education, and cleaning up the environment, in order to ensure the proper level of aggregate demand.

---

[5]This is true for a closed economy, one that does not trade with other nations.

EXHIBIT 5 Equilibrium for a mixed economy

Given the current level of aggregate demand, only the income level Y_e could be maintained over time. What if full employment required an income level greater than Y_e—for example, Y_f? Continual unemployment would result, unless something happened to change the level of aggregate demand.

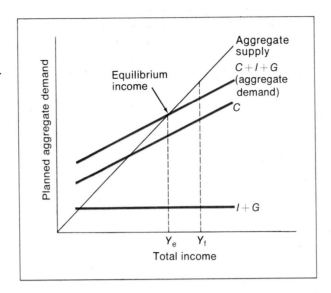

The government's taxing policy can also be utilized to influence demand. In subsequent chapters, we will analyze both the potential for and limitations of public policy as a tool with which to control aggregate demand and promote full employment along with price stability.

LEAKAGES AND INJECTIONS— ANOTHER WAY OF LOOKING AT EQUILIBRIUM

Thus far, we have focused our analysis on the relationship between aggregate demand and total income. But aggregate demand can also be seen as total income minus the leakages (saving and taxes) from the income stream plus the injections (investment and government expenditures) back into the income stream. Instead of focusing on the aggregate demand–total income relationship, we can analyze the relationship between leakages and injections. The leakage–injection approach allows us to look at the concept of aggregate equilibrium from another angle.

Investment and government spending contribute to the aggregate demand for goods and services. They are injected into the income stream. In contrast, saving and government taxes are leakages or withdrawals from the current income stream. These leakages will detract from current demand because they will not be spent on the purchase of current goods and services.

In equilibrium, the planned leakages (saving and taxes) must be equal to the planned injections (investment and government spending). Any level of income for which leakages and injections are not equal cannot be maintained. When planned injections are in excess of planned leakages, government spending and private investment are putting more into the income stream than saving and taxes are taking out. Planned consumption—income minus leakages—would be greater than the current supply of consumer goods. Business inventories would decline, reducing current business investment (including the negative investment in business inventories) below planned levels. During the next period, businesses

EXHIBIT 6 Two ways of looking at equilibrium

In equilibrium, aggregate demand will be equal to aggregate supply. For this to be true, planned leakages (saving plus taxes) and planned injections (investment plus government spending) must also be equal. These are simply two ways of looking at the same thing.

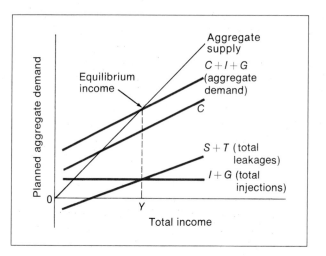

would expand output in order to replenish their inventories. The flow of money income would grow, expanding employment opportunities.

When, on the other hand, planned leakages are in excess of injections, taxes and saving are taking more out of the income stream than investment and government spending are injecting back into it. Production of consumer goods—total output minus investment and government spending—will exceed current consumption demand. Businesses will accumulate undesired inventories. Their actual investment, including inventories, will exceed their desired level. Firms will respond by cutting their future output. Income and employment will decline.

As Exhibit 6 shows, the leakage–injection method is merely another way of looking at aggregate demand relative to aggregate supply. When aggregate demand is equal to aggregate supply, planned injections ($I + G$) will also be equal to planned leakages ($S + T$). Thus, the $I + G$ and $S + T$ schedules will cross each other at the same income level where the aggregate demand function crosses the 45-degree line. When there is excess aggregate demand in comparison with output, injections will also exceed leakages. Thus, the income stream will expand. When output exceeds aggregate demand, leakages will necessarily exceed injections. Income will decline.

THE MULTIPLIER PRINCIPLE

Keynes pointed out that one individual's expenditures become the income of another. Similarly, as the income recipient spends some of his or her additional earnings, that spending will become the income of a third individual. This spending–income linkage may continue through subsequent rounds, causing income to rise by a multiple of the initial injection of spending into the income stream.

Suppose that there were idle unemployed resources and that a business-person decided to undertake a $1 million investment project. Since investment is a component of aggregate demand, the project would increase demand directly by $1 million. This is not the entire story, however. The investment project would require plumbers, carpenters, masons, lumber, cement, and many

EXHIBIT 3 Restrictive fiscal
policy to offset inflationary
pressure

Excessive aggregate demand,
such as that pictured by
$C_2 + I_2 + G_2$, would cause
rising prices. If policy-makers
could anticipate the excessive
demand, its inflationary impact
could be offset by a restrictive
fiscal policy. For example, government expenditures might be
cut in order to maintain
aggregate demand at
$C_1 + I_1 + G_1$.

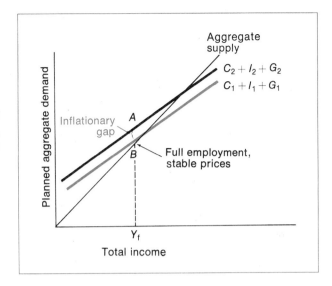

Our analysis highlights the importance of proper timing. If inflationary
forces are anticipated, offsetting restrictive policy is a highly effective weapon
against the inflation. However, if the restrictive fiscal policy is not instituted
until after the inflationary forces are at work, undesired negative side effects
on real output are likely to accompany the anti-inflationary strategy.

FISCAL POLICY AND BUDGET DEFICITS

Most politicians and budget planners in the 1950s thought of taxes as merely
a tool with which to raise revenues for the financing of government expenditures. The budgetary problem, as has been noted, was conceived as one of
matching revenues with expenditures.

According to the Keynesian view, it is often imprudent to seek a balanced
budget. Rather, a planned budget deficit (expansionary fiscal policy) is more
appropriate when economic conditions are slack, and a planned budget surplus
(restrictive fiscal policy) is called for when policy-makers anticipate an inflationary boom. The general economic conditions replace the concept of the
annual balanced budget as the proper criterion for determining budget policy.

**Planned and Actual
Deficits**

Not only does the budget policy of the government exert an influence on
economic conditions, but economic conditions also influence the revenue and
expenditure level of the government, and not always in accordance with policy.
Or, to put it another way, budget policy can have unplanned, counterproductive
effects. When an economy is at less than full employment, a tax reduction may
result in a deficit that is smaller than anticipated. This happens when the
planned government deficit, by stimulating a rise in income, also stimulates an
increase in tax revenues. Thus, despite the reduction in tax *rates,* tax *revenues*
may decline by only a small amount. There is considerable evidence that this
is what happened as a result of the much-heralded 1964 tax cut in the United
States. Beginning in March 1964, the tax rates on personal income were slashed

across the board by approximately 20 percent. The basic tax rate on corporate earnings was reduced from 52 percent to 48 percent. A planned annual deficit of between $10 billion and $15 billion was initially expected during fiscal years 1965 and 1966. However, GNP grew rapidly during the period immediately following the tax cut. Measured in dollars of constant purchasing power, revenues from the personal and corporate income taxes during fiscal year 1965 (which began four months after the tax cut) actually exceeded those of 1963 and 1964! The total taxes collected at the higher income levels were greater than anticipated. The actual government deficits were $1.6 billion in 1965 and $3.8 billion in 1966, much lower than the planned deficits for the two years.

How Not to Reduce the Deficit

In the reverse situation, when taxes are increased or expenditures reduced in an effort to avoid a budgetary deficit, a deficit may still result. Exhibit 4 illustrates why this is true. Suppose that the government is initially running a deficit because total income is at less than the full-employment level. Balanced-budget-minded politicians increase taxes and reduce government expenditures in order to bring the budget into balance. Such a policy will cause economic conditions to deteriorate even further. The tax increase will reduce disposable income, leading to a decline in consumption and aggregate demand. The reduction in government spending will directly reduce aggregate demand. As demand declines, the $C + I + G$ line will shift down, causing the equilibrium level of income to fall by some multiple of the decline in aggregate demand. At the lower income level, tax revenues will be less than expected, even though tax rates have been increased. An *actual* budget deficit may still result, even though the policy was designed to avoid it.

There is strong evidence that the 1958–1959 budgetary policies of the Eisenhower administration resulted in precisely this type of unplanned deficit. In 1958, the unemployment rate was 6.8 percent, and the economy was performing far below capacity. The Eisenhower administration *planned* a balanced budget despite the state of the economy at that time. The result was a continuation of high unemployment levels through 1961, a slow rate of growth in income, and a $12.9 billion budget deficit. Even though a balanced budget was *planned,* the actual deficit for the 1958–1959 fiscal year was the largest of any single year between World War II and 1968. It was primarily the result of *planning* a balanced budget when lower tax rates and a budget deficit were called for to stimulate income and employment.

The Full-Employment Budget Concept

The budget is complex, and no single indicator can reflect its precise impact on the economy. The actual budget deficit (surplus) does not reveal its source: It may or may not be indicative of the direction of economic policy. If a deficit, for example, does exist, it is important to know whether it is a *planned* deficit—the result of expansionary policy—or an *unplanned* deficit—the result of an inappropriate policy in combination with an economic recession, as was the case with the Eisenhower administration deficit in 1958–1959.

In an attempt to solve this problem, economists have devised a summary statistic designed to isolate (a) the impact of the budget on the economy from (b) the impact of the economy on the budget deficit or surplus. This summary

EXHIBIT 4   Trying to balance the budget can make things worse

If an economy were operating at less than full employment, reduced government expenditures and/or higher tax rates would cause aggregate demand to fall (shift to $C_2 + I_2 + G_2$). Income would decline. At the lower level of income, unemployment would rise, and tax revenues would be less than expected. An actual budget deficit would still be likely to result.

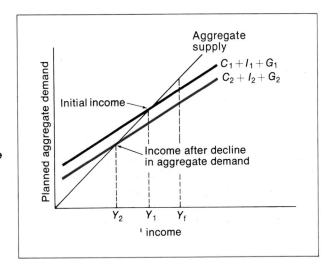

Full-Employment Budget: An estimate of what government revenues and expenditures would be if the economy were at full employment.

statistic, called the **full-employment budget,** is an estimate of what the revenues and expenditures of the government would be if the economy were at full employment, the level of activity associated with 5.0 to 5.5 percent unemployment. The full-employment budget standardizes budget estimates to a long-run, high-employment norm and thereby removes the impact of variations in economic activity that influence the actual budget deficit or surplus.

When the economy is operating at its full-employment norm, the actual budget and the full-employment budget are equal. The full-employment budget concept is most significant when the actual level of economic activity differs substantially from the long-run, full-employment norm. If there is a full-employment budget deficit, this indicates that fiscal policy is expansionary; policy-makers *planned* the budget deficit. Similarly, a surplus in the full-employment budget implies that fiscal policy is restrictive. In contrast, if the estimated full-employment budget is roughly in balance (or running a surplus), this indicates the absence of fiscal stimulus, *even though the actual budget deficit might be substantial.* Under these circumstances, the actual budget deficit is clearly *unplanned* and is not indicative of expansionary fiscal policy.

Economists are not in complete agreement on the precise guidelines to be used for calculating the full-employment budget estimate. Since there is no rigid definition of full employment, calculations based on alternative assumptions are clearly possible. Although the full-employment budget estimate provides us with a somewhat reliable indicator of fiscal policy, it may not be a *perfect* indicator of fiscal stimulus or restraint. Most economists believe that it performs its most useful function when utilized in conjunction with the actual budget deficit or surplus data.

PRACTICAL LIMITATIONS OF DEMAND-MANAGEMENT STRATEGY

Instituting fiscal changes that will promote high employment and at the same time reduce economic instability is far more difficult than most economists envisioned in the mid-1960s. With the benefit of hindsight, it is clear that past fiscal modifications have sometimes been destabilizing. Fiscal restraint, imposed to combat inflation, has sometimes overrestricted the economy and thus has contributed to the onset and the severity of recessions; expansionary macroeconomic policies, on the other hand, have sometimes overstimulated the economy and promoted inflation.

Why have policy-makers failed to create dependable, consistent policies and to achieve economic stability, given what they know about demand management? This question is not easily answered. It is important to recognize that maintaining the proper level of aggregate demand is a highly complex task. Both economic and political factors are involved. Although fiscal policy is an effective tool for combating a serious recession, the likelihood that it will entirely override the business-cycle forces is greatly reduced by the following four factors.

1. Forecasting Errors and Time Lags Make It Difficult to Time Fiscal Policy Properly.
Policy-makers, like other decision-makers, must make choices without perfect information. Our ability to forecast a forthcoming recession or inflationary acceleration is very limited. Thus, the economic conditions that call for a change in fiscal policy may already be present and be worsening before they are widely recognized. Even after the need for a policy change is recognized, there is generally an additional time lag before the change can be instituted. Experts must study the problem. Congressional leaders must hold hearings. Legislators may choose to delay action if they can use their positions to obtain special favors for their constituencies. A majority of the lawmakers must be convinced that a proposed action is in the interest of the country and that of their own districts and supporters. All of these things take time.

Even after a change is instituted, its major impact will not be felt immediately. If government expenditures are going to be increased, time will be required for competitive bids to be submitted and new contracts granted. Contractors may be unable to begin work right away. Although a tax reduction will usually stimulate the economy more quickly, the secondary effects of the multiplier process will only be felt with time.

In summary, it is extremely difficult to synchronize demand-management policies with real-world economic conditions because of the unavoidable delays involved in instituting the policies and interpreting their effects.

2. If the Economic Slump Is Localized within a Specific Geographical Area or Labor Force Group, Generalized Economic Stimuli May Be Relatively Ineffective. The stimulation effects of a tax cut or general increase in government expenditures will tend to be felt throughout the economy, causing an increase in demand for virtually every product. If the economic slowdown is widespread, this generalized economic stimulus will be an advantage. On the other hand, if the depressed economic conditions are localized within a specific industry (such as the aerospace or automobile industry), a specific geographical region (for example, the industrial Northeast or Appalachia), or a specific labor force group (such as youthful blacks or unskilled workers), the general stimulus may generate inflationary pressure in other economic sectors while failing to relieve conditions in the specifically depressed areas. For example, if unemployment is high in West Virginia, a generalized increase in demand will probably do little to relieve the situation.

When depressed economic conditions are localized, a microeconomic approach is necessary. Fiscal policy must be carefully targeted if it is to be

effective. Under such circumstances, well-designed government expenditure projects have a clear advantage over a generalized tax cut. In theory, there is no reason why much or most fiscal stimuli cannot be of this variety. However, the economics of this approach are better than the politics. In the real world, representatives from low-unemployment areas are predictably more concerned with steering government projects toward their own constituencies than with voting funds to assist high-unemployment areas that make up other legislators' constituencies. Political factors impose a constraint on what we can realistically expect to attain through targeted fiscal policy.

3. Public Choice Theory Indicates That Discretionary Fiscal Policy Will Have an Inflationary Bias. If fiscal policy is to exert a countercyclical influence, it must be even-handed and attuned to changing economic conditions. As the economy stops contracting and begins expanding, fiscal policy should be responsive: Ideally, it should shift from stimulus to restraint. But economists sometimes forget that real-world fiscal policy is instituted by means of the legislative decision-making process. Political entrepreneurs are generally interested in how fiscal policy will affect their own election prospects. Like other policy choices, fiscal choices provide incumbent legislators with a tool for furthering their political objectives and personal ambitions. Fiscal policy choices will be influenced by political considerations. It is naive to expect otherwise.

Public choice theory indicates that fiscal policy prescriptions are asymmetrical—that political entrepreneurs are more likely to follow an expansionary course than to institute restrictive budget policy. Tax reductions and spending programs (and, thus, budget deficits) permit political entrepreneurs to provide benefits to their constituents. These benefits, of course, will be popular with voters. Given the popularity of spending programs and tax reductions, we should expect politicians to be quick, perhaps too quick, to institute economic stimuli. In contrast, budget cuts and tax increases will require political entrepreneurs to vote for either a reduction in the dollar amount of public sector goods provided to their constituents or the imposition of higher taxes. Politicians will be reluctant to undertake the unpleasant tasks of imposing higher taxes and cutting government expenditures, even when appropriate.

Thus, political considerations—concerns with popularity among constituents—tend to make expansionary policies more attractive than restrictive policies to political decision-makers. This reduces the likelihood that appropriate, balanced fiscal action will be instituted.[4]

4. Secondary Effects of a Fiscal Policy May Undercut the Policy's Desired Effects. Suppose policy-makers desire to expand government expenditures in order to stimulate demand. If the additional government expenditures are financed by borrowing, the demand for loanable funds will rise. Upward pressure will be exerted on interest rates. The higher interest rates may, especially with the passage of time, cause the level of private investment and purchase of durable goods to decline. Any such decline in private spending will at least partially undercut the expansionary effect generated by the additional government expenditures. Alternatively, if taxes are raised in order to finance the additional spending, this, too, will crowd out private spending. The higher tax rates will reduce disposable income, causing the level of consumer spending to fall.

Secondary effects may also dampen the impact of restrictive fiscal policy. Suppose the government reduces its expenditures and/or increases taxes in order to achieve a budget surplus. As the result of the surplus, the government's demand for loanable funds will decline, placing downward pressure on interest rates. In turn, the lower interest rates will stimulate private investment, at least partially undercutting the government's more restrictive policy.

AUTOMATIC STABILIZERS

There are a few fiscal programs that automatically tend to help stabilize the economy. No discretionary legislative action is needed, and the problem of proper timing can be minimized.

Automatic stabilizers, even without legislative action, tend to contribute to a budget deficit during bad times and to a surplus during an economic boom. When unemployment is rising and business conditions are slow. these stabilizers automatically reduce taxes and increase government expenditures, giving the economy a shot in the arm. On the other hand, automatic stabilizers help to apply the brakes to an economic boom, increasing tax revenues and decreasing government spending. Three of these built-in stabilizers deserve specific mention.

1. Unemployment Compensation. When unemployment is high, the receipts from the unemployment compensation tax will decline because of the reduction in employment. Payments will increase because more workers are now eligible to receive benefits. The program will automatically run a deficit during a business slowdown. In contrast, when the unemployment rate is low, tax receipts from the program will increase because more people are now working. The amount paid in benefits will decline because fewer people are unemployed. The program will automatically tend to run a surplus during good times. Thus, without any change in policy, the program has the desired countercyclical effect on aggregate demand.[5]

Automatic Stabilizers: Built-in features that tend automatically to promote a budget deficit during a recession and a budget surplus during an inflationary boom, even without change in policy.

---

[4]See James M. Buchanan and Richard E. Wagner, *Democracy in Deficit—The Political Legacy of Lord Keynes* (New York: Academic Press, 1977), for additional discussion of this topic.

[5]Although unemployment compensation has the desired countercyclical effects on demand, it also reduces the incentive to accept available employment opportunities. As a result, researchers have found that the *existing* unemployment compensation system actually increases the long-run normal unemployment rate. This issue is discussed in detail in Chapter 16.

When James Tobin was appointed to the Council of Economic Advisers by President John F. Kennedy in 1961, he warned the young president, "I'm a sort of ivory tower economist." "That's all right," replied Kennedy, "I'm a sort of ivory tower president."[6]

Tobin helped design President Kennedy's famous tax-cut program of the 1960s and was responsible for the incorporation of the investment tax credit into the legislation. A former president of the American Economic Association, Tobin was an undergraduate at Harvard in the 1930s, when the ideas of Keynes began to sweep across the United States. To this day, Tobin continues to be an unabashed Keynesian.

Not surprisingly, Tobin is a strong critic of the Reagan economic program of tax reductions coupled with a deceleration in the growth rate of the money supply. He argues that the tax cuts will stimulate consumption and the tight money policies will generate high interest rates that will hold back investment. This, according to Tobin, will lead to feeble growth. In contrast, Tobin favors tight fiscal policy coupled with aggressive monetary policy. He believes that this strategy would lower interest rates, stimulate investment, and promote economic growth.

The Sterling Professor of Economics at Yale University since 1957, Tobin was awarded the Nobel Prize in economics in 1981. His best-known work, and that which caught the attention of the Nobel committee, is his theory of portfolio selection. His work in this area has revolutionized our understanding of how people and institutions choose between various available combinations of risk and yield. By emphasizing the logic of building a diverse "portfolio" of various kinds of financial assets, Tobin forced economists to recognize as simplistic the assumption that investors would always choose the highest rate of return (profit or interest). Characteristically, Tobin refers to his theory as "just the principle of not putting all your eggs in one basket."[7]

The Nobel Prize has not significantly changed Tobin's life. He still enjoys teaching and lunching with Yale undergraduates. Students may not realize that their shy professor is considered by some to be the greatest living Keynesian economist.

[6]Conversation reported in "Keynesian Yalie," *Time*, October 26, 1981, p. 68.

[7]Quoted by William D. Marbach, in "Laurels for an Old Roman," *Newsweek*, October 26, 1981, p. 62.

2. Corporate Profit Tax. Tax studies show that the corporate profit tax is the most countercyclical of all the automatic stabilizers. This results because corporate profits are highly sensitive to cyclical conditions. Under recessionary conditions, corporate profits will decline sharply and so will corporate tax payments. This sharp decline in tax revenues will tend to enlarge the size of the government deficit. During economic expansion, corporate profits typically increase much more rapidly than wages, income, or consumption. This increase in corporate profits will result in a rapid increase in the "tax take" from the business sector during expansion. Thus, the corporate tax payments will go up during expansion and fall rapidly during a contraction if there is no change in tax policy.

3. Progressive Income Tax. During economic expansion, the disposable income of consumers increases less rapidly than total income. This results because, with higher incomes, the progressive income tax pushes more people into the higher tax brackets. Thus, tax revenues increase because (a) income is higher and (b) tax rates on marginal income have increased. On the other hand, when income

PERSPECTIVES IN ECONOMICS

FACT AND FICTION ABOUT THE NATIONAL DEBT

Keynesian analysis suggests that a budget deficit may often be an appropriate means of stimulating the economy. When the federal budget runs a deficit, the difference between expenditures and revenues is financed by borrowing. The U.S. Treasury issues interest-bearing bonds, which are sold to financial investors. These interest-bearing bonds comprise the national debt. In effect, the national debt is a loan from financial investors to the U.S. Treasury.

For years, laymen, politicians, and economists have debated about the burden of the national debt. One side has argued that we are mortgaging the futures of our children and grandchildren. Future generations will pay the consequences of our fiscal irresponsibility. The other side has retorted, "We owe it to ourselves." Since most of the national debt is held by U.S. citizens in the form of bonds, it represents an asset as well as a future liability. Not only will we pass along a tax burden associated with the interest payments on the debt, but we will also bequeath to our children and grandchildren a valuable asset—interest-bearing U.S. bonds. The asset will offset the liability of the debt. Has time, the ultimate judge, declared a winner of this debate? What is fact and what is fiction about the national debt?

1. FACT: *The national debt is owned by U.S. citizens, foreigners, U.S. government agencies, and the Federal Reserve System.* Exhibit 5 gives the breakdown on who owns the debt. The biggest share of it, some 55.5 percent, is held internally by U.S. citizens and private institutions, such as insurance companies and commercial banks. Thirteen percent of the national debt is held by foreigners. The portion owned by foreigners is sometimes referred to as external debt. Approximately 19 percent of the debt is held by agencies of the federal government. For example, surplus social security trust funds are often used to purchase U.S. bonds. When the debt is owned by a government agency, it is little more than an accounting transaction indicating that one government agency (for example, the Social Security Administration) is making a loan to another (for example, the U.S. Treasury). Even the interest payments, in this case, represent little more than an internal government transfer. Approximately one-eighth of the public debt is held by the Federal Reserve System. As we will see in the next chapter, this portion of the debt is an important determinant of the stock of money in the United States.

2. FICTION: *The national debt must be paid off.* Borrowing is an everyday method of doing business. Many of the nation's largest and most profitable corporations continually have outstanding debts to bondholders. Yet these corporations, particularly the profitable

ones, will have no trouble refinancing the outstanding debt if they so wish. What is necessary is that the borrower have sufficient assets or income to pay both the interest and principal as they come due. As long as General Motors has billions of dollars worth of assets and corporate income, it will have no trouble borrowing a few million and refinancing the debt, and refinancing it again and again, because lenders know that GM will be able to pay off the loan. Similarly, as long as the U.S. government can raise huge revenues through taxes, lenders can be very sure that the government will be able to return their money plus interest when due. Therefore, there is no date in the future on which the national debt must be repaid.

3. FICTION: *The national debt has grown so fast that the U.S. government is on the verge of bankruptcy.* As we just indicated, what is important is the government's ability to raise revenues to meet its debt obligation. Actually, by this standard, the debt has declined in recent years. In 1946, the national debt was 120 percent of GNP. By 1955, it was only 70 percent of GNP. By 1974, the national debt was only 35 percent of GNP. In recent years the national debt has risen slightly relative to GNP. As of 1980, it was approximately 37 percent of GNP.

4. FACT: *The interest burden on the debt has risen significantly in recent years.* Exhibit 6 represents the interest payments on the debt as a percentage of GNP for the period from 1954 to 1980. After World War II, interest on the debt declined relative to GNP. During the period from 1954 to 1973, the ratio of interest payments on the national debt divided by GNP was virtually constant at 1.5 percent. The high interest rates and the large deficits during the period from 1974 to 1980 pushed the interest payment/GNP ratio upward. The interest payments

EXHIBIT 5   Ownership of the national debt (February 1982)

Ownership of U.S. Securities	Dollar Value (Billions)	Percentage
U.S. government agencies	201.1	19.2
Federal Reserve Banks	125.4	12.0
Domestic investors	581.7	55.5
Foreign investors	140.0	13.3
Total	1048.2	100.0

Board of Governors of the Federal Reserve System.

on the national debt in 1980 were 2.6 percent of GNP. The federal government must levy taxes in order to meet the interest payments on the debt. If the interest payments should continue to rise relative to total income, additional taxes to meet this obligation could exert a significant negative impact on the incentive to earn taxable income. Clearly, excessive debt can lead to serious economic problems. However, the probability of default by the federal government is vastly different from that for municipal and state governmental units. Unlike the latter, the federal government can create money. Thus, excessive federal debt would be far more likely to lead to inflation than to bankruptcy.

5. FACT: *Since the Korean War, private debt has grown faster than the national debt.* The growth of the national debt should be kept in perspective. During the last 27 years, public debt has increased much more slowly than private debt. Exhibit 7 shows that between 1953 and 1980 the national debt increased 238 percent, compared to a more than 1043 percent increase in private indebtedness. To the extent that excessive debt is a problem, it is clearly a problem for both the public and private sectors.

6. FACT: *For federal debt that is financed internally, future generations of Americans will inherit both a higher tax liability and additional bonds.* The U.S. debt is a liability to future taxpayers, who will pay higher taxes in order to meet the interest payments on the debt. Simultaneously, it is an asset to owners or future owners of U.S. securities, who will receive principal and interest payments. For internal debt, both of these parties are U.S. citizens, either current or future.

7. FACT: *External debt has increased in recent years.* In 1970, only $20 billion of U.S. securities, 5 percent of the total, were held by foreigners. By 1980, the figure had jumped to $138 billion, representing almost 18 percent of the total national debt. Even external debt can potentially improve the economic welfare of future generations. It depends on how the government uses the borrowed funds.

8. FACT: *The true measure of how the debt influences the welfare of future generations requires knowledge of how it influences the future capital stock.* The economic welfare of future generations will be determined by how much capital stock—houses, factories, machines, and other productive assets—is bequeathed to them. When the government borrows, it tends to raise the interest rate and discourage private investment. This reduction in private capital formation can be offset if the government spends the borrowed funds on long-lasting capital assets, such as hospitals, schools, highways, and airplanes, that will yield future income greater than future interest payments. On the other hand, if the borrowed funds are spent primarily on current consumption items (for example, income transfers and administrative expenses), the capital assets available to future generations will be reduced and the burden of the debt increased. This is true for both the internal and the external debt.

9. FACT: *When deficit spending is necessary to push the economy to full employment, it will contribute to the future capital stock and therefore improve the economic welfare of future generations.* If there are unemployed resources that could be used to produce houses, factories, and other assets, as well as current consumer goods, a government deficit may help put these resources to work. When a deficit results in the employment of otherwise idle resources, there can be little doubt that it will help future generations despite the future tax liability. For example, consider the 1930s. Between 1930 and 1934, gross private investment was less than 3 percent of GNP. Once allowance was made for depreciation, the nation's capital stock actually declined. Were future generations helped because the federal government incurred little debt (either with the public or the Federal Reserve) during this period? The answer clearly is no. Future generations would have been better off if the government had incurred a deficit

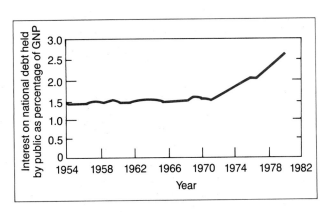

EXHIBIT 6   Interest payments as a percentage of gross national product

During the period from 1954 to 1973, the interest payments on the portion of the national debt held by the public comprised approximately 1.5 percent of GNP. In recent years, the percentage has risen. The interest on the national debt now totals 2.6 percent of GNP.

Budget of the United States (annual).

while using monetary and fiscal tools to put idle manpower and resources to work. The future capital stock would have been greater, to say nothing of current output during that period.

10. FACT: *In the 1970s, deficit spending drained a substantial share of the funds from the private loanable funds market.* There is some evidence that most of these funds were allocated to current consumption rather than to capital formation. The consequence seems to have been a slowing in the U.S. growth rate. In many respects, *changes* in the national debt, particularly in that portion held by private investors, are more important than the actual size of the debt. Rapid growth of the privately held portion of the national debt implies that the government is draining a substantial amount of funds from the private capital market. Potential investment funds are being bid away from businesses and state and local governments in the process. During the period from 1946 to 1966,

U.S. Treasury borrowing from private sources expanded from $208 billion to $219 billion, an $11 billion increase in 20 years. Federal borrowing from the private loanable funds market increased from $219 billion in 1966 to $657 billion in 1980, a $438 billion *increase* in just 14 years! Whereas during the period from 1946 to 1966 less than 1 percent of the funds raised in the domestic loanable funds market were used to cover the Treasury's deficit, more than 15 percent of the funds raised during the period from 1967 to 1980 were allocated to the federal deficit.

As we indicated, if the borrowed funds are directed into capital formation, they will have little negative effect on the U.S. economic growth rate and the well-being of future generations. However, this has not been the case in recent years. The share of federal spending allocated to capital formation has been steadily declining, reflecting a vast increase in transfer payments. The proportion of funds channeled into investment in

the private sector is substantially greater than that for the public sector. Therefore, there is good reason to suspect that the vast expansion of federal borrowing from private sources during the period from 1967 to 1980 drained funds away from capital formation. To the extent that this has been true, our current capital stock is lower than it otherwise would have been. Our growth rate has suffered in the process.

Discussion

1. Can the government or a private corporation have continual debt outstanding? Explain.

2. Do we owe the national debt to ourselves? Does this mean that the size of the debt is of little concern? Why or why not?

3. "The national debt is a mortgage against the future of our children and grandchildren. We are forcing them to pay for our irresponsible and unrestrained spending." Evaluate.

EXHIBIT 7   Private and public debt, 1953 and 1980

Private debt has increased much more rapidly than the national debt.

Federal Reserve Board.

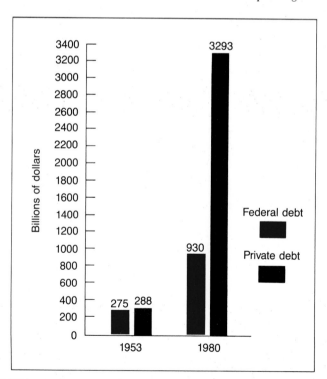

declines, many taxpayers are assigned lower tax rates, reducing the government's tax take. However, when inflation is present during a recession, the normal countercyclical impact on the progressive tax structure is eliminated. The inflation pushes taxpayers into higher tax brackets, even though their *real* incomes are declining. During an inflationary recession, the progressive income tax actually exerts a perverse (negative) effect on aggregate demand.[8]

LOOKING AHEAD

Thus far, we have concentrated on the demand side of the aggregate market for goods and services. We must more fully integrate aggregate supply into our analysis. This will be our goal in Chapter 11.

CHAPTER LEARNING OBJECTIVES

1 Fiscal policy is a tool that can be used to moderate economic disturbances that arise from fluctuations in aggregate demand.

2 When an economy's resources are underutilized, an increase in government expenditures, holding taxes constant, will increase aggregate demand and push the economy to a higher level of real income and employment.

3 A tax reduction can also be used to push an economy toward full employment. When taxes are reduced, the disposable income of consumers will increase, stimulating consumption. At the higher level of consumption, both real income and employment will expand. Tax reductions can usually influence consumption rapidly because the tax-withholding system affects disposable income almost immediately.

4 Restrictive fiscal policy (higher taxes or reduced government expenditures) can be used to combat inflationary pressure. In the face of inflation, a planned government surplus would be in order.

5 The Keynesian view rejects the idea that the government's budget should be balanced annually. Keynesian analysis implies that general economic conditions should be the prime determinant of fiscal policy. When the economy is slack, budget authorities should plan a deficit. In contrast, when the economy is experiencing an inflationary boom, a budget surplus is in order.

6 Proper timing is vital for the success of fiscal policy. If a fiscal action is not properly timed, it may be counterproductive. Restrictive fiscal policy, if applied during a recession, will lengthen the recession's duration and heighten its severity. Similarly, if expansionary fiscal policy is followed despite an ongoing or approaching inflation, the inflationary conditions will worsen.

---

[8]Beginning in 1985, the federal personal income tax is scheduled to be indexed for inflation. Indexing will eliminate the ability of inflation to push individuals into higher tax brackets when their real incomes have not increased. Thus, with indexing, personal income tax revenues, as a share of income, will fall if real personal income declines during an inflationary recession. Similarly, revenues will expand, as a share of income, when *real* incomes increase during an economic boom. Therefore, indexing will make the personal income tax a more consistent automatic stabilizer. (See feature, p. 100).

7 The full-employment budget is a measure of what expenditures and revenues would be if the economy were at full employment. It provides a useful summary statistic on the degree to which deficits or surpluses are the result of fiscal policy. The full-employment budget generally reveals the impact of fiscal policies on the economy more clearly than the actual budget.

8 Economic theory indicates that there are limitations on the expected effectiveness of discretionary fiscal policy as a stabilization tool. There is often a lag between the time when a policy change is needed and the time when legislative authority is granted. Even after a fiscal policy change has been instituted, it may take time for the policy to exert its major effects. If an economic slump is localized to a specific geographical area or labor force group, a generalized fiscal stimulus may be relatively ineffective. The effectiveness and timing of fiscal policy may also suffer as a result of political considerations. Political entrepreneurs find spending attractive but dislike imposing taxes. Thus, they will find budget deficits more attractive than surpluses. Therefore, an inflationary bias is likely to characterize the conduct of fiscal policy. The secondary effects of fiscal policy (for example, higher interest rates due to a budget deficit) may, at least partially, undercut the policy's desired effects. Each of these factors complicates the effective use of countercyclical fiscal policy.

9 Unemployment compensation, corporate taxes, and the progressive income tax act as automatic stabilizers because they automatically contribute to a budget deficit during slack times and to a budget surplus when the economy is at full employment.

10 The burden of the national debt has long been a controversial issue. It is not true that the debt will eventually have to be paid off. Nor does the debt indicate that the federal government is about to go bankrupt. Since the Korean War, private debt has grown more rapidly than the federal debt. The debt affects future generations through its impact on capital formation. During the period from 1946 to 1966, federal borrowing had little impact on the private loanable funds market. In contrast, during the period from 1967 to 1980, there was a vast increase in the growth of Treasury borrowing in the private credit market. Given the declining share of government expenditures allocated to capital investment, there is reason to believe that the borrowing during the period from 1967 to 1980 retarded capital formation and economic growth.

THE ECONOMIC WAY OF THINKING—DISCUSSION QUESTIONS

1 Suppose that you are a member of the Council of Economic Advisers. The president has asked you to prepare a statement on "What is the proper fiscal policy for the next 12 months?" Prepare such a statement, indicating (a) the current state of the economy (that is, unemployment rate, growth in real income, and rate of inflation) and (b) your fiscal policy suggestions. Should the budget be in balance? Present the reasoning behind your suggestions.

2 If an economy were experiencing 7 percent unemployment while prices were rising at a 2 percent annual rate, indicate your view on appropriate fiscal policy. Explain your reasons.

3 "In the real world, it is wrong to expect that fiscal policy will be symmetric. Politicians will be glad to run a deficit during bad times to stimulate the economy, but they will surely fail to plan a surplus when it is needed to halt inflationary pressures. Thus, fiscal policy has an inflationary bias." Do you agree with this view? Why or why not?

4 What are automatic stabilizers? Explain the major advantage of automatic stabilizers.

5 What's Wrong with This Way of Thinking?

"Keynesians argue that a budget deficit will stimulate the economy. The historical evidence is highly inconsistent with this view. A $12 billion budget deficit in 1958 was associated with a serious recession, not expansion. We experienced recessions in both 1961 and 1974–1975, despite budget deficits. The federal budget ran a deficit every year from 1931 through 1939. Yet the economy continued to wallow in the Depression. Budget deficits do not stimulate GNP and employment."

Tax reductions have two principal effects. On the one hand,
individuals and firms will buy
more goods and services [the demand effect]. . . . But tax cuts
also increase the supply of goods
and services. Since lower tax
rates allow individuals and firms
to keep a larger fraction of their
income after taxes, the lower rates
affect incentive to work, to save,
and to invest the savings, increasing potential GNP.[1]
Council of Economic Advisers
    (1980–1981)
Charles L. Schultze, Chairman

11

AGGREGATE SUPPLY, FISCAL POLICY, AND STABILIZATION

For years, microeconomists have recognized that both demand and supply are important and that it is a mistake to focus on one to the near-exclusion of the other. Heavily influenced by the Great Depression, macroeconomists, on the other hand, have generally focused on aggregate demand. Balance is rapidly being restored, however. Like demand, supply is an important component of the macro- as well as the microeconomic way of thinking.

Classical economic analysis of price, output, and employment focused primarily on the supply side of the market. The classical economists believed that total output was determined by the conditions affecting supply. Further-more, they argued that an expansion in aggregate demand would not alter total output but would merely lead to inflation. Similarly, they argued that a reduc-tion in aggregate demand would primarily affect the price level, leaving real output more or less unchanged.

The Great Depression and other economic downturns provide strong evidence that the classical view of aggregate demand was incorrect. Downward price flexibility does not quickly and painlessly restore full employment in the face of declining demand. However, the economic conditions prevalent in the 1970s indicate that the classical view on the importance of aggregate supply was essentially correct. Supply factors *do* limit our ability to expand output. Supply is not the *only* thing that matters, but that it does matter is undeniable.

In this chapter, we will investigate the determinants of aggregate supply and incorporate more fully the concept of a supply constraint into our macro-economic model. We will consider the major factors likely to alter the economy's supply constraint. Finally, we will discuss one of the more controversial current issues, the impact of taxes on output, employment, and prices.

---

[1] *Economic Report of the President, 1981,* p. 79.

THE DETERMINANTS OF AGGREGATE SUPPLY

Goods are not gifts from nature. Human energy and knowledge must be applied to physical resources before goods become available to consumers, investors, and governments. What determines the supply of goods and services? The three major determinants of aggregate supply are (1) the quantity (and quality) of resources used in the production process, (2) the efficiency with which the applied resources are used, and (3) the current state of production technology. Let us take a closer look at each of these three factors.[2]

Resource Utilization

Other things constant, as the quantity (and quality) of resources contributing to the production process expands, aggregate supply will increase. But resources are scarce. At any point in time, the size of the economy's resource base will constrain aggregate supply. With the passage of time, the economy's resource base will change. Capital goods wear out with usage and time. Some investment will be necessary just to replace the machines, structures, and other capital assets worn out during a period. In addition, *net* investment can expand the availability of physical capital, loosening the aggregate supply constraint. The knowledge and skills of the work force—the supply of human labor resources—will also affect the productive capacity of an economy. Investment in education, training, and skill-enhancing experience is an essential ingredient for the maintenance and enlargement of the human resources that play such a vital role in the production process.

Potentially productive resources will not enhance aggregate supply unless they actually become engaged in the productive process. Just as physical-resource scarcity limits the economy's resource base, so, too, do human-imposed restrictions and individual decisions that reduce the *effective* availability of resources. For example, a worker who is unemployed because the combination of unemployment compensation, welfare benefits, and leisure is preferred to any of the available jobs adds no more to current production than a person who is *not* part of the labor force at all. Similarly, a potential youthful worker priced out of employment by minimum wage legislation is *not* part of the *effective* resource base of the economy. Thus, the size of the effective resource base of the economy is influenced by both scarcity and the human-created barriers that discourage the utilization of resources.

Economic Efficiency

The efficiency of resource utilization will also affect aggregate supply. Political and economic institutions that encourage individuals to specialize in those areas where they have the greatest comparative advantage and to engage in mutually advantageous exchange are necessary ingredients for the efficient use of resources. Without the gains from the division of labor and cooperative effort by participants, aggregate supply will fall far short of its potential. Public policy can enhance the efficiency of resource use if it provides (a) a stable environment under which competitive markets can flourish, (b) an effi-

---

[2]The analysis of aggregate supply is closely related to the concept of the production possibilities curve discussed in Chapter 2 (see pp. 21–25). This would be an excellent time to review that material.

cient remedy in instances where externalities (spillover effects) would otherwise be a source of waste, and (c) the desired level of public goods.[3]

However, public policy can also be a source of inefficiency. For example, if the tax structure encourages individuals to purchase goods and services that cost more to produce than their true consumer value, economic waste results. Similarly, regulatory actions that generate greater costs than benefits will reduce the size of the economic pie. As we proceed, we will analyze the impact of public policy on economic efficiency and aggregate supply in greater detail.

Technology

A technological improvement is the discovery of a new and better way of doing something—a new production technique that reduces costs or a new product that is economically superior to those previously available. Scientific breakthroughs play an important role in the advancement of technology. For example, when scientists discovered a new, low-cost method of converting sand into a silicon chip with computing power a thousand times greater than the human brain, our production capacity (aggregate supply) expanded. Sometimes technological advances merely involve the dissemination and adoption of a new idea that enables us to get more out of our existing resources. For example, when Ray Kroc, a West Coast equipment salesman, transformed an idea into a chain of stores to provide fast-service, low-cost hamburgers, his technological advance increased aggregate supply. The consumption opportunities available to millions of persons were improved as Kroc's idea became the fast-food restaurant chain that the world knows today as McDonald's.

An efficient economic system must provide a method of validating and disseminating technological advances. In a market economy, prices and competition serve this function. If consumers are willing to buy a new product at a price that will cover the product's resource cost, the idea behind the product—the technological advance it represents—is validated by the market. In contrast, if resource costs exceed the market price of a product, economic losses provide the decision-maker with swift if painful proof that the idea is unsound or untimely, economically speaking.

THE AGGREGATE SUPPLY CURVE FOR THE CONSTRAINED ECONOMY

Real Aggregate Supply Curve: A curve indicating the relationship between total real output and the price level. The term may also be used to describe the relationship between aggregate expenditures and the real income level of an economy.

Supply-side factors restrain our ability to produce additional output. Exhibit 1 incorporates a **real aggregate supply curve** into the now-familiar Keynesian income–flow model. Until the economy's full-employment supply constraint (income Y_f) is reached, *real* output will be fully responsive to an expansion in aggregate demand. Therefore, in this range, sometimes referred to as the Keynesian range, the real aggregate supply curve is merely the 45-degree line. Since demand stimulus will lead to the employment of additional resources rather than rising prices in the Keynesian range, real aggregate supply and nominal aggregate supply are equal.[4]

[3]See Chapter 4 for additional detail on the potential positive role of government in each of these areas.

[4]As we discussed earlier, the constancy of prices in the Keynesian range reflects both the assumption of downward price inflexibility and the absence of rising prices because unemployed resources are available.

EXHIBIT 1   The constrained aggregate supply curve

Here we illustrate the shape of the *real* aggregate supply curve for a supply-constrained economy within the Keynesian framework. The real aggregate supply curve is merely the 45-degree line until the supply-constrained output rate, Y_f, is attained. Since output rates beyond Y_f cannot be sustained, the real aggregate supply curve becomes vertical at Y_f.

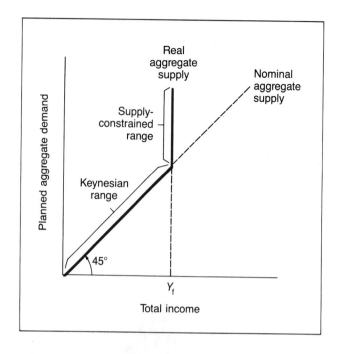

Supply-Constrained Output: The maximum output that can be sustained in the long run, given public policy and the current availability of resources. It is similar to the full-employment constraint, except that it also encompasses the concept of economic efficiency. Public policies that lead to an inefficient use of resources will decrease an economy's supply-constrained output rate.

Microincentive Structure: The incentive factors that influence *if* and *how* resources are used. In addition to market conditions, these factors will be influenced by public policy. For example, the economy's tax and income transfer policies will influence the personal benefits derived from work, saving, and investing and thereby affect the incentive of individuals to undertake these activities.

However, once the **supply-constrained output** (Y_f) is attained, the real aggregate supply curve becomes vertical. It will *not* be possible to sustain real output rates greater than Y_f. As the dotted 45-degree line indicates, nominal supply (income) may expand beyond Y_f as prices rise in response to demand conditions. But the higher levels of nominal income will be unable to push real income beyond the economy's supply capacity.

An economy's supply constraint encompasses the concepts of both full employment and economic efficiency. Given the **microincentive structure** of an economy, the supply constraint indicates the maximum real output that can be sustained by demand-stimulus policies.

It is important to recognize that public policy, as well as resource scarcity, influences an economy's attainable output rate. Idle resources do not always imply deficient aggregate demand.[5] Some resources may remain idle or be used inefficiently because public policy generates an incentive structure that encourages such activity. A supply constraint reflecting the economy's microstructure will be no more responsive to demand-stimulation policies than constraints imposed by the actual unavailability of resources.

Exhibit 2 illustrates how changes in aggregate demand affect the level of output and prices in our supply-constrained model. Given the availability of unemployed resources, "demand creates its own supply" in the Keynesian range. As aggregate demand increases from $C_1 + I_1 + G_1$ to $C_2 + I_2 + G_2$, real output expands via the multiplier process to Y_f. Prices remain constant, since both real and nominal income increase by identical amounts.

---

[5] Remember, full employment, the employment rate associated with the "normal rate of unemployment," reflects both frictional unemployment and the structural conditions of the economy. Thus, public policies that contribute to structural unemployment will influence an economy's full-employment rate. See pp. 135–136 for additional detail on this topic.

EXHIBIT 2 Changes in demand and the aggregate supply constraint

If an economy is currently operating at Y_1, an income level well below its full-employment capacity Y_f, an increase in aggregate demand from $C_1 + I_1 + G_1$ to $C_2 + I_2 + G_2$ will cause both real and nominal income to increase to Y_f. In this Keynesian range, additional demand will lead to additional real (and nominal) output. However, once income has been pushed to the full-employment capacity, still more demand (for example, $C_3 + I_3 + G_3$) will merely cause inflation. Nominal income will increase because of the higher prices, but real income will be constrained at Y_f.

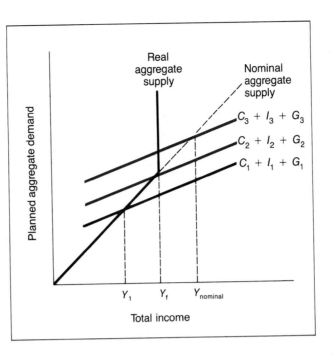

Given the economy's full-employment supply constraint, aggregate demand $C_2 + I_2 + G_2$ elicits the maximum rate of output consistent with stable prices. An increase in aggregate demand beyond this rate (for example, an increase to $C_3 + I_3 + G_3$) leads only to higher prices. Nominal income increases but real income remains unchanged (at Y_f). Employees get more nominal dollars in their paychecks, but these dollars only buy the same amount of goods as before the price increase.

Is it really true that supply constraints will prevent any increase in output beyond Y_f? The 45-degree portion of the aggregate supply curve is a simplification intended to reinforce the idea that changes in demand exert little impact on prices (and a great deal of impact on output) when substantial excess capacity is present. Similarly, the vertical portion of the aggregate supply curve is a simplifying assumption meant to illustrate the concept that there is an attainable output rate beyond which increases in demand will lead almost exclusively to price increases (and only small increases in real output).

The vertical portion of the aggregate supply curve should not be taken to imply that it would be impossible to expand output *temporarily* beyond Y_f. *For a short period of time,* expansionary demand policies may well lead to an output rate greater than Y_f. Unemployment may fall below its long-run normal rate. Employees may work abnormally large amounts of overtime. Employers may operate their plants beyond their normal productive rates. But these abnormally high utilization rates will not continue in the long run. Output rates beyond the supply constraint Y_f will *not* be sustainable. As decision-makers adjust the utilization rates of their resources to their desired long-run level, output will eventually fall back to Y_f.[6]

---

[6]In Chapter 15, we will analyze more fully the implications of utilizing demand-stimulus policies to attain output rates beyond the economy's supply constraint and explain why such a strategy will often be ineffective (and even counterproductive) in the long run. See pp. 306–317.

The 1970s highlighted the importance of aggregate supply. Aggregate demand was strong during the decade, pushing up *nominal* income at a very rapid rate. Nonetheless, *real* income grew slowly. Supply-side factors limited the ability of demand-stimulus policies to promote *real* economic growth.

Shifts in the Aggregate Supply Curve

Changes in (a) the quantity of resources utilized, (b) the efficiency with which they are applied, and/or (c) the level of technology will cause the aggregate supply curve to shift. These determinants of supply will be influenced by individual and collective choices, as well as by the forces of Nature—unfavorable weather conditions, for example.

Let us first consider factors that will increase aggregate supply. With the passage of time, net capital formation may expand the availability of machines and other capital assets. Additional natural resources may be discovered. The size of the labor force may expand. The education and skill level of workers may improve. Technological advancements may make it possible to squeeze a larger output from the available resources. Each of these factors would expand the production possibilities (the supply-constrained output capacity) of the economy.

Exhibit 3 illustrates the impact of an increase in aggregate supply within the framework of our income–flow model. The expansion in aggregate supply (AS) will shift the real AS curve to the right, indicating that a larger real income level (Y_2 rather than Y_1) is now attainable. If aggregate demand increases to $C_2 + I_2 + G_2$, the equilibrium income level Y_2 will be consistent with stable prices. Both real and nominal income of the economy will expand. If aggregate supply did not expand (that is, if it remained at real AS_1), an increase in aggregate demand to $C_2 + I_2 + G_2$ would be inflationary. However, when aggregate supply does increase, the higher level of aggregate demand will be in harmony with both price stability and an expansion in real income (to Y_2).

Sometimes unfavorable natural or economic events or imprudent economic policies cause aggregate supply to decline. A drought reduces the supply of agriculture products. Bad weather slows production on construction projects. Excessive regulatory actions and/or a decline in the competitiveness of markets may reduce the efficiency of an economy and thereby retard aggregate supply.

The sharp increases in crude-oil prices during 1973–1974 and again in 1979–1980 provide a vivid illustration of changing conditions adversely affecting supply. The higher oil prices meant that oil-importing nations like the United States had to give up a larger amount of other goods in exchange for each barrel of imported oil. The result was a transfer of wealth from the oil-importing nations to the oil-exporting countries. The resource base of the oil-importing nations was contracted—cheap oil was no longer available. Thus, aggregate supply fell.

Exhibit 3b illustrates the impact of such a reduction in aggregate supply. The vertical portion of the real aggregate supply curve will shift to the left (to AS_2), reflecting the decline in the attainable output rate. Real income will decline to Y_2. If aggregate demand remains unchanged at $C_1 + I_1 + G_1$, prices will rise.

The implication of our theory is that a reduction in aggregate supply will exert an inflationary impact upon the economy, unless it is offset by a decline in aggregate demand. The experience of the United States during the

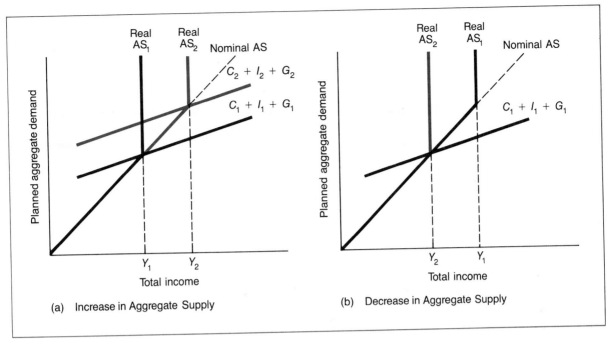

(a) Increase in Aggregate Supply

(b) Decrease in Aggregate Supply

EXHIBIT 3   Shifts in aggregate supply

If aggregate supply increases to real AS_2 (frame a), an accompanying increase in aggregate demand (shift to $C_2 + I_2 + G_2$) will permit the economy to attain a higher equilibrium rate of real output (Y_2) while maintaining price stability. Frame (b) illustrates the impact of a decline in aggregate supply (from AS_1 to AS_2). If aggregate demand remains unchanged at $C_1 + I_1 + G_1$, the reduction in supply will cause prices to rise. *Real* income will decline to Y_2. Unless aggregate demand also declines, inflation will accompany the fall in aggregate supply.

periods of rising crude-oil prices is consistent with this view. Following the oil embargo and sharply rising crude-oil prices of 1973–1974, the U.S. economy slipped into a recession in 1974–1975; at the same time the inflation rate was accelerating to 11 percent in 1974, up from 6.2 percent in 1973. The pattern was repeated during 1979–1980. Real GNP was virtually unchanged during 1979–1980, while the inflation rate rose from 7.6 percent in 1978 to more than 12 percent during 1979 and 1980. Of course, other factors may also have contributed to the inflationary pressures during these periods. Nonetheless, our analysis indicates that the sharp oil price increases and the accompanying decline in aggregate supply played important roles in the acceleration of the inflation rate during 1973–1975 and again during 1978–1980.

FISCAL POLICY, AGGREGATE DEMAND, AND AGGREGATE SUPPLY

In the past, macroeconomists have often ignored the supply-side effects of taxes. However, it has become very clear that alteration of tax rates will affect aggregate supply as well as aggregate demand. Tax rates, in addition to affecting disposable income to be spent on consumption, also alter relative prices and thereby affect the incentive of individuals to work, invest, save, and utilize resources efficiently. The *marginal tax rate* is particularly important because it determines the breakdown of one's additional income into tax payments on the one hand and disposable income on the other. Changes in marginal tax rates will influence the incentive of individuals to use the resources at their disposal.

When marginal tax rates are reduced, there is an increased reward derived from added work, investment, saving, and other activities that become less heavily taxed. People shift into these activities away from leisure (and leisure-intensive activities), tax shelters, consumption of tax-deductible goods, and other forms of tax avoidance. These substitutions both enlarge the effective resource base and improve the efficiency with which the resources are applied.

Other things constant, these incentive effects lead to an increase in aggregate supply. In contrast, higher tax rates reduce the reward derived from productive activities while making tax avoidance more attractive. This encourages a shift of resources from productive activities to tax avoidance, which will retard aggregate supply.

Fiscal policy affects aggregate demand and aggregate supply differently. Fiscal policy affects aggregate demand through its impact on disposable income and the flow of expenditures. It affects aggregate supply through changes in marginal tax rates, which influence the relative attractiveness of productive activity in comparison to leisure and tax avoidance.

Of course, tax revenues provide support for public sector expenditures. Public goods such as police and fire protection, the legal system, national defense, provision of roads, and the monetary system provide the infrastructure for the efficient operation of markets. The efficiency gains derived from collective action in these and other areas may outweigh the negative effects of the tax rates necessary to finance these public goods. In such instances, aggregate supply increases despite the negative effects of the taxation on incentive. However, as the size of the public sector expands, funds are likely to be allocated into areas (increased transfer payments, for example) where they exert less and less positive impact on aggregate supply. Simultaneously, the "disincentive effects" and supply-side inefficiencies will become more important as marginal tax rates rise. Eventually, the adverse impact of the higher tax rates will dominate.

The Supply-Side Effects of Changes in Tax Rates

Let us consider in detail the economic distortions and supply-side effects arising from high marginal tax rates. We will then be able to analyze the impact of various fiscal policies on aggregate supply as well as on aggregate demand. There are three major reasons that rising marginal tax rates may retard aggregate supply.

1. High Marginal Tax Rates May Decrease the Supply of Labor and Reduce Its Productive Efficiency. An increase in marginal tax rates encourages individuals to shift their labor resources away from activities that generate taxable income toward activities that are untaxed. In the process, the gains stemming from specialization, exchange, and the law of comparative advantage will be diminished.[7] Aggregate supply will be retarded, unless the benefits from government-provided goods and services outweigh these disincentive effects.

How will rising marginal tax rates influence labor supply? First, they encourage individuals to substitute leisure for work. Economists refer to this as the **leisure–work substitution effect.** The higher marginal tax rates will induce some individuals to opt out of the labor force.[8] Others will simply work less. People will decide that productive effort yielding so little personal return is

---

[7]Students who do not understand this point should review the material on specialization, exchange, and the law of comparative advantage for a detailed explanation of the impact of these factors on the production possibilities of an economy. See Chapter 2, pp. 25–31.

[8]Empirical studies have suggested that higher marginal tax rates may *not* measurably alter the hours worked of prime-age males. However, the labor supply of married women, older workers, and youthful workers is more responsive. A recent study by Michael Evans estimated that a 10 percent reduction in personal income tax rates increases the hours worked of non-prime-age males by 3.7 percent. See Michael Evans, "An Econometric Model Incorporating the Supply-Side Effects of Economic Policy" (Paper presented at a conference on "The Supply-Side Effects of Economic Policy," Washington University and Federal Reserve Bank of St. Louis, October 24–25, 1980).

simply not worthwhile. Many of them will decide to take more lengthy vacations, forego overtime opportunities, retire earlier, be more particular about accepting jobs when unemployed, or forget about pursuing that promising but risky business venture. These substitutions of "leisure" for taxable work effort will reduce the available labor supply, causing aggregate supply to fall.[9] In addition to hours of work, the effectiveness of work time can also be influenced. Since workers are unable to capture as large a proportion of a larger paycheck, they may be *less willing* to work intensively and productively on a job, accept additional responsibility, work under less pleasant conditions, and make similar sacrifices in order to gain a higher pay rate.

High marginal tax rates will also result in inefficient utilization of labor. Some individuals will substitute less productive activities that are not taxed (or that are taxed at a lower rate) for work that is taxed at a higher rate. Here the possibilities abound. Untaxed household production may be substituted for taxed activities. Self-employment generally affords the individual a greater opportunity to legally consume tax-deductible goods (in this context, they are called "expenses"). Therefore, rising marginal tax rates will encourage individuals to allocate more labor to self-employment activities (because of the tax shelter benefits rather than its high productivity) and away from more productive but more highly taxed employee labor services. Similarly, high marginal tax rates will channel labor resources into the underground economy (see feature, page 101). Waste and economic inefficiency result.

2. High Marginal Tax Rates May Decrease the Supply of Capital and Reduce Its Productive Efficiency. An individual can use disposable income for either additional consumption or for increased savings and investments. The expectation of future income derived from savings and investments provides the reward that induces individuals to forego current consumption. However, high marginal tax rates reduce that reward, making it less attractive for individuals to save and invest: The greater their future income, the more it will be taxed. Correspondingly, the high tax rates make current consumption cheap. Individuals will be encouraged to channel funds away from savings and investments toward current consumption.

Perhaps the following example will make this point clear. Suppose one is considering the purchase of a $30,000 Mercedes for business purposes. If the current interest rate is 10 percent, one would have to give up $3000 of additional *before-tax* income per year in order to purchase the Mercedes. However, if one is in the 50 percent marginal tax bracket, since half of one's additional income is taxed, the Mercedes could be enjoyed at a cost of only $1500 of *after-tax* income per year. Still higher increases in marginal tax rates would make

---

[9]Some economists have argued that higher marginal tax rates may induce individuals to work more in order to maintain their usual standard of living. The problem with this view is that it ignores the reason the taxes are levied. Taxes are levied so that public services can be provided. Higher tax rates and an expansion in public sector goods will generate a negative income effect *only* if the public sector projects are inefficient—that is, only if they reduce real income. If public sector projects are efficient, *on average,* the benefits derived from the public sector spending will at least offset the reduction in income caused by the higher taxes. Persons will *experience* a reduction in income (which might induce them to work more) only if their valuation of what the government provides with the tax revenues is less than their valuation of the revenues given up to the tax collector. Levying taxes to finance true income-destroying activities is hardly defensible, even if it does force those hurt by the inefficiency to work more to regain lost income. See James Gwartney and Richard Stroup, "Labor Supply and Tax Rates: A Correction of the Record," *American Economic Review* (forthcoming), for additional detail on this point.

the cost of the Mercedes to the consumer (but not to society) even lower. As marginal tax rates on investment earnings in England rose to 98 percent in the 1970s, the sales of Rolls-Royces and Mercedes soared.[10] Such marginal tax rates made it cheap, in terms of after-tax future income, for wealthy consumers to enjoy expensive automobiles.

Not only do high marginal tax rates retard the growth of saving and investment; they also encourage investors to turn to projects that shelter current income from taxation and to turn away from projects with a higher rate of return but fewer tax-avoidance benefits. Investments in depreciable assets can often provide substantial tax advantages. Projects that supply investors with rapid depreciation write-offs and paper losses can be utilized to (a) put off tax liability until some future date and (b) transform regular income into capital gains income, which is taxed at a lower rate. Resources with valuable alternative uses are channeled into the **tax shelter industry,** an industry that owes its prosperity, if not its existence, to high marginal tax rates. Many of our most intelligent citizens are becoming tax lawyers, accountants, and investment consultants as the tax shelter industry expands and prospers. Other individuals are going into business largely because of the associated tax advantages. Lawyers, physicians, college professors, plumbers, and electricians, among others, are spending less time working professionally and more time trying to figure out how to reduce their tax liability. All of this activity consumes real resources, which would be applied to more valuable, more productive activities were it not for the high marginal tax rates.

Tax Shelter Industry:
Business enterprises that specialize in offering investment opportunities designed to create a short-term accounting or "paper" loss, which can then be deducted from one's taxable income; at the same time, future "capital gain" income is generated, which is taxable at a lower rate.

3. High Marginal Tax Rates May Encourage Individuals to Substitute Less-Desired, Tax-Deductible Goods for More-Desired, Nondeductible Goods. This is a side effect of high tax rates that often goes unnoticed. High marginal tax rates make **tax-deductible expenditures** cheap for those with large taxable incomes. Of course, people will adjust their expenditure patterns accordingly. By substituting tax-deductible purchases for nondeductible goods, they can reduce their tax burden.

Tax-Deductible Expenditures:
Expenditures that the taxing authorities permit taxpayers to subtract from their income, thereby reducing the size of their taxable income. These are usually either (a) costs associated with one's business or profession or (b) expenditures on goods that public policy designates as meritorious (medical services, interest on home mortgages, and charitable contributions, for example).

Most corporate earnings in the United States are taxed at a 46 percent marginal rate. In addition, the owners of a corporate business must pay personal income tax on the dividends paid out by the firm. For a corporate owner-manager whose marginal personal income tax rate is 44 percent, the implied tax on corporate earnings paid out to the owner is 70 percent, when both the corporate (46 percent) and personal income tax (44 percent of the 54 percent of the corporate earnings remaining after taxation) are considered. Under these circumstances, the *personal cost* of purchasing tax-deductible goods becomes very low. Luxury automobiles for business use, a company airplane, company membership in a country club, a business-related vacation in Hawaii, a plush business office, and numerous other business-related goods can be enjoyed at a fraction of their production cost since they are business expenses. The cost of a tax-deductible item is reduced by the amount of the marginal tax rate. The higher the consumer's tax bracket, the greater the reduction in the item's cost to that consumer. Thus, for example, if one were in the 50 percent marginal tax bracket, the *personal cost* of a $5000 tax-deductible vacation with all the trimmings (accommodations

---

[10]Measured in terms of future after-tax annual income foregone, what is the cost of a $30,000 automobile for a businessperson in the 98 percent marginal tax bracket when the interest rate is 10 percent? How does it compare with the cost of a bicycle that must be purchased with after-tax earnings?

WHAT IS SUPPLY-SIDE ECONOMICS?

As the economic program of the Reagan administration unfolded, we were told that it embodied the principles of supply-side economics. The term was widely used by the mass media. As is often the case with a popularized expression, supply-side economics was used quite loosely. Many people, including policymakers, used the expression without really understanding the idea. The expression began to mean different things to different people.

Supply-side economics stresses the role of relative prices. If a product becomes more expensive relative to an alternative, the supply-side approach emphasizes that people will choose less of the higher-priced product and more of the substitute products that have become relatively cheaper. For example, an increase in the price of beef causes people to choose less beef and more chicken. Similarly, supply-side economists emphasize that fiscal policy, especially the tax and income transfer components, change relative prices and thereby alter aggregate supply. Three relative prices are of particular importance.

First, marginal tax rates affect the allocation of existing income between (a) current consumption and (b) saving and investing for future consumption. Rising marginal tax rates reduce the individual's *after-tax* reward derived from saving and investing. Thus, decision-makers will tend to substitute current consumption for saving and investment

projects that will yield future *taxable* income. The result is a decline in capital formation and future output (aggregate supply).

Second, higher marginal tax rates make it (a) less rewarding for an individual to devote time, effort, and capital more diligently to the production of goods and services most desired by others, and (b) more attractive to employ a more leisurely pace and attitude, centered directly on what the producer personally enjoys. The higher tax rate makes it more difficult for buyers to get what they want, since more of the payment they offer to producers for added value is diverted from producers to the tax collector.

Third, marginal tax rates will influence the relative prices of (a) activities that reduce (shelter) one's current income and (b) projects that yield taxable income. As marginal tax rates rise, the benefit derived from tax shelters increases, while the after-tax rewards to projects yielding taxable income fall. Thus, investment decisions will be distorted. Low productivity projects with tax shelter benefits will be substituted for projects yielding a higher pretax rate of return. Inefficiency results, causing aggregate supply to fall (or grow at a slower rate).

The supply-side view is not monolithic. There are at least two supply-side perspectives. One—we might call it the "quick-fix view"—believes that lower tax rates will stimulate output rapidly and will often lead to an increase in tax revenues. Although this view may

have some validity for exceedingly high marginal tax rates, there is little evidence to support it in the lower range of tax rates, say marginal rates of less than 25 percent. The U.S. experience during 1981–1982 indicates that a tax cut is not a quick fix.

The dominant supply-side view is that the incentive effects emanating from a reduction in marginal rates will work more slowly. In the first place, the decision-makers will have to be convinced that the new incentive structure is permanent rather than temporary before they can be induced to undertake long-term projects. Even after they are convinced, it will take time for them to adjust fully to the new reward structure—to opt out of tax shelters and into more socially productive investments, for example. According to this view, supply-side economics is clearly a long-run strategy.

The supply-side perspective adds another dimension to fiscal policy. The Keynesian view emphasizes that fiscal policy operates on the economy by changing disposable income and thus demand; supply-side economics emphasizes that fiscal policy affects the economy by changing relative prices. While our understanding of the potency of the demand-side income effects and the supply-side relative price effects is incomplete, one thing is certain. The current interest in supply-side economics will trigger additional research designed to help us understand more fully the effects of fiscal policy on both aggregate demand and aggregate supply.

at the finest hotels, dining at the best restaurants, flying first-class, renting a luxury car) would be only $2500. Even if this (business-related) vacation is only worth $3000, it will nevertheless be purchased and supplied at a cost to society of $5000.

Here, the inefficiency stems from the fact that individuals do not bear the full cost of tax-deductible purchases. Since the customers do not bear the full cost of tax-deductible purchases, they are substituted for more highly valued nondeductible goods whose price tags are more directly determined by their production costs. Waste and inefficiency are by-products of this incentive structure.

Fiscal Policy Possibilities Once aggregate supply constrains an economy, it is important to consider both the demand and supply effects of fiscal policy. With regard to the expansionary and restrictive fiscal policies that can be applied to an economy, four general possibilities emerge: (1) a tax reduction coupled with an increase in the planned budget deficit; (2) a tax increase coupled with a planned budget surplus (or decline in the size of the deficit); (3) a tax increase coupled with an increase in the planned deficit; and (4) a tax reduction coupled with a planned budget surplus (or decline in the size of the deficit).

1. Lower Tax Rates and an Expansion in the Budget Deficit. Clearly, this fiscal strategy is expansionary. The budget deficit, as we have seen, stimulates aggregate demand, since government expenditures are injecting more spending into the income stream than tax revenues are draining out. Simultaneously, the lower marginal tax rates enhance aggregate supply, since they increase the incentive to utilize resources productively and efficiently. If the economy is operating below its supply-constrained income level, this fiscal strategy is a sound one. The increase in aggregate demand permits real income and output to expand toward the supply constraint of the economy, and the lower tax rates increase aggregate supply, further enlarging the potential noninflationary output of the economy.

However, once output has increased to the economy's supply constraint, the wisdom of this strategy is questionable. If the expansionary impact of the budget deficit is large, and the positive effects of the lower tax rates on aggregate supply are small, the strategy will be inflationary. Exhibit 4 illustrates this point. Initially, the economy is presumed to be in equilibrium at output level Y_1. The tax reduction coupled with a budget deficit is instituted. The budget deficit stimulates aggregate demand, causing it to expand (to $C_2 + I_2 + G_2$). This increase in aggregate demand triggers the multiplier process and causes nominal income to expand to Y_{2n}. The lower tax rates improve the microstructure of the economy, causing aggregate supply to expand (to AS_2). Real income increases from Y_1 to Y_2. However, the demand effect dominates. Thus, the increase in real income is smaller than the expansion in nominal income, indicating that inflation is a side effect of this fiscal strategy.

It is important to distinguish between changes in tax *rates* and changes in tax *revenues.* Individuals will adjust their work efforts and tax-avoidance activities in response to the lower tax rates. Their response will increase the size of the tax base. Therefore, tax revenues will generally decline by a smaller percentage than that by which the tax rates are reduced. If the supply-side effects are quite strong, the revenue reduction accompanying the lower rates may be small, particularly in the long run.[11] Thus, only a small increase in the size of the deficit may occur. If this is the case, the demand-stimulus effects will be dampened, reducing the inflationary side effects of this policy.

---

[11]When marginal rates are extremely high, a rate reduction *in high tax brackets* might actually lead to an *increase* in tax revenue. See the discussion of the Laffer curve (Chapter 5, pp. 95–96) for additional detail on this issue.

EXHIBIT 4 Impact of budget deficit coupled with lower tax rates—demand effect dominates

Here we illustrate the impact of expansionary fiscal policy when supply constraints are present. The budget deficit stimulates demand, causing the aggregate demand curve to shift to $C_2 + I_2 + G_2$. The lower tax rates induce an increase in real aggregate supply, causing it to shift to AS_2. However, if the demand effects dominate, as illustrated here, this strategy will be inflationary.

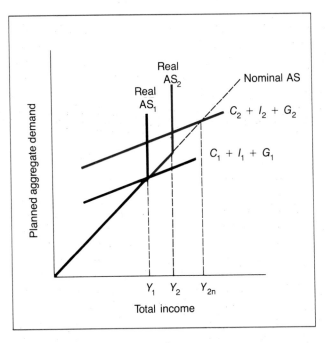

2. *Higher Tax Rates and a Planned Budget Surplus (or Smaller Deficit).* This strategy will cause both aggregate demand and aggregate supply to decline. It has often been advocated to combat inflation. Suppose an economy is experiencing inflation because aggregate demand is greater than aggregate supply. Policy-makers institute a tax increase and plan a budget surplus. The budget surplus causes aggregate demand to decline, since the budget injects less spending into the income stream than tax revenues drain out. Simultaneously, the higher tax rates induce resource users to move away from activities that generate taxable income and toward tax avoidance. Aggregate supply decreases as a result. If the budget surplus is substantial, the demand effects will dominate, and the strategy will retard the inflation. However, real income will also decline. Essentially, this strategy leads to an economic slowdown—a recession—in an effort to control the inflationary pressures.

3. *Higher Tax Rates and a Planned Budget Deficit.* In this case, the impact of the budget on aggregate demand is the reverse of the impact of tax rates on aggregate supply. This strategy depends upon the presence of a budget deficit, even when tax rates are increased. For this to be true, (a) government expenditures must increase sharply, and/or (b) tax revenues must decline (or expand by only a small amount) as tax rates are increased.

Exhibit 5 illustrates the impact of fiscal policy characterized by a budget deficit and rising tax rates. Initially, the economy is assumed to be in equilibrium. Aggregate demand $(C_1 + I_1 + G_1)$ is equal to aggregate supply (real AS_1) at output Y_1. The budget deficit stimulates the economy, causing the aggregate demand curve to shift upward to $C_2 + I_2 + G_2$. Simultaneously, the rising marginal tax rates cause people to substitute leisure and tax avoidance for productive activities. Real aggregate supply declines (shifts to the left) to AS_2. This combination—an increase in aggregate demand coupled with higher tax rates—will be highly inflationary. While nominal income expands to Y_{2n}, real

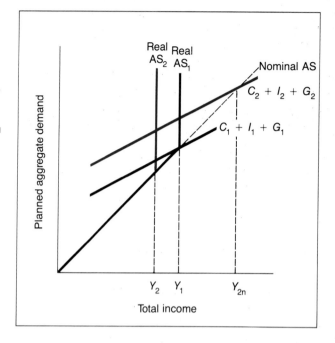

EXHIBIT 5 The impact of a budget deficit coupled with rising tax rates

The budget deficit causes aggregate demand to shift upward to $C_2 + I_2 + G_2$. The higher tax rates alter incentives, causing real aggregate supply to decline, shifting to AS_2. The result is inflation—an increase in nominal income to Y_{2n} and a decline in real income to Y_2. Some economists believe that this is what happened during the 1970s.

Figure labels: Real AS_2, Real AS_1, Nominal AS, $C_2 + I_2 + G_2$, $C_1 + I_1 + G_1$, Planned aggregate demand, Y_2, Y_1, Y_{2n}, Total income

income is slowed (to Y_2) as the result of the negative impact of the high marginal tax rates on aggregate supply. This fiscal policy leads to inflation accompanied by recession and sluggish economic growth.

Some economists believe that this is precisely what happened during the 1970s. Government spending, particularly transfer payments, increased sharply as the Great Society programs of the latter half of the 1960s were put into place and expanded. Budget policy was expansionary. The federal budget was in deficit every year during the 1970s. Simultaneously, the inflation of the decade pushed taxpayers into higher and higher marginal tax brackets (see Chapter 5, Exhibit 10, for evidence on this point). Economists who believe that the adverse incentive effects of high marginal tax rates on aggregate supply are highly significant argue that fiscal policy was a major contributing factor to the economic sluggishness of the 1970s.

Of course, the rising marginal tax rates of the 1970s were not the only factor influencing aggregate supply. As we discussed earlier in this chapter, higher worldwide oil prices reduced the efficiency of much of the capital stock in the United States, further retarding supply. Viewed from this perspective, the 1970s seem much less puzzling. Given (a) the impact of soaring oil-import prices and the rising marginal tax rates on aggregate supply and (b) the impact of the budget deficits on aggregate demand, the inflation and sluggish growth of the 1970s are not particularly surprising.

4. Lower Tax Rates and a Budget Surplus (or Smaller Deficit). A budget surplus tends to retard aggregate demand, while lower tax rates induce an expansion in aggregate supply. In order to institute this strategy, (a) policy-makers must reduce government expenditures (or at least cut expenditure growth significantly), and/or (b) tax *revenues* must remain relatively unresponsive to the reduction in marginal tax rates.

The viability of this strategy is one of today's most divisive issues among

EXHIBIT 6 The Reagan fiscal policy—proponents and critics

When the Reagan administration assumed office; it confronted an economy characterized by both inflation and a high rate of unemployment. A reduction in tax rates coupled with cuts in government expenditures was proposed and adopted. As illustrated by (a) above, the proponents of the Reagan strategy argued that the tax rate reduction would stimulate aggregate supply (to AS_2), while the budget cuts and the planned eventual budget surplus would curtail demand (shift to $C_2 + I_2 + G_2$). The expected outcome: substantial real growth and deceleration in the inflation rate. As illustrated by (b) above, critics argued that the lower tax rates would result in a substantial loss of tax revenues, large budget deficits, and an increase in aggregate demand relative to supply. The result: an acceleration in the inflation rate.

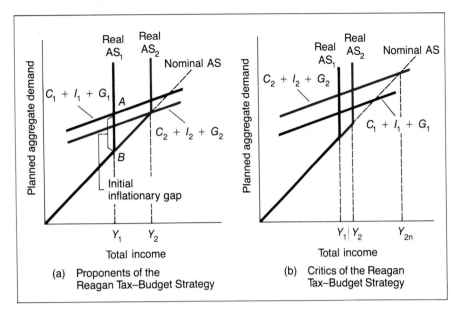

(a) Proponents of the Reagan Tax–Budget Strategy

(b) Critics of the Reagan Tax–Budget Strategy

economists. Economists who believe that the relative price incentive effects are quite important argue that a reduction in tax *rates* will expand the tax base and stimulate substantial economic growth. Therefore, the lower tax rates will *not* lead to a substantial reduction in tax revenues, at least not in the long run.

Traditional Keynesian economists reject this view. They do not believe that lower tax rates will exert much impact on aggregate supply. Thus, they argue that a substantial tax cut will result in a large decline in the Treasury's tax revenues, a huge budget deficit, and an acceleration in the inflation rate.

The Reagan Tax Cut— The Proponents and the Critics

The responsiveness of aggregate supply to lower tax rates lies at the heart of the controversy over the Reagan fiscal policy. When President Reagan assumed office in 1981, he inherited an economy experiencing high rates of both inflation and unemployment. The inflation rate during 1980 exceeded 12 percent. The unemployment rate at the beginning of 1981 stood at 7.5 percent. Following through on a campaign promise, Reagan advocated budget cuts and a 30 percent across-the-board reduction in tax rates spread over three years. Congress modified the Reagan plan, limiting the tax rate reduction to 23 percent and spreading it over 39 months. The proponents of the Reagan strategy believed that the lower tax rates would exert a strong positive impact on aggregate supply, but the critics rejected this view.

Exhibit 6 presents a graphic illustration of the logic behind the views of both the proponents and critics of the Reagan plan. Initially, the economy was assumed to be characterized by excess demand and inflation. An inflationary gap of AB was present. As Exhibit 6a indicates, the proponents of the Reagan policy believed that the reduction in tax rates would lead to a substantial increase in aggregate supply (shift from real AS_1 to AS_2). They expected real income to increase, causing an expansion in the tax base. At the higher rate of real income, they believed that the loss of tax revenue would be relatively small. They also believed that if significant budget cuts were made, the size of the budget deficits could be reduced. The budget cuts would reduce demand-side pressures, causing aggregate demand to decline to $C_2 + I_2 + G_2$, according to this view. The result would be an increase in the real growth rate accompanied by a deceleration in the inflation rate.

Following the traditional demand-side Keynesian view, the critics of the plan argued that the supply-side effects of the tax rate reduction would be small. They believed that the reduction in tax rates would lead to a substantial decline in the tax revenue of the Treasury, causing large budget deficits. As Exhibit 6b illustrates, the critics believed that the budget deficits would overwhelm the supply-side effects; the large deficits would cause aggregate demand to rise (shift upward to $C_2 + I_2 + G_2$), while aggregate supply would expand only to AS_2. As frame (b) illustrates, this increase in aggregate demand relative to aggregate supply would cause the inflationary pressures to worsen. This is why the critics charged that the Reagan strategy would be counterproductive.

The Great Unanswered Question. Who is right—the traditional demand-side Keynesians or the supply-side Reaganites? The answer to this question is critical, but there is no consensus among economists. Some believe that the supply-side incentive effects are quite important and argue that a strategy like Reagan's is at least a step in the right direction. Others believe, as we have seen, that the impact of aggregate demand will always overwhelm any possible supply-side effects and that the Reagan strategy was destined to failure from the outset.

One point is clear. The Reagan experiment is both interesting and important. It should go a long way toward helping us understand one of today's "great unanswered questions" in macroeconomics.

WHAT DO WE KNOW ABOUT FISCAL POLICY?

In light of the experience of the last decade, what do we know about fiscal policy? Four major points emerge.

1. Fiscal Policy Can Be an Effective Weapon with Which to Confront a Serious Recession Generated by Deficient Demand. Tax reductions and/or increases in government expenditures are capable of preventing a recurrence of anything like the experience of the 1930s. This is a major accomplishment that those who grew up during the *relatively* stable post-World War II era often fail to appreciate.

2. The Use of Countercyclical Fiscal Policy Is Difficult and Highly Complex. Both economic and political factors make it difficult. Our limited knowledge of the future and the presence of real-world time lags reduce our ability to time fiscal policy changes properly. The incentive structure under which political decisions are made reduces the likelihood that fiscal policy will be applied evenly. Our knowledge of the relative importance of the demand and supply effects of fiscal policy is inadequate. Thus, our attempts to create and structure fiscal policy that will combat a combination of inflation and unemployment are characterized by uncertainty.

3. Once the Inflation Rate Has Accelerated, It Is Difficult for Fiscal Policy to Return the Economy to a Condition of Stable Prices. If properly timed, restrictive fiscal policy could prevent a demand-induced acceleration in the inflation. However, *once the inflation rate has begun to accelerate,* the application of an anti-inflationary fiscal policy will be more costly. Its initial impact is likely to be on output; its decelerating influence on the price level will be delayed.

4. It Is Important to Consider the Impact of Fiscal Policy on Aggregate Supply. Supply conditions generally inhibit the growth of real output and income. The impact of fiscal policy upon the supply and efficient use of resources must not be ignored. The tools of microeconomics can help us understand the macroeconomic impact of fiscal policy.

THE DUAL PROBLEMS OF MACROECONOMICS

In Chapters 9 and 10, we noted that instability in aggregate demand can be an important source of unemployment and economic inefficiency. In this chapter, we have indicated that limited supply constrains our ability to expand real income. These chapters highlight the twin policy objectives of macroeconomics:

1. The provision of a stable economic environment, characterized by steady economic growth, a high level of employment, and a stable price level.
2. The allocation of resources in an efficient manner that minimizes waste so that the supply of goods and services available can be maximized.

The first could be called the "stability problem" and the second "the efficiency problem." The two are closely intertwined. We will return to these objectives repeatedly. They provide effective criteria for evaluating macroeconomic policy.

LOOKING AHEAD

We are now ready to integrate the monetary system into our analysis. The following chapter will focus on the operation of the banking system and the factors that determine the supply of money. In Chapter 13, we will analyze the ways in which monetary policy affects the interest rate, price level, and output.

CHAPTER LEARNING OBJECTIVES

1 Both aggregate demand and aggregate supply influence the levels of output, employment, and prices.

2 The three major determinants of aggregate supply are (a) the utilization level of resources, (b) the efficiency with which the resources are applied, and (c) the current state of technology. An alteration in any one of these three factors will induce a change in aggregate supply. The constraints on aggregate supply involve both resource scarcity and the incentive structure—the ways in which, and the degree to which, people are motivated to work, save, and invest—resulting from public policy.

3 If an economy is operating at its supply-constrained output level, an increase in aggregate demand will lead to higher prices rather than to a larger sustained rate of real output.

4 It is useful to divide a real aggregate supply curve into two distinct segments: (a) a Keynesian range, within which output can be fully responsive to an increase in aggregate demand, and, beyond this, (b) a supply-constrained range, where an increase in aggregate demand will lead, in the long run, only to an increase in price levels. The Keynesian range is a simplification of the idea that *when excess capacity is present,* an increase in aggregate demand will exert its primary impact on output, and prices will remain relatively stable. Similarly, the supply-constrained portion of the aggregate

supply curve simplifies and reinforces the important concept of an attainable output rate beyond which increases in aggregate demand will lead almost exclusively to price increases and exert little impact on real output.

5 With the passage of time, factors such as net capital formation, discovery of additional natural resources, technological advances, improvements in the skill (and educational) level of the work force, and improvements in the operational efficiency of markets will increase aggregate supply. An increase in aggregate supply will make it possible for real output to expand and price stability to be maintained.

6 Factors such as unfavorable weather conditions, a decline in capital assets, a decline in the average skill (or educational) level of the labor force, higher prices for imported goods, and falling prices for exported goods will cause a decline in aggregate supply. A decrease in aggregate supply will cause real output to fall. It will also lead to inflation, unless it is accompanied by a reduction in aggregate demand.

7 Changes in marginal tax rates alter the incentive of individuals to work, invest, save, and pay taxes. Other things constant, an increase in marginal tax rates will (a) decrease the supply of labor and reduce its productive efficiency, (b) decrease the supply of capital and reduce its productive efficiency, and (c) encourage individuals to substitute less-desired, tax-deductible goods for more-desired, nondeductible goods.

8 When fiscal policy alters marginal tax rates, it will thus exert an impact on aggregate supply as well as on aggregate demand. Other things constant, higher marginal tax rates tend to reduce aggregate supply; lower rates will increase supply.

9 The economic policy of the 1970s was characterized by budget deficits and rising marginal tax rates. The budget deficits added to aggregate demand, while the higher tax rates reduced aggregate supply. This combination of factors contributed to the inflationary pressures of the decade.

10 When the Reagan administration took office in 1981, its fiscal strategy was to reduce government expenditures and tax rates. Since the proponents of the Reagan plan believed that lower tax rates would stimulate income, they expected that the tax cut would lead to only a small reduction in tax revenues. Thus, if government expenditures were reduced, the size of the budget deficit could also be reduced (or at least maintained within manageable proportions). The proponents of this strategy believed it would stimulate aggregate supply while retarding aggregate demand and thereby reduce the inflationary pressures.

11 The critics of the Reagan plan charged that the loss of tax revenues would be substantial, leading to huge budget deficits. They believed that the plan would exert little impact on aggregate supply, while stimulating aggregate demand. Thus, the critics argued that the plan would cause the already high rate of inflation to accelerate.

THE ECONOMIC WAY OF THINKING — DISCUSSION QUESTIONS

1 Indicate the impact of each of the following on aggregate supply in the United States:

(a) An increase in the world price of wheat, a major export product of the United States

(b) The discovery of a major oil field in Utah

(c) A sharp reduction in the import price of Japanese automobiles stemming from the adoption of new, improved production techniques

(d) A drought causing a 40 percent loss of the Midwest corn crop

(e) A 20 percent increase in unemployment compensation benefits to help alleviate hardships of unemployment

(f) A discovery of an additional $20 billion of gold misplaced in the vaults at Fort Knox

2 "An increase in aggregate expenditures will always lead to more income because one person's spending is another person's income. Maintenance of a high level of expenditures is the key to maintenance of a high level of income." Evaluate.

3 If unemployed resources are present, an economy is not operating on the vertical portion of its aggregate supply curve. True, false, or uncertain? Discuss.

4 Empirical studies indicate that males in their prime earning years do not adjust their work time significantly in response to a change in their after-tax wage rates. Do these findings indicate that marginal tax rates exert little influence on aggregate supply? Why or why not? Discuss.

6 When the Reagan administration took office, its fiscal strategy was to cut taxes and government expenditures. The administration believed that this strategy, with time, would effectively combat the high rate of inflation without causing a major recession. Evaluate the Reagan strategy. Has it reduced the inflation rate? The unemployment rate? Has the administration followed its announced strategy or has it changed course? Indicate why you judge the Reagan fiscal policy as either a success or failure. Be specific.

7 Given current economic conditions, how would an increase in aggregate demand influence output, employment, and price? Discuss.

ADDENDUM

MACROEQUILIBRIUM WITHIN THE PRICE–QUANTITY FRAMEWORK

We have utilized the traditional Keynesian income–flow approach to analyze the aggregate market for goods and services. However, the flow of total spending, which comprises aggregate demand in the Keynesian framework, is actually nothing more than the sum of price times quantity for all goods and services produced during a given period. Therefore, the relationship between price (level) and quantity (of output) can also be used to analyze highly aggregated markets. We can view the price and output relationship for the entire economy, if the purchases of consumers, investors, and government are considered as a single market, the market for goods and services. Since the price variable represents the average price of all goods and services, it is really the price level of the economy. An increase in price in the aggregate goods and services market is indicative of inflation. Similarly, the quantity variable in the aggregate goods and services market represents the total real output of the economy. An increase in quantity indicates an expansion in real output.

Using the price–quantity framework, Exhibit A-1 illustrates the general shapes of the aggregate demand and aggregate supply curves for the macro-economic model that we have developed. As Exhibit A-1a reveals, aggregate demand is inversely related to price. As the price level decreases, the value of money and assets representing future income measured in money terms (for example, government bonds and savings deposits) will rise. These monetary assets will buy more goods and services as the price level declines. Thus, other things constant, a lower price level will induce individuals to demand more of everything. For a single good, as we discussed in Chapter 3, there is also an inverse relationship between price and amount demanded; but in that case it is because

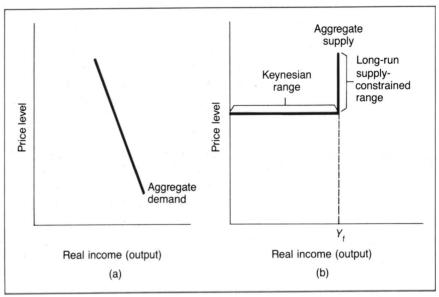

EXHIBIT A-1 Aggregate demand and supply: the price–quantity framework

Here we view the aggregate demand and supply curves within the framework of the price–quantity relationship. The aggregate demand curve (above, left) will slope downward to the right. As prices fall, money (and assets that represent a fixed amount of money) become worth more in purchasing-power terms. Therefore, individuals increase their purchases (amount demanded) as prices decline. The aggregate supply curve (above, right) will (a) have a flat portion reflecting inflexible prices and excess capacity for output rates below the full-employment (Y_f) level and (b) a vertical portion beginning at Y_f, reflecting the supply constraints of the economy.

consumers substitute lower-priced for higher-priced products. When the demand curve is for all goods, this substitution effect is not present. However, though the explanations are somewhat different, both the aggregate demand curve and the demand curve for a single commodity will slope downward to the right, indicating the inverse relationship of amount demanded to price.

Exhibit A-1b illustrates the aggregate supply curve. Remember, our model assumes that the existing level of prices will remain unchanged until the supply-constrained output, Y_f, is reached. Therefore, for output rates less than Y_f, the aggregate supply curve is perfectly horizontal, indicating that an expansion in aggregate demand will induce the flow of available idle resources into the production process at the existing level of prices, P_1. Given the resource base and the economy's incentive structures, it will not be possible to maintain output rates greater than Y_f. Thus, the aggregate supply curve becomes vertical at Y_f.

In Exhibit 2, we illustrated the impact of changing demand conditions within the framework of the Keynesian income–flow diagram. Exhibit A-2 illustrates that same analysis for the price–quantity model. As aggregate demand increases from D_1 to D_2, output is fully responsive to the demand stimulus. Real income expands to Y_f, while prices remain stable at P_1. In this range, the additional output is generated by drawing previously unemployed resources into the production process. However, once the unemployed resources are in use, the supply constraint of the economy is confronted. Although an increase in demand from D_2 to D_3 might expand output temporarily, output levels beyond Y_f cannot be maintained in the long run. An expansion in aggregate demand to

Here we present the changes in aggregate demand from Exhibit 2, as viewed within the price–quantity framework. Initially, the economy is operating at price level P_1 and at output Y_1, well below the full-employment capacity Y_f. Given these Keynesian underemployment conditions, an increase in aggregate demand from D_1 to D_2 will cause real output to expand to Y_f; prices will remain stable. However, once the full-employment output level has been attained, an additional increase in demand to D_3 will merely cause higher prices (price level increases to P_2) rather than additional real output.

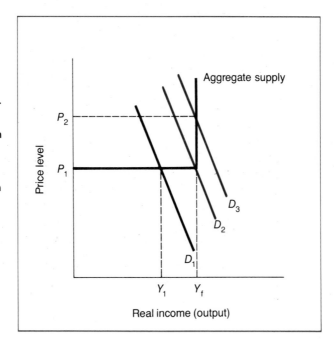

D_3 will be inflationary. When the adjustment process is complete, the new equilibrium will be at a higher level of prices (P_2), and the rate of real output will still be constrained at Y_f.

Suppose that an expansion in demand pushed that price level upward. What would happen if the inflationary rise in prices were followed by a period of declining demand? Our Keynesian assumption of downward price rigidity implies that once a price level is attained, a decline in aggregate demand will induce a fall in real output. Thus, although an increase in demand beyond the supply constraint merely results in inflation—a higher level of prices—a decrease in demand will *not* result in lower prices.

We can also demonstrate the impact of a change in aggregate supply within the price–quantity framework. Exhibit A-3a illustrates the case of an increase in aggregate supply. When accompanied by an increase in aggregate demand (D_2), the increase in aggregate supply (to AS_2) leads to a higher level of real income at Y_2; price stability is maintained.

Exhibit A-3b illustrates the impact of a decline in aggregate supply. If the level of demand remains unchanged (at D), the fall in supply will cause real income to decline (to Y_2). The price level will rise, since the demand (D) has increased *relative* to the new, smaller supply of goods.

The price–quantity framework, like the Keynesian income–flow model, can be utilized to analyze changes in macroeconomic markets. They are simply alternative methods of looking at problems. The price–quantity framework illustrates more clearly what is happening to prices; the income–flow model highlights the importance of equilibrium between total spending and total output. It can often be profitable to employ both approaches when analyzing the impact of macroeconomic changes.

EXHIBIT A-3 Changes in aggregate supply

As frame (a) illustrates, when aggregate supply increases (to AS_2), an expansion in demand (to D_2) leads to an increase in real income (to Y_2); price stability is maintained. Frame (b) illustrates the case of a decline in aggregate supply. A fall in real income and in higher prices results, unless aggregate demand declines also.

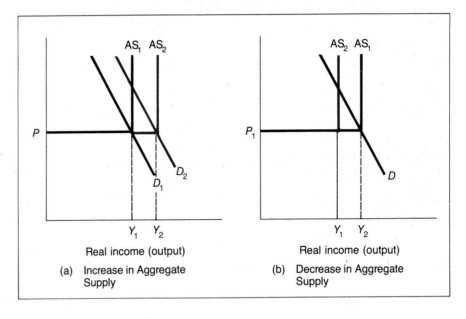

(a) Increase in Aggregate Supply

(b) Decrease in Aggregate Supply

12

There have been three great inventions since the beginning of time: fire, the wheel, and central banking.
Will Rogers

MONEY AND THE BANKING SYSTEM

The purposes of this chapter are to explain the operation of our banking/finance system and to analyze the determinants of the money supply. Later, we will consider the influence of money on prices, employment, output, and other important economic variables.

To many economists, analyzing the determinants of national income without considering money is like playing football without a quarterback. The central moving force has been excluded. Although the majority would assign a somewhat lesser role to money, almost all economists believe that money, and therefore monetary policy, matters a great deal.

WHAT IS MONEY?

Money makes the world go around. Although this is an exaggeration, money is nonetheless an important cog in the wheel that makes trade go around. Without money, everyday exchange would be both tedious and costly. Of course, money today is issued and controlled by governments, but the use of money arose thousands of years ago, not because of government decree, but because money simplified exchange. Money performs three basic functions.

1. Money Serves as a Medium of Exchange. If one desires to exchange labor services for clothing, one first sells one's labor for money and then uses the money to buy clothes. Similarly, if a farmer wants to exchange a cow for electricity and medical services, the cow is sold for money, which is then used to buy the electricity and medical services. In a barter economy, such simple exchange would necessitate finding a buyer for one's goods who was willing to sell precisely those things one wanted to purchase. Exchange would be enormously time-consuming. In an exchange economy with money, money trades in all markets, simplifying exchange and oiling the wheels of trade.

2. Money Serves as an Accounting Unit.   Consumers want to compare the prices of widely differing goods and services so that they will be able to make sensible choices. Similarly, cost-conscious businesspeople want to compare the prices of vastly different productive resources. Since money is widely used in exchange, it certainly makes sense that we also use it as the accounting unit, the yardstick by which we compare the value of goods and resources.

3. Money Is Used as a Store of Value.   Money is a financial asset, a form of savings. There are some disadvantages of using money as a vehicle for storing value (wealth). Most methods of holding money do not yield an interest return. During a time of inflation, the purchasing power of money will decline, imposing a cost on those who are holding wealth in the form of money. However, money has the advantage of being a perfectly **liquid asset.** It can be easily and quickly transformed into other goods at a low transaction cost and without an appreciable loss in its nominal value. Thus, most people hold some of their wealth in the form of money because it provides readily available purchasing power for dealing with an uncertain future.

Liquid Asset: An asset that can be easily and quickly converted to purchasing power without loss of value.

Why Is Money Valuable?

Neither currency nor checking-account deposits have significant intrinsic value. A dollar bill is just a piece of paper. Checkable deposits are nothing more than accounting numbers. Coins have some intrinsic value as metal, but it is considerably less than their value as money.

From what does money derive its value? The confidence of people is important. People are willing to accept money because they are confident that it can be used to purchase real goods and services. This is partly a matter of law. The government has designated currency as "legal tender"—acceptable for payment of debts.

However, the major source of the value of money is the same as that of other commodities. Economic goods are more or less valuable because of their scarcity relative to the amount that people desire. Money is no exception.

If the purchasing power of money is to remain stable over time, the supply of money must be controlled. The value of a dollar is measured in terms of what it will buy. Therefore, its value is inversely related to the level of prices. An increase in the level of prices and a decline in the purchasing power of money are the same thing. Assuming a constant rate of use, if the supply of money grows more rapidly than the growth in the real output of goods and services, prices will rise. This happens because the quantity of money has risen *relative* to the availability of goods. In layman's terms, there is "too much money chasing too few goods."

The linkage between rising prices and a *rapid* growth of the supply of money was demonstrated dramatically in post-World War I Germany. The supply of German marks increased by 250 percent *per month* for a time. The German government was printing money almost as fast as the printing presses would run. Since money became substantially more plentiful in relation to goods and services, it quickly lost its value. As a result, an egg cost 80 billion marks and a loaf of bread 200 billion. Workers picked up their wages in suitcases. Shops closed at lunch hour to change price tags. The value of money was eroded.

How Is the Supply of Money Defined?

Demand Deposits: Deposits in a bank that can either be withdrawn or payable on demand to a third party via check. In essence, they are "checkbook money" because they permit transactions to be paid for by check rather than currency.

NOW Accounts: Interest-earning savings accounts on which the account holder is permitted to write checks. They may be offered by savings and loan associations, credit unions, and mutual savings banks, as well as by commercial banks.

Money Supply (M-1): The sum of (a) currency in circulation (including coins), (b) demand deposits of commercial banks, (c) other *checkable* deposits of depository institutions, and (d) traveler's checks.

Determining what should be included in the supply of money is not as easy as it might appear to be. At one time, only gold and silver coins were considered money. Eventually, paper currency and **demand deposits** (checking-account balances) replaced metal coins as the major means of exchange. In defining money, it makes sense to rely on its basic functions as a medium of exchange, a unit of account, and a store of value. On the basis of these criteria, it is clear that currency (including both coins and paper bills) and demand deposits should be included in the supply of money. Most of the nation's business—more than 75 percent—is conducted by check. Demand deposits are freely convertible to currency. The amount of currency in circulation at any given time is merely a reflection of the public's preferences for "checking-account money" versus cash. In addition to demand deposits, financial institutions also offer combination savings/checking accounts. NOW (negotiable order of withdrawal) accounts are the most common such deposits. **NOW accounts** earn interest, but the depositor is also permitted to write checks against the account. Thus, deposits in NOW accounts and similar combination savings/checking deposits are also part of the money supply. Like currency and demand deposits, funds in these checkable accounts are immediately available for use as a medium of exchange. Traveler's checks can also be freely converted to cash at parity and may be used as a means of payment.

The **money supply (M-1)** in its narrowest definition is composed of (a) currency in circulation, (b) demand deposits, (c) other checkable deposits, and (d) traveler's checks. Economists use the term M-1 when referring to this narrowly defined money supply. As Exhibit 1 shows, the total money supply (M-1) in the United States was $452.3 billion in April 1982. Demand and other checkable deposits account for approximately 70 percent of the total money supply. Unless otherwise noted, throughout this text, when we speak of the money supply, we will be referring to the M-1 definition.

EXHIBIT 1 Composition of the money supply in the United States

Components of the Money Supply	Amount in Circulation, April 1982	
	Total (Billions of Dollars)	Percentage of Total Money Supply (M-1)
Currency (in circulation)	126.3	27.9
Demand deposits	233.0	51.5
Other checkable deposits[a]	88.6	19.6
Traveler's checks	4.4	1.0
Total money supply, M-1	452.3	100.0
Total money supply, M-2	1879.7	
Total money supply, M-3	2256.6	

[a]Includes NOW accounts and automatic transfer system balances in all institutions, credit union share-draft balances, and demand deposits at mutual savings banks.

The Board of Governors of the Federal Reserve System, June 1982.

Thrift Institutions: Traditional savings institutions, such as savings and loan associations, mutual savings banks, and credit unions.

Money Supply (M-2): Equal to M-1 plus (a) savings and time deposits (accounts of less than $100,000) of all depository institutions, (b) money market mutual fund shares, (c) overnight loans from customers to commercial banks, and (d) overnight Eurodollar deposits held by U.S. residents.

Eurodollar Deposits: Deposits denominated in U.S. dollars at banks and other financial institutions outside of the United States. Although this name originated because of the large amounts of such deposits held at banks in Western Europe, similar deposits in other parts of the world are also called Eurodollars.

Money Supply (M-3): Equal to M-2 plus time deposits (accounts of more than $100,000) at all depository institutions and (b) longer-term (more than overnight) loans of customers to commercial banks and savings and loan associations.

Near Monies and Broader Definitions. Several financial assets resemble money in many ways. Noncheckable time deposits in commercial banks and **thrift institutions** are a highly liquid means of holding purchasing power into the future. Although these deposits are not legally available on demand (without payment of a penalty), they can often be withdrawn on short notice. Some noncheckable savings accounts can even be transferred to one's checking account upon request without penalty. Similarly, money market mutual fund shares can generally be quickly transformed to cash at (or very near) their parity value.

The line between money and "near monies" is a fine one. Some economists prefer to use a broader definition of the money supply than M-1. In various degrees, these broader definitions incorporate savings and other liquid assets into the money supply. The most common broad definition of the money supply is M-2. The **money supply (M-2)** includes M-1 plus (a) savings and small-denomination time deposits at all depository institutions, (b) money market mutual fund shares, (c) overnight loans of customers to commercial banks (they are called *repurchase agreements*) and (d) overnight **Eurodollar deposits** of U.S. residents. In each case, these financial assets can be easily converted to checking-account funds. Their owners may perceive them as funds available for use as payment. In some cases, the assets may even be directly used as a means of exchange. Thus, regardless of whether or not they are counted as part of the money supply, it is clear that the additional assets incorporated into M-2 are close substitutes for money.

There is a third method of measuring the money supply, M-3. Under this definition, the **money supply (M-3)** is composed of M-2 plus (a) large-denomination (more than $100,000) time deposits at all depository institutions and (b) longer-term (more than overnight) loans of customers to commercial banks and savings and loan associations. These additional assets included in M-3 are not quite as liquid as the items that comprise M-2.

As Exhibit 1 notes, M-2 and M-3 are roughly four to five times larger than M-1. Exhibit 2 illustrates the paths of the three measures of the money supply during the period from 1964 to 1982. Although all three have increased substantially in recent years, they have not always moved together. In general, the growth rates of M-2 and M-3 have been more rapid than the rate for M-1. We will take note of these differences, but our attention will be focused primarily on the narrowest definition, M-1.

THE BUSINESS OF BANKING

We must understand a few things about the business of banking before we can explain the factors that influence the supply of money. As we have indicated, the banking industry in the United States operates under the jurisdiction of the Federal Reserve System. Not all banks belong to the Federal Reserve, but recent legislation leaves only a nominal difference between member and nonmember banks.

Since 1933, almost all commercial banks—state and national—have had their deposits insured with the Federal Deposit Insurance Corporation (FDIC). The FDIC fully insures each account up to $100,000 against losses due to bank failure. The Federal Savings and Loan Insurance Corporation and the National Credit Union Administration provide identical coverage for deposits of savings

EXHIBIT 2   Three alternative measures of the money supply

The graph illustrates the growth of the money supply (1964–1982) according to three alternative definitions. The narrowest and most widely used definition, M-1, includes currency, demand deposits, other checkable deposits in all institutions, and traveler's checks. M-2 includes M-1 plus money market mutual fund shares, savings and time deposits of less than $100,000, overnight Eurodollar deposits, and overnight repurchase agreements issued by commercial banks. M-3 includes M-2 plus time deposits of $100,000 or more and longer-term repurchase agreements issued by banks and savings and loan institutions.

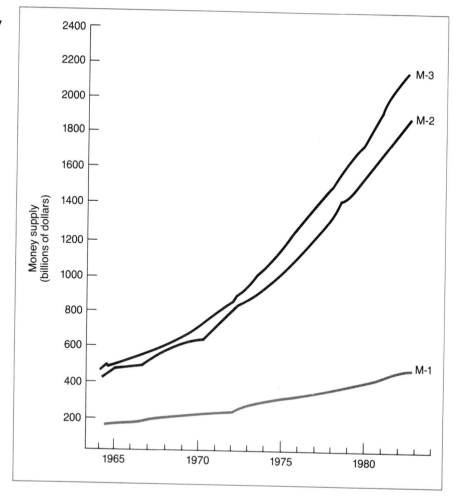

and loan associations and credit unions. Since the establishment of the FDIC, bank failures have become a rare, although not impossible, occurrence.

Banks are in business to make a profit. They provide checking- and savings-account services to their customers. However, interest-earning investments are the major source of income for most banks. Banks use a sizable share of both their demand and time deposits for interest-earning purposes—primarily the extension of loans and the undertaking of financial investments.

The consolidated balance sheet for all commercial banks (Exhibit 3) illustrates the major banking functions. It shows that the major liabilities of banks are demand and time deposits. *From the viewpoint of a bank,* these are liabilities because they represent an obligation of the bank to its depositors. Outstanding interest-earning loans comprise the major class of banking assets. In addition, most banks own sizable amounts of interest-earning securities, both government and private.

Banking differs from most businesses in that a large portion of its liabilities are payable on demand. However, even though it would be possible for all depositors to demand the money in their checking accounts on the same day, the probability of this occurring is quite remote. Typically, while some

EXHIBIT 3 The functions of commercial banks

Banks provide services and pay interest to attract demand and time deposits (liabilities). A portion of their assets is held as *reserves* (either cash or deposits with the Fed) to meet their daily obligations toward their depositors. Most of the rest is invested and loaned out, providing interest income for the bank.

Consolidated Balance Sheet of Commercial Banks—May 1982
(Billions of Dollars)

Assets		Liabilities	
Reserves	43.0	Capital accounts	132.5
Loans outstanding	1007.5	Demand deposits	327.9
U.S. government securities	114.3	Time deposits	958.2
Other securities	236.6	Other liabilities	393.4
Other assets	410.6		
Total	1812.0	Total	1812.0

Federal Reserve Bulletin, June 1982.

individuals are making withdrawals, others are making deposits. These transactions tend to balance out, eliminating sudden changes in demand deposits.

Thus, banks maintain only a fraction of their assets in reserves to meet the requirements of depositors. As Exhibit 3 illustrates, on average, **reserves**—vault cash and deposits with the Federal Reserve—were only 13 percent as large as the demand deposit obligation of member banks in 1982.

Reserves: Vault cash plus deposits of the bank with Federal Reserve Banks.

Recent Changes in Financial Institutions and the Banking System

Commercial Banks: Financial institutions that offer a wide range of services (for example, checking accounts, savings accounts, and extension of loans) to their customers. Commercial banks are owned by stockholders and seek to operate at a profit.

Savings and Loan Associations: Financial institutions that accept deposits in exchange for shares that pay dividends. Historically, these funds have been channeled into residential mortgage loans. Under recent banking legislation, S & L's are now permitted to offer checkable deposits (NOW accounts) and extend a broad range of services similar to those of commercial banks.

Prior to the 1980s, commercial banks, savings and loan associations, and credit unions performed distinctly different functions. If one wanted a checking account, a personal or business loan, or a credit card, one would go to a **commercial bank.** For maximum interest on a savings account, or to obtain funds to buy a home, one would patronize a **savings and loan association. Credit unions** specialized in small personal loans, frequently offering the advantage of automatic deductions from one's paychecks.

In recent years, changes in the rules issued by the authorities regulating depository institutions have blurred the traditional distinctions among commercial banks, savings and loan associations, credit unions, and **mutual savings banks.** Under the Depository Institutions Deregulation and Monetary Control Act of 1980 (see feature, page 250), all of these depository institutions are permitted to offer NOW checking accounts. Simultaneously, the Depository Act lifted various restrictions on the types of loans and investments that savings and loan associations, mutual savings banks, and credit unions could make and provided for the phasing out of interest-rate ceilings on time and savings deposits by 1986. In addition, *all* depository institutions were placed under the jurisdiction of the Federal Reserve System and eventually will be required to meet similar regulatory requirements. As the result of these changes, the functions performed by commercial banks, savings and loan associations, mutual savings banks, and credit unions are now quite similar. In essence, recent legal and regulatory changes have transformed thrift institutions into banks. All of these depository institutions now offer both checking and savings accounts, and extend a wide variety of loans to their customers. Therefore, when we speak

Credit Unions: Financial co-operative organizations of individuals with a common affiliation (such as an employer or labor union). They accept deposits, including checkable deposits, pay interest (or dividends) on them out of earnings, and channel their funds primarily into loans to members.

Mutual Savings Banks: Financial institutions that accept deposits in exchange for interest payments. Historically, home mortgages have constituted their primary interest-earning assets. Under recent banking legislation, these banks, too, are authorized to offer interest-bearing checkable accounts. They exist in only 18 states and are concentrated in the Northeast.

EXHIBIT 4   A thumbnail sketch of the major depository institutions in the United States

Type of Institution	Number (Approximate)	Assets—March 1982 (Billions of Dollars)
Commercial banks	14,700	1819.9
Savings and loan associations	4,700	678.0
Mutual savings banks	500	174.8
Credit unions	22,300	81.1

Federal Reserve Bulletin, June 1982.

of the banking industry, we are referring not only to commercial banks but to savings and loan associations, credit unions, and mutual savings banks as well.

Exhibit 4 provides a thumbnail sketch of the depository institutions that comprise the banking industry. The assets of commercial banks are nearly twice as large as the combined total of those of the other three banking/depository institutions. In turn, the assets of savings and loan associations are substantially greater than those of either mutual savings banks or credit unions. Credit unions are more numerous (22,300) than any other type of depository institution, but their total assets came to only $81.1 billion in 1982.

Fractional Reserve Goldsmithing

Economists often like to draw an analogy between the goldsmith of the past and our current banking system. In the past, gold was used as the means of making payments. It was money. People would store their money with a goldsmith for safekeeping, just as many of us open a checking account for safety reasons. Gold owners received a certificate granting them the right to withdraw their gold anytime they wished. If they wanted to buy something, they would go to the goldsmith, withdraw gold, and use it as a means of making a payment. Thus, the money supply was equal to the amount of gold in circulation plus the gold deposited with goldsmiths.

The day-to-day deposits of and requests for gold were always only a fraction of the total amount of gold deposited. A major portion of the gold simply lay idle in the goldsmiths' "vaults." Taking notice of this fact, goldsmiths soon began loaning gold to local merchants. After a time, the merchants would pay back the gold plus an interest payment for its use. What happened to the money supply when a goldsmith extended loans to local merchants? The deposits of persons who initially brought their gold to the goldsmith were not reduced. Depositors could still withdraw their gold anytime they wished (as long as they did not all try to do so at once). The merchants were now able to use the gold they borrowed from the goldsmith as a means of payment. As goldsmiths lent gold, they increased the amount of gold in circulation, thereby increasing the money supply.

It was inconvenient to make a trip to the goldsmith every time one wanted to buy something. Since people knew that the certificates were redeemable in gold, certificates began circulating as a means of payment. The depositors were pleased with this arrangement because it eliminated the need for a trip to the goldsmith every time something was exchanged for gold. As long as they had confidence in the goldsmith, sellers were glad to accept the gold certificates as payment.

Since depositors were now able to utilize the gold certificates as money, the daily withdrawals and deposits with goldsmiths declined even more. Local goldsmiths would keep about 20 percent of the total gold deposited with them so they could meet the current requests to redeem gold certificates that were in circulation. The remaining 80 percent of their gold deposits would be loaned out to business merchants, traders, and other citizens. Therefore, 100 percent of the gold certificates was circulating as money; and that portion of gold that had been loaned out, 80 percent of the total deposits, was also circulating as money. The total money supply, gold certificates plus gold, was now 1.8 times the amount of gold that had been originally deposited with the goldsmith. Since the goldsmiths issued loans and kept only a fraction of the total gold deposited with them, they were able to increase the money supply.

As long as the goldsmiths held enough reserves to meet the current requests of their depositors, everything went along smoothly. Most gold depositors probably did not even realize that the goldsmiths did not have *their* actual gold and *that of other depositors,* precisely designated as such, sitting in the "vaults."

Goldsmiths derived income from loaning gold. The more gold they loaned, the greater their total income. Some goldsmiths, trying to increase their income by extending more and more interest-earning loans, depleted the gold in their vaults to imprudently low levels. If an unexpectedly large number of depositors wanted their gold, these greedy goldsmiths would have been unable to meet their requests. They would lose the confidence of their depositors, and the system of fractional reserve goldsmithing would tend to break down.

Fractional Reserve Banking

Fractional Reserve Banking: A system that enables banks to keep *less than* 100 percent reserves against their deposits. Required reserves are a fraction of deposits.

Required Reserves: The minimum amount of reserves that a bank is required by law to keep on hand to back up its deposits. Thus, if reserve requirements were 15 percent, banks would be required to keep $150,000 in reserves against each $1 million of deposits.

In principle, our **fractional reserve banking** system is very similar to goldsmithing. The early goldsmiths did not have enough gold on hand to pay all of their depositors simultaneously. Nor do our banks have enough cash and other reserves to pay all of their depositors simultaneously (see Exhibit 3). The early goldsmiths expanded the money supply by issuing loans. So do present-day bankers. The amount of gold held in reserve to meet the requirements of depositors limited the ability of the goldsmiths to expand the supply of money. The amount of cash and other **required reserves** limit the ability of present-day banks to expand the supply of money.

How Bankers Create Money. How do banks expand the supply of money? In order to answer this question, let us consider a banking system without a central bank and in which only currency acts as reserves against deposits. Initially, we will assume that all banks are required by law to maintain vault currency equal to at least 20 percent of the checking accounts of their depositors.

Suppose that you found $1000, which apparently your long-deceased uncle had hidden in the basement of his house. How much would this newly found $1000 of currency expand the money supply? You take the bills to the First National Bank, open a checking account of $1000, and deposit the cash with the banker. First National is now required to keep an additional $200 in vault cash, 20 percent of your deposit. However, they received $1000 of additional cash, so

Excess Reserves: Actual reserves that exceed the legal requirement.

after placing $200 in the bank vault, First National has $800 of **excess reserves,** reserves over and above the amount they are required by law to maintain. Given their current excess reserves, First National can now extend an $800 loan. Suppose that they loan $800 to a local citizen to buy a car. At the time the loan is extended, the money supply will increase by $800 as the bank adds the funds to the checking account of the borrower. No one else has less money. You still have your $1000 checking account, and the borrower has $800 for a new car.

When the borrower buys a new car, the seller accepts a check and deposits the $800 in a bank, Citizen's State Bank. What happens as the check clears? The temporary excess reserves of the First National Bank will be eliminated when it pays $800 to the Citizen's State Bank. But when Citizen's State Bank receives $800 in currency, it will now have excess reserves. It must keep 20 percent, an additional $160, in the reserve against the $800 checking-account deposit of the automobile seller. The remaining $640 could be loaned out. Since Citizen's State, like other banks, is in business to make money, it will be quite happy to "extend a helping hand" to a borrower. As the second bank loans out its excess reserves, the deposits of the persons borrowing the money will increase by $640. Another $640 has now been added to the money supply. You still have your $1000, the automobile seller has an additional $800, and the new borrower has just received an additional $640. Because you found the $1000 that had been stashed away by your uncle, the money supply has increased by $2440.

Of course, the process can continue. Exhibit 5 follows the *potential* creation of money resulting from the initial $1000 through several additional stages. In total, the money supply can increase by a maximum of $5000, the $1000 initial deposit plus an additional $4000 in demand deposits that can be created by the process of extending new loans.

Deposit Expansion Multiplier: The multiple by which an increase (decrease) in reserves will increase (decrease) the money supply. It is inversely related to the required reserve ratio.

The multiple by which new reserves increase the stock of money is referred to as the **deposit expansion multiplier.** In our example, the potential deposit expansion multiplier is 5. The amount by which additional reserves can increase the supply of money is determined by the ratio of required reserves to demand deposits. In fact, the deposit expansion multiplier is merely the reciprocal of the required reserve ratio. In our example, the required reserves are 20 percent, or

EXHIBIT 5 Creating money from new reserves

When banks are required to maintain 20 percent reserves against demand deposits, the creation of $1000 of new reserves will potentially increase the supply of money by $5000.

Bank	New Cash Deposits (Actual Reserves) (Dollars)	New Required Reserves (Dollars)	Potential Demand Deposits Created by Extending New Loans (Dollars)
Initial deposit	1000.00	200.00	800.00
Second stage	800.00	160.00	640.00
Third stage	640.00	128.00	512.00
Fourth stage	512.00	102.40	409.60
Fifth stage	409.60	81.92	327.68
Sixth stage	327.68	65.54	262.14
Seventh stage	262.14	52.43	209.71
All others	1048.58	209.71	838.87
Total	5000.00	1000.00	4000.00

only 10 percent reserves were required, the deposit expansion multiplier would be 10, the reciprocal of 1/10.

The lower the percentage of the reserve requirement, the greater is the potential expansion in the supply of money resulting from the creation of new reserves. The fractional reserve requirement places a ceiling on potential money creation from new reserves.

The Actual Deposit Expansion Multiplier. Will the introduction of the new currency reserves necessarily have a full deposit expansion multiplier effect? The answer is no. The actual deposit multiplier may be less than the potential for two reasons.

First, the deposit expansion multiplier will be reduced if some persons decide to hold the currency rather than deposit it in a bank. For example, suppose that the person who borrowed the $800 in the preceding example spends only $700 and stashes the remaining $100 away for a possible emergency. Then only $700 can end up as a deposit in the second stage and contribute to the excess reserves necessary for expansion. The potential of new loans in the second stage and in all subsequent stages will be reduced proportionally. When currency remains in circulation, outside of banks, it will reduce the size of the deposit expansion multiplier.

Second, the deposit multiplier will be less than its maximum when banks fail to utilize all the new excess reserves to extend loans. However, banks have a strong incentive to loan out most of their new excess reserves. Idle excess reserves do not draw interest. Banks want to use most of these excess reserves so they will generate interest income. Exhibit 6 shows that this is indeed the case. In recent years, excess reserves have comprised less than 1 percent of the total reserves of banks.

Currency leakages and idle excess bank reserves will result in a deposit expansion multiplier that is less than its potential maximum. However, since most people maintain most of their money in bank deposits rather than as currency, and since banks typically eliminate most of their excess reserves by extending loans, strong forces are present that will lead to multiple expansion.

THE FEDERAL RESERVE SYSTEM

The Federal Reserve System is the central monetary authority or "central bank" for the United States. Every major country has a central banking authority. The Bank of England and Bank of France, for example, perform central banking functions for their respective countries.

Central banks are charged with the responsibility of carrying out monetary policy. The major purpose of the Federal Reserve System (and other central banks) is to regulate the supply of money and provide a monetary climate that is in the best interest of the entire economy.

The Fed, a term often used to refer to the Federal Reserve System, was created in 1913. As Exhibit 7 illustrates, the policies of the Fed are determined by the Board of Governors. This powerful board consists of seven members, each appointed to a staggered 14-year term by the president with the advice and consent of the Senate. Since a new member of the governing board is appointed only every other year, each president has only limited power over the Fed.

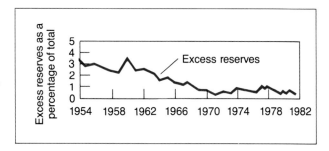

EXHIBIT 6 Banking and excess reserves

Profit-maximizing banks use their excess reserves to extend loans and other forms of credit. Thus, excess reserves are very small, less than 1 percent of the total in recent years.

Because the Fed operates with considerable independence of both Congress and the executive branch, it often becomes the "whipping boy" for legislative leaders and presidents during difficult times.

The Board of Governors establishes rules and regulations applicable to all depository institutions. It sets the reserve requirements and regulates the composition of the asset holdings of depository institutions. The board is the rule-maker, and often the umpire, of the banking industry.

Two important committees assist the Board of Governors in carrying out monetary policy. First, the **Federal Open Market Committee (FOMC)** is a powerful policy-making arm of the system. This committee is made up of (a) the seven members of the Board of Governors, (b) the president of the New York District Bank, and (c) four (of the remaining eleven) additional presidents of the Fed's District Banks, who rotate on the committee. The FOMC determines the Fed's policy with respect to the purchase and sale of government bonds. As we shall soon see, this is the Fed's most frequently used method of controlling the money supply in the United States. Second, the Federal Advisory Council meets periodically with the Board of Governors to express its views on monetary policy. The Federal Advisory Council is composed of 12 commercial bankers, one from each of the 12 Federal Reserve districts. As the name implies, this council is purely advisory.

EXHIBIT 7 The structure of the Federal Reserve System

The Board of Governors of the Federal Reserve System is at the center of the banking system in the United States. The board sets the rules and regulations for the banking system and other depository institutions, thereby controlling the supply of money.

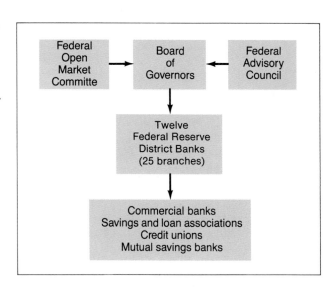

The 12 Federal Reserve District Banks operate under the control of the Board of Governors.[1] These district banks handle approximately 85 percent of all check-clearing services of the banking system. Federal Reserve District Banks differ from commercial banks in several important respects.

1. *Federal Reserve Banks Are Not Profit-Making Institutions.* Instead, they are an arm of the government. All of their earnings, above minimum expenses, belong to the Treasury.

2. *Unlike Other Banks, Federal Reserve Banks Can Actually Issue Money.* Approximately 90 percent of the currency in circulation was issued by the Fed. Look at the dollar bill in your pocket. Chances are that it has "Federal Reserve Note" engraved on it, indicating that it was issued by the Federal Reserve System. The Fed is the only bank that can issue money.

3. *Federal Reserve Banks Act as Bankers' Banks.* Private citizens and corporations do *not* bank with Federal Reserve Banks. Commercial depository institutions and the federal government are the only banking customers of the Fed. Most depository institutions, regardless of their membership status with the Fed, usually maintain some deposits with the Federal Reserve System. Of course, deposits with the Fed count as reserves. The Fed audits the books of depository institutions regularly so as to assure regulatory compliance and the protection of depositors against fraud. The Fed also plays an important role in the clearing of checks through the banking system. Since most banks maintain deposits with the Fed, the clearing of checks becomes merely an accounting transaction.

Initially, the Fed was made independent of the executive branch so that the Treasury would not use it for political purposes. However, the policies of the Treasury and the Fed are usually closely coordinated. For example, the chairman of the Board of Governors of the Federal Reserve, the Secretary of the Treasury, and the chairman of the President's Council of Economic Advisers meet weekly to discuss and plan macroeconomic policy. In reality, it would be more accurate to think of the Fed and the executive branch as equal partners in the determination of policies designed to promote full employment and stable prices.

How the Fed Controls Our Money Supply

The Fed has three major means of controlling the money stock: (a) establishing reserve requirements for depository institutions, (b) buying and selling U.S. government securities in the open market, and (c) setting the interest rate at which it will loan funds to commercial banks and other depository institutions. We will analyze in detail how each of these tools can be used to regulate the amount of money in circulation.

Reserve Requirements. The Federal Reserve System requires banking institutions (including credit unions and savings and loan associations) to maintain reserves against the demand deposits of its customers. The reserves of banking

---

[1] Federal Reserve District Banks are located in Boston, New York, Philadelphia, Cleveland, Richmond, Atlanta, Chicago, St. Louis, Minneapolis, Kansas City, Dallas, and San Francisco. There are also 25 district "branch banks."

institutions are composed of (a) currency held by the bank and (b) deposits of the bank with the Federal Reserve System. A bank can always obtain additional currency by drawing on its deposits with the Federal Reserve. Thus, both cash on hand and the bank's deposits with the Fed can be used to meet the demands of depositors. Therefore, both count as reserves.

Exhibit 8 indicates the **required reserve ratio**—the percentage of each deposit category that banks are required to keep in reserve (that is, their cash plus deposits with the Fed). The reserve requirement for **transaction accounts,** primarily checkable deposits, was set at 3 percent for amounts under $26 million and 12 percent for amounts in excess of $26 million as of June 1982.[2] A reserve ratio of 3 percent is applicable for **nonpersonal time deposits** with a maturity date during the next $3\frac{1}{2}$ years. Currently, no reserves are required against nonpersonal time deposits with a maturity date of more than $3\frac{1}{2}$ years in the future. Banks are also required to maintain 3 percent in reserve against Eurodollar liabilities.

Why are commercial banks required to maintain assets in the form of reserves? One reason is to prevent imprudent bankers from overextending loans and thereby placing themselves in a poor position to deal with any sudden increase in withdrawals by depositors. The quantity of reserves needed to meet such emergencies is not left totally to the judgment of individual bankers. The Fed sets the rules.

However, the Fed's control over reserve requirements is important for another reason. By altering them, the Fed can alter the money supply. The law does not prevent commercial banks from holding reserves over and above those required by the Fed, but, as we have noted, profit-seeking banking institutions prefer to hold interest-bearing assets such as loans rather than large amounts of excess reserves. Since reserves draw no interest, banks seek to minimize their excess reserves.

Exhibit 9 shows the actual reserve position of commercial banks (see also Exhibit 6). Not surprisingly, the actual reserves of these banks are very close to the required level. Since the excess reserves of banks are very small, when the

Required Reserve Ratio: A percentage of a specified liability category (for example, transaction accounts) that banking institutions are required to hold as reserves against that type of liability.

Transaction Accounts: Accounts including demand deposits, NOW accounts, and other checkable deposits against which the account holder is permitted to transfer funds for the purpose of making payment to a third party.

Nonpersonal Time Deposits: Time deposits owned by businesses or corporations.

EXHIBIT 8 **The required reserve ratio of banking institutions**

Banking institutions are required to maintain 3 percent reserves against transaction-account deposits of less than $26 million and 12 percent reserves for transaction deposits over $26 million (in effect June 1982). Other required reserve ratios are also shown below.

	Transaction Accounts		Nonpersonal Time Deposits		Eurocurrency Liabilities
	$0–26 Million	Over $26 Million	Less Than $3\frac{1}{2}$ Years Maturity	$3\frac{1}{2}$ Years or More Maturity	All Types
Required reserves as a percent of deposits	3	12	3	0	3

Federal Reserve Bulletin, June 1982.

[2]The $26 million dividing point is adjusted each year by 80 percent of the change in total transaction account deposits in all banking institutions, beginning in 1982.

EXHIBIT 9   The reserves
of banks

In 1982, the actual reserves of
banks were only slightly in
excess of their required reserves. The required reserves
average out at approximately
9 percent against demand deposits plus 1 percent against
time deposits.

Total—Commercial Banks
March 1982
(Billions of Dollars)

Total demand deposits	350.8
Total time deposits	944.2
Actual reserves	41.09
Required reserves	40.91
Excess reserves	.18

Federal Reserve Bulletin, June 1982.

Open Market Operations: The
buying and selling of U.S. government securities (national
debt) by the Federal Reserve.

Fed changes the required reserve ratio, banks respond in a manner that changes the money supply.

If the Fed reduced the required reserve ratio, it would free additional reserves that banks could loan out. Profit-seeking banks would not allow these excess reserves to lie idle. They would extend additional loans. The extension of the new loans would expand the money supply.

What would happen if the Fed increased the reserve requirements? Since banks typically have very few excess reserves, they would have to extend fewer loans in the future. This reduction in loans outstanding would cause a decline in the money supply.

Reserve requirements are an important determinant of the money supply because they influence both the availability of excess reserves and the size of the deposit expansion multiplier. Higher reserve requirements will reduce the size of the deposit expansion multiplier and force banks to extend fewer loans. Therefore, an increase in the required reserve ratio will reduce the money supply. On the other hand, a decline in the required reserve ratio will increase the potential deposit expansion multiplier and the availability of excess reserves. Banks will tend to extend additional loans, thereby expanding the money supply.

In recent years, the Fed has seldom utilized its regulatory power over reserve requirements to alter the supply of money. Because of the deposit expansion multiplier, small changes in reserve requirements can cause large changes in the money supply. In addition, the precise magnitude and timing of a change in the money stock that will result from a change in reserve requirements are difficult to predict. For these reasons, the Fed has usually preferred to use other monetary tools.

Open Market Operations.   Open market operations, the buying and selling of U.S. securities in the open market, is by far the most important mechanism that the Fed utilizes to control the stock of money. When the Fed enters the market and buys U.S. government securities, it expands the reserves available to banking institutions. The sellers of the securities receive a check drawn on a Federal Reserve Bank. As the check is deposited in a bank, the bank acquires a deposit or credit with the Federal Reserve. The banking system has increased its reserves, and the Fed has purchased part of the national debt. Since the deposit with the Fed, like currency, counts as reserves, banks can now extend more loans. The money supply will eventually increase by the amount of the securities purchased by the Fed times the actual deposit expansion multiplier.

Let us consider a hypothetical case. Suppose that the Fed purchases $10,000 of U.S. securities from commercial bank A. Bank A has fewer securities, but it now has additional excess reserves of $10,000; put another way, $10,000 has been added to the economy's *potential* reserves. The bank can extend new loans of up to $10,000 while maintaining its initial reserve position. This $10,000 expansion of loans will contribute directly to the money supply. Part of it will eventually be deposited in other banks, and they will also be able to extend additional loans. The creation of the $10,000 of new bank reserves will cause the money supply to increase by some multiple of the amount of U.S. securities purchased by the Fed.

The reserve requirements in effect in the early 1980s suggest that the *potential* deposit multiplier could be 9 or 10. Of course, as new reserves are injected into the banking system, there is some leakage either because of potential currency reserves circulating as cash or because some banks may be accumulating

EXHIBIT 10 How big is the actual money deposit multiplier?

In recent years the actual deposit expansion multiplier has been between 2.5 and 3.0. Of course, if the reserve requirements were lowered (raised), the deposit expansion multiplier would rise (fall).

Year (December)	Money Supply (M-1)[a]	Total Potential Reserves[a,b]	Money Deposit Expansion Multiplier
1970	216.8	73.1	2.97
1972	252.4	85.8	2.94
1974	278.0	100.6	2.76
1976	311.1	114.3	2.72
1978	364.2	134.9	2.70
1979	390.5	145.3	2.69
1980	415.6	158.2	2.63
1981	441.9	166.0	2.66

[a]Billions of dollars.

[b]Economists refer to the total potential reserves as the monetary base.

Board of Governors of the Federal Reserve System and *Economic Report of the President, 1982.*

Potential Reserves: The total Federal Reserve credit outstanding. Most of this credit is in the form of U.S. securities held by the Fed.

excess reserves. Exhibit 10 shows that during the 1970s the money supply was between 2.6 and 3.0 times greater than the **potential reserves**[3], suggesting that the actual deposit expansion multiplier is about 2.75. Therefore, when the Fed purchases U.S. securities, injecting additional reserves into the system, *on average,* the money supply tends to increase by approximately $2.75 for each dollar of securities purchased.

Open market operations can also be used to reduce the money stock, or its rate of increase. If the Fed wants to reduce the money stock, it will sell some of its current holdings of government securities. When the Fed sells securities, the buyer will pay for them with a check drawn on a commercial bank. As the check clears, the reserves of that bank with the Fed will decline. The reserves available to commercial banks are reduced, and the money stock will fall.

Since open market operations have been the Fed's primary tool of monetary control in recent years, the money stock and the Fed's ownership of U.S. securities have followed similar paths. When the Fed increases its purchases of U.S. securities at a rapid rate, the money stock will grow rapidly. A slowdown in the Fed's purchases of government bonds will tend to reduce the rate of monetary expansion.

As we indicated earlier, the Federal Open Market Committee (FOMC), a special committee of the Fed, decides when and how open market operations will be used. The members meet every three or four weeks to map out the Fed's policy concerning the purchase and sale of U.S. securities.

The Discount Rate—The Cost of Borrowing from the Fed. Banking institutions can borrow from the Federal Reserve, but when they do they must pay interest on the loan. The interest rate that banks pay on loans from the Federal Reserve is called the **discount rate.** When the newspapers announce that the discount rate has increased by 0.5 percent, many people think this means their

Discount Rate: The interest rate that the Federal Reserve charges banking institutions that borrow funds from it.

[3]Currency in circulation plus the actual reserves of commercial banks comprise the total potential reserves. Economists often use the term "monetary base" when referring to the total potential reserves.

local banker will (or must) now charge them a higher interest rate for a loan.[4] This is not necessarily so. The major source of loan funds of commercial banks is reserves acquired through demand and time deposits. Borrowing from the Fed contributes less than 0.5 of 1 percent to the available loan funds of commercial banks. Thus, an increase in the discount rate does not necessarily cause your local bank to raise the rate at which it will lend money to you.

The Fed does not have to loan funds to banking institutions. Banks rely on this source of funds primarily to meet a short-run shortage of reserves. They are most likely to turn to the Fed as a temporary method of meeting their reserve requirements while they are making other adjustments in their loan and investment portfolios.

An increase in the discount rate makes it more expensive for banking institutions to borrow from the Fed. Borrowing is discouraged, and banks are more likely to build up their reserves to ensure that they will not have to borrow from the Fed. Thus, an increase in the discount rate is restrictive. It will tend to discourage banks from shaving their excess reserves to a low level.

In contrast, a reduction in the discount rate is expansionary. At the lower interest rate, it costs banks less if they have to turn to the Fed to meet a temporary emergency. Thus, banks are more likely to reduce their excess reserves to a minimum, extending more loans and increasing the money supply, as the cost of borrowing from the Fed declines.

However, the general public has a tendency to overestimate the importance of a change in the discount rate. Since it applies to such a small share of total reserves, a 0.5 percent change in the discount rate has something less than a profound impact on the availability of credit and the supply of money. The influence of a change in the discount rate is not completely negligible, but usually the open market operations of the Fed are a much better index of the direction and magnitude of monetary policy.

Also, if a bank has to borrow in order to meet its reserve requirements, it need not turn to the Fed. Instead, it can go to the **federal funds market.** In this market, banks with excess reserves extend short-term (sometimes for as little as a day) loans to other banks seeking additional reserves. If the federal funds rate (the interest rate in the federal funds market) is less than the discount rate, banks seeking additional reserves will tap this source rather than borrow from the Fed. In recent years the Fed has kept its loans to banking institutions at a low level by altering the discount rate to match the federal funds rate more closely. As a result, the federal funds rate and the discount rate tend to move together. If the federal funds rate is significantly above the discount rate, banks will attempt to borrow heavily from the Fed. Typically, when this happens, the Fed will raise its discount rate, removing the incentive of banks to borrow from the Fed rather than from the federal funds market.

Federal Funds Market: A loanable funds market in which banks seeking additional reserves borrow short-term (generally for seven days or less) funds from banks with excess reserves. The interest rate in this market is called the federal funds rate.

Summarizing the Tools of the Fed. Exhibit 11 summarizes the monetary tools of the Federal Reserve. If the Fed wants to follow an expansionary policy, it can decrease reserve requirements, purchase additional U.S. securities, and/or lower the discount rate. If the Fed wants to reduce the money stock, it can

---

[4]The discount rate is also sometimes confused with the prime interest rate, the rate at which banks will loan money to low-risk customers. The two rates are different. A change in the discount rate will not necessarily affect the prime interest rate.

EXHIBIT 11   Summary of the monetary tools of the Federal Reserve

Federal Reserve Policy	Expansionary Monetary Policy	Restrictive Monetary Policy
1. Reserve requirements	*Reduce reserve requirements,* because this will free additional excess reserves and induce banks to extend additional loans, which will expand the money supply	*Raise reserve requirements,* because this will reduce the excess reserves of banks, causing them to make fewer loans; as the outstanding loans of banks decline, the money stock will be reduced
2. Open market operations	*Purchase additional U.S. securities,* which will expand the money stock directly, and increase the reserves of banks, inducing bankers in turn to extend more loans; this will expand the money stock indirectly	*Sell U.S. securities,* which will reduce both the money stock and excess reserves; the decline in excess reserves will indirectly lead to an additional reduction in the money supply
3. Discount rate	*Lower the discount rate,* which will encourage more borrowing from the Fed; banks will tend to reduce their reserves and extend more loans because of the lower cost of borrowing from the Fed if they temporarily run short on reserves.	*Raise the discount rate,* thereby discouraging borrowing from the Fed; banks will tend to extend fewer loans and build up their reserves so they will not have to borrow from the Fed

increase the reserve requirements, sell U.S. securities, and/or raise the discount rate. Since the Fed typically seeks only small changes in the money supply (or its rate of increase), it usually utilizes only one or two of these tools at a time to accomplish a desired objective.

The Fed's Monetary Growth Targets

Prior to October 1979, the Fed judged the appropriateness of monetary policy primarily by looking at interest rates. In the face of rapid inflation and monetary expansion, the Fed announced that henceforth it would seek to control the monetary aggregates more closely while permitting the interest rates to fluctuate according to market forces.

With the passage of time, the money supply, like the GNP, generally expands. In a dynamic setting, therefore, monetary policy might best be gauged by the rate of change in the money supply. When economists say that monetary policy is expansionary, they mean that the rate of growth of the money stock is rapid. Similarly, restrictive monetary policy implies a slow rate of growth or a decline in the money stock.

At the beginning of each year, the Fed announces its target range for the rate of growth of various measures of the money supply. For 1982, the Fed's target growth range for M-1 was 3.5 to 6 percent. The Fed seeks to utilize its policy tools—particularly open market operations—to maintain the supply of

THE DEREGULATION AND MONETARY CONTROL ACT

"This act is the most significant banking legislation before Congress since the passage of the Federal Reserve Act in 1913."
Senator William Proxmire, Chairman, Senate Committee on Banking, Housing, and Urban Affairs (1980)

As Senator Proxmire indicated, the Depository Institutions Deregulation and Monetary Control Act of 1980 was an extremely important piece of legislation. In effect, it restructured the banking industry, eroding the distinction between banking institutions and thrift institutions, such as savings and loan associations and credit unions. The act marked the culmination of several years of study by members of Congress, regulatory agencies, and financial institutions. As the title implies, the legislation had a twofold purpose: (1) deregulation designed to enhance the competitiveness of the financial industry and (2) imposition of uniform rules, applicable to all depository institutions, that would improve the Fed's ability to control the money supply accurately.

Prior to the passage of the act, different types of financial institutions operated under different sets of regulations, which were designed to segment the financial market. There were specific restrictions on the kinds of deposit accounts each type of institution could offer and the variety of loans and investments each could undertake. As a result, competition between depository institutions was limited.

Let us consider the major elements of the act and analyze their impact upon the financial industry.

1. The Fed Sets the Reserve Requirements for All Depository Institutions. The act granted the Federal Reserve the power to regulate the reserves of savings and loan associations, mutual savings banks, credit unions, and nonmember commercial banks, as well as those of the system's member banks. The Fed was instructed to apply reserve requirements uniformly to all depository institutions. The act provided for the phasing in of these requirements over periods of up to eight years. It was believed that expansion of the Fed's power over the reserve requirements of all depository institutions would permit the agency to control the supply of money with greater precision.

2. The Right to Offer NOW Accounts Was Extended to All Depository Institutions. The Banking Act of 1933 granted commercial banks a virtual monopoly over checking accounts. The 1980 act dismantled the earlier legislation and thereby permitted all thrift institutions to compete for checking-account deposits.

3. Various Restrictions on the Types of Loans and Investments That Nonbanking Thrift Institutions Could Make Were Revoked. Most thrift institutions were authorized to hold a larger share of their assets in the form of consumer loans, corporate securities, commercial paper, and various other types of unsecured loans. This removal of restrictions placed depository institutions on a more equal footing; all can now offer a wide range of loanable fund services.

4. Interest-Rate Ceilings on Time and Savings Deposits at Depository Institutions Will Be Phased Out by 1986. Interest rates rose during the 1970s; regulated interest ceilings imposed on the financial industry discouraged people from saving, impeded the ability of many depositors to compete for funds, and created inequities among institutions. The phaseout of these "interest-rate controls" will permit all depository institutions to compete more effectively for funds. The act also provided for the overriding of state usury laws to varying degrees. Thus, it is a move toward a competitive market in the loanable funds industry.

The act removed a number of artificial distinctions among financial institutions. With time, the competitive process should improve the efficiency of the financial industry. However, the transition period may well be fraught with danger and instability. In the short run, some financial institutions may find it difficult to meet the new competitive pressures. In addition, as funds flow in and move out of institutions and different types of accounts, the Fed may find it more difficult, *during the transition period,* to maintain monetary stability. Even positive, desirable change usually involves growing pains.

money within the target range. Currently, the Fed has announced that it plans gradually to reduce the growth rate of the money supply (M-1) by .5 percent a year for the next four to six years. Presumably, this slower rate of growth will help control inflation.

Although the concept of announced monetary targets is generally applauded among economists, there is one problem with it. Thus far, the Fed has not been very good at hitting its announced targets. For short time periods of six to nine months, the growth rate of the money supply in recent years has often either soared above the announced maximum growth target or fallen well short of even the minimum growth rate target. The Federal Reserve has come under intense criticism for these fluctuations, the implication of which we will investigate as we proceed.

The Fed and the Treasury

Many students have a tendency to confuse the Federal Reserve and the U.S. Treasury, probably because both sound like monetary agencies. The Treasury is a budgetary agency. If there is a budgetary deficit, the Treasury will *issue* U.S. securities as a method of financing the deficit. Newly issued U.S. securities are almost always sold to private investors (or invested in government trust funds). Bonds issued by the Treasury to finance a budget deficit are seldom purchased directly by the Fed. In any case, the Treasury is interested primarily in obtaining funds so it can pay Uncle Sam's bills. Except for nominal amounts, mostly coins, the Treasury does not issue money. Borrowing—the public sale of new U.S. securities—is the primary method used by the Treasury to cover any excess of expenditures in relation to tax revenues.

Whereas the Treasury is concerned with the revenues and expenditures of the government, the Fed is concerned primarily with the availability of money and credit for the entire economy. The Fed does not *issue* U.S. securities. It merely purchases and sells government securities issued by the Treasury as a means of controlling the money supply of the economy. The Fed does not have an obligation to meet the financial responsibilities of the U.S. government. That is the domain of the Treasury. The Fed's responsibility is to provide a stable monetary framework for the entire economy. Thus, although the two agencies cooperate with each other, they are distinctly different institutions established for different purposes.

LOOKING AHEAD

In this chapter we focused on the mechanics of monetary control. In the following two chapters we will analyze the impact of monetary policy on output, growth, and prices.

CHAPTER LEARNING OBJECTIVES

1 Money is anything that is widely accepted as a medium of exchange. It also acts as a unit of account and provides a means of storing current purchasing power for the future. Without money, exchange would be both costly and tedious.

2 There is some debate among economists as to precisely how the money supply should be defined. The narrowest and most widely used definition of the money supply (M-1) includes only (a) currency in the hands of the public, (b) demand deposits with commercial banks, (c) other checkable deposits in depository institutions, and (d) traveler's checks. None of these categories of money have significant intrinsic value. Money derives its value from its scarcity relative to its usefulness.

3 Banking is a business. Banks provide their depositors with safekeeping of money, check-clearing services on demand deposits, and interest payments on time deposits. Banks derive most of their income from the extension of loans and investments in interest-earning securities.

4 Recent legislation and regulatory changes have altered the structure of the banking industry. Currently, savings and loan associations, mutual savings banks, and credit unions offer services, including checking accounts, similar to those of commercial banks. The Federal Reserve System now regulates all of these depository institutions and is legally required to apply uniform reserve requirements to each. In essence, these changes have integrated the three classes of thrift institutions into the banking industry.

5 The Federal Reserve System is a central banking authority designed to provide a stable monetary framework for the entire economy. It establishes regulations that determine the supply of money. It issues most of the currency in the United States. It is a banker's bank.

6 The Fed has three major tools with which to control the money supply.

(a) *Establishment of the Required Reserve Ratio.* Under a fractional reserve banking system, reserve requirements limit the ability of banking institutions to expand the money supply by extending more loans. When the Fed lowers the required reserve ratio, it creates excess reserves and allows banks to extend new loans, expanding the money supply. Raising the reserve requirements has the opposite effect.

(b) *Open Market Operations.* The open market operations of the Fed can directly influence both the money supply and available reserves. When the Fed buys U.S. securities, the money supply will expand because bond buyers will acquire money and the reserves of banks will increase as checks drawn on Federal Reserve Banks are cleared. When the Fed sells securities, the money supply will contract because bond buyers are giving up money in exchange for securities. The reserves available to banks will decline, causing banks to issue fewer loans and thereby reducing the money supply.

(c) *The Discount Rate.* An increase in the discount rate is restrictive because it discourages banks from borrowing from the Fed in order to extend new loans. A reduction in the discount rate is expansionary because it makes borrowing from the Fed less costly.

7 At the beginning of each year the Fed announces a target range for the growth of monetary aggregates. In a dynamic setting, monetary policy can best be judged by the rate of change in the money supply. A rapid growth rate in the money supply is indicative of expansionary monetary policy while a slower rate indicates that monetary policy is more restrictive.

8 The Federal Reserve and the U.S. Treasury are two distinct, different agencies. The Fed is concerned primarily with the money supply and the establishment of a stable monetary climate. The Treasury focuses on budgetary matters—tax revenues, government expenditures, and the financing of government debt.

9 The Deregulation and Monetary Control Act of 1980 (a) dismantled many of the regulations that restricted competitiveness among depository institutions and (b) imposed uniform reserve requirements on all depository institutions, placing them under the jurisdiction of the Fed. All depository institutions were granted the right to offer NOW accounts. Various limitations on the types of loans that thrift institutions could extend were relaxed. The act mandated the phasing out of interest-rate ceilings on time and savings deposits. Essentially, it removed many of the artificial distinctions among financial institutions.

1 Why can banks continue to hold reserves that are only a fraction of the demand deposits of their customers? Is your money safe in a bank? Why or why not?

2 What makes money valuable? Does money perform an economic service? Explain. Could money perform its function better if there were twice as much of it? Why or why not?

3 "People are poor because they don't have very much money. Yet central bankers keep money scarce. If poor people had more money, poverty could be eliminated." Explain the confused thinking this statement reveals and why it is misleading.

4 Explain how the creation of new reserves would cause the supply of money to increase by some multiple of the newly created reserves.

5 How will the following actions affect the money supply?
   (a) A reduction in the discount rate
   (b) An increase in the reserve requirements
   (c) Purchase by the Fed of $10 million of U.S. securities from a commercial bank
   (d) Sale by the U.S. Treasury of $10 million of newly issued bonds to a commercial bank
   (e) An increase in the discount rate
   (f) Sale by the Fed of $20 million of U.S. securities to a private investor

6 **What's Wrong with This Way of Thinking?**

"When the government runs a budget deficit, it simply pays its bills by printing more money. As the newly printed money works its way through the economy, it waters down the value of paper money already in circulation. Thus, it takes more money to buy things. The major source of inflation is newly created paper money resulting from budget deficits."

The rate of inflation can be reduced only if fiscal and monetary
policies over the long term aim at
lowering the rate of growth of
nominal GNP.[1]
Economic Report of the President, 1980

13

MONEY, EMPLOYMENT, INFLATION, AND A MORE COMPLETE KEYNESIAN MODEL

Now that we have an understanding of the banking system and the determinants of the money supply, we can introduce money into the Keynesian model. In this chapter, we present the Keynesian view of monetary policy and indicate how it can be used to influence the level of employment, prices, and output.

In Chapter 14, we will present an alternative view of the influence of money on economic activity, that of the monetarists. During the last two decades, the monetarists have often challenged the dominant Keynesian view, particularly with regard to the impact of discretionary monetary and fiscal policy. Taken together, Chapters 13 and 14 outline the nature of the Keynesian–monetarist debate and discuss the consensus view that has emerged from the controversy.

THE DEMAND AND SUPPLY OF MONEY

Demand for Money: At any given interest rate, the amount of wealth that people desire to hold in the form of money balances, that is, cash and checking-account deposits. The quantity demanded is inversely related to the interest rate.

What factors underlie the **demand for money?** That is, why do people want to maintain part of their wealth in the form of cash and checking-account money? Keynes stressed three major reasons. First is the *transactions motive.* Money helps each of us make everyday purchases; we keep a little cash or money in the bank in order to bridge the gap between everyday expenses and payday. Second is the *precautionary motive.* Most of us keep a little money in the bank or in our billfold in case some unforeseen contingency should arise. Keynes felt that these two motives for holding money balances were determined primarily by the level of income. Finally, there is the *speculative motive.* Individuals and businesses may want to maintain part of their wealth in the form of money so that they will be able to take ready advantage of changes in prices, particularly prices of bonds,

---

[1] *Economic Report of the President, 1980,* p. 102.

stocks, and other financial assets. Money is the most liquid form of holding wealth. Unlike land or houses, it can be quickly traded for other assets. Thus, people may want to hold some money so that they can quickly respond to a profit-making opportunity.

The speculative demand for money is strongly affected by the existing and expected level of interest rates. When interest rates are high, the opportunity cost of holding idle money balances is greater. High interest rates induce people to hold less money, whereas low interest rates have the opposite effect.

Exhibit 1a illustrates the inverse relationship between the demand for money and the interest rate. The Keynesian view emphasizes that during normal times the curve representing the demand for money is like the demand curve for any other good. When the price (the interest foregone) of holding money rises, the quantity of money demanded will decline. The supply of money is determined by the monetary authorities, the Fed in the United States. The money supply is not affected by interest rates. Hence as Exhibit 1b shows, it is represented by a vertical line.

When the money market is in equilibrium, the quantity of money demanded at the existing interest rate will just equal the quantity supplied. Monetary policy can influence the rate of interest, *at least in the short run.* High interest rates make it expensive to hold money balances that generally do not pay interest, at least not as high an interest rate as could be derived from bonds, stocks, and savings accounts. Suppose that the money market were initially in equilibrium; the public would be just willing to hold the existing money stock, given the interest foregone when wealth is held in the form of money balances. As Exhibit 2 illustrates, an increase in the supply of money would cause the interest rate to fall. Why? The expansionary monetary policy, shift from M to M', creates an excess supply of money. Money balances are increased. People will find the 10 percent interest rate now too high to merit holding the larger quantity of money. The public will attempt to reduce their money balances by purchasing interest-bearing substitutes, primarily bonds. The demand for bonds will increase, causing bond prices to rise.

There is an inverse relationship between bond prices and interest rates. Higher bond prices are the same thing as lower interest rates (see the boxed feature, "Bonds, Interest Rates, and Bond Prices"). Thus, when people reduce their cash balances by purchasing more bonds, the interest rate will fall, reducing the opportunity cost of holding money. Eventually, at the lower rate of interest, 5 percent in the example of Exhibit 2, the public will be content to hold the larger supply of money (M').

When open market operations are used to expand the money supply, the impact on interest rates is even more straightforward. How do the open market purchases by the Fed affect the money supply? The Fed buys interest-bearing bonds from the public, bidding up bond prices and lowering interest rates. The public acquires money balances, funds that can be used to extend credit to private investors. This increase in the supply of funds *available to finance private investment* will also place downward pressure on interest rates. Of course, lower interest rates will eventually restore equilibrium in the money market.

What happens to interest rates when the Fed sells bonds to the public, thereby reducing the money stock? The Fed's action increases the supply of

EXHIBIT 1   The demand and supply of money

The demand for money is inversely related to the interest rate (a). The supply of money is determined by the monetary authorities (the Fed) through their open market operations, discount rate policy, and reserve requirements (b).

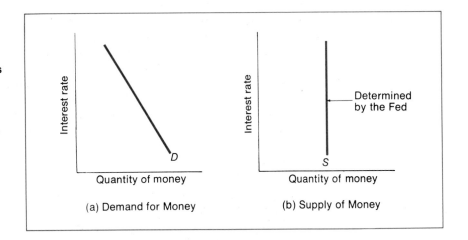

(a) Demand for Money

(b) Supply of Money

bonds, causing lower bond prices (higher interest rates). Temporarily, the reduction in the supply of money will create an excess demand for money balances. The public will attempt to restore their money balances to the desired level. How can this be done? By selling bonds, withdrawing funds from savings accounts, or borrowing. However, all of these actions will place upward pressure on the interest rate. As interest rates rise, the opportunity cost of holding money increases. Eventually, equilibrium will be restored in the money market, since the public will be satisfied with their smaller money balances at a new, higher interest rate.

In summary, monetary policy can influence interest rates in the short run. If the demand for money remains constant, expansionary monetary policy will push interest rates downward. In contrast, a restrictive monetary policy will cause interest rates to rise.[2]

EXHIBIT 2   The determination of interest rates—Keynesian model

If the demand for money remains fixed, an increase in supply will cause interest rates to decline.

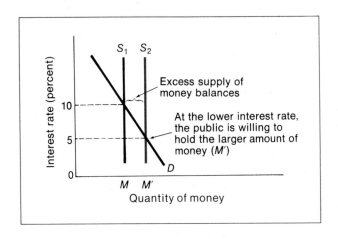

----

[2]Many economists, particularly monetarists, believe that the long-run effect of monetary policy on interest rates is just the opposite of its short-run impact (see Chapter 15, pp. 317–320).

BONDS, INTEREST RATES, AND BOND PRICES

What Is a Bond?

Bonds are simply IOUs issued by firms and governments. Issuing bonds is a method of borrowing money to finance economic activity. The entity issuing the bond promises to pay the bondholder an agreed-upon sum (called the "principal") either on a specific date or in installments over a specified period, during which time a fixed interest rate may be paid with payments due on certain dates. Most bonds pay a fixed return per year until the bond matures, at which time the owner is entitled to receive payment of the face value of the bond. The fixed return is expressed as a percent of the face value. The U.S. Coupon Bond shown here is a typical government bond. The face value of this bond is $100,000, and the bond was issued at an interest rate of 3.5 percent. Until the bond matured, the owner was entitled to a fixed yearly return of $3500 (3.5 percent of $100,000). In this case, interest was payable semiannually (in two payments of $1750) upon redemption of the coupons at the Treasury Department or a designated agency.

Even though most bonds are issued over the long term, the face value of a bond can be redeemed before it matures. Each day, sales of previously issued bonds comprise the majority of bonds bought and sold on the bond market. Like most stocks traded on the stock market, new issues of bonds account for only a small portion of all bond sales.

How Does a Change in the Market Interest Rate Affect Bond Prices?

Suppose that you have just bought a newly issued $1000 bond that pays 8

percent on the issue price. As long as you own the bond, you are entitled to a fixed return of $80 per year. Let us also assume that after you have held the bond for one year and have collected your $80 interest for that year, the market interest rate, for whatever reason, increases to 10 percent.[3] How will the increase in the interest rate affect the market price of your bond? Since bond purchasers can now earn 10 percent interest if they buy newly issued bonds, they will be unwilling to pay more than $800 for your bond, which pays only

$80 interest per year. After all, why would anyone pay $1000 for a bond that yields only $80 interest per year when the same $1000 will now purchase a bond that yields $100 (10 percent) per year? Once the interest rate has risen to 10 percent, your 8 percent, $1000 bond will no longer sell for its original value. The market value of your bond will fall to $800. You have experienced a $200 capital loss on the bond during the year. Rising market interest rates cause bond prices to decline.

On the other hand, falling interest rates will cause bond prices to rise. If the market interest rate had fallen to 6 percent, what would have happened to the market value of your bond? (Hint: $80 is 6 percent of $1333.) Bond prices and interest rates are inversely linked to each other.

---

[3] The astute reader will recognize an oversimplification in this discussion. In reality, the economy supports a variety of interest rates, which usually tend to move together.

Interest Rates and Investment

Interest rates influence the cost of each new investment project. Regardless of whether a business produces doorknobs or razor blades, lamp posts or refrigerators, or any other product, the interest rate will have either a direct or indirect effect on the cost of investment. If one has to borrow, there will be a direct interest cost. Even if borrowing is unnecessary, undertaking an investment project will mean foregoing interest income that could have been earned with the same funds. Since the interest rate contributes to the cost of each new investment, we would expect an inverse relationship between the level of investment and the interest rate.

When entrepreneurs consider an investment, they will compare the expected rate of return with the interest rate. If the expected rate of return exceeds the interest rate, the project is profitable and will be undertaken. In contrast, profit-seeking entrepreneurs will not invest in a project for which the expected rate of return is less than the interest rate.

Exhibit 3 pictures the relationship between investment and the interest rate for both a single firm and the entire economy. As a firm undertakes more investment projects, the expected rate of return from each additional investment opportunity will decline. As more capital is invested (that is, as more projects are undertaken), it will be necessary to include some of the less attractive projects. For the firm illustrated by Exhibit 3a, project A is expected to yield more than a 20 percent rate of return, B about 17 percent, C approximately 15 percent, and so on. If the interest rate were 10 percent, projects A, B, C, and D would be undertaken. If the interest rate fell to 5 percent, E (but not F) would also be carried out. However, if the interest rate rose to 16 percent, only projects A and B would be profitable.

The declining rate of return on *additional* investment will be true both for individual firms and for the entire economy. Thus, as Exhibit 3b shows, for an economy, there is an inverse relationship between total investment and the interest rate.

EXHIBIT 3   When business-people invest

If the interest rate were 10 percent, firm A (graph a) would undertake projects A, B, C, and D. For the entire economy, investment would be *I* (graph b). There is an inverse relationship between the amount of investment and the interest rate for both individual firms and the economy as a whole, other things constant.

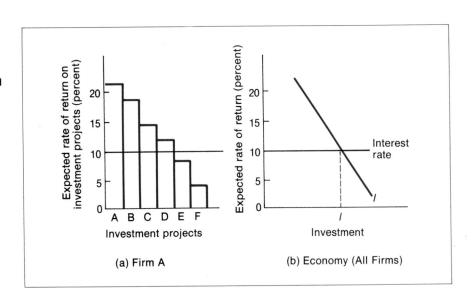

(a) Firm A

(b) Economy (All Firms)

Since the supply of money can be influenced by the Federal Reserve, it presents planners with another policy variable with which to promote full employment and stabilize prices. If the central monetary planners, like the Fed, wanted to follow an **expansionary monetary policy,** they could (a) purchase government bonds, (b) reduce the reserve requirements of banks, and/or (c) reduce the discount rate. All of these changes would tend to increase the supply of money, making credit more readily available to the economy. In contrast, if the Federal Reserve sold government bonds, increased bank reserve requirements, and/or raised the discount rate, the supply of money would tend to decline (or increase at a slower rate). Monetary planners would be following a **restrictive monetary policy,** causing interest rates to rise in the short run.

Expansionary Monetary Policy: A policy that results in a rate of change in the supply of money that exceeds the long-run average rate.

Restrictive Monetary Policy: A policy that results in a rate of change in the money supply that is less than the long-run average rate.

How does monetary policy influence aggregate demand and income? Economists are not in complete agreement on this issue. In fact, it comprises one of the major differences between Keynesians and monetarists. Keynesians believe that monetary policy exerts its major effect indirectly by influencing the interest rate. As we will see later, monetarists believe there is a more direct link between monetary policy and aggregate demand.

How Monetary Policy Works—The Keynesian View

Keynesian economists believe that expansionary monetary policy can be used to reduce interest rates. Because of the lower rate, business entrepreneurs will undertake a larger number of investment projects. The "easy money" policy can thereby stimulate private investment.

Exhibit 4 illustrates the Keynesian view of expansionary monetary policy for an economy that is initially operating below its long-run, supply-constrained output rate (Y_2). The monetary authorities—via open market purchases, for example—expand the supply of money from M to M' (Exhibit 4a). At the initial interest rate i_1, the public has more money than it desires to hold. It will attempt to reduce its money balances by buying bonds and other financial assets. The interest rate will decline. What effect will this decline have on private investment? Investment will rise, as businesspeople find that more projects are profitable at the lower interest rate. Aggregate investment will increase from I_1 to I_2 (ΔI in Exhibit 4b and c) The additional investment ΔI will cause aggregate demand to expand (Exhibit 4c). By how much will the equilibrium level of income go up? The new investment will have a multiplier effect, causing income to rise by a larger amount than the increase in aggregate demand.

Thus, Keynesian theory suggests that expansionary monetary policy will lower the interest rate and induce additional investment. The expansion in investment will increase aggregate demand and, working via the multiplier, cause aggregate income to rise to the supply-constrained output rate.

Of course, it will take time for the process to work. As we discussed in Chapter 9, the multiplier effect will not take place instantaneously. Several months may pass before the full effects of the expansionary monetary policy are felt. Nonetheless, the directional impact of expansionary monetary policy is straightforward. Expansionary monetary policy provides an additional tool that macroplanners can use to ensure sufficient aggregate demand and full employment.

EXHIBIT 4 How monetary policy can stimulate demand

Within the Keynesian model, an increase in the supply of money (shift from S_1 to S_2) would cause the interest rate to decline (from i_1 to i_2), stimulating additional investment (ΔI). Because of the multiplier, the equilibrium level of income would increase by a much larger amount [ΔY, graph (c)] than investment. Since the economy was initially operating below its long-run real aggregate supply level, the expansionary monetary policy would induce an increase in real output. However, once the economy's long-run supply constraint (Y_2) was attained, monetary expansion would be inflationary.

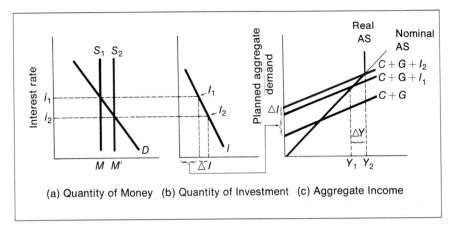

(a) Quantity of Money (b) Quantity of Investment (c) Aggregate Income

What would happen if the money supply were expanded by a larger amount, beyond M' (Exhibit 4)? Suppose that expansionary monetary policy drove the interest rate below i_2, causing investment to increase beyond I_2. Aggregate demand would rise to a higher level than $C + G + I_2$. This policy would lead to inflation. Nominal income would rise beyond Y_2; but real income cannot be permanently expanded beyond the economy's long-run supply constraint. When an economy is operating at its long-run, supply-constrained income level (Y_2), expansionary monetary policy (for example, an acceleration in the rate of growth in the money supply) is inflationary.

Combining Monetary and Fiscal Policies

When the government incurs a budget deficit in an attempt to stimulate demand, it must borrow funds to finance the deficit. There are two ways in which the government can do this. First, the Treasury can sell U.S. securities to the public. When the deficit is financed entirely in this manner, it is a purely fiscal action. The supply of money will be left unchanged.[4] The demand deposits of private parties will decline, but the Treasury's demand deposits will rise by an offsetting amount. With time, the Treasury will use the newly acquired funds to purchase such things as highways, education, bombs, and airplanes. This method of financing the deficit will reduce the supply of loanable funds available for financing private investment. Higher interest rates will result, dampening the expansionary impact of the budget deficit. However, Keynesians believe that, *in the short run,* the negative impact of the higher interest rate on current investment will be relatively minor, particularly if the economy is operating below its long-run, supply-constrained rate of output. Thus, Keynesians stress that the net effect of a budget deficit will be expansionary, even when it is financed by borrowing from the public.[5]

Second, the budget deficit can be financed by issuing bonds that are purchased, perhaps secondhand, by the Federal Reserve. This method of financ-

---

[4]Be careful not to confuse (a) bond sales by the Treasury to the public and (b) bond sales by the Federal Reserve to the public. Only the latter will affect the money supply.

[5]Many monetarists disagree with this view. See Chapter 14, pp. 288–290.

ing combines fiscal and monetary policies. When the Treasury borrows indirectly from the Fed, the budget deficit is financed by newly created money. This action will leave the funds of potential private bondholders undisturbed and available for financing private investment. The monetary expansion will also exert downward pressure on the short-run interest rate, further stimulating investment and aggregate demand. If stimulus is desired, the combination of expansionary fiscal and monetary policies will clearly exert more intense pressure than a budget deficit financed entirely by borrowing from the public.

Money and Inflation

During a period of inflation—when aggregate demand exceeds the long-run supply constraint of the economy and prices are rising—restrictive monetary policy can be utilized to reduce aggregate demand to a level consistent with the economy's long-run supply capacity and stable prices. Within the Keynesian framework, the effect of restrictive monetary policy is transmitted through its impact on the interest rate. Suppose that the Federal Reserve decides to sell government bonds. The private purchasers of the bonds will pay for them by giving up deposits (money). The supply of money will be reduced. The smaller supply of money (and larger supply of bonds) will cause bond prices to fall and interest rates to rise. As the rate of interest increases, investors will choose to forego some of their less profitable investment projects. The higher interest rates will increase the opportunity cost of investing in physical capital. Private investment will decline, as some potential investors choose to purchase bonds instead of capital goods. The decline in private investment will reduce both aggregate demand and the inflationary pressure. Thus, restrictive monetary policy can help to stem the tide of inflation.

How is restrictive monetary policy likely to affect output and employment? Suppose the economy is operating at its long-run, supply-constrained output level (for example, Y_2, Exhibit 4). A restrictive monetary policy that results in a deceleration in the growth rate of the money supply, for example, will cause the interest rate to rise, at least in the short run. The higher interest rate will reduce the rate of investment. Operating through the multiplier, the decline in investment will cause aggregate demand to fall. Remember, the Keynesian model emphasizes that prices are inflexible downward, particularly in the short run. Thus, the decline in aggregate demand will cause both nominal and real output to fall. Unemployment will rise. In the short run, the restrictive monetary policy is likely to lead to an economic slowdown or even to thrust the economy into a recession.

Since monetary policy tends to exert an uneven impact across industries, some economists are critical of excessive reliance upon it as an anti-inflationary weapon. The construction and automobile industries, for example, are highly sensitive to changes in interest rates; higher interest rates make it more expensive for consumers to purchase the houses and automobiles produced by these industries. Many potential consumers will choose to forego the purchase of these goods during a period of high interest rates. Thus, restrictive monetary policy may cause widespread unemployment and recessionary conditions in industries sensitive to interest-rate fluctuations, even while inflationary pressures remain strong in other industries.

Proper Timing

Just as with fiscal policy, monetary policy must be timed properly if it is to help stabilize an economy. When an economy is operating below its long-run supply constraint, expansionary policy can stimulate demand and push the output of the economy to its supply-constrained rate. Similarly, if properly timed, restrictive monetary policy can help control (or prevent) an inflationary boom.

However, proper timing of monetary policy is not an easy task. Some studies indicate that a change in monetary policy may exert its primary impact on aggregate demand anywhere from 6 to 30 months after it is initially instituted. Given our ability to forecast the future overall needs of an economy, such time lags obviously make it extremely difficult to time monetary policy correctly. If improperly timed, monetary policy may actually contribute to economic instability. For example, a restrictive monetary policy whose impact is finally felt during a downturn would intensify the severity of an imminent recession. Similarly, expansionary monetary policy is capable of promoting an inflationary boom. As we will see, one of the major points of contention between Keynesians and monetarists is whether or not monetary planners are likely to apply discretionary monetary policy in a manner that will actually help stabilize the economy.

Limitations of Monetary Policy from the Keynesian Perspective

Against the background of the Great Depression, early Keynesian economists believed that insufficient aggregate demand was the primary problem of macroeconomics. During the two decades following the publication of the *General Theory,* there was widespread concern among Keynesian economists that monetary policy would be ineffective in combating a depression or serious economic recession. They feared that at such a time the mere injection of more money into the system would do nothing to stimulate aggregate demand. They had three major reasons for holding this view.

1. Vertical Investment Schedule. When an economy is in a depression, investors may be very pessimistic about the future. Many plants may be operating below capacity level. Even though an interest reduction lowers their costs, businesspeople may still feel the demand is so low that they could sell few additional units even at a lower price. The existing excess capacity and pessimism about the future *may* result in a vertical (or nearly vertical) investment schedule with respect to the interest rate during times of depression.

Exhibit 5a illustrates this concern of Keynesian economists. When the investment schedule is almost vertical, even if expansionary monetary policy does lower the interest rate, it will lead to only a small increase in investment and will not be a very potent means by which to stimulate aggregate demand. Many economists believed that this was the case during the Great Depression, given the pervasive business pessimism of that period. In contrast, when the investment schedule is more sensitive to a change in the interest rate (Exhibit 5b), expansionary monetary policy will be able to reduce the interest rate. Under these circumstances, the lower interest rate will stimulate additional investment (increase from I_1 to I_2, Exhibit 5b) and, working through the multiplier, induce a substantial increase in aggregate demand.

EXHIBIT 5 Investment and the interest rate

When the investment schedule is insensitive to the interest rate (a), expansionary monetary policy will be an ineffective tool with which to stimulate aggregate demand. In contrast, if investment is sensitive to changes in the interest rate (b), expansionary monetary policy, working through the interest rate, will stimulate investment and thereby exert a substantial impact on aggregate demand.

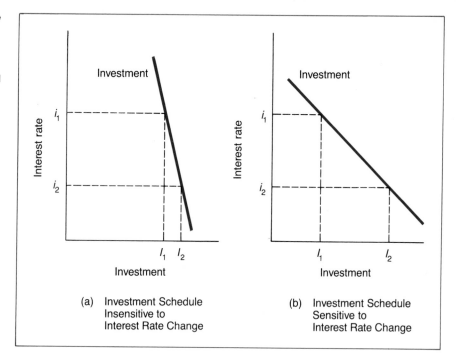

(a) Investment Schedule Insensitive to Interest Rate Change

(b) Investment Schedule Sensitive to Interest Rate Change

2. The Liquidity Trap. Professor Keynes outlined a particular liquidity preference, or demand for money, schedule that would render monetary policy totally ineffective. Suppose that the economy is in a depression and that interest rates are very low. There is little incentive to purchase additional bonds because of their low interest yield. This is particularly true if households think that interest rates may increase in the future. If interest rates rise, one's current decision to buy a bond yielding a 1 percent rate of return will mean foregoing a bond yielding 2 percent next month. Therefore, households may simply decide to stash money away rather than buy bonds at low interest rates. In this case, an increase in the money supply will fail to increase the demand for bonds and to lower interest rates. Since the expansionary monetary policy does not lower interest rates, it cannot induce new investment, which would expand aggregate demand. Monetary policy is rendered ineffective because the **liquidity trap** prevents the interest rate from declining.

Has the U.S. economy ever been caught in the liquidity trap? Today, most economists, both Keynesian and non-Keynesian, do not think so. However, when interest rates are quite low, as was true during the Great Depression, the demand schedule for money may become quite flat. This means that large increases in the supply of money would be necessary to reduce interest rates further and induce any specified amount of investment. Monetary policy would not be totally ineffective, but neither would investment and aggregate demand be very responsive to a specific change in the stock of money.

3. Refusal of Banks to Extend Loans at Low Interest Rates. As we explained in the previous chapter, Federal Reserve policy can inject additional reserves into the banking system. During normal times, profit-seeking banks will use the

Liquidity Trap: Situation in which the demand for money is horizontal with respect to the interest rate. Thus, an increase in the supply of money would not cause the interest rate to decline. Should this situation arise, monetary policy would be unable to stimulate aggregate demand.

OUTSTANDING ECONOMIST
Paul Samuelson (1915–   )

Two generations of economists have been brought up on Paul Samuelson. His best-selling introductory text has gone through eleven editions, and literally millions of students have used it. However, as Professor Samuelson noted, "They don't give Nobel Prizes for writing textbooks." The first American to win the Nobel Prize in economics, he was so honored for "raising the level of analysis in economic science." Samuelson's earlier background was in mathematics. His book, *Foundations of Economic Analysis*,[6] gave precise mathematical meaning to much of economic reasoning. Many graduate students and faculty members have spent months poring over this masterpiece of economics.

Professor Samuelson's interests are wide-ranging, and his contributions to economics reflect this fact. International trade theory, welfare economics, theory of the firm, theory of public goods, and monetary and fiscal theory have all "felt the brush" of this master artist. His *Collected Scientific Papers* have recently been published, and they encompass three lengthy volumes.[7]

Professor Samuelson is an avid modern Keynesian. He believes that discretionary fiscal policy can and should be used to reduce unemployment. Although he accepts the Keynesian view that money exerts an influence on aggregate demand via the interest rate, he has been perhaps the most vociferous critic of the monetarists. His confrontations with Milton Friedman, a well-known monetarist and another Nobel Prize winner, have often enlivened professional meetings.

Professor Samuelson has never held a government position, although he did serve as an adviser to both President Kennedy and President Johnson. Students may be familiar with his column on current economic affairs, which appeared for several years in *Newsweek*. A professor of economics at Massachusetts Institute of Technology for more than three decades, Samuelson favored the temporary wage–price controls when they were introduced by the Nixon administration in 1971. Yet he opposes permanent controls, arguing that they would lead "to long lines, black markets, and consumer desperation." Samuelson does not believe that we will ever again experience a depression such as that of the 1930s. "It's not in the attitude of the consumer. It's not in the attitude of business. The big change since the 1930s is this: In the last analysis, we will not sit by and do nothing when a chronic slump is developing and threatens to feed upon itself. The government, in a democracy, can step in and turn the tide."[8]

Samuelson often criticizes those who perceive economics to be a precise science that yields definitive answers. He argues that economic problems are extremely complex and that generalized conclusions can seldom be drawn. Professor Samuelson is one of the few economists who is well known and respected by both professional economists and the general public. He has bridged the gap between academia and the real world.

---

[6] Paul Samuelson, *Foundations of Economic Analysis* (Cambridge, Massachusetts: Harvard University Press, 1947).

[7] Paul Samuelson, *Collected Scientific Papers of Paul Samuelson* (Cambridge, Mass.: MIT Press, 1966).

[8] Interview in *U.S. News and World Report*, December 14, 1964, p. 65.

---

additional reserves to extend loans, thereby inducing a multiple expansion in the supply of money. But what if the demand for loanable funds were weak during a recession and extending loans were highly risky? Might not banks merely accumulate the additional reserves rather than extend risky loans at a low interest rate?

There was some evidence that banks were reluctant to extend new loans during the Great Depression. Many banks went under during the period from 1930 to 1933. Others were able to survive only because they had substantial excess reserves. Many bankers were anxious to build up their reserves when they had an opportunity to do so. This factor tended to reduce the ability of the Federal Reserve to control directly the supply of money during this period.[9]

However, even in such an extreme case, the monetary authorities have one other tool at their disposal. They can purchase bonds directly from the nonbank public and thereby increase the money supply by at least the amount of the bond purchase. Thus, the building of reserves need not render monetary policy completely ineffective, although it may cause the economy to be less responsive to changes in monetary variables.

The post-World War II experience has greatly reduced the fear of Keynesian economists about the insensitivity of aggregate demand to monetary policy. Numerous studies during the 1950s and 1960s, conducted by both Keynesians and monetarists, have found that monetary policy makes a difference—that aggregate demand is affected by monetary policy even during a recession. In contrast to their predecessors, modern Keynesians generally emphasize the effectiveness of both monetary and fiscal policies. Monetary policy has taken its place alongside fiscal policy as a tool available to macroplanners seeking to steer a stable economic course.

THE MODERN KEYNESIAN VIEW OF MONETARY AND FISCAL POLICY

During the postwar period, the Keynesian view has dominated macroeconomics. As we have indicated, this view has changed over the last several decades. Nonetheless, basic propositions that distinguish the Keynesian perspective remain. We believe that the following four propositions accurately reflect the modern Keynesian position and summarize the major aspects of the Keynesian model we have been constructing.

Proposition 1.   A market-directed capitalist economy is inherently unstable. Minor fluctuations tend to feed on themselves, causing upswings to accelerate into inflationary booms and downturns to decline into major recessions.

Keynesians believe that the investment component of aggregate demand is highly volatile. When business is good, investors respond by expanding their operations. The multiplier magnifies a relatively small increase in investment, causing a significant increase in output. The strong demand, triggered by the expansion in investment, will cause decision-makers to become more optimistic. The business optimism will induce still more investment. During this phase of the business cycle, the upswing feeds on itself, causing output and employment to grow rapidly.

However, as the economy approaches its full-employment supply constraint, the inflation rate accelerates, and the *rate* of growth slows. The reduction in the growth rate will dampen business optimism and investment spending.

---

[9]In the midst of the Great Depression, many banks attempted to build up their reserves so that they would be in a stronger position to deal with a "run" on the deposits of the bank (a situation in which most depositors sought to withdraw their funds because they feared that the bank was close to insolvency). Since the Federal Deposit Insurance Corporation now guarantees the individual deposits of banks up to a maximum of $100,000, the likelihood of a bank run today is extremely low. Recognizing this factor, current-day bankers do not maintain substantial *excess* reserves. Therefore, the probability that modern-day monetary policy will be rendered ineffective as a result of the excess reserve trap is also very low.

Business conditions will worsen because the investment stimulus is absent. Like the upswing, the downswing will feed on itself. Workers will be laid off as investment declines. Personal income will fall, causing households to reduce their consumption, which will further retard aggregate demand. In the Keynesian view, a minor downswing is likely to be magnified into a major recession or even a depression.

Recent economic analysis, including the permanent income hypothesis, has moderated the Keynesian view of the instability of private consumption. However, the cyclical nature of private investment is a continuing problem. According to the Keynesian view, were it not for macropolicy, gyrations in investment spending would cause the market economy to swing between the extremes of economic boom and recession.[10]

> **Proposition 2.** Policy-makers should not attempt to balance the federal budget. Budgetary policy should reflect macroeconomic conditions. During a downswing, countercyclical policy calls for a budget deficit, which will rekindle demand. In contrast, during an inflationary boom, a budget surplus should be planned in order to restrain demand.

Functional Finance: The view that the level of taxation relative to government expenditures —that is, whether stimulus or restraint is needed to promote full employment and price stability—should be determined by the state of the economy rather than by a desire to balance the budget.

The Keynesian revolution temporarily buried the balanced-budget concept. Before Keynes, both laymen and professional economists believed that prudence required the annual balancing of the federal budget. Keynesian analysis replaced the balanced-budget criterion with **functional finance.** The appropriateness of a budget deficit or surplus is dependent on the state of the economy. During an inflationary boom, the budget should be used to restrain demand. Therefore, government withdrawals from the income stream should exceed injections into it. A budget surplus is the appropriate measure. In contrast, when economic stagnation is a problem, budgetary policy should stimulate demand. Injections should exceed withdrawals. Taxes should be less than government expenditures, leaving the budget in deficit. The Keynesian view emphasizes that there is nothing magical about a balanced budget. A balanced budget is clearly of secondary importance to the fiscal needs of the economy.

Keynes believed that functional finance would correct the major defect of capitalism—economic instability. Even before the *General Theory* was published, he stated his belief that his work would provide for economic stability within a capitalist framework and thereby protect all capitalist systems from the "onslaught" of Marxism.

> **Proposition 3.** Both fiscal policy and monetary policy influence economic activity. However, the effects of a change in fiscal policy are more predictable and generally more immediate.

In contrast to their forerunners, late twentieth-century Keynesians believe that monetary policy is quite important. They stress the importance of coordinating monetary and fiscal policies. Thus, when macroexpansion is called for, Keynesians emphasize the need for monetary acceleration to accompany a budget deficit and thereby dampen the tendency of interest rates to rise in response to the Treasury's increase in demand for loanable funds. Similarly, it is appropriate to coordinate monetary restraint with a budget surplus when macroplanners are seeking to moderate an inflationary boom.

---

[10]In contrast, monetarists argue that macropolicy itself is the major source of economic instability. See Chapter 14, pp. 283–288, for a presentation of this view.

However, although modern Keynesians recognize the significance of monetary policy, they continue to place greater faith in the ability of fiscal tools to keep the economy on track. Keynesians argue that during a downturn investment may be relatively insensitive to a decline in interest rates. They stress that investors will probably be reluctant to undertake new projects during a recession, even if expansionary monetary policy pushes interest rates downward. Instead, Keynesians believe that a tax reduction will provide stimulus quickly. When a tax cut is enacted, the amount of taxes withheld from millions of paychecks is reduced, causing disposable income to rise almost immediately. Similarly, an increase in the amount of taxes withheld can cause a rapid reduction in disposable income, thereby retarding aggregate demand.

Proposition 4. Discretionary macroplanning is more likely to lead to economic stability than are fixed rules because discretionary policy permits macroplanners to respond, and to respond quickly, to changing economic conditions.

We live in a dynamic world. The Keynesian view stresses the importance of maintaining planning flexibility that will enable policy-makers to respond to changing economic conditions. In recent years, some economists, particularly those of monetarist persuasion, have advocated various rules and formulas that would restrict the discretionary decision-making powers of macroplanners.[11] Keynesians have generally opposed this approach. Their position is based on the belief that macroplanners, using economic indicators as a guide, are able to reduce the degree of instability below that which would result from an inflexible monetary or budgetary rule. Keynesians are concerned that rigid rules would prohibit macroplanners from responding to unforeseen and extreme economic change. What if we experienced a disastrous crop year or if OPEC nations again quadrupled the price of oil? Keynesians believe that if macroplanners were given a reasonable degree of flexibility, they would follow a course that would minimize the effects of such disruptions.

Economic indicators, such as the rates of inflation and unemployment, can act as guides for macroplanners. During certain periods, economic indicators may give conflicting signals, some indicating economic strength and others suggesting weakness. Of course, macroplanners may not always be correct in their analysis of the future direction of the economy. However, they can easily identify the extremes. According to the Keynesian view, sensible discretionary macroplanning will at least ensure the injection of stimulus during recessionary periods and the exercise of restraint during inflationary booms. Given our forecasting abilities, **macropolicy** may not always be on target; but our knowledge of macroeconomics is continually expanding. Keynesians believe that improvements in our ability to predict the future will enable macroplanners to steer a more stable economic course in the 1980s.

Macropolicy: A combination of fiscal and monetary policy.

THE INFLATION OF THE 1970s—A KEYNESIAN VIEW

During 1967–1980, the inflation rate in the United States averaged almost 7 percent, compared to 2.5 percent during the 20 years following World War II. Most Keynesian economists believe that the high rate of inflation during the

---

[11]The use of monetary rules is discussed in more detail in Chapter 14, pp. 291–292.

1970s was the result of a combination of (a) supply-side economic shocks and (b) demand-side expansionary macropolicy.

Supply-Side Shocks

The supply-side shocks arose from three major sources. First, the oil embargo of late 1973 and the soaring oil prices resulting from the policies of the OPEC cartel during 1973–1974 and again in 1979–1980 disrupted the economy and retarded aggregate supply. Of course, the United States had to export more goods and services in order to pay its bill for imported oil. This reduced the supply of goods available for domestic consumption. In addition, the higher energy prices during the 1970s contributed to economic uncertainty and reduced the productive efficiency of the U.S. capital stock. Energy shortages led to production slowdowns and even plant closings. Structures and equipment designed with little heed for energy efficiency (during a period of low energy prices) became virtually obsolete during the 1970s. Since World War II, the United States has experienced only three years of double-digit inflation—1974, 1979, and 1980. OPEC sharply increased the price of oil during each of these three years. Most economists believe that this linkage was more than a mere coincidence.

Second, the world food market was beset by a number of adverse elements during 1972–1974. Unusual weather patterns led to crop failures in many parts of the world. There was the fabled nonappearance of the normal Peruvian anchovy run in 1972. Soviet grain crops were even worse than usual. Even though the United States was hit less hard than some other nations, these shocks placed upward pressure on food prices in the United States during 1973–1975.

Third, the wage–price controls imposed by the Nixon administration in August 1971 disrupted the economy and generated additional uncertainty. It was hoped that the price freeze would break the inflationary expectations of the period and thereby assist in the control of the wage–price spiral. This did not occur. While the controls were in effect, the incentive to produce some goods was reduced. Inadequate supply and bottlenecks developed. During the freeze, inflation was suppressed, not controlled. When the controls were lifted, the inflation rate accelerated sharply, partially because of pent-up demand generated by the freeze and partially because decision-makers raised their prices to a high level just in case the controls were reimposed.

Expansionary Macropolicy

While economic shocks were adversely affecting aggregate supply, expansionary macropolicy was stimulating aggregate demand. As Exhibit 6 illustrates, during the 1966–1980 period, the national debt expanded at an annual rate of 7.7 percent, compared to 1.4 percent during the 1949–1962 period. Of course, the rapid growth of the national debt reflects the deficit financing and expansionary fiscal policy during the post-1965 period. As the Treasury relied more heavily on deficit financing, the Fed rapidly expanded its holdings of Treasury bonds. The annual rate of growth of the Federal Reserve's Treasury bond holdings was 7.5 percent during the period from 1966 to 1980, compared to only 2.3 percent during 1949–1962. Of course, as the Fed purchases Treasury bonds, newly created money is injected into the economy. The money supply grew nearly three times more rapidly during the period from 1966 to 1980 than it did in the 1950s. Clearly, both monetary policy and fiscal policy were sub-

EXHIBIT 6 How expansionary have monetary and fiscal policies been?

The graph shows the changes in money supply, national debt, and the holdings of U.S. securities by the Federal Reserve for the period from 1940 to 1980. Note that all three have increased more rapidly since 1965 than at any time since World War II. What impact would this have on the price level of a fully employed economy? (Braces indicate the compound annual rate of change for an inclusive period.)

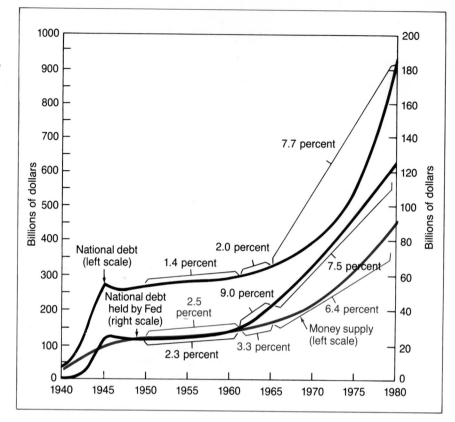

stantially more expansionary during the period from 1966 to 1980 than during any period of comparable length in the post-World War II era.

CAN BUSINESS AND LABOR CAUSE INFLATION?

It is popular to blame inflation on those who raise prices. Politicians, no doubt attempting to distract attention from their own shortcomings, often blame labor unions and big business for inflation. Since both wages and prices rise during an inflation, commentators often debate whether wages are pushing up prices or vice versa. The **cost-push theory of inflation** is based on the view that costs push the price level up. According to this view, powerful labor unions and/or large corporations use their market power to raise wages and profit margins, thereby triggering a wage–price (or price–wage) inflationary spiral. Suppose that an economy were initially experiencing both stable prices and the normal rate of unemployment. What would happen if a major union, that of the automobile workers, for example, could use its monopoly power and the threat of a strike to obtain a very substantial increase in wages? According to the cost-push theory, the generous settlement would have two major consequences. First, the higher labor costs would push up the price of automobiles, trucks, and buses. The consumer price index would rise directly as a result. Automotive products are widely used in the production of other goods (for example, transportation services). The production costs and therefore the price of these

Cost-Push Inflation: The view that labor unions and large corporations cause inflation by using their monopoly power to increase wages and profit margins, thereby triggering a general increase in the price level.

other goods would also rise, providing additional impetus to the inflationary spiral. Second, as other union contracts expired, the leaders of these unions would be under intense pressure to match or exceed the large wage increase of the auto workers. According to the cost-push theory, more lucrative wage settlements in steel, aerospace, electronics, and other basic industries would be triggered as a result of the excessive wage increase obtained by the auto workers. Costs would rise, and product prices would be pushed upward in the process.

Defects of the Simple Cost-Push Theory

Intuitively, the cost-push theory makes a certain amount of sense. Nonetheless, upon close inspection, it suffers from several defects. First, the theory tends to confuse the ability of monopolists to charge a *high* price (or gain a high wage) with their ability to obtain *rising* prices (or wages). According to a well-established proposition in economics, monopoly power will enable a seller to charge a price in excess of the competitive level.[12] However, economic theory does not indicate that a sudden price surge is more likely to occur when unions (or firms) have monopoly power than when competitive conditions are present. Stated another way, both economic theory and empirical studies indicate that strong unions, such as that of the automobile workers, are able to obtain higher wages for their members than would exist in the absence of unionism. However, there is no evidence that union wages *rise* more rapidly than other resource (or product) prices. In order for union or business monopolists to *raise* their wages (prices) more rapidly than other sellers, their monopoly power must be steadily increasing. There is no evidence of a sudden increase in labor and/or business monopoly power that could explain the acceleration in the U.S. rate of inflation that began during the mid-1960s and persisted throughout the 1970s.[13]

Second, it is important to recognize that union wages are also prices. Blaming "price" inflation on "cost" inflation or "wage" inflation involves circular reasoning. It fails to focus on the basic questions. If wages are pushing up prices, what is causing the price of labor (that is, the union wage rate) to rise? Why do prices rise rapidly during some periods, but not in others? Unless the cost-push theory of inflation can answer these questions, it is not a very helpful theory.

Third, proponents of the cost-push theory often ignore the secondary effects. They tend to confuse a change in the relative price of a resource or product with a general rise in the price level. Suppose that the monopoly power of the auto workers (or any other union or business firm) does increase, and thus they are able to obtain a large wage increase at the negotiation table. Will this cause a sustained increase in the rate of inflation? Surprisingly, once we take the secondary effects into account, the answer is no. If the cost of producing automobiles increases as a result of the higher wages, the prices of automobiles will rise. Confronting the higher automobile prices, consumers must either (a) purchase fewer automobiles (quality-constant units) or (b) increase their expenditures on automobiles. Possibly, they will do both.

[12]Those in a microeconomics course will find this proposition explained fully in the chapter on monopoly and high barriers to entry.

[13]Union membership, as a proportion of the total labor force, has actually been declining during the last two decades. Similarly, corporate profits have declined both as a share of GNP and as a percentage of sales during each of the periods of major inflation since World War II.

If consumers purchase fewer (or less expensive) automobiles (a), the amount of labor services required by the automobile industry will decline. Automotive employment will fall (or at least expand by an abnormally small amount). Some workers who would have been able to find jobs in the automobile industry will now be forced into other lines of employment. The labor supply in these alternative employment areas will increase, placing downward pressure on wages and costs in these sectors.

Alternatively, if consumers increase their expenditures on automobiles (b), they will have less income to spend on other things. Consumers will be forced to cut back their spending in other areas. The demand for products, the consumption of which must now be foregone as a result of the increase in expenditures on automobiles, will decline. Market adjustments will place downward pressure on prices in these areas.

Thus, neither (a) nor (b)—that is, neither one of the possible consumer reactions to higher prices—will set off a wage–price spiral. In fact, both will result in downward pressure on prices in other sectors. Relative prices will change. The prices of goods requiring the services of automobile workers will rise, but the prices (and costs) of other goods will decline (or rise less rapidly). Once we consider the secondary effects, there is no reason to expect a generalized, sustained rise in prices merely because the price of one product or resource has risen by a large amount.

Qualifications of the Argument against Cost-Push Inflation

Having indicated the major shortcomings of the cost-push theory, we must now add two qualifications. First, the adjustment process does not take place instantaneously. Continuing with our example, we note that the prices of automobiles may rise long before the secondary effects place downward pressure on prices (and costs) in other sectors. As a result, the rate of inflation may rise *temporarily* above the rate that is consistent with the current rate of monetary growth.

Second, price increases arising from the monopoly power of unions or big business may cause an abnormally high rate of unemployment and/or disrupt the economy. For example, a large wage increase in the automobile industry may adversely affect employment in automobile manufacturing and related industries. Unemployment may rise, and output may decline. Policy-makers may attempt to minimize these effects by pursuing a more expansionary course. Some commentators argue that under such circumstances macroplanners have no choice but to follow an expansionary course. They believe that union monopolies and powerful business interests push their wages and prices above the level that is consistent with full employment. In turn, this induces macroplanners to follow an expansionary course, which eventually generates the inflationary pressure. According to this view, the inflation-causing linkage runs from (a) excessive increases in wages and prices based on monopoly power to (b) unemployment to (c) macroexpansion designed to promote employment.

To date, the advocates of the cost-push theory have failed to present convincing evidence that the monopoly power of business and labor increased significantly during the period from 1967 to 1978 relative to the two decades following World War II. Until this link is made, the theory is certain to remain controversial. Although politicians are likely to find it useful to shift the blame for inflation away from themselves, currently the theory is incapable of explaining satisfactorily the *persistent* increases in the U.S. price level since 1967.

PERSPECTIVES IN ECONOMICS
WHAT CAUSED THE GREAT DEPRESSION?

The Great Depression has exerted an enormous impact upon economic thought and economic institutions. It was a time of massive unemployment, idle factories, and extreme hardship. Many people literally lived from hand to mouth, uncertain of the source of their next meal.

Of course, the United States and other Western economies had experienced recessions prior to the 1930s. During the early stages, most people thought that the economic decline that began with the stock market crash of 1929 would be like previous recessions. They expected that economic conditions would soon begin to improve, just as in the past. But this did not happen—at least, not for several years. For four successive years (1930–1933), real output fell. Unemployment soared. Although recovery did take place during 1934–1937, the economy again fell into the depths of depression in 1938. The depression did not end until the demands of World War II stimulated economic activity.

Why did it happen? The general answer is that the economic exchange system broke down during the 1930s. As Adam Smith pointed out so well in *The Wealth of Nations,* enormous gains are derived from specialization and exchange. For the most part, the comfortable houses, good cars, permanent-press clothing, color television sets, and many other items that we enjoy today are the results of specialization, mass production, and exchange. Without an efficiently operating exchange system, we would not be able to enjoy many of the things that we consider vital to our standard of living.

Disruption of this system leads to a decline in economic growth and the wealth of nations. Several factors contributed to the breakdown

of the exchange system and retarded the potential for economic recovery during the 1930s. Let us consider four of the most important.

1. Monetary Policy: A Sharp Reduction in the Supply of Money Led to a Decline in Aggregate Demand, Deflation, and Economic Uncertainty. In a modern economy, most economic exchange involves money. Money represents the purchasing power that can be used to buy or sell almost any good. Many expensive exchanges also often involve contracts that specify payment *in money terms* over a period of time. When this is the case, it is important that the purchasing power of money does not change in an unexpected manner. If the value of a unit of money changes substantially over time, the actual terms of trade (measured in real terms) will differ from what was intended. Individuals and corporations may not be able to fulfill their contractual obligations. In addition, fear of fluctuations in the value of the monetary unit will discourage individuals from entering into long-term contractual agreements. The volume of exchange will slow, and the potential gains derived from it will be retarded.

This phenomenon was an important cause of the Great Depression. The supply of money expanded slowly but steadily throughout the 1920s.[14] Beginning in 1930, monetary policy suddenly shifted. The supply of money *declined* by 4.2 percent during 1930, by 7.1 percent in 1931, and by 12.3 percent in 1932. Banks failed, and the Fed also failed to act as a lender of last resort in order to head off the huge decline in the supply of money. From 1929 to 1933, the quantity of money in circulation *declined* by 27

percent. Of course, this sharp reduction in the supply of money and the uncertainty that it generated placed downward pressure on wages and prices. The changing purchasing power of money altered the terms of trade of long-term contracts. Farmers, businesspeople, and others who had signed long-term contracts (for example, mortgages) in the 1920s were now unable to meet their fixed money commitments in an economy dominated by falling prices and wages. Bankruptcies resulted. Those trends bred fear and uncertainty, causing still more people to avoid exchanges involving long-term money commitments. Economic exchange came to a standstill. Gains previously derived from comparative advantage, specialization, and exchange were lost.[15]

2. Fiscal Policy: A Tax Increase in the Midst of a Severe Recession Made a Bad Situation Worse. The federal budget had been in surplus throughout the 1920s. Even in 1930, the budget registered a small surplus. But a budget deficit was incurred during 1931, and the prospects were not looking any better for 1932. Of course, prior to the "Keynesian revolution," the dominant view was that the federal budget should be balanced. So the Hoover administration, assisted by the newly elected Democratic majority in the House of Representatives, passed the largest peacetime tax-rate increase in the history of the United States. At the bottom of the income scale, marginal tax rates were raised from 1.5 percent to 4.0 percent in 1932. At the top of the scale, tax rates were raised from 25 percent to 63 percent.

This huge tax increase—a perverse fiscal policy—undoubtedly

---

[14]From 1921 through 1929, the money stock expanded at an annual rate of 2.7 percent, slightly *less rapidly* than the growth in the output of goods and services. Thus, the 1920s were a decade of price stability, even of slight deflation.

[15]For a detailed analysis of the role of monetary policy during the 1930s, see Milton Friedman and Anna J. Schwartz, *A Monetary History of the United States, 1867–1960* (Princeton: Princeton University Press, 1963), particularly the chapter entitled "The Great Contraction."

contributed to the severity of the Depression. Of course, the tax increase reduced disposable income, causing consumption and aggregate demand to fall. During 1932, the year of the tax increase, *real* GNP declined by 14.8 percent. Unemployment rose from 15.9 percent in 1931 to 23.6 percent in 1932. Even after Franklin Roosevelt assumed office, government expenditures only rose from 3.6 percent of GNP in 1930 to 7.9 percent of GNP in 1938. Although budget deficits were present after 1931, they were small in relation to the magnitude of the problem.

3. Tariff Policy: Tariff Increases Retarded International Exchange. Concerned about low agricultural prices and the loss of revenues due to the economic slowdown, the Hoover administration pushed for a substantial increase in tariffs on a wide range of products in early 1930. The tariff legislation took effect in June of 1930. Other countries promptly responded by increasing their tariffs, further slowing the flow of goods between nations. A tariff is, of course, nothing more than a tax on exchanges between parties residing in different countries. Since the increase in tariff rates made such transactions more costly and reduced their volume, additional gains from specialization and exchange were lost.

The high tariff policy of the Hoover administration not only retarded our ability to generate output; it was also ineffective as a revenue measure. The tariff legislation increased the duty (tax) rate on imports into the United States by approximately 50 percent.[16] However, the value of the goods and services imported declined even more sharply. By 1932, the volume of imports to the United States had fallen to $2.1 billion, down from $5.9 billion in 1929. Exports declined by a similar amount. Thus, tariff revenues fell from $602 million in 1929 to $328 million in 1932.[17] Like the monetary and fiscal policies of the era, tariff policy retarded exchange and contributed to the uncertainty of the period.

4. The Stock Market Crash and the Business Pessimism That Followed Reduced Both Consumption and Investment Demand. Economists generally perceive the stock market as an economic thermometer. It registers the temperature but is not the major cause of the fever. However, although historians usually exaggerate the importance of the stock market crash of 1929, there is reason to believe that it was of significance. As the stock market rose substantially during the 1920s, business optimism soared. In contrast, as stock prices plummeted beginning in October of 1929, aggregate demand fell. The falling stock prices reduced the wealth in the hands of consumers. This decline in wealth contributed to the sharp reduction in consumption expenditures in the early 1930s. In addition, the stock market crash changed the expectations of consumers and investors. Both reduced their expenditures as they became more pessimistic about the future. As spending continued to decline, unemployment rose and the situation worsened. Given the impact of both the business pessimism and the perverse policies previously discussed, a minor recession was turned into an economic debacle.

Could It Ever Happen Again?

Of course, we continue to experience economic ups and downs. But most economists believe that it is highly unlikely that we will ever experience a downturn on the scale of the Great Depression again. There are four major reasons for this view.

1. Knowledge of How to Control the Economy. In the 1930s Western nations did not understand how to deal with the business cycle. During that period, both politicians and economists believed that the government should always balance its budget. There was a lack of awareness about the importance of changes in the money supply. As a result, public policy during the 1930s, even under the Roosevelt administration, did little to limit the decline in aggregate demand. Today the situation has changed. We have both the knowledge and the commitment to use the government's expenditure and taxing powers (fiscal policy) and its tools for the control of the money supply (monetary policy) so as to ensure a level of total demand that would preclude a depression.

2. The Federal Deposit Insurance Corporation (FDIC). This government agency insures the deposits of commercial and savings banks. It provides depositors with 100 percent assurance that they will receive the money in their accounts up to the $100,000 ceiling. Since the FDIC protects the depositor, the possibility of bank runs has been eliminated.[18] Because people know their accounts are safe, they do not panic. Before the establishment of the FDIC in 1933, more than 10,000 banks, one-third of the total in the United States, failed during the period between 1922 and 1933. Since then, the number of annual banking failures has seldom exceeded four or five. The establishment of the FDIC,

---

[16]The ratio of duty revenue to the value of imports on which duties were levied rose from 40.1 percent in 1929 to 59.1 percent in 1932. See U.S. Census Bureau, *The Statistical History of the United States from Colonial Times to the Present* (New York: Basic Books, 1976), p. 888.

[17]See Jude Wanniski, *The Way the World Works: How Economies Fail and Succeed* (New York: Basic Books, 1978), pp. 125–148, for additional information on the tariff policy of the period and its impact upon the economy.

[18]A bank run is a situation in which depositors attempt to withdraw their deposits all at once because they fear that the bank is about to go broke. Under a fractional reserve system, of course, the bank will be unable to pay all its depositors at once. Thus, bank runs cause bank failures.

more than any other institutional action, has eliminated a major source of monetary and economic instability.

3. The Increased Importance of Automatic Stabilizers. Our economy is now protected by several built-in forces that tend to counter any reduction in the levels of spending and income. During a recession, welfare payments and unemployment benefits increase automatically. Social security ensures the maintenance of a certain level of income for the elderly even during bad times. Government tax revenues tend to fall and expenditures increase automatically when business conditions are poor. Although some of these stabilizers may have unattractive side effects,

particularly in the long run, these programs serve to cushion the cumulative effects of economic decline.

4. The Size of the Government Sector. Before the Great Depression, government expenditures—federal, state, and local—accounted for one-tenth of our national income. Today they account for more than one-third. The growth in the public sector provides our economy with a large base of stable economic activity that is not determined by expected profits.

Of course, the components of our economy are highly interrelated. Today, as during the 1930s, each of us derives enormous gains from specialization and exchange. If the system

should break down, as it did during the 1930s, our standard of living would plummet. There is no law that can guarantee we will not pursue perverse policies again. However, given our current knowledge of macroeconomics and the presence of built-in stabilization factors, most economists believe that the likelihood of another Great Depression is remote.

Discussion
1. It is commonly held that the stock market crash caused the Great Depression. Do you think this was true? Why or why not? Why has this belief been so widely accepted?
2. Do you think our economy is "depression-proof"? Why or why not?

LOOKING AHEAD

There is no unanimity among economists about how monetary policy works and what it can accomplish. In the following chapter we will present the views of the monetarists, a group of economists who have contributed much to our thinking about monetary policy.

CHAPTER LEARNING OBJECTIVES

1 There is an inverse relationship between the quantity of money demanded and the interest rate. An increase in the supply of money, according to Keynesian theory, will cause people to use their excess money balances to buy bonds. Bond prices will rise, and the interest rate will decline, at least in the short run. On the other hand, restrictive monetary policy will cause the interest rate to rise in the short run.

2 Interest is either a direct or an opportunity cost of every capital investment. *Ceteris paribus,* as the interest rate increases, the quantity of capital investment will decline. Business decision-makers will undertake the projects that they expect to be most profitable. As the interest rate increases, some of the marginal investment projects will be foregone.

3 According to the Keynesian view, expansionary monetary policy will reduce the interest rate, thereby stimulating investment and leading to an increase in aggregate demand. A restrictive monetary policy will increase the interest rate, thereby discouraging investment and reducing aggregate demand. The interest rate is the mechanism that transmits monetary policy in the Keynesian model.

4 If an economy is operating below its long-run supply constraint, expansionary monetary policy will stimulate investment and aggregate demand, causing the equilibrium level of output to rise. Both nominal and real output will expand until the economy's full-employment output rate is reached. Once the economy's supply constraint

is attained, however, monetary acceleration that expands demand further will be inflationary. Expansionary monetary policy, like expansionary fiscal policy, cannot permanently push the equilibrium level of output beyond the economy's long-run supply constraint.

5 As with fiscal policy, proper timing of monetary policy is vital. If properly timed, restrictive monetary policy can dampen aggregate demand and help to control inflationary pressures during an economic boom. On the other hand, when the current level of demand is consistent with stable prices and the economy's supply-constrained output rate, a move to a more restrictive monetary policy will most likely lead to a decline in aggregate demand and real output.

6 There are two ways in which the Treasury can finance a deficit: by borrowing from the public and by borrowing from the Fed. The former method will increase the supply of bonds (and reduce the availability of loanable funds with which to finance private investment), causing the interest rate to rise. In contrast, borrowing from the Fed will increase the money supply and exert downward pressure on interest rates in the short run. It is the more expansionary of the two methods.

7 Early Keynesians feared that expansionary monetary policy might be ineffective during a recession because (a) the interest rate would not decline if the economy was caught in the liquidity trap; (b) investment might be insensitive to a decline in the interest rate; and (c) banks might simply accumulate reserves injected into the system by the Fed. Thus, early Keynesians emphasized fiscal policy almost exclusively. However, the post-World War II experience indicates that both monetary and fiscal policy influence aggregate demand. Modern Keynesians recognize the importance of both.

8 Keynesians charge that a market-directed economy is inherently unstable. However, they believe that fiscal and monetary policy can be utilized to minimize the effects of these unstable tendencies. While recognizing that monetary policy exerts an important influence, modern Keynesians argue that the effects of fiscal policy are more predictable and generally more immediate. They also favor discretionary macropolicy over predetermined rules or formulas.

9 The Keynesian view stresses that both (a) supply-side economic shocks and (b) demand-side expansionary policies contributed to the inflation of the 1970s. Soaring energy prices, worldwide crop failures, and the Nixon wage–price freeze retarded aggregate supply during the decade. Meanwhile, both monetary and fiscal policies were considerably more expansionary than during the 20 years following World War II. This combination—a slow growth in aggregate supply coupled with strong aggregate demand—yielded inflation.

10 Economic analysis indicates that macropolicy, rather than labor unions and large corporations, played the major role in the acceleration of the inflation rate during the 1970s. There is no evidence of a sudden increase in labor and/or business monopoly power that would explain the acceleration of the U.S. inflation rate during this period.

THE ECONOMIC WAY OF THINKING—DISCUSSION QUESTIONS

1 What impact do Keynesians believe that an increase in the supply of money would have on (a) interest rates, (b) the level of investment, (c) aggregate demand, (d) employment, and (e) prices? Explain your answer fully.

2 Will a budget deficit be more expansionary if it is financed by borrowing from the Federal Reserve or from the general public? Explain.

3 Suppose that you have just been appointed chairman of the Council of Economic Advisers. Prepare a press release outlining your views on unemployment, inflation, and proper macropolicy for the next three years.

4 "Macropolicy has been oversold. For years, textbooks told us that it would stabilize the economy and eliminate the business cycle. The historical record is inconsistent with this view. It suggests that improper macropolicy caused the Great Depression, the slow rate of growth during the 1950s, and the inflation of World War II and the 1970s. Macropolicy itself has been the major source of economic instability." Either defend or criticize this view.

5 "The economic stimulus of deficit spending is based on money illusion. When the government issues bonds to finance its deficit, it is promising to levy future taxes so that bondholders can be paid back with interest. Bond financing is merely a substitution of future taxation for current taxation. The stimulus results because taxpayers, failing to recognize fully their greater future tax liability, are deceived into thinking that their wealth has increased Thus, they increase their current spending." Is this view correct? Why or why not?

6 How would each of the following be affected by a 20 percent across-the-board reduction in tax rates?
   (a) Current output
   (b) The rate of inflation
   (c) Tax revenues
   (d) The demand for the services of tax consultants
Be specific, and carefully explain your reasoning.

7 Why did the early followers of Keynes believe that monetary policy would be ineffective during a recession? Why did they believe that at such a time market economies would be plagued by stagnation? Why do most Keynesians reject these views today?

14

INFLATION, INSTABILITY, AND THE CHALLENGE OF THE MONETARISTS

If we cannot achieve our objectives by giving wide discretion to independent experts, how else can we establish a monetary system that is stable, free from irresponsible government tinkering, and incapable of being used as a source of power to threaten economic and political freedom? My choice . . . would be a legislated rule. . . . I would specify that the Reserve System should see to it that the total stock of money rises month by month . . . at an annual rate of X percent, where X is some number between 3 and 5.[1]
Milton Friedman

The ideas of John Maynard Keynes have had a profound effect on almost all economists. His ideas have dominated the thinking of profesional macroeconomists since World War II. Beginning in the 1960s, the Keynesian view has exerted an unmistakable and powerful influence on the economic stabilization policies of the United States. At the same time, however, many professional economists have been engaged in research designed to help us understand the importance of monetary factors. A large part of this research has been undertaken by monetarists, economists who believe that the Keynesian analysis has failed to grasp the significance of erratic monetary policy as a source of economic instability. Led by Nobel Prize-winner Milton Friedman, the monetarists have substantially influenced the direction of macroeconomics.

During the last two decades, the professional debate between the Keynesians and the monetarists has been a focal point of macroeconomics. Of course, many economists—probably most—do not fit neatly into either the Keynesian or the monetarist camp. Neither view is monolithic. Monetarists and Keynesians sometimes differ among themselves on macroeconomic matters. And the actual areas of controversy between the two groups have dwindled. Nonetheless, the monetarist perspective, as much as—if not, recently, more than—that of the Keynesians, has had a powerful influence on modern macroeconomic analysis and deserves our attention. In this chapter, we will discuss the historical roots of monetarism and outline the monetarists' views, which have evolved primarily from the economics literature of the last 20 years.[2] Finally, we will present the consensus view that has emerged from the Keynesian—monetarist debate.

[1] Milton Friedman, "Should There Be an Independent Monetary Authority?" in *In Search of a Monetary Constitution,* ed. Leland B. Yeager (Cambridge, Massachusetts: Harvard University Press, 1962), p. 239.

[2] The origin of the monetarist view as we know it today might well be traced to the monumental work of Milton Friedman and Anna Schwartz, *A Monetary History of the United States, 1867–1960* (New York: National Bureau of Economic Research, 1963).

PREMONETARIST VIEWS: HOW IMPORTANT IS MONEY?

Money is involved in almost every exchange. Usually, the purchaser receives goods, and the seller receives money. If we add together the purchases of all *final products and services,* they are equal to the GNP. The GNP is merely the sum of the price P times the quantity Q of each "final product" purchased. When the existing money stock M is multiplied by the number of times V that money is used to buy final products, this, too, yields the economy's GNP. Therefore,

$$PQ = \text{GNP} = MV$$

Velocity of Money: The average number of times a dollar is used to purchase final goods and services during a year. It is equal to GNP divided by the stock of money.

The V represents velocity, or the annual rate at which money changes hands in the purchase of final products. The **velocity of money** is merely GNP divided by the size of the money stock. For example, in 1981, GNP was $2.92 trillion, and the average money stock (currency plus checkable deposits) was $429 billion. On average each dollar was used 6.8 times to purchase a final product or service. Therefore, the velocity of money was 6.8.

The Classical View— Money Does Not Matter

Equation of Exchange: $MV = PQ$, where M is the money supply, V is the velocity of money, P is the price level, and Q is the quantity of goods and services produced.

The **equation of exchange,** $MV = PQ$, is simply an identity, or a tautology. The equation is defined in such a way that it must be true. Classical economists formulated a theory, the quantity theory of money, using the equation. Put crudely, the **quantity theory of money** hypothesizes that V and Q do not change very much. Thus, an increase in M, the money supply, would cause a proportional increase in prices P. For example, according to the classical view, if the money stock were increased by 5 percent, the price level would rise by 5 percent.

Quantity Theory of Money: A theory, based on the equation of exchange, that hypothesizes that a change in the money supply will cause a proportional change in the price level because velocity and real output are unaffected by the quantity of money.

On what did the classical economists base these conclusions? They thought that institutional factors, such as the organization of banking and credit, the rapidity of transportation and communication, and the frequency of income payments, were the primary determinants of velocity. Since these factors would change very slowly, for all practical purposes the velocity or "turnover" rate of money in the short run was constant. The classicists also thought that flexible wages and prices would ensure full employment. Thus, a change in the money supply could not affect real output.

For classical economists, the link between prices and the money supply was straightforward and quite mechanical. An increase in the money stock meant a proportional increase in prices. The real income of the economy was determined by other factors, such as capital accumulation, technology, and the skill of the labor force. They did not believe that money had any independent effect on real production, income, and employment.

The View of the Early Keynesians—Money Still Does Not Matter Much

For two decades following the publication of the *General Theory,* Keynesians paid little attention to money as a potential vehicle for stimulating demand. During the 1950s, it was popular to draw an analogy between monetary policy and the workings of a string. Like a string, monetary policy could be used to *pull* (hold back) the economy and thereby control inflation. However, just as one cannot *push* with a string, monetary policy could not be used to push (stimulate) aggregate demand.

In the *General Theory,* Keynes offered a plausible explanation of why monetary policy might be an ineffective method of stimulating demand. What if the direction of changes in velocity were opposite to the direction of changes in the money stock? If a 5 percent increase in money led to a 5 percent reduction in velocity, money would fail to change anything. It would directly influence neither real income nor the price level.

Lord Keynes himself was *not* an advocate of the extreme position that money does not matter.[3] However, he did point out that highly atypical conditions could arise that would paralyze the ability of monetary policy to stimulate aggregate demand (see pages 263–264). In the shadow of the Great Depression, many of his early followers took the unusual to be the typical. As we have noted, modern Keynesians believe that money does have an effect on aggregate demand, but as we will see, they disagree with the monetarists about how that effect is transmitted.

THE MODERN MONETARIST VIEW—MONEY MATTERS MOST

Like the classicists, the modern monetarists emphasize that money plays a role in each exchange. Unlike the classicists, however, the monetarists treat money not simply as a medium of exchange but as a valuable good that households demand, just as they demand other goods. Money is valuable because it facilitates exchange *and* is an alternative method of holding wealth. Households make decisions about how much of their wealth they want to hold (or demand) in the form of houses, cars, clothes, stocks, insurance policies, and money. Money, like other goods, is demanded because it yields a stream of services.[4]

What Determines the Demand for Money?

Since monetarists treat money as a good, in general, factors that influence the demand for any good will influence the demand for money balances. Five factors deserve special note.

1. The Price Level. The price level determines the purchasing power of money, or how much it will buy. This means that the amount of money necessary to buy any specific bundle of goods (for example, a week's supply of groceries, gas for the car, or lunches for the kids) will increase with the price level. Thus, as the price level rises, the demand for money balances expands.

2. Income. As real income increases, households demand more of most goods. Money is no exception. People like to reserve a portion of their money balances for conducting transactions. Since the number and magnitude of one's transactions usually increase with income, high-income recipients usually hold (demand) more money than persons of less means. The demand for money is a positive function of income.

---

[3]Keynes thought that money did matter, even during a recession. He stated, "So long as there is unemployment, employment will change in the same proportion as the quantity of money, and when there is full employment, prices will change in the same proportion as the quantity of money." [*The General Theory of Employment, Interest, and Money* (New York: Harcourt, 1936), p. 296].

[4]Be careful not to confuse (a) the demand for money balances with (b) the desire for more income. Of course, all of us would like to have more income, but we may be perfectly satisfied with our holdings of money in relation to our holdings of other goods, given our current level of wealth. When we say that people want to hold more (or less) money, we mean that they want to *restructure* their wealth toward larger (smaller) money balances.

3. The Price of Closely Related Assets. Bonds, stocks, savings accounts, and other liquid forms of holding wealth are close substitutes for money. Although most of these assets are not directly exchanged for goods, they can often be easily transformed into money. Money held in the form of currency, demand deposits, or traveler's checks does not yield an interest return. Even interest-bearing checkable accounts generally pay a lower rate of interest than bonds, for example. Thus, as the interest yield derived from nonmoney financial assets increases, the opportunity cost of holding money rises. Higher interest rates make it less attractive to hold money, particularly in non-interest-bearing forms. Therefore, there is an inverse relationship between the amount of money balances demanded and the interest rate.

4. Expected Rate of Inflation. As the price of goods (houses, cars, stocks, etc.) rises, the value of the dollar declines. Inflation diminishes the relative value of money, increasing the opportunity cost of holding it. People do not want to hold assets that they expect to decline in value. When people expect inflation to diminish the value of money, the attractiveness of holding money is reduced. During an inflation, money becomes something like a hot potato. People do not want to get burned by holding substantial amounts of money while it declines in value. Therefore, when the **expected rate of inflation** rises, the demand for money balances will decline.

Expected Rate of Inflation: The rate at which people anticipate future prices will rise.

5. Institutional Factors. How easily can money be borrowed if one runs short? How difficult is it to "match up" one's current income and expenditures? Does one's income arrive in a steady stream, or does it come once a year at harvest time? The answers to these questions will influence how much money, on average, a household will demand. They, in turn, are determined primarily by institutional factors that influence credit and the timing of one's personal income. These factors change over time and thereby alter the demand for money.

How have changes in institutional factors influenced the demand for money in recent years? Both evidence and logic suggest that they have reduced it. The widespread use of general-purpose credit cards helps households to match up their bills with their receipt of income. Readily available short-term loans have reduced the need to maintain a substantial cash balance for emergencies. The movement away from agriculture means that more families have a steady income every two weeks or once each month, rather than an unpredictable income two or three times per year. This steady income makes planning easier. All these factors have reduced the need for households to maintain large cash balances.

These factors would cause the demand for money balances to:

Increase	Decrease
1. A higher price level	1. A lower price level
2. Expanding real income	2. Falling real income
3. Lower interest rates	3. Higher interest rates
4. Expectation of falling prices	4. Expectation of rising prices
5. Institutional factors that make it more difficult for persons to match up income and spending	5. Institutional factors that make it easier for persons to match up income and spending

Exhibit 1 shows that the velocity of money climbed from less than 3 in the mid-1950s to 6.8 in 1981. Today, each dollar turns over much more frequently in the purchase of final goods and services. Institutional factors like credit cards, regular incomes, and readily available short-term loans allow us to handle a larger volume of transactions with a smaller bank account than was possible 20 years ago. The demand for money balances has been reduced.

Other things constant, there is an inverse relationship between the demand for money balances and velocity. An increase in the velocity of money indicates that each unit of money is being used more intensively. Therefore, an increase in velocity makes it possible to carry out a given level of business activity with a smaller money balance. It is important to note that even though the velocity of money has increased in recent decades, the increase has been steady. This implies that the year-to-year fluctuations in the demand for money have been moderate.

The Impact of Money

Monetarists believe that the basic aggregate markets—current goods and services, labor resources, loanable funds, and money—are highly interrelated. Supply and demand work together to determine both prices and output levels in these markets. Whereas Keynesians believe that monetary policy reduces the interest rate and thereby stimulates private investment, monetarists argue that there is a much more direct link between output and changes in the supply of money.

Monetarists believe that expansionary monetary policy creates an **excess supply of money.** People adjust by increasing their spending on a wide range of goods, causing aggregate demand to expand. Similarly, monetary restriction creates an **excess demand for money,** causing people to reduce their spending. Monetary policy is not dependent on the interest rate for its effectiveness.

Unlike the classical economists, monetarists do not believe that prices adjust easily and rapidly. They believe that the market process will bring about equilibrium only with the passage of time. The role of time in the adjust-

Excess Supply of Money: Situation in which the actual money balances of individuals and business firms are in excess of their desired level. Thus, decision-makers will spend money buying other assets and goods as they reduce their actual balances to the desired level.

Excess Demand for Money: Situation in which the actual balances of individuals and business firms are less than their desired balances. Thus, decision-makers will reduce their spending as they expand their actual balances.

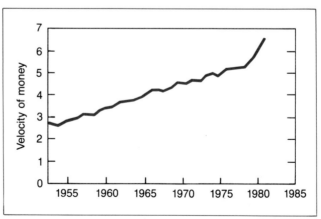

EXHIBIT 1   The increasing velocity of money

The velocity of money (GNP divided by the money stock) increased from less than 3 in the mid-1950s to 6.8 in 1981. Today, each dollar is being used more often to purchase goods and services.

ment process explains why monetarists believe that the short-run impact of monetary policy differs substantially from its impact in the long run. According to monetarists, short-run fluctuations in the trend rate of growth of the money supply will exert their primary effect on output. Although this "output effect" will be significant, it will be temporary. In the long run, as markets have time to adjust more fully, the impact of monetary factors will be almost exclusively on prices. Output will be largely unaffected, since it will be determined by such factors as changes in the labor force, capital stock, natural resources, and technology.

Expanding the Money Supply and Aggregate Demand

What would happen if the Federal Reserve decided to follow a more expansionary policy than it had been following? For example, suppose that it bought bonds at a faster rate, expanding the money supply at an annual rate of 8 percent, up from 4 percent. Exhibit 2 illustrates the impact of this expansionary monetary action on the markets for (a) money balances and (b) current goods and services.[5] In the money market, the monetary expansion would create an excess supply of money balances. People would attempt to adjust by reducing their money holdings. Everybody knows how this could be accomplished—through increased spending! The aggregate demand for current goods would rise as people spent more on consumer goods, capital goods, education, and other items.

If the economy were operating below the economy's full-employment supply constraint, Q_0 for example, the expansionary monetary policy would push the economy toward its long-run capacity (Q_1). Real output would expand as previously unemployed manpower and machinery were brought into use. Since the economy was previously operating below its long-run capacity, prices would not necessarily rise.

What would happen if the monetary acceleration continued once the long-run, full-employment supply constraint of the economy had been reached? Stated another way, what would happen if an expansionary monetary course were followed, even though the economy was already at its long-run, supply-constrained output level (Q_1, Exhibit 2)? According to the monetarist view, in the short run, the long-run, full-employment level of output would be surpassed. The rate of unemployment would temporarily fall below its long-run, normal rate.

In order to understand fully the monetarist position, it is necessary to reflect on the market adjustment process. Suppose that you were a radio manufacturer and that there were an increase in demand for your product. How would you know it? You would probably first note that your monthly sales were up. However, sales sometimes rise for several months and then tumble downward for a month or so. Several good months do not necessarily indicate a *permanent* expansion in demand. Therefore, if you were a typical business decision-maker, you would initially attempt to expand production in order to accommodate the strong demand and keep your inventories from declining sharply. Several months of the strong demand would be necessary to convince you that market conditions merited a price increase. You would not want to raise prices until you were convinced that the expansion in demand for your product was permanent. An unmerited price rise would drive customers to your

---

[5]For additional detail on aggregate demand and aggregate supply within the price–quantity framework, see Chapter 11, Addendum, pp. 229–232.

EXHIBIT 2 Money and ex-panding aggregate demand

An increase in the supply of money [shift from S_0 to S_1 in graph (a)] will generate a temporary excess in holdings of money, which will cause persons to increase their spending on goods and services. Aggregate demand will expand. If the output rate is below the long-run capacity level, for example, Q_0 [graph (b)], full employment with price stability can be attained. However, efforts to push output beyond the long-run supply constraint of the economy (Q_1) will be successful only in the short run. Expansionary monetary policy may *temporarily* push sales to Q_2. Output will expand. But with time, inflation will result (prices will rise to P_1), and output will fall back to the long-run, full-employment output level (Q_1). At this higher level of money income (P_1Q_1), the demand for money will increase (shift from D_0 to D_1), thereby restoring equilibrium in the money market.

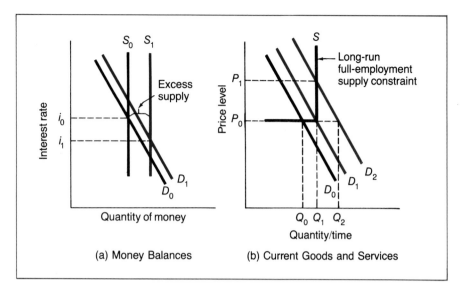

(a) Money Balances   (b) Current Goods and Services

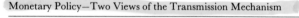

Monetary Policy—Two Views of the Transmission Mechanism

1. *Keynesian view*
   Money supply ⟶ interest rate ⟶ investment ⟶ aggregate demand
2. *Monetarist view*
   Money supply ————————————————⟶ aggregate demand

competitors. In addition, some of your customers would have contracts specifying price and delivery for as many as 6 to 12 months into the future. Thus, contractually you would be unable to raise these prices, even after you became convinced that the demand for your product had increased.

As a result of these forces, the initial impact of the expansion in demand is primarily on output, even when the economy is at its long-run capacity level. *Initially,* business decision-makers will hire more employees, cut down on maintenance time, and assign more overtime. Unemployment will fall below its normal rate. However, this pace cannot be maintained. After 6 to 18 months, the excess demand in markets will cause prices to rise, and output will fall back to a long-run equilibrium level.

Thus, the monetarist view stresses that although expansionary monetary policy can *temporarily* push unemployment below its normal rate (and output beyond the economy's supply constraint), in the long run such a policy will cause inflation without *permanently* reducing the rate of unemployment.

Disaster and a Reduction in the Money Stock

What would happen if someone, perhaps a mischievous Santa Claus, destroyed half of the U.S. money stock? Suppose that when we get up one morning, half of the cash in our billfolds and checkable deposits in our banks is gone. Ignore, for the sake of analysis, the liability of bankers and the fact that the federal government would take corrective action. Just ask yourself, "What has changed because the money supply has been drastically reduced?" The work force is the same. Our buildings, machines, land, and other productive resources are

EXHIBIT 3 A reduction in the supply of money

When the stock of money declines, an excess demand for money balances results. Individuals seek to restore their money balances by spending less. Aggregate demand declines from D_0 to D_1, and sales fall to Q_1 when prices are inflexible downward. With time, the excess supply in the market for goods and services will cause prices to decline, to P_1, for example. However, this method of restoring equilibrium will be a painful process, beset by economic recession or even a depression.

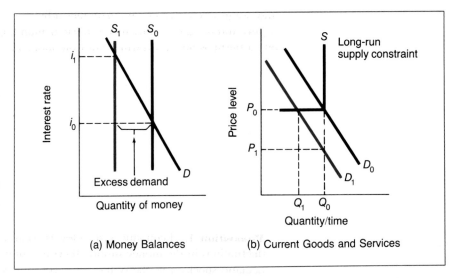

(a) Money Balances

(b) Current Goods and Services

untouched. There are no consumer durables missing. The gold is still in Fort Knox. Only the money, half of yesterday's supply, is gone.

Exhibit 3 sheds some light on the situation. In order to make things simple, let us assume that before the calamity, individuals were holding their desired level of money balances for current needs. The reduction in the supply of money, the shift from S_0 to S_1, would result in an excess demand for money. Individuals would try to restore at least part of their depleted money holdings.

How do people build up their money balances? All poor, struggling college students should know the answer. They spend less. With almost everybody spending less, the aggregate demand for current goods and services would fall (shift from D_0 to D_1, Exhibit 3b).

If prices and wages were perfectly flexible, as the classicists thought, this would not cause any big problem. Both product and resource prices would be cut in half, but real GNP would remain unchanged (that is, it would stay at Q_0). In the real world, however, things are not so simple. In the short run, wages and prices tend to be inflexible, particularly downward. As a result of the decline in aggregate demand, sales would fall to Q_1. An excess supply of many products would exist. Business inventories would rise. Factories would operate at levels far below capacity, and unemployment would rise. Our mischievous Santa Claus would have brought about disaster without even touching any of our real assets. With time, the excess supply would result in declining prices, but recessionary conditions would permeate the economy long before falling prices would be able to restore equilibrium at price level P_1 and output Q_0.

Why is it that prices do not fall in response to the decline in demand? In the first place, several months may pass before business decision-makers recognize that there has been a genuine reduction in demand for their product. Even after they recognize it, additional time will be necessary before contract and catalogue prices can be adjusted to reflect the new demand conditions more accurately.

Similarly, job seekers will not initially recognize that there has been a decline in demand for their services. Thus, they, too, will initially be reluctant to accept jobs paying a lower money wage. Anticipating that they will soon find a job at their old money wage, they will extend their employment-search time, thereby increasing the duration of their unemployment. Therefore, prices and wage rates will not immediately adjust to the reduction in the money supply and the accompanying decline in demand. Rather, rising unemployment and a business slowdown will result from monetary restriction.

DISCRETIONARY POLICY AND THE MONETARIST VIEW

In order to delineate the monetarist position in the clearest way, it is useful to break it down into basic components. Although monetarists believe that money is highly important, it does not follow that they believe monetary policy to be a cure-all for economic ills; in fact, they stress that discretionary monetary policy is more likely than not to be destabilizing. Let us consider the basic propositions of the monetarist position in relation to economic stability and discretionary policy.

> **Proposition 1.** Economic instability is almost exclusively the result of fluctuations in the money supply. If erratic monetary policy did not inject demand shocks into the system, the economy would be relatively stable.

Monetarists believe that the business cycle is generated largely by inappropriate monetary policy. The problem of economic instability stems from the stop–go nature of our past monetary policy. Rapid monetary expansion generates an economic boom and eventually leads to an increase in the rate of inflation. Typically, the monetary authorities then respond to the inflation by applying the monetary brake. This monetary slowdown thrusts the economy into a recession. Milton Friedman, the leading spokesman for monetarists, in his presidential address before members of the American Economic Association in 1967, stated:

Every major contraction in this country has been either produced by monetary disorder or greatly exacerbated by monetary disorder. Every major inflation has been produced by monetary expansion.[6]

Monetarists believe that the market economy contains ingredients that minimize economic instability. Consumption spending, in particular, is a stabilizing element. Since current consumption is largely a function of one's expected future income (see permanent income hypothesis, pages 160–163), consumption spending is relatively stable over the business cycle. The stability of consumption expenditures will assure that a temporary economic expansion does not spiral into a raging economic boom, according to the monetarist view. Similarly, the strength of consumption expenditures will prevent an uncontrolled economic plunge. If disturbances introduced by monetary fluctuations were eliminated, the

---

[6]Milton Friedman, "The Role of Monetary Policy," *American Economic Review* (March 1968), p. 12.

monetarists believe that the economy would be relatively stable, at least in comparison with past performance.

Proposition 2. Expansionary monetary policy cannot permanently reduce the unemployment rate and increase the pace of economic growth. In the long run, efforts to use monetary policy to accomplish these goals will not only fail but will be inflationary.

The distinction that monetarists make between the short-run and long-run impact of a change in monetary policy cannot be overemphasized. Although monetarists concede that changes in the supply of money have important short-run effects on output and employment, they do not believe that monetary policy can effectively alter these real variables in the long run.

Even when the economy is operating at its full-employment output rate, monetarists believe that monetary acceleration will *initially* exert its primary impact on output and employment rather than on prices. For a time, decision-makers will be fooled by monetary acceleration. *Initially,* as they observe the increase in demand for their product, they will not know whether it reflects a temporary or a permanent change. Similarly, they will be unsure whether there has been (a) an increase in demand for *their product relative to other products* or (b) an increase in demand for all products. The former calls for an expansion in output; the latter does not. Confused by the situation, many producers will choose to expand output and employment. But as producers, in general, attempt to follow this course, they will bid up prices. Eventually, decision-makers will discover that there has been a generalized increase in demand, rather than a specific and temporary increase in demand for their product. As they adjust to this situation, incorporating the higher price level (or in the dynamic case, the higher inflation rate) into their market decisions, output and employment will return to their previous rates.

What will happen when the monetary authorities shift gears, deciding to decelerate the growth rate of the money supply in order to fight the inflation? Monetarists stress that, as with monetary acceleration, the initial impact of monetary deceleration will be on output. For a time, many decision-makers will believe that the demand for their product has fallen relative to other products. They will cut back output and lay off workers. In the short run, the unemployment rate will rise above its long-run, normal level.

Monetarists strongly reject the view that inflation can be traded off for a lower rate of unemployment. Although monetary acceleration leads to less unemployment in the short run, it will lead to more unemployment and inflation in the future. According to the monetarists' view, the trade-off is between (a) a lower unemployment rate in the present and the immediate future and (b) an acceleration in the rate of inflation 12 to 24 months in the future, and an abnormally high rate of unemployment when inflation subsides.

Proposition 3. The expansionary impact of pure fiscal policy will be largely offset by reductions in private spending caused by rising interest rates, which are an inevitable result of the government borrowing.

Whereas Keynesians stress the effectiveness of fiscal policy, monetarists argue that budget deficits will have only a moderate impact on aggregate demand

1. *Keynesian view*
   Budget deficit or surplus ⟶ aggregate demand
2. *Monetarist view*
   Budget deficit or surplus ⟶ interest rate ⟶ velocity of money ⟶ aggregate demand

Pure Fiscal Policy: A change in taxes or government spending that is not financed by borrowing from the Federal Reserve. Thus, the policy does not change the supply of money.

unless they are accompanied by a change in the money supply.[7] Monetarists stress that expansion by **pure fiscal policy,** a fiscal action that does not alter the money supply, will lead to rising interest rates, which will retard private spending.

Suppose that the Treasury is running a $25 billion deficit. If the money supply is to remain unchanged, the deficit will have to be financed by borrowing in the private loanable funds market.[8] What will happen when the Treasury borrows an additional $25 billion in the loanable funds market? According to the monetarist view, the expansion in Treasury borrowing will increase the demand for loanable funds and drive interest rates upward. The rising interest rates will cause private investment and consumption to be partially priced out of the market. Private investors will not undertake some construction and business expansion projects because these are now too expensive. Similarly, higher interest rates (and an increase in taxes necessitated by the interest payments on the enlarged debt) will "squeeze out" private spending on housing, automobiles, and a host of other consumer goods. The anticipated reduction in private spending in response to rising interest rates caused by a budgetary deficit is known as the **crowding-out effect.**

Crowding-Out Effect: A reduction in private spending as a result of high interest rates generated by budget deficits that are financed by borrowing in the private loanable funds market. If this effect is strong, pure fiscal policy loses much of its impact.

Monetarists believe that the crowding-out effect will largely offset the impact of an expansionary fiscal action. They argue that deficit spending results mainly in the substitution of public for private sector spending. Of course, if the government could borrow the $25 billion without bidding up the interest rate, private spending would not be crowded out. Monetarists argue that this is unlikely to be the case. Few individuals would have excess funds stuffed away in a pillowcase that they would be willing to make available to finance the government deficit.

The monetarists' view of fiscal policy is symmetrical. Just as they question the effectiveness of fiscal expansion, they deny that a budget surplus exerts a significant restraining influence. As a result of the budget surplus, the Treasury's demand for loanable funds will decline, placing downward pressure on the interest rate. The lower interest rate will stimulate additional private spending, which will largely offset the restraining influence of the budget surplus.

---

[7]Milton Friedman, in his *Newsweek* column of August 7, 1967, made this point clear: "Deficits have often been connected with inflation, but they need not be. Whether deficits produce inflation depends on how they are financed. If, as so often happens, they are financed by creating money, they unquestionably do produce inflationary pressure. If they are financed by borrowing from the public, at whatever interest rate is necessary, they may still exert some minor inflationary pressure. However, their major effect will be to make interest rates higher than they otherwise would be."

[8]The only other method of financing the deficit would be an expansion in borrowing from the Federal Reserve. As we noted in Chapter 12, when the Fed buys bonds, whether from the Treasury or from private dealers, the money supply will expand. Thus, a deficit financed by borrowing from the Federal Reserve is not a pure fiscal action.

Keynesians and Monetarists—A Summary of Their Views

Keynesians	Monetarists
1. Market economy is inherently unstable; macropolicy can correct this deficiency.	1. Erratic monetary policy is the major source of instability; the market economy has self-correcting, stabilizing features.
2. Policy-makers should plan budget deficits during recessions and budget surpluses during inflationary booms in order to promote full employment and economic stability.	2. Macropolicy cannot *permanently* reduce unemployment and stimulate the pace of economic growth. Efforts to do so with demand-stimulus policies will cause inflation.
3. Fiscal policy is both more potent and more predictable than monetary policy.	3. Fiscal policy is relatively impotent because of the crowding-out effect.
4. Discretionary macroplanning is more likely to lead to stability than are fixed rules.	4. A fixed monetary rule is more likely to lead to stability than is discretionary macropolicy.
5. Monetary policy is transmitted indirectly via the interest rate.	5. Monetary policy exerts a direct impact on the demand for goods and services.
6. Fiscal policy exerts a direct impact via the flow of expenditures.	6. Fiscal policy is transmitted indirectly via the interest rate and the velocity of money.

Although monetarists stress the offsetting effects generated by fiscal action, it is not true that fiscal policy is considered *totally* ineffective within the monetarist framework. Remember that the monetarist view emphasizes that a pure fiscal action will cause the interest rate to rise. At the higher interest rate, businesses and households will find it more costly to hold money balances. Since it will now be more expensive to hold money, decision-makers will economize on its use to a greater degree. They will attempt to use their money balances more intensively. The velocity of money will rise. Assuming that the supply of money is constant, an increase in the velocity of money will have an expansionary effect, if only a moderate one, on aggregate demand.

Just as in the case of monetary policy, the difference between the monetarist and Keynesian views of fiscal policy boils down to the transmission mechanism. Keynesians believe that fiscal policy has a direct effect on aggregate demand, whereas monetarists argue that the impact of a fiscal action is transmitted indirectly via the interest rate and the velocity of money to aggregate demand.

Proposition 4. The difficulties of timing macropolicy properly and the nature of the political process lead one to predict that discretionary macropolicy will be destabilizing.

If macropolicy is going to reduce instability, the effects of expansion or restraint must be felt at the proper time. Given our limited ability to forecast the future accurately, it will be extremely difficult to follow a proper stabilization course. A policy change may be needed before political decision-makers recognize the need. The political process will generally lead to additional delays. Even after

EXHIBIT 9   The money interest rate and inflation

The expectation of inflation will cause the demand for loanable funds to increase (shift from D_1 to D_2) and the supply of loanable funds to decrease (shift from S_1 to S_2). The result will be higher money interest rates.

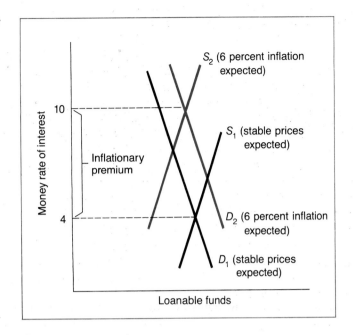

the course of the loan. They may also shift their funds to real assets (for example, land or buildings) that are expected to increase in value with inflation.

Thus, when monetary expansion leads to an acceleration in the inflation rate, the added inflation will cause money interest rates to rise, not fall. Exhibit 10 illustrates the impact of monetary policy on the rates of inflation and interest in the United States for the 1950–1980 period. During the 1950–1963 period, the money supply grew at a moderate rate, 2.2 percent annually. Both the inflation rate and interest rate fluctuated within a very narrow band during this period. The average annual yield on corporate bonds (AAA) never exceeded 4.4 percent during the 14 years. Beginning in the mid-1960s, monetary policy became more expansionary. The annual growth rate of the money supply rose to 4.2 percent during 1964–1967. The monetary acceleration was accompanied by increases in the inflation rate, to 2.9 percent annually, and in the interest rate, to 5.5 percent. The trend continued during 1968–1973. More rapid monetary growth led to still higher rates of both inflation and interest. The monetary acceleration was reversed during 1974–1976. A decline in both the rate of inflation and the rate of interest accompanied the move toward a more restrictive monetary policy. Beginning in 1977, the monetary authorities again reversed their course. The money supply grew at an annual rate of 7.7 percent for 1977–1980. A sharply higher inflation rate and rising interest rates accompanied the monetary acceleration during this period. Just as the incorporation of expectations into our analysis indicates, when monetary expansion leads to inflation, it will also result in rising money rates of interest.

The importance of monetary policy to the rates of inflation and interest can be observed worldwide. The highest interest rates in the world are found in countries like Chile, Brazil, and Argentina, where the supply of money has often expanded at annual rates in excess of 30 percent. Low interest rates will be found

EXHIBIT 10   The money supply, inflation, and interest rates

Time Period	Annual Rate of Change in Money Stock[a]	Annual Rate of Change in Consumer Prices		Interest Rate (AAA Corporate Bond)	
		Initial Year	Terminal Year	Initial Year	Terminal Year
1950–1963	2.2	1.0	1.2	2.6	4.3
1964–1967	4.2	1.3	2.9	4.4	5.5
1968–1973	6.4	4.2	6.2	6.2	7.4
1974–1976	5.0	11.0	5.8	8.6	8.4
1977–1980	7.7	6.5	13.5	8.0	11.9

[a]The money supply data are for M-1.

in countries like Switzerland (or the United States during the 1950s and 1960s), where monetary expansion is moderate, 3 to 4 percent annually.

How quickly will financial markets respond to a change in the direction of monetary policy? The adaptive expectations hypothesis implies that interest rates will lag behind both the monetary acceleration and the inflation rate. In the 1970s, as the inflation rate accelerated, interest rates did appear to lag behind. Thus, looking backward, the real rate of interest was actually negative throughout much of the 1970s.

The rational expectations hypothesis implies that people will adjust rapidly, as soon as they perceive a change in policy direction. There is some recent evidence indicating individuals are beginning to react more promptly to changes in monetary policy. For example, during the six-month period from May to November 1980, there was a rapid acceleration in monetary growth from approximately 6 percent to a 16 percent annual rate. Financial markets, anticipating an acceleration in the inflation rate, responded quickly. The prime interest rate, the rate banks charge their best customers, soared from 11 percent in July 1980 to 21.5 percent in December 1980. In this instance, the temporary period of lower interest rates was quite short. The sharply higher rates lagged behind the monetary acceleration by only a few months, just as would be implied by the rational expectations hypothesis.

PULLING IT ALL TOGETHER

For 30 years following the Keynesian revolution, most economists thought economic conditions would be relatively stable if macropolicy injected demand stimulus into the system during a recession and exercised demand restraint during an inflationary boom. Now expectations theories, public choice analysis, and recent history indicate that stabilization policy is far more complex.

Our knowledge of exactly how expectations are determined and when and why they change is imprecise. Nonetheless, economic theory indicates they are highly important. Incorporation of expectations into our model points to the limitations of macropolicy. To the extent that people eventually adjust to demand-stimulus policies, persistent expansionary macropolicy may generate inflation without *permanently* reducing unemployment below its normal, long-run rate. Similarly, a shift to a more restrictive policy in order to combat inflation is most likely to cause output to slow and unemployment to rise, at least *tempo-*

rarily, to abnormally high rates. There are no easy solutions. Finding ways to accelerate the rate of economic growth and promote a high rate of employment is difficult. Once again, economics might be called the dismal science. The debate between the proponents of adaptive and rational expectations does not greatly alter our understanding of macropolicy's limitations, although it does have important implications for the timing and pattern of the adjustment process. And public choice theory has shown that we can expect discretionary macropolicy to have an inflationary bias and to be used as much for political purposes as for economic stabilization.

The bottom line of our analysis is that steering a stable course is substantially more difficult than was envisioned at the beginning of the 1970s. Recognition that there are limits on what can be accomplished with macropolicy does *not* necessarily mean instability and a high rate of unemployment will persist in the future. It does imply, however, that we must change the focus of our search for solutions. We will look at some possibilities for new directions in the following chapter.

CHAPTER LEARNING OBJECTIVES

1 Prior to the 1970s, there was evidence to suggest that higher rates of inflation were associated with lower rates of unemployment. This relationship could be mapped out on a curve, known as the Phillips curve.

2 Expansionary macropolicy may be able to reduce *temporarily* the rate of unemployment, because decision-makers are (a) unsure whether the increase in current demand is temporary or permanent, (b) unable to adjust previously negotiated long-term contracts *immediately,* and (c) misled into believing that the inflationary price and wage increases reflect a relative increase in demand for *their* product or service.

3 According to the adaptive expectations hypothesis, individuals base their expectations on the immediate past. The expectations in the short run lag behind actual events. In this view, if an inflationary course is pursued, the *short-run* trade-off of lower unemployment for an accelerated inflation rate holds true. However, individuals will *eventually* come to expect the higher inflation rate and alter their decisions accordingly. This will cause the rate of unemployment to return in the long run to its normal level.

4 The initial effects of macrodeceleration, according to the adaptive expectations hypothesis, will also be on output rather than on prices. The macrodeceleration will cause output to slow and the unemployment rate to rise temporarily above its normal, long-run rate. The primary impact of macrorestraint on prices may come later, perhaps several months after the rate of growth of output begins to slow.

5 In the long run, there is no evidence that inflationary policies can reduce the unemployment rate—that inflation can be "traded off" for unemployment. Thus, the long-run Phillips curve is vertical, or nearly vertical.

6 Collective choice theory indicates that strong political pressures exist that are likely to lead to a stop–go macropolicy with an inflationary bias. Such a policy will cause the annual inflation–unemployment points plotted on a Phillips curve diagram to rotate in a clockwise manner and spiral upward. The actual inflation–unemployment data imply that this is what happened during the post-1967 inflation.

7 According to the rational expectations hypothesis, people will (a) comprehend the impact of macropolicy changes on prices and employment and (b) adjust their choices accordingly and rapidly. For example, when confronting an expansionary macropolicy, lenders will demand higher interest rates, union representatives higher money wage rates, and business firms higher prices on long-term contractual sales. According to the rational expectations theory, these actions will cause the inflation rate to rise almost

immediately while largely offsetting the employment and output effects of the expansionary policy.

8 Given rational expectations, the anticipated impact of a macropolicy change is unpredictable. Discretionary macropolicy is likely to be a major source of instability. The implication of this theory is that policy-makers should seek to follow a consistent, stable course.

9 The critics of the rational expectations view argue that it is unrealistic to assume that people possess the knowledge necessary to respond consistently to changes in macropolicy. Thus, they believe decision-making that is based on a simple rule of thumb (in the future, things will be very similar to what they have been in the recent past) is most common and more probable in the real world.

10 Expectations as to the future rate of inflation will influence money interest rates. During a time of inflation, money interest rates will include an inflationary premium. Although expansionary macropolicy may temporarily reduce the money rate of interest, if pursued persistently it will lead to inflation and high interest rates. The high money interest rates in the United States during the 1970s are consistent with this view.

11 Incorporation of expectations into our macroeconomic thinking indicates the limitations of macropolicy. To the extent that decision-makers adjust to demand-stimulus policies, persistent expansionary macropolicy may lead to inflation without *permanently* reducing the unemployment rate below its long-run, normal rate. Recognition of the limitations of macropolicy forces economists to search more diligently for new ways to deal with instability, inflation, and unemployment.

THE ECONOMIC WAY OF THINKING — DISCUSSION QUESTIONS

1 "In order to achieve the nonperfectionist's goal of high enough output to give us no more than 3 percent unemployment, the price index might have to rise by as much as 4 to 5 percent per year." (Paul Samuelson and Robert Solow, American Economic Association meetings, December 1959)

   (a) Do you think that a rate of inflation of 4 or 5 percent would enable us to achieve the nonperfectionist's goal of 3 percent unemployment today? Why or why not?

   (b) Would a rate of inflation of 15 or 20 percent enable us to achieve the goal? If so, could the 3 percent unemployment level be maintained? Why or why not?

2 State in your own words the adaptive expectations hypothesis. Explain why adaptive expectations imply that macroacceleration will only *temporarily* reduce the rate of unemployment.

3 Compare and contrast the rational expectations hypothesis with the adaptive expectations hypothesis. If expectations are formed "rationally" rather than "adaptively," will it be easier or more difficult to decelerate the inflation rate without causing an economic recession? Explain.

4 "The high rates of interest during the 1970s are reflective of the Fed's tight money policies. If the Fed would loosen monetary growth a little more, lower interest rates and more rapid economic growth would result." Indicate why you either agree or disagree with this view.

5 The analysis summarized by Exhibits 7 and 8 assumes adaptive expectations. How would the outcome differ if people adjusted quickly to changes in macropolicy, as the rational expectations hypothesis implies?

6 Outline the major economic problems that plagued the U.S. economy during the 1970s. How would each of the following explain these problems: (a) Keynesians, (b) monetarists, (c) supply-side economists, and (d) proponents of the rational expectations view? Are there substantial points of agreement among these alternative views? Explain.

16

**NEW DIRECTIONS
IN MACROECONOMIC
POLICY**

*The ideas that will influence eco-
nomic policy in the 1980s and
beyond will be very different from
the dominant ideas of the past
35 years.[1]
Martin Feldstein*

The approach of economists to macroeconomic problems has changed dramatically during the last decade. The 1970s, like the 1930s, are sure to exert a lasting
imprint upon macroeconomics. We have already integrated many of the recent
developments into our macroeconomic way of thinking. In this chapter we will
summarize the major problems that plague the U.S. economy and consider
policy alternatives to deal with these problems. As macroeconomists have become
increasingly aware of the limitations of monetary and fiscal policies, their interest
in the microstructure of our economy has grown. For the first time since the
Keynesian revolution, the development of a microeconomic approach to traditional macroeconomic issues is attracting widespread interest among economists.
We will discuss several microeconomic policy suggestions to promote economic
growth, high employment, and stable prices. We will also outline the Reagan
administration's response to the economic problems of the 1980s and consider
the impact of its economic policies.

THE TROUBLED U.S. ECONOMY

As the 1970s began, economists were optimistic about our ability to follow policies
that would generate rapid growth, high employment, and economic stability.
Clearly, the subsequent economic record fell far short of the optimistic expectations. The Reagan administration, assuming office in 1981, inherited a troubled
economy. Five major economic problems confronted the new administration.

---

[1]Martin Feldstein, "The Retreat from Keynesian Economics," *The Public Interest* (Summer 1981),
p. 93.

The Inflation Rate. Exhibit 1 illustrates the inflation rate for the 1960–1981 period as measured by the consumer price index. Beginning from an inflation rate of under 2 percent in the early 1960s, the rate rose to 6 percent in 1969. After receding to approximately 3 percent in 1971–1972, the inflation rate jumped all the way to 12.2 percent during the inflationary recession of 1974–1975. By 1976, the rate had again declined to 4.8 percent. However, it began to climb again in 1977, reaching 13.3 percent in 1979 and 12.4 percent in 1980.

Sluggish Economic Growth. In addition to the inflation problem, the decade of the 1970s was marred by sluggish economic growth. Measured by real GNP, the performance of the U.S. economy during the 1970s was the worst of any decade since the 1930s. Exhibit 2 presents a graphic illustration of the growth rate problem. During the 25 years following World War II, real GNP per capita in the United States expanded at an annual rate of 2.3 percent. At a growth rate like this, per capita GNP doubles approximately every generation. Thus, each successive generation is expected to be about twice as wealthy as the preceding generation. During the 1973–1980 period, this long-term growth rate fell by approximately a third, to only 1.5 percent. At this slower growth rate, nearly two generations are required for real per capita income to double.

One can build a strong case that even the sluggish growth rate of per capita GNP *understates* the economic decline. As the "baby boom" generation, born following World War II, entered the work force during the 1970s, employment grew rapidly. As a result, the annual growth rate of real GNP *per employee* during 1973–1980 fell to only 0.4 percent, down from 2.2 percent during 1947–1972.

Not only was the U.S. growth rate poor by historical standards, but it was also poor compared to other major industrial nations. As Exhibit 3 illustrates, the United States and the United Kingdom rank at the bottom among Western economies. The growth rate of real GNP for Japan, France, West

EXHIBIT 1   The rising inflation rate, 1960–1981

This graph shows the December-to-December change in the consumer price index for all urban consumers. Shaded areas indicate periods of recession. The inflation rate has been spiraling upward since the mid-1960s.

U.S. Department of Labor.

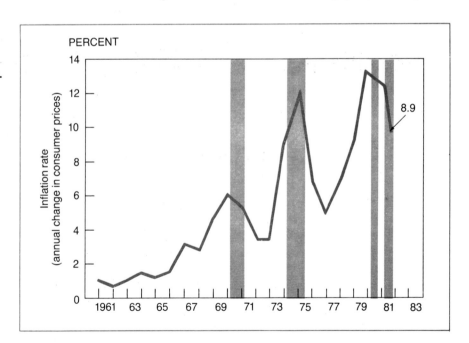

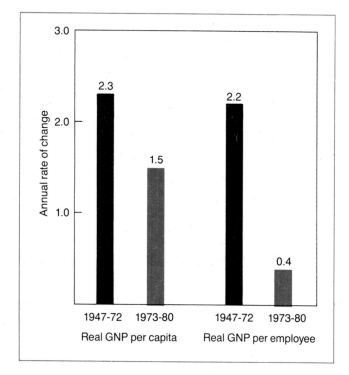

Germany, and Canada surpassed that of the United States during the 1970–1980 period. Only the United Kingdom ranked below the United States. When one focuses on the growth of output per worker, the picture is even bleaker. Japan, West Germany, and France experienced a growth rate of real GNP per employee of 3 percent or more during 1970–1980; the United States lagged far behind, at a rate of only 0.7 percent. Even the growth rate per employed worker of the United Kingdom exceeded that of the United States.

Low Saving and Investment Rates. Saving is important because it provides the funds with which to finance investment. If people do not save, capital investment projects cannot be carried out, and capital formation is an important determinant of economic growth. There are two reasons why a low investment

EXHIBIT 3 **The growth rates of real GNP and GNP per employee for selected countries, 1970–1980.**

Country	Growth Rate of Real GNP, 1970–1980	Growth Rate of Real GNP per Employed Worker, 1970–1980
Japan	5.0	4.2
West Germany	2.8	3.1
France	3.9	3.5
Canada	3.9	1.6
United Kingdom	2.2	2.0
United States	2.5	0.7

Derived from *International Economic Conditions: Annual Data 1961–1980,* Federal Reserve Bank of St. Louis (released June 1981), and *Statistical Abstract of the United States—1980,* Table 1589.

rate will tend to retard economic growth. First, when capital investment expenditures are low, the plant capacity and modern machinery that allow greater output per labor-hour will not be available for workers in the future. Without expanding output (supply) per labor-hour, real wage rates will come to a standstill. Second, a low rate of investment means that the capital stock of a nation will only be able to incorporate new technological breakthroughs very slowly. Thus, when new, improved methods of producing goods are discovered, it takes a long time for them to be widely adopted by low-investment nations. The result: a slower growth of real output and income for the low-investment nations.

Many economists believe the sluggishness of the U.S. economy during the 1970s was largely the result of our failure to allocate a larger share of our aggregate income to saving, investment, and technological development. As Exhibit 4 illustrates, the saving and investment rates of the United States lag well behind other major industrial nations. During the 1970s, the saving rate of the United States was less than one-third that of Japan; it was less than one-half the rates of France and West Germany. The low saving rates restricted the availability of funds for capital formation. The capital formation rate of the United States was also well below the rates of Canada, France, West Germany, and Japan (Exhibit 4b). Only the United Kingdom had saving and investment rates roughly similar to those of the United States. Predictably, the growth of GNP in the United Kingdom, like that of the United States, also lagged well behind that of the "high-investment" major Western economies (see Exhibit 3).

High and Unstable Money Interest Rates. From 1950 through 1965, the interest rate on corporate (AAA) bonds fluctuated within a narrow range—between 2.86 percent and 4.49 percent. In sharp contrast, interest rates have been both high and extremely volatile in recent years. In 1974, short-term money interest rates soared to 12 percent, only to fall back to 6 percent less than 12 months later. In 1980, short-term rates rose to the 15 to 17 percent range in February, plummeted to near 8 percent in July, and jumped back to 18 percent at the year's end. Things were not much better in 1981; short-term rates fluctuated between 12 percent and 21.5 percent throughout the year. Such wide interest-rate fluctuations make business investments very risky and long-range financial planning virtually impossible.

Continual Large Deficits. As we previously discussed, budget deficits, *as a percent of GNP,* rose sharply during the 1970s (see Exhibit 9, Chapter 14, page 298). During the 1975–1981 period, the federal deficit averaged 2.4 percent of GNP, up from 0.2 percent of GNP during the 1960s. Prior to the 1970s, large peacetime deficits had been experienced for a year or two during an economic recession. However, the economy was not beset by *continual* large deficits (relative to GNP) until the mid-1970s.

Large deficits pose two major problems. First, they place upward pressure on interest rates because of the strong government demand for loanable funds. Second, as the national debt increases, the interest payments to finance the debt constantly go up.

By 1981, the interest payments on the debt had risen to 2.5 percent of GNP, up from 1.5 percent throughout most of the 1950–1975 period (see Exhibit 6, Chapter 10, page 205). Obviously, the rising interest payments require the government either to (a) raise tax rates or (b) cut expenditures in other areas.

EXHIBIT 4 The lagging saving and investment rates of the United States

United Nations, *Monthly Bulletin of Statistics* (various issues, 1970–1979).

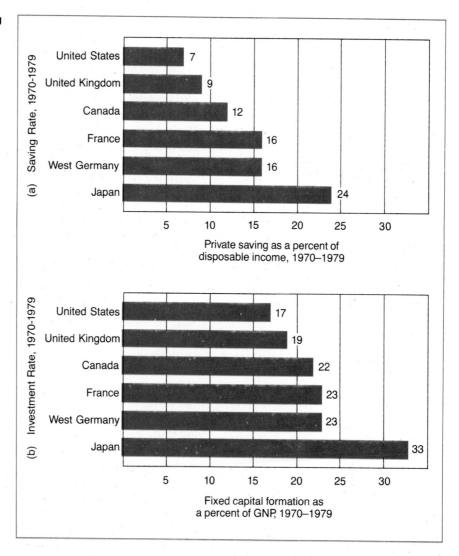

(a) Saving Rate, 1970-1979

United States	7
United Kingdom	9
Canada	12
France	16
West Germany	16
Japan	24

Private saving as a percent of disposable income, 1970–1979

(b) Investment Rate, 1970-1979

United States	17
United Kingdom	19
Canada	22
France	23
West Germany	23
Japan	33

Fixed capital formation as a percent of GNP, 1970–1979

A MICROECONOMIC APPROACH TO MACROECONOMIC PROBLEMS

The 1930s taught us that deficient demand can produce economic recession and high unemployment. The 1970s proved that there can be other causes of sluggish growth and high unemployment. As we search for answers to the economic problems of the 1980s, it is clear that microeconomics will play a far greater role in the shaping of macroeconomic policy than has been true in the past. Economists of all persuasions—Keynesians, monetarists, supply-siders, and various hybrids—are developing an increasing appreciation of the importance of the microstructure underlying aggregate markets.

What are the ingredients of this new microapproach to traditional macroeconomic policy matters? First, much closer attention is being paid to incentives and their importance as determinants of unemployment, investment, long-term growth, and inflation. Changes in relative prices do matter. If rapid growth and price stability cannot be attained with macropolicy, perhaps policies that alter the incentive to save, invest, work, and produce can improve the picture.

Second, the new microapproach analyzes changes in the components of the economy more carefully. Changes in the composition of the labor force, the structure of industry, and/or the functions of government may influence the rates of saving, investment, and economic growth. In the past, the importance of the microcomponents of aggregate markets have often been overlooked.

Third, the new microapproach stresses the importance of the long run. Policy prescriptions that exert positive short-run effects sometimes have harmful side effects in the long run. Since micropolicy prescriptions usually affect the economy by changing relative prices, decision-makers must be given time to adjust to the new incentive structure. Clearly, the microapproach is a long-run strategy, not a quick fix.

The microapproach to the macroeconomic problems of the 1980s yields interesting insights and suggests several policy alternatives. We will proceed to take a closer look at some of the implications of this approach.

A Comparison of Unemployment in the 1930s and 1980s

The unemployment problem of the 1980s differs from that of the 1930s. When the unemployment rate soared to nearly 25 percent in 1933, most of those counted among the unemployed were adult men who had lost their jobs. There were few two-earner families. Unemployment compensation and layoff benefits were virtually nonexistent. There were no food stamp or welfare programs to assist unemployed workers.

The unemployment of the post-World War II period, particularly that of the last decade, was markedly different. In the late 1970s nearly half of the unemployed workers were under age 25. Approximately one in four was a teenager.[2] Another substantial share of the unemployed were members of families with other employed earners. Unemployment compensation and various assistance programs were in place to cushion the effects of unemployment, particularly for job losers. The sluggish growth and high unemployment rate of the 1980s differ considerably from the conditions in the 1930s. A different type of policy approach is required for the 1980s.

Solving the Investment–Saving Problem

The current U.S. tax structure subsidizes borrowing and penalizes saving. Individuals are permitted to deduct interest costs from their taxable income. Thus borrowing, including borrowing for the purchase of consumer goods, is encouraged. In contrast, income allocated to savings will generally be taxed twice, once as regular income when it is earned, and once again when it earns interest. Even the inflation premium built into the interest rate is taxed as though it represented real income instead of a correction for inflation. This incentive structure—subsidizing borrowing and taxing saving—increases consumer demand for loanable funds while discouraging saving and investment.

This proconsumption and antisaving incentive structure is an outgrowth of the Keynesian view of saving. Influenced by the Great Depression, early Keynesians believed that excessive saving and deficient consumption

---

[2]In 1979, 48.7 percent of the total persons unemployed were between the ages of 16 and 24; 26 percent of the unemployed workers were teenagers.

demand were a constant threat to prosperity. The role of saving as a source of funds for capital formation was generally de-emphasized.

Given the current economic situation, excessive saving is not a problem. If the United States wants to accelerate its sagging growth rate, most economists believe that both saving and investment must be increased. In fact, one could argue that the official statistics actually understate the bleak picture of capital formation. The official statistics make no allowance for the impact of energy price increases on the productivity of the U.S. capital stock. The sharp jump in crude-oil prices during the last decade has rendered much of our capital stock economically obsolete long before it would normally have worn out.

How can economic policy encourage saving and capital formation? The microeconomic answer to this question is: Change relative prices in a manner that will make saving and investment more attractive relative to borrowing and current consumption. There are several policy options. For example, income derived from savings could be made wholly or partially exempt from taxation. Individuals might be permitted to deduct the *net additions* to the personal savings (at least up to some maximum amount) from their taxable income.[3] The deductibility of interest expenses, particularly interest incurred through the use of credit cards and borrowing for consumer purchases, might be eliminated. Such proposals would encourage individuals to supply additional funds to the loanable funds market and discourage them from borrowing to finance consumption expenditures. A lower *real* interest rate would result. This strategy, particularly if accompanied by a reduction in government borrowing, would encourage capital formation. Capital and business income might also be treated more favorably from a tax viewpoint. Corporate tax rates could be reduced. The government might rely more heavily on consumption taxes and reduce taxes on personal and business income. All of these actions would affect relative prices in a manner that would promote more saving, lower real interest rates, and higher rates of capital formation.

A low investment (and saving) rate is inconsistent with a rapid growth rate. If we want to grow faster—to enhance the productivity of our work force more rapidly—a high investment rate is essential. If the U.S. investment rate continues to sag, sluggish growth of productivity and real income will result.

Indexing of Government Bonds

The interest cost of the national debt has risen from $31 billion in fiscal 1975 to $99 billion in 1982. Interest payments on the debt now total 2.5 percent of GNP, up from 1.5 percent in the mid-1970s. The major reason for the rapid increase in the interest cost is high *money* interest rates that reflect a high expected rate of inflation.

In the early 1970s, money interest rates were low; most people expected relatively stable prices. As the inflation rate accelerated, government benefited because it was able to pay its bondholders with "inflated" dollars. For several years, Treasury-bond-holders actually received a negative *real* interest rate because the annual rate of inflation exceeded their interest return. In contrast, the federal government received a windfall gain from inflation, even though its policies were the major source of this problem. Of course, this was a short-lived

---

[3]The recent tax legislation providing for favorable tax treatment of funds paid into Individual Retirement Accounts is a step in this direction.

benefit. Once bondholders came to expect the higher inflation rates, they demanded higher rates of interest.

The process works in the opposite direction when government initiates a deceleration of the inflation rate. Bondholders, receiving a high money interest rate because of the high expected rate of inflation, will receive a windfall gain because the inflation rate is lower than was expected. Simultaneously, the interest burden of the debt will expand; the government pays exceedingly high *real* interest rates as the inflation rate decelerates. In fact, this rising real interest burden will reduce the government's ability to move toward stable prices. The government may shift again to an expansionary policy.

Government issue of indexed bonds could prevent such counterproductive effects and the vicious cycles that result. Indexed bonds would pay a market value *real* interest rate, plus the annual rate of inflation. For example, an indexed bond, yielding a 5 percent real interest rate, would pay the bondholder 5 percent if prices were stable, 10 percent if the annual inflation was 5 percent, 15 percent at a 10 percent inflation rate, and so on. Only the income from the real interest component would be taxed, since the indexed adjustment would merely reflect inflation, not additional income.

Indexed bonds have two potential major advantages. First, they would reduce the government's interest payments as the inflation rate declines. For example, rather than paying 15 percent money interest rates and creating a windfall transfer for bondholders as it reduces the inflation rate, the government could pay a 5 percent real interest rate and limit the size of the windfall transfer as we move toward stable prices.

Second, indexed bonds would tend to keep government policy directed toward long-run stable prices and discourage it from following expansionary policies. If the government decelerated the inflation rate, it would benefit *immediately* in the form of lower interest payments on the debt. Similarly, if it accelerated the inflation rate, the government would be penalized *immediately* in the form of higher money interest payments to bondholders. The government would no longer be able to reap a short-run windfall gain by accelerating the inflation rate beyond the previously expected rate. Indexed bonds would help to ensure that the federal government follows a consistent, noninflationary course.

The Macroeconomic Side Effects of Demographic Changes

The microapproach suggests that demographic changes can exert an important influence on saving, unemployment, and growth of real income. There is reason to believe that recent demographic changes exerted an influence on the performance of the U.S. economy during the 1970s. Similarly, analysis of the continuing changes in the age composition during the 1980s will enhance our understanding of what lies ahead.

Exhibit 5 points out the essentials of the demographic changes during the 1970s. There was a tremendous bulge in the 18-to-34 age grouping, in which new job seekers are concentrated and job switching in search of a career path is most common. Undoubtedly, this bulge increased the normal rate of unemployment during the 1970s. Workers in the under-35 age categories are inexperienced and relatively unproductive at this stage of their careers. Growth of real income per capita is retarded when these youthful workers comprise an increasing proportion of the total work force, as was true during the 1970s.

EXHIBIT 5 The changing age composition of the U.S. population, 1970–1980 and 1980–1990

Age	Percent Change in Population Grouping	
	1970–1980	1980–1990
Under 15	−13.8	10.6
15–17	3.4	−20.1
18–24	22.5	−14.6
25–34	45.4	13.5
35–44	11.3	42.4
45–54	−2.2	11.5
55–64	14.0	−1.9
Over 65	25.6	19.6

U.S. Bureau of the Census.

There is also reason to believe that demographic factors during the 1970s adversely affected the saving rate in the United States. In addition to the 18-to-34 age grouping, the number of people aged 65 and over also grew quite rapidly. There is good reason to expect that both of these age groupings have a low saving rate.[4] Youthful individuals often borrow to establish their households, and save only a small percentage of their relatively low incomes. Similarly, the elderly generally dissave in order to meet their current living expenses. In contrast, the 35-to-54 age grouping, which generally saves a high proportion of current income, grew very slowly during the 1970s. These demographic trends contributed to the low saving rate in the United States during the 1970s.

By the end of the 1980s, the situation will differ considerably. As Exhibit 5 shows, there will actually be a decline in the number of people in the 15-to-24 age category and only a moderate expansion in the 25-to-34 age grouping. During the 1980s, the big bulge will be in the 35-to-44 category, where stable employment patterns are far more common. As this latter group acquires a substantial amount of job experience, their incomes will grow rapidly. Economic theory indicates that these demographic trends will both reduce the normal rate of unemployment and contribute to a more rapid growth of real income. In fact, given the sharp decline in the number of workers under age 25, the United States may well experience a relative shortage of unskilled workers by the end of the 1980s. These changing demographic patterns will lead to an increase in demand for labor-saving capital equipment as producers seek to substitute capital for the increasingly scarce unskilled labor. Clearly, this will be a reversal of the trend present during the 1970s.

The demographic trends will also exert a positive impact on the saving rate during the 1980s. Fewer young people and more individuals in the middle-age categories should push the economy's saving rate upward.

In summary, based on life cycle patterns, there is good reason to expect that the maturing and more gradual growth of the U.S. labor force during the 1980s will reduce the normal rate of unemployment while exerting a positive impact on saving, investment, and the growth of real income.

---

[4]See discussion of the life cycle hypothesis of saving and consumption (Chapter 8, p. 163) for additional background on this topic.

Employment and Unemployment Compensation

The unemployment compensation system was designed to reduce the hardships of unemployment. As desirable as this program is from a humanitarian standpoint, it diminishes the opportunity cost of job search, leisure, nonproductive activities, and continued unemployment. The conflict between high benefit levels and low rates of unemployment should therefore not be surprising.

The current unemployment compensation system causes the rate of unemployment to rise for two reasons. First, it greatly reduces, and in some cases virtually eliminates, the personal cost of unemployment. The benefits in most states provide covered unemployed workers with *tax-free* payments of 50 to 60 percent of their *previous gross earnings*. Since these benefits are tax free for most workers,[5] they often replace 75 percent or more of the employee's *net* loss of income. Benefit levels in this range greatly reduce the employee's incentive to accept employment at lower wages or in other locations.

Second, unemployment compensation acts as a subsidy to employers who offer unstable or seasonal employment opportunities. Employees would be more reluctant to work for such employers (for example, northern contractors who generally lay off workers in the winter) were it not for the fact that these employees can supplement their earnings with unemployment compensation benefits during layoffs. The system makes seasonal, temporary, and casual employment opportunities more attractive than would otherwise be the case. Excessive unemployment results, because employers (and employees) are encouraged to adopt production methods and work rules that rely extensively on temporary employees and supplementary layoff benefits.

There is little doubt that the current unemployment compensation system increases the normal rate of unemployment and thereby retards aggregate supply. Most researchers in the area believe that the long-run rate of unemployment is between 0.5 and 1.0 percent higher than it would be if the negative employment effects of the system could be eliminated. Since more than 80 percent of the work force is now covered by the program, compared to 56 percent in 1960, the impact of the system on the normal rate of unemployment has probably been increasing.

How can the unemployment compensation system be reformed without undercutting the original humanitarian objectives of the program? Several policy alternatives exist. After a specified period of time, three months, for example, unemployment compensation recipients might be required to accept available jobs (including public sector employment) that provide wage rates equal to their unemployment compensation benefits. Under current legislation, persons who refuse to accept suitable work are denied benefits. However, "suitable work" is usually defined as a job similar to the claimant's previous employment, in terms of pay rate, occupation, and work responsibilities. Thus, most claimants can draw benefits for up to 26 weeks (or 39 weeks in some cases) without accepting available jobs that differ from their previous positions.

In addition, the tax structure could be changed in a manner that would reduce the perverse incentive effects. Currently, except for a few high-income workers, unemployment compensation income is not taxed when it is received.

---

[5]Persons with incomes in excess of $20,000 ($25,000 if they are filing a joint return) must pay tax on 50 percent of their income derived from unemployment compensation. In addition, social security and state income taxes are not collected on this income.

If such income were taxed, two things would be accomplished. First, unemployed workers would have a greater incentive to accept available jobs, because income received from *both* earnings and unemployment compensation (not just the former) would now be taxable. Second, people with the same annual income would pay the same tax bill. The current system results in lower taxes as the proportion of income received from unemployment compensation increases. Only a perverse concept of equity could justify taxing an employed person more than an unemployed person with the same income.

Dealing with Youth Unemployment

Nearly one-half of all unemployed workers were under 25 years of age in the early 1980s. The teenage unemployment rate usually runs about 2.5 times the rate for adults. The unemployment problem among black teenagers is particularly acute. The unemployment rate of black teenagers rose to 35.8 percent in 1980, compared to an overall rate of 7.1 percent.

As we discussed previously, since youthful workers are still in the process of deciding what career they want to pursue and how much schooling they need or want, they shift back and forth between jobs and educational opportunities more often than their older counterparts. A higher rate of unemployment for youthful workers results. However, many economists believe that other factors also contribute to the enormous gap between the rates of unemployment for older and younger workers. The experience of other countries, notably West Germany and Britain, indicates that high youth unemployment rates can be avoided. Two specific proposals deserve mention.

1. Exemption from Minimum Wage Legislation. Many younger workers are searching for a path to a good job in the future. This is why so many choose formal education. However, training and skill-building experience can also provide the ticket to future success. Often these attributes are best learned on the job, but they are costly for an employer to provide. The minimum wage law often makes it infeasible for an employer to (a) provide training to inexperienced workers and (b) pay the legal minimum wage at the same time. Thus, there are few (temporarily) low-paying jobs offering a combination of informal (or formal) training and skill-building experience. While we subsidize formal education, this aspect of public policy clearly discriminates against on-the-job training.

2. Youth Work Scholarships. Martin Feldstein has suggested that we provide youthful workers, those under 25 years of age, for example, with a **youth work scholarship.** A wide variety of alternatives are possible. At one extreme, individuals could be provided with monthly subsidies, in addition to wage benefits from their employers as long as they are employed. Under this plan, it would be up to each worker to choose his or her most preferred combination of current wage and on-the-job training. A maximum duration, two years, for example, could be established for each scholarship. An additional reward for continual employment could be provided.

Youth Work Scholarship: A proposed scholarship providing subsidies to younger workers who maintain jobs. Some scholarships would limit the subsidies to employment that offered on-the-job training.

Another possibility would be to provide the scholarship only for jobs that involved approved training. Jobs that resulted in the development of craft, clerical, operative, and perhaps even managerial skill could be high-priority targets. The long-run goal would be to improve the quality of the labor force and the quality and quantity of output, so that real income could be increased without inflation.

"And for the jobless, my committee is making a two-million-dollar study on how to survive on welfare."

THE REAGAN PROGRAM

The Reagan administration took office amidst strong public dissatisfaction with the economy. As a candidate, Reagan projected an optimistic image, arguing that our economic conditions were merely the result of a long string of unsound policies; even though some rough times might lie ahead, a sound program would get the economy back on track. The administration's program for economic recovery contains four key elements: (1) the slowing of monetary growth, (2) tax reductions, (3) a reduction in the growth rate of federal spending, and (4) deregulation. We will consider each of these elements of what has come to be known as "Reaganomics" and analyze their probable impact upon the economy.

A Stable, Slower Monetary Growth

Monetary policy is, of course, carried out by the Federal Reserve System. Nonetheless, the executive branch does exert an indirect influence. President Reagan and his economic advisers have called for slower, more stable monetary growth. Reflecting the monetarist viewpoint, the administration has argued that a gradual reduction in the money supply would lead simultaneously to less inflation and lower *money* interest rates.

The Federal Reserve has appeared quite willing to cooperate with the administration on this point. In fact, soon after the new administration took office, the Fed reduced its target growth rates for the money supply (M-1) by one-half of a percent per year for both 1982 and 1983. The Fed is expected

As the economy languished during 1982, President Reagan turned to Martin Feldstein when he filled the vacancy for the chairmanship of the Council of Economic Advisers. Feldstein is the leader of a new generation of economists who believe that the solution to the traditional macroeconomic problems of unemployment and inflation can be attained by altering price incentives. The volume and quality of Feldstein's research had elevated him to positions of professional prominence and respect even before he reached his fortieth birthday. In 1977, he received the John Bates Clark Medal, an award presented by the American Economic Association to the most outstanding economists under the age of 40. Receipt of this biannual award placed Feldstein in a select group that includes Nobel laureates Kenneth Arrow, Milton Friedman, and Paul Samuelson. At the age of 38, Feldstein was elected president of the National Bureau of Economic Research, a prestigious research agency long known for the outstanding quality of its work.

Feldstein's interest in economics was almost accidental. He entered Harvard in 1957, fully intent on following his father into the legal profession. However, he found law "dull" and was soon attracted to economics. After graduating first in his class at Harvard in 1961, he spent a year at Oxford studying health economics on a Fulbright scholarship. It was during his stay at Oxford that he first began to sense the power of empirical work in economics.

"Creative" and "original" are two words that are often used to describe Feldstein's work. In some ways, his views are unorthodox, but they are always backed up with carefully conducted empirical research.

Now a professor of economics at Harvard, Feldstein is a leader among the expanding group of economists who emphasize a microeconomic approach to the twin problems of sluggish growth and inflation. Feldstein argues that "there is a growing recognition that our high permanent rate of unemployment cannot be lowered by expansionary demand policies." He believes the solution will be found through policies that "correct labor market disincentives and distortions."[6]

His own work on the disincentive effects of unemployment compensation and factors retarding capital formation have made an important contribution to the microeconomic approach. Feldstein's research on the unemployment compensation system indicates that it causes workers to lengthen their job-search time and induces employers to make more extensive use of temporary layoffs. The result: a higher rate of unemployment. His work on capital formation indicates that policies such as the "pay-as-you-go" approach to social security and tax legislation that subsidizes borrowing while taxing saving have retarded the economic growth of the United States. Professor Feldstein's research in these areas will be most helpful as he searches for policy solutions to the problems plaguing the social security system.

[6]Martin Feldstein, "The Retreat from Keynesian Economics," *The Public Interest* (Summer 1981), p. 97.

to reduce the rate of monetary expansion until the growth rate of M-1 declines to 3 percent, the approximate real long-run growth rate of the economy.

The Fed's stability record in the recent past has left a great deal of room for improvement. In October 1979, the Fed announced that, henceforth, it would concentrate on controlling the growth of the money supply rather than interest rates. However, as Exhibit 6 illustrates, unstable monetary growth characterized the Fed's subsequent policy. Just as the rational expectations hypothesis implies, monetary acceleration has been associated with rising money interest rates, while falling interest rates have accompanied declines in the money supply during the post-1979 period. As the money supply fell during the February–May period of 1980, the interest rate on three-month Treasury bills tumbled from over 15 percent to under 7 percent (see Exhibit 6). Other short-term interest rates followed a similar path. In May 1980 the Fed shifted gears and expanded the money supply at an annual rate of 16 percent during the six months prior to the 1980 presidential election. Financial markets re-

EXHIBIT 6   Monetary instability and interest rates

In recent years, short-term money interest rates have *risen* sharply when the money supply was expanded rapidly. Similarly, monetary contraction has brought short-term money interest rates downward.

Federal Reserve Bulletin (monthly).

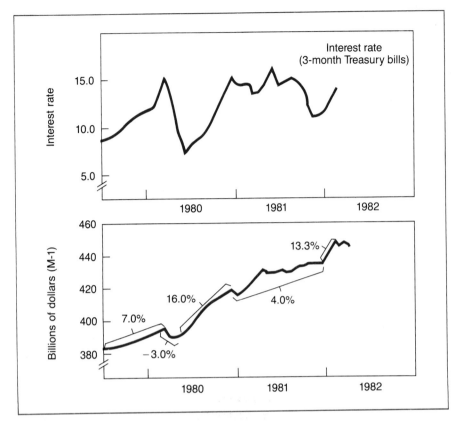

sponded quickly. Short-term interest rates jumped back to the 15 percent range. In 1981, monetary growth (M-1) was a moderate 4 percent. By the latter half of the year, interest rates were again headed downward. By the end of 1981, the three-month Treasury bill rate was under 11 percent. However, in late 1981 and early 1982, there was another surge in the money supply. Short-term interest rates rose accordingly.

Thus, although the overall rate of monetary growth moderated following January of 1981, monetary policy was characterized by short-run instability. Interest rates appear to be highly responsive to monetary instability.

The monetary deceleration in 1981 was an effective weapon against inflation. The inflation rate during 1981 was 8.9 percent, down from 12.4 percent in 1980 and 13.3 percent in 1979. However, as the adaptive expectations view of the Phillips curve implies, rising unemployment and economic recession accompanied the decline in the inflation rate. By the end of 1981, the unemployment rate had soared to more than 9 percent, up from 7 percent earlier in the year. As the layoffs continued, dissatisfaction with Reaganomics grew.

The Reagan Tax Policy

The administration argued that the rising tax rates of the 1970s (see Exhibit 10, Chapter 5, page 98) were a major cause of stagflation. According to this view, high marginal tax rates had reduced the incentive of individuals to work, save, and invest and had encouraged them to channel valuable resources into the tax-shelter industry. As a result, aggregate supply had expanded at a very slow rate, and demand-stimulus policies had exerted their primary impact on the price level, at least in the long run.

With the cooperation of Congress, the Economic Recovery Tax Act of 1981 was passed. The major provisions of the legislation are outlined below.

1. Tax Rate Reductions. By 1984 individual tax rates are scheduled to be reduced "across-the-board" by 23 percent, with cumulative rate reductions of 1.25 percent for 1981, 10 percent for 1982, 19 percent for 1983, and 23 percent for 1984. In addition, the top marginal tax rate was reduced from 70 percent to 50 percent beginning in 1982. Once all reductions have been implemented, marginal tax rates will range from 11 percent to 50 percent, compared with 14 percent to 70 percent under prior law.

2. Indexing. Starting in 1985, tax brackets, personal exemptions, and the zero-bracket amount will be indexed for inflation (see "Indexing," page 100, for details). This means that inflation will no longer push taxpayers with an unchanged real income (but a higher money income) into higher tax brackets and thereby increase their tax burdens.

3. More Rapid Depreciation Allowances. Assets are grouped into broad categories with fixed periods for depreciation write-off. In general, automobiles, light trucks, and mobile tools can be depreciated in 3 years, other equipment and machinery in 5 years, and most buildings in 15 years. Under the new law, businesses will be able to depreciate more quickly the cost of their investment in plant equipment. In addition, liberalized leasing rules will permit companies that are not making a current profit to sell their "depreciation costs" to companies with a tax liability. These provisions will reduce the tax burden of businesses, particularly those undertaking current investment projects.

4. Savings Incentives. All individuals with earnings are permitted to establish an **individual retirement account** (IRA) with a depository institution. Each year, tax-deductible contributions of up to $2000 may be made into these retirement/savings accounts. Self-employed persons who establish a Keogh saving plan, similar to an IRA, may make tax-deductible contributions of up to 15 percent of their income, subject to a $15,000 limitation per year. Under prior law, only a $7500 contribution was allowed.

Individual Retirement Account (IRA): A savings account for one's retirement. Under current law individuals may make tax-deductible contributions of up to $2000 per year from their earnings into such accounts. IRAs are offered by a wide range of financial institutions; the funds may also be invested in bonds, stocks, and other liquid financial assets. There is a penalty for withdrawal before age 59.

The strategy behind the tax package is straightforward. The administration anticipates that lower tax rates, more attractive depreciation allowances, and expanded tax incentives to save will encourage greater work effort, more investment, and additional saving. The package was widely heralded as a supply-side tax plan. In a sense this is true. However, as we will discuss, there are reasons to doubt the strength of the supply-side impact of the package.

The Reagan Budget Strategy

The third component of the Reagan economic plan is a reduction *in the growth rate* of government expenditures. According to the administration's view, the increase in federal spending, as a share of GNP, was a major contributor to the stagflation of the 1970s.

Here, as in other areas, it is important to observe what people do, rather than merely what they say they are going to do. After all, President Carter, as well as others before him, often argued that it was essential to bring federal spending under control. Since the Reagan administration has planned to *increase* national defense expenditures, curbing government spending as intended might prove difficult.

Deregulation

Government regulation of economic activity has expanded rapidly in recent years. Since the mid-1960s, regulatory agencies such as the Consumer Product Safety Commission, the Environmental Protection Agency, the Occupational Safety and Health Administration, and the Department of Energy have been formed. Regulation can often serve a useful purpose, yielding substantial benefits to the public. For example, the automobile emission standards have substantially reduced air pollution from this source.

However, regulatory activity is costly. The regulatory agency must enforce the regulations. This requires additional manpower, time, and effort paid for by your tax dollars. In addition, producers in a regulated industry must not only comply with the regulations but provide proof to the government that they have done so. This requires time and effort to fill out substantial numbers of forms, conduct necessary testing, and in general provide whatever information is requested by the regulating agency. Regulations impose a substantial burden on taxpayers in the form of a larger tax bill and on consumers in the form of higher prices.

If you multiply the cost of the time and effort devoted to regulation on the part of both producers and regulators by the millions of products and services produced every year, you get some idea of the overall cost of the regulation. According to a study by Murray Weidenbaum, former chairman of the Council of Economic Advisers, government regulations added $100 billion to the cost of goods and services bought by consumers in 1980. In addition, the government of the United States spent another $20 billion in the federal paperwork and manpower necessary to monitor and enforce those regulations.

Since the majority of regulatory costs are paid for in the form of higher prices of products, these costs are often overlooked by lay observers. Regulatory compliance is a cost to the producer, just as labor and raw materials are. Regulatory costs, like all other costs, will be reflected in the final price of the good or service when it is sold. Although it makes good political rhetoric to speak of "making business pay," in reality consumers will pay the business cost of regulation, just as they pay for other costs associated with the production of goods.

Are the regulatory costs worth incurring? When the benefits exceed the costs, the answer is clearly yes. But when the costs of enforcement and compliance exceed the benefits, then economic inefficiency results and aggregate supply is reduced. Unfortunately, the benefits and the costs are both to some degree subjective and difficult to measure with precision.

In several areas, the Reagan administration decided that regulatory actions had been counterproductive. Steps toward deregulation were taken. In early 1981 President Reagan accelerated the decontrol of domestic crude-oil prices and eliminated the entitlement tax-subsidy regulatory program. Here, the results were quite successful. Initially, gasoline prices rose by 5 to 10 cents per gallon, but then declined gradually throughout the rest of the year. Some 12 months after decontrol, gasoline and fuel-oil prices had fallen below where they had been prior to decontrol. Under President Reagan, the Executive Office of the President monitors the regulatory actions of federal agencies. The president has pointed to a substantial decline in the number of pages in the *Federal Register* as evidence that his administration has reduced the intrusion of the federal government into the nation's economic life.

However, the regulatory record of the Reagan administration has not been entirely consistent. For example, there is evidence that administrative actions have actually slowed deregulation in the trucking industry. Many believe that President Reagan's initial appointment to the Interstate Commerce Commission, which regulates the trucking industry, was unduly influenced by the Teamsters union, one of the few labor organizations that supported his candidacy.

THE REAGAN PROGRAM—ITS IMPACT ON THE ECONOMY

Is the Reagan program capable of dealing with the stagflation, instability, and high interest rates that have plagued the U.S. economy in recent years? In some ways, there is reason to believe that the program will be constructive. Slowing the rate of monetary growth should help bring both the inflation rate and money interest rates down. Most economists believe that the high money interest rates of 1979–1981 were largely the result of the built-in inflationary premium. Thus, as Exhibit 6 illustrates, monetary expansion will not bring these rates down. Arguments for more rapid monetary growth to lower interest rates do not take into account the rapid adjustments of current financial markets when monetary acceleration raises inflationary expectations.

In the short run, the reduction in monetary growth will temporarily reduce output and cause an increase in unemployment. However, if the monetary deceleration is gradual, it need not cause a *prolonged* recession. Credibility is also important here. If both the Fed and the administration make it clear that monetary policy is going to be *permanently* more restrictive, markets will adjust more quickly. The short-run adverse side effects of restrictive monetary policy will be minimized, and a foundation for strong, noninflationary growth in the future will be established.

As monetary policy slows both the economy and the inflation rate, the budget deficit will expand. Remember, recessions help create deficits by reducing tax receipts and simultaneously increasing spending on unemployment compensation and other social programs. Should taxes be increased to reduce the deficit? According to both Keynesian and supply-side theory, the answer is no. Historically, tax increases during a recession have been ineffective and in a few instances catastrophic.

The huge Hoover tax increase in 1932 failed to balance the budget and plunged the economy into a deeper depression. The Eisenhower efforts to balance the budget during the 1958 recession were largely counterproductive. Large deficits during the recessionary phase should not be viewed with alarm. Business demand will be weak. Therefore, it will be possible to finance a recessionary deficit without an inordinate increase in interest rates.

The large deficit becomes a problem during the recovery phase. The size of the deficit must be reduced if the economy is going to sustain a strong, healthy recovery. This is the major weakness in the Reagan strategy. Even the administration's projections call for budget deficits in the $100 billion range for 1983–1985. Most independent observers project even larger deficits. The "saving incentives" included in the 1981 tax legislation should be helpful. A substantial increase in the personal saving rate might be able to finance the deficits and prevent sharply higher real interest rates from choking off the recovery. However, this is a risky strategy.

From a policy standpoint, there are not any easy ways of reducing the deficit. Basically, there are three options. First, defense spending could be reduced and/or extended farther into the future. Second, the cost-of-living adjustments that automatically increase the benefit levels of **entitlement programs,** such as social security and federal pensions, might be reduced and/or delayed. Third, taxes could be increased, or the scheduled reduction in the nominal rates might be slowed and extended farther into the future.

Defense and entitlement programs consume such a large proportion of the budget that major cuts can obviously not be made and still leave these programs intact. Without cuts in defense, cuts in entitlements, or higher tax rates (or a combination), substantial progress toward reducing the deficit will be impossible. Once the recovery phase begins, it will be crucial that President Reagan and Congress face up to these economic realities. If they do not, huge budget deficits, rising *real* interest rates, and a short, weak, unsustainable recovery phase are likely.

Entitlement Programs: Programs whose benefit levels are established by prior legislation. Unless the earlier legislation is changed, the government has a continuing funding obligation. Social security benefits and federal pensions are examples of entitlement programs.

Problems Confronting the Reagan Strategy— A Summary

During the heat of the political debate over the Reagan tax package, some of the administration's strong supply-side advocates implied that the tax package would stimulate the economy tremendously, making it possible to expand defense expenditures, maintain the current *real* level of transfer payments, and balance the budget. This was to be accomplished even while restrictive monetary policy was decelerating the growth rate of nominal GNP. There are several reasons for believing that these goals are inconsistent and that all of the results expected by the optimistic Reagan strategists are unlikely to be achieved.

1. The Tax Cut Does Not Reduce Marginal Tax Rates on Real Incomes. The rates during 1981–1984 will be lower than they would have been in the absence of the Reagan plan. However, they will be about the same or higher than the 1980 tax rates. Essentially, the Reagan "tax cut" merely offsets **bracket creep** and higher social security taxes.

Bracket Creep: Term used to describe the increase in taxes as a share of income when inflation pushes persons with a constant *real* income but a larger money income into higher tax brackets.

Exhibit 7 illustrates this point. The average and marginal tax rates on income for 1977, 1980, 1982, and 1984 for a two-earner family of four filing a joint return are presented. The second wage earner is assumed to earn one-half the amount of the first. The tax rates include both the federal individual income and payroll taxes (employee's share only). Data are presented for a spectrum of income levels, ranging from $20,000 to $80,000 in 1980 dollars.

In general, the average tax rates for 1982 were slightly *higher* than for 1980 and well above the rates for 1977, the first year of the Carter administration. The picture for marginal rates is about the same. The marginal tax rates on joint incomes of $20,000, $40,000, $60,000, and $80,000 (in 1980 dollars) were all higher in 1982 than in 1980. In each case, the 1982 rates were well above the comparable marginal rate for 1977. By 1984, assuming that the tax legisla-

EXHIBIT 7   Average and marginal tax rates for a two-earner family of four, 1977–1984

Adjusted Gross Income (1980 Dollars)	1977	1980	1982	1984
	Average Tax Rate (Percent)			
$20,000	10.57	11.27	13.36	13.13
$40,000	16.13	19.00	19.53	18.78
$60,000	19.62	23.29	23.56	22.26
$80,000	23.23	27.10	26.87	25.07
	Marginal Tax Rate (Percent)			
$20,000	24.85	24.13	25.7	24.7
$40,000	33.85	38.13	39.7	39.7
$60,000	41.85	49.13	50.7	44.7
$80,000	45.00	49.00	55.7	48.7

The data here are for federal personal income and social security tax liabilities. The calculations are based on the following assumptions: The couple files a joint return, and all income is earned income. The second wage earner earns one-half the amount of the first. Taxpayers take the zero-bracket amount or itemize deductions equal to 23 percent of income, whichever is higher. Finally, an 8 percent inflation rate during 1980–1984 is also assumed.

tion is unchanged, the picture will be only slightly different. The 1984 average federal tax rate on earnings will be moderately lower than the 1980 rates for income above $40,000 but well above the average tax rate for the same real income in 1977. In general, the marginal rates for 1984 are almost identical to the 1980 marginal rates and well above the parallel marginal rates for 1977.

From a supply-side viewpoint, the data of Exhibit 7 are vitally important. Since marginal tax rates will not be lower, there is no reason to expect any significant impact on aggregate supply from tax changes taking effect in the 1981–1984 periods.

The only taxpayers who will experience significantly lower rates will be the small group of high-income individuals who confront the 50 percent marginal tax ceiling. This means that only about 1 percent of all taxpayers will be affected by the tax-reduction aspect of the Reagan program. For most others the Reagan tax package simply keeps tax rates (the combination of federal personal income and social security rates) from rising.

2. The Budgetary Policy Will Be Unable to Increase Defense Spending, Leave the Entitlement Programs Unchanged, and Significantly Slow the Growth of Federal Expenditures Simultaneously.   In fiscal 1982, the three largest items in the federal budget were (a) transfer payments to individuals (41 percent), (b) defense, space, and international affairs (28 percent), and (c) interest payments (13 percent). These three categories comprised 82 percent of federal spending. The Reagan administration hopes to increase *real* defense expenditures 7 percent annually during 1983–1987. This would bring national defense to 7.4 percent of GNP in 1987, up from 5.0 in 1980, but still well below the defense expenditure levels of the 1960s.

The problem with this strategy is that it conflicts with other budgetary objectives, particularly the administration's commitment to reduce the size of federal spending as a share of GNP. Neither interest payments nor transfer payments are likely to decline as a share of GNP. Interest payments will not decline as long as large deficits are incurred and interest rates remain high. If anything, interest payments are likely to *increase* as a share of GNP. The bulk of the transfer payments are entitlement programs that are indexed; the expenditures rise automatically with the price level. In recent years spending on these programs has grown far more rapidly than national income. Exhibit 8 illustrates their growth rate for the 1969–1979 period. Measured in *real* dollars, spending on income transfer programs expanded at an annual rate of 7.2 percent, compared to only a 2.8 percent increase in national income. The rapid growth rate was pretty much across-the-board. Social security benefits, Medicare/Medicaid, unemployment benefits, federal pensions, and worker's compensation all grew more than twice as fast as real income. *Real* expenditures on the food stamp program rose at an annual rate of 28.7 percent during the 1970s—more than ten times as rapidly as national income. Real expenditures on one of the more controversial transfer programs, Aid for Dependent Children, rose at a 5 percent annual rate, somewhat less rapidly than the other major transfer programs. Exhibit 8 illustrates that retirement pension programs comprise the bulk of these expenditures. Recent history suggests that Congress will be reluctant to hold these expenditures to the growth rate of national income and highly unlikely to reduce them as a share of GNP.

EXHIBIT 8   The growth of transfer payments

Expenditures on income transfers, primarily entitlement programs, grew much more rapidly than national income during the 1970s.

Facts and Figures on Government Finance—1981, Table 20.

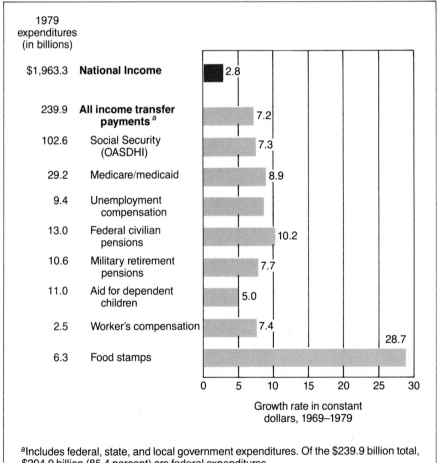

ᵃIncludes federal, state, and local government expenditures. Of the $239.9 billion total, $204.9 billion (85.4 percent) are federal expenditures.

If neither interest payments nor transfer payments are likely to decline as a share of GNP, it is virtually impossible to reduce the relative size of government *and* increase real defense expenditures. Unless Congress and the Reagan administration are prepared to tamper with social security and other pension programs, the likelihood of a significant decline in federal spending *as a share of GNP* is remote.

3. Policy-Makers Will Find That They Cannot Increase Defense Expenditures, Leave the Major Transfer Programs Intact, Cut Tax Rates, and Use Monetary Policy to Slow Down the Economy without Incurring Large Budget Deficits. As we discussed previously, the administration inherited budget deficits that have been running at approximately 2.4 percent of GNP (see Exhibit 9, Chapter 14, page 298). This means that for the $3.5 trillion economy expected in 1983, there will be a base deficit of roughly $84 billion. However, the administration's tax-spending policies will almost certainly increase this figure. Most independent observers are forecasting annual deficits of between $100 and $200 billion for the 1983–1985 fiscal years.

The accompanying Thumbnail Sketch summarizes both the Reagan approach and the possible complications of the administration's policy. Despite the early optimism of some of the proponents of the Reagan program, it is primarily a long-run strategy. For example, even if the monetary policy designed to decelerate the inflation rate is successful in the long run, it will probably exert a negative impact on economic growth and employment in the short run. Similarly, the incentive effects of the tax program will be felt primarily in the long run. The administration should be judged on the basis of its programs. As economic events unfold, time will render a judgment.

Thumbnail Sketch — Reaganomics

The Economic Problem	Primary Reagan Solution	Possible Complications
Inflation	Gradual decline in the growth rate of the money supply	Tight monetary policy may cause a recession; a recession will increase size of budget deficit
Slow rate of economic growth	Lower tax rates; deregulation; reduce the size of the public sector	Unable to reduce government expenditures; therefore tax cut causes huge budget deficit
High interest rates	The saving incentives built into the tax plan; monetary deceleration	Tax package does not stimulate much additional saving, while budget deficits increase the demand for loanable funds
Large budget deficits	Reduce the growth rate of government expenditures; cut tax rates to stimulate economic growth and *eventually* tax revenues	Unable to cut expenditures; tax cut enlarges the deficits; high interest rate and sluggish growth result

MACROECONOMICS IN THE 1980s

Regardless of the success or failure of the Reagan program, the microeconomic approach will continue to exert an important influence on the direction of macroeconomics in the 1980s. The important questions of the 1980s encompass both macro- and microeconomics. How can we alter relative price incentives in a manner that will lower the rates of both unemployment and inflation? How important are the effects of a tax cut (or tax increase) on work incentives? How can the role of time and adjustment lags in highly aggregative markets be integrated into our analysis? Researchers will have to use both macro- and microeconomic tools as they seek answers to these questions.

The distinction between micro- and macroeconomics is becoming increasingly blurred by these developments. This is all to the good. After all, both micro- and macroanalysis are concerned with decision-making and human behavior.

PERSPECTIVES IN ECONOMICS
THE REAGAN TAX CUT AND WELFARE FOR THE RICH[7]

The 1981 tax legislation has often been criticized as "welfare for the rich." It is easy to understand why. Not only is the dollar amount of the tax reduction greater for those with higher incomes, but these people will also receive a larger percentage increase in their after-tax marginal earnings. For example, at the top of the income ladder, marginal tax rates are reduced from 70 percent to 50 percent. Thus, after the tax cut, high-income recipients in the top tax bracket are permitted to keep 50 cents of every *additional* dollar earned, compared to only 30 cents under prior legislation. Their after-tax income from an extra dollar of earning will increase by 66.7 percent as the result of the tax cut. Similarly, the marginal

---

[7]This piece is based on a larger study done by the authors, which was supported by The Center for Political Economy and Natural Resources at Montana State University. See James Gwartney and Richard Stroup, "Tax Cuts: Who Shoulders the Burden?" Federal Reserve Bank of Atlanta *Economic Review* (March 1982), pp. 19–27, for additional details on this topic.

tax rate of a married couple with a joint *taxable* income of $60,000–$85,600 will decline from 54 percent in 1980 to 42 percent in 1984. A couple in this tax bracket will be permitted to keep 58 cents of each *additional* dollar earned in 1984, compared to only 46 percent in 1980—an increase of 26 percent. In contrast, the marginal tax rate in the lowest income category will fall from 14 percent to 11 percent. Thus, the after-tax marginal income in the lowest tax bracket will increase from 86 percent to 89 percent, an increase of only 3 percent.

If *taxable* incomes remain unchanged, tax revenues will decline and high-income taxpayers will reap a disproportionately large "windfall" reduction in the size of their tax bill. Clearly, this is the way that the major news media and most citizens viewed the tax cut. However, the situation is far more complicated. There is good reason to believe that the layperson's view of the distributional aspects of the tax cut is at least misleading, if not incorrect.

The problem arises because of a failure to distinguish between changes in tax *rates* and changes in the *revenues*. Since high-income taxpayers experienced the largest increase in after-tax

income *per additional dollar earned*, the incentive effects of the tax cut will be greatest in this area. The lower rates will also reduce the profitability of tax shelters, inducing high-income taxpayers to allocate less of their income to this area. As a result, more of their income will be taxable. Predictably, *taxable* income in the upper brackets will grow more rapidly than in lower-income brackets. Therefore, lower tax *rates* will not result in a proportional decline in tax *revenues*, at least not in the high marginal tax brackets where the incentive effects of the tax cut will be largest.

The Kennedy–Johnson tax cut provides evidence in support of this view. The 1964 tax cut sliced the top marginal bracket from 91 percent to 70 percent, leading to a 233 percent increase (from 9 cents to 30 cents per additional dollar of earnings) in take-home pay from marginal income in this bracket. The bottom rate was cut from 20 percent to 14 percent. Therefore, after-tax income per dollar of additional earnings in the bottom bracket rose from 80 percent to 86 percent, an increase of only 7.5 percent. Thus, the Kennedy–Johnson tax cut, like the 1981 legislation, resulted in both larger dollar reductions in tax liability and larger increases in after-tax earnings for high-income taxpayers.[8] However, as Exhibits 9 and 10 illustrate, this does not necessarily mean that the proportion of tax revenue collected from high-income recipients declined. Just as one would expect given the incentive effects, *taxable incomes* grew rapidly in the upper tax brackets after the tax cut. Exhibit 9 presents data on the growth of adjusted gross income (AGI) and tax revenues collected from tax returns with an AGI of $50,000 or more for the 1960–1966 period. The adjusted gross income derived from these high-income taxpayers grew at a 7 percent annual rate during the three years

immediately prior to the tax cut. The picture was quite different for 1964–1966. During the three years following the rate reductions, the AGI (measured in constant 1963 dollars) derived from returns on incomes of $50,000 or more rose at an annual rate of 17.5 percent.

The growth rate of tax revenues derived from these taxpayers followed, of course, a similar pattern. For the 1961–1963 period, the real tax revenue collected from returns with an income of $50,000 or more rose at an annual rate of 6.1 percent. In the three years following the tax cut, tax revenues collected from these taxpayers grew at an annual rate of 14.1 percent. Even though the tax rates of these high-income taxpayers were cut sharply, the constant dollar growth rate of revenues collected in this category rose substantially as the result of the rapid growth of taxable income.

Exhibit 10 presents data on tax

revenue before and after the 1964 tax cut according to percentile income groupings. For the bottom 50 percent of income earners, tax revenues (measured in 1963 dollars) declined from $5.01 billion in 1963 to $4.55 billion in 1965, a reduction of 9.2 percent. Clearly, there is no reason to think that this group is on the backward-bending portion of the Laffer curve.[9] Revenue collections from returns in the 50th to 75th percentile and in the 75th to 95th percentile also declined, albeit by a smaller percentage than for the lowest income grouping. In all three of these income categories, the negative impact of the rate reductions on tax revenues was dominant over the positive impact of income growth on tax revenues.

---

[8]This results because both the 1964 and 1981 tax reductions were approximately "across-the-board" tax cuts. Tax rates were cut by a similar *percentage* for all brackets. However, since the percentage reduction of high-income taxpayers is calculated from their higher marginal tax rate, it will be a larger *nominal* rate reduction.

[9]The backward-bending portion of the Laffer curve indicates that for tax rates above a certain level, an increase in tax rates leads to a *reduction* in tax revenues (see Chapter 5, pp. 93–96).

EXHIBIT 9   The growth rate of adjusted gross income and tax revenue for high-income returns

These data are for tax returns reporting incomes of $50,000 or more, prior to and subsequent to the 1964 tax cut. Data are measured in constant 1963 dollars. Note the rapid growth in both income and tax revenue collected from these high-income taxpayers following the 1964 tax cut.

Year	Adjusted Gross Income (Billions of Constant 1963 Dollars) Returns with AGI Greater than $50,000	Tax Revenue Collected (Billions of Constant 1963 Dollars) Returns with AGI Greater than $50,000
1960	11.99	4.54
1961	13.75	5.21
1962	13.62	5.04
1963	14.60	5.38
1964	17.67	6.08
1965	21.33	7.20
1966	23.65	7.97
Average Growth Rate (Percent)		
1961–1963 (before tax cut)	7.0	6.1
1964–1966 (after tax cut)	17.5	14.1

Internal Revenue Service, *Statistics of Income: Individual Income Tax Returns* (annual).

EXHIBIT 10 Tax revenue from various income groupings

The tax revenues are ranked according to adjusted gross income prior to and subsequent to the 1964 reduction in tax rates.

Percentile of All Returns (Ranked from Lowest to Highest Income)	Tax Revenues Collected from Group (in Billions of 1963 Dollars)[a]		Percent Change
	1963	1965	
Bottom 50 percent	$ 5.01	$ 4.55	−9.2
50th to 75th percentile	10.02	9.61	−4.1
75th to 95th percentile	16.00	15.41	−3.7
Top 5 percent	17.17	18.49	+7.7
Total	$48.20	$48.06	−0.3

[a]These estimates were derived by interpolation.

Internal Revenue Service, *Statistics of Income: Individual Income Tax Returns* (1963 and 1965).

Therefore, tax revenues collected in these income categories in 1965 were lower than was true for 1963.

The picture for the 5 percent of taxpayers with the highest incomes was quite different. The tax rates of these high-income taxpayers were reduced from the 30 to 91 percent range in 1963 to the 25 to 70 percent range in 1965. In this highest income category, *real* federal tax revenue collections from personal income rose from $17.17 billion in 1963 to $18.49 billion in 1965, a healthy increase of 7.7 percent. Tax revenues collected from these high-income taxpayers grew because the rapid expansion in their taxable income had more impact than the loss of tax revenue associated with the rate reductions. *The 1964 tax cut actually shifted the tax burden toward the rich,* despite the fact that this group received larger *nominal* rate reductions than other groups. The top 5 percent of taxpayers paid 38.5 percent of the federal personal income tax in 1965, up from 35.6 percent in 1963.

Where are we on the Laffer curve? The correct answer will vary for different income brackets. For persons with low marginal tax rates, 10 percent for example, there is little reason to expect that a 20 percent rate reduction (from 10 percent to 8 percent) will have much impact on their incentive to earn and report additional taxable income. After all, at the margin, take-home pay will only increase from 90 percent to 92 percent in this bracket, not a very large increase. Under these conditions, there is every reason to expect that lower tax rates will lead to an approximately proportional reduction in tax revenues.

However, the implications of the same 20 percent reduction in *high* marginal tax rates are dramatically different. A 20 percent cut in a 70 percent marginal rate (to 56 percent), will increase the taxpayer's after-tax income per additional dollar earned from 30 cents to 44 cents, an increase of 47 percent. In this bracket, the incentive effects of the 20 percent reduction will be substantial.

Thus, there is reason to believe that the *taxable* income of individuals in high marginal tax brackets will be far more sensitive to changes in marginal tax rates than the taxable income of those with lower marginal rates. A reduction in high marginal rates may result in only a small reduction in tax revenues. At very high rates, we may even see an increase in tax revenues, as the backward-bending Laffer curve implies. Therefore, even if the larger *nominal* rate reductions go to high-income (and therefore high-marginal-rate) taxpayers, it does not follow that they will carry a smaller share of the personal income tax burden. In fact, an analysis of the 1964 tax cut indicates that this is unlikely to be the case.

Discussion

1. Do you think the rich should pay a *higher percentage* of their income in taxes than do the poor? Why or why not?

2. Do you think that the marginal earnings of persons with high incomes should be taxed at rates of 50 percent or more? Why or why not?

3. If the highest marginal rates could be reduced 10 percent without any loss of tax revenue to the Treasury, would you favor the reduction? Why or why not?

1 During the 1970s, the economy of the United States was plagued by a declining growth rate and an accelerating inflation rate. The growth rate of the U.S. economy was poor not only by historical standards but also in comparison to other industrial nations.

2 In recent years, there has been an upsurge in interest in microeconomic policy designed to deal with problems of sluggish economic growth, high unemployment, and inflation. The microapproach emphasizes (a) relative price effects, (b) the microstructure of the economy, and (c) long-run rather than short-run policy prescriptions.

3 Unemployment in the 1980s differs from that of the 1930s in several respects. In the 1930s, unemployment generally involved the loss of jobs by prime-age workers who were solely responsible for the income of their families. Unemployment compensation, layoff benefits, and welfare programs were generally unavailable to cushion the impact of unemployment. In contrast, in the early 1980s, nearly half of the unemployed workers were under age 25. Multi-earner families were much more common, and various types of income transfer programs were available to assist the unemployed.

4 If the United States wants to accelerate its sagging growth rate, most economists believe that a higher rate of capital formation will be necessary. Currently, the U.S. tax structure tends to subsidize borrowing and penalize saving. A reversal of this incentive structure would encourage saving, reduce current consumption, and help supply the funds necessary for an expansion in capital formation.

5 Indexing the interest rate of government bonds would reduce the government's cost of borrowing and eliminate the windfall transfer of income to bondholders as the inflation rate falls. Similarly, indexing would prevent the government from gaining at the expense of bondholders, if it should follow inflationary policies in the future.

6 During the 1970s there was a rapid growth in the number of people under age 35 and over age 65. These demographic changes increased the normal rate of unemployment, retarded the growth of real income, and reduced the rate of saving. In contrast, during the 1980s, there will be a decline in the youthful (under age 25) segment of the population, while the 35-to-54 age group will expand rapidly. Other things constant, this will reduce the normal rate of unemployment, lead to a more rapid growth rate of income, and result in a higher rate of saving.

7 The unemployment compensation program was designed to minimize the hardship of unemployment. Unfortunately, the system also encourages unemployment, since it (a) induces employers to make more extensive use of temporary layoffs and (b) makes longer periods of unemployment (and job search) cheaper to workers relative to the acceptance of available employment opportunities. The system could be reformed so as to retain its original objective but minimize its adverse impact on the normal rate of employment.

8 Exemption of youthful workers from minimum wage legislation and the institution of youth work scholarships are two reforms that many economists believe would effectively combat the high rate of unemployment among youthful workers.

9 The Reagan administration proposed a four-part economic program to deal with the stagflation, instability, and high interest rates that plagued the U.S. economy at the beginning of the 1980s. The major components of the program were: (a) slower growth of the money supply; (b) a reduction in tax rates; (c) a reduction in the growth rate of government expenditures; and (d) economic deregulation.

10 In 1981, Congress passed the Economic Recovery Tax Act. This legislation (a) reduced nominal personal income tax rates over a four-year period by approximately 23 percent; (b) mandated the indexing of tax rates beginning in 1985; (c) provided for a more rapid depreciation allowance on investment; and (d) instituted various tax incentives to encourage individuals to save for retirement.

11 The Reagan tax cut will not really reduce marginal tax rates on *real* income unless the inflation rate falls substantially. Essentially, it offsets bracket creep and higher social security taxes. Since the legislation will not significantly reduce marginal tax rates for most people, there is little reason to expect a substantial expansion in aggregate output.

12 The Reagan strategy calls for an increase in national defense expenditures. Since it is likely to be extremely difficult to reduce federal spending on either (a) national debt interest payments or (b) pension/retirement programs, it seems impossible that the administration will be able to increase defense spending *and* reduce the relative size of the federal sector as planned. If spending is not cut and/or taxes increased, large deficits are likely to lead to rising interest rates, which will stall the recovery from the 1981 recession.

THE ECONOMIC WAY OF THINKING—DISCUSSION QUESTIONS

1 The chairman of the Council of Economic Advisers has requested that you write a short paper on how we can permanently reduce the rate of unemployment. Be sure to make specific proposals. Indicate why your recommendations will work. Submit the paper to your instructor, and she or he will pass it along to the CEA.

2 The early part of this chapter outlined the economic conditions present when Ronald Reagan became president. How have conditions changed? Has his program effectively combated inflation, unemployment, instability, and high interest rates? What grade would you give the president's economic program?

3 "The economic events of the 1970s illustrate the failure of macroeconomic policy. If economists were as smart as they let on, we would have experienced neither the high rate of unemployment nor the business instability of the decade." Indicate why you either agree or disagree with this view.

4 How does the microeconomic approach to the problems of unemployment and economic growth differ from the traditional emphasis on monetary and fiscal policy? Is the microeconomic approach a substitute for traditional monetary and fiscal policy? Explain.

5 Why do you think that the economic growth rate of the United States has been so slow compared to that of other industrial nations? Should we be concerned about our sagging growth rate? Why or why not?

6 Why was the unemployment rate so high during the 1970s? Was the high unemployment rate indicative of a sluggish demand for labor? What do you think will happen to the unemployment rate in the late 1980s?

PART THREE

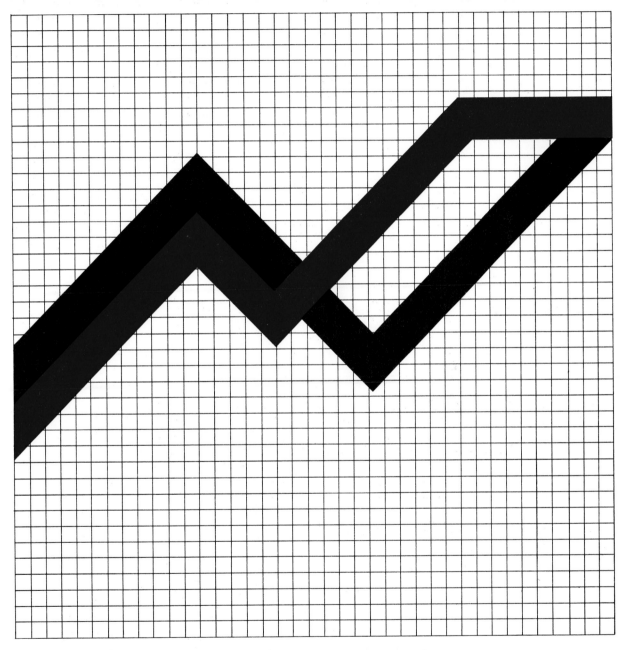

MICROECONOMICS

17

DEMAND AND CONSUMER CHOICE

Macroeconomics focuses on aggregate markets—the big picture. Aggregate outcomes are, of course, the result of many individual decisions. We cannot understand, or successfully influence, the big picture without a solid knowledge of how microeconomic decisions are made. In this section, we will break down the aggregate product market into microeconomic markets for specific products.

Microeconomics focuses on how changes in *relative* prices influence consumer decisions. As we stressed in Chapter 3, the price system guides individuals in their production and consumption decisions.[2] Prices coordinate the vast array of individual economic activities by signaling relative wants and needs and by motivating market participants to bring their own activities into harmony with those of others. Changes in one market affect conditions in others. In this chapter we take a closer look at (a) the interrelationships among markets and (b) the factors underlying the demand for specific products.

CHOICE AND INDIVIDUAL DEMAND

Exhibit 1 shows how consumers allocated their spending among alternative goods in 1950 and 1981. Why did consumers spend more on transportation than medical care, or more on alcoholic beverages than religious and welfare activities? Why have consumer expenditures on food declined (as a percentage of the total) while spending on housing has expanded? If we are to answer these questions, we will need to know something about the factors that influence the behavior of consumers.

---

[1]Henry Fielding, *Tom Jones,* Book VI, Chapter III.

[2]You may want to review Chapter 3 before beginning the study of microeconomics.

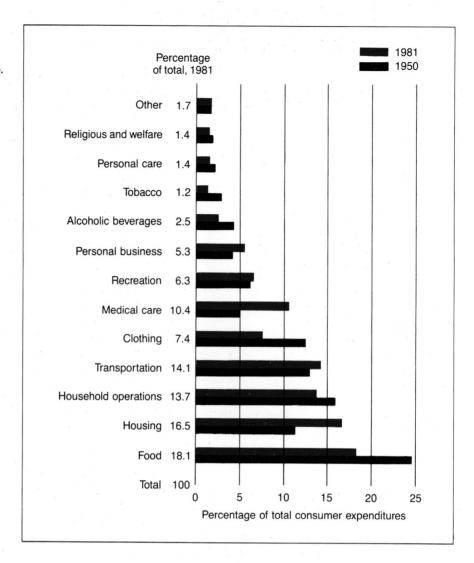

When analyzing the choices of consumers, economists usually make the following assumptions.

1. Limited Income Necessitates Choice.   Most of us are all too aware that our desire for goods far exceeds our limited income. People do not have enough resources to produce everything they would like. A limited income forces each of us to make choices. When one good or service is purchased, many others must be foregone.

2. Consumers Make Decisions Purposefully.   Consumption decisions are made in order to increase personal welfare. A foolish purchase means giving up something more worthwhile. The purpose or goal behind a consumer decision can usually be met in many different ways, so that careful consideration of alternatives is useful. Consumers generally choose the alternative that is expected to increase their personal welfare the most, relative to cost. They do not *consciously* choose a lesser-valued alternative when another of equal cost but projected greater benefit is available.

3. *One Good Can Be Substituted for Another.* Consumers have many goals, each with alternative means of satisfaction. No single good is so precious that some of it will not be given up in exchange for more of other goods. For example, consumers will give up some fried chicken in order to have more pizza, hamburgers, fish, ham sandwiches, or apple pie. Similarly, reading, watching movies and television, or playing cards can be substituted for playing football. How about our "need" for basic commodities such as water or energy? The "need" of a person for an item is closely related to its cost—what must be given up in order to obtain the item. Southern California residents "need" water from the north, but the individual resident, when faced with a high water cost, finds that cactus gardens can be substituted for lawn, a plumber's bill for a faucet drip, and flow constrictors for full-force showers. The need for water depends on its cost. People living in Montana, where household electricity costs about twice as much as in nearby Washington, use half as much electricity per household. Montanans reduce their "need" for electricity by substituting gas, fuel oil, insulation, and wool sweaters for it.

4. *Consumers Must Make Decisions without Perfect Information, but Knowledge and Past Experience Will Help.* No human being has perfect foresight. Napoleon did not anticipate Waterloo; Julius Caesar did not anticipate the actions of Brutus. Consumers will not always correctly anticipate the consequences of their choices.

However, consumer choices are not made in a vacuum. You have a pretty good idea of what to expect when you buy a cup of coffee, five gallons of gasoline, or lunch at your favorite diner. Why? Because you have learned from experience—your own and that of others. When you buy a product, your expectations may not be fulfilled precisely (for example, the coffee may be stronger than expected or the gasoline may make your car knock), but even these experiences will give you valuable information that can be used in making future decisions.

Law of Diminishing Marginal Utility: A basic economic principle which states that as the consumption of a commodity increases, eventually the marginal utility derived from consuming more of the commodity (per unit of time) will decline. Marginal utility may decline even though total utility continues to increase, albeit at a reduced rate.

Marginal Utility: The additional utility received by a person from the consumption of an additional unit of a good within a given time period.

5. *The Law of Diminishing Marginal Utility Applies: As the Rate of Consumption Increases, the Utility Derived from Consuming Additional Units of a Good Will Decline.* Utility is a term that economists use to describe the subjective personal benefits that result from an action. The **law of diminishing marginal utility** states that the **marginal** (or additional) **utility** derived from consuming successive units of a product will *eventually* decline as the rate of utilization increases. For example, the law implies that even though you might like ice cream, your marginal satisfaction from *additional* ice cream will eventually decline. Ice cream at lunchtime might be great. An additional helping for dinner might be even better. However, after you have had it for evening dessert and a midnight snack, ice cream for breakfast will begin to lose some of its attraction. The law of diminishing marginal utility will have set in, and thus the marginal utility derived from the consumption of additional units of ice cream will decline.

Marginal Utility and Consumer Choice

Consumer choices, like other decisions, are influenced by changes in benefits and costs. If a consumer wants to get the most out of her or his expenditures, how much of each good should be purchased? As more of a good is consumed per unit of time, the law of diminishing marginal utility states that the consumer's marginal benefit per unit of time will decline. A consumer will gain by purchasing more of a product as long as the benefit, or marginal utility (MU), derived from the consumption of an additional unit exceeds the costs of the unit (the expected marginal utility from other consumption alternatives that must now be given up).

Given a fixed income and specified prices for the commodities to be purchased, consumers will maximize their satisfaction (or total utility) by ensuring that the last dollar spent on each commodity purchased yields an equal degree of marginal utility. If consumers are to get the most for their money, the last dollar spent on product A must yield the same utility as the last dollar spent on product B (or any other product).[3] After all, if tickets for football games, for example, yielded less marginal utility *per dollar* than opera tickets did, the obvious thing for a consumer to do would to be cut back spending on football games and allocate more funds for opera tickets. If we assume that people really attempt to spend their money in a way that yields the greatest amount of satisfaction, the applicability of the consumer decision-making theory outlined above is difficult to question.

Price Changes and Consumption Decisions

Demand is the schedule of the amount of a product that consumers would be willing to purchase at alternative prices during a specific time period. The first law of demand states that the amount of a product purchased is inversely related to its price. Why? First, as the price of a product declines, the opportunity cost of consuming it will fall. The lower opportunity cost will induce consumers to buy more of it. However, as they increase their rate of consumption, what will happen to the marginal utility derived from the product? It will fall. Thus, as more of the product is consumed, eventually the benefits (marginal utility) derived from the consumption of still more units will again be less than the cost. Purposeful decision-makers will not choose such units. Thus, a price reduction will induce consumers to purchase more of a product, but the response will be limited because of the law of diminishing marginal utility. Economists refer to this tendency to substitute a *relatively* cheaper product for goods that are now more expensive as the **substitution effect**.

Substitution Effect: That part of an increase in amount consumed that is the result of a good being cheaper in relation to other goods because of a reduction in price.

Second, since the money income of consumers is constant, a reduction in the price of a product will increase their real income—the amount of goods and services that they are able to purchase. Typically, consumers will respond by purchasing more of the cheaper product (as well as other products) because they can now better afford to do so. This factor is referred to as the **income effect**.

Income Effect: That part of an increase in amount consumed that is the result of the consumer's real income (the consumption possibilities available to the consumer) being expanded by a reduction in the price of a good.

Of course, the substitution and income effects will generally cause

---

[3]Mathematically, this implies that the consumer's total utility is at a maximum when his limited income is spent on products such that

$$\frac{MU_a}{P_a} = \frac{MU_b}{P_b} = \cdots = \frac{MU_n}{P_n}$$

where MU represents the marginal utility derived from the last unit of a product, and P represents the price of the good. The subscripts a, b, . . . , n indicate the different products available to the consumer. In the continuous case, the above expression implies that the consumer will get the most for his or her money when the consumption of each product is increased only to the point where the marginal utility from one more unit of the good is equal to the marginal utility obtainable from the best alternative purchase that must now be foregone. For more advanced students, this proposition is developed in an alternative, more formal manner in the Addendum on indifference curves.

consumers to purchase less of a good if its price rises. Why will consumers curtail their consumption of a product that has risen in price? The opportunity cost of consuming the product has risen, making it a less attractive buy. As consumption is reduced, however, the consumer's marginal utility derived from the product will rise. If the price rise is not so great as to price the consumer out of the market completely, a sufficient fall in the rate of consumption will cause enough rise in the product's marginal utility that it will again equal its opportunity cost. With moderate increases in price, the consumer's reduction in consumption will be limited. We must also bear in mind that if we assume that the consumer's money income is constant, the price increase will reduce the individual's real income. A reduction in real income will tend to result in a reduction in the consumption of many goods, including the good that has increased in price.

Exhibit 2 illustrates the adjustment of consumers to a change in a price. In 1978–1979, gasoline prices rose rapidly in the United States. As demand theory would predict, consumers reduced their rate of consumption. As gasoline prices rose from 80 cents to $1.20, Joneses weekly consumption fell from 20 gallons to 18 gallons. Initially, consumers eliminated the least valued uses of gasoline. Less valuable trips were discontinued, shopping trips were combined with other business near shopping centers, and television watching was substituted for leisure driving. At the lower consumption level, the marginal utility of gasoline rose, bringing it into line with the higher price.

Still higher gasoline prices would have elicited an even greater reduction in consumption. The additional decline in consumption would have required consumers to forego still higher valued uses of gasoline. However, if the price had risen to $1.60, for example, the response would have again been limited, because the marginal utility of gasoline would have risen as consumption was reduced.

Time Cost and Consumer Choice

The monetary price of a good is not always a complete measure of its cost to the consumer. Consumption of most goods requires time as well as money. Time,

EXHIBIT 2   Gas prices, consumption, and marginal utility

Individuals will increase their rate of consumption of a product as long as MU exceeds its opportunity cost (principally the price of the good). Higher prices will cause individuals to consume less, but the reduction in consumption will be limited because the MU of the product will rise as consumption falls.

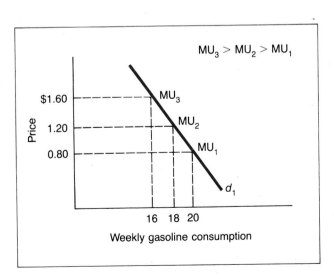

like money, is scarce to the consumer. A lower time cost, like a lower money price, will make a product more attractive to consumers.[4]

Some commodities are demanded primarily because of their ability to reduce the consumer's time cost. Consumers are often willing to pay higher money prices for such goods. The popularity of automatic dishwashers, electric razors, prepared foods, air travel, and taxi service is based on their low time cost in comparison with substitutes.

What is the cost of a college education? Tuition payments and the price of books comprise only a small component. The major cost of a college education is the time cost—approximately 4000 hours. If a student's time is valued at only $3 per hour, the time cost of a college education is $12,000!

Time costs, unlike money prices, differ among individuals. They are higher for persons with greater earning power. Other things being equal, high-wage consumers choose fewer time-intensive (and more time-saving) commodities than persons with a lower time cost. High-wage consumers are over-represented among air and taxicab passengers but underrepresented among television watchers, chess players, and long-distance automobile travelers. Can you explain why? You should be able to if you understand that both money and time cost influence the choices of consumers.

Consumer Choice and Market Demand

The market demand schedule is the amount demanded by all the individuals in the market area at various prices. Since individual consumers purchase less at higher prices, the amount demanded in a market area is also inversely related to price.

Exhibit 3 illustrates the relationship between individual demand and market demand for a hypothetical two-person market. The individual demand curves for both Jones and Smith are shown. At 50 cents per gallon, both Jones and Smith consume 20 gallons of gasoline weekly. The amount demanded in the two-person market is 40 gallons. If the price rises to $1 per gallon, the amount demanded in the market will fall to 28 gallons, 16 demanded by Jones and 12 by Smith. The market demand is simply the horizontal sum of the individual demand curves.

Market demand reflects individual demand. Individuals buy less as price increases. Therefore, the total amount demanded in the market declines as price increases.

Consumer Surplus

Consumer Surplus: The difference between the maximum amount a consumer would be willing to pay for a unit of a good and the payment that is actually made.

The demand curve reveals how many units consumers will purchase at various prices. However, it also reveals consumers' evaluation of units of a good. The height of the demand curve indicates how much consumers value a particular unit. The difference between the amount that consumers would be willing to pay and the amount they actually pay for a good is called **consumer surplus.** As Exhibit 4 illustrates, it is measured by the area under the demand curve but above the market price level.

Previously, we indicated that voluntary exchange is advantageous to both

---

[4]For a technical treatment of the importance of time as a component of cost from the vantage point of the consumer, see Gary Becker, "A Theory of the Allocation of Time," *Economic Journal* (September 1965), pp. 493–517.

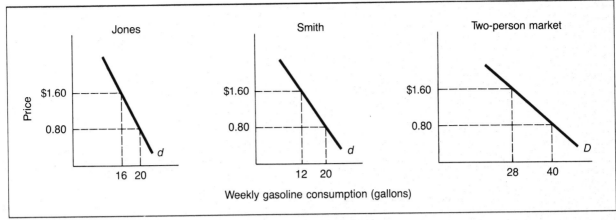

EXHIBIT 3   Individual and market demand curves

The market demand curve is merely the horizontal sum of the individual demand curves. The market demand curve will slope downward to the right just as the individual demand curves do.

buyer and seller. Consumer surplus is a measure of the gain that accrues to the buyer/consumer. Consumer surplus also reflects the law of diminishing marginal utility. Consumers will continue purchasing additional units of a good until the marginal utility is just equal to the market price. Up to that point, however, consumption of each unit will generate a surplus for the consumer, since the valuation of the unit generally exceeds the market price. In aggregate, the total value (utility) consumers place on the units purchased may be far greater than the consumers' total cost.

The size of the consumer surplus is determined by the market price. A reduction in the market price will increase the amount of consumer surplus; an increase in the market price will cause the surplus to decline.

EXHIBIT 4   Consumer surplus

As the shaded area indicates, the difference between the amount consumers would be willing to pay and the price they actually pay is called consumer surplus.

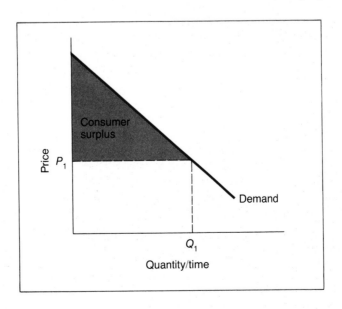

What Causes the Demand Curve to Shift?

The demand schedule isolates the impact of price on amount purchased, assuming other factors are held constant. What are these "other factors"? How do they influence demand?

Changes in the Income of Consumers Influence the Demand for a Product.[5] The demand for most products is positively related to income. As their income expands, consumers typically spend more on consumption. The demand for most products increases. Conversely, a reduction in consumer income usually causes the demand for a product to fall.

Changes in the Distribution of Income Influence the Demand for Specific Products. If more income were allocated to alcoholics and less to vegetarians, the demand for liquor would increase, whereas the demand for vegetables would fall. Consider another example. Suppose that a law were passed that taxed all inheritances over $50,000 at a 90 percent rate. If the law effectively reduced the income of sons and daughters of the wealthy, it would also reduce their demand for yachts, around-the-world cruises, diamonds, and perhaps even Harvard educations. If the revenues from the tax were redistributed to persons with incomes below $5000, the demand for hamburgers, used cars, moderately priced housing, and other commodities that low-income families purchase would increase relative to yachts, cruises, and diamonds.

The Prices of Closely Related Goods Influence the Demand for a Product. Related goods may be either substitutes or complements. When two products perform similar functions or fulfill similar needs, they are **substitutes.** There is a direct relationship between the price of a product and the demand for substitutes. For example, butter and margarine are substitutes. Higher butter prices will increase the demand for margarine as consumers substitute it for the more expensive butter. Similarly, higher coffee prices will increase the demand for such substitutes as cocoa and tea. A substitute relationship exists between beef and pork, pencils and pens, apples and oranges, and so forth.

> **Substitutes:** Products that are related such that an increase in the price of one will cause an increase in demand for the other (for example, butter and margarine, Chevrolets and Fords).

Other closely related products are consumed jointly. Goods that "go together," so to speak, are called **complements.** For complements, there is an inverse relationship between the price of one and the demand for the other. For example, as the experiences of the 1970s illustrate quite well, higher gasoline prices cause the demand for large automobiles to decline. Gasoline and large automobiles are complementary. Similarly, lower prices for portable radios increase the demand for complementary batteries. Ham and eggs are complementary to each other; so are tents and camping equipment, and automatic dishwashers and electricity.

> **Complements:** Products that are usually consumed jointly (for example, lamps and light bulbs). An increase in the price of one will cause the demand for the other to fall.

Changes in Consumer Preferences Influence Demand. Why do preferences change? People are always changing. New information might change their valuation of a good. How did consumers respond to new information linking cigarette smoking to cancer in the mid-1960s? They smoked fewer cigarettes. Annual per capita consumption, which had been increasing, fell more than 6

---

[5]Do not forget that a change in *quantity demanded* is a movement along a demand curve in response to a change in price, but a change in *demand* is a shift in the entire demand curve. Review Chapter 3 if you find this point confusing.

percent between 1965 and 1970. When consumers acquired information that cigarettes were also cancer sticks, many of them changed their preferences.

Changes in Population and Its Composition Influence the Demand for Products. The demand for products in a market area is directly related to the number of consumers. Changes in the composition of the population may also have an impact on demand. If a higher percentage of the population is between 16 and 21 years of age, the demand for movies, stereo equipment and records, sports cars, and college educations will be positively affected. An increase in the number of elderly people will positively affect the demand for medical care, retirement housing, and vacation travel.

Expectations Influence Demand. When consumers expect the future price of a product to rise (fall), their current demand for it will expand (decline). Buy now, before the price goes even higher! When the price of beef rose sharply in 1977–1978, how did shoppers respond? Initially, current sales increased; consumers hoarded the product because they expected its price to continue rising. Conversely, if consumers thought that the price of a product, automobiles, for example, would be 10 percent lower next year, would this influence current actions? Of course; many consumers would defer their purchase of an automobile until next year, so they would be able to buy at bargain prices.

When an economist constructs a demand schedule for a product, it is assumed that factors other than the price of the product are held constant. As Exhibit 5 shows, changes in any of these factors that influence consumer decisions will cause the entire demand curve to shift. The accompanying Thumbnail Sketch (a) points out that *quantity demanded* (but not demand) will change in response to a change in the price of a product and (b) summarizes the major factors that cause a change in *demand* (a shift of the entire curve).

THE ELASTICITY OF DEMAND

If the tuition charges at your school go up 50 percent next year, how many of your classmates will be back? If the price of salt doubles, how much less will you purchase? These are questions about price elasticity of demand.

EXHIBIT 5   Price is not all that matters

Other things constant, the demand schedule will slope downward to the right. However, changes in income and its distribution, the prices of closely related products, preferences, population, and expectations about future prices will also influence consumer decisions. Changes in these factors will cause the entire demand curve to shift (for example, increase from D_1 to D_2).

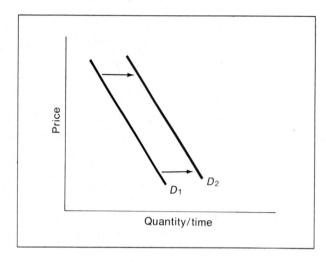

Price Elasticity of Demand: The percent change in the quantity of a product demanded divided by the percent change in its price. Price elasticity of demand indicates the degree of consumer response to variation in price.

Price elasticity of demand[6] is defined as:

$$\frac{\text{Percent change in quantity demanded}}{\text{percent change in price}}$$

This ratio is called the elasticity coefficient. Elasticity of demand refers to the flexibility of consumers' desire for a product—the degree of their responsiveness to a change in a product's price. If the amount of a good that consumers choose falls substantially in response to a small rise in price, the demand for the product is elastic. In contrast, if a substantial increase in price results in only a small reduction in quantity demanded, demand is said to be inelastic. The quantity demanded along an elastic demand curve is highly sensitive to a change in price. In contrast, an inelastic demand curve indicates inflexibility or little consumer response to variation in price.

The precise distinction between elastic and inelastic can be determined by the elasticity coefficient. When the elasticity coefficient is greater than 1 (ignoring the sign), demand is elastic. An elasticity coefficient of less than 1 means that demand is inelastic. "Unitary elasticity" is the term used to denote a price elasticity of 1. The sign of the elasticity coefficient will always be negative, since a change in price will cause the quantity demanded to change in the opposite direction.

---

[6]You might want to distinguish between (a) the elasticity at a point on the demand curve and (b) the *arc* elasticity *between* two points on the demand curve. The formula for point elasticity is:

$$\frac{\text{Change in quantity demanded}}{\text{Initial quantity demanded}} \div \frac{\text{change in price}}{\text{initial price}}$$

The formula for arc elasticity is:

$$[(q_0 - q_1)/\tfrac{1}{2}(q_0 + q_1)] \div [(P_0 - P_1)/\tfrac{1}{2}(P_0 + P_1)]$$

where the subscripts 0 and 1 refer to the respective prices and amounts demanded at two alternative points on a specific demand curve. The arc elasticity is really an average elasticity between the two points on the curve.

Graphic Representation of Demand Elasticity

Exhibit 6 presents demand curves of varying elasticity. A demand curve that is completely vertical is termed "perfectly inelastic." The addict's demand for heroin or the diabetic's demand for insulin might *approximate* perfect inelasticity over a wide range of prices, although no demand curve will be perfectly inelastic at all prices (Exhibit 6a).

The more inelastic the demand, the steeper the demand curve *over any specific price range.* Inspection of the demand for cigarettes (Exhibit 6b), which is highly inelastic, and the demand for portable television sets (Exhibit 6d), which is relatively elastic, indicates that the inelastic curve tends to be steeper. When demand elasticity is unitary, as Exhibit 6c illustrates, a demand curve that is convex to the origin will result. When a demand curve is completely horizontal, an economist would say that it is perfectly elastic. The demand for the wheat of a single wheat farmer, for example, would approximate perfect elasticity (Exhibit 6e).

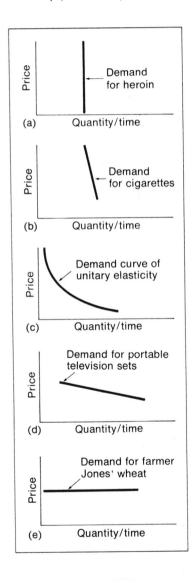

EXHIBIT 6   Demand elasticity

(a) *Perfectly inelastic*—Despite an increase in price, consumers still purchase the same amount. The price elasticity of an addict's demand for heroin or a diabetic's demand for insulin might be approximated by this curve.

(b) *Relatively inelastic*—A percent increase in price results in a smaller percent reduction in sales. The demand for cigarettes has been estimated to be highly inelastic.

(c) *Unitary elasticity*—The percent change in quantity demanded is equal to the percent change in price. A *curve* of decreasing slope results. Sales revenue (price times quantity sold) is constant.

(d) *Relatively elastic*—A percent increase in price leads to a larger percent reduction in purchases. Consumers substitute other products for the more expensive good.

(e) *Perfectly elastic*—Consumers will buy all of farmer Jones's wheat at the market price, but none will be sold above the market price.

Since elasticity is a relative concept, the elasticity of a straight-line demand curve will differ at each point along the line. Thus, as Exhibit 7 illustrates, the elasticity of a straight-line demand curve (one with a constant slope) will range from highly elastic to highly inelastic. For the example of Exhibit 7, when the price rises from $10 to $11, sales decline from 20 to 10. According to the arc elasticity formula, the price elasticity of demand is −7.0. Demand is very elastic in this region. In contrast, demand is quite inelastic in the $1 to $2 price range. As the price increases from $1 to $2, the amount demanded declines from 110 to 100. The arc elasticity of demand in this range is only −0.14; demand is highly inelastic.

Why do we bother with elasticity? Why not talk only about the slope of a demand curve? We use elasticities because they are independent of the units of measure. Whether we talk about dollars per gallon or cents per quart, the elasticities, given in percentages, remain the same. This is appropriate because people do not care what units of measurement are used; they care about what they receive for their money.

Determinants of Elasticity of Demand

Economists have estimated the price elasticity of demand for many products. Exhibit 8 presents some of these estimates. They vary a great deal. The demand for several products—salt, toothpicks, matches, light bulbs, and newspapers, for example—is highly inelastic. On the other hand, the demand for fresh tomatoes, Chevrolet automobiles, and fresh green peas is highly elastic. What factors explain this variation? Why is demand highly responsive to changes in price for some products but not for others?

EXHIBIT 7 The slope of a demand curve is not the same as the price elasticity

With this straight-line (constant-slope) demand curve, demand is more elastic in the high-price range. The formula for arc elasticity (see footnote 6) shows that when price rises from $1 to $2 and quantity falls from 110 to 100, demand is inelastic. A price rise of the same magnitude (but of a smaller percentage), from $10 to $11, leads to a decline in quantity of the same size (but of a larger percentage), so that elasticity is much greater. (Price elasticities are negative, but we typically ignore the sign and look only at the absolute value.)

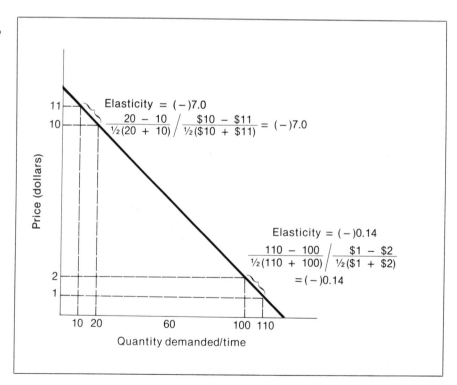

Elasticity = (−)7.0

$$\frac{20 - 10}{\frac{1}{2}(20 + 10)} \Big/ \frac{\$10 - \$11}{\frac{1}{2}(\$10 + \$11)} = (-)7.0$$

Elasticity = (−)0.14

$$\frac{110 - 100}{\frac{1}{2}(110 + 100)} \Big/ \frac{\$1 - \$2}{\frac{1}{2}(\$1 + \$2)}$$
$$= (-)0.14$$

EXHIBIT 8 The estimated price elasticity of demand for selected products

Inelastic	
Salt	0.1
Matches	0.1
Toothpicks	0.1
Airline travel, short run	0.1
Gasoline, short run	0.2
Gasoline, long run	0.7
Residential natural gas, short run	0.1
Residential natural gas, long run	0.5
Coffee	0.25
Cigarettes	0.35
Legal services	0.5
Physician services	0.6
Taxi	0.4
Tires, short run	0.6
Tires, long run	0.4
Automobiles, long run	0.2
Approximate unitary elasticity	
Housing	0.9
Private education	1.1
China and tableware	1.1
Radio and television receivers	1.2
Elastic	
Fresh tomatoes	4.6
Foreign travel, long run	4.0
Airline travel, long run	2.4
Fresh green peas	2.8
Automobiles, short run	1.2–1.5
Chevrolet automobiles	4.0

Hendrik S. Houthakker and Lester D. Taylor, *Consumer Demand in the United States, 1929–1970* (Cambridge, Massachusetts: Harvard University Press, 1966); Douglas R. Bohi, *Analyzing Demand Behavior* (Baltimore: Johns Hopkins University Press, 1981); and U.S. Department of Agriculture.

The Availability of Substitutes. This factor is the most important determinant of demand elasticity. When good substitutes for a product are available, a price rise simply induces consumers to switch to other products. Demand is elastic. For example, if the price of fountain pens rose, many consumers would switch to pencils, ballpoint pens, and felt-tip pens. If the price of Chevrolets increased, consumers would substitute Fords, Dodges, and Volkswagens.

When good substitutes are unavailable, the demand for a product tends to be inelastic. Medical services are an example. When we are sick, most of us find witch doctors, faith healers, palm readers, and cod-liver oil to be highly imperfect substitutes for a physician. Not surprisingly, the demand for physician services is inelastic.

The availability of substitutes increases as the product class becomes more specific, thus enhancing price elasticity. For example, as Exhibit 8 shows, the price elasticity of Chevrolets, a narrow product class, exceeds that of the broad class of automobiles in general.

The Share of Total Budget Expended on the Product. If the expenditures on a product are quite small relative to the consumer's budget, demand tends to be more inelastic. Compared to one's total budget, expenditures on some commodities are almost inconsequential. Matches, toothpicks, and salt are good examples. Most consumers spend only $1 or $2 per year on each of these items. A doubling of their price would exert little influence on the family budget. Therefore, even if the price of such a product were to rise sharply, consumers would still not find it in their interest to spend much time and effort looking for substitutes.

Time and Adjustment to a Price Change. It takes time for consumers to recognize and to respond fully to a change in the price of a product. Initially, all consumers may not be aware of the price change; more will become aware of it as the price change persists into the future. Consumer response to a price change can also be slow because rapid adjustment of individual consumption patterns is often costly.

Generally, the longer a price change persists, the greater the price elasticity of demand will be. The direct relationship between the elasticity coefficient of demand and the length of the time period allowed for consumer adjustment is often referred to as the second law of demand. According to this law, the elasticity of demand for a product is generally greater in the long run than in the short run.

The case of gasoline provides a vivid illustration of the second law of demand. When gasoline prices rose from 35 cents to 60 cents during 1973–1975, did consumers *immediately* stop driving their 350-horsepower, gas-guzzling automobiles? No. But when their full-sized cars wore out, did many consumers switch to compact cars giving higher gas mileage? Yes. In the short run, consumers responded to higher gas prices by reducing speeds, forming car pools, and driving less. Given more time, however, they substituted compact cars for full-sized models, reducing gasoline consumption even more. Thus, as Exhibit 8 shows, the long-run demand for gasoline (0.7) proved more elastic than the short-run demand (0.2).

Although the demand for most products will be more elastic in the long run than in the short run, there are a few exceptions, primarily durable consumer goods. Often such purchases can initially be "lengthened into the future" as prices rise. The old tires can be driven a few more miles or the old washing machine repaired one more time. Thus, higher prices result in a greater reduction in quantity demanded in the short run than is possible over an extended time period.

Elasticity and Total Expenditures

Price elasticity establishes the relationship between a change in price and the corresponding change in the total expenditures on the product. Let us examine how this relationship works. When demand is inelastic, the percent change in price exceeds the percent reduction in sales. The price effect dominates. Suppose that when the price of beef rises from $2 to $2.40 (a 20 percent increase), the quantity demanded, on average, by consumers falls from 100 pounds to 90 pounds (a 10 percent reduction) per year. Since the percent increase in price exceeds the percent reduction in quantity demanded, we know that demand is inelastic.[7] At the $2 price, the average person spends $200 annually on beef. When the price rises to $2.40, the average annual expenditures rise to $216. The higher beef prices cause total expenditures to increase because demand is inelastic.

When demand is elastic, on the other hand, the percent decline in quantity demanded will exceed the percent increase in price. The loss of sales will exert a greater influence on total expenditures than the rise in price. Therefore, total revenues will fall.

Exhibit 9 summarizes the relationship between changes in price and total expenditures for demand curves of varying elasticity. When demand is inelastic, a change in price will cause total expenditures to change in the same direction. If demand is elastic, price and total expenditures will change in opposite directions. For unitary elasticity, total expenditures will remain constant as price changes.

How Does Income Influence Demand?

Income Elasticity: The percent change in the quantity of a product demanded divided by the percent change in consumer income. It measures the responsiveness of the demand for a good to a change in income.

As income expands, the demand for most goods will increase. **Income elasticity** indicates the responsiveness of the demand for a product to a change in income. It is defined as:

$$\frac{\text{Percent change in quantity demanded}}{\text{percent change in income}}$$

As Exhibit 10 shows, the income elasticity coefficients for products vary, although they are normally positive. In general, goods that people regard as "necessities" will have a low income elasticity of demand. Therefore, it is understandable that items such as fuel, electricity, bread, tobacco, economy clothing, and potatoes have a low income elasticity. A few commodities, such as navy beans, low-quality meat cuts, and bus travel, have a negative income elasticity. Economists refer to goods with a negative income elasticity as **inferior goods.** As income expands, the demand for inferior goods will decline.

Inferior Goods: Goods for which the income elasticity is negative. Thus, an increase in consumer income causes the demand for such a good to decline.

Goods that consumers regard as "luxuries" generally have a high (greater than 1) income elasticity. For example, private education, new automobiles, recreational activities, expensive foods, swimming pools, and air travel are all income-elastic. Thus, as income increases, the demand for these products expands rapidly.

EXHIBIT 9 Demand elasticity, change in price, and change in total expenditures

Price Elasticity of Demand	Numerical Elasticity Coefficient[a]	The Impact of a Change in Price on Total Expenditures (and Sales Revenues)
Elastic	1 to ∞	Price and total expenditures change in opposite directions
Unitary	1	Total expenditures remain constant as price changes
Inelastic	0 to 1	Price and total expenditures change in the same direction

[a]The sign of the elasticity coefficient is negative.

[7]Calculate the elasticity coefficient as an exercise. Is it less than 1?

EXHIBIT 10 The estimated income elasticity of demand for selected products

Low income elasticity	
Fuel	0.38
Electricity	0.50
Food	0.51
Tobacco	0.64
Hospital care	0.69
High income elasticity	
Private education	2.46
New cars	2.45
Recreation and	
amusements	1.57
Alcohol	1.54

Hendrik S. Houthakker and Lester D. Taylor, *Consumer Demand in the United States, 1929–1970* (Cambridge, Massachusetts: Harvard University Press, 1966).

DETERMINANTS OF SPECIFIC PREFERENCES— WHY DO CONSUMERS BUY *THAT*?

Did you ever wonder why a friend spent hard-earned money on something that you would not have even if it were free? Tastes differ, and as we have already shown, they influence demand. What determines preferences? Why do people like one thing but not another? Economists have not been able to explain very much about how preferences are determined. The best strategy has generally been to take preferences as given, using price and other demand-related factors to explain and predict human behavior. Still, there are some observations about consumer preferences worth noting.

First, the preferences behind any one choice are frequently complex. The person looking for a house wants far more than just a shelter. An attractive setting, a convenient location, quality of public services, and a great many other factors will enter the housing decision. Each person may evaluate the same attribute differently. Living near a school may be a high priority for a family with children but a nuisance to a retired couple.

Second, the individual consumer's choice is not always independent of other consumers. Not wanting to be left out, a person might buy an item to "get on the bandwagon"—just because others are buying the same item. Or a good may have "snob appeal," setting owners apart from the crowd or elevating them into an exclusive group. Even relatively inexpensive items may have this appeal.[8]

A third factor influencing consumer choice is advertising. Advertisers would not spend tens of billions of dollars each year if they did not get results. But how does advertising affect consumers? Does it simply provide valuable information about product quality, price, and availability? Or does it use repetition and misleading information to manipulate consumers? Economists are not of one opinion. Let us take a closer look at this important issue.

---

[8]See Harvey Leibenstein, "Bandwagon, Snob, and Veblen Effects in the Theory of Consumer Demand," *Quarterly Journal of Economics* (May 1950), pp. 183–207, and R. Joseph Monsen and Anthony Downs, "Public Goods and Private Status," *Public Interest* (Spring 1971), pp. 64–76, for a more complete discussion of bandwagon and snob effects.

Prolific, innovative, controversial, arrogant, and unconventional are all words that have been used to describe Harvard's John Kenneth Galbraith. Professor Galbraith is a philosopher, poet, social critic, political activist, and economic adviser—all at the same time. He was ambassador to India during the Kennedy administration. He helped Lyndon Johnson plan the war on poverty before splitting with him over the Vietnam issue. Galbraith was one of George McGovern's earliest supporters and served as a McGovern delegate to the Democratic National Convention in 1972.

Galbraith has been a long-time critic of consumer theory in general and advertising in particular. In his best-seller, *The Affluent Society,* Galbraith charged, "The fact that wants can be synthesized by advertising, catalyzed by salesmanship, and shaped by discreet manipulations of the persuaders shows that they are not very urgent."[9]

In Galbraith's view, consumers in affluent Western societies are trapped on a merry-go-round. Artificial wants are created so business firms can sell more goods for profit. Whereas economists typically view production as the means of satisfying wants, Galbraith argues that production necessitates the creation of wants. Advertising and the creation of wants are simply the tools of producers in a modern economy.

The solution to the problem in Galbraith's view is a vast expansion in the role of government.[10] Galbraith favors permanent price controls for sectors of the economy dominated by large corporations, redistribution of income toward greater equality, and socialization of several major industries, such as steel, petroleum, and automobiles. Needless to say, he is not exactly the businessperson's friend. Reflecting on his experience as a price fixer with the Office of Price Administration during World War II, he once remarked, "I always thought that any businessman who left my office smiling indicated that I made some kind of mistake."[11]

For many years, Galbraith was either ignored or treated with scorn by most of his fellow economists. In the late 1960s, however, his undisputed popularity among the general populace began to rub off on his professional peers. In 1971, he served as president of the American Economic Association, an honor that many felt was long overdue.

Galbraith's critics charge that he pays no heed to scientific methods. Most economists make ample use of theory, testing, computers, and statistics. Galbraith will have none of it. He expects his listeners and readers to either have faith or do their own "number grubbing." Although his approach is unlikely to transform the methodology of the profession, he has already caused it to reconsider the foundations of economic analysis.

[9]John Kenneth Galbraith, *The Affluent Society* (Boston: Houghton Mifflin, 1958), p. 123.

[10]See J. K. Galbraith, "Conversations with an Inconvenient Economist," *Challenge* (September/October 1973), pp. 28–37, for a short statement of Galbraith's views on a broad range of issues.

[11]*San Francisco Examiner,* December 29, 1974.

Advertising—How Useful Is It?

What does advertising do for Americans? What were the results of the $54 billion spent on advertising in 1980? Advertising is often used as a sponsoring medium; it reduces the purchase price of newspapers, magazines, and, most obviously, television viewing. However, the consumer of the advertised products pays indirectly for these benefits. Thus, advertising cannot be defended solely on the basis of its sponsorship role.

Advertising does convey information about product price, quality, and availability. New firms or those with new products, new hours, new locations, or new services use advertising to keep consumers informed. Such advertising facilitates trade and increases efficiency. But what about those repetitious television commercials that offer little or no information? The critics charge that such advertising is wasteful, misleading, and manipulative. Let us look at each of these charges.

Is Advertising Wasteful? A great deal of media advertising seems simply to say "We are better" without providing supportive evidence. An advertiser may wish to take customers from a competitor or establish a brand name for a product. A multimillion-dollar media campaign by a soap, cigarette, or automobile manufacturer may be largely offset by a similar campaign waged by a competitor. The consumers of these products end up paying the costs of these battles for their attention and their dollars. However, we must remember that consumers are under no obligation to purchase advertised products. If advertising results in higher prices without providing compensating benefits, consumers can turn to cheaper, nonadvertised products.

A good brand name, even if it has been established by advertising, places additional responsibility on the seller. People value buying from sellers in whom they have confidence. Those who bought from anonymous moonshiners during Prohibition trusted mainly in the skill and integrity of the moonshiner to ensure that the beverages did not contain dangerous impurities. Those who buy Jack Daniels or Jim Beam whiskey today know that besides skill and integrity, distillers have an enormous sum of money tied up in their brands. A distiller would spend a large amount of money, if necessary, to avoid even one death from an impure batch of a brand-name product. Is a brand name, promoted by costly advertising, worth it to the customer? The customer must decide.

Is Advertising Misleading? Unfair and deceptive advertising—including false promises, whether spoken by a seller or packaged by an advertising agency—is illegal under the Federal Trade Commission Act. The fact that a publicly advertised false claim is easier to establish and prosecute than the same words spoken in private is an argument for freedom in advertising. But what about general, unsupported claims that a product is superior to the alternatives or that it will help one enjoy life more? Some believe that such noninformational advertising should be prohibited. They would establish a government agency to evaluate the "informativeness" of advertising. There are dangers in this approach. Someone would have to decide what was informative and what was not, or what was acceptable and what was not. If we could be assured that the special agency would be staffed by "regulatory saints" (borrowing a phrase from George Stigler), it would make sense to follow this course. Past experience, however, indicates that this would not be the case. Eventually, the regulatory agency would most likely be controlled by established business firms and advertising interests. Firms that played ball with the political bloc controlling the agency would be allowed to promote their products. Less powerful and less political rivals would be hassled. Costs would rise as a result of the paperwork created by compliance procedures. If consumers are misled by slick advertisers to part with their money without good reason, might they not also be misled by a slick media campaign to support politicians and regulatory policies that are not in their interest? Why should we expect consumers to make poor decisions when they make market choices but wise decisions when they act in the political (and regulatory) arena? Clearly, additional regulation is not a cure-all. Like freedom in advertising, it has some defects.

Does Advertising Manipulate the Preferences of Consumers? The demand for some products would surely be much smaller without advertising. Some people's preferences may, in fact, be shaped by advertising. However, in evaluating the manipulative effect of advertising, we must keep two things in mind. First, business decision-makers are likely to choose the simplest route to economic gain. Generally, it is easier for business firms to cater to the actual desires of consumers than attempt to reshape their preferences or persuade them to purchase an undesired product. Second, even if advertising does influence preferences, does it follow that this is bad? Economic theory cannot provide an answer. Economic theory does not rank people's desires; it does not assign different values to a person's desires before and after a change in preferences. Suppose that several students of classical music spend an evening at a disco and suddenly find that they like disco music more than Brahms. Were the students' tastes "more natural" or better before being shaped by the disco? Economists may have an opinion, but they have no analytical answer to that question.

LOOKING AHEAD

In this chapter we outlined the mechanism by which consumers' wants and tastes are communicated to producers. Consumer choices underlie the market demand curve. It is the market demand for a product that tells producers how strongly consumers desire each commodity relative to others. In the following chapter, we turn to costs of production, which arise because resources have alternative uses. In fact, the cost of producing a good tells the producer how badly the resources are desired in *other* areas. An understanding of these two topics—consumer demand and cost of production—is essential if we are to understand how markets allocate goods and resources.

CHAPTER LEARNING OBJECTIVES

1 The demand schedule indicates the amount of a good that consumers would be willing to buy at each potential price. The first law of demand states that the quantity of a product demanded is inversely related to its price. A reduction in the price of a product reduces the opportunity cost of consuming it. At the lower price, many consumers will substitute the now cheaper good for other products. In contrast, higher prices will induce consumers to buy less as they turn to substitutes that are now *relatively* cheaper.

2 The market demand curve reflects the demand of individuals. It is simply the horizontal sum of the demand curves of individuals in the market area.

3 In addition to price, the demand for a product is influenced by the (a) level of consumer income, (b) distribution of income among consumers, (c) price of related products (substitutes and complements), (d) preferences of consumers, (e) population in the market area, and (f) consumer expectations about the future price of the product. Changes in any of these six factors will cause the *demand* for the product to change (the entire curve to shift).

4 Consumers usually gain from the purchase of a good. The difference between the amount that consumers would be willing to pay for a good and the amount they actually pay is called consumer surplus. It is measured by the area under the demand curve but above the market price.

5 Time, like money, is scarce for consumers. Consumers consider both time and money costs when they make decisions. Other things constant, a reduction in the time cost of consuming a good will induce consumers to purchase more of the good.

6 Price elasticity reveals the responsiveness of the amount purchased to a change in price. When there are good substitutes available and the item forms a sizable component of the consumer's budget, its demand will tend to be more elastic. Typically, the price

elasticity of a product will increase as more time is allowed for consumers to adjust to the price change. This direct relationship between the size of the elasticity coefficient and the length of the adjustment time period is often referred to as the second law of demand.

7   Both functional and subjective factors influence the demand for a product. Some goods are chosen because they have "snob appeal." Goods may also have a "bandwagon appeal," fulfilling a consumer's desire to be fashionable. Observation suggests that goods are demanded for a variety of reasons.

8   The precise effect of advertising on consumer decisions is difficult to evaluate. The magnitude of advertising by profit-seeking business firms is strong evidence that it influences consumer decisions. Advertising often reduces the amount of time consumers must spend looking for a product and helps them make more informed choices. However, a sizable share of all advertising expenditures is for largely noninformational messages. Although this is a controversial area, it is clearly much easier to point out the short-comings of advertising than to devise an alternative that would not have similar imperfections.

THE ECONOMIC WAY OF THINKING—DISCUSSION QUESTIONS

1   What impact did the substantially higher gasoline prices of the 1970s have on (a) the demand for big cars, (b) the demand for small cars, (c) the incentive to experiment and develop electric and other non-gas-powered cars, (d) the demand for gasoline (*Be careful*), and (e) the demand for Florida vacations?

2   "As the price of beef rises, the demand of consumers will begin to decline. Economists estimate that a 5 percent rise in beef prices will cause demand to decline by 1 percent." Indicate the two errors in this statement.

3   The following chart presents data on the price of fuel oil, the amount of it demanded, and the demand for insulation. (a) Calculate the price elasticity of demand for fuel oil as its price rises from 30 cents to 50 cents; from 50 cents to 70 cents. (b) Are fuel oil and insulation substitutes or complements? How can you tell from the figures alone?

Fuel Oil		Insulation
Price per Gallon (Cents)	Quantity Demanded (Millions of Gallons)	Quantity Demanded (Millions of Tons)
30	100	30
50	90	35
70	60	40

4   What are the major factors that influence a product's price elasticity of demand? Explain why these factors are important.

5   Do you think that television advertising—as it is conducted by the automobile industry, for example—is wasteful? If so, what would you propose to do about it? Indicate why your proposal would be an improvement over the current situation.

6   In 1971, residential electricity in the state of Washington cost about 1 cent per kilowatt-hour. In nearby Montana, it cost about 2 cents. In Washington, the average household used about 1200 kilowatt-hours per month, whereas Montanans used about half that much per household. Do these data provide us with two points on the average household's demand curve for residential electricity in this region? Why or why not?

7   **What's Wrong with This Way of Thinking?**

"Economics is unable to explain the value of goods in a sensible manner. A quart of water is much cheaper than a quart of oil. Yet water is essential to both animal and plant life. Without it, we could not survive. How can oil be more valuable than water? Yet economics says that it is."

ADDENDUM

CONSUMER CHOICE AND INDIFFERENCE CURVES

In the text of this chapter, we used marginal utility analysis to develop the demand curve of an individual. In developing the theory of consumer choice, economists usually rely on a more formal technique, indifference curve analysis. Since this technique is widely used at a more advanced level, many instructors like to include it in their introductory course. In this addendum, we use indifference curve analysis to develop the theory of demand in a more formal—some would say more elegant—manner.

WHAT ARE INDIFFERENCE CURVES?

Indifference Curve: A curve, convex from the origin (representing the individual's current consumption), that separates the consumption bundles that are more preferred by an individual from those that are less preferred. The points *on* the curve represent combinations of goods that are equally preferred by the individual.

There are two elements in every choice: (a) preferences (the desirability of various goods) and (b) opportunities (the attainability of various goods). The **indifference curve** concept is useful for portraying a person's preferences. An indifference curve simply separates better (more preferred) bundles of goods from inferior (less preferred) bundles. It provides a diagrammatic picture of how an individual ranks alternative consumption bundles.

In Exhibit A-1, we assume that Robinson Crusoe is initially consuming 8 fish and 8 breadfruit per week (point *A*). This initial bundle provides him with a certain level of satisfaction (utility). However, he would be willing to trade this initial bundle for certain other consumption alternatives if the opportunity presented itself. Since he likes both fish and breadfruit, he would especially like to obtain bundles to the northeast of *A*, since they represent more of both goods. However, he would also be willing to give up some breadfruit if in return he received a compensatory amount of fish. Similarly, if the terms of trade were

EXHIBIT A-1   The indifference curve of Robinson Crusoe

The curve generated by connecting Crusoe's "I do not care" answers separates the combinations of fish and breadfruit that he prefers to the bundle *A* from those that he judges to be inferior to *A*. The *I* points map out an indifference curve.

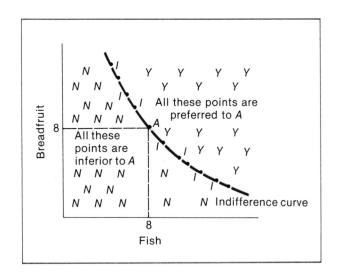

right, he would be willing to exchange fish for breadfruit. These trade-offs would occur *along* the indifference curve.

Starting from point *A* (8 fish and 8 breadfruit), we ask Crusoe if he is willing to trade that bundle for various other bundles. He answers "Yes" (*Y*), "No" (*N*), or "I do not care" (*I*). Exhibit A-1 illustrates the pattern of his response. Crusoe's "I do not care" answers indicate that the original bundle (point *A*) and each alternative indicated by an *I* are valued equally by Crusoe. These *I* points, when connected, form the indifference curve. This line separates the preferred bundles of fish and breadfruit from the less valued combinations. Note that such a curve may be entirely different for any two people. The preferences of different individuals vary widely.

We can establish a new indifference curve by starting from any point not on the original curve and following the same procedure. If we start with a point (a consumption bundle) to the northeast of the original indifference curve, all points on the new curve will have a higher level of satisfaction for Crusoe than any on the old curve. The new curve will probably have about the same shape as the original.

Characteristics of Indifference Curves

In developing consumer theory, economists assume that the preferences of consumers exhibit certain properties. These properties enable us to make statements about the general pattern of indifference curves. What are these properties, and what do they imply about the characteristics of indifference curves?

1. More Goods Are Preferable to Fewer Goods—Thus, Bundles on Indifference Curves Lying Farthest to the Northeast Are Always Preferred. Assuming the consumption of only two commodities, since *both* commodities are desired, the individual will always prefer to have more of at least one of the goods without loss of any of the other. This means that combinations in the northeast region of an indifference curve diagram will always be preferred to points in the southwest region.

2. Goods Are Substitutable—Therefore, Indifference Curves Slope Downward to the Right. As we indicated in the text of this chapter, individuals are willing to substitute one good for another. Crusoe will be willing to give up some breadfruit if he is compensated with enough fish. Stated another way, there will be some amount of additional fish such that Crusoe will stay on the same indifference curve, even though his consumption of breadfruit has declined. However, in order to remain on the same indifference curve, Crusoe must always acquire more of one good in order to compensate for the loss of the other. Thus, the indifference curve for goods will always slope downward to the right (run northwest to southeast).

Marginal Rate of Substitution: The change in the consumption level of one good that is just sufficient to offset a unit change in the consumption of another good without causing a shift to another indifference curve. At any point on an indifference curve, it will be equal to the slope of the curve at that point.

3. The Valuation of a Good Declines As It Is Consumed More Intensively—Therefore, Indifference Curves Are Always Convex When Viewed from Below. The slope of the indifference curve represents the willingness of the individual to substitute one good for the other. Economists refer to the amount of one good that is just sufficient to compensate the consumer for the loss of a unit of the other good as the **marginal rate of substitution.** The marginal rate of substitution is equal to the slope of the indifference curve. Reflecting the principle of diminishing marginal utility, the marginal rate of substitution of a good will decline as the

an exam is typically less than the gain from the first or second hour of studying.[2] Similarly, if a farmer applies fertilizer more and more intensively to an acre of land (a fixed factor), the application of additional 100-pound units of fertilizer will expand the wheat yield by successively smaller amounts.

Essentially, the law of diminishing returns is a constraint imposed by nature. If it were not valid, it would be possible to raise all of the world's foodstuffs on an acre of land, or even in a flowerpot. Suppose that we did *not* experience diminishing returns when we applied more labor and fertilizer to land. Would it ever make sense to cultivate any of the less fertile land? Of course not. We would be able to increase output more rapidly by simply applying another unit of labor and fertilizer to the world's most fertile flowerpot! But, of course, that would be a fairy tale; the law of diminishing returns applies in the real world.

Exhibit 3 illustrates the law of diminishing returns numerically. Column 1 indicates the quantity of the variable resource, labor in this example, that is combined with a specified amount of the fixed resource. Column 2 shows the **total product** that will result as the utilization rate of labor increases. Column 3 provides data on the **marginal product,** the change in total output associated with each additional unit of labor. Without the application of labor, output would be zero. As additional units of labor are applied, total product (output) expands. As the first three units of labor are applied, total product increases by successively larger amounts (8, then 12, then 14). However, beginning with the fourth unit, diminishing returns are confronted. When the fourth unit is added, marginal product—the change in the total product—declines to 12 (down from 14, when the third unit was applied). As additional units of labor are applied, marginal product continues to decline. It is increasingly difficult to

Total Product: The total output of a good that is associated with alternative utilization rates of a variable input.

Marginal Product: The change in the total product resulting from a unit change in the employment of a variable input. Mathematically, it is the ratio of (a) change in total product divided by (b) change in the quantity of the variable input.

EXHIBIT 3   The law of diminishing returns (hypothetical data)

(1) Units of the Variable Resource, Labor (per Day)	(2) Total Product (Output)	(3) Marginal Product	(4) Average Product
0	0		—
1	8	8	8.0
2	20	12	10.0
3	34	14	11.3
4	46	12	11.5
5	56	10	11.2
6	64	8	10.7
7	70	6	10.0
8	74	4	9.3
9	75	1	8.3
10	74	−1	7.4

[2]Why does each additional hour of study time improve your grade less than previous ones? What do you study first? The most important material. As you continue studying, you allocate more and more time to less important tasks, the study of less relevant material. Thus, your return from *additional* hours of study will diminish.

squeeze a larger total product from the fixed resources (for example, plant size and equipment). Eventually, marginal product becomes negative (beginning with the tenth unit).

Column 4 of Exhibit 3 provides data for the **average product** of labor. The averge product is simply the total product divided by the units of labor applied. Note the average product increases as long as the marginal product is greater than the average product. This is true through the first four units. However, the marginal product of the fifth unit of labor is 10, less than the average product for the first four units of labor (11.5). Therefore, beginning with the fifth unit, average product declines as additional labor is applied.

Utilizing the data from Exhibit 3, Exhibit 4 illustrates the law of diminishing returns graphically. Initially, the total product curve (Exhibit 4a) increases quite rapidly. As diminishing marginal returns are confronted (beginning with the fourth unit of labor), total product increases more slowly. Eventually a

Average Product: The total product (output) divided by the number of units of the variable input required to produce that output level.

EXHIBIT 4   The law of diminishing returns

As units of variable input (labor) are added to a fixed input, total product will increase, first at an increasing rate and then at a declining rate (graph a). This will cause both the marginal and average product curves (graph b) to rise at first and then decline. Note that the marginal product curve intersects the average product curve at its maximum.

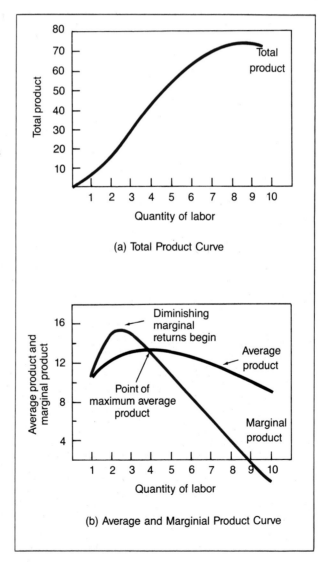

(a) Total Product Curve

(b) Average and Marginial Product Curve

maximum output (75) is reached with the application of the ninth unit of labor. The marginal product curve (Exhibit 4b) reflects the total product curve. Geometrically, marginal product is the slope of the total product curve. Marginal product reaches its maximum with the application of three units of labor. Beyond three units, diminishing returns are present. Eventually, marginal product becomes negative at ten units of labor. When marginal product becomes negative, total product is necessarily declining. The average product curve will rise as long as the marginal product curve is above it. Average product will reach its maximum at four units of labor. Beyond that, average product will decline as the utilization of labor increases.

Diminishing Returns and Cost Curves

What impact will diminishing returns have on a firm's costs? Once a firm confronts diminishing returns, successively larger amounts of variable factors will be required to expand output by an additional unit. Marginal costs will rise until, eventually, they exceed average total cost. When marginal costs are greater than ATC, ATC will increase. It is easy to see why. What happens when an above-average student is added to a class? The class average goes up. What, then, would happen if a unit of above-average cost were added to output? Average total cost would rise. Therefore, the firm's marginal cost curve crosses the ATC curve at the ATC's lowest point. For output rates beyond the minimum ATC, the rising marginal cost will cause average total cost to increase. Again, we will find the average total cost curve to be U-shaped.

Exhibit 5 illustrates numerically the implications of the law of diminishing returns for a firm's short-run cost curves. Here, we assume that Royal Roller Skates, Inc., combines units of a variable input with a fixed factor to produce units of output (skates). Columns 2, 3, and 4 indicate how total cost schedules are altered as output is expanded. Total fixed costs, representing the opportunity cost of the fixed factors of production, are $50 per day. For the first four units of output, total variable costs increase at a *decreasing rate*. This

EXHIBIT 5 Numerical short-run cost schedules of Royal Roller Skates, Inc.

(1)	Total Cost Data (per Day)			Average/Marginal Cost Data (per Day)			
	(2)	(3)	(4)	(5)	(6)	(7)	(8)
Output per Day	Total Fixed Cost	Total Variable Cost	Total Cost, (2)+(3)	Average Fixed Cost, (2)÷(1)	Average Variable Cost, (3)÷(1)	Average Total Cost, (4)÷(1)	Marginal Cost, Δ(4)÷Δ(1)
0	$50	$ 0	$ 50	—	—	—	
1	50	15	65	$50.00	$15.00	$65.00	$15
2	50	25	75	25.00	12.50	37.50	10
3	50	34	84	16.67	11.33	28.00	9
4	50	42	92	12.50	10.50	23.00	8
5	50	52	102	10.00	10.40	20.40	10
6	50	64	114	8.33	10.67	19.00	12
7	50	79	129	7.14	11.29	18.43	15
8	50	98	148	6.25	12.25	18.50	19
9	50	122	172	5.56	13.56	19.11	24
10	50	152	202	5.00	15.20	20.20	30
11	50	202	252	4.55	18.36	22.91	50

occurs because, in this range, increasing returns to the variable input are present. However, beginning with the fifth unit of output, diminishing marginal returns are present. From this point on, total variable costs and total costs increase by successively larger amounts as output is expanded.

Columns 5 through 8 of Exhibit 5 reveal the general pattern of the average and marginal cost schedules. For small output rates the average total cost of producing skates is high, primarily because of the high AFC. Initially, marginal costs are less than ATC. However, when diminishing returns set in for output rates beginning with five units, marginal cost will rise. Eventually marginal cost will exceed average variable cost (beginning with the sixth unit of output), causing AVC to rise. Beginning with the eighth unit of output, MC will exceed ATC, causing it to rise also. Thus, ATC will be a minimum at seven units of output. Observe the data of Exhibit 5 carefully to make sure that you fully understand the relationships among the various cost curves.

Utilizing the numeric data of Exhibit 5, Exhibit 6 illustrates graphically both the total and the average/marginal cost curves. Note that the marginal cost curve intersects both the average variable cost and average total cost curves at the minimum points (Exhibit 6b). As marginal costs continue to rise above average total cost, unit costs rise higher and higher as output is expanded (beyond seven units).

In sum, the firm's short-run cost curves are merely a reflection of the law of diminishing marginal returns. Assuming that the price of the variable resource is constant, marginal costs will decline as long as the marginal product of the variable input is rising. This results because, in this range, less and less of the variable input is required to produce each additional unit of output. However, this situation is eventually reversed when diminishing returns are confronted. Once diminishing returns set in, more and more units of the variable factor are required to generate each additional unit of output. Marginal cost will rise, because the marginal product of the variable resources is declining.

EXHIBIT 6   Costs in the short-run

Using data of Exhibit 5, graph (a) illustrates the general shape of the firm's short-run total cost curves; graph (b) illustrates the general shape of the firm's average and marginal cost curves. Note that when output is small (for example, 2 units), average total cost will be high because the average fixed costs are so high. Similarly, when output is large (for example, 11 units) per unit cost (ATC) will be high because it is extremely costly to produce the marginal units. Thus, the short-run ATC curve will be U-shaped.

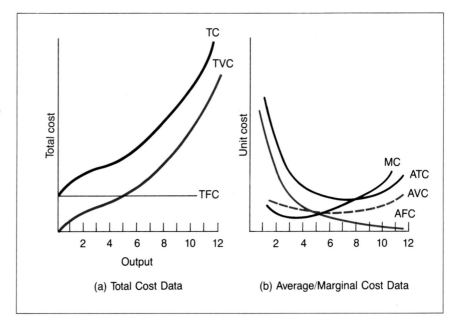

(a) Total Cost Data

(b) Average/Marginal Cost Data

Second, we have emphasized the role of competition as the taskmaster forcing sellers to obey the desires of consumers. As is generally the case with those under the thumb of a tough taskmaster, sellers have a strong incentive to escape the discipline imposed by competitive forces. Business participants can be expected to attempt to avert the discipline of competition. Much of the material on industrial structure will provide a framework within which to analyze both the likelihood of a business firm escaping the directives of competition and the economic implications of its doing so.

THE PURELY COMPETITIVE MODEL

Pure Competition: A model of industrial structure characterized by a large number of small firms producing a homogeneous product in an industry (market area) that permits complete freedom of entry and exit.

Homogeneous Product: A product of one firm that is identical to the product of every other firm in the industry. Consumers see no differences in units of the product offered by alternative sellers.

Barriers to Entry: Obstacles that limit the freedom of potential rivals to enter an industry.

Pure competition presupposes that the following conditions exist in a market.

1. All Firms in the Market Are Producing a **Homogeneous Product.** The product of firm A is identical to the product offered by firm B and all other firms. This presupposition rules out advertising, locational preferences, quality difference, and other forms of nonprice competition.

2. A Large Number of Independent Firms Produce the Product. The independence of the firms rules out joint actions designed to restrict output and raise prices.

3. Each Buyer and Seller Is Small Relative to the Total Market. Therefore, no single buyer or seller is able to exert any noticeable influence on the market supply and demand conditions. For example, a wheat farmer selling 5000 bushels annually would not have a noticeable impact on the U.S. wheat market, where 1,800,000,000 bushels are traded annually.

4. There Are No Artificial **Barriers to Entry** *into or Exit from the Market.* Under pure competition, any entrepreneur is free either to produce or fail to produce in the industry. New entrants need not obtain permission from the government or the existing firms before they are free to compete. Nor does control of an essential resource limit market entry.

The purely competitive model, like other theories, is abstract. Keep in mind that the test of a theory is not the realism of its assumptions but its ability to make predictions that are *consistent* with the real world (see Chapter 1). Assumptions are made and ideas are simplified so that we can better organize our thoughts. Models, based on simplifications and assumptions, can often help us develop the economic way of thinking.

Why Is Pure Competition Important?

Previously, we discussed how supply and demand jointly determine market price. The model of pure competition is another way of looking at the operation of market forces. The model will help us understand the relationship between the decision-making of individual firms and the market supply. If we familiarize ourselves with the way in which economic incentives influence the supply decisions of firms within the competitive model, we will be better able to understand the behavior of firms in markets that are less than purely competitive.

There are other reasons for the model's importance. Its conditions are approximated in a few important industries, most notably agriculture. The model will help us understand these industries. In addition, as we will show later, the equilibrium conditions in the competitive model yield results that are identical to ideal static efficiency conditions. Thus, many economists use the competitive model as a standard by which to judge other industrial structures.

THE WORKINGS OF THE COMPETITIVE MODEL

Price Takers: Sellers who must take the market price in order to sell their product. Because each price taker's output is small relative to the total market, price takers can sell all of their output at the market price but are unable to sell any of their output at a price higher than the market price. Thus, they face a horizontal demand curve.

Since a competitive firm by itself produces an output that is small relative to the total market, it is unable to influence the market price. A purely competitive firm must accept the market price if it is to sell any of its product. Thus, competitive firms are sometimes called **price takers,** because they must take the market price in order to sell.

Exhibit 1 illustrates the relationship between market forces [graph (b)] and the demand curve facing the pure competitor [graph (a)].

If a pure competitor sets a price above the the market level, consumers will simply buy from other sellers. Why pay the higher price when the identical good is available elsewhere at a lower price? For example, if the price of wheat were $4 per bushel, a farmer would be unable to find buyers for wheat at $4.50 per bushel. A firm could lower its price, but since it is small relative to the total market, it can already sell as much as it wants at the market price. A price reduction would merely reduce revenues. Thus, a purely competitive *firm* confronts a perfectly elastic demand for *its* product.

Deciding How Much to Produce—The Short Run

The firm's output decision is based on comparison of benefits with costs. If a firm produces at all, it will continue expanding output as long as the benefits (additional revenues) from the production of the additional units exceed their marginal costs.

How will changes in output influence the firm's costs? In the last chapter, we discovered that the firm's short-run marginal costs will *eventually* increase as

EXHIBIT 1   The firm's demand curve under pure competition

The market forces of supply and demand determine price (b). Under pure competition, individual firms have no control over price. Thus, the demand for the product of the firm is perfectly elastic (a).

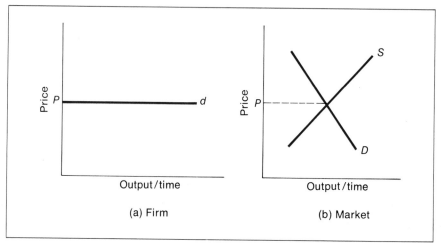

(a) Firm   (b) Market

output is expanded, by working the firm's fixed plant facilities more intensively. The law of diminishing marginal returns assures us that this will be the case. *Eventually*, both the firm's short-run marginal and average total costs will rise.

What about the benefits or additional revenues from output expansion? **Marginal revenue** (MR) is the change in the firm's total revenue per unit of output. It is the additional revenue derived from the sale of an additional unit of output. Mathematically,

Marginal Revenue: The incremental change in total revenue derived from the sale of one additional unit of a product.

$$MR = \frac{\text{total revenue}}{\text{change in output}}$$

Since the purely competitive firm sells all units at the same price, its marginal revenue will be equal to the market price.

In the short run, the purely competitive firm will expand output until marginal revenue (which equals price) is just equal to marginal cost. This decision-making rule will maximize the firm's profits (or minimize its losses).

Exhibit 2 helps to explain why. Since the firm can sell as many units as it would like at the market price, the sale of one additional unit will increase revenue by the price of the product. As long as price exceeds marginal cost, revenue will increase more than cost as output is expanded. Since profit is merely the difference between total revenue and total cost, profit will increase as output is expanded as long as price exceeds MC. For the pure competitor, profit will be at a maximum when $P = MR = MC$. This would be output level q for the firm of Exhibit 2.

Why would the firm not expand output beyond q? The cost of producing such units is given by the height of the MC curve. The sale of these units would increase revenues by only P, the price of the product. Production of units beyond q would add more to cost than to revenue. Therefore, production beyond q, the $P = MC$ output level, would reduce the firm's profits.

A profit-maximizing firm with the cost curves indicated by Exhibit 2 would produce exactly q. The total revenue of the firm would be the sales price P multiplied by output sold q. Geometrically, the firm's total revenues would be $POqB$. The firm's total cost would be found by multiplying the average total cost by the output level. Geometrically, total costs are represented by $COqA$.

EXHIBIT 2 Profit maximization and the purely competitive firm

The purely competitive firm would maximize profits by producing the output level q, where $P = MC$.

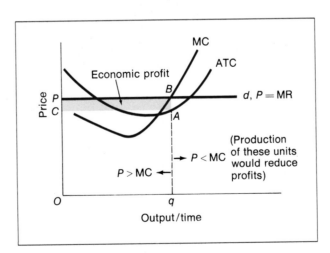

The firm's total revenues exceed total costs, and the firm is making short-run economic profit (the shaded area).

In the real world, of course, decisions are not made by entrepreneurs who sit around drawing curves labeled MC and P. Many have not even heard of these concepts. Also, our model ignores the problem of uncertainty. Very often, businesspeople must make decisions without complete knowledge of what costs or product price will be. In addition, there may be problems of "lumpiness." The manager may prefer to use 1.7 machines and 2.5 people to carry out a production process. However, managers know that both machines and people come in discrete "lumps," or whole units. They may not always be able to approximate what they want by renting, or changing the machine size they use, or hiring part-time employees.

Despite the inconvenient and uncertain facts of real life, our simple model makes fairly accurate predictions. A business decision-maker who has never heard of the $P = $ MC rule for profit maximization probably has another rule that yields approximately the same outcome. For example, the rule might be: Produce those units, and only those units, that add more to revenue than to cost. This ensures maximum profit (or minimum loss). It also takes the firm to the point at which $P = $ MC. Why? To stop short of that point is to fail to produce units that add more (the sales price) to revenue than they do to cost. Similarly, refusal to produce units that cost more than they add to revenue ensures that production will not exceed the $P = $ MC output level. Thus, this commonsense rule leads to the same outcome as the competitive model, even when the decision-maker knows nothing of the technical jargon of economics. This shows why economics is often described as organized common sense.

Exhibit 3 uses numeric data to illustrate the profit-maximizing decision-making for a competitive firm. The firm's short-run total and marginal cost schedules have the general characteristics that we discussed in the previous chapter. Since the firm confronts a market price of $5 per unit, its marginal revenue is $5. Thus, total revenue *increases* by $5 per additional unit of output. The firm maximizes its profit when it supplies an output of 15 units.

There are two ways of viewing this profit-maximizing output rate. First, we could look at the difference between total revenue and total cost, identifying the output rate at which this difference is greatest. Column 6, the profit data, provides this information. For small output rates (less than 11), the firm would actually experience losses. But at 15 units of output, an $11 profit is earned ($75 total revenue minus $64 total cost). Inspection of the profit column indicates that it is impossible to earn a larger profit than $11 at any other rate of output.

Exhibit 4a presents the total revenue and total cost approach in graph form. Profits will be maximized when the total revenue line exceeds the total cost curve by the largest vertical amount. Of course, that takes place at 15 units of output.

The marginal approach can also be used to determine the profit-maximizing rate of output for the competitive firm. Remember, as long as price (marginal revenue) exceeds marginal cost, production and sale of additional units will add to the firm's profit (or reduce its losses). Inspection of columns 4 and 5 of Exhibit 3 indicates that MR is greater than MC for the first 15 units of output. Production of these units will expand the firm's profit. In contrast, the production of each unit beyond 15 adds more to cost than to revenue. Therefore, profit will decline if

EXHIBIT 3   Profit maximization of a competitive firm—a numeric illustration

(1) Output (per Day)	(2) Total Revenue	(3) Total Cost	(4) Marginal Revenue	(5) Marginal Cost	(6) Profit (TR–TC)
0	$ 0.00	$ 25.00	$0.00	$ 0.00	−20.00
1	5.00	29.80	5.00	4.80	−24.80
2	10.00	33.75	5.00	3.95	−23.75
3	15.00	37.25	5.00	3.50	−22.25
4	20.00	40.25	5.00	3.00	−20.25
5	25.00	42.75	5.00	2.50	−17.75
6	30.00	44.75	5.00	2.00	−14.75
7	35.00	46.50	5.00	1.75	−11.50
8	40.00	48.00	5.00	1.50	− 8.00
9	45.00	49.25	5.00	1.25	− 4.25
10	50.00	50.25	5.00	1.00	− 0.25
11	55.00	51.50	5.00	1.25	3.50
12	60.00	53.25	5.00	1.75	6.75
13	65.00	55.75	5.00	2.50	9.25
14	70.00	59.25	5.00	3.50	10.75
15	75.00	64.00	5.00	4.75	11.00
16	80.00	70.00	5.00	6.00	10.00
17	85.00	77.25	5.00	7.25	7.75
18	90.00	85.50	5.00	8.25	4.50
19	95.00	95.00	5.00	9.50	0.00
20	100.00	108.00	5.00	13.00	− 8.00
21	105.00	125.00	5.00	17.00	−20.00

EXHIBIT 4   Profit maximization—the total and marginal approaches

Utilizing the data of Exhibit 3, here we provide two alternative ways of viewing profit maximization. As graph (a) illustrates, the profits of the competitive firm are maximized at the output level at which total revenue exceeds total cost by the maximum amount. Graph (b) demonstrates that the maximum-profit output can also be identified by comparing marginal revenue and marginal cost.

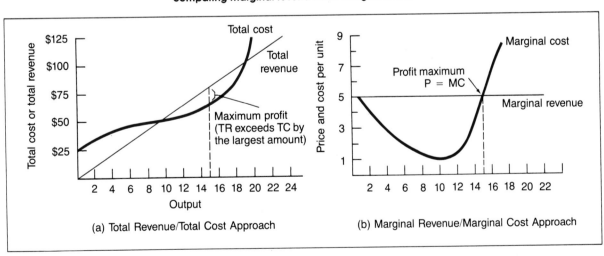

(a) Total Revenue/Total Cost Approach

(b) Marginal Revenue/Marginal Cost Approach

output is expanded beyond 15 units. Given the firm's cost and revenue schedule, the profit-maximizing manager will choose to produce 15, and only 15, units per day.

Exhibit 4b illustrates the marginal approach graphically. Note here that the output rate (15 units) at which the marginal cost and marginal revenue curves intersect coincides with the output rate in Exhibit 4a at which the total revenue curve exceeds the total cost curve by the largest amount.

Losses and Going Out of Business

Suppose that changes take place in the market that depress the price below a firm's average total cost. How will a profit-maximizing (or loss-minimizing) firm respond to this situation? The answer to this question depends on both the firm's current sales revenues relative to its *variable cost* and its expectations about the future. The firm has three options—it can (a) continue to operate in the short run, (b) shut down temporarily, or (c) go out of business.

If the firm anticipates that the lower market price is temporary, it may want to continue operating in the short run as long as it is able to cover its variable cost.[3] Exhibit 5 illustrates why. The firm shown in this exhibit would minimize its loss at output level q, where $P = \mathrm{MC}$. At q, total revenues ($OqBP_1$) are, however, less than total cost ($OqAC$). The firm confronts short-run economic losses. However, if it shuts down completely, it will still incur fixed costs,

EXHIBIT 5 Operating with short-run losses

A firm will operate in the short run if it (a) can cover its variable costs now and (b) expects price to be high enough in the future to cover all its costs.

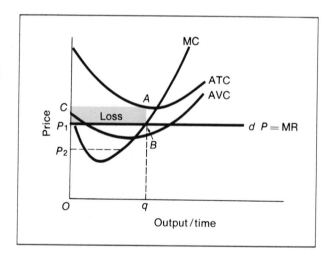

[3]In discussing this issue, it is vital that we keep the opportunity cost concept in mind. The firm's fixed costs are opportunity costs that do not vary with output. However, they can be avoided if, and only if, the firm goes out of business. Fixed costs are *not* (as some economics texts have stated) the depreciated value of the firm's fixed assets. Accounting depreciation "costs" may bear little resemblance to the firm's actual fixed cost. The proper specification of fixed cost relates (a) to how much the firm's assets would bring if they were sold or rented and (b) to other costs, such as operating license fees and debt, which could be avoided if the firm declared bankruptcy and/or went out of business. Since fixed costs can be avoided if the firm goes out of business, the firm will not operate even in the short run if it does not anticipate that market conditions will improve. See Marshall Colberg and James King, "Theory of Production Abandonment," *Revista Internazionale di Scienze Economiche e Commerciali* 20 (1973), 961–1072.

unless it goes out of business. If the firm anticipates that the market price will increase so that it will be able to cover its average total costs in the future, it may not want to sell out. It may choose to produce q units in the short run, even though losses are incurred. At price P_1, production of output q is clearly better than shutting down because the firm is able to cover its variable costs and pay some of its fixed costs. If it were to shut down, *but not sell out,* the firm would lose the entire amount of its fixed cost.

What if the market price declines below the firm's average variable cost (for example, P_2)? Under these circumstances, a temporary **shutdown** is preferable to short-run operation. If the firm continues to operate in the short run, operating losses merely supplement losses resulting from the firm's fixed costs. Therefore, even if the firm expects the market price to increase, so that it will be able to survive and prosper in the future, it will shut down in the short run when the market price falls below its average variable cost.

The firm's third option is **going out of business** immediately. After all, even the losses resulting from the firm's fixed costs (remember that if they are costs at all, they must be avoidable) can be avoided if the firm sells out. If it does not expect market conditions to change for the better, this is the preferred option.

The Competitive Firm's Short-Run Supply Curve

The competitive firm that intends to stay in business will maximize profits (or minimize losses) when it produces the output level at which $P = \mathrm{MC}$ and variable costs are covered. Therefore, the portion of the firm's short-run marginal cost curve that lies above its average variable cost is the short-run supply curve of the firm.

Exhibit 6 illustrates that as the market price increases, the competitive firm will expand output along its MC curve. If the market price were less than P_1, the firm would shut down immediately because it would be unable to cover even its variable costs. However, if the market price is P_1, a price equal to the firm's average variable cost, the firm may supply output q_1, *in the short run.* Economic losses will result, but the firm would incur similar losses if it shut down completely. As the market price increases to P_2, the firm will happily expand output along its MC curve to q_2. At P_2, price is also equal to average costs. The

Shutdown: A temporary halt in the operation of a business. The firm does *not* sell its assets. Its variable cost will be eliminated, but the firm's fixed costs will continue. The shutdown firm anticipates a return to operation in the future.

Going Out of Business: The sale of a firm's assets, and its permanent exit from the market. By going out of business, a firm is able to avoid fixed cost, which would continue during a shutdown.

EXHIBIT 6   The supply curve for the firm and the market

The short-run market supply is merely the sum of the supply produced by all the firms in the market area (b).

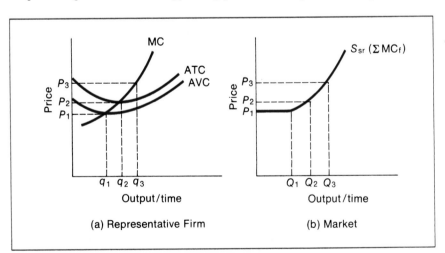

(a) Representative Firm   (b) Market

firm is making a "normal rate of return," or zero economic profits. Higher prices will result in a still larger short-run output. The firm will supply q_3 units at market price P_3. At this price, economic profits will result. At still higher prices, output will be expanded even more. As long as price exceeds average variable cost, the firm will expand supply along its MC curve, which therefore becomes becomes the firm's short-run supply curve.

The Short-Run Market Supply Curve

The short-run market supply curve corresponds to the total amount supplied by each of the firms in the industry.

For a purely competitive industry, the short-run market supply curve is the horizontal summation of the marginal cost curves (above the level of average variable cost) for all the firms in the industry. Since individual firms will supply a larger amount at a higher price, the short-run market supply curve will slope upward to the right.

Exhibit 6 illustrates this relationship. As the price of the product rises from P_1 to P_2 to P_3, the individual firms expand their output along their marginal cost curves. Since the individual competitive firms supply a larger output as the market price increases, the total amount supplied to the market also expands.

Our construction of the short-run market supply curve assumes that the prices of the resources used by the industry are constant. When the entire industry (rather than just a single firm) expands output, resource prices may rise. If this does happen, the short-run market supply curve will be just slightly more inelastic (steeper) than the sum of the supply curves of the individual firms.

The short-run market supply curve together with the demand curve for the industry's product will determine the market price. At the short-run equilibrium market price, each of the firms will have expanded output until marginal costs have risen to the market price. They will have no desire to change output, *given their current size of plant.*

OUTPUT ADJUSTMENTS IN THE LONG RUN

In the long run, firms have the opportunity to alter their plant size and enter or exit from an industry. As long-run adjustments are made, output in the whole industry may either expand or contract.

Long-Run Equilibrium

In addition to the balance between quantity supplied and quantity demanded necessary for short-run equilibrium, the firms in a competitive industry must earn the normal rate of return, and only the normal rate, before long-run equilibrium can be attained. If economic profit is present, new firms will enter the industry, and the current producers will have an incentive to expand the scale of their operation. This will lead to an increase in supply, placing downward pressure on prices. In contrast, if firms in the industry are suffering economic losses, they will leave the market. Supply will decline, placing upward pressure on prices.

Therefore, as Exhibit 7 illustrates, when a competitive industry is in long-run equilibrium, (a) the quantity supplied and the quantity demanded will be equal at the market price, and (b) the firms in the industry will be earning normal (zero) economic profit (that is, their minimum ATC will just equal the market price).

EXHIBIT 7 Long-run equilibrium in a competitive market

The two conditions necessary for equilibrium in a competitive market are depicted here. First, quantity supplied and quantity demanded must be equal in the market (b). Second, the firm must earn zero economic profit, that is, the "normal rate of return," at the established market price (a).

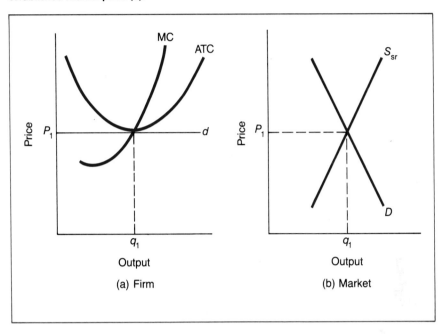

(a) Firm

(b) Market

Adjusting to an Expansion in Demand

Suppose that a purely competitive market is in equilibrium. What will happen if there is an increase in demand? Exhibit 8 presents an example. An entrepreneur introduces a fantastic new candy product. Consumers go wild over it. However, since it sticks to one's teeth, the market demand for toothpicks increases from D_1 to D_2. The price of toothpicks rises from P_1 to P_2. What impact will the higher market price have on the output level of toothpick-producing firms? It will increase (from q_1 to q_2, Exhibit 8) as the firms expand output along their marginal cost curves. In the short run, the toothpick producers will make economic profits. The profits will attract new toothpick producers to the industry and cause the existing firms to expand the scale of their plants.[4] Hence, the market supply will increase (shift from S_1 to S_2) and eventually eliminate the short-run profits. If cost conditions are unchanged in the industry, the market price for toothpicks will return to its initial level, even though output has expanded to Q_3.

Adjusting to a Decline in Demand

Economic profits attract new firms to an industry; economic losses (those that are expected to continue) encourage capital and entrepreneurship to move out of the industry and into other areas where the profitability potential is more

[4]If the *long-run* average total cost curve results in only one possible minimum-cost output level (see Exhibit 9a of the previous chapter), the expansion in long-run supply will be generated entirely by the entry of new firms. However, when the long-run average total cost is such that a wide range of minimum-cost output levels is possible (see Exhibit 9b of the previous chapter), both the entry of new firms and expansion by the established firms will contribute to the increase in supply.

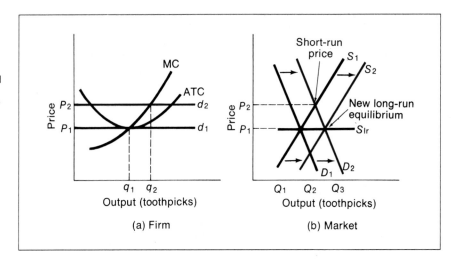

(a) Firm

(b) Market

favorable. Economic losses mean that the owners of capital in the industry are earning less than the market rate of return. The opportunity cost of continuing in the industry exceeds the gain.

Exhibit 9 illustrates how market forces react to economic losses. Initially, an equilibrium price exists in the industry. The firms are just able to cover their average costs of production. Now suppose that there is a reduction in consumer income, causing the market demand for the product to decrease and the market price to decline. At the new, lower price, firms in the industry will be

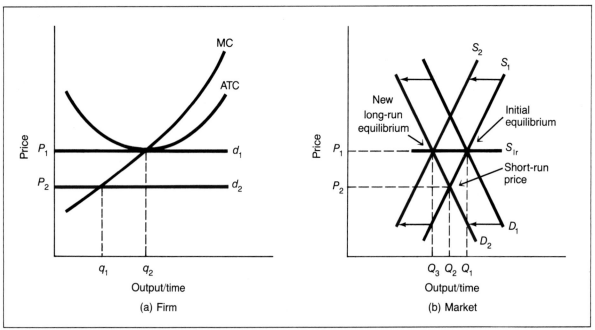

(a) Firm

(b) Market

unable to cover their costs of production. In the short run, they will reduce output along their MC curve. This reduction in output by the individual firms results in a reduction in the quantity supplied in the market.

In the face of short-run losses, there will be a reduction even in replacement capital into this industry. Some firms will leave the industry. Others will reduce the scale of their operation. These factors will cause the industry supply to decline, to shift from S_1 to S_2. What impact will this have on price? It will rise. In the long run, the market supply will decline until the price rises sufficiently to permit "normal profits" in the industry.

THE LONG-RUN SUPPLY CURVE

The long-run market supply curve indicates the minimum price at which firms will supply various market output levels, given sufficient time both to adjust plant size (or other fixed factors) and to enter or exit from the industry. The shape of the long-run market supply curve is dependent upon what happens to the cost of production as the output of an industry is altered. Three possibilities emerge, although one is far more likely than the other two.

Constant Cost Industries

Constant Cost Industry: An industry for which factor prices and costs of production remain constant as market output is expanded. Thus, the long-run market supply curve is horizontal.

If factor prices remain unchanged, the long-run market supply curve will be perfectly elastic. In terms of economics, this describes a **constant cost industry**. Exhibits 7 and 8 both picture constant cost industries. As Exhibit 7 illustrates, an expansion in demand causes prices to increase *temporarily*. The high prices and profits stimulate additional production. The short-run market supply continues to expand until the market price returns to its initial level and profits to their normal level. In the long run, the larger supply will not require permanent price increase. Thus, the *long-run* supply curve is perfectly elastic. Exhibit 8 illustrates the impact of a decline in demand on a constant cost industry. Again, the long-run supply curve is perfectly elastic, reflecting the basically unchanged cost at the lower rate of industry output.

A constant cost industry is most likely to arise when the industry's demand for the resources is quite small relative to the total demand for these resources. For example, since the demand of the matches industry for wood, chemicals, and labor is so small relative to the total demand for these resources, doubling the output of matches would exert only a negligible impact on the price of the resources used by the industry. Thus, matches approximate a constant cost industry.

Increasing Cost Industries

Increasing Cost Industries: Industries for which costs of production rise as the industry output is expanded. Thus, the long-run market supply is directly related to price.

For most industries, called **increasing cost industries** by economists, an expansion in total output causes a firm's production cost to rise. As the output of an industry increases, the demand for the resources used by the industry expands. This usually results in higher resource prices, which cause the firm's cost curves to shift upward. For example, an increase in demand for housing places upward pressure on the prices of lumber, roofing, window frames, and construction labor, causing the cost of housing to rise. Similarly, an increase in the demand (and market output) for beef may cause the prices of feed grains, hay, and grazing land to rise. Thus, the production costs of beef rise as more of it is produced.

In some industries, additional demand may lead to industrial congestion, which will reduce the efficiency of the industry and cause costs to rise, even

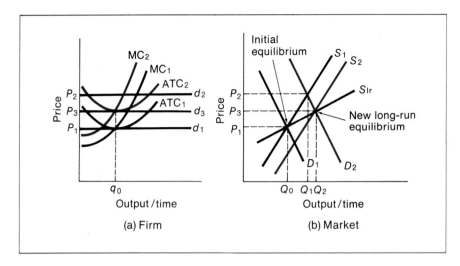

EXHIBIT 10 Increasing costs and the long-run supply

Most often, higher factor prices and industrial congestion will cause costs to rise as the *market* output increases. For such increasing cost industries, the long-run supply curve (S_{lr}, graph b) will slope upward to the right.

though resource prices are constant. For example, as the demand for lobster increases, additional fishermen are attracted to the industry. However, the increase in the number of fishermen combing lobster beds typically leads to congestion, which reduces the catch per hour of individual fishermen. Thus, the production cost in the lobster industry rises as output per labor-hour declines.

For an increasing cost industry, an expansion in market demand will bid up resource prices and/or lead to industrial congestion, causing the per unit cost of the firms to rise. As a result, a larger market output will be forthcoming only at a higher price. Thus, the long-run market supply curve for the product will slope upward.

Exhibit 10 depicts an increasing cost industry. An expansion in demand causes higher prices and a larger market output. The presence of short-run profit attracts new competitors to the industry, expanding the market output even more. *As the industry expands,* factor prices rise and congestion costs increase. What happens to the firm's cost curves? Both the average and marginal cost curves rise (shift to ATC_2 and MC_2). This increase in production cost necessitates a higher long-run price. Hence, the long-run supply curve slopes upward to the right.

Decreasing Cost Industries

Decreasing Cost Industries: Industries for which costs of production decline as the industry expands. The market supply is therefore inversely related to price. Such industries are atypical.

Conceivably, factor prices could decline if the market output of a product were expanded. Since a reduction in factor prices would lead to a lower long-run competitive market price for the product, economists refer to such industries as **decreasing cost industries.** The long-run (but not the short-run) market supply curve for a decreasing cost industry would slope downward to the right. For example, as the electronics industry expands, suppliers of components may be able to adopt large-scale techniques that will lead to lower component prices. If this occurs, the cost curves of the electronics firms may drift downward, causing the industry supply curve for electronics products to slope downward to the right (at least temporarily). However, since expansion of an industry is far more likely to cause rising rather than falling input prices, decreasing cost industries are atypical.

Market Adjustments to Changing Costs of Production

We have analyzed the impact that changes in market demand conditions have on both the short- and long-run market price. Often, disequilibrium is the result of changes in costs of production. Suppose that a technological advancement makes it possible for the firms of an industry to produce a given output level with fewer inputs. Therefore, costs are reduced. The market price will decline, but in the short run, price will decline less than costs. The firms will make short-run economic profits. The profits, however, will attract new firms into the industry, and the short-run market supply curve will continue shifting to the right until the profits have been eliminated. Price will decline. In long-run equilibrium, firms are just able to cover their average (and marginal) costs.

An increase in costs of production can be traced in a similar manner. Higher costs of production will cause an increase in the short-run market price, but the immediate increase will not be sufficient to cover the higher per unit cost of production completely. Short-run losses will result. Some firms will exit from the industry. This exodus of resources from the industry will continue until the reduction in market supply is sufficient to push the market price upward to the long-run, normal profit equilibrium.

Can you graphically depict the market adjustment that would result from a reduction (or increase) in costs or production? Try it and see. (Remember to assume that demand is unchanged.)

Supply Elasticity and the Role of Time

The market supply curve is more elastic in the long run than in the short run because the firm's short-run response is limited by the "fixed" nature of some of its factors. The short- and long-run distinction offers a convenient two-stage analysis, but in the real world there are many intermediate production "runs." Some factors that could not be easily varied in a one-week time period can be varied over a two-week period. Expansion of other factors might require a month, and still others, six months. To be more precise, the cost penalty for quicker availability is greater for some production factors than for others. In any case, a faster expansion usually means that greater cost penalties are necessary in order to provide for an earlier availability of productive factors.

When a firm has a longer time period to plan output and adjust all of its productive inputs to the desired utilization levels, it will be able to produce any specific rate of output at a lower cost. Because it is less costly to expand output slowly, the expansion of output by firms will increase with time, as long as price exceeds cost and up to the point at which returns begin to diminish. Therefore, the elasticity of the market supply curve will increase as more time is allowed for firms to adjust control.

Exhibit 11 illustrates the important effect of time on the supply response of producers. When the price of a product increases from P_1 to P_2, the *immediate* suppiy response of the firms is small because it is costly to expand output hastily. After one week, firms are willing to expand output only from Q_1 to Q_2. After one month, due to cost reductions that are possible because of the longer production planning period, firms are willing to offer Q_3 units at the price P_2. After three months, the rate of output expands to Q_4. In the long run, when it is possible to adjust all inputs to the desired utilization levels (within a six-month time period, for example), firms are willing to supply Q_5 units of output at the market price of P_2. The supply curve for products is typically more elastic over a long time period than for a shorter period.

EXHIBIT 11 Time and the elasticity of the supply

The elasticity of the market supply curve usually increases as more time is allowed for adjustment to a change in price.

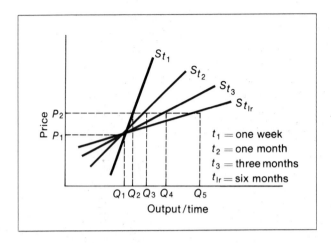

The Role of Profits in the Competitive Model

In the competitive model, profits and losses are merely signals sent out by consumers to producers. Economic profits will be largest in those areas where consumer wants are greatest *relative to costs of production.* Profit-seeking entrepreneurs will guide additional resources into these areas. Supply will increase, driving prices down and eliminating the profits. Free entry and the competitive process will protect the consumer from arbitrarily high prices. In the long run, competitive prices will reflect costs of production.

Economic profits result because a firm or entrepreneur increases the value of resources. The successful business decision-maker combines resources into a product that consumers value more than the sum of the resources used to produce it. That is why consumers are willing to pay a price in excess of the cost of producing the good. In contrast, losses result when the actions of a producer reduce the value of resources. The value of the resources used up by such unsuccessful firms exceeds the price consumers are willing to pay for their product. Losses and bankruptcy are the market's way of bringing such wasteful activities to a halt.

Of course, producers, like other decision-makers, confront uncertainty and dynamic change. Entrepreneurs, at the time they must make investment decisions, cannot be sure of either future market prices or costs of production. They must base their decisions on expectations. Within the framework of the competitive model, however, the reward–penalty system is clear. Firms that produce efficiently and anticipate correctly the products and services for which future demand will be most urgent (relative to production cost) will make economic profit. Those that are inefficient and incorrectly allocate resources into areas of weak future demand will be penalized with losses.

EFFICIENCY AND THE COMPETITIVE MODEL

Economists often seem to be enchanted by the purely competitive model. Sometimes they hold it up as the standard by which to judge other models. What accounts for the special significance of pure competition? Most economists agree that under rather restrictive assumptions the resource allocation within the purely competitive model is ideal from society's viewpoint. In what sense can we say that it is "ideal"?

Production Efficiency (P = ATC)

In the long run, competition forces firms to minimize their average total cost of production and charge a price that is just sufficient to cover production costs. Competitive firms must use production methods that minimize costs if they are going to survive. In addition, they must choose a scale of operation that minimizes their long-run average total cost of production. Consumers of competitively produced goods will benefit, since they will receive the largest quantity at the lowest possible price, given the prevailing cost conditions. Competitive markets will eliminate waste and production inefficiency. Inefficient, high-cost producers will confront economic losses and be driven from a competitive industry.

Allocative Efficiency (P = MC)

Allocative Efficiency: The allocation of resources to the production of the goods and services most desired by consumers. The allocation is "balanced" in such a way that reallocation of resources could not benefit anyone without hurting someone else.

Allocative efficiency refers to the balance achieved by the allocation of available resources to the production of the goods and services most desired by consumers, given their income. Allocative efficiency is present when all markets are in long-run competitive equilibrium. Each good is produced as long as consumers value it more than the alternative goods that might be produced with the same resources. No unit of the good is produced if a more valuable alternative must be foregone; and any reallocation of resources toward different goods or different combinations of goods—any disturbance of the allocative balance—would not benefit any one person without hurting someone else.

The profit-maximization rule ($P = MC$) assures allocative efficiency within the competitive model. The market demand (price) reflects consumers' valuation of an additional unit of a good. The seller's marginal cost indicates the value of the resources (in their alternative uses) necessary to produce an additional unit of the good. When the production of each good is expanded as long as price exceeds marginal cost, each good will be produced if, and only if, consumers value it more than the alternatives that might have been produced. Thus, in purely competitive markets, profit-maximizing producers will be led to produce the combination of goods most desired by consumers.

Pure Competition and the Real World

In the purely competitive model, the "invisible hand" that Adam Smith spoke of does its job very well indeed. Producers who are motivated purely by the desire to make a profit act no differently than they would if they cared only about the efficient satisfaction of consumers' desires. Because of the resulting price structure, even the desire of a highly selfish consumer for a consumption item is balanced against the value of the good (price relative to that of other goods) to other people. In other words, prevailing prices provide each person with the incentive to heed the wishes of others. An incredibly complex array of consumer desires, production possibilities, and resource availabilities can be optimally coordinated in the model. No central person or group need know or understand all the aspects of the model. A few market prices condense the needed information and convey it to each decision-maker.

However, pure competition is merely a hypothetical model. It can only exist under very restrictive conditions. For better or for worse, these conditions are often absent in the real world, for several reasons. First, in many industries, the production costs of large firms are less than for small firms, due to economies

OUTSTANDING ECONOMIST
**Friedrich A. von Hayek
(1899–   )**

For six decades Professor Hayek has been a consistent and eloquent defender of classical liberalism, even as most of the world has moved increasingly toward central planning and big government. Born in Vienna, Hayek was a lecturer in Austria during the 1920s. In 1931, he accepted a professorship of economics at the London School of Economics. After World War II, he joined the faculty of the University of Chicago, where he taught for many years. He is currently on the faculty of the University of Freiburg in Germany. In 1979 Hayek was the joint recipient (along with Gunnar Myrdal) of the Nobel Prize in economics.

Hayek studied under Ludwig von Mises at the University of Vienna. The two eventually became the most powerful spokesmen in this century for what is known as the "Austrian school" of economics. Hayek has made important contributions in areas as diverse as monetary theory, markets and knowledge, capital theory, and the theory of business cycles. With *The Road to Serfdom* (1944), Hayek emerged as a scholar of international repute. The major thesis of his book is that a centrally planned economy eventually destroys both the economic and political freedom of individuals. Hayek argues:

Economic control is not merely control of a sector of human life which can be separated from the rest; it is the control of the means for all our ends. And whoever has sole control of the means must also determine which ends are to be served, which values are to be rated higher and which lower—in short, what men should believe and strive for.[5]

Hayek believes the meaning of competition is a major source of confusion among economists. Many economists classify markets as either perfectly or imperfectly competitive. Perfect competition is believed to be both "ideal" and rarely achievable, and imperfect competition is viewed as both widespread and undesirable. Hayek argues that markets will be competitive when the government does not create artificial obstacles restricting the entry of firms. According to Hayek, competition is a process that "creates the views people have about what is best and cheapest." In the absence of entry barriers created by government, the lowest possible prices will exist in markets—that is, prices will be driven down to the level of production costs. Producers will be unable to take advantage of consumers. "The practical lesson of all this," Hayek states, "is that we should worry much less about whether competition in a given case is perfect and worry much more whether there is competition at all."[6]

His most recent publications include a three-volume work entitled *Law, Legislation, and Liberty,* in which he articulates his views on the importance of rules over discretionary authority, the interrelationship of economic and political freedom, and the illusory concept of social justice. Hayek is much more than an economist—he is a social critic, philosopher, political theorist, and scholar.

[5]Friedrich A. Hayek, *The Road to Serfdom* (Chicago: University of Chicago Press, 1944), p. 92.

[6]Friedrich A. Hayek, *Individualism and Economic Order* (Chicago: University of Chicago Press, 1948), pp. 105–106.

of scale. Under these circumstances, it is neither feasible nor economical to have the industry's output divided among a large number of small producers. Second, the preferences of consumers differ widely with regard to such factors as product design, quality, and location of purchase. In short, they desire variety, not the homogeneous products implied by the purely competitive model. Third, we live in a dynamic world. Changes in knowledge and technology often alter both the availability and cost of alternative products. Disequilibrium, rather than a stable, purely competitive equilibrium, is the dominant characteristic. The purely competitive hypothetical ideal loses some of its relevance in a world characterized by rapid technological change, constant introduction of new products, and continual discovery of new information. Fourth, competition (in the rivalry sense) is multidimensional. Pure competition emphasizes one of the dimensions—price. But competition for the approval of consumers that is based on product quality, producer reliability and honesty, convenience of location, and quickness of service is also of tremendous importance. This nonprice competition may be just as intense as the price competition of the purely competitive model.

Nevertheless, pure competition is important because it can help us understand real-world markets characterized by low barriers to entry and a substantial number of independent sellers. At the opposite end of the spectrum lie markets characterized by high barriers to entry and a single seller. The following chapter focuses on the hypothetical model that economists have developed to analyze markets of this type—pure monopoly.

CHAPTER LEARNING OBJECTIVES

1 Competition as a process should not be confused with pure competition, a model of industrial structure. Competition as a process implies rivalry. Rival firms use quality, style, location, advertising, and price to try to attract consumers. On the other hand, pure competition is a model of industrial structure that assumes the presence of a large number of small (relative to the total market) firms, each producing a homogeneous product in a market for which there is complete freedom of entry and exit.

2 The competitive process places producers under strong pressure to operate efficiently and heed the views of consumers. Those who do not offer quality goods at economical prices lose customers to rivals. As Adam Smith recognized long ago, self-interest is a powerful motivator of human beings. If it is bridled by competition, self-interest leads to economic cooperation and productive effort.

3 Under pure competition, firms are price takers—they face a perfectly elastic demand curve. Profit-maximizing (or loss-minimizing) firms will expand output as long as the additional output *adds* more to revenues than to costs. Therefore, the competitive firm will produce the output level at which marginal revenue (and price) equals marginal cost.

4 The firm's short-run marginal cost curve (above its average variable cost) is its supply curve. Under pure competition, the short-run *market* supply curve is the horizontal sum of the marginal cost curves (when MC is above AVC) for all the firms that comprise the industry.

5 If a firm (a) is covering its average variable cost and (b) anticipates that the "below-average total cost" price will be temporary, it may operate in the short run even though it is experiencing a loss. However, even if it anticipates more favorable market conditions in the future, loss minimization will require the firm to shut down if it is unable to cover its average variable cost. If the firm does not anticipate that it will be able to cover its average total cost even in the long run, loss minimization requires that it immediately go out of business (even if it is covering its average *variable* cost) so that it can at least avoid its fixed cost.

6 When price exceeds average total cost, a firm will make economic profits. Under pure competition, profits will attract new firms into the industry and stimulate the existing firms to expand. The market supply will increase, pushing price down to the level of average total cost. Competitive firms will be unable to make long-run economic profits.

7 Losses exist when the market price is less than the firm's average total cost. Losses will cause firms to leave the industry or reduce the scale of their operation. The market supply will decline, until price rises sufficiently so that firms can earn normal (that is, zero economic) profits.

8 As the output of an industry expands, marginal costs will increase in the short run, causing the short-run market supply curve to slope upward to the right. If cost conditions

in the industry remain unchanged as the market output is expanded, the long-run supply curve will be perfectly elastic. However, as the output of an industry expands, rising factor prices and industrial congestion will normally cause the firm's cost curves to shift upward. The long-run market supply curve for such an increasing cost industry will slope upward to the right.

9 Within the framework of the purely competitive model, firms that produce efficiently and anticipate correctly those goods for which future demand will be most urgent (relative to costs of production) will make profits. Firms that produce inefficiently and allocate resources incorrectly to the production of goods for which future demand turns out to be weak (relative to costs of production) will be penalized with losses. In the short run, firms might make either profits or losses, but in the long run, competitive pressures will eliminate economic profits (and losses).

10 Economists often argue that pure competition leads to ideal economic efficiency because (a) average costs of production are minimized and (b) output is expanded to the level at which the consumer's evaluation of an additional unit of a good is just equal to its marginal cost.

THE ECONOMIC WAY OF THINKING—DISCUSSION QUESTIONS

1 Farmers are often heard to complain about the high cost of machinery, labor, and fertilizer, suggesting that these costs drive down their profit rate. Does it follow that if, for example, the price of fertilizer fell by 10 percent, farming (a highly competitive industry with low barriers to entry) would be more profitable? Explain.

2 If the firms in a competitive industry are making short-run profits, what will happen to the market price in the long run? Explain.

3 What factors will cause the supply curve for a product to slope upward in the long run? Be specific.

4 A sales tax, collected from the seller, will shift the firm's cost curves upward. Outline the impact of a sales tax within the framework of the competitive model. Use diagrams to indicate both the short-run and long-run impact of the tax. Who will bear the burden of the sales tax?

5 What do economists mean when they say that resource allocation is ideal or efficient? Why is it sometimes argued that a purely competitive economy will allocate goods ideally? Explain.

6 The following table presents the expected cost and revenue data for the Tucker

Cost and Revenue Schedules—Tucker Tomato Farm, Inc.

Output (Tons per Month)	Total Cost	Price per Ton	Marginal Cost	Average Variable Cost	Average Total Cost	Profits (Monthly)
0	$1000	$500	—	—	—	—
1	1200	500				
2	1350	500				
3	1550	500				
4	1900	500				
5	2300	500				
6	2750	500				
7	3250	500				
8	3800	500				
9	4400	500				
10	5150	500				

Tomato Farm. The Tuckers produce tomatoes in a greenhouse and sell them wholesale in a purely competitive market. (a) Fill in the firm's marginal cost, average variable cost, average total cost, and profit schedules. (b) If the Tuckers are profit maximizers, how many tomatoes should they produce when the market price is $500 per ton? Indicate their profits. (c) Indicate the firm's output level and maximum profit if the market price of tomatoes increases to $550 per ton. (d) How many units would the Tucker Tomato Farm produce if the price of tomatoes declined to $450? Indicate the firm's profits. Should the firm continue in business? Explain.

20

MONOPOLY AND HIGH BARRIERS TO ENTRY

In the last chapter we analyzed pure competition, a hypothetical market structure characterized by numerous sellers. We now turn to the other extreme of market structure, pure monopoly. The word "monopoly," derived from two Greek words, means "single seller." When there is only a single seller, the firm will exert more control over price and output. This does not mean that the monopolist is completely free from competitive pressures. As Professor Wilcox implies, varying degrees of competition are present even under conditions of monopoly.

However, the absence of numerous rivals and the existence of substantial entry barriers will influence the nature of a market. What price will a monopolist charge? How does the domination of an industry by a single firm affect the efficiency of resource allocation? Can we improve the expected outcome of free markets under these circumstances? In this chapter we will discuss these issues in relation to both static and dynamic market conditions.

DEFINING MONOPOLY

Monopoly: A market structure characterized by a single seller of a well-defined product for which there are no good substitutes and by high barriers to the entry of any other firms into the market for that product.

We will define **monopoly** as a market structure characterized by (a) high barriers to entry and (b) a single seller of a well-defined product for which there are no good substitutes. Even this definition is ambiguous because "high barriers" and "good substitutes" are both relative terms. Are the barriers to entry into the automobile or steel industries high? Many observers would argue that they are. After all, it would take a great deal of financial capital to compete successfully in these industries. However, there are no *legal* restraints that prevent you or anyone else from producing automobiles or steel. In addition, if you can convince others that you are likely to be successful in any industry,

---

[1]Clair Wilcox, *Competition and Monopoly in American Industry,* Monograph no. 21, Temporary National Economic Committee, Investigation of Concentration of Economic Power, 76th Cong., 3rd sess. (Washington, D.C.: U.S. Government Printing Office, 1940), p. 8.

it will be possible to raise large amounts of financial capital. The concept of barriers to entry is, in part, subjective.

Similarly, there is always some substitutability among products, even those produced by a monopolist. Is a letter a good substitute for telephone communication? For some purposes, legal correspondence for example, it is a very good substitute. In other cases, when the speed of communication and immediacy of response are important, telephone communication has a tremendous advantage over letter writing. Are there any good substitutes for electricity? Most of the known substitutes for electric lighting (candles, oil lamps, and battery lights, for example) are inferior to electric lights. However, natural gas, fuel oil, and wood are often excellent substitutes for electric heating.

Monopoly, then, is always a matter of degree. Pure monopoly, like pure competition, is a rare phenomenon. Nonetheless, there are two reasons why it is important to understand how markets work under pure monopoly. First, the monopoly model will help us understand markets dominated by only a few sellers. A dominant firm in an industry often has a tendency to behave like a monopolist. When there are only two or three producers in a market, they may seek to collude rather than compete with each other and thus together behave like a monopoly. Second, there is only a single producer in a few important industries. Local telephone and electricity services provide examples. The monopoly model will illuminate the operation of such markets.

Barriers to Entry

What makes it difficult for potential competitors to enter a market? Three factors are of particular importance.

1. Legal Barriers. Legal barriers are the oldest and most effective method of protecting a business firm from potential competitors. Kings once granted exclusive business rights to favored citizens or groups. Today, governments continue to establish barriers, restricting the right to buy and sell goods. In the United States, in order to compete in the communications industry (for example, in order to operate a radio or television station), one must obtain a government franchise. The Post Office, a government corporation, is granted the exclusive right to deliver first-class mail, although this is currently being challenged. Potential private competitors are eliminated by law.

Licensing, a process by which one obtains permission from the government to enter a specific occupation or business, often limits entry. In many states, a person must obtain a license before operating a liquor store, barbershop, taxicab, funeral home, or drugstore. Sometimes, these licenses cost little and are designed to ensure certain minimum standards. In other cases, they are expensive and designed primarily to limit competition.

Patent: The grant of an exclusive right to use a specific process or produce a specific product for a period of time (17 years in the United States).

Another legal barrier to entry is a **patent,** which grants the owner a legal monopoly on the commercial use of a newly invented product or process for a limited period of time, 17 years in the United States. Once a patent has been granted, other persons are prevented from using the procedures or producing the product unless they obtain permission from the patent holder. Essentially, the patent system is designed to permit inventors to reap the benefits of their inventions. Nonetheless, patents are often used to restrict the entry of rivals into a broad market area. For example, Polaroid's control over patent rights enabled it to exclude all rivals from the instant-picture market for years, until Eastman Kodak developed a new process.

2. Economies of Scale. In some industries, a firm is unable to produce at a low cost unless it is quite large, both in absolute terms and relative to the market. Under these circumstances, economies of scale prevent small firms from entering the market, building a reputation, and competing effectively with large firms. The existing firms are thus protected from potential competitors.

3. Control over an Essential Resource. If a single firm has sole control over a resource that is essential for entry into an industry, it can eliminate potential competitors. The famous DeBeers Company of South Africa is a classic case. Since this company has almost exclusive control over all of the world's diamond mines, it can effectively prevent other firms from entering the diamond-producing industry. Its ability to raise the price of new diamonds is limited only by the availability of substitute gems, and by the potential sales by current owners of previously produced diamonds.

THE HYPOTHETICAL MODEL OF MONOPOLY

Suppose that you invent, patent, and produce a microwave device that locks the hammer of any firearm in the immediate area. This fabulous invention can be used to immobilize potential robbers or hijackers. Since you own the exclusive patent right to the device, you are not concerned about a competitive supplier in the foreseeable future. Although other products are competitive with your inventions, they are poor substitutes. In short, you are a monopolist.

What price should you charge for your product? Like the purely competitive firm, you will want to expand output as long as marginal revenue exceeds marginal cost. However, unlike the purely competitive firm, you will face a downward-sloping demand curve. Since you are the only firm in the industry, the industry demand curve will coincide with your demand curve. Consumers will buy less of your product at a higher price. At high prices, even a monopolist will have few customers.

Total Revenue, Marginal Revenue, and Elasticity of Demand

Since the demand curve of a monopolist slopes downward, there will be two conflicting influences on total revenue when the seller reduces price in order to expand output and sales. As Exhibit 1 illustrates, the resultant increase in sales (from q_1 to q_2) will positively influence the total revenue of the monopolist; additional units can now be sold at the lower price that could not have been sold at the higher price. The sale of these units will increase total revenue. However, a price reduction will also tend to *lower* the monopolist's total revenue, simply because the units of the product that *could* have been sold at the higher price are now sold at a lower price (P_1 rather than P_2, as illustrated). The marginal revenue derived from the additional sales will be less than the sales price. Thus, as shown in Exhibit 1, the marginal revenue curve of the monopolist will lie inside (below) the demand curve of the firm.[2]

---

[2]For a straight-line demand curve, the marginal revenue curve will bisect any line parallel to the *x*-axis. For example, the MR curve will divide the line P_2F into two equal parts, P_2E and EF.

EXHIBIT 1 The effect of increases in sales on revenue

When a firm faces a downward-sloping demand curve, a price reduction that increases sales will exert two conflicting influences on total revenue. First, total revenue will rise because of an increase in the number of units sold (from q_1 to q_2). However, revenue losses from the lower price (P_2) on units that could have been sold at a higher price (P_1) will at least partially offset the additional revenues due to increased sales. Therefore, the marginal revenue curve will lie inside the firm's demand curve.

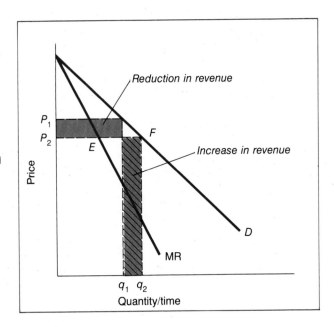

While the demand curve shows the number of units that can be sold at different prices, it also reveals how revenues vary as price and output are altered. Using a straight-line demand curve, Exhibit 2 illustrates how total and marginal revenue are related to elasticity of demand. At very high prices, the sales of the monopolist will be small. As price is reduced and output is expanded on the elastic portion of the monopolist's demand curve, total revenue will rise. Marginal revenue will be positive. Suppose the monopolist charged $15 for a product and sold 25 units, yielding a total revenue of $375. If the monopolist reduced price to $10, sales would expand to 50 units. Total revenue would rise to $500. Thus, a price reduction from $15 to $10 would increase the total revenue of the monopolist.

Consider the output rate at which elasticity of demand is equal to unity. At that point, total revenue reaches its maximum. Marginal revenue is equal to zero. As price falls below $10 into the inelastic portion of the monopolist's demand curve, total revenue declines as output is expanded. For this range of price and output, marginal revenue will be negative. Thus, marginal revenue goes from positive to negative as the elasticity of demand changes from elastic to inelastic (at output 50 of Exhibit 2).

This analysis has obvious implications. For a monopolist operating on the inelastic portion of its demand curve, a price increase would lead to more total revenue *and* less total cost (since fewer units would be produced and sold). Thus, we would never expect a profit maximizing monopolist to push the sales of a product into the range where the product's demand curve becomes inelastic.

The Profit-Maximizing Output

Both cost and revenues must be considered when we analyze the profit-maximization decision rule for the monopolist. The profit-maximizing monopolist will continue expanding output until marginal revenue equals marginal cost. The price corresponding to that output level is given by the demand curve of the monopolist.

EXHIBIT 2   Price, total revenue, and marginal revenue of a monopolist

In the elastic portion of the monopolist's demand curve (prices greater than $10), a price reduction will be associated with rising total revenue (frame b) and positive marginal revenue. At unitary elasticity (output of 50 units), total revenue will reach a maximum. When the monopolist's demand curve is inelastic (output beyond 50 units), lower prices will lead to declining total revenue and negative marginal revenue.

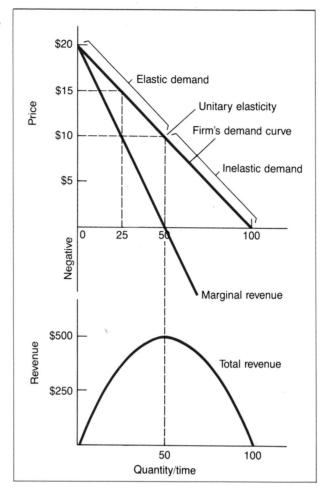

EXHIBIT 3   The short-run price and output of a monopolist

The monopolist will reduce price and expand output as long as MR exceeds MC. Output Q will result. When price exceeds average cost at the output level, profit will accrue.

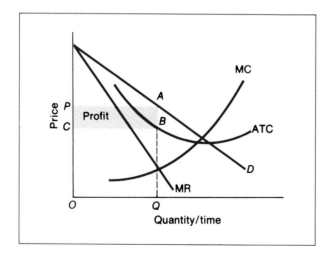

Exhibit 3 provides a graphic illustration of profit maximization. The monopolist will continue to expand output as long as marginal revenue exceeds marginal cost. Therefore, output will be expanded to Q, where MR = MC.

The monopolist will be able to sell the profit-maximizing output Q for a price indicated by the height of the demand curve. At any output less than Q, the benefits (marginal revenue) of producing the *additional* units will exceed their cost. The monopolist will gain by expanding output. For any output greater than Q, the monopolist's cost of producing *additional* units will be greater than the benefits (marginal revenue). Production of such units will reduce profits.

Exhibit 3 also depicts the profits of a monopolist. At output Q, the monopolist would charge price P. Price times the number of units sold yields the firm's total revenue ($PAQO$). The firm's total cost would be $CBQO$, the average per unit cost multiplied by the number of units sold. The firm's profits are merely total revenue less total cost, the shaded area of Exhibit 3.

Although both competitive and monopolistic firms expand output until $MR = MC$, there is one important difference. For the competitive firm, price will also equal marginal cost at the maximum-profit output. This will not be true for the monopolist. A profit-maximizing monopolist will choose an output rate where price is greater than marginal cost. Later we will consider the implications of this difference.

Exhibit 4 provides a numeric illustration of profit-maximizing decision-making. At low output rates, marginal revenue exceeds marginal cost. The monopolist will continue expanding output as long as MR is greater than MC. Thus, an output rate of eight units per day will be chosen. Given the demand for the product, the monopolist can sell eight units at a price of $17.25 each. Total revenue will be $138, compared to a total cost of $108.50. Thus, the monopolist will make a profit of $29.50. The profit rate will be smaller at all other output rates. For example, if the monopolist reduces the price to $16 in order to sell nine units per day, marginal revenue will increase by $6. However, the marginal cost of producing the ninth unit is $6.25. Since the cost of producing the ninth unit is greater than the revenue it brings in, profits will decline.

EXHIBIT 4   Profit maximization for a monopolist

Rate of Output (per Day) (1)	Price (per Unit) (2)	Total Revenue (1) × (2) (3)	Total Cost (per Day) (4)	Profit (3) − (4) (5)	Marginal Cost (6)	Marginal Revenue (7)
0	—	—	$ 50.00	$ −50.00	—	—
1	$25.00	$ 25.00	60.00	−35.00	$10.00	$ 25.00
2	24.00	48.00	69.00	−21.00	9.00	23.00
3	23.00	69.00	77.00	− 8.00	8.00	21.00
4	22.00	88.00	84.00	4.00	7.00	19.00
5	21.00	105.00	90.50	14.50	6.50	17.00
6	19.75	118.50	96.75	21.75	6.25	13.50
7	18.50	129.50	102.75	26.75	6.00	11.00
8	17.25	138.00	108.50	29.50	5.75	8.50
9	16.00	144.00	114.75	29.25	6.25	6.00
10	14.75	147.50	121.25	26.25	6.50	3.50
11	13.50	148.50	128.00	20.50	6.75	1.00
12	12.25	147.00	135.00	12.00	7.00	−1.50
13	11.00	143.00	142.25	.75	7.25	−4.00

group decreases, the group purchases substantially more units. Thus, the lower price P_b maximizes the profit from this group.

What easily identifiable characteristics might be linked to the customer's elasticity of demand? Sometimes factors such as age, income, and sex will influence elasticity of demand. For example, the demand of children for movies, airline tickets, and football games is often believed to be more elastic than the demand of adults.

Can you think of any examples of price discrimination? Airlines often offer discount fares to individuals willing to travel during off-peak hours, make reservations well in advance, or travel with another person paying a full fare. The demand of these consumers is thought to be more elastic than that of other customers, such as business travelers. Thus, the group with the more elastic demand is given the discount, while other customers are required to pay the full fare. Why do professional journals usually charge individual subscribers lower rates than libraries? They generate more revenue by charging higher prices to subscribers with an inelastic demand (libraries). Why are women often charged lower prices for attending nightclubs and baseball games? Again, price discrimination apparently leads to greater increases in revenues than in costs.

A seller need not be a pure monopolist in order to gain from price discrimination. Any firm that faces a downward-sloping demand curve for its product may employ the technique. In fact, competitive weapons such as discounts and economy fares are often indicative of price discrimination. We introduce the concept while discussing monopoly merely to illustrate the general point.

DEFECTS AND PROBLEMS OF MONOPOLY

The monopolists, by keeping the market constantly under-stocked, by never fully supplying the effectual demand, sell their commodities much above the natural price, and raise their emoluments, whether they consist of wages or profit, greatly above their natural rate.[3]

What types of problems arise under monopoly? Can public policy improve resource allocation in markets characterized by monopoly?

Three Defects of Monopoly

From Adam Smith's time to the present, economists have generally considered monopoly a necessary evil at best. There are three major reasons for this view.

Monopoly Severely Limits the Options Available to Consumers. If you do not like the food at a local restaurant, you can go to another. If you do not like the wares of a local department store, you can buy good substitutes somewhere else. The competition of rivals protects the consumer from the arbitrary behavior of a single seller. But what are your alternatives if you do not like the local telephone service? You can send a letter or deliver your message in person, or you can write to your legislative representative and complain. However, these

---

[3]Adam Smith, *An Inquiry into the Nature and Causes of the Wealth of Nations* (1776; Cannan's ed., Chicago: University of Chicago Press, 1976), p. 69.

are not very satisfactory alternatives to the service of the monopolist. If the monopolist "pushes you around," often you have no feasible alternative but to accept poor service, rude treatment, or high prices.

In the absence of monopoly, the consumer can buy a product either from firm A or from another firm. In the presence of monopoly, the option is to buy from the monopolist or do without. This reduction in the options available to the consumer greatly reduces the consumer's ability to discipline monopolists.

Monopoly Results in Allocative Inefficiency. Allocative efficiency requires a community to undertake an activity when it generates additional benefits that are in excess of the cost. This would require a firm to expand output as long as price exceeded marginal cost. A profit-maximizing monopolist, however, would restrict output below this level, in order to maintain marginal revenue in excess of marginal cost. Marginal cost would be equal to marginal revenue (the cut-off level for maximum profits in a monopoly) at a *lower* level of output than that at which price would be equal to marginal cost.

The logic of this criticism is pictured in Exhibit 7. The demand is a measure of how much consumers value additional units of a product. The marginal cost curve represents the opportunity cost of the resources utilized to produce the additional units. Ideally, economic efficiency would require output to be expanded as long as the height of the demand curve exceeded the marginal cost. From the viewpoint of the entire community, output level Q_i would be best.

The monopolist, however, would produce only Q_m units. If output were expanded beyond Q_m to Q_i, how much would consumers gain? The area under the demand curve, ABQ_iQ_m, reveals the answer. How much would it cost the monopolist to produce these units? CBQ_iQ_m reflects the monopolist's costs. The benefits of producing the units would exceed the cost to consumers. Yet the monopolist would not produce these additional units because they would add less to the monopoly's revenues (assuming that all consumers are charged the same price) than to its costs. As Adam Smith observed 200 years ago, the monopolist understocks the market and charges prices that are too high.

EXHIBIT 7 Understocking in the market

A monopolist will produce only output Q_m, even though Q_i is best for the entire community.

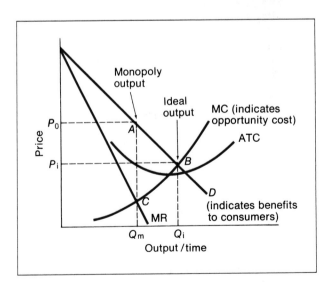

Under Monopoly, Profits and Losses Do Not Properly Induce Firms to Enter and to Exit from Industries. When barriers to entry are low, profits induce firms to produce goods for which consumers are willing (because of the expected benefits) to pay prices sufficient to cover costs of production. Losses constrain firms from the production of goods for which consumers are unwilling to cover costs of production. Profits and losses are able to direct resources into those activities for which consumer valuation is highest.

For the monopolist, profits play a smaller role because entry barriers are high. Although losses will induce exit from the market, a monopolist's profits are a premium enjoyed at the expense of the consumer.

When Can a Monopolized Industry Be Competitive?

In a nutshell, the most serious problems raised by a monopoly would be avoided if the monopolist faced the threat of rivals producing the same product or even close substitutes. The presence of competitors would prevent independent firms from restricting output and raising prices.

Why not break up the monopolist into several rival units, substituting competition for monopoly? If it were not for economies of scale, this would be a very good strategy.

Exhibit 8 compares competition and monopoly, assuming that economies of scale are unimportant in the industry. Thus, the minimum-cost production conditions for purely competitive firms would not differ from those of a monopolist. If the industry were purely competitive, price would be determined by supply and demand. As Exhibit 8a illustrates, under these conditions competition would drive price down to P_c in the long run. An industry output of Q_c would result. The market price would just equal the *marginal* opportunity costs of production.

In contrast, if the industry were monopolized, the profit-maximizing monopolist would equate marginal revenue with marginal cost (Exhibit 8b). This would lead to an output level of Q_m. The monopolist would charge P_m, a higher price than would exist in a competitive industry. When economies of scale are unimportant, imposition of competitive conditions on a monopolized

EXHIBIT 8 Pure competition and pure monopoly in the absence of economies of scale

Here we assume that a product can be produced by either numerous small firms or a monopolist at the same average total and marginal costs. When there are no cost disadvantages for small-scale production, competition serves to reduce price. For a purely competitive industry (a), supply and demand would dictate price P_c. The firms would just be able to cover their cost. If all the firms merged into a monopoly and *cost conditions remained the same*, the monopolist would restrict output to Q_m (where MC would equal MR). Price would rise to P_m.

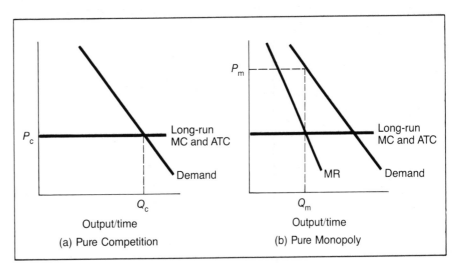

(a) Pure Competition

(b) Pure Monopoly

industry would result in lower prices, a larger output, and improved economic efficiency.

Economies of Scale and Natural Monopoly

Unfortunately, it is often unrealistic to expect similar cost conditions for pure competition and monopoly. Economies of scale are often the reason that certain industries tend to be monopolized. If economies of scale are important, larger firms will have lower per unit cost than smaller rivals. Sometimes economies of scale may be so important that per unit cost of production will be lowest when the entire output of the industry is produced by a single firm. In the absence of government intervention, the "natural" tendency will then be toward monopoly, because increases in firm size through merger or "survival of the fittest" will lead to lower per unit cost.

Natural Monopoly: A market situation in which the average costs of production continually decline with increased output. Thus, a single firm would be the lowest-cost producer of the output demanded.

Exhibit 9 depicts the **natural monopoly** case. The long-run average cost in the industry declines and eventually crosses the demand curve. In order to take full advantage of the economies of scale, given the demand for the product, the total output of the industry would have to be produced by a single firm. If the firm were an unregulated monopolist, it would produce output Q_m and charge price P_m. The firm would realize economic profits, because average costs would be less than price at the profit-maximizing output level. It would be very difficult for any firm to begin to compete with the natural monopolist; initially, while the new competitor was still small, it would have very high costs of production and would be unable to make profits at price P_m. The "natural" monopoly conditions of the industry would act as an entry barrier to potential competitors.

Therefore, when "natural" monopoly exists, a "competitive" market structure will be both costly and difficult to maintain. Suppose that the output of an industry were divided among ten firms of size Q_c (see Exhibit 8). These small firms would have per unit average costs of P_c. Even if they charged a price that was equal to their average cost, the price would be higher than the monopolistic price P_m. In addition, since firms larger than Q_c would always be

EXHIBIT 9   Monopoly and competition with economies of scale

When economies of scale are important, efforts to impose a competitive market structure are self-defeating. For an industry with cost (and demand) curves like those indicated here, prices (and costs) would be lower under monopoly than if there were ten competitors of size Q_c.

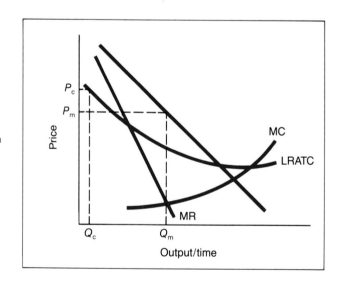

at a competitive advantage, there would be a strong tendency for firms to merge and become larger. Imposition of a competitive structure would be self-defeating in cases in which monopoly "naturally" exists because of the economies of scale.

The telephone industry and local public utilities (water and electricity, for example) approximate natural monopoly conditions. If there were several telephone companies operating in the same area, each with its own lines, transmission equipment, and home phones, costly duplication would result. In such industries, a large number of firms would not be feasible.

POLICY ALTERNATIVES TO NATURAL MONOPOLY

When monopoly or near monopoly results because of economies of scale, there are only three feasible policy alternatives. First, monopolists could be permitted to operate freely. We have already pointed out that this option limits consumer choice and results in a higher product price (and smaller output) than is consistent with ideal economic efficiency. Second, government regulation could be imposed on the monopolists. Third, the government could completely take over production in the industry. Government operation is an alternative to private monopoly. Let us take a closer look at the last two alternatives so that we can compare them with private monopoly.

Regulating the Monopolist

Can government regulation improve the allocative efficiency of unregulated monopoly? In theory, the answer to this question is clearly yes. Government regulation *can* force the monopoly to reduce its price; at the lower government-imposed price ceiling, the monopolist will voluntarily produce a larger output.

Exhibit 10 illustrates why ideal government price regulation would improve resource allocation. The profit-maximizing monopolist sets price at P_0 and produces output Q_0, where MR = MC. Consumers, however, would value *additional* units more than the opportunity cost. How can the regulatory agency improve on the situation that would result from unregulated monopoly?

1. Average Cost Pricing. If a regulatory agency forces the monopolist to reduce price to P_1, the intersection of the firm's ATC curve and the market (and firm) demand curve, the monopolist will expand output to Q_1. Since the firm cannot charge a price above P_1, it cannot increase revenues by selling a smaller output at a higher price. Once the price ceiling is instituted, the firm can increase revenues by P_1, and by only P_1, for each unit that it sells. The regulated firm's MR is constant at P_1 for all units sold until output is increased to Q_1. Since the firm's MC is less than P_1 (and therefore less than MR), the profit-maximizing, regulated monopolist will expand output from Q_0 to Q_1. The benefits from the consumption of these units (ABQ_1Q_0) clearly exceed their costs (CEQ_1Q_0). Social welfare has improved as a result of the regulative action (we will ignore the impact on the distribution of income). At that output level, revenues are sufficient to cover costs. The firm is making zero economic profit (or, "normal" accounting profit).

2. Marginal Cost Pricing. Ideally, since even at the Q_1 output level marginal

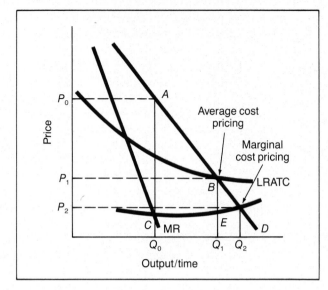

cost is still less than price, additional welfare gains are possible if output is increased to Q_2. However, if a regulatory agency forced the monopolist to reduce price to P_2 (so that price would equal marginal cost at the output level Q_2), economic losses would result. Even a monopolist, unless subsidized, would not undertake production if the regulatory agency set the price at P_2 or any price below P_1. Usually, problems associated with determining and allocating the necessary subsidy would make this option infeasible.

"And though in 1969, as in previous years, your company had to contend with spiralling labor costs, exorbitant interest rates, and unconscionable government interference, management was able once more, through a combination of deceptive marketing practices, false advertising, and price fixing, to show a profit which, in all modesty, can only be called excessive."

Drawing by Lorenz; © 1970 The New Yorker Magazine, Inc.

Why Regulation May Go Astray

Analysis of economic incentives suggests that government regulation of monopolies is usually a less than ideal solution. Why?

Lack of Information. In discussing ideal regulation, we assumed that we knew what the firm's ATC, MC, and demand curves looked like. In reality, of course, this would not be the case.

Because estimates of demand and marginal costs are difficult to obtain, regulatory agencies usually use profits (or rate of return) as a gauge to determine whether the regulated price is too high or too low. The regulatory agency, guarding the public interest, seeks to impose a "fair" or "normal" rate of return on the firm. If the firm is making profits (that is, an abnormally high rate of return), the price must be higher than P_1 (Exhibit 9) and should be lowered. If the firm is incurring losses (less than the fair or normal rate of return), the regulated price must be less than P_1, and the firm should be allowed to increase price.

However, the actual existence of profits is not easily identified. Accounting profit, even allowing for a normal rate of profit, is not the same as economic profit. In addition, regulated firms have a definite incentive to adopt reporting techniques and accounting methods that conceal profits. This will make it difficult for a regulatory agency to identify and impose the price that is consistent with allocative efficiency.

Cost Shifting. To a large degree the owners of the regulated firm can expect the long-run rate of profit to be essentially fixed regardless of whether efficient management reduces costs or inefficient management allows costs to increase. If costs decrease the "fair return" rule imposed by the regulatory agency will force a price reduction; if costs increase, the fair return rule will allow a price increase. Thus, the *owners* of the regulated firm have less incentive to be concerned about costs than the owners of unregulated firms. Managers will have a freer hand to pursue personal objectives. They will be more likely to fly first-class, entertain lavishly on an expense account, give their relatives and friends good jobs, grant larger wage increases, and perform many other such actions that increase the firm's costs but yield personal benefits to the managers.

Essentially, the managers will capture some of the gains that would otherwise go to consumers in the form of lower prices (or to owners as higher profits). Normally, these activities would be policed by the owners, but since the firm's rate of return is established by the regulatory agency, the owners have little incentive to be concerned.

Exhibit 11 demonstrates the impact of such activities. If the firm's costs were effectively policed, average total cost curve ATC_1 would result. Because of production inefficiency, however, the firm's average total cost curve shifts to ATC_2. A regulatory agency, granting the firm a fair return, would then allow a price increase to P_2.[4] Although P_2 might still be less than the unregulated profit-maximizing monopolist would charge, some of the gains of the regulatory policy would be lost.[5]

---

[4]Alternatively, the regulatory agency might permit the firm to maintain price P_2 because the firm's costs are ATC_2, even though ATC_1 could be attained with efficient operation.

[5]If the regulatory agency did not *immediately* force the monopolist to reduce prices after a cost reduction, the incentive of the monopolist to operate efficiently would be increased, since any improvement in operational efficiency would then result in *short-run* economic profits.

EXHIBIT 11   Cost shifting and monopoly regulation

Managers of a regulated firm have a greater incentive to follow policies that yield personal gain at the expense of higher cost. With time, this may cause the cost curves of the regulated monopolistic firm to rise, resulting in higher prices even though monetary profits are still normal.

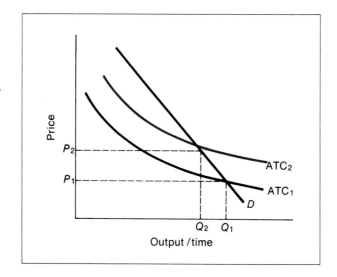

The Impact of Inflation.   Regulation based on normal rate of return will encounter serious difficulties during inflationary times. If the costs of labor, energy resources, and other factors of production rise along with other prices, the cost of producing the product or service of the regulated firm will increase during the period of inflation. A rate structure based on *last year's cost figures* will not permit the firm to earn a normal rate of return. Of course, as its rate of return drops below normal, the firm's case for a rate increase *next* year will be strengthened. However, if the inflation continues, the regulated firm's rate of return will continue to be below normal. The firm will be unable to earn the normal rate of return during inflationary times as long as its rate structure is based on historical costs. As a result of its low earnings, the regulated firm will have difficulty raising funds in the capital market. If the normal rate of return on capital is 12 percent, who will want to invest with a firm that is able to earn only 9 percent? Many regulated utilities were caught in precisely this cost-regulated price squeeze as the price of energy and other resources soared during the inflation of the 1970s.

Quality Regulation.   It is much easier to regulate product price than to regulate quality. Regulated firms desiring to raise the price of their product can often do so by taking cost-reducing steps that result in quality deterioration. Consider the quality dimension of a seemingly uniform good such as telephone service. The speed at which your call goes through, the likelihood that you will have to dial the desired number more than once, the number of times your phone is out of order, and the rapidity with which you are able to get it repaired are determinants of the quality of telephone service. Since these factors are hard to control, it is extremely difficult for a regulatory agency to impose a price *per constant quality unit*. During inflationary times, regulated firms caught in a cost-regulated price squeeze may be particularly tempted to lower the quality of their product.

Special Interest Effect.   The difficulties of government regulation discussed thus far are practical limitations that a regulatory agency, seeking to perform its duties efficiently, would confront. But the special interest effect suggests that regulatory authorities cannot necessarily be expected to pursue efficiency. Regulated firms are dependent upon the agencies that regulate them. They have a strong incentive to ensure that "friendly people" serve as regulators, and they will invest political and economic resources to this end.

What about consumer interests? Do you know who serves on the Interstate Commerce Commission or the public utility regulatory boards? Do you know any consumer who voted against a politician because of his or her appointments to a regulatory commission? Chances are that you do not. Consumer interests are widely dispersed and disorganized. Ordinarily, consumers cannot be expected to invest time, resources, votes, and political contributions to ensure that regulatory commissions represent their views. The firms that are regulated can, however, be expected to make such investments.[6] Even though the initial stimulus for a regulating agency might come from consumer interests, economic theory suggests that such agencies will eventually reflect the views of the business and labor interests they are supposed to regulate.

The Government-Operated Firm

Government-operated firms—socialized firms such as the Post Office, the Tennessee Valley Authority, and many local public utilities—present an alternative to both private monopoly and regulation. How do socialized firms operate in the real world? The decision-makers of firms owned by the government are influenced by both political and economic factors. With the rise of public sector action, economists have recently expressed renewed interest in the socialized firm.

The ideal theoretical solution is straightforward. The socialized firm should (a) operate efficiently and (b) set price equal to marginal cost. When cost conditions are like those illustrated by Exhibit 6, the government-operated monopoly firm will ideally expand output to Q_i (where $P = MC$) and charge price P_i. The firm will make profits that can be channeled into the public treasury. On the other hand, marginal cost pricing may sometimes result in economic losses, requiring a subsidy for the government-operated firm. Exhibit 9 illustrates this possibility. Output should be expanded to Q_2 if the potential marginal welfare gains are to be fully realized. Price P_2 will be charged. The consumer's valuation of the marginal unit (P_2) will equal its marginal cost. Since losses result at this price and output, it will be necessary to subsidize the public enterprise.

This analysis is based on the assumptions that the socialized firm will both operate efficiently and set the proper price. How realistic are these assumptions? The same "perverse" managerial incentives—incentives to ignore efficiency and pursue personal gain at the firm's expense—that regulated firms confront also tend to plague the government-operated firm. Professor John Kenneth Galbraith and others have argued that dispersed ownership rights limit the ability of poorly informed stockholders to police management inefficiency. Managers have more freedom to pursue their own objectives at the expense of "owners." The socialized firm presents the extreme case of disorganized, uninformed "owners" who are in a weak position to assert their ownership rights. No

---

[6]The special interest effect will be weaker when regulatory commissions are elected rather than appointed. This will allow the voter to separate this issue from other issues of greater importance.

small group of owners will be able to increase its wealth if the public enterprise operates more efficiently. The disorganized owners (voters and taxpayers) will have neither the incentive nor the information to police the managerial decision-making of public enterprises effectively—to reward efficiency and penalize inefficiency. Higher costs result.

In much the same way, special interests also affect incentives—usually in terms of political or group gain—and result in inefficiency. The managers, employees, and specialized users of public enterprises often comprise special interest groups, particularly if the employees are well organized (for example, unionized) for political action. Should the wages of public sector employees be raised and their working conditions improved? Should comfortable offices, lengthy coffee breaks, and lucrative fringe benefits be provided to employees? Should attractive positions in the public enterprise be provided to the politically faithful? Should management resist pressures to lay off unneeded workers (particularly at election time), abandon unprofitable service areas, and charge users low prices (that is, less than the marginal cost) when the opportunity cost of providing the service is high? On all of these issues, the interests of public sector special interest groups will be in conflict with the interests of the disorganized, uninformed taxpayers. Under these circumstances, economic theory suggests that the views of the special interest groups will usually dominate, even when inefficiency and higher costs result.

Thus, public enterprises can be expected to use at least some of their monopoly power, not to benefit the wide cross section of disorganized taxpayers and consumers, but as a cloak for inefficient operation and actions that advance the personal and political objectives of those who exercise control over the firm. Government ownership, like unregulated monopoly and government regulation, is a less than ideal solution. It is not especially surprising that those who denounce monopoly in, for instance, the telephone industry seldom point to a government-operated monopoly—such as the Post Office—as an example of how an industry should be run.

Summary

The policy implications that can legitimately be drawn from an analysis of monopoly are more limited than might initially appear. We may not like monopolistic power or its effects, but the alternatives are not terribly attractive. Monopoly power based on economies of scale poses a particularly troublesome problem. Clearly, in that instance, something approximating pure competition is not a viable alternative. Much of the criticism of monopoly is based on the assumption that cost conditions in an industry would be the same if there were several competing firms in the market. In practice this is often untrue. Any restructuring of an industry with public policy is likely to affect both cost conditions and incentives for innovation and efficiency.

DYNAMIC CHANGE, MONOPOLY POWER, AND RESOURCE ALLOCATION

We have analyzed monopoly within a static framework and emphasized the lack of competition (sellers of alternative products) *within the industry*. However, no firm is an island unto itself. Each firm competes with every other firm for the

PERSPECTIVES IN ECONOMICS
PRODUCT OBSOLESCENCE, MONOPOLY POWER, AND THE DYNAMICS OF PRODUCT DEVELOPMENT

Many Americans believe that business firms can gain by producing shoddy merchandise that wears out quickly, particularly during inflationary times. It is often charged that business firms, over the objections of consumers, produce goods with a short life expectancy so they can sell replacements. Economists have sometimes been at the forefront of those deploring such planned obsolescence.

Yet a solid majority of economists believe that price indexes overstate the measured rate of inflation because they fail to make an adequate allowance for actual improvements in product quality that have been observed. Why has the quality of products, on the average, risen, if firms have an incentive to produce shoddy, nondurable goods?

Should a Car Last a Lifetime?

There are three important points to keep in mind. First, the production of longer-lasting, higher-quality goods will increase costs. There are no free lunches. A car that lasts 15 years will be more expensive than one with a shorter life expectancy. We should expect consumers to trade off lower prices for more durability. At some point, the greater durability will not be worth the price.

Second, "newness," product variability, and style changes are often valued by consumers. For example, operational reliability aside, many consumers would prefer three differently styled, new-model cars lasting 5 years each to a single car of equal cost that lasts 15 years. *Under these conditions,* the production of goods with less than maximum life expec-

tancy is perfectly consistent with consumer tastes.[7]

Third, goods engineered to last a relatively short time put their owners in a more adaptable position. For example, buyers of new American cars in 1971–1972 preferred large cars. At the time, this made good sense because gasoline prices were not only low (relative to post-1974 real prices) but had been declining in real terms for many years. However, the market value of large, gas-guzzling cars dropped sharply in 1974 as gasoline prices soared and spot shortages developed. If those who bought large cars in 1971–1972 had paid for years of extra durability, their losses (and the nation's) would have been greater. In a dynamic world, one decision every ten years is less flexible (and, if wrong, more costly to correct) than a decision every five years.

Clearly, there are both positive and negative sides to product obsolescence. Durability has both advantages and disadvantages. We should expect consumers to attempt to balance their desire for product durability against its cost in terms of higher prices, less diversity, and less flexibility.

Durability of Products and Producer Choices

In a competitive environment, producers have a strong incentive to cater to the preferences of consumers. Product quality, including durability, is a competitive weapon. If customers really want longer-lasting products, competitive firms have a strong incentive to introduce them. If consumers are willing to pay the price for greater durability, firms that cater to their views can gain. However, durability is

---

[7]Both the authors and reader may disagree with such "vulgar taste." However, we should be aware that such disagreement stems from our views about how consumers should behave and does not necessarily mean that the system that caters to that taste is defective.

only one facet of a product that is attractive to consumers. Low prices, newness, and product variation are also preferred by many people. Much of our planned obsolescence undoubtedly stems from the choice of consumers to give up some of the former (durability) in order to have more of the latter.

The Monopolist and the Durability of Products

Will a monopolist ever introduce a new, improved, longer-lasting product, even if the new product is expected to drive the existing, profitable product off the market? Strange as it may seem, a monopolist will introduce the new product if two conditions are met.

1. The product must be a genuine improvement—it must give the consumer more service per dollar of opportunity cost (to the monopolist) than the monopolist's current product.

2. The monopolist must be able to enforce property rights over the gains from the new product. A patent preventing others from copying the innovative idea serves this purpose.

If these two conditions are met, the monopolist will be able to price the new product such that it will be profitable to introduce, even though it may eventually replace the monopolist's current product line. Two examples will help to clarify this point.

Super Sharp: The Better Blade

Suppose that Super Sharp Razor, Inc., has a monopoly on razor blades, which sell for 5 cents and give one week of comfortable shaves. Currently, Super Sharp makes a 3-cent profit (return above opportunity cost) on each blade. Assume that the firm discovers (and quickly patents) a blade made with the same machines at the same cost but with a slightly different metal alloy.[8] It gives two weeks of comfortable shaves instead of one. Will the firm market the new blade, even though it will lose one-half of its weekly sales of blades? Yes! Customers will gladly pay up to 10 cents per blade for the new blades, which last twice as long. Instead of making 3 cents per customer per week, the firm now will make up to 8 cents per customer every two weeks. Profits will rise. In fact, a price of 9 cents per blade will benefit *both* the buyer *and* Super Sharp.

Would Monopoly Oil Sell the Miracle Carburetor?

For years it has been rumored that a much more efficient "miracle carburetor" for automobiles has been discovered but that the big oil companies have plotted to keep it off the market because it would reduce their profits from the sale of gasoline.

Suppose that an oil cartel, Monopoly Oil, sells all the oil and gasoline in the world. This hypothetical organization has also obtained the patent on a miracle carburetor. The real improvement is simply a little plastic gizmo that can be inserted into ordinary carburetors. The gizmo can be made in quantity for 1 cent each, and each gizmo lasts just long enough (one year, on average) to save its buyer 1000 gallons of gas. If Monopoly Oil makes 5 cents per gallon economic profit on each gallon of gasoline, the sale lost *per gizmo* will cost the firm $50 per year. Will Monopoly Oil sell the gizmo? Of course! If gas sells for 95 cents per gallon (but the opportunity cost of crude oil, refining, etc., is only 90 cents), the cartel will *increase* its profit by selling the gizmo (cost 1 cent), which replaces 1000 gallons of gasoline, as long as the price of the gizmo exceeds $50.01. Certainly the consumer would pay far more than $50.01 in order to save 1000 gallons of gas. Indeed, any price below $950 per gizmo would help the motorist.[9]

Do Patents Help or Hurt the Consumer?

Of course, a patent right is crucial to both of the above examples. If firms could not at least partially capture the gains to be made from introducing a new product, they might prefer to keep it off the market and thereby prevent other firms from cutting into their profits by copying the new idea.

The patent system has a dual impact on the allocation of resources. First, the patent monopoly grants, as any monopoly does, the patent owner the ability (for a limited time) to keep the price of the patented item higher than costs of production warrant. Thus, *for patented inventions that have already been introduced,* consumers would be better off if competition replaced patent monopolies.

However, there is also a second effect. The fact that one can patent a new product or production process encourages the development of improved, lower-cost goods. Public policy in the United States allows temporary patent monopolies, which are costly to consumers in the short run, in order to provide firms (and individuals) with a strong incentive to undertake the risk and effort involved in the development of technological improvements, which may lead to lower costs and greater efficiency in the long run.

---

[8]If the blade requires new and different machines that render the firm's current machines obsolete, the firm will still introduce the product. It will do so, however, at a slower pace, because the cost associated with new machines is higher than the zero *opportunity cost* (assuming the old machines have no alternative use) of using existing machines. Phasing in the new product so that the existing machines may be more fully used may be a cheaper alternative for Super Sharp. If so, it will also be cheaper for consumers.

[9]If the gizmo were invented by someone other than Monopoly Oil, the inventor would have an even stronger incentive to introduce the product. However, the introduction of the product *by someone else* would detract from the net profit of Monopoly Oil. The latter would have an incentive to suppress the product, if possible. The cartel might attempt to use political power or extralegal methods to keep the product off the market. Of course, these two actions could well lead to counterproductive economic activity.

---

dollar votes of the consumer. Dynamic change is present in the real world and the expectation of monopoly profit may influence its speed. Competitors will seek to develop and market substitutes for products offered by profitable firms. If a monopoly is profitable, it will attract rivals that produce substitute products. Actual and potential substitutes exist for almost every product. With the passage of time, the development of substitutes is a threat to the market power of even an entrenched monopoly.

High monopoly prices will encourage development of substitutes. For example, the high price of natural rubber spurred the development of synthetic rubber. High rail-shipping rates accelerated the development of long-distance trucking. The strong exercise of monopoly power by the Organization of Petroleum Exporting Countries (OPEC) has subjected oil to vastly intensified competition from coal, solar energy, and other nonpetroleum energy sources.

This dynamic competition from substitute products, both actual and potential, is important for two reasons. First, a monopolist will sometimes choose to produce a larger output and charge a lower price—lower than the short-run profit-maximizing price—in order to discourage potential rivals from developing substitutes. When this happens, the allocative inefficiency associated with monopoly will be less than our static model implies. Second, the expectation of monopoly profits may spur product development. In fact, the patent system is based on this premise. When a new product or production method is patented, monopoly power is granted to the patent owner for a period of 17 years. Others are prohibited from copying the product or technique. If this "reward" of at least temporary monopoly power and profit did not exist, it is probable that businesses would be less inclined to undertake research designed to reduce costs and improve product quality (see Perspectives in Economics on product obsolescence). Thus, even though these dynamic competitive forces will operate more slowly than when barriers to entry into an industry are low, the development of substitutes will nonetheless tend with the passage of time to erode the market power of a monopolist.

LOOKING AHEAD

Most markets do not fit neatly into either the pure competition or pure monopoly models. Many markets are characterized by low barriers to entry and competition on the basis of product quality, design, convenience of location, and producer reliability. Other markets involve a small number of rival firms, operating under widely varying entry conditions. In the following chapter we will investigate market structures that lie between pure competition and pure monopoly.

CHAPTER LEARNING OBJECTIVES

1 Pure monopoly is a market structure characterized by (a) high barriers to entry and (b) a single seller of a well-defined product for which there are no good substitutes. Pure monopoly is at the opposite end of the market-structure spectrum from pure competition.

2 Analysis of pure monopoly is important for two reasons. First, the monopoly model will help us understand the operation of markets dominated by a few firms. Second, in a few important industries, for example, telephone service and utilities, there is often only a single producer in a market area. The monopoly model will help us understand these markets.

3 The three major barriers to entry into a market are legal restrictions, economies of scale, and control of an essential resource.

4 The monopolist's demand curve is the market demand curve. It slopes downward to the right. The marginal revenue curve for a monopolist will lie inside the demand curve because of revenue losses from the lower price for units that could have been sold at a higher price.

5 For the elastic portion of a monopolist's demand curve, a lower price will increase total revenue. For the inelastic portion of the monopolist's demand curve, a price reduction will cause total revenue to decline. A profit-maximizing monopolist will not operate on the inelastic portion of the demand curve because in that range it is always possible to increase total revenue by raising the price and producing fewer units.

6 A profit-maximizing monopolist will lower price and expand output as long as marginal revenue exceeds marginal cost. At the maximum-profit output, MR will equal MC. The monopolist will charge a price along its demand curve for that output rate.

7 If losses occur in the long run, a monopolist will go out of business. If profit results, high barriers to entry will shield a monopolist from competitive pressures. Therefore, *long-run* economic profits for a monopoly are sometimes possible.

8 Economists are critical of a monopoly because (a) it severely limits the role of demand in the market for a good and thus consumers' "control" over the producer; (b) the unregulated monopolist produces too little output and charges a price in excess of the marginal cost; and (c) profits are less able to stimulate new entry, which would expand the supply of the product until price declined to the level of average production costs.

9 Natural monopoly exists when long-run average total costs continue to decline as firm size increases (economies of scale). Thus, a larger firm always has lower costs. Cost of production would be lowest when a single firm generated the entire output of an industry.

10 In the presence of natural monopoly, there are three policy alternatives: (a) private, unregulated monopoly; (b) private, regulated monopoly; and (c) government ownership. Economic theory suggests that each of the three will fail to meet our criteria for ideal efficiency. Private monopoly will result in higher prices and less output than would be ideal. Regulation will often fail to meet our ideal efficiency criteria because (a) the regulators will not have knowledge of the firm's cost curves and market demand conditions; (b) firms have an incentive to conceal their actual cost conditions and take profits in disguised forms; and (c) the regulators often end up being influenced by the firms they are supposed to regulate. Under public ownership, managers often can gain by pursuing policies that yield them personal benefits and by catering to the views of special interest groups (for example, well-organized employees and specialized customers) who will be able to help them further their political objectives.

11 Even a monopolist is not completely free from competitive pressures. All products have some type of substitute. Monopolists who raise the price of their products lower entry barriers and provide encouragement for rival firms to develop substitutes, which may eventually erode the market power of the monopolist. Some monopolists may charge less than the short-run, profit-maximizing price in order to discourage *potential* competitors from developing substitute products.

12 Monopoly profits derived from patents have two conflicting effects on resource allocation. *Once a product or process has been discovered,* the monopoly rights permit the firm to restrict output and raise price above the current marginal (and average) cost of production. However, the monopoly rights granted by a patent encourage entrepreneurs to improve products and develop lower-cost methods of production.

THE ECONOMIC WAY OF THINKING—DISCUSSION QUESTIONS

1 Which of the following are monopolists: (a) your local newspaper, (b) Boston Celtics, (c) General Motors, (d) U.S. Postal Service, (e) Johnny Carson, (f) American Medical Association? Is the definition of an industry or market area important in the determination of a seller's monopoly position? Explain.

2 What are barriers to entry? Give three examples. Why are barriers to entry essential if a firm is to make profits in the long run?

3 Do monopolists charge the highest prices for which they can sell their products? Do they maximize their average profit per sale? Are monopolistic firms always profitable? Why or why not?

4 The retail liquor industry is potentially a competitive industry. However, the liquor retailers of a southern state organized a trade association that sets prices for all firms.

For all practical purposes, the trade association transformed a competitive industry into a monopoly. Compare the price and output policy for a purely competitive industry with the policy that would be established by a profit-maximizing monopolist or trade association. Who benefits and who is hurt by the formation of the monopoly?

5 Does economic theory indicate that a monopoly forced by an ideal regulatory agency to set prices according to either marginal or average cost would be more efficient than an unregulated monopoly? Explain. Does economic theory suggest that a regulatory agency *will* follow a proper regulation policy? What are some of the factors that complicate the regulatory function?

6 Is a monopolist subject to any competitive pressures? Explain. Would an unregulated monopolist have an incentive to operate and produce efficiently? If so, why?

7 What is the purpose of the patent system? Is the patent system efficient or inefficient? Explain.

21

THE INTERMEDIATE CASES: MONOPOLISTIC COMPETITION AND OLIGOPOLY

Differences in tastes, desires, incomes and locations of buyers, and differences in the uses which they wish to make of commodities all indicate the need for variety and the necessity of substituting for the concept of a "competitive ideal" an ideal involving both monopoly and competition.[1]
Edward H. Chamberlin

Most real-world firms operate in markets that fall between the extremes of pure competition and pure monopoly. These firms do not confront numerous competitors all producing a homogeneous product sold at a single price; neither do most firms produce a good or service that is unavailable from other sellers. Instead, most firms face varying degrees of competition. In some cases, there are competitors offering roughly the same product; in other instances, the competitor's product is merely an attractive substitute. There may be numerous competitors; or there may be only a few other sellers in a given market. The models of monopolistic competition and oligopoly have been developed by economists to describe markets that are neither purely competitive nor purely monopolistic.

Monopolistically competitive and oligopolistic firms have different degrees of freedom in setting prices, altering quality, and choosing a marketing strategy than firms in purely competitive or purely monopolistic markets. Most firms, unlike those under purely competitive conditions, will lose some *but not all* of their customers when they increase the price of their product. These firms face a downward-sloping demand curve. They are sometimes called **price searchers** because they must search for the price that is most consistent with their overall goal—maximum profit, for example. But as we have indicated, just as they are not pure competitors, most price searchers are not monopolists, either. Thus, their freedom to raise price is limited by the existence of both actual and potential competitors offering similar products. The difference between monopolistic competition and oligopoly is in one sense a difference in the degree to which a price searcher is limited by competition.

Price Searchers: Firms that face a downward-sloping demand curve for their product.

[1]Edward H. Chamberlin, *The Theory of Monopolistic Competition* (Cambridge, Massachusetts: Harvard University Press, 1948), p. 214.

CHARACTERISTICS OF MONOPOLISTIC COMPETITION

Monopolistic Competition: A situation in which there are a large number of independent sellers, each producing a differentiated product in a market with low barriers to entry. Construction, retail sales, and service stations are good examples of monopolistically competitive industries.

During the 1920s, many economists felt that neither pure competition nor pure monopoly was descriptive of markets such as retail sales, construction, service businesses, and small manufacturing, which were generally characterized by numerous firms offering different but closely related products or services. The need for a more accurate model for markets of this type led to the theory of **monopolistic competition.** The theory was developed independently by Joan Robinson, a British economist, and Edward Chamberlin, an American economist. The major work of both Robinson and Chamberlin was published in 1933.[2] Both economists outlined three distinguishing characteristics of monopolistic competition.

Product Differentiation

Differentiated Products: Products that are distinguished from similar products by such characteristics as quality, design, location, and method of promotion.

Monopolistic competitors offer **differentiated products** to consumers. Goods and services of one seller are differentiated from those of another by convenience of location, product quality, reputation of the seller, advertising, and various other product characteristics.

Since the product of each monopolistic competitor is slightly different from that of its rivals, the individual firm faces a downward-sloping demand curve. A price reduction will enable the firm to attract new customers. Alternatively, the firm will be able to increase its price by a small amount and still retain many of its customers, who prefer the location, style, dependability, or other product characteristics offered by the firm. However, the demand curve confronted by the monopolistic competitor is highly elastic. Although each firm has some control over price, that control is extremely limited, since the firm faces competition from rivals offering very similar products. The availability of close substitutes and the ease with which consumers can turn to rival firms (including new firms that are free to enter the market) force a monopolistically competitive firm to think twice before raising its price.

Low Barriers to Entry

Under monopolistic competition, firms are free to enter into or exit from the market. There are neither legal barriers nor market obstacles hindering the movement of competitors into and out of a monopolistically competitive market. Monopolistic competition resembles pure competition in this respect; firms in both these types of markets confront the constant threat of competition from new, innovative rivals.

Many Independent Firms

A monopolistic competitor faces not only the potential threat posed by new rivals but competition from many current sellers as well. Each firm is small relative to the total market. No single firm or small group of firms is able to dominate the market.

Retailing is perhaps the sector of our economy that best typifies monopolistic competition. In most market areas, there are a large number of retail

[2]See Joan Robinson, *The Economics of Imperfect Competition* (1933; reprint ed., New York: St. Martin's, 1969), and Edward H. Chamberlin, *The Theory of Monopolistic Competition* (Cambridge, Massachusetts: Harvard University Press, 1933).

stores offering similar products and services. Rivalry is intense, and stores are constantly trying new combinations of price and quality of service (or merchandise) in their effort to win customers. The *free entry* that typifies most retailing makes for rapid change. Yesterday's novelty can quickly become obsolete as new rivals develop still better (or more attractive) products and marketing methods.

PRICE AND OUTPUT UNDER MONOPOLISTIC COMPETITION

How does a monopolistic competitor decide what price to charge and what level of output to produce? Like a pure monopolist, a monopolistic competitor will face a downward-sloping demand curve for its product. Additional units can be sold only at a lower price. Therefore, the marginal revenue curve of the monopolistic competitor will always lie below the firm's demand curve.

Any firm can increase profits by expanding output as long as marginal revenue exceeds marginal cost. Therefore, a monopolistic competitor will lower its prices and expand its output until marginal revenue is equal to marginal cost.

Exhibit 1 illustrates the profit-maximizing price and output under monopolistic competition. A profit-maximizing monopolistic competitor will expand output to q, where marginal revenue is equal to marginal cost. It will charge price P, the highest price at which output q can be sold. For any output level less than q (for example, R), a price reduction and sales expansion will add more to total revenues than to total costs. At output R, marginal revenue exceeds marginal costs. Thus, profits will be greater if price is reduced so output can be expanded. On the other hand, if output exceeds q (for example, S), sale of additional units beyond q will *add* more to costs (MC) than to revenues (MR). The firm will therefore gain by raising the price to P, even though the price rise will result in the loss of customers. Profits will be maximized by charging price P and producing the output level q, where MC = MR.

The firm pictured by Exhibit 1 is making economic profit. Total revenues $PAqO$ exceed the firm's total cost $CBqO$ at the profit-maximizing output level. Since barriers to entry in monopolistically competitive markets are low, profits will attract rival competitors. Other firms will attempt to duplicate the product (or service) offered by the profit-making firms.

EXHIBIT 1   The monopolistic competitor's price and output

A monopolistic competitor maximizes profits by producing output q, for which MR = MC, and charging price P. The firm is making economic profits. What impact will they have?

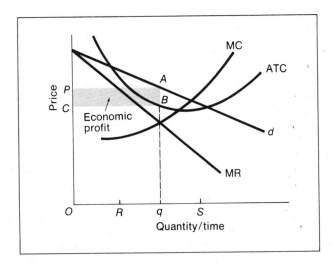

EXHIBIT 2 Monopolistic competition and long-run normal profit

Since entry and exit are free, competition will eventually drive prices down to the level of average total cost.

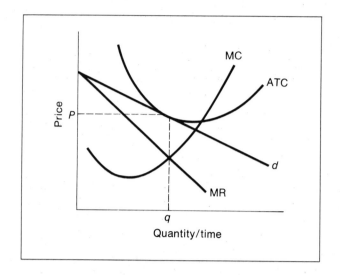

What impact will the entry of new rivals have on the demand for the products of profit-making firms already in the market? These new rivals will draw customers away from existing firms. As long as monopolistically competitive firms can make economic profits, new competitors will be attracted to the market. Eventually, the competition among rivals will shift the demand curve for monopolistic competitors inward and eliminate the economic profits. In the long run, as illustrated by Exhibit 2, a monopolistically competitive firm will just be able to cover its production costs. It will produce to the MR = MC output level, but the entry of new competition will force the price down to the average per unit cost.

If losses exist in a monopolistically competitive industry, some of the existing firms in the industry will go out of business over a period of time. As such firms leave the industry, some of their previous customers will buy from other firms. The demand curve facing the remaining firms in the industry will shift out until the economic losses are eliminated and the long-run, zero-profit equilibrium illustrated by Exhibit 2 is again restored.

Under monopolistic competition, profits and losses play precisely the same role as they do under pure competition. Economic profits will attract new competitors to the market. The increased availability of the product (and similar products) will drive the price down until the profits are eliminated. Conversely, economic losses will cause competitors to exit from the market. The decline in the availability of the product (supply) will allow the price to rise until firms are once again able to cover their average cost.

In the short run, a monopolistic competitor may make either economic profits or losses, depending on market conditions. In the long run, however, only a normal profit rate (that is, zero economic profits) will be possible because of competitive conditions and freedom of entry.

COMPARING PURE AND MONOPOLISTIC COMPETITION

As you can see, determination of price and output under monopolistic competition is in some ways very similar to that under pure competition. Also, since the long-run equilibrium conditions under pure competition are consistent with ideal economic efficiency, it is useful to compare and contrast other market structures with pure competition. There are both similarities and differences between pure and monopolistic competition.

Similarities between Pure and Monopolistic Competition

Since barriers to entry are low, neither pure nor monopolistic competitors will be able to earn long-run economic profit. In the long run, competition will drive the price of both pure and monopolistic competitors down to the level of average total cost.

In each case, entrepreneurs have a strong incentive to manage and operate their businesses efficiently. Inefficient operation will lead to losses and forced exit from the market. Both pure and monopolistic competitors will be motivated to develop and adopt new cost-reducing procedures and techniques because lower costs will mean higher profits (or at least smaller losses).

The response of pure and monopolistic competitors to changing demand conditions is very similar. In both cases, an increase in market demand leads to higher prices, short-run profits, and the entry of additional firms. With the entry of the new producers, and the concurrent expansion of existing firms, the market supply will increase until the market price falls to the level of average total cost. Similarly, a reduction in demand will lead to lower prices and short-run losses that will force firms from the market. As firms leave the market, supply will decline, permitting the remaining firms to raise prices. Eventually, the short-run losses will be eliminated. Profits and losses will direct the activities of firms under both pure and monopolistic competition.

Differences between Pure and Monopolistic Competition

As Exhibit 3 illustrates, the pure competitor confronts a horizontal demand curve; the demand curve faced by a monopolistic competitor is downward-sloping. This is important because it means that the marginal revenue of the monopolistic competitor will be less than, rather than equal to, price. Thus, when the profit-maximizing monopolistic competitor expands output until

EXHIBIT 3 Comparing pure and monopolistic competition

The long-run equilibrium conditions of firms under pure and monopolistic competition are illustrated here. In both cases, price is equal to average total cost, and economic profit is absent. However, since the monopolistically competitive firm confronts a downward-sloping demand curve for its product, its equilibrium price exceeds marginal cost, and equilibrium output is not large enough to minimize average total cost. *For identical cost conditions,* the price of the monopolistic competitor will be slightly higher than that of the pure competitor. Chamberlin referred to this slightly higher price as the premium a society pays for variety and convenience (product differentiation).

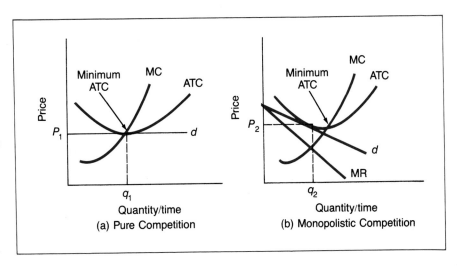

(a) Pure Competition

(b) Monopolistic Competition

MR = MC, price will still exceed marginal cost (Exhibit 3b). In contrast, in the long-run equilibrium, the price charged by the pure competitor will *equal* marginal cost (Exhibit 3a). Thus, the zero economic profit equilibrium for a monopolistically competitive firm, unlike that for a pure competitor, occurs at an output rate that fails to minimize the firm's long-run average total cost, as Exhibit 3 illustrates. The monopolistic competitor would have a lower per unit cost if a larger output were produced.

Under monopolistic competition, firms produce differentiated products; pure competitors produce homogeneous products. A monopolistically competitive firm will seek to increase the demand for a product by taking steps to convince consumers that the product is both different from and superior to products offered by rivals. Monopolistic competitors often engage in competitive advertising as a means of attracting additional customers. Purely competitive firms do not need to use advertising, since they can already sell all they can produce at the market price.

Allocative Efficiency under Monopolistic Competition

The efficiency of monopolistic competition has been the subject of debate among economists for years. At one time, the dominant view seemed to be that allocative inefficiency results because monopolistic competitors fail to operate at an output level that minimizes their long-run average total cost. Due to the proliferation in the number of monopolistic competitors, the sales of each competitor fall short of their optimal (lowest per unit cost) capacity level. The potential social gain associated with the expansion of production to the P = MC output rate is lost, according to this view, whose advocates point out that if there were fewer producers, they would each be able to operate at a minimum-cost output rate. Instead, there is wasteful duplication—too many producers each operating below their minimum-cost output capacity. According to this traditional view, the location of two or more filling stations, restaurants, grocery stores, or similar establishments side by side is indicative of the economic waste generated by monopolistic competition.

In addition, the critics of monopolistic competition argue that it often leads to self-defeating, wasteful advertising. Firms have an incentive to use advertising to promote artificial distinctions between similar products. Each firm bombards consumers with advertisements proclaiming (or implying) that its own product is fancier, has greater sex appeal, and/or brings quicker relief than any product of rival firms. Firms that do not engage in such advertising can expect their sales to decline. However, advertising results in higher prices for consumers and thus from society's point of view can be argued to be too costly.

In recent years, this traditional view has been seriously challenged. Many economists now believe that such a view is mechanistic and fails to take into account the significance of dynamic competition. Most important, the traditional view assumes that consumers place no value on the wider variety of qualities and styles that results from monopolistic competition. Prices might very well be slightly lower if there were fewer gasoline stations, located farther apart, and offering a more limited variety of service and credit plan options. Similarly, the prices of groceries might very well be slightly lower if there were fewer supermarkets, each a bit more congested and located somewhat less conveniently

Along with Edward Chamberlin, Joan Robinson is given credit for developing the theory of monopolistic competition. In her book *The Economics of Imperfect Competition* (1933), she redefined the market demand curve to account for interdependence among firms.[3] Following Alfred Marshall, she

[3] Joan Robinson, *The Economics of Imperfect Competition* (1933; reprint ed., New York: St. Martin's, 1969).

used differences among products to define an industry. Essentially, she viewed each firm as a monopolist facing a downward-sloping demand curve that is affected by the behavior of other "monopolists" in the industry. Unlike Chamberlin, she did not introduce product differentiation and quality competition *within an industry* into her analysis.

Professor Robinson's contribution to economics goes far beyond her role in developing the theory of monopolistic competition. Now professor emerita of economics at Cambridge University, she was one of a select group of economists who worked with Keynes during the developmental stage of his *General Theory*. She fully accepts the Keynesian view that the market economy is inherently unstable. Furthermore, she argues that market economies suffer from other serious defects—income inequality, pollution, business concentration, and manipulation of demand.

Professor Robinson has played a prominent role in continuing the Cambridge tradition of dissent from the traditional orthodoxy. Delivering the Richard T. Ely Lecture to the American Economic Association in

1971, she argued that the economics profession faces a second major crisis. Just as pre-Keynesian economists failed to develop a theory of aggregate employment, Professor Robinson charges that current economists have failed to develop a meaningful theory of "what employment should be for." In her view, "this primarily concerns the allocation of resources between products, but it is also bound up with the distribution of products between people." She feels that the relative earnings of individuals depend on bargaining power and union influence, not primarily on market conditions.

In recent years, she has become a vocal critic of the capitalist system. In many ways, she is something of an English Galbraith. The *Collected Economic Papers* of Professor Robinson now fill four volumes.[4] Her work in economics runs the gamut. Capital theory, international trade, Marxian economics, growth theory, and comparative systems are among the many areas that have felt the touch of her pen.

[4] Joan Robinson, *Collected Papers,* 4 vols. (New York: Humanities Press, 1960–1972).

for many customers. However, since customers value diversity in product selection as well as lower prices, it does not follow that consumers are worse off under the conditions created by monopolistic competition. Edward Chamberlin, one of the developers of the theory, argues that the higher prices (and costs) are simply the premium consumers pay for variety and convenience. When consumers receive utility from product diversity, one cannot conclude that pure competition (and the reduction in diversity that would accompany it) would be preferable to monopolistic competition.

The defenders of monopolistic competition also deny that it leads to excessive, wasteful advertising. They point out that advertising often reduces the consumer's search time and provides valuable information on prices. If advertising really raises prices, it must provide the consumer with something that is valuable. Otherwise, the consumer will purchase lower-priced, nonadvertised goods. When consumers really prefer lower prices and less advertising, firms offering that combination do quite well. In fact, the proponents argue, monopolistic competitors actually do often use higher-quality service and lower prices to compete with rivals that may advertise more heavily.

The debate among economists has helped to clarify the issues on this topic. Nonetheless, the efficiency of monopolistic competition continues to be one of the unresolved issues of economics.

REAL-WORLD MONOPOLISTIC COMPETITORS

In our model, we assume that firms have perfect knowledge of both their costs and demand conditions. Real-world firms do not have such information. They must rely on past experience, market surveys, experimenting, and other business skills when they make price, output, and production decisions.

Could profits be increased if prices were raised, or would lower prices lead to larger profits? Real-world business decision-makers cannot go into the back room and look at their demand—cost diagram in order to answer these questions. They must search. They might raise prices for a time and see what would happen to their sales. Or they might lower prices and see if additional sales would expand revenues more than costs. Note that if maximum profit is the goal of the firm, charging prices that are too high can be just as costly as charging prices that are too low. The successful, astute business decision-maker will search and find the profit-maximizing price—the MR = MC output level—that our model assumes is common knowledge.

For real-world entrepreneurs, the problem of uncertainty goes well beyond setting the profit-maximizing price. When considering entry into a monopolistically competitive field, how can entrepreneurs decide whether demand and cost conditions will permit them to make a profit? Just what combination of qualities should be built into the firm's product or service? What location will be best? What forms of advertising will be most effective? Again, past experience, trial and error, and business skill will guide profit-seeking entrepreneurs. Those who have exhibited skill on the basis of past successful experiences will be encouraged to stay and expand. Newcomers can learn by working with others, hiring expert help, or contracting with existing firms, perhaps on a franchise basis.

Despite their high hopes, many firms go out of business every year. In recent years, among corporate establishments alone, the number of firms going out of business has generally exceeded 200,000 annually. A great many of these unsuccessful businesses are small, monopolistically competitive firms that are forced out of business by losses stemming from market competition.

Why do losses result in the real world? Since business decisions must be made without perfect information, mistakes sometimes result. A firm may mistakenly produce a good for which consumers are unwilling to pay a price that will enable the producer to cover the costs of production. Losses are the market's method of bringing such activities to a halt. Economic losses signal that the resources would be valued more highly if they were put to other uses. Losses also provide the incentive to correct this allocative inefficiency.

Oligopoly: **A market situation in which a small number of sellers comprise the entire industry. It is competition among the few.**

"Oligopoly" means "few sellers." Thus, when there are only a few firms in an industry, the industrial structure is called an **oligopoly**. In the United States, the vast majority of output in such industries as automobiles, steel, cigarettes, and aircraft is produced by only four or five dominant firms. In addition to a small number of producers, there are several other characteristics that oligopolistic industries have in common.

Interdependence among Firms

Since the number of sellers in an oligopolistic industry is small, each firm must take the potential reactions of rivals into account when it makes business decisions. The business decisions of one seller often have a substantial impact on the price of products and the profits of rival firms. The welfare of each oligopolistic seller is dependent on the policies followed by its major rivals.

Substantial Economies of Scale

In an oligopolistic industry, large-scale production (relative to the total market) is necessary to attain a low per unit cost. Economies of scale are significant. A small number of the large-scale, cost-efficient firms will meet the demand for the industry's product.

Using the automobile industry as an example, Exhibit 4 illustrates the importance of economies of scale as a source of oligopoly. It has been estimated that each firm must produce approximately 1 million automobiles annually before its per unit cost of production is minimized. However, when the selling price of automobiles is barely sufficient for firms to cover their costs, the total quantity demanded from the industry as a whole is only 6 million. Thus, in order to minimize costs, each firm must produce approximately one-sixth (1 million of the 6 million) of the output demanded. In other words, the industry can support no more than five or six firms of cost-efficient size.

EXHIBIT 4   Economies of scale and oligopoly

Oligopoly exists in the automobile industry because firms do not fully realize the cost reductions from large-scale output until they produce approximately one-sixth of the total market.

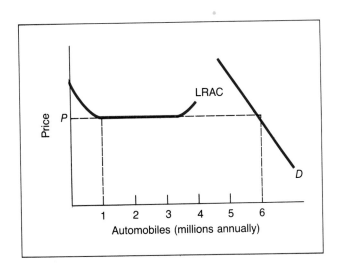

As with monopoly, barriers to entry limit the ability of new firms to compete effectively in oligopolistic industries. Economies of scale are probably the most significant entry barrier. A potential competitor will be unable to start out small and gradually grow to the optimal size, since, as we just explained, a firm in an oligopolistic industry must gain a large share of the market before it is able to minimize per unit cost. Patent rights, control over an essential resource, and government-imposed restraints may also prevent additional competitors from entering oligopolistic industries. Without substantial barriers to entry, oligopolistic competition would be similar to monopolistic competition.

**Products May Be
Either Homogeneous
or Differentiated**

The products of sellers in an oligopolistic industry may be either homogeneous or differentiated. However, although the nature of the product does not help us to identify an oligopoly, it influences the competitive strategies of rival firms. When firms produce identical products, there is less opportunity for nonprice competition. On the other hand, rival firms producing differentiated products are more likely to use style, quality, and advertising as competitive weapons.

PRICE AND OUTPUT UNDER OLIGOPOLY

Unlike a monopolist or a pure competitor, an oligopolist cannot determine the product price that will deliver maximum profit simply by estimating demand and cost conditions. An oligopolist must also predict how rival firms (that is, the rest of the industry) will react to price (and quality) adjustments. Since each oligopolist confronts such a complex problem, it is impossible to determine the precise price and output policy that will emerge in oligopolistic industries. However, economics does give signposts that suggest certain behavioral patterns. We can outline the potential range within which prices will lie. We can discuss the factors that will determine whether prices in the industry will be high or low relative to costs of production.

Consider an oligopolistic industry in which seven or eight rival firms produce the entire market output. Substantial economies of scale are present. The firms produce identical products and have similar costs of production. Exhibit 5 depicts the market demand conditions and long-run costs of production of the individual firms for such an industry.

What price will prevail? We can answer this question by making two extreme assumptions. First, suppose that each firm sets its price independently of the other firms. There is no collusion, and each competitive firm acts independently, seeking to maximize profits by offering consumers a better deal than its rivals. Under these conditions, the market price would be driven down to P_c. Firms would just be able to cover their per unit costs of production. What would happen if a *single firm* raised its price? Its customers would switch to rival firms, which would now expand to accommodate the new customers. The firm that raised its price would lose out. It would be self-defeating for any one firm to raise its price if the other firms did not raise theirs.

What would happen if supply conditions were such that the market price was above P_c? Since the demand curve faced by each *individual firm* is highly elastic, rival sellers would have a strong incentive to reduce their price. Any firm that reduced its price slightly, by 1 percent, for example, would gain numerous

EXHIBIT 5 The range of price and output under oligopoly

If oligopolists competed with one another, price-cutting would drive price down to P_c. In contrast, perfect cooperation among firms would lead to a higher price P_m and a smaller output (Q_m rather than Q_c).

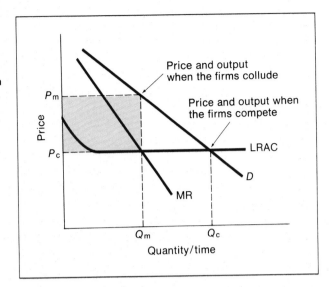

Cartel: An organization of sellers designed to coordinate supply decisions so that the joint profits of the members will be maximized. A cartel will seek to create a monopoly in the market.

customers. The price-cutting firm would attract some new buyers to the market, but, more important, that firm would also lure many buyers away from rival firms charging higher prices. Total profit would expand as the price-cutter gained a larger share of the total market. But what would happen if all firms attempted to undercut their rivals? Price would be driven down to P_c, and the economic profit of the firms would be eliminated.

When rival oligopolists compete (pricewise) with one another, they drive the market price down to the level of costs of production. However, this is not always the case. There is a strong incentive for oligopolists to collude, raise price, and restrict output.

Suppose that the oligopolists, recognizing their interdependence, acted cooperatively in order to maximize their joint profit. They might form a **cartel,** such as OPEC, in order to accomplish this objective. Alternatively, they might collude without the aid of a formal organization. Under federal antitrust laws, collusive action to raise price and maximize the joint profit of the firms would, of course, be illegal. Nonetheless, let us see what would happen if oligopolists followed this course. Exhibit 5 shows the marginal revenue curve that would accompany the market demand D for the product. Under perfect cooperation, the oligopolists would refuse to produce units for which marginal revenue was less than marginal cost. Thus, they would restrict joint output to Q_m, where MR = MC. Market price would rise to P_m. Thus, with collusion, substantial joint profits (the shaded area of Exhibit 5) could be attained. The case of perfect cooperation would be identical with the outcome under monopoly.

In the real world, however, the outcome is likely to fall between the extremes of price competition and perfect cooperation. Oligopolists generally recognize their interdependence and refuse to engage in vigorous price competition, which would drive price down to the level of per unit costs. But there are also obstacles to collusion. Thus, prices in oligopolistic industries do not rise to the monopolistic level. Oligopolistic prices are typically above the purely competitive level but below that for pure monopoly.

EXHIBIT 6   Gaining from cheating

The industry demand (D_i) and marginal revenue curves are shown in graph (b). The joint profits of oligopolists would be maximized at Q_i, where $MR_i = MC$. Price P_i would be best for the industry as a whole. However, the demand curve (d_f) facing each firm (graph a) would be much more elastic than D_i. Given the greater elasticity of its demand curve, an individual firm would maximize its profit by cutting its price to P_f and expanding output to q_f, where $MR_f = MC$. Thus, individual oligopolists could gain by secretly shaving price and cheating on the collusive agreement.

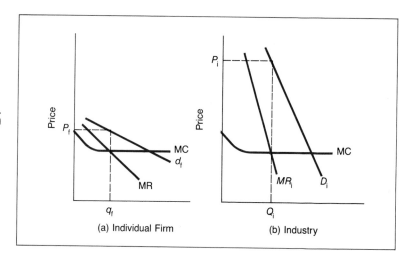

(a) Individual Firm   (b) Industry

Obstacles to Collusion

Collusion: Agreement among firms to avoid various competitive practices, particularly price reductions. It may involve either formal agreements or merely tacit recognition that competitive practices will be self-defeating in the long run. Tacit collusion is difficult to detect. The Sherman Act prohibits collusion and conspiracies to restrain interstate trade.

Collusion is the opposite of competition. It involves cooperative actions by sellers to turn the terms of trade in their own favor against that of buyers. Since oligopolists can profit by colluding to restrict output and raise price, economic theory suggests that they will have a strong incentive to do so.

However, each *individual* oligopolist also has an incentive to cheat on collusive agreements. Exhibit 6 will help us to understand why. An undetected price cut will enable a firm to attract both (a) customers who would not buy from any firm at the higher price *and* (b) those who would normally buy from other firms. Thus, the demand facing the oligopolistic *firm* will be considerably more elastic than the industry demand curve. As Exhibit 6 shows, the price P_i that maximizes the industry's profits will be higher than the price P_f that is best for each individual oligopolist. If a firm can find a way to reduce its price below the collusive agreement prices, expanded sales will more than make up for the reduction in per unit profit margin.

In oligopolistic industries, there are two conflicting tendencies. An oligopolistic firm has a strong incentive to cooperate with its rivals so that joint profit can be maximized. However, it also has a strong incentive to cheat secretly on any collusive agreement in order to increase its share of the joint profit. Oligopolistic agreements therefore tend to be unstable. This instability exists whether the cooperative behavior is informal or formal, as in the case of a cartel.

There are certain situations that work against the tendency of oligopolists to collude. Five major obstacles can limit collusive behavior.

When the Number of Oligopolists Is Fairly Large, Effective Collusion Is Less Likely. Other things constant, as the number of major firms in an industry increases, it becomes more costly for the oligopolists to communicate, negotiate, and enforce agreements among themselves. Developing and maintaining collusive agreements become more difficult. In addition, the greater the number of firms, the more likely it is that the objectives of individual firms will conflict with those of the industry. Each firm will want a bigger slice of the pie. Costs and the extent of unused plant capacity may differ among firms. Aggressive, less mature firms may want to expand their share of total output. These conflicting interests contribute to the breakdown of collusive agreements.

When It Is Difficult to Eliminate Secret Price Cuts, Collusion Is Less Attractive. Unless a firm has a way of policing the pricing policy of its rivals, it may be the "sucker" in a collusive agreement. Firms that secretly cut prices may gain a larger share of the market, while others maintain their higher prices and lose customers as well as profits. Sometimes price-cutting can be accomplished in ways that are difficult for the other firms to identify. For example, a firm might provide better credit terms, faster delivery, and other related services "free" in order to improve slightly the package offered to the consumer.[5]

When firms sell a differentiated product, improvements in quality and style can be used as competitive weapons. "Price cuts" of this variety are particularly attractive to an oligopolist because they cannot be easily and quickly duplicated by rivals. Competitors can quickly match a reduction in money price, but it will take time for them to match an improvement in quality. When firms can freely use improvements in quality to gain a larger share of the market, collusive agreements on price are of limited value. When cheating (price-cutting) is both profitable and difficult for rivals to police, it is a good bet that oligopolistic rivals will be induced to cheat.

Low Entry Barriers Are an Obstacle to Collusion. Unless potential rivals can be excluded, oligopolists will be unable to make unusually large profits. Temporarily successful collusion will merely attract competitors into the industry, which will eliminate the profits. Even with collusion, long-run profits will not be possible unless entry into the industry can be blocked.

Local markets are sometimes dominated by a few firms. For example, many communities have only a small number of ready-mix concrete producers, bowling alleys, accounting firms, and furniture stores. However, in the absence of government restrictions, entry barriers into these markets are usually low. The threat of potential rivals reduces the gains from collusive behavior under these conditions.

Unstable Demand Conditions Are an Obstacle to Collusion. Demand instability may lead to honest differences among oligopolists about what is best for the industry. One firm may want to expand because it anticipates a sharp increase in future demand. A more pessimistic rival may want to hold the line on existing industrial capacity. Differences in expectations about future demand create still another area of potential conflict among oligopolistic firms. Successful collusion is more likely when demand is relatively stable.

Vigorous Antitrust Action Increases the Cost of Collusion. Under existing antitrust laws, collusive behavior is prohibited. Of course, secret agreements are possible. Simple informal cooperation might be conducted without discussions or collusive agreements. However, like other illegal behavior, all such agreements would be unenforceable by any firm. Vigorous antitrust action can discourage

---

[5]See Marshall R. Colberg, Dascomb Forbush, and Gilbert R. Whitaker, *Businesss Economics,* 5th ed. (Homewood, Illinois: Irwin, 1975), for an extensive discussion of the alternative methods by which business firms are able to alter price.

firms from undertaking such illegal agreements. As the threat of getting caught increases, participants will be less likely to attempt collusive behavior.

The Kinked Demand Curve

As we noted earlier, since the demand for an oligopolistic firm's product is dependent not only upon market conditions but also upon the reaction of rival firms, the oligopolist must include the possible and probable reactions of rivals in its decisions. How will rivals react to a price change? When there is a dominant firm in an industry, rivals may be willing to follow the leadership of the larger firm. For example, if General Motors raises its prices by 5 percent, the other major automobile manufacturers may cooperate by raising their prices by a similar amount. However, oligopolists can never be sure what rivals will do. Sometimes prospective price increases are announced simply in order to observe the reactions of competitors.

The probable response of rivals is more difficult to determine when there is no single dominant firm in an industry. However, it does appear that rivals will be more likely to match a price reduction than a price increase. If a nondominant firm increases its price, other firms will be able to expand their market share if they maintain their current price. The sales of the firm that increases its price may fall substantially. On the other hand, when a single oligopolist lowers its price, it can be almost certain that rivals will respond. If they do not, their sales will fall sharply. But since the price reduction will be matched by the other firms of the industry, it is not likely to increase sales substantially for any single firm.

The hypothesis of the **kinked demand curve** is based on these projected reactions. The essential idea of the kinked demand curve is that the oligopolist's demand curve will be (a) very *elastic* for a price increase because other firms will maintain their prices but (b) very inelastic for a price reduction because the other firms will respond by reducing their prices also. The kinked demand curve hypothesis thus implies that prices in oligopolistic industries are likely to be quite stable.

Exhibit 7 illustrates the kinked demand curve. Since the demand curve is kinked at output Q, the marginal revenue curve will be discontinuous. This means that marginal costs could vary substantially at output Q while continuing

Kinked Demand Curve: A demand curve that is highly elastic for a price *increase* but inelastic for a price *reduction*. These differing elasticities are based on the assumption that rival firms will match a price reduction but not a price increase. This demand curve is thought to be descriptive of the situation faced by many oligopolistic firms.

EXHIBIT 7   The kinked demand curve

If an oligopolistic firm increases its price, it will lose many customers to rival firms. In contrast, a price reduction, since it will be matched by competitors, will lead to few additional customers. Thus, the oligopolist's demand curve is kinked, and the corresponding MR curve is discontinuous, as shown. The oligopolist will not change price even if MC fluctuates between E and F.

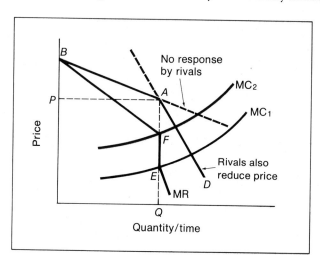

to equal marginal revenue. For example, both MC_1 and MC_2 intersect the MR curve at output Q. Therefore, despite these changes in cost, the profit-maximizing price of the oligopolist will remain at P. When the demand curve of a firm is kinked, the firm's profit-maximizing price may remain unchanged even though there are substantial changes in cost conditions.

Economists continue to debate the importance of the kinked demand curve hypothesis. Initially, the widespread use of price lists and categories that established prices in oligopolistic industries for a significant time period was thought to be consistent with the concept of a kinked demand and stable prices. However, recent studies suggest that price stability in oligopolistic industries may be more apparent than real. These studies have found that even when the *list* price of a product is stable, firms use such factors as discounts, credit terms, and delivery conditions to alter "price" in response to changing market conditions. In any event, it is clear that the kinked demand theory does not offer a complete explanation of price determination. Although the theory predicts tendencies *once a price is established*, it does not explain how the initial price is set.

Limits of the Oligopoly Model

Market Power: The ability of a firm that is not a pure monopolist to earn unusually large profits, indicating that it has some monopoly power. Because the firm has few (or weak) competitors, it has a degree of freedom from the discipline of vigorous competition.

Uncertainty and imprecision characterize the theory of oligopoly. We know that firms will gain if they can successfully agree to restrict output and raise price. However, collusion also has its costs. We have outlined some of the conflicts and difficulties (costs) associated with the establishment of perfect cooperation among oligopolistic firms. In some industries, these difficulties are considerable, and the **market power** of the oligopolists is therefore relatively small. In other industries, oligopolistic cooperation, although probably less than perfect, may permit the firms to turn the terms of trade in their favor. Economists would say that such firms have market power, indicating that even though these firms are not pure monopolists, they do have some monopoly power. Analysis of the costs and benefits of collusive behavior at least allows us to determine when discipline by competitive pressures is more likely for an oligopolist.

CONCENTRATION AND REAL-WORLD OLIGOPOLISTIC POWER

Which industries are dominated by a small number of firms? How important is oligopoly? Economists have developed a tool, the concentration ratio, that will help us to answer these questions.

Concentration Ratio: The total sales of the four (or sometimes eight) largest firms in an industry as a percentage of the total sales of the industry. The higher the ratio, the greater is the market dominance of a small number of firms. The ratio can be seen as a measure of oligopolistic power.

The **concentration ratio** is the percentage of total industry sales that are accounted for by the four (or sometimes eight) largest firms of an industry. This ratio can vary from nearly zero to 100, with 100 indicating that the sales of the four largest firms comprise those of the entire industry.

The concentration ratio can be thought of as a broad indicator of competitiveness. In general, the higher (lower) the concentration ratio, the more (less) likely that the firms of the industry will be able to collude successfully against the interests of consumers. However, this ratio is by no means a perfect measure of competitiveness. Since the sales of foreign producers are excluded, it overstates the degree of concentration in industries for which foreign competition is important. It does not reveal the elasticity of demand for products, although concentration is not as great a problem if good substitutes for a product are available. For example, the market power of aluminum producers is partially, limited by competition from steel, plastics, copper, and similar products. Similarly, the monopoly power of commercial airlines is substantially reduced by the availability of automobiles, buses, chartered private flights, and even conference telephone calls. Concentration ratios tend to conceal such competitiveness among products.

The concentration ratio can also overstate the competitiveness in instances in which the relevant market area is a city or region. For example, consider the case of newspaper publishing companies. In 1977, there were more than 7800 such companies in the United States. The sales of the four largest amounted to only 17 percent of the national market. However, most cities were served by only one or two newspapers. In most market areas, newspaper publishing is a highly concentrated industry, even though this is not true nationally. In this instance, the concentration ratio for the nation in the newspaper publishing industry probably overstates the actual competitiveness of the industry.

What do concentration ratios reveal about the U.S. economy? Exhibit 8 presents concentration data for several manufacturing industries in 1947 and 1977. Several industries, including the automobile, steel, aircraft, telephone and telegraph, computer equipment, and soap industries, are dominated by a few

EXHIBIT 8   Concentration ratios for selected manufacturing industries in 1947 and 1977

Industry	1947	1977	Change
High concentration (40 or more)			
Motor vehicles and car bodies	71	93	+22
Blast furnaces and steel mills	50	45	−5
Tires and inner tubes	70[a]	70	—
Aircraft and parts	72	59	−13
Telephone and telegraph	92	99	+7
Farm machinery	36	46	+10
Soap and other detergents	72[a]	59	−13
Photographic equipment and supplies	61	72	+11
Electronic computing equipment	66[a]	44	−22
Medium concentration (20–39)			
Petroleum	37	30	−7
Bread, cake, and related products	16	33	+17
Periodicals	34	22	−12
Gray iron foundries	16	34	+18
Toilet preparations	24	40	+16
Pharmaceuticals	28	24	−4
Low concentration (less than 20)			
Newspapers	21	19	−2
Meat packing	41	19	−22
Bottled and canned soft drinks	12[a]	15	+3
Commercial printing	13[a]	14	+1

[a]Data are for 1963.

U.S. Bureau of the Census, *Census of Manufacturing, 1947* and *1977.*

firms. They are oligopolistic. At the other end of the spectrum, the "big four" accounted for less than 20 percent of the sales of newspapers, meat packing, bottled and canned soft drinks, and commercial printing.

Most research suggests that, on balance, there has been little change in the patterns of business competitiveness over the last several decades. Of course, there have been some changes *within specific industries*. For example, concentration increased in the motor vehicle and photographic equipment industries between 1947 and 1977. The degree of concentration in aircraft, computer equipment, and meat packing has declined significantly in recent years.

Concentration and Mergers

Horizontal Merger: The combining under one ownership of the assets of two or more firms engaged in the production of *similar products*.

During the early stages of the development of American manufacturing, mergers had an important influence on the structure of our economy. The desire of oligopolistic firms to merge is not surprising. A **horizontal merger,** the combining of the assets of two or more firms under the same ownership, provides the firms with an alternative to both the rigors of competition and the insecurity of collusion.

There have been two great waves of horizontal mergers. The first occurred between 1887 and 1904, the second between 1916 and 1929. Many corporations whose names are now household words—U.S. Steel, General Electric, Standard Oil, General Foods, General Mills, and American Can, for example—are the products of mergers formed during these periods. Mergers led to a dominant firm in manufacturing industries such as steel, sugar refining, agricultural implements, leather, rubber, distilleries, and tin cans.

Analysis of these horizontal mergers leads to two interesting observations. First, horizontal mergers can create a highly profitable dominant firm, even if there is freedom of entry into an industry. The entry of new competitors takes time. A firm formed by merger that controls a substantial share of the market for a product can often realize oligopolistic profits for a period of time before the entry of new firms drives prices back down to the level of average cost. Of course, if entry barriers can be established to limit or retard the entry of new rivals, the incentive to merge is further strengthened.[6] Second, with the passage of time, competitive forces have generally eroded the position of the dominant firms created by horizontal mergers. Almost without exception, the market share of the dominant firms created by horizontal mergers began to decline soon after the mergers were consummated. Smaller firms gained ground relative to the dominant firm. This suggests that temporary profits stemming from market power, rather than economies of scale, were the primary motivation for the horizontal mergers. In 1950, the Celler–Kefauver Act made it substantially more difficult to use horizontal mergers as a means of developing oligopolistic power. Today, mergers involving large firms seldom involve former competitors.

Vertical Merger: The creation of a single firm from two firms, one of which was a supplier or customer of the other—for example, a merger of a lumber company with a furniture manufacturer.

Another type of merger, the **vertical merger,** joins a supplier and a buyer—for example, an automobile maker and a steel producer. A vertical merger might simplify the long-range planning process for both firms and reduce the need for costly legal contracting between the two. Even though vertical mergers generally do not increase concentration within industries, some econo-

---

[6]See George Stigler, "Monopoly and Oligopoly by Merger," *American Economic Review* (May 1950), pp. 23–34, for a detailed analysis of this issue.

mists are concerned that such mergers may reduce competition if either the buyer or the supplier grants a market advantage to the other.

A **conglomerate merger** combines two firms in unrelated industries. The stated intent is usually to introduce new and superior management into the firm being absorbed. This type of merger results in increased size but not necessarily in reduced competition. Since the 1960s, when some very large corporations were formed by conglomerate merger, some observers have expressed concern that the concentration of political power created by such mergers and the enormous financial assets available to the operating units may be potentially dangerous. Others have argued that the conglomerate mergers often lead to more efficient management and increased competitiveness within specific industries. The impact of conglomerate mergers on our economy is a topic of current research among economists.

Concentration and Profits

The model of oligopoly implies that if the firms in concentrated industries cooperate with one another, *jointly* they can exercise monopoly power. Is there a relationship between industrial concentration and profitability in the real world? Researchers in this area have not been able to arrive at a definite conclusion. An early study by Joe Bain showed a distinctly positive relationship between concentration and profitability. George Stigler, in a detailed study of manufacturing industries, found that from 1947 to 1954 "the average [profit] rate in the concentrated industries was 8.00 percent, while that in the unconcentrated industries was 7.16 percent." Later, both a study by William Shepherd covering the period from 1960 to 1969 and the White House Task Force on Antitrust Policy presented evidence that the rate of profitability is higher in concentrated industries.

Nonetheless, other researchers remain unconvinced. Sam Peltzman argues that the alleged link "between profitability and concentration is, in fact, attributable to other factors which happen to be correlated with concentration." Yale Brozen argues that the proper test is between concentration and future (not past) profitability. His work indicates that "rates of returns in concentrated industries at a later time . . . turn out to be insignificantly different from those in less concentrated industries."[7]

The weight of the evidence on this topic suggests that the profit rate of firms in concentrated industries is just slightly higher than the profit rate of other firms. The link between industrial concentration and profitability is a weak one. Other factors, such as demand conditions, management efficiency, and entrepreneurship, are the major determinants of business profitability. Thus, the odds are only a little better than 50–50 that a more concentrated industry will be more profitable than a less concentrated one.

---

[7]For a detailed analysis of this issue, see Joe S. Bain, "Relation of Profit Rate to Industry Concentration: American Manufacturing 1936–40," *Quarterly Journal of Economics* (August 1951); Yale Brozen, "Concentration and Profits: Does Concentration Matter?" in *The Impact of Large Firms on the U.S. Economy,* ed. J. Fred Weston and Stanley I. Ornstein (Lexington, Massachusetts: Heath, 1973); George Stigler, *Capital and Rates of Return in Manufacturing Industries* (Princeton, New Jersey: Princeton University Press, 1963); H. M. Mann, "Seller Concentration, Barriers to Entry, and Rates of Return in Thirty Industries, 1950–1960," *Review of Economics and Statistics* (August 1966); Sam Peltzman, "Profits, Data, and Public Policy," in *Public Policies toward Mergers,* ed. J. Fred Weston and Sam Peltzman (Pacific Palisades, California: Goodyear, 1967); W. G. Shepherd, "Elements of Market Structure," *Review of Economics and Statistics* (February 1972); and "White House Task Force on Antitrust Policy," Report 1, in *Trade Regulation Reports,* Suppl. 415 (May 26, 1969).

Market Power and Profit—
The Early Bird Catches
the Worm

In the last chapter, we saw that under certain conditions an unregulated monopolist can earn economic profit, even in the long run. Similarly, our analysis of oligopoly suggests that if barriers to entry are high, firms may sometimes be consistently able to earn above-average profits, even in the long run. Suppose that a well-established firm, such as Exxon or General Motors, is able to use its market power to earn consistent economic profits. Do its current stockholders gain because of its monopoly power? Surprisingly, the answer is no. The ownership value of a share of corporate stock for such a corporation long ago began to reflect its market power and profitability. Many of the *present* stockholders paid high prices for their stock because they expected the firm to be highly profitable. In other words, they paid for any above-normal economic profits that the firm might be expected to earn because of its monopoly power.

Do not expect to get rich buying the stock of highly profitable monopolistic or oligopolistic firms. You are already too late. The early bird catches the worm. Those who owned the stock when these firms initially developed their market position have already captured the gain. The value of their stock increased at that time. After a firm's future prospects are widely recognized, subsequent stockholders fail to gain a high rate of return on their financial investment.

MYTHS OF ECONOMICS
"The prices of most goods are unnecessarily inflated by at least 25 percent as a result of the high rate of profit of producers."

During the recent period of inflation, profits have been about as popular with consumers as failing grades are with students at the end of a semester. When food prices rise, the profits of farmers, meat processors, and food store chains are heavily publicized by the news media. When gasoline prices jump, many people believe that they are being pushed up by greedy profiteering on the part of the major oil companies. The casual observer might easily be left with the impression that large profits were the major source of the high rate of inflation of the 1970s.

This issue is clouded by the fact that both the size of profits and their function are largely misunderstood by most people. Surveys show that young people believe that the after-tax profits of corporations comprise between 25 and 30 percent of sales. A recent national sample poll of adults conducted by Opinion Research of Princeton found that the average person thought that profits comprised 29 cents of every dollar of sales in manufacturing. In reality, as Exhibit 9b shows, the after-tax accounting profits of manufacturing corporations are approximately 5 percent of sales. Thus, the public believes that the rate of profit as a percentage of sales is nearly six times greater than the actual figure!

Why are people so misinformed on this issue? The popular media are one source of confusion. The media nearly always report the accounting profits of firms in dollar terms, instead of comparing them to sales, stockholder equity, or the value of the firms' assets. A favorite device is to report that profits, either annually or quarterly, were up by some astonishing percentage.[8] Unless we know

whether profits were high, normal, or low during the previous period, this type of statement tells little or nothing about the firm's earnings rate on its capital assets. For example, suppose that a corporation with $100 million of assets earned a profit of $2 million last year, a 2 percent rate of return on its capital assets. Now suppose that the firm's earnings this year are $4 million, generating only a 4 percent rate of return. It would not be unusual for the popular media to report, "The profits of corporation X soared to $4 million, a 100 percent increase over last year." What this statement conceals is that the profits of the firm as as a percentage of its capital assets were less than what you or I could earn on a savings account.

Not only is the average person misinformed about the size of profits, but most individuals do not understand their function. Many believe that if profits were eliminated, our economy would continue to operate as if nothing had happened. This erroneous view indicates a misunderstanding of what accounting profits are. Accounting profits are primarily a monetary return to persons who have

---

[8]This is equally true for large wage increases. Apparently, the extreme example rather than the norm helps to sell newspapers. We should note that such reports do not imply an antibusiness bias. The *Wall Street Journal*, not noted for such bias, regularly headlines its stories in the same manner.

EXHIBIT 9 How great are profits?

After-tax corporate profits average about 12 percent of stockholder equity and 5 percent of sales in the United States.

Economic Report of the President, 1982. As the result of changes in definitions, the data for 1975–1980 are not, strictly speaking, comparable to the figures for the earlier periods.

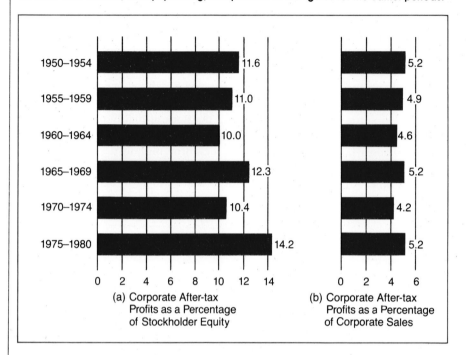

(a) Corporate After-tax Profits as a Percentage of Stockholder Equity

(b) Corporate After-tax Profits as a Percentage of Corporate Sales

invested in machines, buildings, and nonhuman productive resources. Investment in physical capital involves both risk and the foregoing of current consumption. If profits were eliminated, the incentive of persons to invest and provide the tools that make the American worker the most productive in the world would be destroyed. Who would invest in either physical or human capital (for example, education) if such investments did not lead to an increase in future income—that is, if investment did not lead to accounting profit?

Profits play an important role in our economy. Persons who increase the value of resources—who produce something that is worth more than the resources that went into it—will be rewarded with economic profit (and generally an above-average accounting profit). Those who allocate resources to a venture that consumers value less than the opportunity cost of the project will experience economic losses (below-average accounting profits). Without this reward–penalty system, individuals (and firms) would not have the incentive to use resources wisely in the development and production of goods that are most desired by consumers relative to the goods' opportunity cost.

LOOKING AHEAD

The competitiveness of a market economy is influenced not only by the various market structures operating within it but also by public policy. Business activity is often directly regulated by the government. In the following chapter, we will investigate the business structure of the U.S. economy and consider the impact of regulatory activities.

1 The distinguishing characteristics of monopolistic competition are (a) firms that produce differentiated products, (b) low barriers to entry into and exit from the market, and (c) a substantial number of independent, rival firms.

2 Monopolistically competitive firms face a gently downward-sloping demand curve. They often use product quality, style, convenience of location, advertising, and price as competitive weapons. Since all rivals within a monopolistically competitive industry are free to duplicate one another's products (or services), the demand for the product of any one firm is highly elastic.

3 A profit-maximizing firm will expand output as long as marginal revenue exceeds marginal cost. Thus, a firm under monopolistic competition will lower its price so that output can be expanded until MR = MC. The price charged by the profit-maximizing monopolistic competitor will be greater than its marginal cost.

4 If monopolistic competitors are making economic profits, rival firms will be induced to enter the market. They will expand the supply of the product (and similar products), enticing some of the customers away from established firms. The demand curve faced by an individual firm will fall (shift inward) until the profits have been eliminated.

5 Economic losses will cause monopolistic competitors to exit from the market. The demand for the products of each remaining firm will rise (shift outward) until the losses have been eliminated.

6 Since barriers to entry are low, firms in a monopolistically competitive industry will make only normal profits in the long run. In the short run, they may make either economic profits or losses, depending on market conditions.

7 Traditional economic theory has emphasized that monopolistic competition is inefficient because (a) price exceeds marginal cost at the long-run equilibrium output level; (b) long-run average cost is not minimized; and (c) excessive advertising is sometimes encouraged. However, other economists have argued more recently that this criticism is misdirected. According to the newer view, firms under monopolistic competition have an incentive to (a) produce efficiently; (b) undertake production if and only if their actions will increase the value of resources used; and (c) offer a variety of products.

8 Oligopolistic market structure is characterized by (a) an interdependence among firms, (b) substantial economies of scale that result in only a small number of firms in the industry, and (c) significant barriers to entry. Oligopolists may produce either homogeneous or differentiated products.

9 There is no general theory of price, output, and equilibrium for oligopolistic markets. If rival oligopolists acted totally independently of their competitors, they would drive price down to the level of cost of production. Alternatively, if they used collusion to obtain perfect cooperation, price would rise to the level that a monopolist would charge. The actual outcome lies between these two extremes.

10 Collusion is the opposite of competition. Oligopolists have a strong incentive to collude and raise their prices. However, the interests of individual firms will conflict with those of the industry as a whole. Since the demand curve faced by individual firms is far more elastic than the industry demand curve, each firm could gain by cutting its price (or raising product quality) by a small amount so that it could attract customers from rivals. If several firms tried to do this, however, the collusive agreement would break down.

11 Oligopolistic firms are less likely to collude successfully against the interests of consumers if (a) the number of rival firms is large; (b) it is costly to prohibit competitors from offering secret price cuts (or quality improvements) to customers; (c) entry barriers are low; (d) market demand conditions tend to be unstable; and/or (e) the threat of antitrust action is present.

12 The kinked demand curve helps to explain why oligopolistic prices may tend to be inflexible. Under the basic assumption of the kinked demand curve—rivals will match price reductions but not increases—a firm's price rise leads to a sharp reduction in its sales, but a price reduction attracts few new customers. Thus, once a price is established, it remains inflexible for extended periods of time.

13 Analysis of concentration ratios suggests that, on balance, there has been little change in the competitiveness of the U.S. economy in several decades.

14 Accounting profits as a share of stockholder equity are probably slightly greater in highly concentrated industries than in those that are less concentrated. The relationship between profits and concentration, however, is not a close one. This suggests that several other factors, such as changing market conditions, quality competition, risk, and ability to exclude rivals, are the major determinants of profitability.

15 The after-tax accounting profits of business firms average about 5 cents of each dollar of sales, substantially less than most Americans believe to be the case. Accounting profits average approximately 12 percent of stockholder equity. This rate of return (accounting profit) provides investors with the incentive to sacrifice current consumption, assume the risk of undertaking a business venture, and supply the funds to purchase buildings, machines, and other assets.

THE ECONOMIC WAY OF THINKING—DISCUSSION QUESTIONS

1 Explain in your own words the meaning of product differentiation. What tactics might be used to differentiate one's product?

2 Why do many economists argue that monopolistic competition is inefficient? If there were fewer small firms in a monopolistically competitive industry (for example, retail groceries), would the *average* selling prices in the industry decline? Why or why not? Would convenience, location, and other quality factors change? Why or why not? Do you think monopolistic competition is inefficient? Explain.

3 It is often charged that competitive advertising among monopolistically competitive firms is wasteful. (a) Do you think that advertising in the following industries is wasteful: retail grocery sales, retail furniture sales, cigarettes, local restaurants, cosmetics, movie theaters, retail department stores? Explain. (b) Does this advertising result in higher prices? (c) Is the advertising valuable to consumers? Explain. (d) Why is it that more firms do not compete by eliminating their advertising and charging lower prices?

4 Explain why decision-makers for firms in an oligopolistic industry have an incentive to collude. What are the factors that influence the success or failure of their collusive efforts?

5 "Effective collusion requires firms to agree on both price and quality. A firm can lower price by raising quality, or it can raise price by lowering quality, even without changing the actual monetary sale price. Unless a firm can keep its competitors from adjusting quality, the gains from price collusion will be short-lived." Do you agree? Why or why not?

6 "High concentration leads to either overt or tacit collusion. Thus, prices in oligopolistic industries will almost surely be rigged against the consumer and to the benefit of the producer." Do you agree? Why or why not?

7 Are profits important in a market economy? Why or why not? Can you think of policies designed to reduce profitability that are consistent with economic efficiency? Explain. Do not forget to consider any secondary effects.

8 **What's Wrong with This Way of Thinking?**

"Firms such as General Motors, AT&T, and General Electric have been using their monopoly power to realize economic profit for years. These high profit rates benefit the current stockholders of these corporations at the expense of the consumers."

22

BUSINESS STRUCTURE, REGULATION, AND DEREGULATION

Most contemporary economists believe, just as Adam Smith did, that competition and rivalry among business firms provide benefits to both consumers and workers. Competition forces producers to operate efficiently and supply consumers with the goods that they desire most intensely (relative to costs). Similarly, competition for resources forces each producer to treat workers and other resource suppliers fairly, offering them pay rates and work environments that are attractive relative to those available elsewhere.

But in spite of widespread agreement on the desirability of competition, there are two major aspects of competition about which there is a great deal of disagreement: the strength and extent of real-world competitive pressures and the actual effectiveness of governmental regulatory policy. As we have discussed, both the nature of competition and its intensity vary according to the structure of the industry under consideration. For example, as we have seen, competitive elements will eventually be introduced into even highly concentrated oligopolistic industries; at the same time, tendencies toward collusion must also be considered. Economists often disagree on the ability of unregulated markets to provide for a strong competitive environment.

As for the argument over the effects of regulation on competition, some economists point out that regulatory policy, by limiting various types of non-competitive behavior, effectively increases the discipline of the market. Others charge that past regulatory policies have often reduced market competitiveness, contributed to economic inefficiency, and, in general, ignored major concerns of consumers and workers.

In this chapter we will analyze the structure of the U.S. economy and consider the effects of regulatory policy on economic behavior in the light of

---

[1]Donald F. Turner, "The Antitrust Chief Dissents," *Fortune* (April 1966), p. 113.

these controversies. How competitive is our economy? Has regulatory policy added to or detracted from its competitiveness? Why have some industries been deregulated? What are the effects of the new "social regulation" designed to provide us with a cleaner, safer, and healthier environment?

THE STRUCTURE OF THE U.S. ECONOMY

The structure of the U.S. economy is extremely diverse. There are approximately 15 million business firms in the United States. Owner-operated farming and service businesses account for more than 6 million of the firms. These businesses are, of course, quite small. In contrast, there are roughly 300,000 corporations with annual business receipts in excess of $1 million. Some of these are giants with thousands of employees and annual sales running into the billions.

The structure of our economy is also continually changing. A century ago, over half of all workers were employed in agriculture, and less than 20 percent worked in manufacturing. Throughout the first half of this century, the relative size of the agricultural sector steadily declined and manufacturing output grew, as a share of total output. By 1950, the manufacturing sector accounted for 30 percent of the total U.S. output; agriculture had declined to less than 10 percent.

Since 1950, a new trend in industrial structure has evolved. The relative sizes of *both* the agricultural and manufacturing sectors have declined, and the government and service sectors (for example, health care, education, professional and repair workers) have expanded. As a share of the total, employment in the government and service sectors rose from 23 percent to more than 34 percent between 1950 and 1980. In contrast, manufacturing employment fell from 30 percent in 1950 to 22 percent in 1980.

During the last two decades, there has also been a movement of industry from the northeast urban centers to the Sunbelt. The composition of the labor force has also changed. Less than a third of all workers were female in 1960; by 1981 more than 43 percent of those at work were women.

How Much of Our Economy Is Competitive?

This is a difficult question to answer. As we have discussed, competition is multidimensional. Dynamic innovation, entrepreneurship, and product-quality competition may be important even in highly concentrated industries. Although the concentration ratio of an industry provides an indication of competitiveness, it is an imperfect measure. The availability of substitutes may substantially limit the monopoly power of firms in some concentrated industries. Other firms may be restrained by the threat of entry from potential rivals. Still other firms in concentrated industries face stiff competition from foreign producers. The relative importance of competitive and noncompetitive sectors within the economy may change with time. Moreover—and perhaps most important—it is not clear where the line should be drawn between competitive and noncompetitive. Most economists would probably classify unregulated industries in which the four largest firms produce less than 20 or 25 percent of the market as competitive. On the other hand, industries in which the largest firms produce more than half of the output would generally be classified as oligopolistic, suggesting the presence of noncompetitive elements. These categories, however, are arbitrary.

Exhibit 1 sheds some light on the competitiveness of the U.S. economy.

EXHIBIT 1   The competitiveness of the U.S. economy, 1980

Gross National Product Originating from:	Billions of Dollars	Percentage of Total
Low barriers to entry	1116	42
Agricultural, forestry, and fisheries	77	
Construction	120	
Wholesale and retail trade	422	
Service	344	
Manufacturing (industries with concentration ratios of less than 20 percent)[a]	153	
Medium barriers to entry	95	4
Manufacturing (industries with concentration ratios between 20 and 40 percent)[a]	95	
High barriers to entry (unregulated)	437	17
Manufacturing (industries with concentration ratios greater than 40 percent)[a]	343	
Mining	94	
Primarily regulated industries	626	24
Transportation, communications, and utility	234	
Finance, insurance, and real estate	392	
Government	303	12
All other	49	2
Total	2626	100

[a]The concentration ratios were for the U.S. Bureau of the Census's two-digit industrial classification. The following industries had four-firm concentration ratios of greater than 40 percent: tobacco, chemicals, rubber products, stone, clay, and glass products, primary metals, electrical equipment, transportation equipment (aircraft and automobiles), machinery (except electrical), and instruments and related products.

Derived from the *Statistical Abstract of the United States—1981,* Tables 703, 1423, and 1427.

The table breaks our gross national product down by sector and industrial concentration. Agriculture, construction, wholesale and retail trade, and service industries have traditionally been characterized by small firms and low barriers to entry.[2] These sectors plus manufacturing industries with four-firm concentration ratios of less than 20 percent accounted for more than two-fifths of the total national output in 1980. They now comprise roughly one-half of the private sector. This suggests that competitive forces still play a highly important role in our economy.

On the other hand, business concentration and regulated sectors are also important. Regulated industries and government generate more than one-third of our total output. Highly concentrated manufacturing industries such as tobacco, chemicals, automobiles, aircraft, primary metals, and electrical equipment accounted for 17 percent of our national income in 1980. Most economists believe that firms in these industries are the most capable of escaping the disciplines of competition. Of course, many of these concentrated industries confront stiff foreign competition. For example, although General Motors, Ford,

---

[2]In 1971, proprietorships, partnerships, and corporations with sales of less than $1 million accounted for 81 percent of the income generated by agriculture, 64 percent of income from service, 44 percent of construction income, and 25 percent of wholesale and retail trade income.

Chrysler, and American Motors share a monopoly on *domestic production,* more than one out of every four automobiles sold in the United States is bought from a foreign producer. Foreign competition is also important in other industries, such as steel and petroleum. Product-quality competition may also account for strong rivalry even among a limited number of competitors. Moreover, in a firm as big as General Motors, even the rivalry among the divisions (Buick versus Oldsmobile, for example) may be intense. Direct price competition within the firm is presumably controlled, but competition involving quality remains. Leaders in each division compete for recognition and advancement, and each is judged by monthly sales and profit figures. Thus, competitive forces are not entirely absent even in a concentrated industry.

These data on the U.S. industrial structure indicate that competitive, concentrated, and highly regulated sectors are all sizable. Approximately two-fifths of our national output is generated by roughly competitive industries—that is, industries in which rivalry exists among a substantial number of firms. Another one-fifth of our output originates from industries characterized by a significant degree of industrial concentration. Highly regulated industries account for nearly a quarter of the total output. The government sector generates the remainder of the total output.[3]

Does Big Business Dominate the U.S. Economy?

Bigness and absence of competition are not necessarily the same thing. A firm can be big and yet function in a highly competitive industry. For example, Sears and Montgomery Ward are both large, but they are also part of a highly competitive industry—retail sales.

Exhibit 2 shows the percentage of the U.S. labor force that is employed by the largest corporations. In 1980, the 100 largest corporate giants employed 10 percent of the labor force. More than one in six labor force participants was employed by a corporation that ranked in the top 1000. Other measures of corporate power, such as share of total assets or value added, paint a similar picture.

Has the relative size of the largest corporations grown? As Exhibit 3 shows, the value added[4] of the 200 largest industrial firms grew relative to both manufacturing and total output (GNP) during the 1947–1967 period. Since 1967, the value added of the 200 largest corporations has expanded slightly as a proportion of manufacturing output. However, the relative size of the manufacturing sector has been shrinking in relation to the economy as a whole. As a share of total output, the value added of the 200 largest industrial corporations declined from 11.8 percent in 1967 to 10.6 percent in 1977 (the most recent data available).

What caused the rapid growth of the largest firms during the 1947–1967 period? A study by the Federal Trade Commission found that mergers accounted

---

[3]These data reflect the research on this topic. See George Stigler, *Five Lectures on Economic Problems* (New York: Longman, 1949); G. Warren Nutter and Henry A. Einhorn, *Enterprise Monopoly in the United States: 1899–1958* (New York: Columbia University Press, 1969); and Solomon Fabricant, "Is Monopoly Increasing?" *Journal of Economic History* (Winter 1953), for additional detail on this topic.

[4]Value added is the total value of the firm's sales less the cost of materials and services purchased from resource suppliers and subcontractors. It is a measure of how much the firm's productive efforts have added to the value of its product.

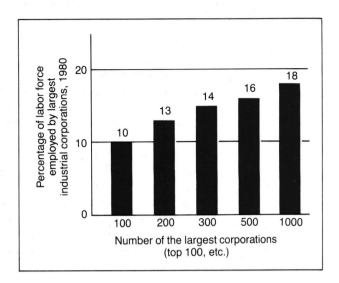

for three-fourths of the relative growth of the 200 largest industrial firms during this period. Most of the mergers were of the conglomerate variety—a collection of diverse enterprises were combined under a single management. Were it not for these mergers, the size of the largest corporations relative to the total economy would have been virtually unchanged during the entire post-World War II period.

The stated objective of public policy has been to restrain various aspects of big business activity, especially when competition seems threatened. Many believe that antitrust action can help to promote efficiency and to keep political power and income more equally distributed. To what extent does the economic and political power of large corporations threaten competitiveness? To what extent does this power need to be restrained? Some observers argue that large firms threaten our decentralized economic institutions and our democratic political structure. Certainly, public choice theory indicates that concentrated business interests, like other special interest organizations, often exert a disproportional influence on the political process. However, we should keep three points in mind as we evaluate this issue and the effectiveness of the government's antitrust policies.

EXHIBIT 3   How big are the giants?

Year	The Value Added of the 200 Largest Industrial Corporations	
	Percentage of Manufacturing	Percentage of GNP
1947	30	8.6
1958	38	10.5
1962	40	11.3
1967	42	11.8
1972	43	10.8
1977	44	10.6

Statistical Abstract of the United States—1981, Tables 703 and 918.

First, since the growth of large corporations has resulted mainly from conglomerate mergers, it does not follow that competitiveness within industries has been reduced. In fact, the evidence indicates that there has not been a similar increase in concentration *within* industries (see Exhibit 8 of the previous chapter).

Second, bigness does not ensure greater profitability. The real-world data do not indicate that profits as a percentage of stockholder equity are linked to corporate size.[5] Many of the conglomerates discovered this when their earnings took a nose dive during the 1970s.

Third, the firms that comprise the largest 100 corporations are heterogeneous and constantly changing. As successful management and the vagaries of business fortune exert their influence, some firms are pushed out of the top group and others enter. Of the 100 largest manufacturing corporations in 1909, only 36 remained on the list in 1948. Of the 50 largest manufacturing firms in 1947, only 25 remained in that category in 1972. Of those that dropped out during the period from 1947 to 1972, 5 failed to make even the top 200. With time, even giants stumble and fall, and new competitors arise to take their place. In a world of changing technology and consumer preferences, bigness does not guarantee success or sticking power.

ANTITRUST LEGISLATION—THE POLICY OBJECTIVES

Predatory Pricing: The practice by which a dominant firm in an industry temporarily reduces price in order to damage or eliminate weaker rivals, so that prices can be raised above the level of costs in a later period.

Exclusive Contract: An agreement between manufacturer and retailer that prohibits the retailer from carrying the product lines of firms that are rivals of the manufacturer. Such contracts are illegal under the Clayton Act when they "lessen competition."

Reciprocal Agreement: An agreement between firms whereby the buyer of a product requires the seller to purchase another product as a condition of sale. The practice is illegal under the Clayton Act when it substantially reduces competiton.

Antitrust legislation seeks to (a) ensure that the economy is structured such that competition exists among firms in the same industry (or market area) and (b) prohibit business practices that tend to stifle competition. Once these objectives are accomplished, it is assumed that market forces can be relied on to allocate goods and services.

There are numerous tactics that business entrepreneurs might use in an effort to avoid the rigors of competition. We have already stressed that collusion and price agreements are potential weapons with which to turn the terms of trade in favor of the seller. Potential competitors might also decide to divide a market geographically, agreeing not to compete in certain market areas. Large, diversified firms might use **predatory pricing,** a practice by which a firm *temporarily* reduces its price below cost in certain market areas in order to damage or eliminate the competition of weaker rivals. Once the rivals have been eliminated, the firm uses its monopoly power to raise prices above costs. A competitor might also use exclusive contracts and reciprocal agreements in an effort to maintain an advantage over rivals. An **exclusive contract** (or dealership) is an arrangement whereby the manufacturer of a line of products prohibits retailers from selling any of the products of rival producers. Thus, an established firm, offering many product lines, might use this tactic in order to limit the entry into retail markets of rivals offering only narrow product lines. A **reciprocal agreement** is a situation in which the buyer of a product requires the seller to purchase another product as a condition of sale. For example, General Motors was charged in 1963 with telling railroads that if they did not buy GM locomotives, GM would ship its automobiles by other means. All of these business practices involve the use of market power rather than superior performance to gain at

---

[5]See William G. Shepherd, *The Economics of Industrial Organization* (Englewood Cliffs, New Jersey: Prentice-Hall, 1979), pp. 270–272, for evidence on this issue. Shepherd found that large corporate size had a mild *negative* impact on the rate of profit of firms during the period from 1960 to 1969.

the expense of rivals. In one form or another, they are all illegal under current antitrust legislation.

Major Antitrust Legislation

A society that wishes to organize economic activity on the basis of competitive markets rather than detailed regulation or socialized planning may need to pursue an antitrust policy. The United States, to a greater extent than most Western countries, has adopted antitrust legislation designed to promote competitive markets. Three major legislative acts—the Sherman Act, the Clayton Act, and the Federal Trade Commission Act—form the foundation of antitrust in the United States.

The Sherman Act. This act was passed in 1890, largely in response to a great wave of mergers. The infamous tobacco, sugar, and Standard Oil trusts enraged Congress and the American people. Action was taken against business concentration. The most important provisions of the act are the following:

Section 1: Every contract, combination in the form of trust or otherwise, or conspiracy, in restraint of trade or commerce among the several states or with foreign nations, is hereby declared illegal.
Section 2: Every person who shall monopolize, or conspire with any other person or persons to monopolize any part of the trade or commerce among the several states, or with foreign nations, shall be guilty of a misdemeanor.

The language of the Sherman Act is vague and subject to interpretation. What does it mean to "attempt to monopolize" or "combine or conspire with another person"? Initially, the courts were hesitant to apply the act to manufacturing corporations. In 1911, however, the Supreme Court ruled that Standard Oil and American Tobacco had used "unreasonable" tactics to restrain trade. At the time, the Standard Oil trust controlled 90 percent of the country's refinery capacity. American Tobacco controlled three-fourths of the tobacco manufacturing market. Both of these firms were broken up into several smaller rival firms.

The Supreme Court, however, did not prohibit monopoly per se. It was the tactics used by Standard Oil and American Tobacco that caused the Court to rule against them. In later cases, the Supreme Court refused to break up other trusts (U.S. Steel and American Can, for example) because it could not be proved that they had followed "unfair or unethical" business practices. But the Sherman Act does not clearly define unfair or unethical business practices, and the courts have been reluctant to enforce it. The ineffectiveness of the act led to the passage of two other antitrust laws in 1914.

The Clayton Act. This act was passed in an effort to spell out and prohibit specific business practices. The following are prohibited by the Clayton Act when they "substantially lessen competition or tend to create a monopoly": (a) *price discrimination*—charging purchasers in different markets different prices that are unrelated to transportation costs; (b) *tying contracts*—a practice whereby the seller requires that the buyer purchase another item; (c) *exclusive dealings*—agreements whereby the seller of a good is forbidden to sell to a competitor of the purchaser; (d) *interlocking stockholding*—one firm purchasing the stock of a competing firm; (e) *interlocking directorates*—the same individual(s) serving on the board of directors of competing firms.

Although somewhat more specific than the Sherman Act, the Clayton Act is still vague. At what point do the prohibited actions actually become illegal? Under what circumstances do these actions "substantially lessen competition"? The task of interpreting this ambiguous phrase still remains with the courts.

The Federal Trade Commission Act. This act declared unlawful all "unfair methods of competition in commerce." The Federal Trade Commission (FTC), composed of five members appointed by the president to seven-year terms, was established to determine the exact meaning of "unfair methods." However, a 1919 Supreme Court decision held that the courts, and not the FTC, had the ultimate responsibility for interpreting the law. Today, the FTC is concerned primarily with (a) enforcing consumer protection legislation, (b) prohibiting deceptive advertising, a power it acquired in 1938, and (c) preventing overt collusion.

When a complaint is filed with the FTC, usually by a third party, the commission investigates. If there is a violation, the FTC initially attempts to settle the dispute by negotiation between the parties. If the attempts to negotiate a settlement fail, a hearing is conducted before one of the commission's examiners. The decision of the hearing examiner may be appealed to the full commission, and the FTC's decision may later be appealed to the U.S. Court of Appeals. The great majority of cases brought before the FTC are now settled by mutual consent of the parties involved.

More Recent Antitrust Legislation

Additional antitrust legislation was passed in the 1930s. The Robinson–Patman Act of 1936 prohibits selling "at unreasonably low prices" when such practices reduce competition. The section of the Clayton Act dealing with price discrimination was aimed at eliminating predatory prices. The Robinson–Patman Act went beyond this. It was intended to protect competitors not just from stronger rivals who might temporarily sell below cost but from more efficient rivals who are actually producing at a lower cost. Chain stores and mass distributors were the initial targets of the legislation. Economists have often been critical of the Robinson–Patman Act, since it has tended to eliminate price competition and protect inefficient producers.

In 1938, Congress passed the Wheeler–Lea Act, which was designed to strengthen sections of the Federal Trade Commission Act that had been weakened by restrictive court decisions. Before the passage of the act, the courts were reluctant to prohibit unfair business practices, such as false and deceptive advertising, unless there was proof of damages to either consumers or rival firms. The Wheeler–Lea Act removed this limitation and gave the FTC extended powers to prosecute and ban false or deceptive advertising.

In 1950, Congress passed the Celler–Kefauver Act (sometimes referred to as the antimerger act), which prohibits a firm from acquiring the assets of a competitor if the transaction substantially lessens competition. The Clayton Act, though it prohibits mergers through stock acquisition, proved unable to prevent business combinations from being formed by sale of assets. The Celler–Kefauver Act has closed this loophole, further limiting the ability of firms to combine in an effort to escape competitive pressures.

Since the intent of the Celler–Kefauver Act is to maintain industrial competition, its applicability to mergers between large firms in the same industry is obvious. The act also prohibits vertical mergers between large firms if competition is reduced by such mergers. For example, the merger of a publishing company with a paper producer is now illegal if the courts find that it lessens competition. However, the applicability of the Celler–Kefauver Act to conglomerate mergers remains ambiguous, primarily because there has not been a clear-cut court decision in this area.

Thumbnail Sketch—Antitrust Legislation

Antitrust laws prohibit the following:
1. Collusion—contracts and conspiracies to restrain trade (Sherman Act, Sec. 1)
2. Monopoly and attempts to monopolize any part of trade or commerce among the several states (Sherman Act, Sec. 2)
3. Persons serving on the board of directors of competing firms with more than $1 million of assets (Clayton Act, Sec. 8)
4. Unfair and deceptive advertising (Federal Trade Commission Act as amended by Wheeler–Lea Act)
5. Price discrimination if the intent is to injure a competitor (Robinson–Patman Act)

The following practices are also illegal when they substantially lessen competition or tend to create a monopoly:
1. Tying contracts (Clayton Act, Sec. 3)
2. Exclusive dealings (Clayton Act, Sec. 3)
3. Interlocking stockholdings and horizontal mergers (Clayton Act, Sec. 7, as amended by Celler–Kefauver Act)
4. Interlocking directorates (Clayton Act, Sec. 8)

The Effectiveness of Antitrust Policy— The Dominant View

Few economists are completely satisfied with all aspects of antitrust policy, but most observers believe that it has exerted a positive, although probably not dramatic, influence on competitive markets. The Sherman and Clayton Acts prohibit the most efficient methods of collusion (for example, mergers, interlocking boards of directors, and interlocking stockholdings) and thereby raise the costs of colluding. Also, since current collusive agreements must thus be tacit and unenforceable, rivals are more likely to cheat. The expected benefits of collusion have been effectively reduced, and economic theory suggests that the magnitude of anticompetitive collusive business practices should therefore be reduced. In addition, counterproductive (from the viewpoint of society) competitive tactics—exclusive contracts, price discrimination, and tying contracts, for example—have been made more costly. Prohibiting such practices has probably served to reduce entry barriers into markets. Since the passage of the Celler–Kefauver Act, most observers believe that antitrust legislation has effectively limited the power of firms to reduce competition *within an industry* through merger. Today, in contrast with earlier periods in American history, the probability of mergers contributing to industrial concentration—and hindering the competition that tends to erode it—is substantially lower.

**Antitrust Policy—
The Dissenting Views**

Like most other areas of policy, antitrust has its critics. Some of the dissenting views are only partially critical. Many economists, though in agreement with overall objectives, disagree with specific aspects of antitrust policy. Many people in business argue that current legislation is vague and that therefore it is difficult to determine whether a firm is in compliance.

There are three major schools of dissent on antitrust policy, which include (a) those individuals who would like deconcentration policies to be pursued more vigorously, (b) those who believe that the strength of competitiveness renders antitrust policy unnecessary, and (c) those who believe that antitrust policy is simply incapable of attacking industrial concentration. We will look briefly at each of these views.

Antitrust Policies Should Be More Vigorously Enforced. The proponents of this position argue that greater effort is required to ensure the existence of competitive markets. They often point out that antitrust policy has functioned primarily as a holding action. That is, it prevents large firms from *increasing* their market share, but it is ineffective as a means for *reducing* industrial concentration. Policy can end up working against its own objectives. For example, established firms controlling 50 or 60 percent of a market are generally left untouched, whereas two smaller firms with a combined market share of as little as 10 percent may be prohibited from merging. Therefore, current policy often protects strong, established firms while weakening their smaller rivals. Those who see current policy as self-defeating typically favor an antitrust policy that would more thoroughly restructure concentrated industries, dividing large firms in such industries into smaller, independent units.

Antitrust Policy Is Unnecessary. The advocates of this position argue that antitrust legislation places too much emphasis on the number of competitors without recognizing the positive role of dynamic competition. They believe that an antitrust policy that limits business concentration will often promote inefficient business organization and therefore higher prices. They reject the notion that pure competition is a proper standard of economic efficiency.[6] As Joseph Schumpeter, an early proponent of this view of competition and regulation, emphasized two decades ago:

It . . . is a mistake to base the theory of government regulation of industry on the principle that big business should be made to work as the respective industry would work in perfect competition.[7]

Like Schumpeter, the current advocates of this position believe that innovative activity is at the heart of competition. An ingenious innovator may forge ahead of competitors, but competition from other innovators will always be present. Competition is a perpetual game of leapfrog, not a process that is dependent on the number of firms in an industry. Bigness is a natural outgrowth of efficiency and successful innovation. One of the leading proponents for this

---

[6]See Dominick T. Armentano, *Antitrust and Monopoly: Anatomy of a Policy Failure* (New York: John Wiley, 1982), for an excellent presentation of this viewpoint.

[7]Joseph Schumpeter, *Capitalism, Socialism and Democracy* (New York: Harper Torchbooks, 1950), p. 106.

position, John McGee, of the University of Washington, argues that concentration is neither inefficient nor indicative of a lack of competition:

Take an industry of many independent producers, each of which is efficiently using small scale and simple methods to make the same product. . . . Suppose that a revolution in technology or management techniques now occurs, so that there is room in the market for only one firm using the new and most efficient methods. Whether it occurs quickly through merger or gradually through bankruptcy, an atomistic industry is transformed into a "monopoly," albeit one selling the same product at a lower price than before. If expected long-run price should rise, resort can still be had to the old and less efficient ways, which were compatible with . . . small firms. It would be incomplete and misleading to describe that process as a "decline of competition." [8]

Antitrust Policy Is Incapable of Dealing with Big Business. The third group of critics argues that antitrust policy is simply incapable of dealing with a modern economy already dominated by a few hundred industrial giants. The leading proponent of this position, John Kenneth Galbraith, charges that monopoly power is far too prevalent for one to expect that market forces could be imposed on large corporations. Galbraith argues that even if this were possible, competition would hinder, not help, economic development. Galbraith states his case against antitrust and competition as follows:

But it will also be evident that the antitrust laws, if they worked as their proponents hoped, would only make problems worse. Their purpose is to stimulate competition, lower prices, otherwise unshackle resource use and promote a more vigorous expansion of the particular industry. But the problem of the modern economy is not inferior performance of the planning system—of the monopolistic or oligopolistic sector, to revive the traditional terminology. The problem is the greater development here as compared with the market system. And the greater the power, the greater the development. Where the power is least—where economic organization conforms most closely to the goals envisaged by the antitrust laws—the development is least. If they fulfilled the hopes of their supporters and those they support, the antitrust laws would make development more unequal by stimulating development further in precisely those parts of the economy where it is now greatest. [9]

New Directions in Antitrust Policy—The AT&T and IBM Cases

Since the days of the Standard Oil trust nearly a century ago, antitrust policy has been strongly influenced by the notion that ideal competitive conditions are characterized by a large number of small firms. This emphasis on the number and size of rival firms has sometimes been pursued with little regard as to how well the interests of consumers are served by a given industry or firm. The Reagan administration seems to be trying to alter the course of antitrust policy. The administration holds the position that bigness does not necessarily mean badness. Under the Reagan antitrust policy, the sheer size of a firm will be less important than has been true in the past. In the enforcement of antitrust legislation, business efficiency and consumer welfare are presumably to be given greater, and industrial concentration less, consideration.

---

[8] John S. McGee, *In Defense of Industrial Concentration* (New York: Praeger, 1971), pp. 21–22.

[9] John Kenneth Galbraith, *Economics and the Public Purpose* (Boston: Houghton Mifflin, 1973), pp. 216–217.

The thrust of the Reagan policy became clear with the settlements in the IBM and AT&T cases on the same day, January 8, 1982. In both of these cases, the government sought to disaggregate the firms into a larger number of smaller firms. Both of the cases had dragged on for years. The filing of the case against IBM in 1969 was one of the last significant acts of the Johnson administration. The AT&T case was filed in 1975 by the Ford administration. The estimated combined costs of these suits to the government and the companies ran in excess of $500 million.

As part of its settlement, AT&T agreed to divest itself of its 22 local telephone companies with assets of $80 billion. These companies are to continue to operate as regulated public utilities. In return, AT&T is to be permitted to enter the fast-growing electronic data and computer fields, from which it had been barred since 1956. After the final divestiture plan is drafted and approved, AT&T is to have 18 months to separate itself from its local operating telephone companies.

In the early 1980s, foreign competitors were severely testing the dominance of AT&T in the telecommunications industry. Although AT&T had maintained substantial market power in the telephone communication industry, technological developments were eroding its position in the broader electronic communications area. Thus, under the terms of the settlement, the research and development arm of AT&T will operate within the forces of market pressure, while the telephone communication arm will be separated and continue to operate in the regulated sector.

Although AT&T operated as a regulated utility, IBM did not. By the late 1960s, IBM was far and away the dominant firm in the computer-manufacturing industry. Like AT&T, IBM had established an image as an aggressive, innovative company. According to the government's position, IBM was hindering competition by charging prices that were too low for the corporation's smaller rivals to meet. However, the government failed to prove adequately that consumers had been harmed by IBM's dominant share of the market.

The passage of time and the competitive process played important roles in the resolution of both of these cases. In the late 1960s, it was quite possible that the competitiveness of the computer-manufacturing industry was being endangered by the near-monopoly position of IBM, but by the latter half of the 1970s this was no longer true. Technological innovations, foreign competition, and the presence of strong rivals (Prime Computer, Wang, Digital, Control Data, Fujitsu, Hitachi, Burroughs, Cray Research, Olivetti, Siemens, and Philips, for example) were eroding IBM's market position. It was not even clear that any American firm would be the leader in the future computer-manufacturing market. It was against this background that the Reagan administration laid the IBM case to rest.

THEORIES OF REGULATION AND REGULATORY POLICY

Antitrust policy seeks to assure that the structure of an industry is competitive. Regulatory policies tend to be somewhat more direct and specific, often dictating pricing or operational policies for business firms. How does regulation work? To date, economists have been unable to develop a complete theory of regulation. Given the complex array of political and economic factors that are involved, this should not be surprising. In regulated markets, predicting what sellers will offer and how much consumers will be willing to buy at various prices is not enough. The regulatory process also represents (a) buyers who are unwilling to pay the full cost, (b) sellers who are inefficient producers, (c) politicians who are simultaneously considering thousands of pieces of legislation, and (d) voters, many of whom are "rationally uninformed" on regulatory issues. It is not easy to predict how such a complex system will deal with economic problems.

We can, however, facilitate our discussion of regulation by breaking it down into two major types: traditional economic regulation and the newer social regulation. We can also draw some conclusions about the decision-making of both economic and political participants in the regulatory process. Economic analysis indicates that decision-makers in the regulatory process, like those in other areas, respond to incentives. There are three incentive-related characteristics of the regulatory process that are important to keep in mind.

1. The Demand for Regulation Often Stems from the Special Interest Effect and Redistribution Considerations Rather Than from the Pursuit of Economic Efficiency. The wealth of an individual (or business firm) can be increased by an improvement in efficiency and an expansion in production. Regulation introduces another possibility. Sellers can gain if competition in their market is restricted. Buyers can gain, at least in the short run, if a legal requirement forcing producers to supply goods below cost is passed. Regulation opens up an additional avenue whereby those most capable of bending the political process to their advantage can increase their wealth.

Our earlier analysis suggested that special interest groups, such as well-organized, concentrated groups of buyers or sellers, exert a disproportionate influence on the political process. In addition, the regulators themselves often comprise a politically powerful interest group. Bureaucratic entrepreneurs are key figures in the regulatory process. Their cooperation is important to those who are regulated. In exchange for cooperation, politicians and bureaucrats are offered all manner of political support.

These factors suggest that there will be demand for economic regulation even if it contributes to economic inefficiency. The wealth of specific groups of buyers, sellers, and political participants may be enhanced, even though the total size of the economic pie is reduced. This is particularly true if the burden of economic inefficiency is widely dispersed among rationally uninformed taxpayers and groups of consumers.

2. Regulation Is Inflexible—It Often Fails to Adjust to Changing Market Conditions. Dynamic change often makes regulatory procedures obsolete. The introduction of the truck vastly changed the competitiveness of the ground transportation industry (previously dominated by railroad interests). Nonetheless, the regulation of price, entry, and route continued for years, even though competitive forces had long since eliminated the monopoly power of firms in this industry. Similarly, city building codes that may have been appropriate when adopted have become obsolete and now retard the introduction of new, more efficient materials and procedures. For example, in many cities, regulatory procedures have prevented builders from introducing such cost-saving materials as plastic pipes, preconstructed septic tanks, and prefabricated housing units. Why does the process work this way? In contrast with the market process, regulatory procedures generally grant a controlling voice to established producers. The introduction of new, more efficient products would reduce the wealth of the existing

"OF COURSE YOU MAY REGISTER A COMPLAINT ABOUT ALL THE GOVERNMENT PAPERWORK, SIR... BUT IT HAS TO BE IN WRITING."

producers of protected products. The political (regulatory) process is often responsive to these producers' charges that substitute materials (or new producers) would create unfair competition, violate safety codes, or be generally unreliable. Hearings are held. Lawsuits are often filed. Regulatory commissions meet and investigate—again and again. All of these procedures result in cost, delay, and inflexibility.

3. With the Passage of Time, Regulatory Agencies Often Adopt the Views of the Business Interests They Are Supposed to Regulate. Although the initial demand for regulatory action sometimes originates with disorganized groups seeking protection from practices that they consider unfair or indicative of monopolistic power, forces are present that will generally dilute or negate the impact of such groups in the long run. Individual consumers (and taxpayers) have little incentive to be greatly concerned with regulatory actions. Often they are lulled into thinking that since there is a regulatory agency, the "public interest" is served. In contrast, firms (and employees) in regulated industries are vitally interested in the structure and composition of regulatory commissions. Favorable actions by the commission could lead to larger profits, higher-paying jobs, and insulation from the uncertainties of competition. Thus, firms and employee groups, recognizing their potential gain, invest both economic and political resources in an effort to influence the actions of regulatory agencies.

How do vote-maximizing political entrepreneurs behave under these conditions? The payoffs from supporting the views of an apathetic public are small. Clearly, the special interest effect is present. When setting policy and making appointments to regulatory agencies, political entrepreneurs have a strong incentive to support the position of well-organized business and labor interests—often the very groups that the regulatory practices were originally designed to police.

There is evidence that regulatory activity in the United States has grown in importance in recent years. The number and the size of regulatory agencies have expanded substantially since the mid-1960s. Murray Weidenbaum, a former chairman of the Council of Economic Advisers, estimated that the various forms of regulation imposed a cost of approximately $500 per person on the U.S. economy during 1979. As Exhibit 4 illustrates, the number of employees involved in the regulatory process has been increasing rapidly.

Traditional Economic Regulation

Economic Regulation: Regulation of product price or industrial structure, usually imposed on a specific industry. By and large, the production processes utilized by the regulated firms are unaffected by this type of regulation.

Regulation of business activity is not a new development. In 1887, Congress established the Interstate Commerce Commission (ICC), providing it with the authority to regulate the railroad industry and, later, the trucking industry. Commissions were established to regulate the commercial airline and the broadcasting industries (the Civil Aeronautics Board and the Federal Communications Commission, respectively). State commissions have regulated the generation of electrical power for many years. All these activities focus on what has been called **economic regulation.**

There are several important elements of traditional economic regulation. First, it is generally industry-specific. For whatever reason, it is deemed that unregulated market forces create various problems in an industry. Sometimes the problem is monopoly. In other cases, excess supply stemming from "cut-throat" competition is alleged to be a problem. In general, it is believed that

EXHIBIT 4   The growth of the regulatory work force

The rate at which regulation is growing can be seen by the rapidly growing size of the regulatory work force.

Center for the Study of American Business, in *Nation's Business* (February 1981), p. 27.

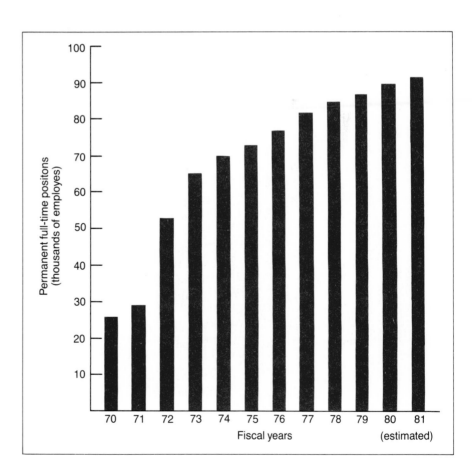

regulation of the industry is necessary to protect the interests of the public and provide for orderly competition. Second, traditional regulation often involves *both* the fixing of price (rates) and the protection of existing firms from potential rivals. Third, as the regulation evolves, it often takes on a cartel-like structure. This is not surprising. As we have discussed, two factors limit the effectiveness of collusive agreements among cartel members. Means must be found to (a) block the entry of potential new competitors and (b) prevent cartel members from cheating on agreements to fix prices. Regulatory agencies are sometimes used to help business firms in a specific industry accomplish both of these objectives.

During the 1970s, widespread dissatisfaction with the traditional regulatory approach developed in several industries. Major steps toward deregulation were taken in the ground and air transportation industries.

Deregulation in the Trucking Industry.   The ICC was initially established to regulate rates in the railroad industry. Actually, much of the railroad industry supported the ICC's establishment. For many years, the commission regulated rates and allocated hauls to various rail shippers. However, beginning in the 1930s, the railroads began to confront stiff competition from the developing trucking industry. Since the trucking industry could be entered with relative ease, competitive forces were pushing rates downward. In response to the demands of railroad and large trucking interests, the regulatory control of the ICC was extended to include the trucking industry in 1935.

The ICC influenced the structure of the ground transportation industry in several ways. First, it limited the number of shippers in interstate commerce. Both rail and truck shippers were required to obtain a license from the ICC before they were permitted to compete in the interstate transportation industry. The ICC issued such licenses only when the proposed new service was deemed "necessary for the public convenience." Established shippers were granted the opportunity to present the ICC with counterevidence attesting that the entry of a new shipper was unnecessary or even harmful. The ICC's policies severely limited entry into the trucking industry.

Second, the ICC regulated shipping rates and permitted the rail and truck industries to establish price-fixing rate bureaus. Competitors who wanted to *reduce* their prices below the schedule established by the rate bureau had to ask the ICC to hear their cases. Typically, it would take six to eight months to obtain a ruling from the ICC. These arrangements strongly discouraged price competition in interstate shipping.

Third, the ICC limited the products that carriers could haul, the routes they could travel, and the number of cities along the route that they could serve. Carriers were prohibited from using price reductions as a means to arrange a "return haul." A carrier that was granted a license to haul from St. Louis to Denver might simultaneously have been prohibited from hauling a return shipment from Kansas City. A carrier's assigned route from New Orleans to Chicago might have required an intermediate stop in Atlanta. The result: miles of wasteful travel and trucks that were empty nearly 40 percent of the time.

The ICC's strict regulation of the trucking industry has been relaxed considerably in recent years. The Motor Carrier Act of 1980 now requires established firms opposing the entry of new rivals to show proof that the rivals would fail to serve the public interest. Generally, the act permits competitors to reduce rates as much as 10 percent without obtaining the ICC's approval.

The ICC was instructed to eliminate its prohibition of carriers from serving intermediate points along a route and its restrictions that limited the ability of carriers to arrange return-trip haulage. The antitrust immunity of the rate-setting bureaus was removed.

A recent study by the Federal Trade Commission indicates that the relaxation of entry barriers and rate-fixing policies has exerted a significant impact on the trucking industry.[10] During the first year after passage of the trucking deregulation legislation, the ICC granted 27,960 additional routes to new and existing carriers, compared to only 2710 during fiscal year 1976. Some 2452 new firms entered the trucking industry. Discount rates were widespread, and in general, freight rates fell between 5 and 20 percent during 1980–1981. There was an influx of small, primarily nonunion carriers into the industry. Price competition led to the acceptance of a temporary wage freeze by the Teamsters union. The influx of competition may well eventually lead to a shakedown in the trucking industry. As the profitability rates of trucking firms fall sharply, renewed pressure for stricter regulatory control will be felt. However, as James Miller, chairman of the FTC, has stated, the likelihood of effective noncompetitive practices being reimposed is low because "the deregulation genie is out of the bottle."[11]

Deregulation in the Airline Industry.   The history of the airline industry has followed a similar pattern. For decades, the airline business was operated under the close supervision of the Civil Aeronautics Board (CAB).[12] In effect, the regulatory powers of the CAB imposed a monopolistic structure on the industry. The CAB blocked competitive entry and outlawed competitive pricing. Any carrier that wanted to compete in an interstate route had to convince the CAB that its services were needed. To say that the CAB limited entry on major routes would be an understatement. Despite more than 150 requests, the CAB did not grant a single trunk (long-distance) route to a new carrier between 1938 and 1978. CAB policy also stifled price competition. Carriers that wanted to lower prices were required to present an application to the CAB. A hearing would be held, at which time the firm's competitors would have ample opportunity to indicate why the impending rate reduction was unfair or potentially harmful to their operation.

At least partially in response to evidence that regulatory policies were leading to excessive fares, half-empty planes, and a uniform product offering, airline regulatory policies in the United States were substantially relaxed in the late 1970s. Under the direction of economist Alfred Kahn, the CAB moved toward deregulation. Carriers were permitted to raise prices by as much as 10 percent and lower them by as much as 70 percent merely by giving the CAB notice 45 days in advance. In 1978, Congress passed the Airline Deregulation Act, which reduced the restrictions on price competition and entry into the industry.

---

[10]See James C. Miller III, "First Report Card on Trucking Deregulation," *Wall Street Journal,* March 8, 1982.

[11]James C. Miller III, "First Report Card on Trucking Deregulation," *Wall Street Journal,* March 8, 1982.

[12]Many people incorrectly associate the CAB with regulation of air safety, a function that it did perform in the past. However, since 1958, the Federal Aviation Agency has been responsible for air safety rules.

What has been the result of the move toward deregulation? The number of special plans (night-coach discount fares, preplanned charters, seasonal discounts, and so on) has vastly increased. During 1978, on average, air fares dropped an estimated 20 percent, and the number of passenger-miles traveled shot up by nearly 40 percent. Even corporate airline profits rose initially.[13]

Deregulation also led to an increase in the number of firms. In 1982, there were roughly 70 commercial airlines in the United States, up from 33 prior to deregulation. The major established airlines' share of domestic traffic fell from 92 percent in 1979 to 86 percent in 1981. Air traffic is quite cyclical. The recessions of 1979 and 1981, along with the increased competitiveness of the industry, have hit several airline firms quite hard. Braniff, for example, was forced into bankruptcy; other carriers may well follow. However, as some firms go out of business, the remaining firms in the industry are strengthened. When the economy recovers, there is no reason to believe that a competitive airline industry will not recover as well.

The New Social Regulation

Social Regulation: **Legislation designed to improve the health, safety, and environmental conditions available to workers and/or consumers. The legislation usually mandates production procedures, minimum standards, and/or product characteristics to be met by producers and employers.**

Along with movement toward deregulation of industrial structure and prices, there has been a sharp increase in what economists call **social regulation.** The new social regulation is comprised of a series of laws in the areas of health, safety, and the environment. Agencies such as the Occupational Safety and Health Administration (OSHA), Consumer Product Safety Commission (CPSC), Food and Drug Administration (FDA), and Environmental Protection Agency (EPA) have grown rapidly. These new agencies as a group are now larger, in terms of both number of employees and size of budgets, than the older regulatory agencies.

There are several significant differences between the two types of regulation. The older economic regulation focuses on a specific industry, whereas the new social regulation applies to the entire economy. Also, though more broadly based, social regulation is much more involved than economic regulation in the actual details of an individual firm's production. Economic regulation confines its attention to price and product quality—the final outcomes of production. The social regulatory agencies, on the other hand, frequently specify in detail the engineering processes to be followed by regulated firms and industries.

The major cost of social regulation is generally felt in the form of both higher production costs and higher prices. Social regulation requires producers to alter production techniques and facilities in accordance with dictated standards—to install more restrooms, to emit less pollution, or to reduce noise levels, for example—and most of the mandated changes increase costs. Of course, there are costs associated with the process of the regulation itself; employment and operating costs of regulatory agencies must be met, which means higher taxes. The higher cost stemming from mandated regulations

---

[13]Even though the regulatory policies stifled both entry and price competition, they did not eliminate other forms of competitive activity. Since firms were generally free to offer additional flights on *existing* routes, the availability of numerous daily flights on a route was often used as a competitive weapon. Given price regulation, this was wasteful, resulting in excessive flights and half-empty planes. This factor, along with the compliance cost of regulatory procedures, drained off much of the potential monopoly profits of the airline companies. Thus, it is not especially surprising that initially the firms' profits increased with deregulation, even though competitive pressures increased and air fares declined.

can also be seen as a tax. As Exhibit 5 illustrates, the higher cost shifts the supply curve for a good affected by the regulation to the left. Higher prices and a decline in the output of the good result.

The primary goal of social regulation is the attainment of a cleaner, safer, healthier environment. Nearly everyone agrees that this is a worthy objective. However, there is considerable disagreement about the procedures that are most likely to accomplish this objective and the price that should be paid to make even marginal improvements. Resources are scarce. More social regulation will mean less of other things. It should not be any more surprising that people differ with regard to the proper consumption level of environmental amenities than it is that they differ with regard to the proper consumption level of ice cream, for example. If one asked 100 people the best rate of consumption for strawberry ice cream, one would expect a wide variety of answers. Similarly, the extent to which we should give up other things to make automobile travel safer, for example, is a question that each person may answer quite differently. One's preferred consumption rate for auto safety, like the preferred rate for strawberry ice cream, will depend in part on expected cost and who pays that cost. Those who expect others to foot the bill will naturally prefer more of any good or amenity, whether it is ice cream or safe highways.

Differing preferences as to how many other goods should be given up in order to attain a safer, cleaner, healthier environment, comprise only part of the problem faced by regulators. An important characteristic of most socially regulated activities is a lack of information about their effects. This is no accident. In most cases, the lack of information contributes directly to the demand for the regulation. For example, if consumers knew exactly what the effect of a particular drug would be, there would be little need for the Food and Drug Administration to keep that drug unavailable. But many people are unaware of the precise effects of drugs, air pollution, or work-place hazards, even when the information is available to experts. It is costly to communicate information, particularly highly technical information. Thus, sometimes there is a potential payoff from letting the experts decide which drugs, how much air pollution, and what forms of work-place safety should be sought. A lack of solid informa-

EXHIBIT 5   The regulation "tax"

Regulation that requires businesses to adopt more costly production techniques is similar to a tax. If the regulation increases per unit costs by t, the supply curve shifts upward by that amount. Higher prices and a smaller output result.

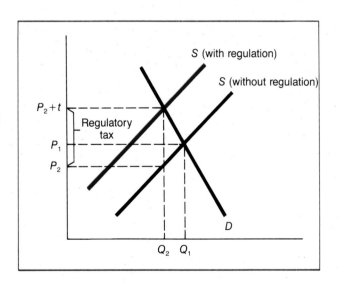

tion generates much of the demand for social regulation. Of course, the lack of information also makes it difficult to evaluate the effectiveness of the regulatory activity (see the feature, "The Regulatory Effects of Motor Vehicle Inspection").

Future Directions. Nearly everyone concedes that regulation, both economic and social, is an imperfect solution. However, it is often difficult to separate beneficial regulations from those that are counterproductive. Although there is strong support for the continuation and expansion of social regulatory activities, recent experience indicates forces favoring deregulation are also present. Improved empirical evidence on the effectiveness of specific social regulation programs may very well emerge during the next decade.

THE REGULATORY EFFECTS OF MOTOR VEHICLE INSPECTION

As of 1980, 27 states and the District of Columbia imposed some form of mandatory vehicle inspection. The rationale for the required inspections is that improved operational effectiveness of motor vehicles is expected to reduce the incidence of traffic accidents and fatalities. Given that there are approximately 18 million motor vehicle accidents and 50,000 traffic fatalities each year, certainly the objectives of this program are laudable.

However, a recent detailed empirical study by Mark Crain of the Center for Public Choice at George Mason University suggests that the vehicle-inspection programs are failing to exert any detectable impact on the safety of motor vehicle travel. According to Crain, there is no statistical relationship between the number of travel-related accidents, injuries, and deaths in states *with* inspection programs and the number in states *without* such programs. Whether the inspections are required once or twice yearly and whether they are performed by publicly or privately operated inspection stations seem to have no perceptible influence on this finding.

Crain believes there are several reasons why the programs are

ineffective. First, it is not obvious that vehicle inspection is a feasible method of detecting the important potential sources of mechanical failure. Although bad tires and faulty headlights can be observed, drivers are usually well aware of these problems and adjust their driving accordingly. The really important sources of mechanical failure, such as a brake line that will leak or a steering mechanism that will fail *sometime in the near future*, are much more difficult to detect. Given the inspectors' lack of incentive—and the absence of a specific mandate for identifying such potential problems—the inspection system can probably do little to improve the actual operational safety of motor vehicles. Second, Crain points out that even if vehicle inspection *does* initially improve vehicle safety, the potential effect on traffic and travel safety may be offset by drivers who take more risks than they would otherwise because they assume the vehicle to be mechanically sound by virtue of having been inspected. Therefore, they may drive faster and place more confidence in the mechanical ability of the vehicle. These factors may offset the positive effects of the inspections.

Crain places the annual costs of safety-inspection programs at $200 million in fees, $2 to $7 billion in unneeded repairs, $30 million in lost

time for vehicle owners, and $200 million in resources necessary to carry out the inspection program. Given these costs, if the programs are ineffective, why have they not been repealed? Lack of information is, of course, one explanation. Crain's study has had some impact. Thus far, five states have abolished their inspection programs, at least partially in response to Crain's findings. However, it should be noted that the inspection programs do generate beneficiaries. At least some of the expenditures on the program represent gains to various groups and industries involved in providing the inspections, supplying replacement parts, and performing maintenance services. As might be expected, interest groups and trade associations, representing those businesses that perform inspection-related services, have been the most vocal in opposing repeal of the programs and advocating instead a nationally standardized inspection program. Crain's analysis of the inspection program emphasizes the importance of differentiating between stated goals and actual results when evaluating regulatory policy.[14]

---

[14]See W. Mark Crain, *Vehicle Safety Inspection Systems—How Effective?* (Washington, D.C.: American Enterprise Institute, 1980).

EXHIBIT 2   The short-run demand schedule of a firm

SunKissed, Inc., sells and installs swimming pools in a competitive industry. The pools are sold separately. When a pool is sold, the firm receives a $1000 installation fee. Given the firm's current fixed capital, column 2 shows how total output changes as additional units of labor are hired. The marginal revenue product schedule of labor (column 6) is the firm's short-run demand curve for that input.

(1) Units of the Variable Factor (Skilled Labor)	(2) Total Output (Pools Installed per Month)	(3) Marginal Product, Change in (2) Change in (1)	(4) Product Installation Price	(5) Total Revenue, (2) × (4)	(6) Marginal Revenue Product, (3) × (4)
0	0	—	$1000	$ 0	—
1	5.0	5.0	1000	5,000	$5000
2	9.0	4.0	1000	9,000	4000
3	12.0	3.0	1000	12,000	3000
4	14.0	2.0	1000	14,000	2000
5	15.5	1.5	1000	15,500	1500
6	16.5	1.0	1000	16,500	1000
7	17.0	0.5	1000	17,000	500

Employment of labor, as well as other resources, will be expanded as long as MRP exceeds resource costs. Thus, as Exhibit 3 illustrates, the marginal revenue product curve is also the firm's demand curve for the resource.[3] At a monthly wage of $5000, SunKissed would hire only one worker. If the monthly wage dropped to $4000, two workers would be hired. At still lower wage rates, additional workers would be hired.

The location of the firm's MRP curve depends upon (a) the price of the product, (b) the productivity of the resource, and (c) the amount of other resources with which the resource is working. Changes in any other of these three factors will cause the MRP curve to shift. For example, if SunKissed obtained a new machine that made it possible for the workers to install more pools each month, the MRP curve for labor would increase. This increase in the quantity of the other resources working with labor would increase labor's productivity.

Adding Other Factors of Production

Thus far, we have analyzed the firm's hiring decision assuming that it employed one variable resource (labor) and one fixed resource. Of course, production usually involves the use of many resources. When a firm employs multiple resources, how should the resources be combined to produce the product? We can answer this question by considering either the conditions for profit maximization or the conditions for cost minimization.

Profit Maximization When Multiple Resources Are Employed.   The same decision-making considerations apply when the firm employs several factors of production. The profit-maximizing firm will expand its *employment of a resource* as long as the marginal revenue product of the resource exceeds its employment

---

[3]Strictly speaking, this is true only for a variable resource that is employed with a fixed amount of another factor.

EXHIBIT 3   The firm's demand curve for a resource

The firm's demand curve for a resource will reflect the marginal revenue product of the resource. In the short run, it will slope downward because the marginal product of the resource will fall as more of it is used with a fixed amount of other resources. The location of the MRP curve will depend on (a) the price of the product, (b) the productivity of the resource, and (c) the quantity of other factors working with the resource.

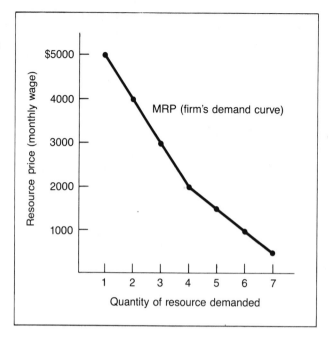

cost. If we assume that resources are perfectly divisible, the profit-maximizing decision rule implies that, in equilibrium, the marginal revenue product of each resource will be equal to the price of the resource. Therefore, the following conditions will exist for the profit-maximizing firm:

$$\text{MRP of skilled labor} = P_{SL} \text{ (wage rate of skilled labor)}$$
$$\text{MRP of unskilled labor} = P_{UL} \text{ (wage rate of unskilled labor)}$$
$$\text{MRP of machine} = P_M \text{ (explicit or implicit rental price of machine A)}$$

and so on, for all other factors.

Cost Minimization When Multiple Resources Are Employed.   If the firm is maximizing profits, clearly it must produce the profit-maximizing output at the least possible cost. If the firm is minimizing costs, the marginal dollar expenditure for each resource will have the same impact on output as every other marginal resource expenditure. Factors of production will be employed such that the marginal product per last dollar spent on each factor is the same for all factors.

Suppose that a dollar expenditure on labor caused output to rise by ten units, whereas an additional dollar expenditure on machines generated only a five-unit expansion in output. Under these circumstances, five more units of output would result if the firm spent $1 less on machines and $1 more on labor. The firm's total (and per unit) cost would be reduced if it substituted labor for machines. If the marginal dollar spent on one resource increases output by a larger amount than a dollar expenditure on other resources, costs can always be reduced by substituting resources with a high marginal product *per dollar* for those with a low marginal product *per dollar expenditure.* This substitution should continue until the marginal product per dollar expenditure is equalized—that is, until the resource combination that minimizes cost is attained. When this is true, the proportional relationship between the price of each resource and its marginal product will be equal for all resources. Therefore, the following condition exists when per unit costs are minimized:

$$\frac{\text{MP of skilled labor}}{\text{price of skilled labor}} = \frac{\text{MP of unskilled labor}}{\text{price of unskilled labor}}$$

$$= \frac{\text{MP of machine A}}{\text{price (rental value) of machine A}}$$

and so on, for the other factors.

In the real world, it is sometimes difficult to measure the marginal product of a factor. Businesspeople may not necessarily think in terms of equating the marginal product/price ratio for each factor of production. Nonetheless, if they are minimizing cost, this condition will be present. Real-world decision-makers may use experience, trial and error, and intuitive rules that are nevertheless consistent with cost-minimization and profit-maximizing criteria. However, when profits are maximized and the cost-minimization method of production is attained, regardless of the procedures used, the outcome will be *as if* the employer had followed the profit-maximization and cost-minimization decision-making rules that we have just discussed.

MARGINAL PRODUCTIVITY, DEMAND, AND ECONOMIC JUSTICE

According to the law of diminishing marginal returns, as the employment level of a resource increases, other things constant, the marginal product (and marginal revenue product) of the resource will decline. As we have just seen, a profit-maximizing employer will expand the use of a resource until its marginal revenue product is equal to the price of the resource. If the price of the resource declines, employers will increase their utilization level of that resource. Therefore, as Exhibit 4 shows, the marginal productivity approach can be used to illustrate the inverse relationship between quantity demanded and resource price.

Some observers, noting that under pure competition the price of each resource is just equal to the value of what it produces (that is, input price equals marginal product of the input multiplied by the price of the product), have argued that competitive markets are "just" or "equitable" because each resource gets paid exactly what it is worth. However, there is a major defect in this line of reasoning. The "marginal productivity" of labor (or any other factor) cannot be determined independently of the contribution of other factors. When a product is produced by a combination of factors, as is almost invariably the case, it is impossible to assign a *specific proportion of the total output* to each resource. For example, if one uses a tractor, an acre of land, and seed to produce wheat, one cannot accurately state that labor (or the seed or the land) produced one-half or any other proportion of the output. Hence, those who argue that the factor payments generated by competitive markets are just, because each resource gets paid according to its productive contribution, are assuming one can assign a *specific* proportion of the total output to each resource, which is

EXHIBIT 4   Marginal productivity and demand

Other things constant, an increase in the employment level will cause the MRP of a resource to decline. The larger quantity of the resource can be employed only at a lower price.

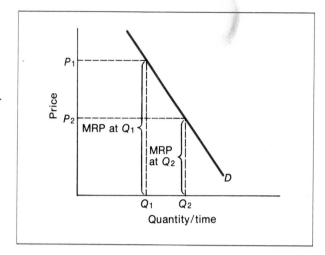

not possible. The marginal product can be used as a measure of the change in total output *associated* with the use of an additional unit of a resource; but this measurement does not *directly* link one resource with one segment of output.

The marginal productivity theory is really a theory about the demand for resources. The central proposition of the theory is that profit-maximizing employers will never pay more for a unit of input, whether it is skilled labor, a machine, or an acre of land, than the input is worth to them. The worth of a unit of input to the firm is determined by how much additional revenue (marginal revenue product) is generated (or seems to be generated) when the unit is used. That is, pursuit of profit will induce employers to hire additional units of each resource as long as the units' marginal productivity generates revenues in excess of costs. Resource prices will tend to reflect—though somewhat roughly in the real world—the marginal productivity of the resource.

However, the price of each resource is determined by conditions of supply as well as demand. Although marginal productivity theory helps us to understand the demand side of the market, it reveals nothing about the *share of the total product* produced by a resource or the justice of a resource price. We must analyze the supply of resources to factor markets in order to complete the picture.

THE SUPPLY OF RESOURCES

In the immediate short-run period, the *total supply* of specific resources, both human and nonhuman, will be virtually fixed. However, resources usually have alternative uses; they can typically be used to help produce a variety of products. Within the fixed total supply there will be some flexibility. The principle of utility maximization implies that resource owners will use their factors of production in a manner that leads to the greatest net advantage to themselves. Of course, both monetary and nonpecuniary considerations will influence their decisions.

In the short run, the quantity of a resource supplied *to a specific use* is directly related to price. Resource owners will shift factors of production toward uses for which compensation has risen and away from areas where resource prices have fallen. Thus, the supply curve for a specific resource (skilled labor, engineering service, or farm land, for example) will slope upward to the right.

The elasticity of supply to a particular use will be dependent on **resource mobility.** Resources that can be easily transferred from one use to another in response to changing price incentives—in other words, those resources with a great many alternative uses or locations—are said to be highly mobile. The supply of such factors to any specific use will be elastic. Factors that have few alternative uses are said to be immobile and will have an inelastic short-run supply.

What can we say about resource mobility in the real world? First, let us consider the mobility of labor. When labor skills can be transferred easily and quickly, human capital is highly mobile. Within skill categories (for example, plumber, store manager, accountant, and secretary), labor will be highly mobile *within the same geographical area.* Movements between geographical areas and from one skill category to another are more costly to accomplish. Thus, labor will be less mobile for movements of this variety.

What about the mobility of land? Land is highly mobile among uses *when location does not matter.* For example, the same land can often be used to raise either corn, wheat, soybeans, or oats. Thus, the supply of land allocated to the production of each of these commodities will be highly responsive to changes in their relative prices. Undeveloped land on the outskirts of cities is particularly mobile among uses. In addition to its value in agriculture, such land might be quickly subdivided and used for a housing development or shopping center. However, since land is totally immobile physically, supply is unresponsive to *changes in price that reflect the desirability of a location.*

Typically, machines are not very mobile among uses. A machine developed to produce airplane wings is seldom of much use in the production of automobiles, appliances, and other products. Steel mills cannot easily be converted to produce aluminum. Of course, there are some exceptions. Trucks can typically be used to haul a variety of products. Building space can often be converted from one use to another. In the short run, however, immobility and inelasticity of supply are characteristic of much of our physical capital.

Resource Mobility: A term that refers to the ease with which factors of production are able to move among alternative uses. Resources that can easily be transferred to a different use or location are said to be highly mobile. In contrast, when a resource has few alternative uses, it is immobile. For example, the skills of a trained rodeo rider would be highly immobile, since they cannot easily be transferred to other lines of work.

Long-Run Supply

In the long run, the supply of resources is not fixed. Machines wear out, human skills depreciate, and even the fertility of land declines with use and erosion. These factors reduce the supply of resources. However, through investment, the supply of productive resources can be expanded. Current resources can be invested to expand the stock of machines, buildings, and durable assets. Alternatively, current resources can be used to train, educate, and develop the skills of future labor force participants. The supply of both physical and human resources in the long run is determined primarily by investment and depreciation.

Price incentives will, of course, influence the investment decisions of both firms and individuals. Considering both monetary and nonmonetary factors, investors will choose those alternatives they believe to be most advantageous. Higher resource prices will induce utility-maximizing investors to supply a larger amount of the resource. In contrast, other things constant, lower resource prices will reduce the incentive to expand the future supply by investing. Therefore, the long-run supply curve for a resource, like the short-run curve, will slope upward to the right.

The theory of long-run resource supply is general. The expected payoff from an investment alternative will influence the decisions of investors in human, as well as physical, capital. For example, the higher salaries of physical and space scientists employed in the expanding space program during the early 1960s induced an expanding number of college students to enter these fields. Similarly, attractive earning opportunities in accounting and law led to an increase in investment and quantity supplied in these areas during the period from 1965 to 1975. When government space efforts tapered off in the late 1960s, the salaries and employment opportunities in physics, aerospace engineering, and astronomy declined. As college enrollments in these areas in the early 1970s attest, human capital investment declined accordingly. In the late 1970s, the demand for petroleum engineers increased. Predictably, salaries rose sharply, as did the number of students graduating in the field of petroleum engineering. As in other markets, people were responding to changes in relative prices.

Considering both monetary and nonmonetary factors, investors will not knowingly invest in areas of low return when higher returns are available elsewhere. Of course, since human capital is embodied in the individual, non-pecuniary considerations will typically be more important for human than for physical capital. Nonetheless, expected monetary payoffs will influence investment decisions in both areas.

The long run, of course, is not a specified length of time. Investment can increase the availability of some resources fairly quickly. For example, it does not take very long to train additional bus drivers. Thus, in the absence of barriers to entry, the quantity of bus drivers supplied will expand rapidly in response to higher wages. However, the gestation period between expansion in investment and an increase in quantity supplied is substantially longer for some resources. It takes a long time to train physicians, dentists, lawyers, and pharmacists. Higher earnings in these occupations may have only a small impact on their *current* availability. Additional investment will go into these areas, but it will typically be several years before there is any substantial increase in the quantity supplied in response to higher earnings for these resources.

Because supply can be substantially expanded over time by investment, the supply of a resource will be much more elastic in the long run than in the short run. This is particularly true when there is a lengthy gestation period between an increase in investment and an actual increase in the availability of a resource. Using nursing services as an example, Exhibit 5 illustrates the relationship between the short- and long-run supply of resources. An increase in the price (wage rate) of nursing services will result in some immediate increase in quantity supplied. Trained nurses may choose to work more hours. Nurses not in the labor force may be drawn back into nursing. With time, the more attractive employment opportunities in nursing will cause the level of investment in human capital in this area to expand (for example, more student nurses). However, since most nursing programs take two to four years, it will be several years before the additional investment will begin to have an impact on supply. In the long run, the quantity of nurses supplied may be quite elastic, but in the short run it is likely to be highly inelastic.

EXHIBIT 5 **Time and the elasticity of supply for resources**

The supply of nursing services (and other resources that require a substantial period of time between current investment and expansion in the future quantity supplied) will be far more inelastic in the short run than in the long run.

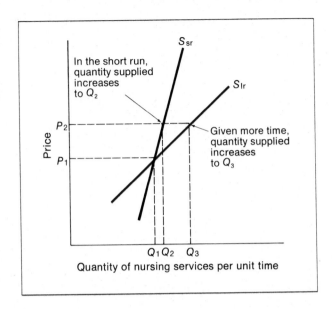

In the short run, quantity supplied increases to Q_2

Given more time, quantity supplied increases to Q_3

Quantity of nursing services per unit time

SUPPLY, DEMAND, AND RESOURCE PRICES

The theories of both supply and demand for resources have been analyzed. This is all we need to develop the theory of resource pricing in competitive markets. When factor prices are free to vary, resource prices will bring the choices of buyers and sellers into line with each other. The forces of supply and demand operate in precisely the same manner for both resource and product markets. Pressures are present that will push resource prices toward equilibrium, where quantity supplied and quantity demanded are equal. An above-equilibrium price will generate an excess supply, that is, unsold resource services. Since they are unable to sell their services at the above-equilibrium price, some resource owners will reduce their price, pushing the market price toward equilibrium. When a resource price is below equilibrium, excess demand will be present. Rather than do without the resource, employers will bid up the price, eliminating the excess supply.

Resource markets, like product markets, generally go through a series of operations in response to changes. Complete adjustment does not take place instantaneously. Depending on the nature of the resource, a substantial period of time may be necessary before the availability of the resource can be greatly increased. However, the nature of the process is straightforward. For example, at a higher level of demand the price of a resource initially would rise sharply, particularly if the short-run supply was quite inelastic. However, at the higher price, *with time*, the quantity of the resource supplied would expand. If it was a natural resource, individuals and firms would put forth a greater effort to discover and develop the now more valuable productive factor. If it was physical capital, a building or machine, current suppliers would have greater incentive to work intensively to expand production. New suppliers would be drawn into the market. Higher prices for human capital resources would also lead to an expansion in the quantity supplied. With time, more people would acquire the

EXHIBIT 6   Adjusting to dynamic change

An increase in demand for a resource will typically cause price to rise more in the short run than in the long run. Can you explain why?

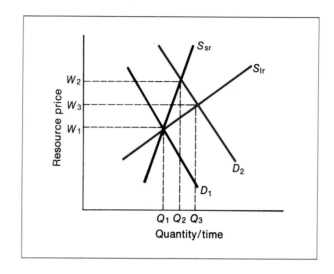

OUTSTANDING ECONOMIST

Gary Becker (1930–   )

This innovative economist is perhaps best known for his ingenious application of economics to several areas that many had previously considered to be noneconomic by nature. Before his pioneering book, *The Economics of Discrimination,*[4] the research of economists

in this area was scanty. Apparently, many felt that something as irrational as prejudice was beyond the realm of a rational science like economics. Becker's book proved otherwise. He developed a general theory that could be used to analyze (and measure) the impact of discrimination in several areas on the status of minorities and women. His work laid the foundation for the burgeoning of research interest in the economics of discrimination that took place during the 1960s and 1970s.

Later, Becker applied economic analysis to such seemingly noneconomic subjects as crime prevention, family development, an individual's allocation of time, and even the selection of a marriage partner.[5] His imaginative work earned him the J. B. Clark Award (1967), granted by the American Economic Association to the "outstanding economist under 40."

The human capital approach

underlies much of Becker's research. His widely acclaimed book, *Human Capital,*[6] is already a classic. This work developed a theoretical foundation for human investment decisions in education, on-the-job training, migration, and health. Becker looks at the individual as a "firm" that will invest in human resources if it is "profitable" to do so. Considering both monetary and nonmonetary factors, the human capital decisions of these profit-maximizing (or utility-maximizing) individuals will be based on the attractiveness (rate of return) of alternative investment opportunities. High rates of return will attract human capital investment to an area, whereas low rates of return will repel it.

Becker has estimated the rate of return for both a high school and college education. His work, along with that of others, suggests that, *on average,* human capital investments in education are highly profitable. A professor at the University of Chicago, Becker also taught at Columbia University for several years.

[4]Gary Becker, *The Economics of Discrimination* (Chicago: University of Chicago Press, 1957).

[5]Gary Becker, *The Economic Approach to Human Behavior* (Chicago: University of Chicago Press, 1976), and Gary Becker and W. M. Landes, *Essays in the Economics of Crime and Punishment* (New York: Columbia University Press, 1974).

[6]Gary Becker, *Human Capital* (New York: Columbia University Press, 1964).

necessary training, education, and experience to develop the skills that would now command a higher price. The expansion of the supply would eventually moderate the price rise. Because of these forces, as Exhibit 6 illustrates, the long-run price increase would be less than the short-run increase.

Similarly, a reduction in demand would cause the price of the resource to fall further in the short run than over a longer period of time. At the lower price, some resource suppliers would use their talents in other areas. The incentive for potential new suppliers to offer the resource would be reduced by the fall in price. With time, the quantity of the resource supplied would become more elastic, moderating the long-run decline in price. Those with the poorest alternatives (that is, lowest opportunity cost) would continue to provide the resource at the lower prices. Those with better alternatives would move to other areas.

LOOKING AHEAD

Now that we have outlined the theoretical underpinnings of factor markets, we can apply the analysis to a broad range of economic issues. The next chapter will focus on the labor market and the determination of wage rates. Later we will focus on the capital market and the allocation of resources over time. The operation of these two markets plays an important role in determining the distribution of income, a topic that will also be analyzed in detail in a subsequent chapter.

CHAPTER LEARNING OBJECTIVES

1 Factor markets, where productive goods and services are bought and sold, help to determine what is produced, how it is produced, and the distribution of income (output). There are two broad classes of productive resources—nonhuman capital and human capital. Both are durable in the sense that they will last into the future, thereby enhancing future productive capabilities. Both yield income to their owners. Investment can expand the future supply of both.

2 The demand for resources is derived from the demand for the products that the resources help to produce. The quantity of a resource demanded is inversely related to its price. If the price of a resource increases, less of it will be used for two reasons. First, producers will substitute other resources for the now more expensive input (substitution in production). Second, the higher resource price will lead to higher prices for products that the resource helps to make, causing consumers to reduce their purchases of those goods (substitution in consumption).

3 The short-run market demand curve will be more inelastic than the long-run curve. It will take time for producers to adjust their production process in order to use more of the less expensive resources and less of the more expensive resources.

4 The demand curve for a resource, like the demand for a product, may shift. The major factors that can increase the demand for a resource are (a) an increase in demand for products that use the resource, (b) an increase in the productivity of the resource, and (c) an increase in the price of substitute resources.

5 Profit-maximizing firms will hire additional units of a resource as long as the marginal revenue product of the resource exceeds its hiring cost, usually the price of the resource. If resources are perfectly divisible, firms will expand their utilization of each resource until the marginal revenue product of each resource is just equal to its price.

6 When a firm is minimizing its costs, it will employ each factor of production up to the point at which the marginal product per last dollar spent on the factor is equal for all factors. This condition implies that the marginal product of labor divided by the

price of labor must equal the marginal product of capital (machines) divided by the price of capital and that this ratio (MP_i/P_i) must be the same for all other inputs used by the firm. When real-world decision-makers minimize per unit costs, the outcome will be *as if* they had followed these mathematical procedures, even though they may not consciously do so.

7 Resource owners will use their factors of production in the manner that they consider most advantageous to themselves. Many resources will be relatively immobile in the short run. The less mobile a resource, the more inelastic its short-run supply. There will be a positive relationship between amount supplied and resource price even in the short run.

8 In the long run, investment and depreciation will alter resource supply. Resource owners will shift factors of production toward areas in which resource prices have risen and away from areas where resource prices have fallen. Thus, the long-run supply will be more elastic than the short-run supply.

9 The prices of resources will be determined by both supply and demand. The demand for a resource will reflect the demand for products that it helps to make. The supply of resources will reflect the human and physical capital investment decisions of individuals and firms.

10 Changing resource prices will influence the decisions of both users and suppliers. Higher resource prices give users a greater incentive to turn to substitutes and stimulate suppliers to provide more of the resource. Since these adjustments take time, when the demand for a resource expands, the price will usually rise more in the short run than in the long run. Similarly, when there is a fall in resource demand, price will decline more in the short run than in the long run.

THE ECONOMIC WAY OF THINKING—DISCUSSION QUESTIONS

1 What is the meaning of the expression "invest in human capital"? In what sense is the decision to invest in human capital like the decision to invest in physical capital? Is human capital investment risky? Explain.

2 (a) "Firms will hire a resource only if they can make money by doing so." (b) "In a market economy, each resource will tend to be paid according to its marginal product. Highly productive resources will command high prices, whereas less productive resources will command lower prices."
Are (a) and (b) both correct? Are they inconsistent with each other? Explain.

3 Use the information of Exhibit 2 to answer the following:
(a) How many skilled laborers would SunKissed hire at a monthly wage of $1200 if it were attempting to maximize profits in its pool installation business?
(b) What would the firm's maximum profit be if its fixed costs were $7000?
(c) Suppose that there was a decline in demand for pools, reducing the market price for installation service to $750. At this demand level, how many employees would SunKissed hire at $1200 per month in the short run? Would SunKissed stay in business at the lower market price? Explain.

4 Are productivity gains the major source of higher wages? If so, how does one account for the rising real wages of barbers, who by and large have used the same technique for half a century? (*Hint:* Do not forget opportunity cost and supply.)

5 "However desirable they might be from an equity viewpoint, programs designed to reduce wage differentials will necessarily reduce the incentive of people to act efficiently and use their productive abilities in those areas where demand is greatest relative to supply." Do you agree or disagree? Why?

6 What's Wrong with This Way of Thinking?

"The downward-sloping marginal revenue product curve of labor shows that better workers are hired first. The workers hired later are less productive."

Properly conceived, education produces a labor force that is more skilled, more adaptable to the needs of a changing economy, and more likely to develop the imaginative ideas, techniques, and products which are critical to the processes of economic expansion and social adaptation to change. By doing so—by contributing to worker productivity—the education process qualifies handsomely as a process of investment in human capital.[1]
Burton Weisbrod

24

EARNINGS, SKILL ACQUISITION, AND THE JOB MARKET

The wages of U.S. workers are the highest in the world—and they have been increasing. The compensation for a day of work by the average labor force participant buys far more today than it did 30 years ago. Individual wages, however, vary widely. An unskilled laborer may earn the $3.35 minimum wage, or something close to it. Lawyers and physicians often earn $60 per hour. Dentists and even economists might receive $40 per hour.

Why do some earn more than others? Why are earnings, measured in terms of their purchasing power, so high for Americans? Can high wages be legislated? In this chapter, we analyze these questions.

WHY DO EARNINGS DIFFER?

The earnings of paired individuals in the same occupation or with the same amount of education very often differ substantially. The earnings of persons with the same family background also vary widely. For example, one researcher found that the average earnings differential between brothers was $5600, compared to $6200 for men paired randomly.[2] In addition, the earnings of persons with the same IQ, level of training, or amount of experience typically differ. How do economists explain these variations? Several factors combine to determine the earning power of an individual. Some seem to be the result of good or bad fortune. Others are clearly the result of conscious decisions made by individuals. In the previous chapter, we analyzed how the market forces of supply and demand operate to determine resource prices. The subject of earnings differentials can be usefully approached within the framework of this model.

If (a) all individuals were homogeneous, (b) all jobs were equally attractive, and (c) workers were perfectly mobile among jobs, the earnings of all employees in a competitive economy would be equal. If, given these conditions,

---

[1]Burton A. Weisbrod, "Investing in Human Capital," *Journal of Human Resources* (Summer 1966), pp. 5–21.

[2]Christopher Jencks, *Inequality* (New York: Basic Books, 1972), p. 220.

higher wages existed in any area of the economy, the supply of workers to that area would expand until the wage differential was eliminated. Similarly, low wages in any area would cause workers to exit until wages in that area returned to parity. However, earnings differentials cannot be avoided in the real world, because the conditions necessary for earnings equality do not exist.

Earnings Differentials Due to Nonhomogeneous Labor

Clearly, all workers are not the same. They differ in several important respects, which influence both the supply of and demand for their services.

Worker Productivity. The demand for employees who are highly productive will be greater than the demand for those who are less productive. Persons who can operate a machine more skillfully, hit a baseball more consistently, or sell life insurance policies with greater regularity will have a higher marginal revenue product than their less skillful counterparts. Because they are more productive, their services will command a higher wage from employers.

Workers can increase their productivity by investment in human capital. Formal education, vocational training, skill-building experience, and proper health care to maintain physical fitness can enhance worker productivity. Of course, native ability and motivation will influence the rate at which an individual can transform educational and training experience into greater productivity. Most of us would not be able to hit a baseball with the skill of Steve Garvey even if we practiced every day from the time we were old enough to walk. Individuals differ in the amount of valuable skills they develop from a year of education, vocational school, or on-the-job training. We should not expect a rigid relationship to exist between years of training (or education) and skill level.

In general, more able persons appear to receive more education and training. Not surprisingly, greater investment in human capital leads to higher average annual earnings *once the person enters the labor force full-time*. As Exhibit 1 shows, persons with more education have higher earnings. Similarly, economic research has shown that a positive relationship exists between training and earnings.

Specialized Skills. Investment in human capital and development of specialized skills can protect high-wage workers from the competition of others willing to offer their services at a lower price. Few persons could develop the specialized skills of a Johnny Carson or Tracy Austin. Similarly, skill (and human capital) factors also limit the supply of heart surgeons, trial lawyers, engineers, and business entrepreneurs. As Exhibit 2 illustrates, when the demand for a specialized resource is great relative to its supply, the resource will be able to command a high wage. In 1979, the earnings of engineers were $31,300, almost three times the figure for laborers. Since engineers possess specialized skills that have been developed by both formal education (usually between 16 and 18 years) and experience, laborers are unable to compete directly in the engineering market. In contrast, the training and skill requirements for laborers are possessed by many. Since the supply of laborers is large relative to the demand, their earnings are substantially less.

It is important to keep in mind that wages are determined by demand *relative to supply*. Other things constant, a skilled specialist will command a higher wage than one with less skill, but high skill will not *guarantee* high wages

EXHIBIT 1 Education and earnings, 1979

Investment in education leads to a higher income. On average, individuals with more years of schooling earn more during their lifetimes.

U.S. Department of Commerce, *Current Population Reports,* P-60 Series, no. 129, Table 52.

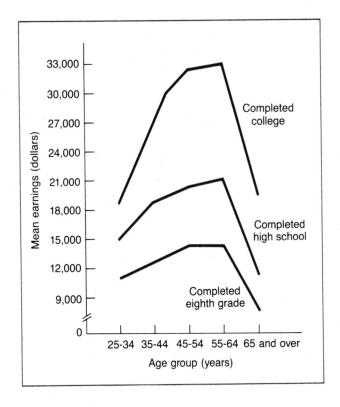

EXHIBIT 2 Supply, demand, and wage differentials

The mean number of years of education for engineers is 16.6 compared to 10.6 for laborers. Because of their specialized skills, high-wage engineers are protected from direct competition with laborers and other persons who do not possess such skills.

Earnings data are from the U.S. Department of Commerce.

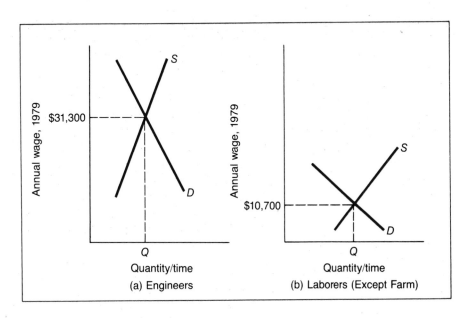

in the absence of demand. For example, expert harness makers and blacksmiths typically command low wages today, even though the supply of these workers is small—because demand even for the services of experts in these areas is low.

Worker Preferences.   This very important source of earnings differentials is sometimes overlooked. People have different objectives in life. Some want to make a great deal of money. Many are willing to work long hours, undergo agonizing training and many years of education, and sacrifice social and family life in order to make money. Others may be "workaholics" because they enjoy their jobs. Still others may be satisfied with enough money to get by, preferring to spend more time with their family, the Boy Scouts, the television, or the local tavern keeper.

Economics does not indicate that one set of worker preferences is more desirable than another, any more than it suggests that people should eat more vegetables and less meat. However, economics does indicate that these factors contribute to differences in wages and earnings. Other things constant, persons who are more highly motivated by monetary objectives will be more likely to do the things necessary to command higher wage rates.

Race and Sex.   Discrimination on the basis of race or sex contributes to earnings differences among individuals. Employment discrimination may directly limit the earnings opportunities of minorities and women. **Employment discrimination** exists when minority or women employees are treated in a different manner than are similarly productive whites or men. Of course, the earnings of minority employees, for example, may differ from whites for reasons other than employment discrimination. Nonemployment discrimination may limit the opportunity of minority groups and women to acquire human capital (for example, quality education or specialized training) that would enhance both their productivity and earnings. If we want to isolate the impact of current employment discrimination, we must (a) adjust for the impact of education, experience, and skill factors and (b) then make comparisons between *similarly qualified* groups of employees who differ with regard to race (or sex) only.

There are two major forms of employment discrimination—wage rates and employment restrictions. Exhibit 3 illustrates the impact of wage discrimination. When majority employees are preferred to minority and female workers, the demand for the latter two groups is reduced. The wages of blacks and women decline relative to those of white men.

Essentially, there is a dual labor market—one market for the favored group and another for the group against which the discrimination is directed. The favored group, whites for example, are preferred, but the less expensive minority employees are a substitute productive resource. Both white and minority employees are employed, but the whites are paid a higher wage rate.

Exclusionary practices may also be an outlet for employment discrimination. Either in response to outside pressure or because of their own views, employers may hire primarily whites and males for certain types of jobs. When minority and female workers are excluded from a large number of occupations, they are *crowded* into a smaller number of remaining jobs and occupations. If entry restraints prevent people from becoming supervisors, bank officers, plumbers, electricians, and truck drivers, they will be forced to accept other

Employment Discrimination: Unequal treatment of persons on the basis of their race, sex, or religion, restricting their employment and earnings opportunities compared to others of similar productivity. Employment discrimination may stem from the prejudices of employers, consumers, and/or fellow employees.

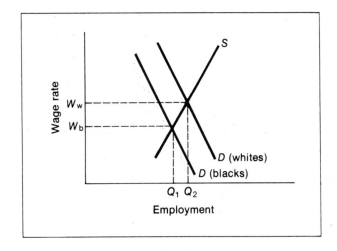

EXHIBIT 3 The impact of direct wage discrimination

If there is employment discrimination against blacks or women, the demand for their services will decline, and their wage rate will fall from W_w to W_b.

alternatives. The supply of labor in the restricted occupations will increase, causing wage rates to fall. The exclusionary practices will result in higher wages for white males holding jobs from which blacks and females are excluded. The outcome will be an overrepresentation of white males in the higher paying occupations, while a disproportionate number of blacks and women will occupy the low-paying, nonrestricted positions. The impact will be a reduction in the earnings of minorities and women relative to white males.

Earnings Differentials Due to Nonhomogeneous Jobs

Nonpecuniary Job Characteristics: Working conditions, prestige, variety, location, employee freedom and responsibilities, and other nonwage characteristics of a job that influence how employees evaluate the job.

When individuals evaluate employment alternatives, they consider working conditions as well as wage rates. Is a job dangerous? Does it offer the opportunity to acquire the experience and training that will enhance future earnings? Is the work strenuous and nerve-racking? Are the working hours, job location, and means of transportation convenient? All of these factors are what economists call **nonpecuniary job characteristics.** Workers are willing to trade off higher wage rates for more favorable nonpecuniary job characteristics. There are numerous examples of this. Because of the dangers involved, aerial window washers (those who hang from windows 20 stories up) earn higher wages than other window washers. Sales jobs involving a great deal of out-of-town travel typically pay more than similar jobs without such inconvenience. Electricians in contract construction are paid more than equally skilled electricians with jobs in which the work and pay are more steady. Because the majority of economists prefer the more independent work environment and intellectual stimulation offered by colleges and universities, the earnings of economists in academia are typically lower than those of economists in business.

Substantial wage differentials exist between similar jobs in (a) large and small firms and (b) urban and rural areas. Nonpecuniary factors, such as transportation costs and locational preferences help to explain these differentials. Large firms must typically draw their labor force from a wider geographical area, resulting in longer average travel time to and from work. Congestion problems are more severe. These factors make employment with large firms less desirable. Thus, they must pay higher wage rates in order to attract the desired size of labor force. Similarly, the lower wages in rural areas probably reflect, at least partially,

IS DISCRIMINATION PROFITABLE TO THE EMPLOYER?

Most people assign the title of "chief discriminator" to the employer. This is because it is the employer who pays lower wages or hires very few minority or female employees even if only in response to consumers, majority employees, union practices, or community pressures. Undoubtedly, however, many employers have followed discriminatory practices of their own volition. Economic theory suggests that it is costly for employers to discriminate when they are merely reflecting their own prejudices. If employers can hire equally productive blacks (or women) at lower wages than for whites (or men), the profit motive gives them a strong incentive to do so. The costs of a discriminator who continues to hire high-wage whites, when similar minority employees are available at a lower wage, will increase. The higher cost will reduce profits.

Major league baseball provides an interesting and easily documented case of an employer paying the cost of discrimination. In the mid-1940s, there were no black players in the "big leagues." Simultaneously, a pool of readily available, proven baseball talent existed in the Negro leagues. The services of most of these players could be purchased at a fraction of the cost of obtaining comparable white players.

Two inputs, white and/or black players, could be used in an effort to win games (an output variable), but the price of an equally productive black player was much lower. Other things constant, firms had an incentive to substitute the less expensive blacks for the higher-priced white players.

After major league baseball had become integrated, the less discriminating employers moved rapidly to employ black players, whereas the highly discriminating teams continued to employ exclusively (or almost exclusively) whites. By the mid-1950s, five teams—the Brooklyn Dodgers, New York Giants, Cleveland Indians, Boston (Milwaukee) Braves, and Chicago White Sox—employed substantially more blacks than the other eleven major league teams.[3] During the period from 1952 to 1956, these five teams were among the top six teams according to won–lost percentage. They won 58 percent of their games, compared to only 46 percent for the highly discriminating teams. Among the teams with few black players, only the New York Yankees were able to compete effectively with the less discriminating teams.

Baseball fans like to watch a winner play. Not only did the less discriminating teams win more games, but their games were also more highly attended. Hiring blacks, largely because of their impact on team performance, paid off nicely at the box office. The less discriminating teams gained, whereas the highly discriminating teams paid a price for their prejudice.

---

[3] See James Gwartney and Charles Haworth, "Employer Cost and Discrimination: The Case of Baseball," *Journal of Political Economy* (June 1974), for a detailed analysis of this topic.

---

employees' willingness to trade off higher wages for jobs in preferred living areas. All of these differences in the nonpecuniary characteristics of jobs contribute to earnings differences among individuals.

Earnings Differentials Due to Immobility of Labor

It is costly to move to a new location or train for a new occupation in order to obtain a job. Such movements do not take place instantaneously. In the real world, labor, like other resources, does not possess perfect mobility. Thus, some wage differentials result from an incomplete adjustment to change.

Since the demand for labor resources is a derived demand, it is affected by changes in product markets. An expansion in the demand for a product causes a rise in the demand for specialized labor to produce the product. Since resources are often highly immobile (that is, the supply is inelastic) in the short run, the expansion in demand may cause the wages of the specialized laborers to rise sharply. This is what happened in the oil-drilling industry in the late 1970s. An expansion in demand triggered a rapid increase in the earnings of petroleum engineers and other specialized personnel. A decline in product demand has the opposite effect. The tapering off of the space program in the late 1960s depressed the wages of engineers, physicists, and space scientists. Demand shifts in the product market favor those in expanding industries but work against those in contracting industries.

Institutional barriers may also limit the mobility of labor. Licensing requirements limit the mobility of labor into many occupations—medicine, taxicab driving, architecture, and undertaking among them. Unions may also follow policies that limit labor mobility and alter the free-market forces of supply and demand. Minimum wage rates may retard the ability of low-skill workers to obtain employment in certain sectors of the economy. All of these restrictions on labor mobility will influence the size of wage differentials among workers.

Thumbnail Sketch—Sources of Earnings Differentials

Differences in workers:
1. Productivity (for example, skills, human capital, native ability, motivation)
2. Specialized skills (primarily human capital plus native ability)
3. Worker preferences (trade-off between money earnings and other things)
4. Race and sex discrimination

Differences in jobs:
1. Location of jobs
2. Nonpecuniary job characteristics (for example, convenience of working hours, job safety, likelihood of temporary layoffs, and working conditions)

Immobility of resources:
1. Temporary disequilibrium resulting from dynamic change
2. Institutional restrictions (for example, occupational licensing and union-imposed restraints)

Summary of Wage Differentials

As the Thumbnail Sketch shows, wage differentials stem from many sources. Many of them play an important allocative role, compensating people for (a) human capital investments that increase their productivity or (b) unfavorable working conditions. Other wage differentials reflect, at least partially, locational preferences or the desire of individuals for higher money income rather than nonmonetary benefits. Still other differentials, such as those related to discrimination and occupational restrictions, are unrelated to worker preferences and are not required to promote efficient production.

PRODUCTIVITY AND THE GENERAL LEVEL OF WAGES

It is also important to understand why the general level of wages varies from one country to another and from one period to another within the same country. Real earnings are vastly greater in the United States than in India or China. In addition, the average real earnings per hour in the United States have approximately doubled during the past 25 years. What factors account for these variations in the general level of wages?

Differences in labor productivity—output produced per worker-hour—are the major source of variation in real wages between nations and between time periods. When the amount produced per worker-hour is high, real wages will be high.

Exhibit 4 illustrates the relationship between real wages and output per

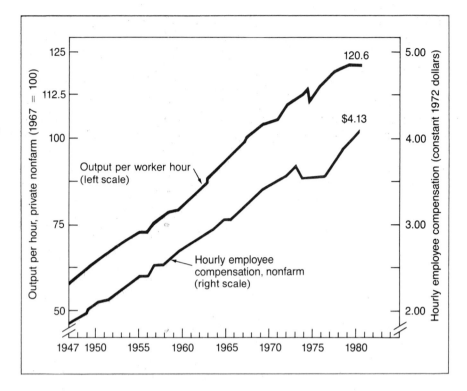

worker-hour since World War II. Between 1947 and 1980 output per worker-hour rose 111 percent in the nonfarm private sector. What happened to employee compensation? During the same time period, the hourly compensation of employees, measured in constant 1972 dollars, increased from $1.94 to $4.13, an increase of 113 percent.

The close relationship between amount produced and real wages should not be surprising. Do not forget that real income and real output are simply two ways of viewing the same thing. Expansion in real income is totally dependent on expansion of output. Without expansion of output, our money incomes, whatever they may be, will not enable us to purchase more goods and services in aggregate.

In the last chapter, we showed that the productivity of a resource, including labor, is dependent on the amount of the other resources with which it works. Contrary to what many believe, physical capital (for example, modern labor-saving machines) is not the enemy of high real wages (see Myths of Economics, "Automation is the major cause of unemployment"). In fact, just the opposite is true.

Machines make it possible for labor to produce more per worker-hour. Are jobs destroyed in the process? Sometimes *specific* jobs are eliminated, but this merely releases human resources so they can be used to expand output in other areas. Output and productivity, not jobs, are the source of high real wages.

Increasing productivity is brought about by a cooperative process. Investment, both in human and nonhuman capital, is vital to the growth of productivity. For several decades, the educational level of members of the work force in the United States has steadily increased. The median number of years of schooling of persons in the labor force in 1980 was 12.8 compared to 10.6 years in 1949. Simultaneously, the nonhuman capital per worker has expanded (although the *growth rate* of capital investment per worker has slowed considerably in recent years). Both the development and innovative application of improved technological methods are also important determinants of the growth of productivity. Technological improvements make it possible to obtain a larger output from the same resource base. Of course, modern technological advancements are often linked to investments in both physical and human capital.

Investment and the Sagging Rate of Growth of Productivity in the United States

Since investment is so important for the growth of future output (and real income), it is useful to compare investment and growth rates in various countries. Ideally, we should analyze investment in both human and physical capital, including resources utilized to improve the available technology. Investment requires that current consumption be sacrificed in order for more resources to be allocated to the production of nonhuman capital, human capital, and technical knowledge with which to expand future production. Other things constant, countries that allocate more to current *investment* will expand their stock of valuable productive assets more rapidly and experience a more rapid growth in income.

Unfortunately, comparable international investment data for human capital have not been developed. However, Exhibit 5 presents International Monetary Fund data for gross fixed capital formation (physical capital) as a percentage of domestic production for several nations. During the period from 1960 to 1980, the share of GNP allocated to investment was considerably lower for the United States than for other major Western nations. Growth in worker compensation in the United States lagged accordingly. On the other hand, countries such as Japan, West Germany, and France, which allocate a much larger share of their domestic product to capital formation, experienced more rapid wage increases during the period.

Even the data of Exhibit 5 probably understate the lag in capital investment *per worker* in the United States. During the period from 1965 to 1980, there was a vast influx of workers into the labor force as the rate of labor force participation among women increased and the children of the post-World

EXHIBIT 5   Investment and the rate of growth in employee compensation, 1960–1979

Country	Gross Fixed Capital Formation as a Percentage of Gross National Product	Growth Rate of Hourly Employee Compensation Deflated by Consumer Price Index (Percent)
United States	17.8	1.3
United Kingdom	18.5	2.7
Italy	20.5	5.0
Canada	22.7	1.7
France	23.3	5.4
West Germany	24.2	10.5
Japan	32.9	8.6

Capital formation data are from *International Financial Statistics,* 1981 supplement (Washington, D. C.: International Monetary Fund, 1978); the compensation data are from *Economic Report of the President, 1982,* Table B–111.

Automation: A production technique that reduces the amount of labor required to produce a good or service. It is beneficial to adopt the new labor-saving technology only if it reduces the cost of production.

"Automation is the major cause of unemployment. If we keep allowing machines to replace people, we are going to run out of jobs."

Machines are substituted for people if, and only if, the machines reduce costs of production. Why has the automatic elevator replaced the operator, the tractor replaced the horse, and the power shovel replaced the ditch digger? Because each is a cheaper method of accomplishing a task.

The fallacy that **automation** causes unemployment stems from a failure to recognize the secondary effects. Employment may decline in a specific industry as the result of automation. However, lower per unit costs in that industry will lead to either (a) additional spending and jobs in other industries or (b) additional output and employment in the specific industry as consumers buy more of the now cheaper good.

Perhaps an example will help to illustrate the secondary effects of automation. Suppose that someone develops a new toothpaste that actually prevents cavities and sells for half the current price of Colgate. At last, we have a toothpaste that really works. Think of the impact the invention will have on dentists, toothpaste producers and their employees, and even the advertising agencies that give us those marvelous toothpaste commercials. What are these people to do? Haven't their jobs been destroyed?

These are the obvious effects; they are seen to be the direct result of the toothpaste invention. What most people do not see are the additional jobs that will indirectly be created by the invention. Consumers will now spend less on toothpaste, dental bills, and pain relievers. Their real income will be higher. They will now be able to spend *more* on other products they would have foregone had it not been for the new invention. They will in-

crease their spending on clothes, recreation, vacations, swimming pools, education, and many other items. This additional spending, which would not have taken place if dental costs had not been reduced by the technological advancement, will generate additional demand and employment in other sectors.

It is undeniable that jobs have been eliminated in the toothpaste and dental industries because of a reduction in consumer spending in these areas. However, *new* jobs have been created in other industries in which consumers have increased their spending as a result of the savings attributable to the new invention.

When the demand for a product is elastic, a cost-saving invention can even generate an increase in employment in the industry affected by the invention. This was essentially what happened in the automobile industry when Henry Ford's mass production techniques reduced the cost (and price) of cars. When the price of automobiles fell 50 percent, consumers bought three times as many cars. Even though the worker-hours *per car* decreased by 25 percent between 1920 and 1930, employment in the industry increased from 250,000 to 380,000 during the period, an increase of approximately 50 percent.

Even if the demand for automobiles had been inelastic, automation would not have caused long-run unemployment. When demand is inelastic, less will be spent on the lower-cost, lower-priced commodity, leaving more to be spent on other goods and services. This spending on other products, which would not have resulted without the new invention, will ensure that there is not a net reduction in employment.

Of course, technological advances that release labor resources may well harm specific individuals or groups. The automatic elevators reduced the job opportunities of elevator operators. Computer technology has reduced the demand for telephone operators. In the future, videotaped lectures may even reduce the job opportunities available to college professors. Thus, the earnings opportunities of specific persons may, at least temporarily, be adversely affected by cost-reducing automated methods. It is understandable why groups directly affected fear and oppose automation.

But focusing on jobs alone can lead to a fundamental misunderstanding about the importance of machines, automation, and technological improvements. Automation neither creates nor destroys jobs. The real impact of cost-reducing machines and technological improvements is an increase in production. Technological advances make it possible for us to produce as much with fewer resources, thereby releasing valuable resources so that production (and consumption) can be expanded in other areas. Other tasks can be accomplished with the newly available resources. Since there is a direct link between improved technology and rising output, automation exerts a positive influence on economic welfare from the viewpoint of society as a whole. In aggregate, running out of jobs is unlikely to be a problem. Jobs represent obstacles, tasks that must be accomplished if we desire to loosen the bonds of scarcity. As long as our ability to produce goods and services falls short of our consumption desires, there will be jobs. A society running out of jobs would be in an enviable position: It would be nearing the impossible goal—victory over scarcity.

War II "baby boom" came of working age. Simultaneously, inflation and the tax treatment of returns to physical capital discouraged private investment.

Economics suggests that a rapid growth in the labor force, accompanied by a sagging rate of capital formation, will adversely affect worker productivity and compensation per worker-hour. As Exhibit 6 shows, this has been precisely the case. During the period from 1948 to 1965, both output per hour and hourly compensation grew annually at a rate slightly in excess of 3.0 percent. Since 1974, there has been a sharp decline in productivity per hour. As the growth rate of output per hour declines, worker compensation per hour must also decline. Real incomes cannot continually increase unless there is an expansion in the production of goods and services. As the growth of productivity sagged during the 1970s, worker compensation per hour, adjusted for inflation, also sagged (Exhibit 6). This lag in the growth rate of productivity is a serious matter. Several leading economists believe that unless the United States begins to allocate a somewhat larger share of its national output to investment, worker productivity and the growth of real income will continue to stagnate.

HOW IS THE ECONOMIC PIE DIVIDED?

We have emphasized that wage rates generally reflect the availability of tools (physical capital) and the skills and abilities of individual workers (human capital). Wages tend to be high when physical capital is plentiful, technology

EXHIBIT 6   The sagging growth of productivity in the United States

Period	Increase in Output per Hour, Private Business Sector (Average Annual Rate)	Increase in Real per Hour Compensation, Private Business Sector (Average Annual Rate)
1948–1955	3.5	3.1
1956–1965	3.1	3.0
1966–1973	2.4	2.8
1974–1981	0.7	1.1

Derived from *Economic Report of the President, 1982*, Table B-41.

is advanced, and the work force is highly skilled. When the equipment available to the typical worker is primitive and most workers lack education and skills, wages are low. Both human capital and physical capital contribute to the productive process.

How is the pie divided between these two broad factors of production in the United States? Exhibit 7 provides an answer. In 1950, approximately 81 percent of the national income was earned by employees and self-employed proprietors, the major categories that reflect the earnings of human capital. In 1980, the share of national income allocated to human capital was also 81 percent. Income earned by nonhuman capital—rents, interest, and corporate profits—currently comprises 18 to 20 percent of the national income.

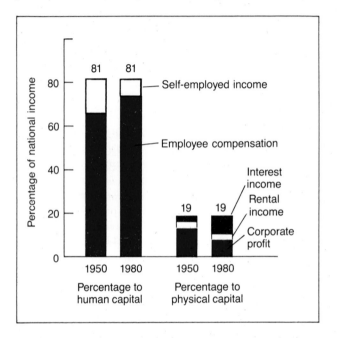

PERSPECTIVES IN ECONOMICS

THE MINIMUM WAGE— AN ECONOMIC APPRAISAL

The legislated minimum wage rates have destroyed beginning jobs for teenagers. These are the jobs in which they normally acquire the skills which make them more productive and enable them to earn far more than the minimum. These [mimimum wage] increases have destroyed the stepping-stones to higher wage jobs.[4]

Minimum Wage Legislation: Legislation requiring that all workers in specified industries be paid at least the stated minimum hourly rate of pay.

---

[4]Yale Brozen, statement before the Illinois Legislature's House Committee on Industrial and Labor Relations, Springfield, Illinois, March 10, 1971.

In 1938, Congress passed the Fair Labor Standards Act, which provided for a national minimum wage of 25 cents per hour. Approximately 43 percent of the private, nonagricultural work force was covered by this legislation. During the last 40 years, the minimum wage has been increased several times, and coverage now extends to 84 percent of the nonagricultural labor force. Currently, federal legislation requires most employers to pay wage rates of at least $3.35 per hour.

Labor Markets and the Minimum Wage

Minimum wage legislation is intended to help the working poor. However, there is good reason to believe that such legislation has the opposite effect. Economic theory indicates that the quantity demanded of labor, particularly a specific skill category of labor, will be inversely related to its wage rate. If a higher minimum wage increases the wage rates of unskilled workers above the level that would be established by market forces, the quantity of unskilled workers employed will fall. The minimum wage will price the services of the least productive (and therefore lowest-wage) workers out of the market.

Exhibit 8 provides a graphic illustration of the direct effect of a $3.35 minimum wage on the employment opportunities of low-skill workers. Without a minimum wage, the supply of and demand for these low-skill workers would be in balance at a wage rate of $2.50. The $3.35 minimum wage makes the low-skill labor service more expensive. Employers will substitute machines and highly skilled workers (whose wages have not been raised by the minimum) for the now more expensive low-productivity employees. Jobs in which low-skill employees are unable to produce a marginal revenue product that is equal to or greater than the minimum will be eliminated. As the cost (and price) of goods and services produced by low-skill employees rises, consumers will rely more heavily on substitute goods produced by highly skilled labor and foreign markets. The net effect of this substitution process will be a reduction in the quantity demanded of low-skill labor.

Of course, some low-skill workers will be able to maintain their jobs, but others will be driven into sectors not covered by the legislation or onto the unemployment and welfare rolls. Workers who retain their jobs will gain. The most adverse effects will fall on those workers who are already most disadvantaged—those whose market earnings are lowest relative to the minimum wage—because it will be so costly to bring their wages up to the minimum.

In summary, the direct results of minimum wage legislation are clearly mixed. Some workers, most likely those whose previous wages were closest to the minimum, will enjoy higher wages. Others, particularly those with the lowest prelegislation wage rates, will be unable to find work.[5] They will often be pushed into the ranks of the unemployed. Many persons in the latter group will eventually give up and drop out of the labor force.

The Minimum Wage, Experience, and Job Training

Minimum wage rates also affect the ability of low-skill workers to acquire experience and training. Many inexperienced workers face a dilemma. They cannot find a job without experience (or skills), but they cannot obtain experience without a job. This is particularly true for youthful workers. Employment experience obtained at an early age, even on seemingly menial tasks, can help one acquire work habits (for example, promptness and self-confidence), skills, and attitudes that will enhance one's value to employers in the future. Since minimum wage legislation prohibits the payment of even a temporarily low wage, it substantially limits the employer's ability to offer employment to inexperienced workers.

---

[5]The impact of minimum wage legislation could differ from the theoretical results that we have outlined if labor markets were dominated by a single buyer. Economists refer to this situation as "monopsony." We choose not to present the monopsony model here because (a) in a modern society, where labor is highly mobile, the major assumptions of the model are seldom met; and (b) the bulk of the empirical evidence in this area is consistent with the competitive model.

EXHIBIT 8 Employment and the minimum wage

If the market wage of a group of employees were $2.50 per hour, a $3.35-per-hour minimum wage would (a) increase the earnings of persons who were able to maintain employment and (b) reduce the employment of others (E_0 to E_1), pushing them onto the unemployment rolls or into less-preferred jobs.

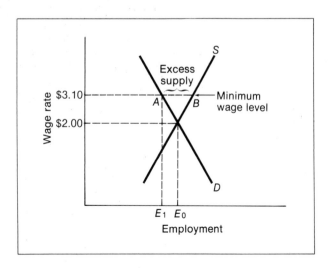

Minimum wage legislation also limits the range of jobs available to low-skill workers. Consider a construction firm that hires "helpers" at $2.50 per hour to work with carpenters and electricians. Since the helpers require close supervision, often make mistakes, and are used on odd jobs during slack periods, initially they are able to command only a low wage. After the minimum wage is introduced, the contractor will receive more applications—including those of workers with experience and past training—but will hire fewer workers at the higher wage. The contractor, now able to be more selective, will hire and train fewer inexperienced helpers. Some **entry-level jobs** will be eliminated.

As entry-level jobs that offer training opportunities to low-productivity workers are eliminated in many sectors of the economy, the positions available to inexperienced workers will be primarily **dead-end jobs.** As Martin Feldstein has pointed out, the minimum wage acts as an institutional barrier limiting the opportunity to acquire on-the-job training.[6] Many leading economists believe that minimum wage legislation is the major reason for the almost complete lack of skill-building jobs at the lower end of the wage spectrum.

Qualifications and Employability

Some people incorrectly argue that inexperienced, low-skill workers have few employment opportunities because they have so few qualifications. Low productivity (skill level) results in low wages, but, in the absence of legal barriers, it need not result in high levels of unemployment. No worker is either qualified or unqualified in an absolute sense. One's qualifications must be considered in relation to one's wage rate. For example, a carpenter may be "qualified" and in great demand at an hourly wage rate of $5. However, the same carpenter may be "unemployable" at $10 per hour. A $10 minimum wage rate would obviously make many workers unemployable, since many would lack the qualifications (skills) necessary to command such high wages. Although the effects are less widespread, a $3.35 minimum wage does precisely the same thing to low-skill workers; it makes them unqualified, that is, unemployable, at such a high wage rate.

The Impact of the Minimum Wage

Most empirical studies of the minimum wage in the United States have focused on teenagers, since there is a higher proportion of low-wage workers (reflecting their lack of skill-building experience) in this age group. This does not mean that most low-skill workers are teenagers—they are not. However, since the skill level of a *higher proportion* of teenagers is low, researchers are better able to isolate the impact of the minimum wage if they focus on this group.

Not all sectors of the economy are covered by minimum wage legislation. But one of the major effects of the legislation has been to reduce the job opportunities available to teenagers (and presumably other low-skill workers) in industries to which the minimum is applied. In a recently published study, Finis Welch found that after the passage of the 1938 minimum wage, there was a distinct shift in the industrial pattern of teenage employment. Employment among teenagers dropped more than the national average in every industry with above-average coverage by minimum wage legislation. In contrast, every industry with below-average coverage experienced a decline in teenage employment that was less than the national average.[7]

There have been several stud-

Entry-Level Jobs: Jobs that require little training or experience and therefore allow untrained or inexperienced job seekers to enter the work force. These jobs frequently are stepping-stones to better jobs.

Dead-End Jobs: Jobs that offer the employee little opportunity for advancement or on-the-job training.

---

[6]It is ironic that although we subsidize formal education, we establish barriers that restrict a worker's ability to acquire training. See Martin Feldstein, "The Economics of the New Unemployment," *Public Interest* (Fall 1973), pp. 3–42.

ies on the impact of the minimum wage on the employment opportunities of youth. Most studies indicate that a 10 percent increase in the minimum wage reduces teenage employment by 1 to 3 percent. Of course, the teenage unemployment rate is well above the average for adult workers. Since one would expect youthful workers searching for a career to change jobs more frequently, the teenage–adult unemployment differential is not surprising. However, it is interesting that as the minimum wage has risen and, more importantly, as more fields of employment are covered by the minimum wage, the teenage–adult unemployment differential has widened. For example, the teenage unemployment rate averaged 11.8 percent in 1954–1955, compared to an overall rate of 5 percent—a differential of 6.8 percent. In contrast, throughout most of the 1970s, the teenage minus adult differential exceeded 10 percent.

Is Minimum Wage Legislation Racist?

On the surface, this question may appear to be absurd. However, a closer look at the data reveals that the minimum wage severely restricts the abil-ity of minorities to acquire experience and skill-building employment opportunities. At the legislated higher minimum, there is an excess supply of low-skill, inexperienced workers. Employers have the opportunity to choose among a surplus of applicants for each opening. They generally choose those workers, *within the low-productivity group,* who have the most skill, experience, and education. If they want to discriminate against minorities, they can do so with impunity. Many low-skill white applicants are available at the artificially high minimum wage. Since all workers must be paid the minimum, the employer's incentive to hire less skilled and less favored groups is destroyed.

Much of the research documenting the adverse impact of the minimum wage on the employment opportunities of blacks has been done by black economists. Walter Williams, economics professor at Temple University, has been at the forefront of those condemning the minimum wage.[8] Andrew Brimmer, a former member of the Federal Reserve Board, has also been among the leading critics of the minimum wage. Brimmer argues:

A growing body of statistical and other evidence accumulated by economists shows that increases in the statutory minimum wage dampen the expansion of employment and lengthen the lineup of those seeking jobs. Advances in the minimum wage have a noticeably adverse impact on young people—with the effects on black teenagers being considerably more severe.[9]

There is strong empirical evidence that the higher rates and expanded coverage of minimum wage legislation have imposed an additional burden on the youthful members of minorities. As Exhibit 9 illustrates, between 1974 and 1981, the average annual rate of unemployment for black teenagers was 35.1 percent, compared to 15.5 percent for white teenagers. This enormous differential has not always existed. Before the minimum wage was raised from 75 cents to $1 in 1956—a 33 percent increase—the rates of unemployment for black and white teenagers were similar (see Exhibit 9, data for 1948–1955). During the period from 1956 to 1981, the black–white unemployment gap steadily widened as the minimum wage rose and as coverage was extended to more and more sectors of our economy.

[7]Finis Welch, "The Rising Impact of the Minimum Wage," *Regulation* (November/ December 1978), pp. 28–37. See particularly Table 2.

[8]See Walter E. Williams, "Government Sanctioned Restraints That Reduce Economic Opportunities for Minorities," *Policy Review* (Fall 1977), pp. 7–30.

[9]Andrew Brimmer, quoted in Louis Rukeyser, "Jobs Are Eliminated," Naught News Service (August 1978).

EXHIBIT 9   The black–white teenage unemployment differential

Period	Minimum Wage (Dollars)	Percentage of Private Nonagricultural Work Force Covered[a]	Rate of Unemployment for Men, Ages 16–19 (Annual Average Percentage during Period)		
			White	Black	Black Minus White
1948–1949	0.40	53	12.0	13.3	1.3
1950–1955	0.75	53	11.0	11.7	0.7
1956–1960	1.00	58	13.1	21.9	8.8
1961–1962	1.15	62	14.7	24.4	9.7
1963–1966	1.25	69	13.5	24.1	10.6
1967–1973	1.40–1.60	79	12.3	25.4	13.1
1974–1981	2.00–3.35	84	15.5	35.1	19.6

[a]Estimated from data of Employment Standards Administration, U.S. Department of Labor.

Economic Report of the President, 1982, Table B–33.

Not only has the rate of unemployment for black teenagers soared, but the rate of labor force participation for youthful blacks has also been adversely affected. As Exhibit 10 shows, before the large increase in the minimum wage (and expansion in coverage) in 1956, the labor force participation rate for blacks, ages 16 to 24, actually exceeded the rate for whites. During the last two decades, that situation has changed dramatically. By January 1982, the labor force participation rate for blacks, ages 16 and 17, was only 49 percent of the rate for whites of the same age group. Similarly, the participation rates for blacks ages 18 to 19 and 20 to 24 fell substantially below the rates for whites in these age groupings. This suggests that many youthful workers, particularly minority workers, have given up their search for employment at the minimum wage. Since they are no longer searching for employment, they are not counted among the unemployed.

Exhibits 9 and 10 illustrate the tragic facts. Approximately 35 percent of all black teenagers in the labor force are unemployed. Even that figure understates the bleakness of the employment picture for inexperienced black workers, since it does not include those who dropped out of the labor force because they were unable to find a job at the minimum wage. Most labor economists believe that if these discouraged workers were counted, the rate of unemployment for black teenagers would approach 50 percent, twice the rate for the total labor force in the midst of the Great Depression.

Persons from disadvantaged backgrounds are precisely those who are most in need of the employment experience and entry-level, skill-enhancing jobs that are unavailable to them as a result of the minimum wage. Members of disadvantaged minority groups are generally least able to afford formal training beyond high school. What are the long-run implications of a policy that prices low-skill workers out of the job market and thereby prevents them from acquiring the experience and skills necessary for economic success in our modern world? Among other things, future poverty statistics and crime rates will certainly be affected.

The Subminimum Wage for Teenagers

Several bills currently before Congress would provide for a lower minimum wage for teenagers. These proposals would permit employers to pay teenagers wage rates of between 60 percent and 75 percent of the adult minimum wage. Advocates believe this type of legislation will help to alleviate an important side effect of the minimum wage—the low availability of both training and employment opportunities for youthful, inexperienced workers. The major opposition to this legislation comes from labor organizations. This should not be surprising. Low-skill—often nonunion—labor is a substitute for high-skill, (union) labor; a lower minimum wage would enhance the attractiveness of substitute, nonunion labor. Stated another way, the demand for union workers might not be as strong if low-skilled labor were not priced out of the market by the minimum wage.

Discussion

1. How will an increase in the minimum wage affect the welfare of each of the following groups: (a) high-income recipients, (b) food service operators and customers, (c) black teenagers, (d) white teenagers, and (e) college students?

2. Do you think the subminimum wage for teenagers is a good idea? Why or why not?

EXHIBIT 10 The black/white rate of labor force participation for persons 16 to 24 years old

| Period | Black/White Labor Force Participation Rate for Youthful Men | | |
	Ages 16–17	Ages 18–19	Ages 20–24
1954–1955	1.00	1.06	1.05
1956–1960	0.96	1.03	1.03
1961–1962	0.94	1.05	1.02
1963–1966	0.87	1.00	1.04
1967–1973	0.73	0.91	1.00
1974–1976	0.60	0.80	0.93
1977–1980	0.58	0.77	0.90
1982 (January)	0.49	0.72	0.88

Derived from Walter Williams, *Youth and Minority Employment*, a study prepared for the Joint Economic Committee, Congress of the United States (Washington, D.C.: U.S. Government Printing Office, 1977), Table 5, and U.S. Department of Labor, *Employment and Earnings* (February 1982), Table A-3.

Payments to resources are of vital importance because individual incomes are determined by (a) resource prices and (b) the amount of resources that one owns. However, the purchasing power of the income received by resource owners is dependent on productivity. There is nothing magical about the growth of real income; it is dependent on the growth of real output. The real output of a nation is strongly influenced by the capital equipment with which people work. The following chapter analyzes the factors that underlie the availability of capital and the investment choices of decision-makers.

CHAPTER LEARNING OBJECTIVES

1 There are three major sources of wage differentials among individuals: differences in workers, differences in jobs, and degree of labor mobility. Individual workers differ with respect to productivity (skills, human capital, motivation, native ability, and so on), specialized skills, employment preferences, race, and sex. All these factors influence either the demand for or the supply of labor. In addition, differences in nonpecuniary job characteristics, changes in product markets, and institutional restrictions that limit labor mobility contribute to variations in wages among workers.

2 Productivity is the ultimate source of high wages. High wages in the United States are the result of large amounts of both human and physical capital.

3 The share of GNP allocated to the formation of physical capital is less for the United States than for most other countries. Many economists believe that this low rate of investment is largely responsible for the sluggish growth of income in the United States. Growth in employee compensation is slower in the United States than in other Western nations where the rate of capital formation is higher.

4 Approximately 80 percent of national income in the United States is allocated to human capital (labor) and 20 percent to owners of physical (nonhuman) capital.

5 Automated methods of production will be adopted only if they reduce cost. Although automation *might* reduce revenues and employment *in a specific industry,* the lower cost of production will increase real income, causing demand in other industries to expand. These secondary effects will cause employment to rise in other industries. Improved technology expands our ability to produce. It is expanded production, not the number of jobs, that contributes to our economic well-being.

6 Minimum wage legislation increases the earnings of some low-skill workers, but others are forced to accept inferior employment opportunities, join the ranks of the unemployed, or drop out of the labor force completely. Minimum wage legislation reduces the ability of employers to offer (and low-skill employees to find) work with on-the-job training and skill-building experience. Thus, the jobs available to low-skill workers tend to be primarily dead-end jobs. The most disadvantaged workers, particularly members of minority groups and teenagers, are the hardest hit. Tragically, many youthful workers, particularly blacks, have been priced out of the job market by the minimum wage. Denied the opportunity to obtain entry-level jobs at an early age, many are unable to acquire the job experience and on-the-job training that would provide for more favorable future employment opportunities.

THE ECONOMIC WAY OF THINKING — DISCUSSION QUESTIONS

1 What are the major reasons for the differences in earnings among individuals? Why are wages in some occupations higher than in others? How do wage differentials influence the allocation of resources? How important is this function? Explain.

2 Why are real wages in the United States higher than in other countries? Is the labor force itself responsible for the higher wages of American workers? Explain.

3 What are the major factors that would normally explain earnings differences between

(a) a lawyer and a minister, (b) an accountant and an elementary-school teacher, (c) a business executive and a social worker, (d) a country lawyer and a Wall Street lawyer, (e) an experienced, skilled craftsperson and a 20-year-old high school dropout, (f) a fire fighter and a night security guard, and (g) an upper-story and a ground-floor window washer?

4 What's Wrong with This Way of Thinking?

"Higher wages help everybody. Workers are helped because they can now purchase more of the things they need. Business is helped because the increase in the workers' purchasing power will increase the demand for products. Taxpayers are helped because workers will now pay more taxes. Union activities and legislation increasing the wages of workers will promote economic progress."

5 What's Wrong with This Way of Thinking?

"Jobs are the key to economic progress. Unless we can figure out how to produce more jobs, economic progress will be stifled."

A greater result is obtained by producing goods in roundabout ways than by producing them directly. . . . That roundabout methods lead to greater results than direct methods is one of the most important and fundamental propositions in the whole theory of production.[1]
Eugen von Böhm-Bawerk

25

CAPITAL, INTEREST, AND PROFIT

Consumption is the objective of all production. We undertake the production of goods because we wish to consume either the good directly or the service it provides. All goods and services are produced by changing the form, condition, or location of raw materials through the application of human energy (human capital) and tools (physical capital).

ROUNDABOUT METHODS OF PRODUCTION

As the Austrian economist Eugen von Böhm-Bawerk pointed out in 1884, physical capital can magnify the productivity of human beings. We can often produce a larger amount of a product with the same quantity of labor (or the same amount of a product with a lesser quantity of labor) if we first apply human energy and ingenuity to the construction of tools, machines, and even factories and later use these man-made capital resources to produce the desired product. Economists refer to this procedure as a **roundabout method of production.**

Through the ages, human beings have expanded their use of tools (physical capital) while developing and applying innovative, roundabout methods of production. This combination—more (and better) tools and the development of superior methods of production—has made it possible for us to attain the standard of living we enjoy today.

In order to use tools and innovative methods of production to expand total production in the future, we are required to make current sacrifices. Generally speaking, we must divert resources from the production of current consumption goods in order to expand the quantity and quality of capital

Roundabout Method of Production: The use of productive effort to make tools and other capital assets, which are then used to produce the desired consumer good.

---

[1]Eugen von Böhm-Bawerk, "Capitalist Production," in *The Capitalist Reader,* ed. Lawrence S. Stepelevich (New Rochelle, New York: Arlington House, 1977), pp. 26–27.

goods available in the future. Costs are associated with the expansion of capital and the utilization of roundabout methods of production. Economic efficiency requires that these costs be balanced against future benefits. How can this be accomplished? How are future goods and future income valued? How do we know whether a capital investment is worth the cost? Are roundabout methods of production always more efficient? What are the incentives to experiment with, develop, and apply innovative, roundabout methods? We will consider each of these questions.

THE INTEREST RATE

Interest is the additional amount that a person is willing to pay in order to obtain a good or resource *now* rather than later. Since people generally acquire goods earlier by borrowing from a third party rather than by simply paying the seller a larger amount at a designated date in the future, the interest rate is often defined as the price of loanable funds. This definition is entirely proper. However, we should keep in mind that it is the *earlier availability* of goods and services that can be purchased with money, not the money itself, that is desired. In other words, the loanable funds can be seen as representing the desired earlier availability.

Interest would exist even in a nonmonetary economy. Consider the economic life of a primitive economy. Suppose that Robinson Crusoe wanted to obtain additional breadfruit now. If the price of breadfruit were 2 fish, Crusoe could obtain 5 breadfruit now in exchange for 10 fish. Alternatively, suppose some natives from another island would be willing to supply Crusoe the 5 breadfruit now in exchange for some amount of fish, let's say 11 fish, to be supplied one year from now. In effect, Crusoe would be paying 11 fish one year from now, rather than 10 fish now, to obtain the 5 breadfruit. Implicitly, he would be paying interest at a rate of 10 percent, since the breadfruit seller would not require him to pay the price (10 fish) now if he were willing to pay the price *plus a 10 percent premium* one year from now.

Loanable Funds: Demand and Supply

Positive Rate of Time Preference: The desire of consumers for goods now rather than in the future.

The demand of both consumers and investors underlies the market demand for loanable funds.

Consumers demand loanable funds because they prefer earlier availability of goods. On average, individuals possess a **positive rate of time preference.** By this we mean that people subjectively value goods obtained in the immediate or near future (including the present) more highly than goods obtained in the distant future. Most people would rather have a new automobile now rather than the same automobile ten years from now.

There may be some exceptions. For example, a person with a large quantity of a perishable good, bananas, for example, might be willing to exchange 100 bananas now for *fewer* bananas in the future. However, in a modern economy, perishable goods can be exchanged for money, a nonperishable commodity.[2]

There is nothing irrational or even shortsighted about a positive rate of

---

[2]Of course, inflation may cause the purchasing power of money to diminish. The impact of inflation on the interest rate is discussed later in this chapter.

time preference. Given the uncertainties of the world in which we live, it is perfectly reasonable to prefer the reality of current consumption to the uncertainty of some larger amount (in physical or monetary terms) of future consumption. As the saying goes, "A bird in the hand is worth two in the bush." Of course, the premium that one must pay for earlier availability—the interest rate—will influence the relative amounts of current and future consumption.

Investors demand loanable funds so that they can invest in capital goods and finance roundabout methods of production that are potentially productive. Since roundabout methods of production often make it possible to produce a larger output at a lower cost, decision-makers can gain even if they have to pay an interest premium in order to purchase the machines, buildings, and other resources required by the production process. Perhaps a simple example will clarify the link between the demand for loanable funds and the productivity of capital. Robinson Crusoe could pursue his fishing occupation by either (a) combining his labor with natural resources (direct production) or (b) constructing a net and *eventually* combining his labor with this tool (a roundabout method of production). Let us assume that Crusoe could catch 2 fish per day by hand fishing but 3 per day if he constructed and used a net that would last for 360 days. Suppose that it would take Crusoe 5 days to build the net. The opportunity cost of constructing the net would be 10 fish (2 per day for each of the 5 days Crusoe spent building the net). If Crusoe used the roundabout method of production, his output during the next year (including the 5 days required to build the net) would be 1080 fish (3 per day for 360 days). Alternatively, hand fishing during the year would lead to an output of only 730 (2 fish per day for 365 days). The capital-intensive, indirect method of production would be highly productive. Total output during the year would be expanded by 350 fish if the roundabout method of production were used.

However, Crusoe's fish production would decline during the time in which he was constructing the net. Crusoe might be on the verge of starvation. Suppose that a fishing crew from a neighboring island visited Crusoe and offered to lend him 10 fish so that he could undertake the capital investment project (building the net). Crusoe could gain. If Crusoe could borrow the 10 fish (the principal) in exchange for, say, 20 fish (a 100 percent interest rate) a year later, the investment project would be highly profitable.

Crusoe's—or the investor's—demand for loanable fish (or funds) stems from the productivity of the capital investment. Since construction of the net enables Crusoe to expand his total output during the year, he is willing to pay an interest premium for current availability. Crusoe's willingness to pay an interest premium for earlier availability stems directly from the productivity of capital.

As Exhibit 1 illustrates, the amount of funds demanded is inversely related to the interest rate. As the interest rate rises, the cost of earlier availability increases. As a result of this increase in the price of current goods relative to that of future goods, consumers will cut back on current consumption; some will be unwilling to pay a higher premium for the earlier availability of consumer goods. In addition, some investment projects that would lead to gain at a lower interest rate will not be profitable at higher rates. Therefore, both consumers and investors will demand fewer funds at higher interest rates.

Although higher interest rates cause the amount of borrowing to decline, they encourage lenders to provide a larger supply of funds to the market. Even individuals with a positive rate of time preference will give up current

EXHIBIT 1 **The determination of the interest rate**

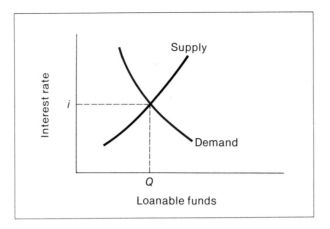

consumption in order to supply funds to the loanable funds market if the price is right—that is, if the interest rate is attractive. Although people generally prefer earlier consumption, they also prefer more goods to fewer goods. A rise in the interest rate is equivalent to an expansion in the quantity of future goods, which will go to those who sacrifice current consumption. This increase in the quantity of future goods that one can obtain for each dollar supplied to the loanable funds market will result in a supply curve that slopes upward to the right.

The interest rate brings the plans of borrowers into harmony with the plans of lenders. In equilibrium, the quantity of funds demanded by borrowers is equal to the amount supplied by lenders, as Exhibit 1 shows.

Money Rate of Interest and Real Rate of Interest

Money Rate of Interest: The rate of interest in monetary terms that borrowers pay for borrowed funds. During periods of inflation, the money rate exceeds the real rate of interest.

Real Rate of Interest: The money rate of interest minus the inflationary premium. The real rate of interest indicates the interest premium, in terms of real goods and services, that one must pay for earlier availability.

We have emphasized that the interest rate is a premium that borrowers are willing to pay for earlier availability. During periods of inflation, the **money rate of interest,** determined by the forces of supply and demand in the loanable funds market, may be a misleading indicator of how much borrowers give up to obtain earlier availability. Suppose that the money rate of interest is 10 percent at a time when prices are rising at an annual rate of 5 percent. A person borrowing $100 will have to pay back $110 one year later. However, during that year, the level of prices will have increased by 5 percent. The $110 paid to the lender one year later will not buy 10 percent more goods. Instead, it will buy only 5 percent more goods than the $100 provided to the borrower one year earlier. Therefore, when the rate of inflation is taken into account, the **real rate of interest** is only 5 percent.

Once decision-makers anticipate rising prices, the money rate of interest will include an inflationary premium compensating lenders for the expected decline in the purchasing power of their principal and interest over the duration of the loan. The real rate of interest is equal to the money rate of interest minus the inflationary premium. Recognizing the decline in the purchasing power of the dollars with which they will be repaid, lenders will reduce the amount of money supplied to the loanable funds market unless they are compensated for the anticipated rate of inflation. Simultaneously, once borrowers become fully aware that they will be paying back their loans with dollars of less purchasing power, they will be willing to pay the inflationary premium as well as the real rate of interest. If both borrowers and lenders fully anticipate, for example, a 5 percent rate of inflation, they will be just as willing to agree on a 10 percent interest rate as they were to agree on a 5 percent interest rate when both anticipated stable prices. Therefore, under inflationary conditions, the money rate of interest will incorporate an inflationary premium reflecting the anticipated rate of inflation as well as the real rate of interest. As the inflationary premium increases, money interest rates will rise. Thus, it should not be surprising that high money interest rates are often associated with high rates of inflation.

Prior to the 1970s, a 15 percent money interest rate was thought to be exceedingly high. However, this notion changed as the inflation rate rose to 12 percent or more several times during the decade. Actually a 15 percent money rate of interest will yield only a 3 percent real rate of return if the annual inflation rate is 12 percent. Even though the money interest rates during the 1970s were high by historical standards, the real interest rates were often quite low.

The Multiplicity of Interest Rates

So far, we have proceeded as though a single interest rate existed. Of course, in the real world, there are many interest rates. For example, there is a mortgage rate, a prime interest rate (the rate charged to business firms with strong credit ratings), a consumer loan rate, and a credit card rate, to name only a few. Generally, all of these interest rates are different. The interest rate on a given loan is influenced by (a) the cost of processing, (b) the risk associated with the borrower, and (c) the duration of the loan.

The accounting costs associated with a loan of several hundred thousand dollars may actually be smaller than those for a consumer loan of a few hundred dollars, if, for example, the large loan is paid back in a lump sum at a designated time in the future and the small loan is paid monthly. Since the bookkeeping costs *per dollar loaned* are generally higher for small loans, interest rates will be higher for such loans.

The interest rate on a loan is also influenced by the credit standing of the borrower and the risk associated with lending to that borrower. Banks are likely to charge an unemployed worker a higher interest rate than they charge General Motors. Since the probability of default is considerably greater for the unemployed worker than for General Motors, the former will have to pay a risk premium, which will be incorporated into the interest rate of the loan. Similarly, the interest rate on a "secured loan," such as a mortgage on a house, will be less than that on an unsecured loan, such as a credit card purchase.

The degree of risk involved in a loan also varies with the loan's duration. Lenders usually require higher interest rates for longer-term loans since they involve greater risk. The longer the time period, the more likely that the financial standing of the borrower will deteriorate substantially or that market conditions will change dramatically. Also, unless rates are believed to be unusually high, borrowers are willing to pay a premium to keep the funds for a longer period of time. Thus, long-term loans usually carry a premium that compensates for the additional uncertainties and additional benefits of the longer time period.

The Components of an Interest Rate—A Short Summary

The money rate of interest on a loan has three components. The pure interest component is the market price one must pay for earlier availability. The inflationary premium component reflects the expectation that the loan will be repaid with dollars of less purchasing power as a result of inflation. The third component can be broken down into a premium that reflects the cost of monitoring and processing the loan and premiums that reflect the risk of the borrower defaulting and the risk incurred over time.

THE VALUE OF FUTURE INCOME

Suppose that one year from now, you will have $100 in receipts. How much would that $100 be worth today? Clearly, it would be worth less than $100. If you deposited $100 today in a savings account earning 6 percent interest, you would have $106 one year from now. The interest rate connects the value of dollars (and capital assets) today with the value of dollars (and expected streams of receipts) in the future. The interest rate is used to discount the value of a dollar in the future so that its present worth can be determined today. The **net present value** (NPV) of a payment received one year from now can be expressed as follows:

Net Present Value: The current worth of future income after it is discounted to reflect the fact that revenues *in the future* are valued less highly than revenues *now.*

$$NPV = \frac{\text{receipts one year from now}}{1 + \text{interest rate}}$$

If the interest rate is 6 percent, the current value of the $100 to be received one year from now is

$$NPV = \frac{\$100}{1.06} = \$94.34$$

If one invested $94.34 in a savings account yielding 6 percent interest, one year from now the account would be valued at $100.

Discounting: The procedure used to calculate the present value of future income. The present value of future income is inversely related to both the interest rate and the amount of time that passes before the funds are received.

Economists use the term **discounting** to describe this procedure of reducing the value of a dollar to be received in the future to its present worth. Clearly, the value of a dollar in the future is inversely related to the interest rate. For example, if the interest rate were 10 percent, the net present value of $100 received one year from now would be only $90.91 ($100 divided by 1.10).

The net present value of $100 received two years from now is:

$$NPV = \frac{\$100}{(1 + \text{interest rate})^2}$$

If the interest rate were 6 percent, $100 received two years from now would be equal to $89 today ($100 divided by 1.06^2). In other words, $89 invested today would yield $100 two years from now.

The net present value procedure can be used to determine the current value of any future income stream. If R represents the receipts received at year-end and i the interest rate, the net present value of the future income stream[3] is

---

[3]For a specific annual income stream in perpetuity, the net present value is equal simply to R/i, where R is the annual revenue stream and i the interest rate. For example, if the interest rate is 10 percent, the NPV of a $100 income stream in perpetuity is equal to $100/.10, or $1000.

$$\text{NPV} = \frac{R_1}{1+i} + \frac{R_2}{(1+i)^2} + \cdots + \frac{R_n}{(1+i)^n}$$

Exhibit 2 shows the net present value of $100 received at various times in the future at several different discount rates. The chart clearly illustrates two points. First, the present value of the $100 declines as the interest rate rises. For example, the present value of $100 received one year from now, when discounted at a 4 percent interest rate, is $96.15, compared to $98.04 when a 2 percent discount rate is applied. Second, the present value of the $100 declines as the date of its receipt is set farther into the future. If the applicable discount rate is 6 percent, the present value of $100 received one year from now is $94.34, compared to $89 if the $100 is received two years from now. If the $100 is received five years from now, its current worth is only $74.73. So the present value of a future dollar payment is inversely related to both the interest rate and how far in the future the payment will be received.

MAKING INVESTMENT DECISIONS

Since investment projects (roundabout methods of production) involve a current sacrifice in order to generate a flow of output (and revenue) in the future, the discounting procedure is particularly important for investors. The value of the net receipts derived from an investment project over the years can be estimated and the receipts discounted in order to determine their current worth. This determination of the net present value of the project provides the decision-maker with an estimate of how much the project is worth now. A worthwhile investment

EXHIBIT 2   The net present value of $100 to be received in the future

The columns indicate the net present value of $100 to be received a designated number of years in the future for alternative interest rates. For example, at a discount rate of 2 percent, the net present value of $100 to be received five years from now is $90.57. Note that the net present value of the $100 declines as either the interest rate or the number of years in the future increases.

| Years in the Future | Net Present Value of $100 to Be Received a Designated Number of Years in the Future for Alternative Interest Rates | | | | | |
	2 Percent	4 Percent	6 Percent	8 Percent	12 Percent	20 Percent
1	98.04	96.15	94.34	92.59	89.29	83.33
2	96.12	92.46	89.00	85.73	79.72	69.44
3	94.23	88.90	83.96	79.38	71.18	57.87
4	92.39	85.48	79.21	73.50	63.55	48.23
5	90.57	82.19	74.73	68.06	56.74	40.19
6	88.80	79.03	70.50	63.02	50.66	33.49
7	87.06	75.99	66.51	58.35	45.23	27.08
8	85.35	73.07	62.74	54.03	40.39	23.26
9	83.68	70.26	59.19	50.02	36.06	19.38
10	82.03	67.56	55.84	46.32	32.20	16.15
15	74.30	55.53	41.73	31.52	18.27	6.49
20	67.30	45.64	31.18	21.45	10.37	2.61
30	55.21	30.83	17.41	9.94	3.34	0.42
50	37.15	14.07	5.43	2.13	0.35	0.01

project must be expected to yield a rate of return equal to or greater than the opportunity cost of loanable funds. The investment discount rate, the rate at which the firm can borrow and lend funds, represents the opportunity cost of funds to the firm. If the current estimated worth (present value) of the project exceeds its cost, undertaking the project makes sense. On the other hand, if the cost of the project exceeds the discounted value of the future net receipts, a profit-seeking firm should reject the prospective project.

Let us consider an example. Suppose that a truck rental firm is contemplating the purchase of a new $40,000 truck. Past experience indicates that after the operational and maintenance expenses have been covered, the firm can rent the truck for $12,000 per year (received at the end of each year) for the next four years, the expected life of the vehicle.[4] Since the firm can borrow and lend funds at an interest rate of 8 percent, we will discount the future expected income at an 8 percent rate. Exhibit 3 illustrates the calculation. Column 4 shows how much $12,000 available at year-end for each of the next four years is worth today. In total, the net present value of the expected rental receipts is $39,744—less than the purchase price of the truck. Therefore, the project should not be undertaken.

The decision to accept or reject a prospective project is highly sensitive to the discount rate. If the discount rate in our example had been 6 percent, reflecting lower interest rates, the net present value of the future rental income would have been $41,580.[5] Since it pays to purchase a capital good whenever the net present value of the income generated exceeds the purchase price of the capital good, the project would have been profitable at the lower interest rate.

After allowance is made for risk factors, the competitive process tends to equalize the net present value of a machine (or some other capital investment

EXHIBIT 3   The discounted present value of $12,000 of truck rental for four years

Year (1)	Expected Future Income (Received at Year-End) (2)	Discounted Value (8 Percent Rate) (3)	Present Value of Income (4)
1	$12,000	0.926	$11,112
2	12,000	0.857	10,284
3	12,000	0.794	9,528
4	12,000	0.735	8,820
			$39,744

[4]For the sake of simplicity, we assume that the truck has no scrap value at the end of four years.
[5]The derivation of this figure is shown in the following tabulation:

Year	Expected Future Income (Dollars)	Discounted Value per Dollar (6 Percent Rate)	Present Value of Income (Dollars)
1	12,000	0.943	11,316
2	12,000	0.890	10,680
3	12,000	0.840	10,080
4	12,000	0.792	9,504
			41,580

project) and the purchase price of the machine (or the cost of the investment project). If the net present value of an investment project exceeds its current cost, the investor will make a profit. As more and more business decision-makers learn about the attractive opportunities for profit, they will enter the market as competitors. The entry of new competitors generally results in an increase in the price of the investment project and/or a reduction in the price of the service it provides. As we discussed previously, this process tends to erode the economic profit and equalize the net present value of the expected future revenues and the current price (or cost) of the investment.

INVESTING IN HUMAN CAPITAL

In earlier chapters, we discussed the concept of human capital. A decision to invest in human capital—to continue in school, for example—involves all the ingredients of other investment decisions. Since both the returns and some of the costs normally accrue in the future, the discounting procedure helps one to assess the present value of expected costs and revenues associated with a human capital investment.

Consider the case of an undergraduate contemplating the pursuit of a master's degree in business administration. The knowledge and certification acquired by completing the MBA program will enable the graduate to earn a higher future income (just as the truck generated net future income in the example of Exhibit 3). Costs will be incurred in the attainment of the MBA. Tuition payments, books, and the reduction in the student's income during the period of study must be allocated to the cost side of the ledger. Will the higher future income be worth the cost? The potential MBA student must discount each year's *additional* income stemming from completion of the master's program and compare that with the discounted value of the cost, including the opportunity cost of earnings foregone during the period of study. If the discounted value of the *additional* future income exceeds the discounted value of the cost, acquiring an MBA degree is a worthwhile human capital investment.

Of course, nonmonetary considerations may also be important. Someone contemplating the rental truck investment might weigh such things as the relative amounts of pride and enjoyment to be derived from dealing with the trucking business. If the nonmonetary elements are attractive, the investment carries a bonus above and beyond the monetary yield. If many investors find the trucking industry attractive *compared with other investment alternatives,* the entry of additional competitors into the industry will drive the rate of return for trucking below that for other industries. Since the investors enjoy the business, they will accept a somewhat lower rate of monetary return.

Nonmonetary considerations are particularly important—probably *more* important—in human capital investment decisions, since the capital is embodied in the individual. One can undertake many physical capital investments without being directly involved, but this is impossible with human capital (training, education, skills, and so on); direct involvement is obviously a given. Although human capital investments can be analyzed in the same terms as any other investment, the analysis is likely to be less precise, since it is difficult to isolate the nonmonetary aspects of these decisions. However, the same methods—the discounting procedures and the comparison of the present value of future revenues (or benefits) with costs—can apply to both human and physical capital investment decisions.

THE COMPONENTS OF THE RETURNS TO CAPITAL

Why do individuals purchase long-lasting capital assets? They do so because they expect to earn a rate of return on their investment. There are three components to the rate of return on capital investment projects.

Pure Interest

Pure Interest Yield: The yield that one can expect to receive on loanable funds without taking any significant risk.

Suppose that you have $1000 to invest. You can take it to the local bank, deposit it in a savings account, and earn 5 percent interest. One year from the day of deposit, you can go to the bank and pick up a check for $1050. You receive $50 for allowing the bank to use your $1000 for one year. The $50 (5 percent) that you earn is a **pure interest yield.** It reflects the market rate at which a borrower in excellent financial standing can obtain loanable funds and the rate at which a lender can expect to receive payment without taking any significant risk. It represents the opportunity cost of capital when the lender bears negligible risk.

Alternatively, you could purchase a capital asset (a building, machine, or plot of land, for example) with your funds. However, if you do not expect that the capital investment will return at least the pure interest yield, you have no incentive to undertake the project. Again, the pure interest yield will be that part of the return on investment that compensates you, the investor, for the opportunity cost of investing. The pure interest yield reflects the costs associated with foregoing current consumption.

The Risk Premium

Owners of capital assets, unless they rent or lease them out, are residual income recipients. For example, the common stockholders of a corporation get what is left over after payments have been made to all persons who supplied resources at a contractually agreed-upon price. If the business venture is successful, the residual income may be large. If the project turns out badly, the residual income recipients may lose a great deal, including their initial investment.

Ownership always involves risk. Owners of capital assets bear the risk of a possible loss of those assets. If people were indifferent to risk, the expected rate of return from the ownership of capital would just equal the pure interest yield. However, most people dislike taking risks. They prefer the certain receipt of $1000 to a 50–50 chance of receiving either nothing or $2000. Generally, the owners of capital will have to be paid a premium to induce them to undertake the risks of capital ownership. If capital ownership did not yield an expected rate of return above that of the pure interest yield, most people would choose not to make such an investment. An imbalance of funds between investments yielding a fixed rate of return, such as savings accounts and bonds, and the more risky ownership rights would result. Thus, part of the rate of return to capital ownership performs the important function of inducing investors to bear the risk associated with these ownership rights.

Economic Profit

Almost an infinite number of potential investment projects are present. Some will increase the value of resources and therefore lead to a handsome rate of return on capital. Others may reduce the value of resources, generating economic losses. Economic loss is the result of uncertainty or miscalculation on the part of investors, who do not willingly undertake projects they do not expect to benefit from. **Economic profit** is the result of uncertainty, unawareness, or lack of knowledge on the part of people other than the investor—those who did not think of the investment project, could not see the benefits of risking it, could not accurately predict market changes that would contribute to it, and so on. In a world of perfect knowledge and communication and no uncertainty, profits (and losses) would be completely absent. However, the real world is one of change, disequilibrium markets, uncertainty, and imperfect knowledge. As a result, undiscovered economic opportunities abound. At any given time, there are numerous investment projects that, if acted upon, would generate revenues in excess of the opportunity cost (including interest and risk premium) of the capital necessary to carry out the task. However, since we cannot all know what these projects are and how they might be carried out, they often lie dormant, waiting to be undertaken by some future entrepreneur. Other opportunities are discovered and acted upon by astute entrepreneurs. These decision-makers are rewarded with profit for discovering a lower-cost method of production, introducing a new product, developing a new marketing technique, or correctly anticipating a future market change.

Economic profit is a return granted to those who recognize and undertake economically beneficial projects that have gone largely unnoticed by others—in short, it is a return for entrepreneurship. It is the result of imperfect knowledge. If knowledge of a profitable opportunity were widespread, competition would eliminate the profit. A successful entrepreneur must make decisions that will lead to an increase in the value of resources in the future. In order to make a profit, an entrepreneur uses roundabout methods of production, transforming resources into a product or service of greater value than the sum of its parts (the opportunity cost of the resources). Originality, quickness to act, and imagination are important aspects of entrepreneurship. Successful entrepreneurship involves leadership; most profits will be gone by the time the imitators arrive on the scene.

The great Harvard economist Joseph Schumpeter believed that entrepreneurship and innovative behavior were the moving forces behind capitalism. According to Schumpeter, this entrepreneurial discovery of new, improved ways of doing things led to a continual improvement in the standard of living of a nation:

The fundamental impulse that sets the capitalist engine in motion comes from the new consumers' goods, the new methods of production or transportation, the new markets, and the new forms of industrial organization that capitalist enterprise creates.[6]

Entrepreneurial decision-making is always conducted in an atmosphere of uncertainty. It is important to be first and to be innovative, but it is also important to be correct. Frequently, the entrepreneur's vision turns out to have been a mirage. What appeared to be a profitable opportunity often turns out to have been an expensive illusion.

Economic Profit: A return to investors who undertake projects that increase the value of the resources used. It stems from imperfect knowledge. As soon as the profitable opportunities are widely recognized by others, the competitive process tends to eliminate the profit. The discovery of opportunities that have gone unnoticed by others is the major source of profit.

---

[6]Joseph A. Schumpeter, *Capitalism, Socialism, and Democracy* (New York: Harper Torchbooks, 1950), p. 83.

Entrepreneurship, like other resources, is scarce. Just as people differ with regard to other skills, so, too, do they possess differing amounts of entrepreneurial ability. Potential entrepreneurs are confined to using their own wealth and that of coventurers, in addition to whatever can be borrowed. Entrepreneurs with a past record of success will be able to attract funds more readily for investment projects. Therefore, in a market economy, previously successful entrepreneurs will exert a disproportionate influence over decisions as to which projects will be undertaken and which will not.

OUTSTANDING ECONOMIST
Joseph Schumpeter
(1883–1950)

Born in Austria, Schumpeter began his career practicing law, but he soon turned to the teaching of economics. After a brief term (1919–1920) as the Austrian Minister of Finance, he taught economics during the 1920s at several European universities and was a visiting professor at Harvard University in 1927–1928 and again in 1930. In 1932, he emigrated to the United States, accepting a professorship at Harvard.

Although Schumpeter was widely respected for his scholarly achievements, he was a maverick among economists. He rejected the view that pure competition was the proper standard by which to judge the economic efficiency of markets. At a time when mathematical economics was asserting itself, he had little use for analysis that reduced economic decision-making to a set of mathematical equations. During the Age of Keynes, Schumpeter was an unabashed non-Keynesian.

A former president of the American Economic Association (1949), Schumpeter is perhaps best known for his views on entrepreneurship and the future of capitalism. He believed that the progressive improvement in the economic well-being of the mass of people was the result of the creative and innovative behavior of business entrepreneurs. Schumpeter believed that in the early stages of its development capitalism provided an almost ideal environment for the innovator. Entrepreneurs willing to risk their livelihood in order to pursue an innovative idea could be counted on to provide a steady stream of improved products at a reduced cost. Profits would accrue to those who successfully instituted innovative ideas. Losses would eliminate the less capable. These forces would generate widespread prosperity. As Schumpeter put it:

Queen Elizabeth owned silk stockings. The capitalist achievement does not typically consist in providing more silk stockings for queens but in bringing them within the reach of factory girls in return for steadily decreasing amounts of effort.[7]

Despite his admiration for a dynamic capitalist system, Schumpeter thought that the system would generate the seeds of its own destruction. Unlike Marx, who argued that capitalism would break down under the weight of its own failures, Schumpeter thought that the success of capitalism would eventually "undermine the social institutions which protect it."[8] He believed that the growth of large, technologically efficient organizations would dampen innovative zeal. The daring entrepreneur would be replaced by the organization person, the committee, and the board of directors. Compromise and organizational survival would replace innovation and creativity as the major objectives of business decision-making.

In addition, the affluence produced by a capitalist system would generate the wealth necessary to support a large intellectual class, which would neither understand nor appreciate the system. It would also breed a generation of flabby business leaders incapable of defending the system against its intellectual critics, who would turn the masses toward socialism. Is Schumpeter's indictment of capitalism correct? Only the future will tell.

[7]Joseph A. Schumpeter, *Capitalism, Socialism, and Democracy* (New York: Harper Torchbooks, 1950), p. 67.

[8]*Ibid.*, p. 61.

MONOPOLY PROFITS

As we discussed in previous chapters, profits may also originate from sole owner-ship of a key resource (as in the diamond industry), government regulation (as in the trucking industry), or a legally granted property right to a technical innovation (as for patented products). In such cases, the monopoly rights to the key resource, privileged license, or patent are worth the present value of the future return that is in excess of what could be earned in competitive markets. What does economics say about monopoly profit? Two factors must be con-sidered. First, as we pointed out previously, monopolists can gain from a "contrived" scarcity. They may choose to supply less of a product so that the price can be raised and profits increased. They may well forego the production of units even though their marginal cost is less than the product price. If one considers only the static economic effects, allocative inefficiency will result.

Second, monopoly profit does not exist in a vacuum. In a dynamic economy, potential monopoly profit will induce competitors to follow pathways that lead to monopoly profit. If dynamic efficiency indicates that the investment resulting in monopoly profit is actually beneficial, this advantage must be weighed against the *static* allocative inefficiency. The protection of property rights to inventions, new products, and innovative production techniques falls in this category—economic activities of this variety, though they result in monopoly profits, can clearly lead to improvements in economic welfare. In order to encourage innovative activities, most countries have established a patent system, even though a temporary grant of monopoly power results.

Regardless of their source, the present value of future monopoly profits is incorporated into the value of the assets that provide the "monopoly rights." Licenses that protect their owners from competitors command high prices if they guarantee an above-market rate of return. Similarly, the market value of patent rights and specialized resources incorporates the present value of any future monopoly profits that these assets might bestow on their owners. Once the monopoly profits are recognized by others, the market value of the monopoly-granting asset will rise until the monopoly profits have been eliminated.

RESOURCE ALLOCATION AND THE RETURNS TO CAPITAL

Each of the three major components of the returns to capital in a competitive economy has an important allocative function.[9] Interest induces persons to

---

[9]In addition to wages, interest, and profits, economists often discuss "rent" as a return to a factor of production. Economists define rent as a return to a factor the supply of which is perfectly inelastic. We have not included this discussion for two reasons. First, one can legitimately argue that the supply of all factors of production has some elasticity. After all, even the supply of usable land can be expanded through drainage, clearing, and conservation. Therefore, rent is always a matter of degree. Second, the term "rent" is used in a variety of ways, even by economists. The macroeconomic usage differs substantially from the usage in microeconomics. The term is sometimes used to define the returns to a specialized resource, such as an actor's talent, even though training plays an integral part in the supply of the resource. Rent is also sometimes applied to a factor the supply of which is temporarily fixed, even though it can clearly be expanded in the future. Since the returns to capital can be adequately discussed without introducing rent, we concluded that the cost of the ambiguity of the term exceeded the benefits of an extended discussion.

forego current consumption, a sacrifice that is a necessary ingredient for capital formation. The risk premium induces individuals to undertake the risk of owning capital assets in a dynamic, uncertain world. Pure economic profit induces human and physical capital decision-makers, whose knowledge is imperfect, to discover and develop opportunities for beneficial and productive projects.

Although nonmonetary factors are more important in human capital decision-making, profits and losses guide human capital investors just as they guide physical capital investors. Choosing a human capital investment project (obtaining a law degree, for example) involves the same risk and opportunity for profit (or loss) as the choice to purchase a new machine. In both instances, profit performs the same function. It is a return to the entrepreneur who discovers and undertakes better ways to utilize resources.

LOOKING AHEAD

The agricultural price support program illustrates the importance of many of the concepts incorporated into this chapter. The competitive process and the normal rate of return, the relationship between the *expected* future income and the present value of an asset, and capitalization of the future value of monopoly profit—all of these concepts will help us understand the impact of agricultural price supports. We conclude this chapter with an analysis of this issue.

PERSPECTIVES IN ECONOMICS
CAN AGRICULTURAL PRICE SUPPORTS MAKE FARMING MORE PROFITABLE?

Legislative action establishing a minimum price for an agricultural product. The government pledges to purchase any surplus of the product that cannot be sold to consumers at the support price.

For several decades, the mean income of farmers has been below the national average. There are several reasons for this. Some people enjoy the life-style—type of work, choice of working hours, self-employment status—of farming and therefore are willing to accept a lower *monetary* income in order to derive the accompanying nonpecuniary benefits. Agriculture provides greater opportunity for household production and self-sufficiency (for example, self-provision of meats, vegetables, and other products) than can be found in most other occupations. Thus, money income data tend to understate living standards in the agricultural sector. In addition, the income elasticity of most agricultural products is low. Thus, the demand for farm products has lagged behind the growth rate of the economy as a whole.

Since the 1930s, the government has instituted various types of **price support programs.** Price supports are designed to increase the prices of crops such as wheat, cotton, tobacco, peanuts, rice, and feed grains and thereby to increase farmers' incomes. However, there is good reason to question the programs' effectiveness.

Using wheat as an example, Exhibit 4 illustrates the nature of the early price support programs. These programs established a price floor for wheat above the market equilibrium

---

EXHIBIT 4 Impact of
agricultural price
supports

When a price support
program pushes the
price of an agricul-
tural product, such as
wheat, above the market
equilibrium, an excess
supply of the product
results. Initially, the excess supply may be
small [A_1B_1 of frame (a)].
However, as farmers ad-
just their planting and
cultivation, the long-run
supply of wheat be-
comes increasingly elas-
tic, causing the excess
supply to expand [to
A_2B_2, frame (b)].

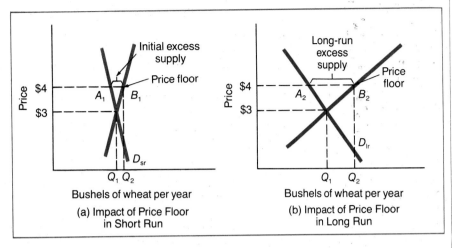

(a) Impact of Price Floor
in Short Run

(b) Impact of Price Floor
in Long Run

Acreage Restriction Program:
**A program designed to raise
the price of an agricultural
product by limiting the acreage planted with the product.**

level and pledged that any wheat that could not be sold at the support price would be purchased by the government. Of course, the above-equilibrium price led to an excess supply of wheat. As Exhibit 4a illustrates, *initially* the excess supply was relatively small (A_1B_1), since both the demand for and the supply of wheat were highly inelastic in the short run. However, with the passage of time, both the demand and supply curves became more elastic. Given sufficient time to adjust, farmers both culti-vated wheat land more intensively and increased the amount of land al-lotted to wheat. Therefore, the ex-cess supply that the government had pledged to purchase continued to in-crease. (Compare the size of the ex-cess supply of Exhibit 4b with 4a.)

The costs of storing the excess supply expanded rapidly. In fact, dur-ing the 1950s, these storage costs be-came a national scandal. The public outcry over the huge costs, economic waste, spoilage, and fraud eventually lead to alteration of the program.

In an effort to maintain a pol-icy of support for farmers without cre-ating surplus crops and the attendant problems, Congress adopted an **acre-age restriction program** designed to reduce the output of agricultural prod-ucts. Under this plan, price is still fixed above the market equilibrium, but the number of acres that farmers

can plant is reduced in order to de-crease supply and bring it into bal-ance with demand at "reasonable" prices. Each farm is granted an acre-age allotment for wheat (and other supported products), based on the acres planted during a base year. The allotments are attached to the farm. Owners of farms are prohibited from planting more than the specified num-ber of acres for each product.

Exhibit 5 illustrates the eco-nomics of the acreage restriction pro-gram. By restricting the number of acres planted, the supply of the prod-uct is reduced until the price of the product rises to the support level. If the government has to purchase the product at the support price, it can reduce the acreage allotments of farm-ers during the next period. In contrast, if the market price rises above the support level, the government can re-lax the allotment a little during the next period. In this manner, the gov-ernment is able to bring the amount demanded and amount supplied into balance at the supported price level (for example, as Exhibit 5 illustrates, at the $4 price floor for wheat).

The acreage restrictions make it more costly to grow any given amount of a product. Normally, farm-ers would minimize their cost of grow-ing more wheat (or any other product) by using a little more of *each* of the factors of production (land, labor, fer-

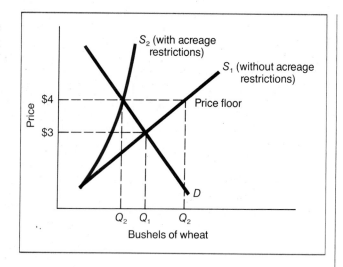

EXHIBIT 5   Acreage restrictions and limiting output

Rather than permit farmers to raise an amount of wheat that would generate an excess supply at the support price, under the acreage restriction program the government restricts the number of acres allocated to the growing of wheat, causing the supply of wheat to decline to S_2. With the acreage restrictions, the excess supply is eliminated, and the $4 support price is maintained.

tilizer, machinery, and so on). The acreage restriction program prohibits them from using more land. The support price provides farmers with an incentive to produce more wheat, for example, but they must do so by using factors of production other than land more intensively. Higher costs result, shifting the supply curve of Exhibit 5 to the left (to S_2). Supply curve S_1 is unattainable once the acreage restrictions are imposed, since it would require a larger amount of land than is permissible under the allotment program.

Is farming more profitable in the long run after the imposition of the acreage restrictions and price support programs? Surprisingly, the answer is no. To the extent that price supports make farming more profitable *in the short run,* the demand for land with acreage allotments increases (see Exhibit 6). Competition bids up the price of land with acreage allotments until the investors receive only the normal rate of return. Just as one cannot earn an abnormally high rate of return by purchasing stock ownership rights of a firm already earn-

ing monopoly profit, neither can a farmer earn an abnormally high rate of return by purchasing the ownership rights of farms with acreage allotments.

Suppose that the price support program permitted wheat growers to earn an additional $100 each year from an acre of land planted in wheat. If that were true, the net present value (NPV) of the *land with a wheat allotment* would rise by $100 divided by the interest rate. At a 10 percent rate of interest, the value of the additional $100 per year would equal $1000

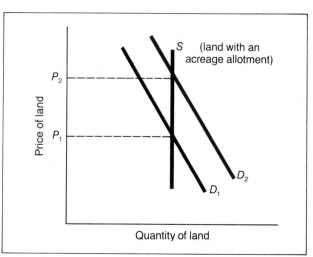

EXHIBIT 6   Rising land values and capitalizing profit

Since land with an acreage allotment permits one to plant wheat and sell it at the above-market-equilibrium price, the price support program makes such land more valuable. Competition drives the price of land *with an allotment* upward until the higher land values fully capture the larger profits resulting from the program. But once land values have risen, the farmer's rate of return on investment is no higher with the program than it was prior to the program's establishment. The major beneficiaries of price support programs have been those who owned land with acreage allotments *at the time the programs were established.*

(NPV $= R/i =$ \$100/.10 $=$ \$1000). The value of an acre of land with a wheat allotment would rise by \$1000. Essentially, the value of the monopoly-profit income stream derived from the price support program would be capitalized into the value of *land with a wheat allotment*.

The major beneficiaries of the price support/acreage restriction program have been the owners of land with an allotment *at the time of the program's establishment*. Competition for land with acreage allotments has driven the price of such land up until the rate of return on agricultural land with allotments is equal to the market rate of return. Thus, the profit rate of the current owners of the land is no higher than it would have been had Congress never adopted any kind of price support system in the first place.

Discussion

1. Suppose the current price support/acreage allotment program for wheat were abolished. What would be the impact on (a) the value of land with wheat allotments, (b) the cost of producing wheat, (c) the market price of wheat, and (d) the profitability of wheat farming?

2. Farmers are often heard to complain that they are not helped by the price support/acreage allotment program, and yet they oppose its repeal. Explain why these seemingly contradictory views are not surprising.

CHAPTER LEARNING OBJECTIVES

1 The extensive use of tools, machinery, and other forms of physical capital sets human beings apart from other animals. An increase in the quantity (and quality) of tools and the adoption of innovative, roundabout methods of production have made our current standard of living possible.

2 Roundabout methods of production require the sacrifice of current production because resources that might otherwise be used to produce consumption goods directly are employed in the construction of tools, machines, and other man-made capital assets designed to increase future productive capabilities.

3 Interest is the price that people are willing to pay to obtain goods and services now rather than in the future. Since earlier availability is usually attained through borrowing in the loanable funds market, the interest rate is often defined as the price of loanable funds.

4 Both consumers and investors demand loanable funds and are willing to pay the price—the interest rate. This is because consumers have a positive rate of time preference, and investors are willing to pay a premium for the loanable funds required to undertake potentially productive capital investment projects. If consumers did not prefer earlier availability and if capital investments were not productive, there would be no reason to expect a positive interest rate.

5 During inflationary times, the money rate of interest incorporates an inflationary premium reflecting the expected future decline in the purchasing power of the monetary unit. Under these circumstances, the money rate of interest exceeds the real rate of interest.

6 The money rate of interest on a specific loan reflects three basic factors—the pure interest rate, an inflationary premium, and a premium associated with the risk and processing cost of the loan.

7 Since a dollar in the future is valued less than a dollar today, the value of future receipts must be discounted in order to calculate their current worth. The discounting procedure can be used to calculate the net present value of an expected income stream from a potential investment project. The discount rate should reflect both the risk and the pure interest elements. The project should be undertaken only if the net present value of the expected income from the project exceeds its current cost (purchase price).

8 The returns to capital are (a) a pure interest return reflecting the opportunity cost of investment funds, (b) a risk premium reflecting the desire of individuals, on average, to avoid the risks of capital ownership and noncontractual income, and (c) pure eco-

nomic profit or loss, reflecting the owner-entrepreneur's ability to identify and carry out projects in a manner that increases the value of resources.

9 Human capital investments are analyzed in the same way in which other investments are analyzed, although nonmonetary factors are more important in human capital decisions.

10 Monopoly profits accrue when entry barriers shield an entrepreneur from competitive pressure. Sole ownership of a vital resource, legal restraint of entry, and patents can bestow monopoly rights on owners of assets. Monopoly profits encourage entrepreneurs to invest resources in order to acquire a monopoly privilege.

THE ECONOMIC WAY OF THINKING—DISCUSSION QUESTIONS

1 Suppose that U.S. investors are considering the construction of bicycle factories in two different countries, one in Europe and the other in Africa. Projected costs and revenues are at first identical, but the chance of guerilla warfare (and possible destruction of the factory) is suddenly perceived in the African nation. In which country will the price of bicycles (and the current rate of return to bicycle factories) probably rise? Will the investors be better off in the country with the higher rate of return? Why or why not?

2 How would a change in each of the following factors influence the rate of interest in the United States?
   (a) The time preference of lenders
   (b) The time preference of borrowers
   (c) Domestic inflation
   (d) Uncertainty about a nuclear war
   (e) Investment opportunities in Europe

3 Can you discover ways to make pure economic profits from an investment by reading about currently profitable investments in the *Wall Street Journal?* Why or why not?

4 "Any return to capital above the pure interest yield is unnecessary. The pure interest yield is sufficient to provide capitalists with the earnings necessary to replace their assets and to compensate for their sacrifice of current consumption. Any return above that is pure gravy; it is excess profit." Do you agree with this view? Why or why not?

5 How are human and physical capital investment decisions similar? How do they differ? What determines the profitability of a physical capital investment? Do human capital investors make profits? If so, what is the source of profit? Explain.

6 Suppose that you are contemplating the purchase of a minicomputer at a cost of $1000. The expected lifetime of the asset is three years. You expect to lease the asset to a business for $400 annually (payable at the end of each year) for three years. If you can borrow (and lend) money at an interest rate of 8 percent, will the investment be a profitable undertaking? Is the project profitable at an interest rate of 12 percent? Provide calculations in support of your answer.

7 How do the accounting profits of corporations differ from economic profits? Do corporate profits incorporate an interest return? A risk return? A pure profit return? A monopoly profit return? As a percentage of corporate assets, how large do you think each of these returns is in most manufacturing industries? Explain.

26

LABOR UNIONS AND COLLECTIVE BARGAINING

Approximately 22 million Americans, a little more than one out of every five workers, belong to labor unions (see Exhibit 1). A labor union is an organization of employees in which the majority have consented to joint bargaining with an employer about wages, grievance procedures, and other conditions of employment. Historically, unions have been controversial. Some believe that the actions of unions are the major source of several economic ills, particularly unemployment and inflation. Others argue that unions are the source of improved economic conditions for working people, their shield against the beast of employer greed. Who is right? What has been the role of the labor union? How does collective bargaining influence the operation of labor markets? This chapter addresses these and related questions.

WHAT IS A COLLECTIVE-BARGAINING CONTRACT?

Collective-Bargaining Contract: A detailed contract between (a) a group of employees (a labor union) and (b) an employer. It covers wage rates and conditions of employment.

Each year, **collective-bargaining contracts** covering wages and working conditions for 6 million to 9 million workers are negotiated. The union negotiators, acting as agents for a group of employees, bargain with management about the provisions of a labor contract. If the union representatives are able to obtain a contract they consider acceptable, they will typically submit it to a vote of the union members. If approved by the members, the contract establishes in detail wage rates, fringe benefits, and working conditions for a future time interval, usually the next two or three years. During that time interval, both union and management must abide by the conditions of the contract. Although the labor contract is between management and the union, it also applies to the nonunion bargaining unit members who are employed by the firm or industry.

---

[1]Irving Kristol, "Understanding Trade Unionism," *Wall Street Journal* (October 23, 1978). Reprinted with permission of the *Wall Street Journal.*

EXHIBIT 1   Union membership

Union membership grew quite rapidly between 1930 and 1950. During the 1960s, it leveled off at approximately one out of every four workers. During the 1970s, union membership as a share of the labor force declined.

Year	Union Membership	Percentage of Labor Force
1900	791	2.6
1910	2,116	5.6
1920	5,034	12.1
1930	3,632	7.4
1940	8,944	15.9
1950	15,000	22.9
1960	18,117	25.1
1970	20,752	24.2
1980	22,400	20.9

Lance E. Davis et al., *American Economic Growth* (New York: Harper & Row, 1972), and *Monthly Labor Review* (January 1982), p.26.

Union Shop: The requirement that all employees join the recognized union and pay dues to it within a specified length of time (usually 30 days) after their employment with the firm begins.

Some labor–management contracts contain a **union shop** provision. A union shop contract requires all workers to join the union after a specified length of employment, usually 30 days. Union proponents argue that since all workers in the bargaining unit enjoy the benefits of collective bargaining, all should be required to join and pay dues. In the absence of a union shop, individual workers can reap the gains brought about by the union's actions without incurring the cost.

Opponents of the union shop argue that all employees are not helped by a union. Some unions lack the necessary power to obtain wage increases. Some employees may feel that they would be better off if they could bargain for themselves. In addition, unions often engage in political activities, either directly or indirectly. These activities may run counter to the views of individual employees. Why should an employee be forced, as a condition of employment, to support activities of which he does not approve? In 1947, Congress passed the Taft–Hartley Act; Section 14-B allows states to enact **right to work laws** prohibiting union shop contracts. Currently, some 20 states have such laws.

Right-to-Work Laws: Laws that prohibit the union shop. Each state has an option to adopt (or reject) such legislation.

THE STRIKE — A "BIG STICK" OF THE UNION

Typically, management and labor negotiators begin the bargaining process for a new labor contract several months, or even a year, before the termination of the current agreement. Usually, the new contract is approved before the old contract has terminated. However, at the termination of the old labor–management agreement, if the bargaining process has broken down and there is no agreement on a new contract, either side may use its economic power to try to bring the other to terms.

Employers can withhold employment from workers at the expiration of the old contract. This is called a **lockout.** Since employers can unilaterally announce their terms for continued employment, however, they will seldom lock out employees. Generally, a lockout occurs only when a union is striking a single member of an employer association, causing that member to lose sales to

Lockout: An action taken by an employer to deny employment to current employees.

competitors. When this is the case, the employers may have an agreement to discontinue work in the entire industry until the labor dispute is settled. Under these circumstances, competitors of the firm may use the lockout.

The major source of work stoppages is the strike. A **strike** consists of two major actions by a union: (a) Employees, particularly union employees, refuse to work, and (b) steps are taken to prevent other employees from working for the employer. Both conditions are essential to a strike. Without efforts to prevent other employees, often referred to as "scabs" or "strikebreakers," from accepting jobs with the employer, a strike would merely be a mass resignation. However, a strike also involves picketing to restrict and discourage the hiring of other workers, actions to prevent free entry and exit from a plant, and perhaps even violence or the threat of violence against workers willing to cross the picket lines.

The purpose of a strike is to impose economic costs on an employer so that the terms proposed by the union will be accepted. When the strike can be used to disrupt the production process and interfere with the employer's ability to sell goods and services to customers, it is a very powerful weapon. Under such conditions, the employer may submit to the wage demands of the union, as a means of avoiding the costs of the strike.

Given the nature of the strike, it is not surprising that the "right to strike" has had an uneven history. At times, striking was prohibited because it was considered to interfere with the rights of nonunion workers. In some countries, the Soviet Union, for example, strikes are prohibited. In others, they are permitted only in certain industries. In the United States, before the passage of legislation in the early 1900s clearly establishing the right to strike, the courts were sometimes willing to intervene and limit certain types of strikes. The role of law enforcement in strikes also has had a mixed history. In some areas, the police have given nonstrikers, who desire to continue working, protection to and from their jobs. In other cases, they have permitted pickets to block entry and have turned their backs on the violence between strikers and nonstrikers. Even today, the protection a nonstriker can expect from the police varies from location to location.

The United States has established some limitations on the right to strike. Several states limit the right of public employees to strike. The Taft–Hartley Act allows the president to seek a court injunction prohibiting a strike for 80 days when it is believed that the strike would create a "national emergency." During the 80-day period, work continues under the conditions of the old contract. However, if a settlement has not been reached during this "cooling-off" period, employees again have the option of using the strike weapon. President Nixon used the 80-day injunction in 1971 when the country was faced with a longshoremen's strike. President Eisenhower applied it during a steel industry strike in 1959. Strikes by federal employees are also prohibited by law. When the air-traffic controllers' union called a strike during the summer of 1981, striking workers who refused to return to work were fired and eventually replaced.

The Strike and Serious Bargaining

A strike can be costly to both the union and management. From the firm's viewpoint, a work stoppage may mean that it will be unable to meet the current demand for its product. It may lose customers, and they may be difficult to win back once they have turned to competitors during the strike. A strike will be more

Strike: An action of unionized employees in which they (a) discontinue working for the employer and (b) take steps to prevent other potential workers from offering their services to the employer.

costly to the firm when (a) demand for its product is strong, (b) it is unable to stockpile its product, and (c) its fixed costs are high even during the strike. If the firm can stockpile its product in anticipation of a strike, a work stoppage may not have much impact on current sales. For example, automobile producers, particularly during slack times, often have an inventory of new cars that allows them to meet current demand during a 60- or even 90-day strike. In contrast, the shipping revenues of a trucking firm may be completely eliminated by a truckers' strike. The firm would be unable to deliver its service because of the strike, and potential customers would therefore turn to rail, air, postal, and other forms of shipping. The firm could suffer a permanent loss of sales.

Careful timing can also magnify the cost of a strike. Agricultural unions can threaten farmers with the loss of an entire year's income by striking at harvest time. Similarly, major league umpires can strengthen their position by striking at World Series time.

The nature of the product, the level of current demand, and the ability of the firm to continue to meet the requests of its customers during a strike all influence the effectiveness of the strike as a weapon. The more costly a work stoppage would be to a firm, the greater the pressure on it to yield to the demands of the union.

Strikes, particularly if they are long, are also quite costly to employees. Although a carnival attitude often prevails during the early days of a strike, a few weeks without paychecks impose an extreme hardship on most families. Strike funds are usually inadequate to deal with a prolonged strike. In recent years, welfare benefits have been used to reduce the cost imposed on workers by the strike.[2] Temporary employment in other areas can sometimes be arranged, but as a strike continues, pressures build on the union to arrive at a settlement.

The strike, or the threat of it, forces both management and labor to bargain seriously. The potential cost of a strike to both union and management provides them with an incentive to settle without a work stoppage. Each year, an estimated 120,000 labor contracts are terminated. Thus, during the course of a year, 120,000 labor and management bargaining teams sit across the bargaining table from each other. They deal with the important issues of wages, fringe benefits, grievance procedures, and conditions of employment. More than 96 percent of the time, labor–management contracts are agreed to without the use of the strike. One seldom hears about these contracts because peaceful settlements are back-page news, at best. It is the strikes that rate the headlines.

The Bureau of Labor Statistics estimates the amount of working time lost because of strikes. These data, presented in Exhibit 2, indicate that during the last 30 years, the number of worker-hours lost because of strikes was less than three-tenths of 1 percent of the total working time, far less than the work time lost because of absenteeism. The amount of work time lost due to strikes has been declining.

How Does the "Big Stick" Affect the Public?

It is often difficult to place work stoppages in proper perspective—to balance the significance and usefulness of the strike with its deleterious effects on the public. Some strikes have a substantial impact on parties other than the union–management participants. For example, a prolonged strike in the steel industry

---

[2]The availability of welfare benefits to strikers varies among areas.

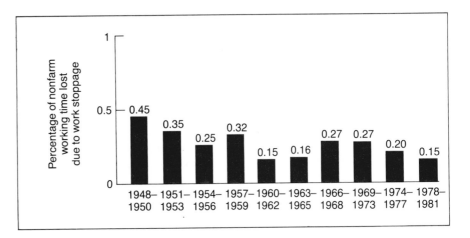

might cause a loss of work time in automobile, construction, and other industries. A teachers' strike might force a working parent to quit his or her job in order to care for the children. A public transit strike in New York can paralyze Fun City. A coal miners' strike can leave Londoners without heat.

Innocent parties, who are unable to influence the labor–management agreement, are often harmed because a vital community service is discontinued. Substantial financial losses are sometimes absorbed by wholesalers, retailers, shippers, and secondary manufacturers (and their employees) who are critically dependent on the material or service that has been interrupted by a strike. The public interest is affected. How can one measure the economic loss from such strikes? Should not third parties be protected when strikes involve the public interest? Many would answer the latter question in the affirmative. But how can the public be protected without interfering with the bargaining process? These questions have not yet been fully answered.

GETTING MORE FOR UNION MEMBERS

How can unions influence wages? The collective-bargaining process often gives one the impression that wages are established primarily by the talents of the union–management representatives who sit at the bargaining table. It might appear that market forces play a relatively minor role. However, as both union and management are well aware, market forces provide the setting in which the bargaining process is conducted. They often tip the balance of power one way or the other.

When the demand for a product is strong, the demand for labor will be high, and the firm will be much more willing to consent to a significant wage increase. However, when demand is weak, the product inventory level of the firm (or industry) is more likely to be high. The firm's current demand for labor will be weakened. It will be much less vulnerable to a union work stoppage. Under such conditions, wage increases will be much more difficult to obtain.

As we have already indicated, collective-bargaining agreements cover both wages and fringe benefits (vacation time, sick leave, accident benefits, and so on). Fringe benefits are an indirect component of employee compensation.

Thus, when we speak of wage rates, we include both direct money wages and employer-provided fringe benefits.

A union can use three basic strategies in order to increase the wages of its members.

Supply Restrictions

If a union can successfully reduce the supply of competitive labor, higher wage rates will result automatically. Licensing requirements, long apprenticeship programs, immigration barriers, high initiation fees, refusal to admit new members to the union, and prohibition of nonunion workers from holding jobs are all practices that unions have used in order to limit the supply of labor to various occupations and jobs. Craft unions, in particular, have often been able to obtain higher wages because of their successful effort to limit the entry of competitive labor. In the 1920s, unions successfully lobbied for legislation that reduced the torrent of worker-immigrants from abroad to a mere trickle. The tighter immigration laws considerably reduced the influx of new workers, reducing the growth of supply in U.S. labor markets and thus causing higher wages to prevail.

Exhibit 3 illustrates the impact of supply restrictions on wage rates. Successful exclusionary tactics will reduce supply, shifting the supply curve from S_0 to S_1. Facing the supply curve S_1, employers will consent to the wage rate W_1. Compared with a free entry market equilibrium, the wage rate has increased from W_0 to W_1, but employment has declined from E_0 to E_1. At the higher wage rate, W_1, an excess supply of labor, AB, will result. The restrictive practices will prevent this excess supply from undercutting the above-equilibrium wage rate. Because of the exclusionary practices, the union will be able to obtain higher wages for E_1 employees. Other employees who would be willing to accept work even at wage rate W_0 will now be forced into other areas of employment.

Bargaining Power

Must unions restrict entry? Why can they not simply use their bargaining power, the strike threat, as a vehicle for raising wages? If they have enough economic power, this will be possible. A strike by even a small percentage of vital employees can sometimes halt the flow of production. For example, a work stoppage by airline mechanics can force major airlines to cancel their flights. Because the mechanics perform an essential function, an airline cannot operate without their services, even though they constitute only 10 percent of all airline employees.

If the union is able to obtain an above-free-entry wage rate, the impact on employment will be similar to a reduction in supply. As Exhibit 3 illustrates, employers will hire fewer workers at the higher wage rate obtained through bargaining power. Employment will decline below the free entry level (from E_0 to E_1) as a result of the rise in wages. An excess supply of labor, AB, will exist, at least temporarily. More employees will seek the high-wage union jobs than employers will choose to hire. Nonwage methods of rationing jobs will become more important.

Increase in Demand

The demand for union labor is usually determined by factors outside the union's direct control, such as the availability of substitute inputs and the demand for

EXHIBIT 3 Supply restrictions, bargaining power, and wage rates

The impact of higher wages obtained by restricting supply is very similar to that obtained through bargaining power. As illustrated by graph (a), when union policies reduce the supply of one type of labor, higher wages result. Similarly, when bargaining power is used in order to obtain higher wages (graph b), employment declines and an excess supply of labor results.

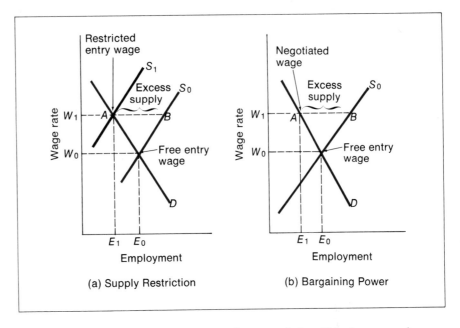

(a) Supply Restriction

(b) Bargaining Power

the product. However, unions can sometimes use their political power to increase the demand for their services. They may be able to induce legislators to pass laws requiring the employment of certain types or amounts of labor for a task (for example, unneeded firemen on trains, allegedly for safety reasons, or a certain number of stage engineers). Unions often seek the protection of tariffs as a means of increasing the demand for domestic labor. For example, automobile workers strongly support high tariffs on foreign-made automobiles. Garment workers seek a tariff policy that limits the import of foreign clothing. Such practices increase the demand for domestic automobiles and clothing, thereby increasing the demand for domestic auto and garment workers. It is not surprising that the management and union representatives of a specific industry often join hands in demanding government tariff protection from foreign competition. As Exhibit 4 illustrates, successful union actions to increase the demand for the services of union members result in both higher wages and an expansion in employment, usually at the expense of consumers.

A union in a strong bargaining position may shift the firm *off* its demand curve. This can happen if the union offers an "all-or-none" settlement in which the union specifies both wage *and* the quantity of labor (or restrictive work rules). In order to get *any* labor, the firm must hire more labor at the union wage than it wants. For example, the International Typographical Union has stipulated that after a page of newspaper type has been set and run automatically (to save time and to get late news in before a deadline), the same page must later be set, proofread, and corrected in the newspaper's composing room. This is called "bogus type" and is discarded. If the newspaper wants *any* work—and no picket lines—from typesetters, it must either pay them to do "bogus" work or make other bargaining concessions that will induce the union to withdraw the rule. This type of "make-work rule" is another way in which a union may be able to loosen the connection between higher wages and lower levels of employment.

EXHIBIT 4 Rising demand and wage increases

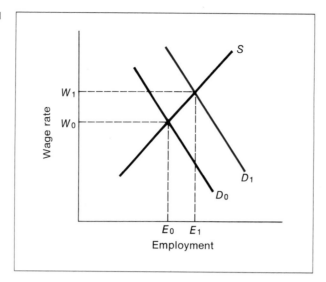

UNION POWER, EMPLOYMENT, AND MONOPSONY

Is unionization necessary to protect employees from the power of employers? When there are a large number of employers in a market area, the interest of employees will be protected by competition among employers. Under these circumstances, each employer must pay the market wage to employees in order to keep them from shifting to higher-paying alternative employers. In a modern society, labor is highly mobile. Most employees work in a labor market where there are many employers. However, a few workers may confront a situation where there is only a single employer of labor, at least for the specific skill category of labor supplied by the workers. For example, if a single large employer—perhaps a textile manufacturer or lumber mill—dominates the labor market of a small town, local workers may have few alternative employment opportunities.

> **Monopsony:** A market in which there is only one buyer. The monopsonist faces the market supply curve for the resource (or product) bought.

Analysis of resource markets under conditions of **monopsony** will help us to understand situations where the market is dominated by a single employer or a small number of employers. Monopsony refers to a market situation in which there is a single buyer for a specific resource, for example, a specific skill category of labor. As we previously discussed, when the *seller* has a monopoly, the seller can profit by restricting output and charging a price above the marginal cost of production. Under monopsony, the *buyer* has a monopoly. Since the alternatives available to sellers are limited, the monopsonist-buyer will be able to profit by restricting the purchase of the resource and paying a price (wage rate) that is less than the marginal revenue generated by the resource.

> **Marginal Factor Cost:** The cost of employing an additional unit of a resource. When the employer is small relative to the total market, the marginal factor cost is simply the price of the resource. In contrast, under monopsony, marginal factor cost will exceed the price of the resource, since the monopsonist faces an upward-sloping supply curve for the resource.

Exhibit 5 illustrates the impact of monopsony in the labor market. Since the monopsonist is the only employer (purchaser of labor), its supply curve for the resource in question will coincide with the market supply curve for that resource. The supply curve for the resource will slope upward to the right because higher wages are necessary to attract the additional workers desired. For now, we will assume that both the old and new employees will be paid the higher wage rates if employment is expanded. The **marginal factor cost** (MFC) curve indicates the marginal cost of labor to the monopsonist. The marginal factor

EXHIBIT 5   Labor market monopsony and unionization

As frame (a) illustrates, the monopsonist's supply curve for labor will slope upward to the right. The marginal factor cost curve for labor will be steeper than the labor supply curve. The monopsonist will hire E_1 units of labor and pay a wage rate, W_1, along its labor supply curve. If a union establishes a wage floor, W_2 of frame (b), for example, the monopsonist may hire additional workers (E_2 rather than E_1) at the higher wage rate.

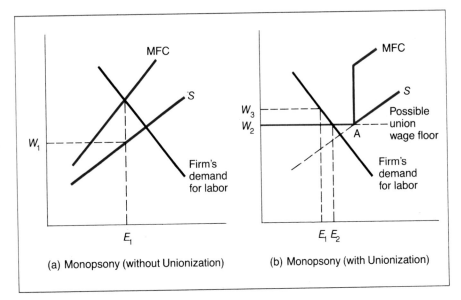

(a) Monopsony (without Unionization)   (b) Monopsony (with Unionization)

cost of labor will exceed the wage rate because the higher wages necessary to attract each additional worker must be paid to *all* employees. As illustrated by Exhibit 5, this means that the monopsonist's marginal factor cost curve will be steeper than the labor supply curve.

How many workers should a profit-maximizing monopsony employ? The monopsonist's demand curve for labor indicates how much each additional worker adds to the firm's total revenue. The monopsonist will continue to expand employment as long as hiring additional workers adds more to total revenue than to total costs. This means that the monopsonist will choose employment level E_1, where the firm's demand curve, reflecting the marginal revenue product of labor, is just equal to the marginal factor cost of labor. A wage rate of W_1 will be sufficient to attract E_1 employees. For employment levels beyond E_1, it would cost (MFC) the monopsonist more to hire an additional worker than that worker would add to total revenue. As the result of this cost, the monopsonist firm will hire fewer employees than it would if it were not the only buyer in the labor market.

Exhibit 5b illustrates what would happen if a union established a wage floor—W_2, for example—for a monopsonist. The wage floor would prohibit the monopsonist from paying low wages even if employment dropped. The union would confront the employer with the supply curve W_2AS. In essence, the wage floor would become the firm's marginal factor cost curve until the wage floor intersected the labor supply curve at A. As long as the marginal factor cost of additional units of labor was less than the firm's demand curve, additional workers would continue to be employed. Thus, if a union imposed wage rate W_2, the monopsonist would expand employment to E_2. In this case, unionization would result in both higher wages and an expansion in employment. If the union expanded the wage rate above W_3, employment would fall below E_1, the level employed by a nonunion monopsonist. But for any wage floor less than W_3, the monopsonist would expand employment beyond E_1.

While this analysis is sound as far as it goes, there are three additional factors that should be considered.[3] First, a higher wage rate will obviously increase the firm's total costs of production. In the long run, when the firm sells its product in a competitive market, higher per unit cost will almost certainly force the firm to raise its price in order to cover costs. A decline in the firm's market share and output is a likely result. As the firm's market share declines, employment of all factors of production, including labor, will fall.

Second, a monopsonist will often be able to confine the higher wage rates to new employees only. When this is the case, the marginal factor cost curve of the monopsonist will not differ from its labor supply curve. Rather than restricting employment in order to keep wages low, the firm may simply offer the new employees (but not the old ones) higher job classifications and more attractive employment conditions in order to obtain their services.

Third, given the speed of transportation, employers often draw workers from 30 to 50 miles away. In addition, many employees (particularly skilled workers, professionals, and managers) compete in a much broader labor market, a national labor market in some cases. Over a peiod of time, such workers will flow into and away from local labor markets. Thus, given the mobility of labor, most employers will be small *relative to their labor market,* and their decisions to expand or contract their work force will not exert much impact on the market wage rate. Under these circumstances marginal factor cost is nearly the same as the wage rate in the competitive market model. Therefore, a rise in the wage rate will almost certainly reduce employment.

WHAT GIVES A UNION STRENGTH?

Not all unions are able to raise the wages of their workers. What are the factors that make a union strong? Why are some unions able to maintain employee wages above free entry level, while others have a negligible impact on wage rates?

Simply stated, if a union is to be strong, the demand for its labor must be inelastic. This will enable the union to obtain large wage increases while suffering only modest reductions in employment. In contrast, when the demand for union labor is quite elastic, a substantial rise in wages will mean few, if any, jobs.

There are four major determinants of the demand elasticity for a factor of production: (a) the availability of substitutes, (b) the elasticity of produce demand, (c) the share of the input as a proportion of total cost, and (d) the supply elasticity of substitute inputs.[4] We now turn to the importance of each of these conditions as a determinant of union strength.

The Availability of Good Substitute Inputs

When it is difficult to substitute other inputs for unionized labor, the union is strengthened. Since nonunion labor is a good substitute for union labor, the

---

[3]See Armen Alchian and William Allen, *Exchange and Production: Competition, Coordination, and Control* (Belmont, California: Wadsworth, 1977) p. 407, for additional theoretical analysis of monopsony.
[4]See Alfred Marshall, *Principles of Economics,* 8th ed. (New York: Macmillan, 1920). Also see Outstanding Economist: Alfred Marshall, p. 48.

power of unions to exclude nonunion labor is an important determinant of union strength. Unless a union can prevent nonunion employees from entering an occupation and cutting wages below the union level, it will be unable to raise wages significantly above the free entry level.

Even if a union can successfully restrict competition from nonunion employees, the availability of machines that are good substitutes for labor will greatly reduce the power of the union. Wage increases will induce employers to mechanize. Thus, a substantial wage increase can mean a sharp reduction in employment. Many workers may be laid off.

A comparison of the experiences of elevator operators and airline pilots highlights the importance of substitute inputs. When the elevator operators of many large cities unionized and negotiated substantial wage increases, their gains were short-lived. Employers quickly turned to automated elevators, and the employment of elevator operators fell drastically. Airline pilots, however, are able to maintain above-free-entry wage rates without much substitution in production. People do not object to riding an automated elevator, but they are not likely (at least not in the foreseeable future) to tolerate an automated airplane. Because a low-cost substitute was available for elevator operators, their union was weakened. Since there is a lack of low-cost substitutes for airline pilots, the pilots' union is one of the strongest in the United States.

The Elasticity of Product Demand

Wages are a component of costs. An increase in the wage of union members will almost surely lead to higher prices for goods produced with union labor. If produce demand is inelastic, higher produce price will exert only a small negative influence on production and employment in the industry. However, if product demand is elastic, higher produce prices will lead to sharply reduced sales and a substantial cut in employment.

An example will help to illustrate the point. Suppose that the garment workers in New York City negotiate a 50 percent increase in wages. The higher wage rates make it more costly to produce clothing products in New York. The New York firms must raise their price if they are to cover costs. When they do so, however, their customers turn to good substitutes, namely, clothing produced by nonunion labor in the South, Puerto Rico, Japan, and other parts of the world. The sales of New York firms fall drastically. Since the demand for their product is highly elastic, New York garment workers are laid off in droves.

The garment industry case points out why unionization of an entire industry is an important determinant of union strength. The demand for the product of a single firm, or even a group of firms in an industry, will almost certainly be quite elastic. When only a portion of an industry is unionized, similar goods produced by the nonunion firms offer consumers a very good substitute. Thus, higher wages in the union sector would have a drastic impact on employment.

Events in the real world are consistent with the theory. In the 1920s, the United Mine Workers obtained big wage gains in unionized coal fields. However, these fields soon lost their major share of the market to nonunionized fields, leading to a sharp reduction in the employment of union members. In more recent times, unionized employment in the trucking industry has declined because of the product market competition of nonunion firms (see boxed feature, following page). The existence of good substitutes, particularly similar products made by nonunion labor, greatly restricts the union's power to raise wages above the open market level.

Union Labor as a Share of Cost of Production

If the unionized labor input comprises only a small share of total production cost, demand for that labor will tend to be relatively inelastic. For example, since the wages of plumbers and pilots comprise only a small share of the total cost of production in the housing and air travel industries, respectively, a doubling or even tripling of the wages of plumbers or airline pilots would result in only a 1 or 2 percent increase in the cost of housing or air travel. A large increase in the price of such inputs would have little impact on product price, output, and employment. This factor has sometimes been called "the importance of being unimportant," because it is important to the strength of the union.

The Supply Elasticity of Substitute Inputs

We have just explained that if wage rates in the unionized sector are pushed upward, firms will look for substitute inputs, and the demand for these substitutes will increase. But if the supply of these substitutes (such as nonunion labor) is inelastic, their price will rise sharply in response to an increase in demand. The higher price will reduce the attractiveness of the substitutes. Thus, an inelastic supply of substitutes will strengthen the union by making the demand for union labor more inelastic.

WAGES OF UNION AND NONUNION EMPLOYEES

Even a strong union must contend with market forces. The precise impact of unions on the wages of their members is not easy to determine. Nonetheless, several studies have examined the effect of unionism on wages.[5]

H. Gregg Lewis, in a pioneering study published in 1963, estimated that, *on average*, union workers received wages between 10 and 15 percent higher than those of nonunion workers *with similar productivity characteristics*. Of course, some unions had an even greater impact. Lewis estimated that strong unions, such as the electricians', plumbers', tool and diemakers', metal craft workers', truckers' (this was prior to moves toward deregulation), and commercial airline pilots' unions, were able to raise the wages of their members by 25 percent or more. In general, Lewis's evidence indicates that craft unions are stronger than industrial unions. From the standpoint of economic theory, this is not surprising. Craftspeople usually perform a vital service for which there are few good substitutes.

Unionization appears to have had the least impact on the earnings of cotton textile, footwear, furniture, hosiery, clothing, and retail sales workers. In these areas, the power of the union has been substantially limited by the existence of readily available nonunion workers. Even when a union shop exists, the demands of the union are moderated by the fear of placing the unionized employer at a competitive disadvantage in relation to the nonunion employers of the industry.

The data for Lewis's study were gathered primarily in the 1940s and

---

[5] See H. Gregg Lewis, *Unionism and Relative Wages in the United States* (Chicago: University of Chicago Press, 1963), for a discussion of many of these studies. Also see Albert Rees, *The Economics of Trade Unions* (Chicago: University of Chicago Press, 1967).

COMPETITION FROM PRODUCTS SUPPLIED BY NONUNION LABOR—THE CASES OF THE UAW AND THE TEAMSTERS

Unless a union can limit the consumers' access to products made by nonmember employees, product market competition is a serious threat to the union. The recent experiences of both the United Automobile Workers (UAW) and the Teamsters illustrate this point. Throughout the 1970s, these two unions were believed to be among the most powerful labor organizations. However, changing market conditions subjected the products of both unions to greater competition in the early 1980s.

As the chart below shows, the hourly earnings of production workers in the motor vehicle industry were 34.8 percent greater in 1969 than the average hourly earnings in the private sector. During the 1970s, the UAW pushed member wages up rapidly. By 1980, the hourly earnings in the motor vehicle industry were 55.6 percent greater than those in the private sector.

Beginning in the late 1970s, the strength of the United Automobile Workers began to be undermined. Two factors were responsible. First, higher fuel prices made small foreign automobiles much more competitive and attractive in the U.S. market. Lower labor costs contributed to the competitive prices of imports. As of late 1981, the average wage rate in the Japanese automobile industry was $6.15 per hour, only a little more than half the comparable rate in the U.S. auto industry. Recent studies indicate that, as of 1980, Japanese manufacturers could build a car and ship it to the United States for $1300 to $1700 less than it would cost U.S. manufacturers to build the equivalent automobile. Thus, imported models grabbed an increasing share of the U.S. market in the late 1970s and early 1980s. By 1981, imports accounted for one-third of U.S. automobile sales, up from 20 percent in 1978. U.S. manufacturers began purchasing more and more automobile components from nonunion suppliers, in an effort to reduce costs. The second reason for the UAW's weakening was the sharp decline in the inflation rate and the accompanying recession during 1979–1981. By 1981, the sales of American-made automobiles had declined to about 6 million, down from roughly 9 million in 1978.

This combination of factors—increased competition from imports, and the recession—threw the automobile industry into a virtual depression in 1981. Employment declined from 1.01 million in 1979 (February) to 704,000 in 1981 (November). Between 1978 and 1980, the UAW lost 142,000 members, a nearly 10 percent decline. In early 1982, the UAW agreed to several concessions in their existing contract, including the foregoing of various paid vacation days and scheduled cost-of-living wage increases. Confronted with massive layoffs, the union became much more concerned about jobs than higher wage rates.

Although reasons for loss of strength differed, the experience of the Teamsters Union was not unlike that of the UAW. Deregulation subjected the unionized segment of the trucking industry to much more intense competition in the early 1980s than it had faced before. As the ICC relaxed the entry restraints into the interstate trucking business, new firms entered the industry. Many of these firms were nonunion employers, and their labor costs were therefore often lower than the established (primarily unionized) firms in the industry. Given their labor-cost advantage, many of the new entrants cut prices in order to gain a larger share of the market. The market share of the unionized firms declined. By late 1981, 117,000 Teamster members were on indefinite layoff. Given the sharp reduction in the employment of their members, the Teamsters Union, like the UAW, agreed to wage concessions and a reduction in their fringe-benefit package.

Thus, we can see that the bargaining position of a union will always be subject to market conditions. Whenever union labor is subject to even *indirect* competition with nonunion labor, it will be difficult for union employees to maintain above-market-equilibrium wage rates.

Average hourly earnings (nonsupervisory production workers)

Year	Private Sector	Automobile Industry	Auto Industry Divided by Private Sector
1969	$3.04	4.10	1.348
1975	4.53	6.44	1.421
1977	5.25	7.86	1.497
1980 (December)	6.94	10.80	1.556

1950s. Studies using more recent data suggest that the union–nonunion wage differential may be increasing. Frank Stafford estimated that when the employee characteristics were held constant, the annual earnings of unionized craft and operative workers were 25 percent greater than those of their nonunion counterparts. Michael Boskin, using 1967 data, placed the union–nonunion differential at between 15 and 25 percent. In a more recent study, Paul Ryscavage estimated that, in 1973, the wages of union workers exceeded those of nonunion workers with *similar productivity characteristics* by more than 25 percent. Ryscavage placed the union–nonunion wage differential at 29 percent for craftspeople, 23 percent for operatives, 44 percent for truck drivers (primarily Teamsters), and 36 percent for laborers.[6]

Above and beyond wage differences for union and nonunion workers, it is important to note that higher wages for union members do not necessarily mean an increase in the share of income going to labor in general—in other words, higher union wages do not necessarily benefit all workers. (The featured Myths of Economics addresses this issue.) In the final analysis, a *general* increase in the level of wages is dependent on an increase in productivity per hour. Of course, improvements in (a) technology, (b) the machines and tools available to workers (physical capital), (c) worker skills (human capital), and (d) the efficiency of economic organization provide the essential ingredients for higher levels of productivity. Higher real wages can be obtained only if the production of goods and services is expanded. Although unions can increase the wages of union workers, they cannot increase the wages of all workers unless their activities increase the total productivity of labor.

The wages of American workers are high because their productivity is high. If the productivity of American workers, their output per worker-hour, ever lagged, their real wages would also lag. Unions cannot alter the relationship between high real wages and high productivity for an entire economy. If the real wages of workers could be increased by union activities, the earnings of Italian, British, and Australian workers would be substantially higher than the wages of American workers. They are not, because real wages reflect productivity, not unionization.

UNIONS AND INFLATION

There is little evidence that unions, *acting independently*, can cause inflation. However, some economists believe that unions can and do generate conditions that induce macroplanners to follow an inflationary course. If union power is able to push wage rates above competitive levels in the union sector, employment in that sector will fall (or fail to expand as rapidly). Unemployment will increase, causing more and more employees who are equipped for employment in the union sector to search for jobs in the nonunion sector. If wages in the nonunion sector were completely flexible downward, they would decline until full employment was attained. But remember that even competitive markets do

---

[6]F. P. Stafford, "Concentration and Labor Earnings: Comment," *American Economic Review* (March 1968), pp. 174–181; M. J. Boskin, "Unions and Relative Wages," *American Economic Review* (June 1972), pp. 466–472; and P. M. Ryscavage, "Measuring Union–Nonunion Earnings Differences," *Monthly Labor Review* (December 1974), pp. 3–9.

MYTHS OF ECONOMICS
"Unions have increased the share of income going to labor."

Unions have increased the earnings of their members, but there is no evidence that they have had a significant impact on the share of income going to labor (human capital) relative to the income of property owners. Exhibit 6 presents data on labor's share of income over the last five decades. Wages and salaries and total employee compensation (including the social security contribution of the employer) have increased slightly since World War II. However, this is primarily a reflection of the decline in the number of self-employed persons in agriculture and the corresponding increase in the proportion of employed workers.

A major share of the earnings of self-employed, unincorporated business proprietors is clearly a return on their labor services. When the earnings of farmers, salespeople, distributors, lawyers, accountants, and other self-employed proprietors are counted as labor income, a clearer picture of the labor–property-owner components of income emerges. This measure of labor's share, employee compensation plus the earnings of self-employed workers, has been amazingly constant. It suggests that between 81 and 83 percent of the national income has gone to labor during each five-year period since 1935. The figure was just slightly higher during the depression of 1930–1934. Union membership increased substantially between 1930 and 1950 (see Exhibit 1). Yet the data of Exhibit 6 do *not* indicate any upward trend in the share of national income going to all workers, including those self-employed, during this period. There is increasing evidence that, during the last decade or so, union wages have increased relative to the wages of nonunion workers with similar productivity characteristics. However, the share of national income going to all labor (all employees plus self-employed workers) continues to hold steady.[7]

These findings are not surprising in light of economic analysis. If unions are able to use monopoly power, supply restrictions, and bargaining power to push union wages above the competitive level, who will pay for these benefits? Most laypeople and many businesspeople, who should know better, typically reply, "They will come out of the employer's profits." Analysis of market forces strongly contradicts this view.

First, wages are a resource cost. Higher wages mean higher costs. If a *product* made by union labor is sold

---

[7]Also see Clark Kerr, "Labor's Income Share and the Labor Movement," in *New Concepts in Wage Determination*, ed. G. W. Taylor and Frank C. Pierson (New York: McGraw-Hill, 1957); Sidney Weintraub, "A Law That Cannot Be Repealed," *Challenge* (April 1962), pp. 17–19; and W. H. Hutt, *The Strike-Threat System* (New Rochelle, New York: Arlington House, 1973).

EXHIBIT 6 Is labor's share constant?

The share of national income allocated to human capital has been virtually constant during the last 50 years.

Derived from the national income estimates of the U.S. Department of Commerce published in *Survey of Current Business*.

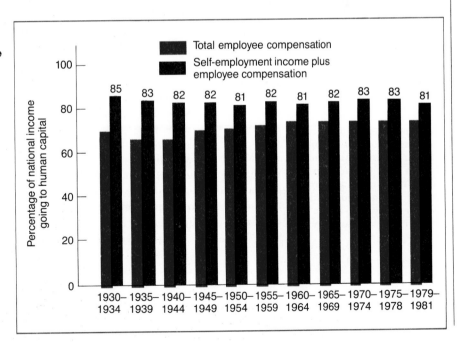

---

under conditions of competition (either pure or monopolistic), it is the *consumer* who pays for any above-market wage gains that a union has won for its members. When the firm hiring union labor has some monopoly power, higher costs may partially be subtracted from profits. Even in this case, however, higher costs will push the prices of union-made products upward.

Second, regardless of the competitive conditions in the product market, higher union wages (and costs) will lead to a reduction in the output of products that use union labor intensively. This factor, along with the substitution of physical capital for labor at the higher wage rate, will cause employment in the unionized sectors to fall. What will happen to employees who are unable to find jobs in the unionized sector? They will compete for nonunion jobs, increasing supply and depressing nonunion wages.

Despite the appearances to the contrary, the major burden (incidence) of any noncompetitive wage gains won by union members will almost surely fall on consumers and nonunion employees, not on employ-ers. In general, the real wages of nonunion employees will fall, because as prices for union-made products increase and union output declines, the supply of labor in the nonunion sector will expand. Labor economist Gregg Lewis has estimated that the real wages of nonunion workers, three-fourths of the labor force, are 3 to 4 percent lower than they would be in the absence of unionism.[8]

---

[8]H. Gregg Lewis, *Unionism and Relative Wages in the United States* (Chicago: University of Chicago Press, 1963).

---

not adjust instantaneously. The unemployment is likely to persist for a significant period of time.[9]

Typically, macroplanners will react to the higher rate of unemployment with a more expansionary macropolicy. Inflation will result, partially eliminating the wage gains that are incorporated into long-term union contracts. During the period of inflation, wages in the nonunion sector will rise more rapidly. Thus, the expansionary (and inflationary) macropolicy will help to reduce the union–nonunion wage differential and restore full employment.

However, with time, union negotiators (and management) will incorporate the inflationary bias of macropolicy into their bargaining strategy. As this happens, it will become increasingly difficult for macropolicy to promote full employment, at least in the absence of high rates of inflation, which will certainly have other harmful side effects. Thus, even though unions cannot directly cause *continuing* inflation, many leading economists believe that unions' monopoly power does tend to give macropolicy an inflationary bias.

THE GROWTH OF BIG LABOR IN THE UNITED STATES

Yellow-Dog Contract: A contract that requires an employee to promise, as a condition of employment, not to join a union. The Norris–LaGuardia Act (1932) declared such contracts illegal.

Injunction: A court order requiring a party (for example, a labor union) to refrain from a certain practice, such as a strike. The Norris–LaGuardia Act made it much more difficult for employers to obtain such an injunction during a labor dispute.

In an earlier era, unions in the United States were quite weak. Employers had several antiunion tactics at their disposal. Employees who were suspected of organizing a union could be fired. A prospective worker could be required to sign a **yellow-dog contract,** which stated that as a condition of employment the employee would not join a union. The courts were often willing to grant employers an **injunction,** a court order prohibiting a union from striking. In the 1930s, a series of legislative acts, of which the Norris–LaGuardia and Wagner

---

[9]Since the union–nonunion wage gap is now larger, a union member who is laid off will be willing to wait longer in the hope of getting a job back, because it pays substantially more than the next-best alternative job. This raises the rate of unemployment. However, the unemployed worker, who is choosing not to seek other work immediately, is not worse off. Even though the economy has lost some work services, the higher union pay scale more than compensates the worker for the lost work time while unemployed.

Acts were the most important, prohibited management from using such tactics. The bargaining position of labor was greatly strengthened. During the subsequent two decades, union membership and strength grew rapidly.

Clearly, the image of a weak union attempting to gain a fair shake for helpless workers is obsolete today. Previously, we discussed the monopolistic power of big business. As we have seen, many labor unions, like business firms with monopoly power, are able to gain higher prices (wages) by restricting supply, usually the supply of nonunion labor. National labor unions, organized along industrial lines, can halt production in an entire industry. Like big business firms, big unions possess considerable political clout. Since unions are well-organized, financially powerful special interest groups, there is good reason to expect that the political process will be responsive to their requests. Unions have been known both to make and to break the careers of political entrepreneurs.

Unions have been at the forefront of the mid-twentieth-century fight for civil rights and welfare legislation, greater social security benefits, and increased benefits for the unemployed, and the benefits (as well as costs) of these programs are certainly felt by the general populace. However, unions have also not hesitated to use their political muscle to gain benefits at the expense of the general populace. Legislation such as that granting food stamp benefits to strikers, licensing requirements restricting the entry of unapproved (nonunion) workers into craft occupations, high tariffs on goods produced by union labor, and high minimum wage rates without any exemption for teenagers bear the "union power" label. In each case, the major beneficiaries are union members, while consumers, taxpayers, and nonunion employees bear the costs.

Are General Motors and the AFL–CIO too strong? Economics cannot answer this question directly, but it can point out the misleading nature of the view that big labor is necessary to offset the power of big business. The power of big labor is used at the expense of the unorganized general populace, with business firms merely acting as intermediaries Using economic efficiency as the criterion, what is good for General Motors, the AFL–CIO, or the Teamsters may not be good for the country.

THE CONTRIBUTION AND SIGNIFICANCE OF UNIONS

Economists generally focus on wages and employment when discussing the impact of unions. The data suggest that many unions are able to raise the wages of their members, but, as we have seen, there is little evidence that unions have been able to influence significantly labor's share of total income. It is also clear that rising production, not union power, is the primary source of the increasing real wages of modern industrial society.

Yet the union movement continues to be almost sacrosanct in the minds of many workers, particularly blue collar workers. Even workers who belong to a weak union, as determined by its impact on wage rates, often have a strong loyalty to the union. Older workers in particular often spin stories about how things used to be. Are they wrong? Would the American economy be different if there were no unions? Wage and income data cannot give full answers to these questions. In perhaps the most important sense, the contribution of unions to American life cannot be statistically measured.

The great contribution of unions in the United States has been their role in defending employees against a sense of powerlessness, unimportance, alienation, and insecurity. The union movement has established a system of on-the-job civil rights and what Summer Slichter has called "industrial jurisprudence" to protect the worker's rights. A union provides the worker with a strong defense against the whim, arbitrary actions, and excesses of a foreman or management representative. Because of the power of the union, even in cases where only a portion of the workers are unionized, management has a greater incentive to treat workers with dignity and to grant them a sense of individual importance. These worker benefits are, for the most part, nonpecuniary and difficult to measure, but they are nevertheless extremely important.

In an industrial society, it is easy to see how individual employees could acquire a sense of helplessness. After all, what does one employee mean to General Motors, General Electric, or Boeing? If workers were unorganized, foremen, supervisors, and personnel managers would possess a great deal of power. In such a case, it would not be difficult to believe stories about employees being fired because they refused to contribute to the foreman's personal Christmas fund or because they won half of their supervisor's paycheck in a lunch-hour crap game. Analysis of economic incentives suggests that when the foreman is king and the worker is a replaceable cog in the wheel, management arbitrariness, worker insecurity, and alienation will result.

The union movement set out nearly a century ago to relieve the helplessness of the individual worker. Today, labor contracts define a worker's civil rights and provide the worker with a series of industrial appeal courts. Specifically, a worker cannot be fired without good cause, which must be proved to the satisfaction of his or her union representative. Actions the worker considers arbitrary or unfair can be taken to a shop steward, appealed through labor–management channels, and eventually brought to an objective outside arbitrator. When a union brings a grievance to the attention of management, management listens. But it takes positive action to ensure that foremen and supervisors treat employees fairly. Production at multimillion-dollar plants has been brought to a halt because a single worker's civil rights, as specified by the labor contract, were violated. Collective bargaining gives management a greater incentive to see that supervisors use discretion in dealing with each worker.[10]

This is not to say that the worker is always right in disputes involving labor and management. But it is important for the self-esteem, morale, and human dignity of workers that they are able to have their say, that they are not powerless, that they can take their grievances to a neutral third party. Unions have played a vital role in establishing these worker rights and in promoting a sense of community among workers. Is it any wonder that some workers, even nonunion employees, think that George Meany, Walter Reuther, and John L. Lewis are of the same stature as the president of the United States?

What is the future of the union movement? There is much concern today about worker alienation and the meaninglessness of assembly line work. Many

---

[10]Of course, when a union is large enough to deal effectively with management and the government, individual workers may not exert much control within the union. There are occasional problems with corrupt and arbitrary actions by union officials, at both the local and the national levels. Opposition to union leadership from within the union is sometimes risky. On the whole, however, unions have worked effectively to give their members a greater voice in determining how their place of work is managed. For a discussion of these problems and how they are handled, see Lloyd G. Reynolds, *Labor Economics and Labor Relations,* 7th ed. (Englewood Cliffs, New Jersey: Prentice-Hall, 1978), Chapter 16.

authorities tell us that these issues are the current major concerns of American workers. Mechanical, boring methods of production have been adopted because of their efficiency and because more "dignifying" production techniques are more costly. But no one can pretend that physical production efficiency is everything. Each of us must make some trade-off between physical production efficiency and the benefits derived from certain types of work. Many of today's workers may be willing to accept a slower rate of growth in real wages in exchange for more fulfilling jobs. If this is so, we can expect the union movement to play an important role in inducing management to adopt alternative methods of production.

CHAPTER LEARNING OBJECTIVES

1   Approximately one out of every four workers in the United States belongs to a union. Union membership grew rapidly between 1930 and 1950. During the 1960s and 1970s, it declined slightly as a share of the labor force.

2   Agreement on most collective-bargaining contracts is reached without a work stoppage. The strike is a major source of union power. A strike can cause the employer to lose sales while incurring continuing fixed cost. The threat of a strike, particularly when inventories are low, is an inducement for the employer to consent to the union's terms.

3   A strike is also costly to employees. Strike funds are usually inadequate to deal with a prolonged strike. The loss of just a few paychecks can impose extreme hardship on most families. The potential cost of a strike to both union and management provides each with an incentive to bargain seriously in an effort to avoid a work stoppage.

4   Since World War II, approximately three-tenths of 1 percent of the total nonfarm working time has been lost because of work stoppages. When the availability of a good or service to the general public is interrupted, strikes can also impose a high cost on secondary parties.

5   There are three basic methods a union can use to increase the wages of its members: (a) restrict the supply of competitive inputs, including nonunion workers; (b) apply bargaining power enforced by a strike or threat of one; and (c) increase the demand for the labor service of union members.

6   When there are a large number of employees competing for labor services, each employer will have to pay the market wage rate in order to keep employees from shifting to higher-wage alternatives. However, when monopsony is present, the single purchaser of labor may be able to profit by restricting employment and paying a wage rate that is less than the marginal revenue generated by the labor. Under these circumstances, a wage floor established by a union can result in both higher wages and increased employment.

7   The strength of a union depends on the elasticity of demand for its service. For a union to be strong, the demand for its labor services must be inelastic. Thus, the strength of a union is enhanced if (a) there is an absence of good substitutes for its service, (b) the demand for the good it produces is highly inelastic, (c) the union labor input is a small share of the total cost of production, and/or (d) the supply of any available substitute is highly inelastic. An absence of these conditions weakens the power of the union.

8   Studies suggest that the earnings of union members exceed those of *similar nonunion members* by between 10 and 25 percent. Research using more recent data tends to place the differential closer to the higher figure. The most powerful unions have been able to obtain even larger wage gains for their members. Some weaker unions, unable to restrict the supply of nonunion workers (or products made by them), have had little impact on wages. Most of the real wage increases of union workers have probably been obtained at the expense of nonunion workers and consumers.

9 There is no indication that unions have significantly increased the share of national income going to labor in general. The real wages of workers are a reflection of their productivity rather than the result of union action or power. There is little reason to believe that unions enhance worker productivity—they may even retard it.

10 Many economists believe that union policies tend to give macropolicy an inflationary bias. They suggest that above-equilibrium union wage rates lead to unemployment, which induces macroplanners to follow a more expansionary course, thereby causing inflation.

11 Unions in the United States have helped to defend employees both against a sense of powerlessness, unimportance, alienation, and insecurity and against arbitrary behavior by management. The union movement is primarily responsible for our system of "industrial jurisprudence." Many think these nonpecuniary factors are far more important than the impact of unions on wages.

THE ECONOMIC WAY OF THINKING—DISCUSSION QUESTIONS

1 Assume that the primary objective of a union is to raise wages. (a) Discuss the conditions that will help the union to achieve this objective. (b) Why might a union be unable to meet its goal?

2 Suppose that Florida migrant farm workers are effectively unionized. What will be the impact of the unionization on (a) the price of Florida oranges, (b) the profits of Florida fruit growers in the short run and in the long run, (c) the mechanization of the fruitpicking industry, (d) the employment of fruit pickers?

3 Unions in the North have been vigorously involved in efforts to organize lower-wage workers in the South. Union leaders often express their compassion for the low-money-wage southern workers. Can you think of a reason, other than compassion, for northern union leaders' (and workers') interest in having the higher union scale extended to the South? Explain.

4 "Unions have brought a decent living to working men and women. Without unions, employers would still be paying workers a starvation wage." Analyze.

5 (a) "An increase in the price of steel will be passed along to consumers in the form of higher prices of automobiles, homes, appliances, and other products made with steel." Do you agree or disagree?
(b) "An increase in the price of craft-union labor will be passed along to consumers in the form of higher prices of homes, repair and installation services, appliances, and other products that require craft-union labor." Do you agree or disagree?
(c) Are the interests of labor unions in conflict primarily with the interests of union employers? Explain.

6 "The purpose of unions is to push the wage rate above the competitive level. By their very nature, they are monopolists. Therefore, they will necessarily cause resources to be misallocated." Do you agree or disagree? Explain.

27

INEQUALITY, INCOME MOBILITY, AND THE BATTLE AGAINST POVERTY

In a market economy, the distribution of income is determined by the sale price of factor services, the resources of individuals, and the choices of individuals as to how their resources are to be employed. Because market income stems from the productive contribution of one's human and physical resources, owners have an incentive to employ their resources efficiently. However, leisure and fulfillment are also goods. Depending on the payoff derived from employment, persons may choose to sacrifice earnings in order to consume leisure or to undertake more satisfying work activities. Taxes and subsidies aside, individuals must pay the full opportunity cost of sacrificing leisure and nonpecuniary job benefits for production. Thus, a market system leads to the careful use of resources, high productivity, and freedom for individuals to do as they choose, since they bear the costs and reap the benefits.

However, the system also leads to a good deal of income inequality. The distribution of income that results may conflict with our sense of fairness. People may want to redistribute income in order to achieve egalitarian objectives.

Economics does not tell us which distribution of income is best. However, it can help us to understand the benefits and costs of income redistribution. How unequal are incomes in the United States? What are the characteristics of the poor? How difficult is it to escape poverty? This chapter focuses on these issues and related topics.

INCOME INEQUALITY IN THE UNITED STATES

Money income is only one component of economic well-being. Such factors as leisure, the nonpecuniary advantages and disadvantages of a job, and the expected stability of future income are also determinants of economic welfare.

[1]Arthur M. Okun, *Equality and Efficiency: The Big Tradeoff* (Washington, D.C.: Brookings Institution, 1975), p. vii.

Nonetheless, since income represents command over market goods and services, it is highly significant. Moreover, it is readily observable. It is the most widely used measure of economic well-being and inequality.

Most income in the United States is generated by persons who are neither rich nor poor. In 1979, 59 percent of all families had incomes in excess of $15,000 but less than $50,000. These middle- and upper-middle-income recipients received 70 percent of the aggregate income. Families with incomes of more than $50,000 comprised 5 percent of all income recipients, and they received 16 percent of the aggregate income. At the other end of the spectrum, the 36 percent of all families with an income of less than $15,000 received 14 percent of the total income.

Exhibit 1 presents data on the distribution of income in the United States by quintile. There was little change in the distribution of actual income *before taxes and transfers* between 1952 and 1979. Throughout most of the period, the bottom 20 percent of family income recipients received approximately five percent of the aggregate income. In contrast, the 20 percent of families with the highest actual incomes earned slightly more than 40 percent of the total. Thus, the top 20 percent of family income recipients received more than eight times as much income as the bottom 20 percent.

Are the Actual Income Data an Accurate Measure of Inequality?

Observers have often argued that the actual income data of Exhibit 1 support two general propositions. First, there is a great deal of income inequality in the United States; and second, the degree of income inequality has remained virtually unchanged during the last several decades. Closer inspection of the data indicates that there are several reasons to doubt both these propositions.

Adjustment for In-Kind Transfers, Taxes, and Family Size Yields a More Equal Distribution of Income and Suggests That There Has Been a Trend toward Greater Income Equality. The actual incomes listed in Exhibit 1 are before-tax incomes, do not include in-kind transfers, and do not account for differences in family size.

Edgar Browning, a University of Virginia economist, has attempted to isolate the impact of these factors on the distribution of income.[2] Browning added the in-kind transfers, such as food stamps, housing subsidies, and publicly provided medical care, and subtracted income taxes and social security taxes from the actual income figures. He also adjusted the data for family size, so that they reflected actual income per person rather than per family.

As Exhibit 1 illustrates, these adjustments are important. Browning found that after adjustments were made for taxes, in-kind transfers, and family size, the "net income" of the lowest quintile of income recipients was 11.7 percent of the total in 1972, more than twice the share indicated by the unadjusted data. At the other end of the spectrum, the top 20 percent of income recipients received only 32.8 percent of the net income in 1972, compared to 41.4 percent before taxes, transfers, and family size were considered.

The adjusted data also illustrate a second major point—there has been a substantial movement toward equality. In recent years, in-kind transfer pay-

[2]Edgar Browning, "The Trend toward Equality in the Distribution of Net Income," *Southern Economic Journal* (July 1976), pp. 912–923, and "How Much More Equality Can We Afford?" *Public Interest* (Spring 1976), pp. 90–110.

EXHIBIT 1 Income inequality and the importance of taxes, income transfers, and family size

	Percentage of Income Received by:				
	Lowest 20 Percent	Second Quintile	Third Quintile	Fourth Quintile	Top 20 Percent
Actual income before taxes and in-kind transfers					
1952	4.9	12.2	17.1	23.5	42.2
1962	5.0	12.1	17.6	24.0	41.3
1972	5.4	11.9	17.5	23.9	41.4
1979	5.2	11.6	17.5	24.1	41.6
Adusted data[a]					
1952	8.1	14.2	17.8	23.2	36.7
1962	8.8	14.4	18.2	23.1	35.4
1972	11.7	15.0	18.2	22.3	32.8

[a]The actual income data were adjusted in the following way: (a) In-kind transfers were added, (b) social security and income taxes were subtracted, and (c) data were converted to per capita.

The data for 1952, 1962, and 1972 are from Edgar K. Browning, "How Much More Equality Can We Afford?" *Public Interest* (Summer 1976), p. 93. The data for 1979 are from Bureau of the Census, *Current Population Reports,* Series P. 60, no. 129, Table 3.

ments have grown rapidly. The income taxes and social security taxes of middle- and high-income recipients have also risen. As a result, the after-tax and transfer income share of the bottom quintile rose from 8.1 percent in 1952 to 11.7 percent in 1972. Simultaneously, the share of income going to the highest 20 percent of family income recipients declined between 1952 and 1972. Although Browning's study has not been updated, most researchers believe that the picture in the early 1980s differs little from the 1972 data.

A Substantial Amount of the Inequality in the Unadjusted Actual Income Data Reflects Differences in Age and Family Characteristics.   If all families were similar except in the amount of income received, the use of the unadjusted annual income data as an index of inequality would be far more defensible. However, this is not the case. The aggregate data lump together (a) small and large families, (b) prime-age earners and elderly retirees, (c) multiearner families and families without any current earners, and (d) husband–wife families and single-parent families. Even if *lifetime incomes* were exactly equal, many of these factors would result in substantial inequality in *annual income* data.

Consider just one factor, the impact of age on the pattern of lifetime income. Typically, income will be low when one is young. This will be particularly true when an individual is undertaking additional education and/or training. As people obtain additional work experience, income will tend to rise, reaching a peak during middle age. Finally, annual income will decline during retirement, as families draw upon pensions and savings from previous earnings. The actual income data illustrate this pattern. In 1979, the mean income of families headed by a person aged 18 to 24 years was $15,000, compared to $29,315 for families headed by a 45- to 54-year-old person. Similarly, income dipped to $15,140 for households in which the head was age 65 or over. Clearly, even if the distribution of lifetime income were roughly equal, annual income would still vary considerably.

Exhibit 2 highlights the differences between high- and low-income fami-

EXHIBIT 2   The differing characteristics of high- and low-income families, 1979

Characteristic	Annual Income	
	Under $7500	Over $50,000
Mean years of schooling (householder)	9.4	15.0
Age of family head (percent distribution)		
Under 34	34	10
35–64	36	84
65 and over	30	6
Family size (percent distribution)		
Two members	54	27
Three members	20	20
Four or more members	26	53
Single-parent family (percent distribution)	45	4
Mean number of earners in family	0.72	2.46

Derived from Bureau of the Census, *Current Population Reports*, Series P-60, no. 129, Tables 1, 21, and 23.

lies in 1979. The typical high-income family (over $50,000) was headed by a well-educated person in the prime-earning-age category whose income was supplemented by the incomes of other family earners. In contrast, nonworking retirees, youthful workers, and persons with little education were substantially overrepresented among low-income families (incomes of less than $7500). The mean number of years of schooling for the household heads of high-income families was 15.0 years, compared to only 9.4 years for heads of families with annual incomes of less than $7500. Eighty-four percent of the high-income families had household heads aged 35 to 64. In contrast, only 36 percent of the low-income families had heads in prime-earning-age categories. There was also wide variation in the size of the family. Whereas a majority (54 percent) of the low-income families had economic responsibility for only two family members, there were four or more family members in 53 percent of the high-income families. Single-parent families comprised 45 percent of the low-income (under $7500) group, whereas 96 percent of the high-income group were husband–wife families. The mean number of earners in high-income families was 2.46, compared to only 0.72 for low-income families. No family members held jobs in more than 40 percent of the low-income families.

Drawing conclusions about inequality from *annual* income data must be done with care. Many high-income families were numbered among low-income families just a few years before. As family members retire in the years just after data are gathered, many of the current high-income families will return to low-income categories. Many of those currently considered low-income recipients can either (a) look forward to higher incomes when schooling is completed and prime-earning age is reached or (b) look back after retirement to higher-income years.

The Difference in the After-Tax and Transfer Income per Hour of Work between High- and Low-Income Recipients Is Quite Small.   In order to eliminate the impact of grouping together households of varying sizes and at various

EXHIBIT 3 The distribution of income among three-person households.

Household heads in these data were 35 to 44 years old.

Income Grouping (1)	Market Earnings (in Billions) (2)	Percent Distribution of Market Earnings (3)	Cash and In-Kind Transfers minus Taxes (in Billions) (4)	Net Income (in Billions) (5)	Percent Distribution, Net Income (6)	Net Income per Hour (7)
Lowest fifth	2.29	5.3	+0.73	3.02	9.2	5.78
Second fifth	5.42	12.6	−0.86	4.56	13.8	5.77
Third fifth	7.76	18.1	−1.84	5.92	17.9	5.68
Fourth fifth	9.90	23.0	−2.34	7.56	22.9	6.66
Top fifth	17.60	41.0	−5.61	11.99	36.3	9.82

Edgar K. Browning and Jacquelene M. Browning, *Public Finance and the Price System* (New York: Macmillan, 1983), Chapter 8.

stages of lifetime earnings, Edgar Browning did a detailed study for 1976 of three-person households headed by a 35- to 44-year-old. Exhibit 3 presents his findings. As column 3 shows, the distribution of pretax market earnings was highly unequal, not unlike the distribution of actual income presented in Exhibit 1. The top fifth of the households surveyed, the high-income households, received 41.0 percent of the aggregate income, compared to only 5.3 percent for the lowest one-fifth (column 3). However, the low-income families paid fewer taxes on their income and received more income transfers as supplements. Once adjustment was made for cash and in-kind transfers, as well as for income tax, the distribution of net income was considerably more equal. As column 6 shows, the top group of income recipients received 36.3 percent of the aggregate *net* income, compared to 9.2 percent for the bottom quintile. However, perhaps the most surprising finding of Browning's work is that most of the differences in net income reflected hours of work. In fact, the net income per hour of work was almost identical for the bottom 60 percent of the income recipients surveyed. However, the net income per hour of the top quintile was $9.82, approximately 70 percent higher than the net income per hour of the quintile of households with the lowest incomes.[3]

---

[3]The importance of time worked as a source of income inequality is also observable in the aggregate annual income data for families. The chart below presents the 1979 data on the distribution of money income and weeks worked by quintile:

Income Grouping	Percentage of Aggregate Income	Percentage of Weeks Worked
Lowest fifth	5.2	7.8
Second fifth	11.6	15.6
Third fifth	17.5	21.2
Fourth fifth	24.1	25.1
Top fifth	41.6	30.3

While the top fifth of families with the highest annual incomes received 41.6 percent of the total income in 1979, they also contributed 30.3 percent of the total weeks worked. In contrast, the bottom one-fifth contributed only 7.8 percent of the total weeks worked. The annual income of the top 20 percent of family income recipients was eight times that of the bottom quintile; but the income *per week worked* for the top group was only two times greater than the income *per week worked* of the lowest income grouping.

**Sources of
Income Inequality**

These findings illustrate that both time worked and life-cycle factors are important sources of inequality in annual income. These data are consistent with the results of a study by Alan Blinder of Princeton University.[4] As Exhibit 4 illustrates, Blinder estimated that approximately 30 percent of the differences in annual income are due to differences in the earnings of people at different stages of their lives. For example, low annual earnings (and hours worked) are typical of students and retirees during the early and late stages of their lifetime income cycles. Blinder estimated that another 28 percent of income inequality is the result of differing preferences in leisure time in proportion to work time. Together, according to Blinder, these two factors exert a substantial influence on the amount of time worked during a year and account for 58 percent of the inequality in annual income in the United States.

How important is capital ownership and inheritance as a source of income inequality? Blinder found that only 2 percent of the inequality in income is based on differences in the inheritance of wealth. Since ownership of physical capital is distributed more unequally than income,[5] this finding is at first quite surprising. Upon reflection, however, it is less so. Most income stems from human, not physical, capital. Only about one-sixth of all income is derived from property (rents, dividends, and interest). Much of the current income from real assets originates from previous labor earnings that were saved or invested. Thus, even the confiscation of all inherited property would influence the degree of income equality only slightly. Differences in wage rates explain 40 percent of the total income inequality, according to Blinder. As we discussed previously, wage differentials result from differences in workers (skills, education, natural abilities, etc.), differences in jobs, and the immobility of resources.

INCOME INEQUALITY IN OTHER COUNTRIES

How does income inequality in the United States compare with that in other nations? Exhibit 5 presents a summary of *household income* data compiled by the World Bank. These data indicate that the distribution of income in the United States, Japan, and West Germany is similar. The degree of income equality in Sweden and the United Kingdom is slightly greater than that in the three major industrial nations. In light of the welfare-state policies of Sweden and the United Kingdom and these nations' relatively homogeneous populations—that is, uniform with respect to race and ethnicity—these findings are not surprising.

---

[4]Alan S. Blinder, *Toward an Economic Theory of Income Distribution* (Cambridge, Massachusetts: MIT. Press, 1974); see particularly pp. 136–138.

[5]The distribution of wealth holdings of households grouped by income is presented below.

Income Grouping	Percentage of Net Wealth
Bottom 20 percent	8
Second quintile	10
Third quintile	10
Fourth quintile	13
Top 20 percent	59

These figures are taken from Richard A. Musgrave and Peggy Musgrave, *Public Finance in Theory and Practice,* 2nd ed. (New York: McGraw-Hill, 1976), Table 14-2.

The share of income going to the wealthy is usually greater in less developed countries. According to the World Bank study, the top 20 percent of income recipients received 66.6 percent of the aggregate income in Brazil and 57.7 percent in Mexico. Although the degree of inequality was somewhat less pronounced for India, Korea, and Indonesia, income inequality in these countries was still greater than for the major industrial nations of Exhibit 5.

INCOME MOBILITY—DO THE POOR STAY POOR AND THE RICH STAY RICH?

Income inequality data do not tell us much about the degree of movement among income groupings over time. Are high income and wealth passed from generation to generation? Do the sons and daughters of low-income parents have an opportunity to escape poverty and attain high-income status? Some observers argue that reducing inequality at the starting line is as important, perhaps even

EXHIBIT 4 Sources of inequality

Source of Inequality in Annual Income	Percentage of Inequality Stemming from Source
Life-cycle factors (new labor force entrant, prime-age worker, retirement, etc.)	30
Work—leisure preference	28
Inheritance	2
Difference in wage rates	40

Alan S. Blinder, *Toward an Economic Theory of Income Distribution* (Cambridge, Massachusetts: MIT Press, 1974), pp. 137–140.

EXHIBIT 5 Equality and inequality around the world

Country (Year)	Percentage of Income Received by:				
	Bottom 20 Percent	Second Quintile	Third Quintile	Fourth Quintile	Top 20 Percent
Developing nations					
India (1975–1976)	7.0	9.2	13.9	20.5	49.4
Korea (1976)	5.7	11.2	15.4	22.4	45.3
Indonesia (1976)	6.6	7.8	12.6	23.6	49.4
Brazil (1972)	2.0	5.0	9.4	17.0	66.6
Mexico (1977)	2.9	7.0	12.0	20.4	57.7
Developed nations					
Japan (1969)	7.9	13.1	16.8	21.2	41.0
United Kingdom (1977–1978)	7.4	11.7	17.0	24.7	39.5
Sweden (1972)	6.6	13.1	18.5	24.8	37.0
United States (1979)	5.2	11.6	17.5	24.1	41.6
West Germany (1973)	6.5	10.3	15.0	22.0	46.2

The World Bank, *World Development Report, 1981,* Table 25, and Bureau of the Census, *Current Population Reports,* Series P-60, no. 129, Table 3.

more important, than equalizing incomes. Many Americans, probably most, see nothing wrong with high incomes that reflect hard work, competence, and superior abilities. They are not opposed to income inequality per se. They are, however, opposed to inequality that simply reflects inheritance of a socio-economic position.

For obvious reasons, reliable data on intergenerational income mobility are difficult to obtain. Nevertheless, researchers have begun to develop the data necessary for tackling this problem. Christopher Jencks summarized the findings of a study conducted by the Center for Educational Policy Research at Harvard University as follows:

Among men born into the most affluent fifth of the population, . . . we estimate that less than half will be part of the same elite when they grow up. Of course, it is also true that very few will be in the bottom fifth. Rich parents can at least guarantee their children that much. Yet if we follow families over several generations, even this will not hold true. Affluent families often have at least one relatively indigent grandparent in the background, and poor families, unless they are black or relatively recent immigrants, have often had at least one prosperous grandparent.[6]

A more recent study by Bradley Schiller is highly consistent with the findings of Jencks. In a study of almost 75,000 male workers (ages 30 to 34) who earned at least $1000 in 1957 and were still working in 1971, Schiller found that the earnings of more than 70 percent of these workers changed by at least 10 percentiles during the period.[7] (*Note:* If earnings placed a worker in the 40th percentile in 1957, a 10-percentile change would require that his or her 1971 earnings be either below the 30th percentile or above the 50th percentile.)

The average change was 21 percentiles, over one-fifth of the distance from one extreme of the income distribution scale to the other. Those near the bottom moved upward to a somewhat lesser extent, however, and blacks were less upwardly mobile than whites. Still, even among blacks starting at the lower extreme of the income distribution scale in 1957, the majority rose at least 10 percentiles. Among whites starting in the top 5 percent, the majority moved downward at least 10 percentiles.

Schiller summarized his findings as follows:

The American economy is characterized by a very high degree of individual income mobility. Specifically, individuals move significant distances up and down the earnings distribution, implying tremendous mobility of relative economic status. The rigid shape of the aggregate income distribution is a misleading index of opportunity stratification because it camouflages a great deal of individual mobility between the separate points of that distribution. The inequalities observed at any particular time are reduced over time as individuals exchange relative economic position.[8]

---

[6]Excerpt from *Inequality: Reassessment of the Effect of Family and Schooling in America,* p. 216, by Christopher Jencks et al. © 1972 by Basic Books, Inc., Publishers, New York.

[7]Bradley R. Schiller, "Equality, Opportunity, and the 'Good Job,'" *Public Interest* (Spring 1976), pp. 111–120, and "Relative Earnings Mobility in the United States," *American Economic Review* 67, no. 5 (1977), pp. 926–939.

[8]Schiller, "Equality, Opportunity, and the 'Good Job,'" pp. 118–119.

In an affluent society such as the United States, income inequality and poverty are related issues. Poverty could be defined in strictly relative terms—as the economic condition of the bottom one-fifth of all income recipients, for example. However, this definition would not be very helpful, since that would mean that poverty would always be with us.

The official definition of poverty in the United States is the standard developed by the Social Security Administration. The cost of an economical and nutritional food plan is determined. Then, since low-income families typically spend approximately one-third of their income on food, the cost of the food plan is multiplied by 3 to obtain the **poverty threshold income level.** Families with less than the poverty threshold income are defined as poor. With the passage of time, the consumer price index is used to adjust the threshold level for inflation.

For a particular family, the poverty income threshold level is also adjusted for family size, sex of the family head, number of children under the age of 18, and location of the family residence (farm or nonfarm). There are 124 poverty threshold income levels, which differ according to these family characteristics. The poverty threshold income in June of 1979 was $6500 per year for a nonfarm family of four and $10,000 for a nonfarm couple with five children.

How many people are poor? According to the official definition of poverty, there were 25.3 million poor people in 1979. As Exhibit 6 illustrates, 11.6 percent of all persons were classified as poor in 1979, compared to 12.6 percent in 1970 and 22.4 percent in 1959.

Poverty Threshold Income Level: The level of money income below which a family is considered to be poor. It differs according to family characteristics (for example, number of family members) and is adjusted when consumer prices change.

Who Are the Poor?

There is diversity among the 25.3 million poor people in the United States. Blacks and Hispanics are overrepresented among the poor. Nonetheless, in 1979, two-thirds of the poor were white.

Exhibit 7 breaks down the poverty population into various subgroups. Children comprise the largest subcomponent—nearly 40 percent of the total poverty population. More than one-half of these children reside in female-headed households. For children, the home environment often provides a more

EXHIBIT 6 The score in the war on poverty

According to the official poverty statistics, the percentage of poor persons continues to decline, although at a slower rate in recent years. These figures do not reflect in-kind transfers, such as food stamps, medical services, and subsidized housing benefits. *Statistical Abstract of the United States—1981.*

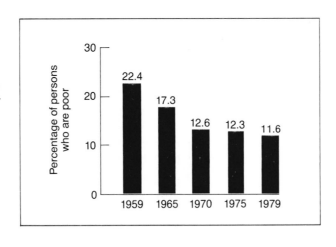

EXHIBIT 7 Who are the poor?

Poverty Population Group	Percentage of Total Group, 1979
All persons (25.3 million)	
Children in female-headed families	21.7
Children in male-headed families	16.6
Elderly	14.2
Other adults in families	34.1
Unattached individuals	13.4
	100.0
Female family heads (2.6 million)	
Worked full-time, year-round	6.4
Worked at some time during year	33.3
Did not work—disabled	12.8
Did not work—other	47.5
	100.0
Male family heads (2.7 million)	
Worked full-time, year-round	25.7
Worked at some time during year	32.3
Did not work—disabled	19.3
Did not work—other	22.7
	100.0

Statistical Abstract of the United States—1981, Tables 748, 749, and 754.

serious handicap than the lack of material goods. Anxiety, neglect, and abuse are often spawned by divorce, parental conflict, or alcoholism, which tend to be rife among the poor. Parents concerned with personal problems and survival have little time to help their children with homework. One of the tragedies of poverty is the handicap it imposes on children.

The elderly comprise another sizable segment of the poverty population, approximately 14 percent of the total. Many are among the 10 percent of elderly persons who are ineligible for social security. The income of others who do qualify for social security is still below the poverty threshold level.

Exhibit 7 helps to explain why many families are poor. Approximately one-half of the poverty-level families are headed by a woman. In 1979, 12.8 percent of these female family heads did not work because they were ill or disabled; another 47.5 percent failed to work even though they were not disabled. Only 6.4 percent of female family heads worked full-time, year-round. Not surprisingly, the incomes of nonworking persons are low. Among the male household heads who had poverty-level earnings, 25.7 percent worked full-time, year-round. In 1979, 19.3 percent of the male household heads of poverty-level families were unable to work because of disability, and another 22.7 percent failed to work for other reasons.

In recent years, the problem of poverty has become increasingly interwoven with family instability. In 1979, there were 2.3 million husband–wife poverty families, compared to 6.1 million in 1959, a 62 percent reduction in two decades. In contrast, the number of poverty families headed by a woman increased from 1.6 million in 1959 to 2.6 million in 1979. Thus, the number of husband–wife poverty families declined sharply, and female-headed poverty families increased both in absolute number and as a percentage of the total.

Government Transfers and the Shrinking Poverty Population

The data of Exhibit 6 suggest that although there was a reduction in the proportion of poor persons during the 1970s, the reduction was modest. These findings are surprising, given the vast expansion in social welfare expenditures since 1960. As Exhibit 8 illustrates, *in dollars of constant purchasing power,* social welfare expenditures increased from $117.6 billion in 1960 to $427.4 billion in 1979, a 263 percent increase. As a share of GNP, these expenditures jumped from 10.5 percent in 1960 to 15.2 percent in 1972, and to 18.5 percent in 1979. Between 1970 and 1979, *in dollars of constant purchasing power,* federal outlays for in-kind transfers more than doubled. Federal expenditures on the food stamp program alone jumped from $1.0 billion (in 1979 dollars) to $6.3 billion between 1970 and 1979, more than a sixfold increase.

Given the vast increases in antipoverty expenditures, why, according to the official figures, has the relative size of the poverty population remained virtually constant? Has the antipoverty effort been a failure? The relatively small decline in the number of people classified as poor is not quite as puzzling once one recognizes that the official poverty statistics do not include gifts and in-kind transfers. During the 1970s, the fast-growing transfer payments were for in-kind income transfers—Medicaid, food stamps, and public housing.[9]

How important are these omissions? In a study by the Congressional Budget Office (CBO), the official poverty figures were corrected for underreported income and the transfer benefits of food stamps, day-care service, public housing, school lunches, Medicaid, and Medicare. On the basis of the revised figures, the CBO estimated that the net income of only 6 percent of the U.S. population fell below the poverty threshold during 1975–1976. Reflecting on the study, Alice Rivlin, the director of the CBO, pronounced, "The nation has come a lot closer to eliminating poverty than most people realize."[10]

In a more recent study, Morton Paglin, professor of economics at Portland State University, refined the earlier estimates of the CBO. Paglin corrected for in-kind transfers and the failure of the Bureau of the Census to apply the income-sharing procedures for family and household data to persons living in the same

EXHIBIT 8 The expansion in social welfare expenditures, 1960–1979

	Federal Transfer Payments			Federal, State, and Local Social Welfare Expenditures	
	Cash Income Transfers (Billions of 1979 Dollars)	In-Kind Transfers (Billions of 1979 Dollars)	Total Transfers (Billions of 1979 Dollars)	Billions of 1979 Dollars	As a Percentage of GNP
1960	54.7	3.0	57.7	117.6	10.5
1970	63.2	21.7	112.6	255.2	15.2
1979	161.7	53.7	215.4	427.4	18.5

Statistical Abstract of the United States—1981, Tables 520 and 522, and Barry Blechman, Edward Gramlich, and Robert Hartman, *Setting National Priorities: The 1975 Budget* (Washington, D.C.: Brookings Institution, 1974), Table 1-1.

---

[9]In 1979, in-kind government transfers totaled $53.7 billion. If targeted to the officially poor, and valued by them at cost, these federal transfers *alone* would have meant $2122 *per person* in uncounted income. The average amount that each low-income person needed to rise above the official level of poverty was approximately $900.

[10]Quoted in Mark R. Arnold, "We're Winning the War on Poverty," *National Observer,* February 19, 1977, p. 1.

household but not related by blood or marriage. According to Paglin's calculations, only 3 percent of Americans were poor in 1976. He also found that when in-kind transfers were considered, the size of the poverty population declined by 80 percent between 1959 and 1975. In contrast, as Exhibit 6 illustrates, the official poverty statistics indicated that the number of persons living in poverty declined by less than 40 percent during the same period.

Paglin summarized his findings as follows:

The [welfare] transfers have been on a sufficiently massive scale to effect a major reduction in the poverty population. It would have been surprising if they had not done so. What is disquieting is the failure to recognize this accomplishment. Social scientists have generally accepted and have given wide currency to the official poverty estimates. It is time for the statistical veil to be lifted so that the poverty problem can be seen in its true dimensions. [11]

Incentives and the Economics of Redistributing Income

Despite the victories that economic growth and redistribution programs have won in the war against poverty, many people—an estimated 6 million, according to Paglin—remain poor. How do the poor react to the programs designed to help them? It is not easy to help the poor by redistributing the national income pie without substantially diminishing the incentives on which the size of the pie depends.

In 1979, the discrepancy between the poverty threshold income level and the income of persons living in poverty (according to the official estimates) was $22.7 billion. Suppose that the persons with incomes above the poverty level were taxed an additional $22.7 billion in order to guarantee the threshold income for everyone. Could such a policy eliminate poverty?

Surprisingly, the answer is no. If the poverty threshold income were guaranteed to all, persons would alter their behavior so that larger payments (relative to earnings) would be necessary to bring their income up to the poverty level. Suppose that the poverty level for single persons were $5000. Put yourself in the position of a student/part-time worker who earned $3000 last year. (Some of you may be in this position.) *If you earned $3000 next year,* a $2000 income transfer would bring your income to the poverty threshold. Would you work and earn the $3000? Unless you are highly unusual, you would not, because if you earned nothing, you would receive a $5000 subsidy, which would bring your income to the poverty threshold. If you earned $4900, you would receive a $100 income transfer. For each dollar earned, one's transfer payments would be reduced by $1, so one's earnings after taxes and transfers would be exactly the same whether one worked (until earnings of $5000 were attained) or not. Under this plan, for all earnings between zero and $5000, single persons would face an implicit **marginal tax rate** of 100 percent. A high marginal tax rate—100 percent in this example—would cause many people living below (and just above) the poverty level to reduce their work effort. Therefore, expenditures far greater than the $22.7 billion poverty threshold shortfall of 1979 would be necessary to finance this program.

Marginal Tax Rate: The amount of one's *additional* (marginal) earnings that must be paid *explicitly* in taxes or *implicitly* in the form of a reduction in the level of one's income supplement. Since it establishes the fraction of an *additional* dollar earned that an individual is permitted to keep, it is an important determinant of the incentive to work.

---

[11] Morton Paglin, *Poverty and Transfers in Kind: A Reevaluation of Poverty in the United States* (Stanford, California: Hoover Institution Press, 1979), Chapter 6, and Morton Paglin, "Poverty in the United States: A Reevaluation," *Policy Review* (Spring 1979), pp. 7–24.

SOCIAL SECURITY AND THE INTERGENERATIONAL REDISTRIBUTION OF INCOME

"Social security"—officially known as Old Age Survivors, Disability and Health Insurance (OASDHI)—is the largest federal program providing for income redistribution. It offers protection against the loss of income that usually accompanies old age or death or dismemberment of a breadwinner. Its Medicare provisions are designed to offset the heavier health care expenses often incurred by the elderly and the disabled. In 1983, more than $150 billion will be paid out to 38 million recipients under the various provisions of OASDHI.

Social Security Is Not an Insurance Program

When social security legislation was passed in 1935, it was envisioned by many as a kind of compulsory national retirement insurance that would operate much like a pension program. Even today, many people believe that *their* social security tax contributions go into an actuarially sound reserve fund, where these payments are set aside for *their* retirement. This is not the case. In contrast with private insurance programs, the tax revenues paid into the OASDHI trust fund are not set aside or invested to pay for the contributor's future benefits. The social security system operates on a "pay-as-you-go" basis. The tax revenues paid into the system are distributed almost immediately to retirees and other beneficiaries of the program. The present social security system is an intergenerational income transfer program. It collects tax revenues from the present generation of workers and redistributes the money to current retirees. Each worker must trust that the next generation will bear the future tax burden necessary to keep the system going.

Problems for the Social Security System

The social security system is financed by a payroll tax, of which the employer and the employee each pay half. The tax is levied on the earnings of employees up to a maximum limit. In 1960, employees and their employers each paid a 3 percent tax on the first $4800 of employee earnings. The maximum combined employee–employer tax was $288. By 1982, both employee and employer were paying a 6.7 percent tax rate on the first $31,800 of earnings. The maximum employee–employer tax had risen to $4262, nearly 15 times the amount of the tax in 1960. Both the tax rate and the maximum taxable base are scheduled to continue rising. By 1987, the combined employee–employer rate will rise to 14.3 percent (7.15 percent on both the employee and the employer) of the first $42,600 of earnings.

Despite these huge tax increases, the social security system is in financial trouble. Most observers believe that under current legislation all trust funds of the system will be exhausted by the late 1980s. What accounts for the financial trouble of the system? The answer to this question is not really complicated. There are two major reasons for the troubles of the system.

1. The Number of Beneficiaries Has Risen Substantially Relative to the Number of Workers. As with any new retirement program, only a few persons reached retirement age in the years just after social security was initiated (1935). However, as the social security system matured, more and more of the nation's retired workers became eligible for payments. The declining birth rate after the post-World War II baby boom and the increased life expectancy of retirees also contributed to the decline in the number of workers paying taxes to finance each social security beneficiary. As Exhibit 11 illustrates, in 1950, there were 16 tax-

paying workers to finance the benefits of each retired social security recipient. By 1970, there were only 4 workers per social security recipient. The ratio of workers per social security beneficiary has now fallen to 3.

Demographic factors indicate that the situation will worsen. When the generation born during the post-World War II baby boom reaches retirement soon after the year 2010, the number of workers per retiree is expected to be about 2 taxpayers per beneficiary.

2. The Level of Social Security Retirement Benefits Has Risen More Rapidly Than the Earnings Base That Supports Them. Measured in dollars of constant purchasing power, social security retirement benefits have risen quite rapidly (Exhibit 12). Between 1970 and 1979, the *real* average monthly benefits of social security recipients rose by almost 40 percent. In contrast, during the same period, the average constant-dollar gross earnings in the private sector declined by 2 percent. As a result, social security benefits rose not only more rapidly than prices but more rapidly than the wages of the workers paying the benefits. In 1965, the average monthly social security benefits of a male retired worker were 25.1 percent of the average gross monthly earnings. By 1979, the average monthly social security benefits had risen until they exceeded 40 percent of the average gross earnings of private sector workers.

The rapid increase in social security benefits was not entirely the result of a planned strategy. Rather it reflected, at least partially, a number of errors. When the benefits were indexed in 1972, a faulty indexing formula caused benefits to rise more rapidly than the consumer price index (CPI). In addition, most observers agree that the CPI itself tends to overstate the inflation rate during a time of rising interest rates, such as were experienced during the

In 1950, there were 16 workers for each Social Security beneficiary.

In 1970, there were 4 workers for each Social Security beneficiary.

In 1982, there were 3 workers for each Social Security beneficiary.

By 2025, there will be just 2 workers for each Social Security beneficiary.

Result: An increasing burden on each worker whose Social Security taxes support the program.

EXHIBIT 11   The declining number of workers per social security recipient

1970s; again, such an overstatement caused benefits to increase too rapidly.

Social Security and the Low Rate of Savings in the United States

To the extent that workers believe that through the social security tax they are setting aside current income for their retirement needs, they will be likely to cut back on savings. However, because social security is not a pension fund, no increase in savings (or, ultimately, loanable funds) is forthcoming from the government or from insurance companies. According to Harvard economist Martin Feldstein (later made chairman of the President's Council of Economic Advisors), the program has caused aggregate private saving to decline by

approximately 50 percent.[18] This reduction in private saving leads to higher interest rates, which retard investment and the rate of capital formation. In turn, the lower rate of capital formation places a drag on economic growth. Thus, many economists believe that during the years the pay-as-you-go social security system has been maturing and expanding, the growth rate of the United States has been retarded.

---

[18]Martin Feldstein, "Social Security Induced Retirement and Aggregate Capital Accumulation," *Journal of Political Economy* (September/October 1974), pp. 905–926.

The Politics of Social Security

The early popularity of social security is easy to understand. Before the program "came of age"—while there were still 10 to 20 taxpayers for each recipient—pay-as-you-go financing enabled Congress to grant substantial benefits to retired and near-retired workers while increasing taxes by only very small amounts *at the time of passage.* Whenever coverage was expanded or benefits increased, future benefits were financed by writing *future* tax increases into the law. Usually the added benefits were scheduled to begin accruing just before election time, and the tax increases were postponed until after the election. In addition, the growing numbers of workers entering the

EXHIBIT 12   The rising social security benefits and the earnings that support them

Year	Average Monthly Benefits (Male Retiring at Age 65)	Real Average Monthly Benefits	Average Monthly Benefits as a Percent of Gross Average Monthly Earnings[a]
1960	$ 82	$201	25.8
1965	96	221	25.1
1970	139	260	29.0
1975	247	333	37.8
1979	359	359	40.8

[a]The gross average earnings are for production employees in the private sector.

system added immediately to the pool of taxpayers but did not increase the drain on the trust funds until later. The political gains were enormous, since Congress could grant immediate benefits to a relatively concentrated group (composed primarily of older people, who are quite likely to vote in elections), while the cost of the program was widely dispersed and would be incurred (or at least felt) primarily in the future.[19]

However, the political profiteering of earlier Congresses has exacted its price from present and future legislators. By now, the inevitable tax increases have become very large. There is no big trust fund from which benefits for the increasing number of social security participants can be paid. The work force is not growing in size (or productivity) as rapidly as before. Taxes must be increased still further if past promises of benefits are to be kept. A program that was a boon to political careers is now a serious political problem. Sizable

[19]In the election of 1976, 62.2 percent of eligible voters over 65 reported that they voted, as compared to 59.2 percent among all those of voting age. For those nearing retirement (age 45–64) the figure was 68.7 percent. See *Statistical Abstract of the United States—1978*, Table 836.

tax increases *without* the promise of larger real benefits are a politician's nightmare.

The Future of Social Security

It seems clear that changes in the social security system must be made if the system is to survive at all. Even the large scheduled tax increases throughout the 1980s will not be sufficient to finance the current benefit levels. Three major changes have been widely discussed.

1. Raise the Normal Eligibility Age from 65 to 68.   This would both (a) increase the number of workers, since people would retire later in life, and (b) decrease the number of recipients. Since life expectancy continues to rise, future beneficiaries would still be able to draw benefits for a timespan similar to that of prior recipients. The plan could be phased in over several years so as to avoid any disruptive influence.

2. Remove the Full Indexing of Future Benefits.   This plan would gradually reduce the benefit rates. The nominal benefits of retirees would continue to be adjusted upward but at a slower rate than the CPI. As benefit levels decline to rates consistent with planned future tax rates and income growth,

full indexing, hopefully to an accurate measure of inflation, could be reinstituted.

3. Gradually Phase the System into an Insurance Program.   This idea, suggested by Michael Boskin of Stanford, would require still higher taxes so that a trust fund could accumulate to finance *earmarked* future benefits for current taxpayers. Instead of taking a chance that future generations will levy higher taxes in order to pay for benefits, current taxpayers would be paying earmarked funds into a trust system to finance their own retirement benefits. No big leap in taxes would be necessary when the post-World War II baby boom generation reaches retirement around 2010. The trust fund would add to the nation's savings, eliminating one of the defects of the current system.

Discussion

1. Explain the major problems confronting the social security system. What solutions would you suggest?

2. Why do you think the social security system is operated by the government? Could a private insurance company establish the same type of plan? Why or why not?

1 The annual income data before taxes and transfers indicate that the bottom 20 percent of families receive approximately 5 percent of the aggregate income, while the top 20 percent receive slightly more than 40 percent. There has been little change in the distribution of actual annual income during the past three decades.

2 Adjustment for in-kind transfers, taxes, and size of family significantly reduces the measured inequality of income.

3 A substantial percentage of the inequality in annual income distribution reflects differences in age and labor-force status. The annual incomes of youthful, inexperienced workers, students, and retirees tend to be low; those in their prime-earning years will have higher incomes. Given the stages of the life-earnings cycle, annual incomes would vary considerably even if lifetime incomes were equal.

4 Differences in time worked are an important source of inequality in both annual and lifetime incomes. The difference in annual after-tax and after-transfer income per hour between high- and low-income recipients is small.

5 In general, income is distributed more equally in the advanced industrial nations than in less developed nations. The degree of income equality is similar for the United States, West Germany, and Japan. Compared to these three nations, there is slightly more income equality in welfare states, such as Sweden and the United Kingdom.

6 There is substantial income mobility in the United States. Studies indicate that persons move up and down the income distribution ladder over their lifetimes. Of the children born to parents who are in the top 20 percent of all income recipients, fewer than half are able to attain that high-income status themselves.

7 Economic analysis alone cannot objectively indicate that one income distribution is better than another, but it can help to predict the outcomes of alternative redistribution policies.

8 According to the official data, poverty is a fact of life for approximately 12 percent of the people in the United States. Those living in poverty are generally younger, less educated, less likely to be working, and more likely to be living in families headed by a female than those who are not poor.

9 In recent years, in-kind transfers, such as medical, housing, and food stamp benefits, have grown far more rapidly than national income. Since the official definition of poverty does not include in-kind benefits, these expanded expenditures fail to reduce poverty *as officially defined*. Once the official data are adjusted to incorporate in-kind transfers and unreported income, research indicates that between 3 and 6 percent of Americans still live in poverty. In contrast with the official data, studies incorporating in-kind income indicate that the size of the poverty population has declined *sharply* in recent years.

10 Many persons with incomes below the poverty level confront very high implicit marginal tax rates. Since their transfer benefits decline as their income rises, additional earnings often cause the *net income* of the poor to rise by only a small amount. This system clearly diminishes the incentive and ability of the poor to earn and escape their dependency on welfare.

11 Income redistribution programs retard the growth of real output, since they increase both the explicit tax rate of the taxpayer-producer and the implicit tax rate of the transfer recipient. At the higher marginal tax rates, *both* the donor and the recipient have an incentive to substitute leisure (which is now cheaper) for work effort (which now is more expensive).

12 Some economists believe that the cost of redistribution could be substantially lowered if the negative income tax were substituted for current social welfare programs. The major advantages of the negative income tax (relative to present programs) are (a) its simplicity and (b) its provision for the transfer of income to people because they are poor, rather than on the basis of other selective characteristics.

1   Do you think the current distribution of income in the United States is too unequal? Why or why not?

2   Do you think it is proper for a tax–transfer system to redistribute income from (a) households making between $25,000 to $30,000 per year to (b) households with incomes between $12,000 and $15,000 per year? Suppose the high-income household head is a prime-earning-age construction worker and the low-income household head is a retired medical doctor. How would this affect your answer?

3   "Welfare is a classic case of conflicting goals. Low welfare payments continue to leave people in poverty, but high welfare payments attract people to welfare roles, reduce work incentives, and cause higher rates of unemployment." (quoted from the *There Is No Free Lunch Newsletter*)

   (a) Evaluate. (*Hint:* Apply the opportunity cost concept.)

   (b) Can you think of a plan to resolve the dilemma? Is the dilemma resolvable? Why or why not?

4   What do you think would be the major effects of the negative income tax? Do not forget the secondary effects.

5   Since income transfers to the poor typically increase the marginal tax rate confronted by the poor, does a $1000 additional transfer payment necessarily cause the income of poor recipients to rise by $1000? Why or why not?

6   Explain how high marginal tax rates affect the decisions of workers to undergo additional training and the willingness of investors to undertake risk.

28 THE ENERGY MARKET

Price controls have . . . had a detrimental impact on the supply of petroleum products and the construction of refinery capacity, essential to increasing domestic energy supplies. Due to the pressure to keep prices below what the free market would specify, shortages of petroleum products have occurred at both the retail and wholesale levels. Had prices been allowed to rise, the quantity supplied would have expanded to meet the quantity demanded; and each consumer would have had direct incentive to economize on usage.[1]
Phillip Gramm

Organization of Oil Exporting Nations (OPEC): A worldwide cartel made up of 13 major oil-exporting countries. The cartel was able to make sharp increases in the price of crude oil during the 1970s.

In many ways, the events in the energy market during the 1970s have provided us with a fascinating—though sometimes painful—laboratory experiment in economics. The quote from Congressman Gramm (also a professor of economics, on leave from Texas A & M University) makes a critical point about the energy market: Energy prices matter, and they matter a great deal. As we will see, the incentive structure created by the energy prices of the 1960s and early 1970s left the United States and most other industrial nations extremely vulnerable to the policies of the **Organization of Oil Exporting Countries (OPEC).** Following the Arab oil embargo of 1973, the prices of many energy products in the United States were fixed below the open market level. Again, prices mattered—the controls led to shortages, long lines at gasoline stations, and nonprice rationing.

Economics indicates that three results can be expected from an increase in the free market price of a product. First, consumers will use the higher-priced product more judiciously. Second, producers will apply resources, technology, and entrepreneurship more intensively to the task of increasing the output of the product and substitute products. Third, both consumers and producers who use the product will search more diligently for cheaper substitutes. However, these adjustments do not take place instantaneously in any kind of market. In this chapter, we will analyze how energy markets work and why the adjustment process is often lengthy.

During the 1970s, the energy crisis was blamed on various villains—for example, the big oil companies, OPEC, allegedly wasteful consumers, and/or manufacturers of gas-guzzling automobiles. What *did* cause the energy crisis? Why did it persist? What lies ahead—will dwindling energy supplies bring economic progress to a grinding halt, or can the energy crisis be relegated to the history books? These questions are at the heart of our discussion in this chapter.

---

[1]W. Phillip Gramm, "The Energy Crisis in Perspective," *Wall Street Journal,* November 30, 1973.

THE NATURE OF THE ENERGY MARKET

As with other resources, supply and demand are important in the energy markets. However, the nature of energy markets sometimes conceals the significance of these forces. Four characteristics are important in understanding the operation of energy markets.

Demand Is Far More Elastic in the Long Run Than in the Short Run

The *immediate* response of consumers to higher energy prices is likely to be relatively weak. In the short run, individuals will find it costly to reduce their consumption of electricity, fuel oil, and gasoline by a large amount, even if the prices of these energy products rise sharply. Of course, some energy-saving measures can be adopted immediately. More care can be taken to turn off the lights in unoccupied rooms. Warmer clothing can be substituted for heating oil in the winter, and fans can be substituted for air conditioning in the summer. Nonessential driving can be curtailed. However, the immediate reduction in energy consumption is likely to be small *relative to the potential reduction over a longer period of time.*[2]

With time, higher energy prices can be expected to result in a substantially greater reduction in energy consumption. Both old and newly constructed homes will be better insulated. New buildings will be constructed with fewer glass windows and with more and improved insulating materials. As gasoline prices rise, new car buyers will exchange some power and size for more fuel economy. The energy efficiency of newly developed heating systems and home appliances will be improved. It will take time to make these changes. Several years will pass before all the energy-saving adjustments triggered by the higher energy prices will be fully instituted.

As Exhibit 1a illustrates, the demand for energy products is often highly inelastic in the short run. However, we should not be deceived by the seemingly weak link between energy prices and consumption in the short run. In the long run, a variety of energy-saving adjustments are possible. Just as the second law of demand predicts, the demand for energy products will be considerably more elastic in the long run than in the short run.

The Short-Run Supply Will Be Inelastic Because of the Lengthy Production Cycle

It generally takes a substantial time period to develop new energy sources. Consider the case of crude oil. Both major and independent oil companies will search more diligently for additional crude-oil supplies in response to higher prices. However, promising areas must be tested, exploratory wells drilled, and production equipment set into place. In some cases, new pipelines must be built. All of these operations are time-consuming. Usually, it takes three to five years from the time the search begins until the refined product can be brought to market. Even though development and delivery can be accelerated slightly, higher product prices will have only a small impact on output in the short run.

With time, however, the higher prices will elicit a greater increase in quantity supplied (Exhibit 1b). Additional exploratory and development ac-

---

[2]Of course, other energy-saving steps (for example, curtailing the use of television and other electrical appliances, bicycling rather than driving on short trips, and enduring even lower temperatures in the winter) are possible, but most consumers are likely to consider them too costly.

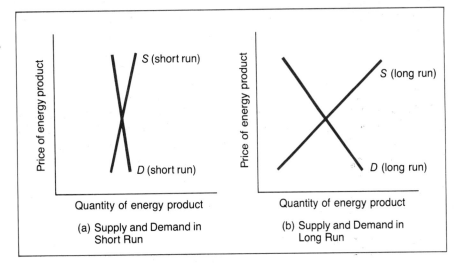

(a) Supply and Demand in Short Run

(b) Supply and Demand in Long Run

tivities will *eventually* lead to an expansion in output. Higher price will also stimulate efforts to achieve more complete extraction from a petroleum pool. Currently, about two-thirds of the oil in a pool is left when a field is abandoned. Extracting the rest is simply too expensive. The share of recovered oil has slowly increased, however, as oil prices have risen. Higher prices make it more attractive to develop new and more elaborate means of recovery, such as flooding a field with water or injecting wells with steam or chemicals. Again, it takes time for producers to install the necessary equipment, extract the extra oil, and transport it to the refinery, even after a price rise is noticed or expected.

Proved Reserves Are Inventories

Proved Reserves: The verified quantity of a resource that can be recovered at current prices and levels of technology.

Petroleum reserves are frequently misunderstood by observers outside the industry. **Proved reserves** are the verified quantity of the resource that producers believe they can recover *at current prices and levels of technology.* In the oil and gas industry, proved reserves are essentially the same as inventories in other areas of business. They allow a firm to adapt to uncertain future market conditions.

It is costly to identify, purchase, and hold petroleum reserves, just as it is costly to hold inventories in other businesses. Thus, at any given time, energy producers will choose to verify and hold only a limited amount of the earth's total energy-producing reserves. The fact that domestic oil and gas producers generally hold only a 10- or 15-year supply at current consumption rates is neither alarming nor surprising. It would be uneconomical for petroleum producers to incur the cost of holding substantially larger amounts, just as it would be uneconomical for an automobile dealer to hold more than a two- or three-month supply of automobiles.

Absolute Reserves: The total amount of a resource in existence. Absolute reserves are unknown and unknowable, although crude estimates (scientific guesses) can be made.

Proved reserves should not be confused with **absolute reserves**—the total amount of reserves in existence. Absolute reserves are the concern of geologists, not economists. No one knows the size of the absolute reserves of oil, gas, and other minerals. Indeed, knowing the quantity of absolute reserves would be of limited value. The valuation of those absolute reserves is dependent on demand, future technology, and the cost of extraction. However, no one knows what products we will want or which technology we will use or how much it will cost to recover a resource 50 or 100 years from now. Therefore, we do not know whether reserves of petroleum and other products that might be available at that time will be as valuable as gold or as worthless as ashes.

The OPEC Cartel

The most significant development in the worldwide petroleum market during the 1970s was the emergence of a strong producer cartel, the Organization of Petroleum Exporting Countries. The major petroleum-exporting countries belong to the cartel. By imposing taxes and decreeing higher prices on petroleum and petroleum products, the OPEC nations increased their revenues substantially. The sharp increase in energy prices during the period after the Arab embargo did not reflect any major rise in worldwide costs of production or sudden increases in demand. Rather, these price rises were the result of the tax–price policy of the OPEC cartel.

The 13 OPEC nations exert an important influence on the world oil market because they produce approximately 40 percent of the world's oil and hold over half of the proved reserves. During 1973–1974, OPEC was able to quadruple the world price of crude oil without being forced to curtail its output significantly. Given the nature of energy markets, this should not be too surprising. As we have pointed out, the demand for energy products is relatively insensitive to price, as is the supply of alternative energy sources (including competitively produced oil from non-OPEC nations) *in the short run*.

Again during 1978–1980, the OPEC cartel sharply increased the export price of oil. Why were the oil-importing nations, including the United States, so vulnerable to OPEC price increases? Is OPEC largely immune from market forces? We will now consider these important questions.

THE HISTORICAL ROOTS OF THE ENERGY CRISIS

One cannot fully understand the energy crisis of the 1970s without having some knowledge of the market conditions and policies that existed in the 1950s and 1960s. As Exhibit 2 illustrates, during the period from 1950 to 1970 the **real price** of energy was declining, thereby stimulating consumption. During these two decades, energy consumption in the United States doubled. The energy prices and consumption pattern of other countries followed suit.

As a result of low energy prices and rising incomes, the construction of homes and office buildings emphasized uniqueness, style, and living space rather than energy conservation. Skyscrapers with an accent on windows were in vogue. Poorly insulated homes featuring sliding glass doors and huge picture windows were popular. This nonconservation of energy was efficient only because energy was cheap and supply was plentiful. Similarly, our automobiles were designed with an eye to power, speed, and size but with little emphasis on saving energy. And after long-term capital assets of this type have been constructed, it is costly to make alterations that improve their energy efficiency. Thus, the low energy prices of the 1950s and 1960s not only encouraged current energy consumption but led to the construction of energy-intensive capital assets that necessarily increased the future (1975–1985) consumption of energy.

Against this backdrop of falling real prices and rapid expansion in energy utilization, public policy in three important areas—price regulation, import

Real Price: The price of a product, such as gasoline, *relative to* a general index of prices—the consumer price index, for example. If the price of the product rises less (more) rapidly than the general price index, the real price of the product has declined (increased). For example, if the price of gasoline rises 10 percent while the general level of prices rises 20 percent, the real price of gasoline has fallen.

EXHIBIT 2 The price of energy, 1950–1981

| Year | Real Energy Prices Paid by Consumers (1976 Dollars) | | |
	Gasoline, Including Tax (Cents/Gallon)	Residential Electricity (Dollars/Million BTUs)	Residential Natural Gas (Dollars/Million BTUs)
1950	63.3	20.00	2.01
1955	61.9	16.53	1.91
1960	59.9	13.92	1.92
1965	56.2	11.90	1.82
1970	52.3	9.02	1.55
1972	49.2	9.13	1.62
1973	49.7	8.94	1.60
1974	60.5	9.57	1.64
1975	60.6	10.00	1.79
1976	59.0	10.93	1.95
1977	58.4	11.17	2.16
1978	54.6	11.01	2.20
1979	67.2	10.65	2.29
1980	82.3	10.85	2.49
1981	82.1	11.36	2.76

Data for 1950–1975 are from Milton Russell, "Energy," in *Setting National Priorities: The 1978 Budget,* ed. J. Pechman (Washington, D.C.: Brookings Institution, 1977); 1976–1981 figures are from U.S. Department of Energy, *Monthly Energy Review* (March 1982), p. 16.

restrictions, and tighter environmental regulation—provided additional stimulus to the forces that culminated in the energy crisis.

Energy Shortages and the Regulation of Natural Gas Prices

Permian Basin Method: An areawide system of price controls on natural gas instituted by the Federal Power Commission in 1961. Under this system, the wellhead price of all natural gas in an area was set at the average historical cost of production for wells in the area.

Proved Reserves/Consumption Ratio: Proved reserves divided by consumption, for the current year.

Beginning in 1954, the Federal Power Commission (FPC) fixed the wellhead price of natural gas. During the 1950s, the FPC used a case-by-case approach to establish a wellhead price that reflected the cost of production of the well. However, it soon accumulated an enormous backlog of cases. As a result, in 1961, the FPC adopted the **Permian Basin method** of areawide rate-making. Under this procedure, the FPC used the average historical cost of producers in an area to establish the price at which producers were permitted to sell gas to interstate pipelines. This price ceiling was imposed on *all* wells in the locality. Under these circumstances, it became unprofitable to exploit natural gas resources when the expected cost of production of a well exceeded the area average. Only the large, easily accessible deposits of natural gas were exploited. Needless to say, this incentive structure retarded the growth of natural gas supply.

During the period from 1954 to 1961, the price of natural gas, even though it was regulated by the FPC, rose relative to both the price of crude oil and the consumer price index. The **proved reserves/consumption ratio** for natural gas remained relatively steady.[3] However, beginning with the FPC's adoption of the Permian Basin method, the real price of natural gas began to

---

[3]See Jai-hoom Yang, "The Nature and Origins of the U.S. Energy Crisis," Federal Reserve Bank of St. Louis *Monthly Review* (July 1977), pp. 2–12.

decline. Throughout most of the 1960s and well into the 1970s, the FPC fixed the price of natural gas at approximately one-third the price of its energy equivalent in crude oil. This below-equilibrium price encouraged consumers to use more natural gas, and at the same time, it greatly reduced the incentive of producers to discover more natural gas.

Needless to say, encouraging consumption while retarding production is the perfect formula for the creation of shortages. By 1974, the proved reserves/consumption ratio of natural gas had declined to 10, compared to its level of just over 20 before the Permian Basin decision. The worsening supply conditions for natural gas caused demand for electricity and oil to increase, putting upward pressure on costs and prices in those markets. The policy seemed almost tailor-made for the OPEC cartel.

Import Restrictions and the Origin of OPEC

Before 1948, the United States was a net exporter of oil. It was in a position of dominance, holding 31 percent of the world's proved reserves. After the discovery and development of petroleum resources in the Persian Gulf states, however, producers in that region began to make inroads into the U.S. position. By the late 1950s imports comprised one-fifth of U.S. domestic consumption. More to the point, the costs of developing foreign oil were generally less than the costs of developing domestic sources. Thus, domestic producers were under intense competitive pressure from "cheap foreign oil." They argued that oil imports were endangering our national security. In 1959, a coalition of domestic producers and refiners argued successfully for mandatory import quotas, limiting the importation of cheap foreign oil into the United States.

The import restrictions, imposed in 1959, were designed to expand the demand for domestic petroleum resources and thereby reduce the trend toward lower petroleum prices. The restrictions also led to an unplanned secondary effect. The demand for foreign oil fell sharply, as did the price of oil in the international export market. The abundance of oil on the world market and falling prices increased the desire of oil exporters to form a cartel, and OPEC was born in September 1960. However, under such conditions a cartel would have been impossible to manage without an effective means of enforcing production quotas, and OPEC had none.

During the 1960s, the world supply of oil was abundant. The United States, with its import restrictions in effect, followed a "drain America first" policy. There was a virtual flood of surplus oil on the international market. The availability of cheap foreign oil reduced the incentive of internationally based American oil producers to explore and develop *new,* more costly domestic sources—if *we* ran out of oil, *they* would have plenty; the restrictions could simply be lifted. Producers permitted their domestic proved reserves to decline (relative to consumption), expecting low-cost foreign reserves to be abundantly available in the future. Even though the abundance of the world oil supply prevented OPEC from exerting much influence during the 1960s, the stage was being set for OPEC's response to the restrictive import policy of the United States.

Energy Markets and Environmental Regulations

Beginning in the late 1960s, the United States began to take steps to preserve its environment. Stringent pollution emission standards, along with the falling *real* price of gasoline, resulted in a substantial decline in the miles per gallon of fuel for the average automobile. This, together with rising incomes and a growing population, generated an increase in the demand for gasoline.

Simultaneously, the United States began to reduce an implicit subsidy to oil refineries—the right to use and pollute water and air resources without paying for them. The way in which this implicit subsidy was reduced aggravated the situation more than was necessary. Instead of seeking to bring about pollution abatement wherever the benefits of doing so would exceed the costs, political authorities in many places simply denied permission to build added refinery capacity. This, of course, reduced incentive to expand refinery capacity. Incentive was further diminished by the uncertainty associated with the import quotas. Since changes in the import quota legislation could dramatically alter the supply cost of oil—for instance, if the import restrictions were lifted and foreign oil wells became the cheapest and most readily available oil sources—oil companies were reluctant to build facilities costing many millions of dollars in locations that five years later might be far from the cheapest sources of crude oil.

THE ENERGY CRISIS AND OUR POLICY RESPONSE

The outbreak of the 1973 Middle East War and the oil embargo that accompanied it provided the backdrop for the energy crisis of the 1970s. Declining domestic prices had encouraged domestic energy consumption and led to the construction of energy-intensive capital assets that would continue to promote energy consumption in the future. The import restrictions encouraged the rapid drain of U.S. domestic oil reserves, and the apparent abundance of proved reserves in foreign countries discouraged domestic exploration. The price controls on natural gas substantially reduced the inventories (proved reserves) of this alternative source of energy. Meanwhile, environmental regulations added to the demand for energy and slowed the construction of refinery facilities, thereby reducing supply. The situation was also aggravated by the imposition of domestic price controls on petroleum during the Nixon price freeze of 1971–1973.

In October 1973, the U.S. domestic consumption of energy was at a high level and could not be reduced easily. Simultaneously, the domestic supply of proved petroleum reserves had dwindled to a low level. These conditions made it possible for the OPEC cartel to raise the price of crude oil from $2.50 to over $10.00 per barrel in less than two years. The short-term impact of this sharp rise in price was predictable. Given the long production lags and the demand for energy as a complement to the currently available stock of assets (buildings, homes, automobiles, etc.), both the supply of and demand for crude oil were highly inelastic in the short run. Therefore, OPEC was able to raise petroleum prices in the short run without confronting a sharp decline in the amount demanded.

During the nationwide debate that followed the OPEC price increases of 1973–1974, many public leaders mistakenly believed that the weak short-run supply and demand response to the higher prices indicated that price did not exert much impact on the allocation of energy. Most news reports referred to energy "needs" and "requirements" as if these grew in fixed proportion to population or the GNP. The impact of price on the supply of energy was also disregarded. Data on *proved* reserves were mistakenly taken as indicating the quantity of *absolute* reserves. Americans were warned that the supply of fossil fuels was only sufficient to last 10 or 15 years into the future.

Exhibit 3 presents a graphic illustration of this widespread view. Here, both the supply of and demand for nonrenewable energy products are assumed to be vertical, and an energy "gap" is present because demand has outrun supply. Of course, this view of the supply of and demand for energy does not stand up under serious examination. Almost without exception, energy products are demanded, not for their own sake, but because they are factors in the production of a desired good or service. For example, electricity is used in the production of lighting and air conditioning. Gasoline is used in the production of transportation services. It follows that these productive resources cannot be any less sensitive to price than the goods that they produce. Energy-intensive goods are no different than other products and resources. Higher prices induce consumers to seek substitute products and motivate producers to supply a larger amount of energy and energy-substitute products.

The proponents of the "energy gap" view exerted a strong impact on U.S. policy during the 1970s. Price controls, production quotas, and federal allocation procedures were characteristic of the approach the United States took to the energy crisis.

Price Controls on Energy Resources

Although the Nixon price controls were removed from other products in 1973, they remained in effect on petroleum resources. As we have noted, the price of natural gas sold in interstate markets was fixed well below market equilibrium. As energy prices rose, natural gas producers sold more and more of their product in the uncontrolled intrastate market. This created shortages in nonproducer states. Congress responded by extending the controls to intrastate markets and raising the controlled price to more realistic levels.

Congress also enacted a complex set of price and allocation rates for crude oil and refined products. In order to encourage producers to search for and develop domestic crude-oil resources, a two-tier pricing system for old and new oil was established in 1974. The price of "old oil"—oil produced from established wells—was fixed at $5.25 per barrel in order to keep the "big oil" companies from making "windfall profits." In contrast, the price of "new oil"—oil

EXHIBIT 3 The mythical vertical demand and supply curves for energy

Leaders of popular opinion often assume that the demand and supply curves for energy resources resemble those presented here. Both economic reasoning and real-world data indicate that this view is incorrect.

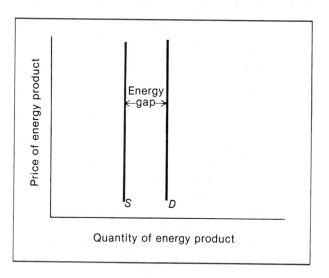

PART FIVE

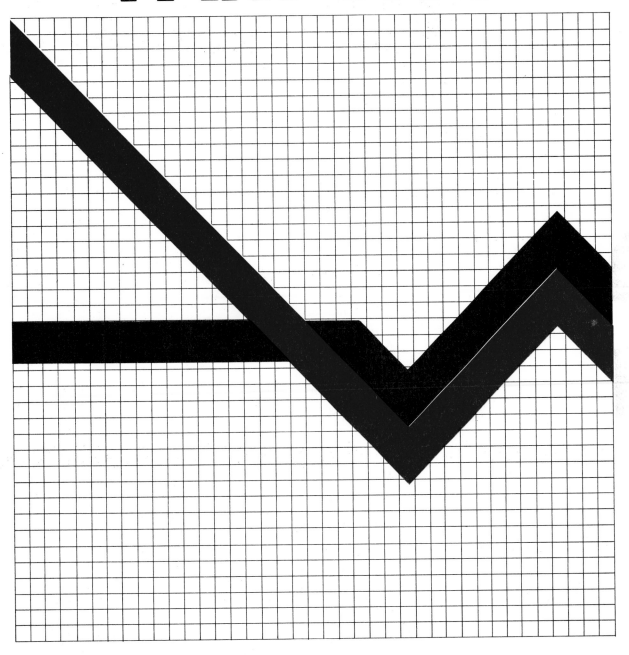

PUBLIC CHOICE

View A: The market coordinates the self-interest of individuals, inducing them to produce a diverse menu of housing structures and food products, convenient shopping centers, completely planned communities with their own police and fire protection, beautiful golf courses, and even the fairyland entertainment center that we call Disney World. The market is a kind of computer that must surely be called one of the wonders of the world.

View B: Personal self-interest working within the framework of a market economy has led to stripped mountainsides, destruction of scenic beauty, pollution of lakes and rivers, air that is a menace to our health, and junkyards that blot our landscape. Unless the market behavior of firms and individuals is altered, environmental disaster cannot be avoided.

Is it possible for the same person to adhere to both of these views? This chapter will help to explain why they need not be inconsistent.

Market Failure: The failure of the market system to attain hypothetically *ideal* allocative efficiency. This means that potential gain exists that has not been captured. However, the cost of establishing a mechanism that could *potentially* capture the gain may exceed the benefits. Therefore, it is not always possible to improve the situation.

We have emphasized that the pricing system coordinates the decisions of buyers and sellers. However, if a market economy is to allocate goods and resources efficiently, certain conditions must be met. First, property rights must be defined so that economic participants will be prohibited from imposing costs on nonconsenting parties. Second, voluntary market behavior requires that productive activity and personal reward be closely linked. Third, both buyers and sellers must be reasonably well informed. Otherwise, one of the parties to an exchange who is misinformed, may unwittingly consent to arrangements that will later be regretted. Fourth, as we emphasized earlier, competition among buyers and sellers must exist.

In this chapter, we focus on **market failure,** economic activity that results in allocative inefficiency relative to the hypothetical ideal of economists. The sources of market failure can be grouped into four general classes: (a) externalities, (b) public goods, (c) conflicts between buyers and sellers *after an exchange,* stemming from poor information and misrepresentation, and (d) monopoly. Since we have already investigated the impact of monopoly on both product and factor markets, we will focus in this chapter on the three other categories of market failure.

Keep in mind that market failure is merely a failure to attain conditions of *ideal* efficiency. Alternative forms of economic organization will also have defects. Market failure creates an opportunity for government to improve the situation. However, in some circumstances, public sector action will not be corrective. Sometimes there may even be good reason to expect that it will be counterproductive. We will analyze market failure in this chapter and focus on the operation of the public sector in the following chapter.

EXTERNAL EFFECTS AND THE MARKET

The genius of a market exchange system lies in its ability to bring personal and social welfare into harmony. Individuals produce and exchange goods because they derive mutual gain from doing so. When only the trading parties are affected, production and voluntary exchange also promote the *social* welfare. Smoothly operating competitive markets lead to economic efficiency as long as all resources and products can be used only with the consent of their owners. Every decision-maker must bear the opportunity cost of any use (or misuse) of scarce resources. Under these conditions, Adam Smith's invisible hand performs its magic.

When production and exchange affect the welfare of nonconsenting secondary parties, externalities are present. The external effects may be either positive or negative. If the welfare of nonconsenting secondary parties is adversely affected, the spillover effects are called **external costs.** A steel mill that belches smoke into the air imposes an external cost on surrounding residents ·who prefer clear air. A junkyard creates an eyesore, making an area less pleasant for passersby. Similarly, litterbugs, drunk drivers, speeders, muggers, and robbers impose unwanted costs on others. If the spillover effects enhance the welfare of secondary parties, they are called **external benefits.** A beautiful rose garden provides external benefits for the neighbors of the gardener. A golf course generally provides spillover benefits to surrounding property owners.

When external costs and external benefits are present, market prices will not send the proper signals to producers and consumers. This situation results in market failure.

External Costs: Harmful effects of an individual's or a group's action on the welfare of nonconsenting secondary parties. Litterbugs, drunk drivers, and polluters, for example, create exernal costs.

External Benefits: Beneficial effects of group or individual action on the welfare of nonpaying secondary parties.

Market Failure: External Costs

Social Costs: The sum of (a) the private costs that are incurred by a decision-maker and (b) any external costs of the action that are imposed on nonconsenting secondary parties. If there are no external costs, private and social costs will be equal.

From the viewpoint of economic efficiency, an action should be undertaken only if it generates benefits in excess of its social costs. **Social costs** include both (a) the private cost borne by the consenting parties and (b) any external cost imposed on nonconsenting secondary parties.

When external costs are present, market prices may fail to register correctly the social cost generated by the use of resources or consumption of products. Decision-makers may not be forced to bear fully the cost associated with their actions. Motivated by self-interest, they may undertake actions that generate a net loss to the community. The harm done to the secondary parties may exceed the net private gain. In such circumstances, private interest and economic efficiency are in conflict.

The hypothetical situation represented in Exhibit 1, which concerns the establishment of a mobile home park in a residential area, highlights the potential conflict. The trading partners—the park owner and those who rent park

EXHIBIT 1   External cost and market failure

Mr. and Mrs. Jones own ten acres of land. If they use it to raise wheat, which they eventually sell to the miller, both the Joneses and the miller gain (a). There are no external costs. However, when external costs are present (b), a market exchange may reduce total welfare, even though the consenting parties gain. For example, suppose that the Joneses decide to use their ten acres for a mobile home park. Both the Joneses and their customers gain by establishing the trailer park. Suppose that the joint net monthly gain is $500. The Joneses' neighbors, however, are harmed because the trailer park is jammed with noisy children and is poorly kept. Overall monthly costs of $1000 are imposed on the Joneses' nonconsenting neighbors. The $500 gain that accrues to Mr. and Mrs. Jones and their customers (the net private benefit) is less than the cost imposed on the neighbors. The action adversely affects the welfare of the community.

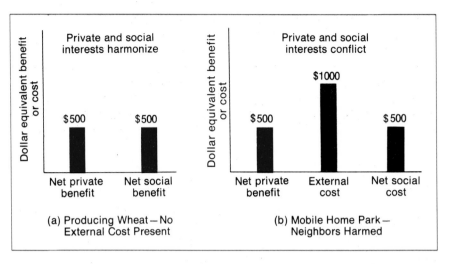

(a) Producing Wheat—No External Cost Present

(b) Mobile Home Park— Neighbors Harmed

space—gain. Their actions, however, generate congestion and noise (external costs). The harm to the neighboring residents exceeds the private benefits of the park owner and the renters. Social costs exceed social benefits. However, since the residents do not have noise or noncongestion rights, the market fails to register their views. The park owner and renters have an incentive to undertake the project even though it will reduce the community's social welfare.

Why not simply prohibit activities that result in external cost? After all, why should we allow nonconsenting parties to be harmed? This approach has a certain appeal, but closer inspection indicates that it is often an unsatisfactory solution. Automobile exhaust imposes an external cost on bicyclists—and, for that matter, on everyone who breathes. Dogs are notorious for using the neighbor's lawn for bone burying and relief purposes. Motorboats are noisy and frighten fish, much to the disgust of fishermen. Yet few would argue that we do away with cars, dogs, and motorboats. From a social viewpoint, prohibition is often a less desirable alternative than tolerating the inconvenience of the external costs. The gains from the activity must be weighed against the costs imposed on those who are harmed, as well as against practical problems associated with controlling the activity.

External Costs and Ideal Output.   Externalities may result from the actions of either consumers or producers. When the actions of a producer impose external costs on others, the costs of the firm, reflecting only private costs, are not an accurate indicator of the total social costs of production.

Exhibit 2 illustrates the impact of external costs on the socially desirable price and output. Suppose that there are a large number of copper-producing firms. They are able to discharge their waste products (mainly sulfur dioxide) into the air without charge, even though the pollution damages people, property, and plants downwind from the discharge. These air pollution costs are external to the copper producers. If allowed to operate freely, the producers have little incentive to adopt either production techniques or control devices that would limit the costs inflicted on other parties. These alternatives would only increase their private production cost.

Since pollutants can be freely discharged into the atmosphere, each copper producer expands output as long as marginal private costs (MC_p) are less than price. This leads to market supply curve S_1, the horizontal summation

EXHIBIT 2 Supply, externality, and minimum-cost production

The supply curve S_1 is the summation of *private* marginal costs when polluting is not costly *to the copper producer*. Since pollution imposes external costs, the social marginal cost is at the level of S_3. Actual output is Q_1 and price is P_1, even though the marginal social cost MC_s is much higher. Curve S_2 shows where social costs could be if producers recognized all social costs and chose production and pollution control methods to minimize private *plus* external costs. *Ideal* output Q^* and price P^* would result if the producers were forced to bear the full cost of resources used, including air pollution damages.

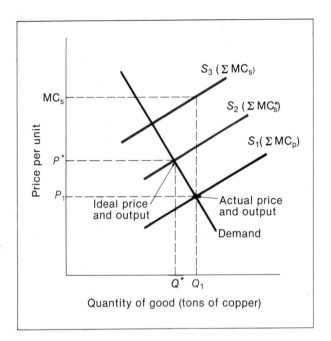

of the *private* marginal cost curves of the copper producers. Given the demand, the equilibrium market price for copper is P_1. Producers supply Q_1 units of copper. However, at output level Q_1, the *social* marginal cost of copper is MC_s, an amount substantially in excess of both the private cost and the consumer's valuation (as indicated by the height of the demand curve at Q_1) of copper. As a result of the external costs, output is expanded beyond the ideal efficiency level. From the standpoint of efficiency, the market price, which fails to reflect the external cost, is too low. Additional units of copper are produced even though the value of the resources, as measured by the social marginal costs (and supply curve S_3) required to produce the units, exceeds the consumer's valuation of the units. A deterioration in air quality is a by-product.

If, on the other hand, copper producers used different production techniques and/or efficient pollution control methods, supply curve S_2 (Exhibit 2) would result. Ideal output would be Q^* at price P^*. Customers would buy only the copper for which they were willing to pay all the costs, including the costs imposed on third parties. Since the consumer's benefit derived from the marginal units of copper would be equal to the marginal cost to society of producing copper ($P^* = MC_s^*$), production would be socially efficient.

When a producer's action imposes external costs on secondary parties, the producer's marginal costs will be understated. Therefore, the producer will choose to produce more of a good and charge less for it than the amounts consistent with ideal economic efficiency.

External Costs and Property Rights.   Clearly defined and enforced property rights are essential for the efficient operation of a market economy. The problems caused by externalities stem from a failure (or an inability) to define clearly and enforce property rights. Property rights help to determine how resources will be used and who will be allowed to use them. **Private property rights** give owners the exclusive right to control and benefit from their resources as long as their

Private Property Rights: A set of usage and exchange rights held *exclusively* by the owner(s).

actions do not harm others. It is important to recognize that private property rights do not include the right to use one's property in a manner in which injury is inflicted on others. For example, property rights do not grant the owners of rocks the right to throw them at automobiles.

Property rights also provide individuals with legal protection against the actions of parties who might damage, abuse, or steal their property. Although often associated with selfishness on the part of owners, property rights could thus more properly be viewed as a means by which owners (including corporate owners) are protected against the selfishness of others. However, if adequately compensated, property owners often allow others to use their assets, even though the value of the assets will subsequently be lower. Rental car firms sell individuals the right to use their automobiles despite the reduction in the resale value of the car. Housing is often rented, even though normal use by the renter imposes a maintenance and upkeep cost on the homeowner. However, since property rights are clearly defined in these cases, the market exchange system forces persons who use the property to consider fully the costs of their actions.

Some people argue that property should be owned communally. **Communal property rights** (sometimes called common property rights) grant anyone the right to use a resource that is not currently being used by someone else. The rights to use highways, city parks, rivers, and the atmosphere are effectively held communally. If there is more of a resource than persons wish to use, communal property rights work well enough. However, problems arise when scarce resources are owned jointly by all. Since no one has exclusive ownership rights, all individuals (and firms) are free to use communal property as intensively as they wish. Invariably, communal property rights lead to the overutilization of scarce resources (see "The Importance of Communal and Private Property Rights," on the following page).

The problems of air and water pollution stem from the nature of the ownership rights to these resources. Since the atmosphere, rivers, streams, and many lakes are, in effect, owned communally, the users of these resources have little incentive to practice conservation or to use less pollution-intensive methods of production. Any *single user* of our commonly owned air and water resources would be foolish to incur control costs voluntarily in order to reduce the pollutants that that particular user puts into the air (or water). The general level of pollution would be virtually unaffected by one user's actions. However, when *all* users fail to consider how their actions affect air and water quality, the result is overutilization, excessive pollution, and economic inefficiency.

The characteristics of some commodities make it costly or nearly impossible for the government to establish property rights in a manner that will ensure that private parties bear the entire cost or reap all of the benefits of an activity. Exclusive ownership can easily be granted for such commodities as apples, cabbages, waterbeds, cars, and airline tickets, but how would one assign property rights to salmon or whales, which travel thousands of miles each year? Similarly, who owns an oil pool that is located under the property of hundreds of different landowners? In the absence of clearly assigned property rights, spillover costs and overutilization are inevitable. Certain whales are on the verge of extinction because no single individual (or small group) has an incentive to reduce the current catch so that the future catch will be larger. Each tries to catch as many whales as possible now; someone else will catch those whales, the argument goes, if the first person (or group) does not. The same principle applies to oil-pool rights. In the absence of regulation, each oil-well operator

Communal Property Rights: Rights to property that can be used by all citizens as intensively as they desire. No one has the right to exclude another from the use of such property. These rights are sometimes referred to as common property rights.

has an incentive to draw the oil *from a common pool* as rapidly as possible, but when all operators do so, the commonly owned oil is drawn out too rapidly.

External Benefits and Missed Opportunities

Spillover effects are not always harmful. Sometimes the actions of an individual (or firm) generate external benefits, gains that accrue to nonparticipating (and nonpaying) secondary parties. When external benefits are present, the personal gains of the consenting parties understate the total social gain, including that of secondary parties. Activities with greater social benefits than costs may not be undertaken because no single decision-maker will be able to capture all the gains fully. Considering only personal net gains, decision-makers will allow potential social gains to go unrealized.

THE IMPORTANCE OF COMMUNAL AND PRIVATE PROPERTY RIGHTS

What is common to many is taken least care of, for all men have greater regard for what is their own than for what they possess in common with others.[1]

The point made by Aristotle more than 2000 years ago is as true now as it was then. It is as important in primitive cultures as it is in developed ones. When the property rights to a resource are communally held, the resource invariably is abused. In contrast, when the rights to a resource are held by an individual (or family), conservation and wise utilization generally result. The following examples from sixteenth century England, nineteenth century American Indian cultures, and modern Russia illustrate the point.

Cattle Grazing on the English Commons

Many English villages in the sixteenth century had commons, or commonly held pastures, which were available to any villagers who wanted to graze their animals. Since the benefits of grazing an additional animal accrued fully to the individual, whereas the cost of overgrazing was an external one, the pastures were grazed extensively. Since the pastures were communal property, there was little incentive for an *individual* to conserve grass in the present so that it would be more abundant in the future. When everyone used the pasture extensively, there was not enough grass at the end of the grazing season to provide a good base for next year's growth. What was good for the individual was bad for the village as a whole. In order to preserve the grass, some people organized enclosure movements. After these movements established private property rights, overgrazing no longer occurred.

The Property Rights of American Indians

Among American Indian tribes, common ownership of the hunting grounds was the general rule. Because the number of native Americans was small and their hunting technology was not highly developed, the hunted animals seldom faced extinction. However, there were at least two exceptions.

One was the beaver hunted by the Montagnais Indians of the Labrador Peninsula. When the French fur traders came to the area in the early 1600s, the beaver increased in value and therefore became increasingly scarce. Recognizing the depletion of the beaver population and the animal's possible extinction, the Montagnais began to institute private property rights. Each beaver-trapping area on a stream was assigned to a family, and conservation practices were adopted. The last remaining pair of beavers was never trapped, since the taker would only be hurting his own family the following year. For a time at least, the supply of beavers was no longer in jeopardy. However, when a new wave of European trappers invaded the area, the native Americans, because they were unable to enforce their property rights, abandoned conservation to take the pelts while they could.[2] Individual ownership was destroyed, and conservation disappeared with it.

The second animal that faced extinction was the communally owned buffalo. Once native Americans gained access to both the gun and the white man's market for hides, their incentive and ability to kill the buffalo increased. By 1840, Indians had emptied portions of the

---

[1]Aristotle, as quoted by Will Durant in *The Life of Greece* (New York: Simon and Schuster, 1939), p. 536.

[2]For an economic analysis of the Montagnais management of the beaver, together with historical references, see Harold Demsetz, "Toward a Theory of Property Rights," *American Economic Review* (May 1967), pp. 347–359.

Great Plains of the area's large buffalo population.[3] In this case, the communal property problem could not be solved by the Indians. Unlike the beaver, the buffalo ranged widely over the Great Plains. Individual, family, and even tribal rights were impossible to establish and enforce. Like oil in a common pool or the sperm whale on the high seas, buffalo were a "fugitive resource," the mobility of which made property rights (and therefore sound management) unattainable. Only the later fencing of the range solved the problem, after most buffalo herds had already been destroyed by both Indians and whites.

Property Rights in the Soviet Union

In the Soviet Union, 97 percent of the farmland is cultivated collectively. The output of the collective farms goes to the state. As a result, most of the benefits derived from wise conservation practices and efficient production techniques accrue to secondary parties (the state) rather than to the individual workers. Families living on collective farms are permitted to cultivate a private plot, the area of which is not to exceed one acre. The "owners" of these private plots are allowed to sell their produce in a relatively free market. Although the private plots constitute approximately 1 percent of the land under cultivation in the Soviet Union, the Communist press reported that about one-quarter of the total value of agricultural output was generated by these plots in 1980. The productivity per acre on the private plots was approximately 40 times higher than that on the collectively farmed land![4] Property rights make a difference even in the Soviet Union. Clearly, the farm workers take better care of the plots they own privately than the land they own communally. Aristotle would surely be satisfied with the long-range accuracy of his observation.

---

[3]This fascinating part of native American history has been recorded in Francis Haines, *The Buffalo* (New York: Crowell, 1970).

[4]See Hedrick Smith, *The Russians* (New York: New York Times Book Co., Quadrangle, 1976), pp. 199–214, for an informative account of the life on collective farms in the Soviet Union.

As in the case of external costs, external benefits occur when property rights are undefined or unenforceable. Because of this, it is costly—or impossible—to withhold these benefits from secondary parties and retain them for oneself at the same time. The producer of a motion picture has rights to the film and can collect a fee from anyone who sees or rents it. In contrast, a person who produces a beautifully landscaped lot that is visible from the street cannot collect a fee for the enjoyment that others derive from it. Some of the benefits of the landscaper's efforts accrue to secondary parties who will probably not help to cover the cost.

Why should we be bothered if others benefit from our actions? Most of us are not—although it is quite possible, for example, that more people would improve the maintenance of their property if those who derived benefits from it helped pay for it. Generally, external benefits become important only when our inability to capture these potential gains forces us to *forego* a socially beneficial activity. Exhibit 3 illustrates this point. Education adds to students' productivity, preparing them to enjoy higher future earnings. In addition, at least certain types of education reduce the future cost of welfare, generate a more intelligent populace, and perhaps even lower the crime rate. Thus, some of the benefits of education, particularly elementary and secondary education, accrue to the citizenry as a whole. The private market demand curve understates the total social benefits of education. In the absence of government intervention, as shown in Exhibit 3, Q_1 units of education result from the market forces. However, when the external benefits MB are added to the private benefits, the social gain from additional units of education exceeds the cost until output level Q_S is produced. Social welfare could thus be improved if output were expanded beyond Q_1 to

EXHIBIT 3 Adding external benefits

The demand curve *D*, indicating only private benefits, understates the social benefits of education. At output Q_1, the social benefit of an additional unit of education exceeds the cost. Ideally, output should be expanded to Q_S, where the social benefit of the marginal unit of education would be just equal to its cost. A public subsidy of *AB*, per unit of education, would lead to this output level.

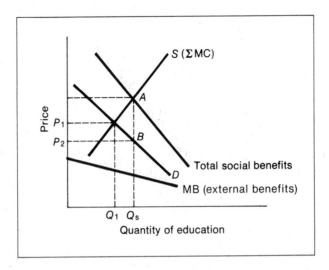

Q_S, but since educational consumers cannot capture these external gains, they fail to purchase units beyond Q_1. The free market output is too small. A subsidy is required if the ideal output level Q_S is to be achieved.

When external benefits are present, the market demand curve understates the social gains of conducting the beneficial activity. Potential social gains go unrealized because no single decision-maker can appropriate or capture the gains fully; they are seen as "lost" when bestowed on nonpaying secondary parties. Thus, decision-makers lack the incentive to carry an activity far enough to capture the potential social gains.

PUBLIC SECTOR RESPONSES TO EXTERNALITIES

What can the government do to improve the efficiency of resource allocation when externalities are present? Sometimes private property rights can be more clearly defined and more strictly enforced. The granting of property rights to ranchers and homesteaders greatly improved the efficiency of land utilization in the Old West during the 1800s. More recently, the establishment of enforceable property rights to the oyster beds of the Chesapeake Bay improved the efficiency of oyster farming in the area. However, in many instances, it is difficult to delineate boundaries for a resource and determine who owns what portion. This is clearly the case with air and water rights. The air rights of property owners often overlap. Property owners cannot go to court and enforce their property rights to clean air or gain compensation for abuse of clean air unless they can demonstrate three things in court: (a) the extent of the damage inflicted by the pollution, (b) the fact that the pollutant in question actually caused the damage, and (ç) the identity of the party whose emissions caused the damage. It is difficult and costly for property owners to prove these things.

When it is impractical (or impossible) to establish and enforce property rights, as in the case of our air resources, an alternative strategy is necessary. There are two general approaches that government might take. First, a government agency might act as a resource manager, charging the users of the resource a fee. Second, a regulatory agency might establish a maximum pollution emission standard and require all firms to attain at least that standard. We will consider each of these alternatives.

The Pollution Tax Approach

Economists generally favor a user's charge, which we will refer to as a pollution tax. Exhibit 4 utilizes the actual data of a copper smelter to illustrate the economics of this approach. The copper-producing firm has minimum costs of production when it spends nothing on pollution control. The marginal control cost curve reveals the cost savings (control costs avoided) that accrue to the firm when it pollutes. The marginal damage cost curve shows the cost ($32.50 per ton) imposed on parties downwind from the smelter. Without any tax or legal restraints, the smelter would emit 190,000 tons of sulfur dioxide into the air per year, causing $6.2 million in damage. A tax equal to the marginal damage cost of $32.50 per ton emitted would cause the firm to reduce its emissions to 17,100 tons per year and reduce pollution damage from $6.2 million to about $0.6 million per year. The control cost of reducing emissions to this level would be about $2.9 million per year. Total social costs each year would fall from $6.2 million (all borne by those suffering pollution damage) to $3.5 million (combined costs of pollution damage and control, paid entirely by the firm and its customers).

How are the costs of pollution—the damage it causes—and the benefits of controlling pollution to be measured? Any pollution control strategy requires that the control agency make estimates of pollution damage caused by various levels of emission. The agency must be able to compare the benefits gained by controlling emissions at different levels. Unfortunately, the damage inflicted on secondary parties is not easy to measure. It varies among areas. The emission of additional units of sulfur oxides into the environment in Four Corners, Wyoming, is far less damaging than similar emissions in New York City or St. Louis. Economic efficiency requires that a pollution tax rate based on pollution damages be directly related to the population of the area. Thus, densely populated areas would have higher pollution taxes, encouraging high-pollution firms to locate in areas where fewer people would be harmed.

At least in theory, the tax approach would promote efficient resource allocation. Several economic incentives would be altered in a highly desirable way. First, the pollution tax would increase the cost of producing pollution-

EXHIBIT 4 Taxing a smelter's emissions

The marginal control cost curve shows that the firm, if it pays no damage costs itself, will emit 190,000 tons per year while spending nothing on control costs. However, if taxed according to the marginal damages it imposes ($32.50 per ton), it will voluntarily cut back its emissions to 17,100 tons per year, which is the socially efficient level. Further control would cost more than its social benefit.

Richard L. Stroup, "The Economics of Air Pollution Control" (Ph.D. diss., University of Washington, 1970).

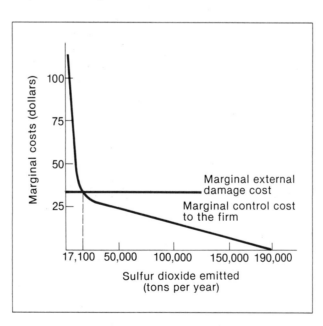

"In other words, what you'll have us believe, sir, is that all the fish in the river next to your plant suddenly died of old age."

intensive goods, causing the supply in these industries to decline. If the tax was properly set, the ideal price and output conditions illustrated by Exhibit 2 would be approximated. The revenues generated by the tax could be used to compensate the secondary parties harmed by the pollutants or to finance a wide range of projects, including applied research on alternative methods of improving air quality. Second, the pollution tax would give firms an economic incentive to use methods of production (and technology) that would create less pollution. As long as it was cheaper for the firm to control harmful emissions than to pay the emission fee (tax), the firm would opt for control. Third, since firms would be able to lower their tax bills by controlling pollution, a market for new emission-control devices would exist. Entrepreneurs would be induced to develop low-cost control devices and market them to firms that would now have a strong incentive to reduce their level of emissions. Note that measuring levels of emissions is an easier task than measuring the damage done by the emissions.

Given the damage and control cost estimates of Exhibit 4, would it make sense for regulatory authorities to follow a policy that fully eliminated pollution emissions? Clearly, the answer is no. At pollution emission levels of less than 17,100 tons per year, the marginal costs of pollution control would exceed the marginal benefits of the control. In cases such as that illustrated by Exhibit 4, substantial improvement can be made at a modest cost. At some point, however, it will become extremely costly to make additional improvements.

Cleaning up the environment is like squeezing water from a wet towel. Initially, a great deal of water can be squeezed from the towel with very little effort, but it becomes increasingly difficult to squeeze out still more. So it is with the environment. At some point, the benefit of a cleaner environment will simply be less than its cost.

People want clean air and water. Since they want other things as well, those entrusted with the authority to control pollution would have to ask themselves two crucial questions: How many other goods and services are we willing to give up in order to fight the battle against pollution? How much would the public like us to spend, from its pockets, to achieve additional freedom from pollution? Since we all want to obtain the maximum benefit from expenditures on pollution control, it is important that these questions be answered carefully, no matter which control strategy we adopt.

The Maximum Emission Standard Approach

Maximum Emission Standard: The maximum amount of pollution that a polluter is permitted to emit, established by the government or a regulatory authority. Fines are generally imposed on those who are unwilling or unable to comply.

Although economics suggests that the pollution tax approach is highly efficient, in the real world a **maximum emission standard** is generally imposed. In this case, the regulatory agency forces all producers to reduce their emissions to a designated level. Producers who are unable to meet the standard are required to terminate production.

The problem with this approach is that the costs of eliminating pollution emissions generally vary widely among firms. Since the maximum emissions standard approach fails to take account of differences in control costs among polluters, it is generally inefficient in that it results in less pollution control per dollar than, for example, the pollution tax strategy. Many economists consider the maximum emission standard too broad and unspecific for use in attaining minimum-cost pollution control or reduction.

Exhibit 5 illustrates why the standard emissions approach is an inefficient method of reducing the level of pollution. A hypothetical emission control cost schedule is presented for three different producers. In the absence of regulation, each producer will emit 6 units of emissions into the air, for a total of 18 units. Suppose that the regulatory agency wants to reduce the total pollution emissions to six units, one-third of the current level. This can be accomplished by requiring each firm to meet a maximum emission standard of two units. Each producer will have to reduce emissions by four units. However, the cost of meeting this standard will differ substantially among the firms; it will cost producer A $500, producer B $700, and producer C $10,000. If this method is adopted, it will cost society $11,200 in control cost to meet the two-unit maximum pollution standard.

Alternatively, the regulatory agency can levy a pollution tax of $350 per unit and eliminate the same amount of pollution. Confronting the tax, producer A will reduce pollution emissions by six units at a control cost of $1050. Producer B will also cut back emissions by six units, at a cost of $1350. Since it is so costly for producer C to reduce emissions, producer C will choose to pay the tax of $350 per unit and emit six units of pollution into the air. Under the tax strategy, the social cost of eliminating the 12 units of pollution will be only $2400, approximately one-fifth of the cost incurred in the elimination of the same amount of pollution under the maximum control strategy.

Since each polluter would have a different control cost schedule, the pol-

EXHIBIT 5   Controlling pollution—the pollution tax versus the maximum emission standard approach

Consider three firms, each of which currently emits 6 units of pollution. If a maximum standard of 2 units of emissions per producer were imposed, it would cost producer A $500, producer B $700, and producer C $10,000 to meet the standard. The cost of eliminating 12 units of pollution by this method would be $11,200. Alternatively, a pollution tax of $350 would induce the producers to eliminate the same amount of pollution (12 units) at a cost to society of only $2400.

	Units Emitted without Regulation		
	Producer A = 6	Producer B = 6	Producer C = 6
Cost of eliminating first unit	$ 50	$100	$1000
Cost of eliminating second unit	100	150	2000
Cost of eliminating third unit	150	200	3000
Cost of eliminating fourth unit	200	250	4000
Cost of eliminating fifth unit	250	300	5000
Cost of eliminating sixth unit	300	350	6000

Total cost of eliminating 12 units of pollution emissions when:
   (a) Maximum emission standard of 2 units is
       imposed $500 + $700 + $10,000 = $11,200
   (b) Emission tax of $350 is imposed $1050 + $1350 + 0 = $2400

lution tax strategy would result in the most pollution control per dollar. This outcome could be attained because the tax would induce firms that could cut their emissions at the least cost to do so and avoid the tax, but the tax would also permit firms with high control cost to compensate society (pay the tax) and pollute. Some people object to the pollution tax strategy because they believe that it would grant producers a license to pollute. In a sense this is true. Some firms would find it cheaper to pay the tax than to control their emissions. However, the firms with a lower pollution control cost would adopt control techniques. If the tax reflected damage cost at the margin, the remaining damages would impose a lower cost on society than would the cost of control.

In its 1976 report, the President's Council on Environmental Quality estimated that firms (and indirectly the consumers of their products) would spend $250 billion between 1975 and 1984 meeting the requirements of the major federal environmental laws. These laws currently reflect the maximum emission standard approach. They make no use of the pollution tax strategy. How much difference would it make if the tax strategy were substituted for the maximum standard approach? Allen Kneese and Charles Schultze have estimated that pollution taxes could save society between 40 and 90 percent of the costs of pollution control.[5] A savings, over ten years, of from $100 billion to $225 billion seems worthy of serious consideration.

---

[5]Allen V. Kneese and Charles Schultze, *Pollution, Prices, and Public Policy* (Washington, D.C.: Brookings Institution, 1975).

Should the Government Always Try to Control Externalities?

Whenever an externality is present, ideal efficiency of resource allocation cannot be attained. However, it does not follow that the government can always improve the situation and bring the economy closer to its ideal allocation level. In evaluating the case for a public sector response to externalities, one should keep in mind the following three points.

1. Sometimes the Economic Inefficiency Resulting from Externalities Is Small. Therefore, Given the Cost of Public Sector Action, Net Gain from Intervention Is Unlikely.   The behavior of individuals often influences the welfare of others. The length of hair, choice of clothing, and personal hygiene care of some individuals may affect the welfare of secondary parties. Should an agency in charge of personal appearance and hygiene be established to deal with externalities in these areas? Persons who value personal freedom would answer with a resounding no. From the standpoint of economic efficiency, their view is correct. The effects of externalities in these and similar areas are small. Thus, the misallocation that results is usually inconsequential. Exhibit 6 provides a graphic illustration. In this instance, if the cost imposed on the secondary parties were fully registered, supply curve S_2 would result. Conditions of ideal efficiency require that output Q_2 be produced and sold at price P_2. Since private decision-makers do not fully consider the economic cost their actions impose on others, a larger output Q_1 and lower price P_1 result from market allocation. However, the difference is small. In fact, the small triangle ABC represents the loss that results from the inefficiency created by external cost.

Government intervention would require the use of scarce resources. A regulatory agency would have to be established. No doubt, suits and counter-suits would be filed. These actions would require the use of scarce legal resources. Most public sector decision-makers would lack the information necessary to determine which activities should be taxed and which should be subsidized. Administrative problems such as these greatly reduce the attractiveness of public sector action. When the external effects are small, the cost of government intervention is likely to exceed the loss due to market inefficiency, *relative to the*

EXHIBIT 6 Trivial externalities

Sometimes externalities have only a small impact on the price and output of a good. This graph illustrates the presence of an external cost. Output is slightly larger and price slightly lower than would be ideal, but the loss that results from the inefficiency generated by the externality is only the small triangle *ABC*. Given the costs of the public decision-making process, government intervention would probably not result in a net gain in instances such as this.

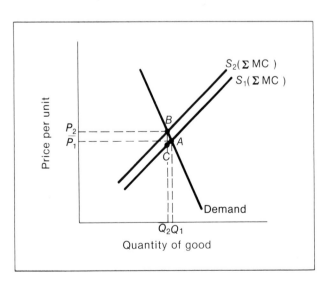

hypothetical ideal. From the standpoint of overall efficiency, under these circumstances, the best approach is to do nothing.

2. The Market Often Finds a Reasonably Efficient Means of Dealing with Externalities. The existence of externalities implies the presence of *potential* gain. If the external effects are significant, market participants have an incentive to organize economic activity in a manner that will enable them to capture the potential gain. If the number of parties affected by the externality is small, they may be able to arrive at a multiparty bargain that will at least partially negate the inefficiency and loss resulting from the externality. Some entrepreneurs have devised ingenious schemes to capture benefits that were previously external to private parties. Community housing developments make it possible to capture benefits that arise when houses are located near a country club, golf course, and/or public park. In these cases, otherwise nonpaying secondary parties can be made to pay for the benefits of trees, gardens, manicured lawns, and so on. If consumers are willing to pay for these amenities, as they often are, developers who provide such services will be able to capture benefits in the form of higher prices on the sale of surrounding lots.[6] Thus, market forces sometimes devise efficient arrangements for dealing with external effects.

3. Government Action May Also Impose an External Cost on Secondary Parties. We have already mentioned that government intervention designed to correct the inefficiencies created by externalities is costly. Often, the costs of public sector intervention exceed the benefits. Therefore, on efficiency grounds, intervention should be rejected. In addition, we should recognize that even democratic public sector action results in the imposition of an externality—the majority imposes an external cost on the minority, which is opposed to the action. Just as an individual may carry an activity too far when some of the costs are borne by others, a majority may also carry an action beyond the point of ideal efficiency. The gains that accrue to the majority may be less than the costs imposed on the minority. Thus, although the government can potentially take corrective measures, counterproductive economic action by the democratic majority may result if the external costs imposed on the minority are not fully considered.

MARKET FAILURE: PUBLIC GOODS

Public goods comprise the extreme case of commodities, the consumption of which results in spillover benefits to secondary parties. In the original formulation by Paul Samuelson, there are two distinctive characteristics of public goods. First, the availability of a public good to one person makes it equally available to all others. Public goods must therefore be consumed jointly by

---

[6]The development of Disney World in Florida is an interesting case in which entrepreneurial ingenuity made it possible to capture external benefits more fully. When Walt Disney developed Disneyland in California, the market value of land in the immediate area soared as a result of the increase in demand for services (food, lodging, gasoline, etc.). Since the land in the area was owned by others, the developers of Disneyland were unable to capture these external benefits. However, when Disney World was developed near Orlando, Florida, the owners purchased an enormous plot of land, far more than was needed for the amusement park. As was the case with Disneyland in California, the operation of Disney World caused land values in the immediate area to rise sharply. However, since the developers of Disney World initially purchased a large amount of land near the attraction, they were able to capture the external benefits by selling prime property to hotels, restaurants, and other businesses desiring a nearby location.

Currently a senior fellow at Resources for the Future (RFF) and adjunct professor of economics at the University of New Mexico, Kneese is a leading authority on environmental economics. He is the author or coauthor of many articles and nearly a dozen books on environmental policy. His recent work in this area has focused on alternative pollution control strategies and quantitative models of environmental economics.[7]

---

[7]See Kneese and Schultze, *Pollution, Prices, and Public Policy,* and Allen V. Kneese, *Economics and the Environment* (London: Penguin, 1977).

Kneese received his doctorate from Indiana University in 1956. He has spent much of his career at RFF, a nonprofit research organization based in Washington, D.C. Currently, he is chairman of the board for the minerals and energy resources program of the prestigious National Academy of Sciences.

Kneese has applied the theory of external cost and public goods to a wide range of environmental problems. In the policy area, in general, he tends to favor an emission charge (pollution tax) control strategy over more direct regulation, such as uniform emission standards.

Kneese recognizes that formulating an efficient control strategy is not an easy task. Control of automobile exhaust, a major source of pollution in many urban areas, presents several special problems. The current approach forces automobile manufacturers to meet certain uniform emission standards on all *new cars* produced. This strategy is highly inefficient for two reasons. First, it forces automobile consumers in sparsely populated areas to pay for the emission control systems on new cars, even though pollution is often not a problem in these areas. Second, the uniform standards approach fails to provide individuals with a personal incentive to keep the control devices operational and their automobiles well tuned in order to reduce exhaust emissions.

In his widely used introductory-level textbook, *The Economics of Environmental Policy* (coauthored with Myrick Freeman and Robert Haveman),[8] Kneese suggests that we control automobile emissions by means of a "smog tax" rather than national uniform standards. Under the smog tax plan, automobiles would be checked periodically and rated according to their emission levels. The smog tax would then be levied *according to the emissions rating of the vehicle* when gasoline was purchased. The owners of cars with high emission levels would pay higher taxes than the owners of automobiles with lower emission levels.

The smog tax approach would permit regional variation, so that drivers in areas in which pollution was not a problem would not be forced to pay for something that yielded little benefit. Unlike the current system, the tax approach would give individuals a personal incentive to adopt effective pollution control devices (on both new and used cars), keep them in good working order, and keep the motor in tune. If policy planners are interested in adopting effective, efficient control strategies, they would do well to listen to the ingenious ideas of Professor Kneese and other economists who understand the necessity of bringing private and social interests into harmony.

---

[8]A. Myrick Freeman III, Robert Haveman, and Allen V. Kneese, *The Economics of Environmental Policy* (New York: Wiley, 1973).

all. Second, because of this joint consumption, it is impossible to exclude nonpayers from the receipt of public goods.[7]

Examples of *pure* public goods are not numerous. National defense is one. The defense system that protects you provides similar protection to all other citizens. Our legal and monetary systems are also public goods. The laws and

---

[9]Note that public and private goods are determined by the characteristics of the good. The consumption benefits of a private good are derived entirely by the individual consumer. The benefits are private. In contrast, the consumption of a public good by a single party makes the benefits of the good equally available to others. Whether the good is produced in the public or private sector of the economy is *not* the factor that determines how the good is classified.

individual rights that are available to one citizen are also provided to others. The policies of the Federal Reserve are provided equally to all citizens. The quality of the atmosphere, and, to a lesser extent, that of rivers and waterways can also be classified as public goods.

The Free Rider Problem

Free Rider: One who receives the benefit of a good without contributing to its costs. Public goods and commodities that generate external benefits offer people the opportunity to become free riders.

Since nonpaying consumers cannot be excluded (at least not at a reasonable cost), a sufficient amount of public goods cannot be provided by the market mechanism. If public goods were provided through the market, each of us would have an incentive to become a **free rider,** one who receives the benefits of a good without contributing to its cost. Why contribute to the cost of supplying a public good? Your actions will have a negligible impact on the supply of clean air, pure water, national defense, and legal justice. The sensible path will lead you to do nothing. As long as you travel that path alone, you will ride along, free and easy. If everyone else joins you, however, the aggregate lack of action will lead to an insufficient quantity of public goods.

Suppose that national defense were provided entirely through the market. Would you voluntarily help to pay for it? Your contribution would have a negligible impact on the total supply of defense available to each of us, even if you made a *large personal* contribution. Many citizens, even though they might value defense highly, would become free riders, and few funds would be available to finance the necessary supply. If the military–industrial complex were dependent on market forces, it would be small indeed!

The harmony between private and social interests tends to break down for public goods. The amount of a public good available to an individual (and others) will be virtually unaltered by whether or not the individual pays for it. Thus, each individual has an incentive to become a free rider. But when numerous individuals become free riders, less than the ideal amount of the public good is produced.

Perhaps another hypothetical example will clarify this important point. Suppose that plans are developed for a flood-control dam. Estimates indicate that the costs of the project will be only one-fifth as great as the benefits to be derived from a reduction in the expected future damage from floods. How will the dam be marketed? Without government action, it will be difficult, because each individual will prefer to be a free rider.

Suppose the flood-control project were proposed for your community. Exhibit 7 shows the options available to you in responding to this public-good project, and the outcomes of each option. The best outcome for you would be the result of option 1. Others would pay the price of the flood-control project, and you would contribute nothing. You would obtain the benefits but would not pay for them. Since others could not provide flood protection for themselves without providing it equally to you, they would have no way of ensuring that you would help pay for the project voluntarily, even though you would derive substantial benefits from it. You would have a strong incentive to become a free rider. However, if everyone, or almost everyone, tried to ride free, the community would fail to purchase the dam because of insufficient funds. This would be the result of option 3.

Unlike option 1, option 2 would be available to all people of the community. If others had preferences like yours, they would prefer option 2 to option 3.

EXHIBIT 7 Everybody rides free — and loses

Personal Ranking of Alternative Plans for the Purchase of the Flood-Control Dam (A Public Good)	Personal Alternatives
Option 1	Others pay the purchase price of the flood-control project. You contribute nothing and receive the benefits of flood control. You are a free rider.
Option 2	Jointly, the downstream community residents undertake the flood-control project. You pay your fair share.
Option 3	You fail to contribute. Because others also fail to pay their share, the community does not undertake the project.
Option 4	Because others fail to contribute, the community has insufficient funds to undertake the project. You pay your share but do not receive any protection against future flood damages.

Government action to finance the project through taxation would be preferable to no action at all. However, if the government did not intervene and each person followed personal interests, the community would be left with option 3.

Near Public Goods

Few commodities are pure public goods, but a much larger set of goods are jointly consumed even though nonpaying customers can be excluded. For example, such goods as radio and television broadcasts, national parks, interstate highways, movies, and football games are jointly consumed. Assuming that there is not a congestion problem, additional consumption of these "near public goods," *once they are produced,* is costless to society.

Should nonpaying customers be excluded when the marginal cost of providing the good to them is zero? Many economists argue that such near public goods as highways, national parks, and television programming should be provided free to consumers, at the expense of the taxpayer. Why exclude people from the consumption of these near public goods when their use of the goods does not add to the cost? The argument has a certain appeal.

However, we must be careful. Television programs, highways, parks, and other public goods are scarce. The consumption of other products must be foregone in order to produce such goods. If a zero price is charged, how does one determine whether consumers value additional units enough to cover their opportunity cost? How can an intensely concerned minority communicate its views as to the types of near public goods that should be produced? Taxes will be necessary to cover the costs of making near public goods freely available. Will such taxes lead to inefficiency? All of these factors reduce the attractiveness of public sector provision of jointly consumed commodities when exclusion of nonpaying consumers is possible.

MARKET FAILURE: POOR INFORMATION

In the real world, market choices, like other decisions, are made with incomplete information. Consumers do not have perfect knowledge about the quality of a product, the price of alternative products, or side effects that may result. They may make incorrect decisions, decisions that they will later regret, because they do not possess good information.

The reality of imperfect knowledge is, of course, not the fault of the market. In fact, the market provides consumers with a strong incentive to acquire information that will help produce satisfying long-run decisions. Because consumers must bear the consequences of their mistakes, they certainly will seek to avoid the deliberate purchase of "lemon" products.

Getting Your Money's Worth

Repeat-Purchase Item: An item purchased often by the same buyer.

The consumer's information problem is minimal if the item is purchased regularly. Consider the problem of purchasing a brand of soap. There is little cost associated with trying out brands. Since soap is a product that is regularly purchased, trial and error is an economical means of determining which brand is most suitable to the consumer's personal needs. It is a **repeat-purchase item.** The consumer can use past experience to good advantage when buying repeat-purchase items, such as soap, toothpaste, most food products, lawn service, and gasoline.

What incentive does the producer have to supply accurate information that will help the customer make a satisfying long-run choice? Is there a conflict between consumer and producer interests? The answers to these questions are critically affected by the seller's dependence on return customers.

If dissatisfaction of *current* customers is expected to have a strong adverse effect on *future* sales, a business entrepreneur will attempt to provide accurate information to help customers make wise choices. The future success of business entrepreneurs who sell repeat-purchase products is highly dependent on the future purchases of currently satisfied customers. There is a harmony of interest because both the buyer and seller will be better off if the customer is satisfied with the product purchased.

Let the Buyer Beware

Major problems of conflicting interests, inadequate information, and unhappy customers arise when goods either (a) are difficult to evaluate on inspection and are seldom repeatedly purchased from the same producer or (b) are potentially capable of serious and lasting harmful side effects that cannot be detected by a layperson. Human nature being what it is, under these conditions, we would expect some unscrupulous producers to sell low-quality, defective, and even harmful goods.

Since customers typically are unable to tell the difference between high-quality and low-quality goods under these conditions, their ability to police quality and price is weakened. Business entrepreneurs have a strong incentive to cut costs by reducing quality. Consumers get less for their dollars; since sellers are not dependent on repeat customers, they may survive and even prosper in the marketplace. The probability of customer dissatisfaction is thus increased because of inadequate information and unexpected poor quality, and the case for an unhampered market mechanism is weakened.[10]

Consider the consumer's information problem when an automobile is purchased. Are most consumers capable of properly evaluating the safety equipment? Except for a handful of experts, most people are not very well equipped to make such decisions. Some consumers might individually seek expert advice. However, it may be more efficient to prevent market failure by having the government regulate automobile safety and require certain safety equipment.

As another example of the problem of inadequate consumer information, consider the case of a drug manufacturer's exaggerated claims for a new product. Until consumers have had experience with the drug or have listened to others' experiences, they might make wasteful purchases. Government regulation might benefit consumers by forcing the manufacturer to modify its claims. Of course, there is no guarantee that the benefits of government action will outweigh the costs. Indeed, as we previously discussed, government regulation itself may be harmful to consumers. Nonetheless, when consumers find it prohibitively expensive to acquire crucial information, the results of government action may be superior to the results of the market.

LOOKING AHEAD

In this chapter, we focused on the failures of the market. In the next chapter, we will use economic analysis to come to a better understanding of the workings of the public sector. We will also discuss some of the expected shortcomings of public sector action. Awareness of both the strengths and weaknesses of alternative forms of economic organization will help us to make more intelligent choices in this important area.

CHAPTER LEARNING OBJECTIVES

1 The sources of market failure can be grouped into four major categories: (a) externalities, (b) public goods, (c) poor information, and (d) monopoly.

2 When externalities are present, the market may fail to confront decision-makers with the proper incentives. Since decision-makers are not forced to consider external cost, they may find it personally advantageous to undertake an economic activity even though it generates a net loss to the community. In contrast, when external benefits are present, decision-makers may fail to undertake economic action that would generate a net social gain.

3 When external costs originate from the activities of a business firm, the firm's cost curve will understate the social cost of producing the good. If production of the good generates external costs, the price of the product under competitive conditions, will be too low and the output too large to meet the *ideal requirements* of economic efficiency.

---

[10]Brand names provide a market solution to information problems that arise from a lack of repeat business. How much would the Coca Cola Company pay to avoid a dangerous bottle of Coke being sold? Surely the answer is, a very large sum. Their reputation is at stake. It is a hostage to quality control. Similarly, franchised food chains make repeat customers of buyers who may never see specific stores twice. The franchise owner polices the control of quality in order to preserve the franchise reputation. That reputation draws customers who are just passing by but know, from reputation, what is being sold. Reputation stimulates repeat business even when a customer only buys once from a *specific* establishment.

4 External costs result from the failure or inability of a society to establish private property rights. Clearly established private property rights enable owners to prohibit others from using or abusing their property. In contrast, communal property rights normally result in overutilization, since most of the cost of overutilization (and misuse) is imposed on others.

5 When external benefits are present, the market demand curve will understate the social gains of conducting the activity. The consumption and production of goods that generate external benefits will tend to be lower than the socially ideal levels.

6 The efficient use of air and water resources is particularly troublesome for the market because it is often impossible to apportion these resources and determine ownership rights. A system of emission charges (a pollution tax) is capable of inducing individuals to make wiser use of these resources. Emission charges (a) increase the cost of producing pollution-intensive goods, (b) grant firms an incentive to use methods of production that create less pollution, and (c) provide producers with an incentive to adopt control devices when it is economical to do so.

7 When the marginal benefits (for example, cleaner air) derived from pollution control are less than the social gains associated with a pollution-generating activity, prohibition of the activity that results in pollution (or other external cost) is not an ideal solution.

8 When the control costs of firms vary, the emission charge (pollution tax) approach will permit society to reduce pollution by a given amount at a lower cost than will the maximum emission standard method, which is currently widely used. The marginal cost of attaining a cleaner environment will rise as the pollution level is reduced. At some point, the economic benefits of a still cleaner environment will be less than the costs.

9 In evaluating the case for government intervention in situations involving externalities, one must consider the following factors: (a) the magnitude of the external effects relative to the cost of government action; (b) the ability of the market to devise means of dealing with the problem without intervention; and (c) the possibility that the political majority may carry the government intervention too far if the external costs imposed on the minority are not fully considered.

10 When it is costly or impossible to withhold a public good from persons who do not or will not help pay for it, the market system breaks down because everyone has an incentive to become a free rider. When everyone attempts to ride free, production of the public good will be lower than the socially ideal level.

11 The market provides an incentive for consumers to acquire information. When a business is dependent on repeat customers, it has a strong incentive to promote customer satisfaction. However, when goods are either (a) difficult to evaluate on inspection and seldom purchased repeatedly from the same producer or (b) have potentially serious and lasting harmful effects, consumer trial and error may be an unsatisfactory means of determining quality. The interests of the consumer and producer are in conflict.

THE ECONOMIC WAY OF THINKING—DISCUSSION QUESTIONS

1 Why may external cost be a cause of economic inefficiency? Why is it important to define property rights clearly? Explain.

2 Devise a tax plan that would (a) reduce the extent of automobile pollution, (b) provide an incentive for entrepreneurs to develop new products that would limit pollution, and (c) permit continued automobile travel for those willing to bear the total social costs. Explain how your plan would influence incentives and why it would work.

3 "When goods generate external benefits, the market is unable to produce an adequate supply. This is why the government must provide such goods as police and fire protection, education, parks, and vaccination against communicable diseases."

(a) Do you agree? Explain.

(b) Does governmental provision necessarily ensure "an adequate supply"? How would you define "adequate supply"?

(c) Such goods as golf courses, shopping centers, country clubs, neckties, and charity also generate some spillover external benefits. Do you think the government should provide these goods in order to ensure an adequate supply?

4   Which of the following goods are most likely to result in a large number of dissatisfied customers: (a) light bulbs, (b) food at a local restaurant, (c) food at a restaurant along an interstate highway, (d) automobile repair service, (e) used cars, (f) plumbing services, (g) used automatic dishwashers, (h) used sofas, (i) television repair service? Explain your answer.

5   What are public goods? Why does a decentralized pricing system have trouble producing an adequate amount of public goods?

6   Are people more likely to take better care of an item they own jointly (communally) or one they own privately? Why? Does the presence of private property rights affect the behavior of persons in noncapitalist nations? Why or why not?

7   What's Wrong with This Way of Thinking?

"Corporations are the major beneficiaries of our lax pollution control policy. Their costs are reduced because we permit them free use of valuable resources—clean water and air—in order to produce goods. These lower costs are simply added to the profits of the polluting firms."

Nothing is more certain than the indispensable necessity of government; and it is equally undeniable that wherever and however it is instituted, the people must cede to it some of their natural rights, in order to vest it with requisite power [to conduct its assigned responsibilities].[2]
John Jay (1787)

30

PUBLIC CHOICE: GAINING FROM GOVERNMENT AND GOVERNMENT FAILURE[1]

Traditionally, economists have focused on how the market works and what ideal public policy can do to improve economic efficiency. The actual operation of the public sector has been virtually ignored. However, this traditional neglect has become less and less satisfactory in dealing with economics today. Each day, millions of economic decisions are made in the public sector. Approximately two-fifths of our national income is channeled through the various governmental departments and agencies. In addition, the legal framework establishes the "rules of the game" for the market sector. The government's role in defining property rights, enforcing contracts, fixing prices, and regulating business and labor practices has a tremendous impact on the operation of an economy.

This chapter analyzes how various types of economic issues are dealt with through the political process. In studying collective decision-making, we seek to understand the link between individual preferences and political outcomes. The political process is simply an alternative method of making economic decisions. Like the market, it is likely to have defects. When we evaluate the costs and benefits of public sector action, we must also compare the likelihood of achieving our goals through that collective action with the expected outcome of market allocation. In other words, for any economic activity, we must ask ourselves: In which sector will the defects stand least in the way of our goals?

Most political decisions in Western countries are made legislatively. We will focus on a system in which voters choose legislators, who in turn institute public policy. Let us see what the tools of economics reveal about the political process.

VOTERS' DEMAND FOR POLITICAL REPRESENTATION

Individuals express their preferences for types of governmental action through the voting process. Under a legislative system, citizens must express their views through a representative. The impact of voters on the quantity and price of political goods is indirectly felt through their impact on the composition of the body of elected representatives.

How do voters decide whom to support? Many factors undoubtedly

---

[1] Before proceeding with this chapter, you may want to review Chapter 4, which provides an overview of public sector decision-making and introduces the central concepts developed here.

[2] John Jay, "The Dangers of Foreign Force and Influence Threatening the United States," *The Federalist Papers,* no. 2 (New York: Washington Square Press, 1964), pp. 5–6.

influence their decision. The personal characteristics of the candidates are important influences. Criteria such as which candidate is the most persuasive, which presents the best television image, and which appears to be the most honest may determine a voter's choice of whom to support in an election.

The perceived views of candidates on issues, particularly on issues of importance to the individual voter, will also influence the voter's decision. According to economic theory, other things constant, each voter will support the candidate who offers the voter the greatest expected net subjective benefits. Factors other than expected direct economic gain will influence the voter's expected benefits, but personal gain will certainly be an important component.

The greater the perceived net personal economic gain from a particular candidate's platform, the more likely it is that the individual voter will favor that candidate. The greater the perceived net economic cost imposed on a voter by a candidate's positions, the less inclined the voter will be to favor the candidate.

Thus, economics implies that dairy farmers are more likely to prefer candidates who support high prices for dairy products. Support of tax breaks for the oil industry makes a candidate more attractive to oil producers. Welfare recipients typically prefer a candidate who supports increased welfare benefits. And, of course, support of higher teachers' salaries and expanded research funds adds to a politician's rating among college professors and other educators.

Although each of us may have a streak of altruism and concern for the public interest, the opportunity for personal gain influences our evaluation of both political and market alternatives. The greater the expected personal gain, the more likely it is that personal interests will dominate. Moreover, each of us sees the public interest from a different perspective. Since many of us consider our own activities to be important and to contribute to the public interest, we have little trouble equating the benefits to be granted in the name of the public interest with the benefits that would aid us in our individual activities. "rational ignorance effect." (See Chapter 4, pages 75–76.)

The Rational Ignorance Effect

When decisions are made collectively, the direct link between the choice of an individual and the outcome of the issue is broken. The choice of a single voter is seldom decisive when the size of the decision-making group is large. Recognizing that the outcome will not depend on one vote, the individual voter has little incentive to seek information in order to vote more intelligently. Typically, the voter relies on information that is freely supplied by others (candidates, political parties, news media, friends, and interest groups). As we pointed out earlier, economists refer to voters' lack of incentive to acquire information as the "rational ignorance effect." (See Chapter 4, pages 75–76.)

The low probability that one's vote will make any difference also explains why many citizens fail to vote. In the 1980 presidential election, approximately one-half of the eligible population took the time to register and vote. When there is not a presidential election, only about one-third of the eligible voters participate in congressional elections.[3] Voter turnouts for city and county elections are often even lower. These findings should not surprise us; they are precisely what we would expect because the *personal* payoffs from voting are low.

---

[3]Since the probability that a single vote will be decisive is almost zero, one may wonder why even one-third to one-half of U.S. citizens vote. The puzzle is probably explained by the fact that many citizens, maybe even most, receive personal utility from the act of voting.

How does the rational ignorance effect influence the decision-making of voters? Lacking the incentive to acquire information, voters typically consider only a subset of issues about which they feel most strongly. The views of the candidates on these issues of "vital personal importance" influence voting decisions. However, most of the several hundred issues confronting Congress each year are virtually ignored by the typical voter. For example, despite their importance to the nation as a whole, the views of political decision-makers on such things as Japanese fishing rights, appointments to the Interstate Commerce Commission, and allocation of licenses for the operation of television stations are not important enough to command the scrutiny of most citizens. Generally, these issues fail to influence their choices.

Even a voter who manages to follow a politician's previous stands on the hundreds of issues arising each year cannot anticipate all the issues to be faced by elected candidates during their terms of office. In this complex situation, labels such as conservative, liberal, Democrat, and Republican become attractive to the voter. Though oversimplified, such categories allow the rationally ignorant voter to hazard a guess as to a candidate's future stands on future issues. In the world of politics, a candidate's "image," however vague or incorrect, is very important to political success. The details of his or her stand on particular issues simply are not known to most voters. That fact strongly influences the actions of suppliers in the political marketplace.

SUPPLY, PROFITS, AND THE POLITICAL ENTREPRENEUR

The market entrepreneur is a dynamic force in the private sector. The entrepreneur seeks to gain by undertaking potentially profitable projects. In the competitive market process, business entrepreneurs produce commodities that are intensely desired relative to their supply. Similarly, the *political entrepreneur* (or politician) is a dynamic force in the collective decision-making process. The political entrepreneur seeks to offer voters an image and a bundle of political goods that will increase the chances of winning elections. Those who are successful survive and may achieve private power, fame, and even fortune. These goals are as important in the political arena as in the private sector. To increase the chance of being elected, the political entrepreneur must be alert to which political goods and services can attract the most voters. Put another way, in order for the politician to choose and to supply any given political good, the cost, measured in votes lost, must be smaller than the benefits—the votes gained.

This does not mean that politicians always favor the viewpoint of the majority of their constituents on a *specific* issue. In some cases, a candidate may gain more votes among an intensely active minority of people who favor the candidate's position than from a dispassionate and rationally uninformed majority opposed to that position.

Money, Political Advertising, and the Successful Politician

Votes win elections, but the rationally uninformed voters must be convinced to "want" a candidate. What is required to win the support of voters? Both one's positive attributes (for example, honesty, compassion, and effectiveness) and one's position on issues, as we have stressed, are important. However, candidates must bring their strengths to the attention of the voters. Money, manpower, and expertise are required to promote a candidate among the voting population.

"I want NEW promises, Fenwick! When you keep making the same ones over and over, people wise up that you're not keeping them!"

Professor Galbraith and others have stressed the role of product advertising and the mass media in affecting consumer preferences. Since voters have little incentive to acquire information, the impact of the media on the political consumer is even greater than it is on market decisions. The image of a political entrepreneur is determined primarily by an ability to acquire mass media resources and to use these resources to promote his or her positive attributes. Candidates without the financial resources to provide television and other media advertising to rationally ignorant voters are seriously handicapped.[4] Similarly, candidates who are unacceptable to the major communications media face a severe disadvantage.

Being Successful Means Being Political

What does our analysis suggest about the motivation of political decision-makers? Are we implying that they are highly selfish, that they consider only their own pocketbooks and ignore the public interest? The answer is no. When people act in the political sphere, they may genuinely want to help their fellow citizens. Factors other than personal political gain, narrowly defined, influence the actions of many political suppliers. On certain issues, one may feel strongly that one's position is best for the country, even though it may not currently be popular. The national interest as perceived by the political supplier may conflict

---

[4]Political expenditures on advertising and other persuasion techniques indicate that candidates are fully aware of the importance of media exposure. On average, contested candidates for the U.S. Senate or House of Representatives spend between 70 and 80 percent of their campaign resources in this area.

with the position that would be most favorable to reelection prospects. Some politicians may opt for the national interest even when it means political defeat. None of this is inconsistent with an economic view of political choice.

However, the existence of political suicide does not change the fact that *most* political entrepreneurs prefer political life. There is a strong incentive for political suppliers to stake out positions that will increase their vote total in the next election. A politician who refuses to give major consideration to electoral gain increases the risk of replacement by a more astute (and less public-minded) political entrepreneur. Competition — the competition of vote-maximizing political candidates — presents even the most public-spirited politician with a strong incentive to base his decisions primarily on political considerations. Just as neglect of economic profit is the route to market oblivion, neglect of potential votes is the route to political oblivion.

THE DEMAND FOR PUBLIC SECTOR ACTION

People participate in market activity in an effort to obtain more goods and services. People turn to the government for much the same reason.

Voters demand public sector action for two major reasons: (a) to improve economic efficiency and thus capture potential gains lost to market failure, and (b) to redistribute income.

As we discussed in the previous chapter, government can attempt to correct market failure with action that results in more total benefits than costs. Corrective action can increase the size of the economic pie, generating personal benefits for individual voters. Pursuit of this potential gain motivates individuals to turn to government when the market fails. Other things constant, the greater the potential gain accruing to voters from corrective government action, the stronger is the demand for collective action.

Voters may also seek to use the government's taxing, spending, and rule-making powers in order to redistribute income. Government can break the link between what an individual earns and what that individual may consume. Therefore, individual voters may be able to use government action to obtain goods for themselves or favored groups while imposing the cost of the goods on taxpayers in general.

Market Failure and Gaining from Government

Much government action that we take for granted stems from market failure. Government crime-prevention activities provide an example. Of course, there are moral reasons for a society's desire to prohibit crimes such as robbery, arson, and murder. However, these activities can also be viewed from a strictly economic perspective. Clearly, such activities involve external costs. Robbers do not consider the welfare of nonconsenting secondary parties when they seek to transfer wealth from others to themselves. Nonetheless, their actions often impose enormous costs on victims and potential victims. Those who do not have to bear fully the costs that their actions impose on secondary parties will tend to engage in an excessive amount of the activity. There would be more robbers robbing if there were no costs for the criminal. Public policy that imposes costs on criminals — that apprehends and prosecutes robbers and other criminals, reducing the incidence of crime — is socially beneficial.

Almost all individuals, even many of those who occasionally commit crimes, gain from this government action that makes it much more costly for a person to commit such crimes as murder, robbery, kidnapping, rape, arson, and assault. The external costs that these crimes impose on victims are so high that most citizens of the community are quite willing to incur substantial cost in order to obtain the benefits of police protection. Groups could organize in order to pay a private police force cooperatively, but there would be a free-rider problem. Each person would want the others to provide the protection. Anyone whose neighbors were protected would automatically gain without having to pay. Thus, market organization would result in less than the desired amount of police protection. Governmentally provided police protection, paid for by taxes levied on everyone, leads to large personal gains for nearly everyone.

From time to time, politicians debate the merits of terminating government farm price supports, various antipoverty programs, or the minimum wage, but when did you last hear a politician advocate leaving crime prevention to the market? The benefit/cost ratio of government action in this area is very large. Political suppliers have responded to the voters' views.

Government Provision of Public Goods

As we discussed previously, the market fails to allocate public goods efficiently, simply because it is impossible to exclude nonpaying consumers. National defense is probably the most important public good that approximates these conditions. Most people favor some national defense. Because it is a public good, however, it will be produced in less than the desired amount if production is left to the market. There is no feasible way in which nonpaying citizens could be restricted from the consumption of their neighbors' (in this case all of us are neighbors) national defense. There would be few paying customers because personal consumption of national defense would not depend on personal payment. Everyone would have an incentive to become a free rider, but if everybody tried to ride free, little national defense would be produced. As a result, an overwhelming majority of the nation's citizens favor government provision of *some* national defense. Political entrepreneurs who support government action to correct the failure of the market in this area reap more political gain than those who favor leaving defense to the market.

Government Action on Air Pollution. Air quality is also a public good. There is no way in which clean air can be provided to some persons in a neighborhood but not to others. As we explained earlier, the problem of air pollution results from the nature of property rights in this area. Because the atmosphere is, in effect, owned communally, an excessive amount of waste is emitted into it, causing a reduction in air quality. Market signals force users to respond properly to the scarcity of most resources, but this is not the case with communally owned air. For example, an electric utility company will use society's scarce coal resources wisely, since the private owners of coal must be compensated for each ton of the resource consumed. However, without regulation, the same utility will probably fail to conserve air resources, since these are "free" to the firm (but not to the community at large).

If public sector action can bring the private and social costs of using air resources more closely into line, social gain will result. During the last two decades, government intervention in the environmental area has increased.

As industrial output and urbanization have expanded, the problem of pollution has become more severe. At the same time, rising real incomes have encouraged consumers to demand cleaner air. This set of forces has led to a strong environmental movement.

Prompted by the public demand for environmental improvement, Congress passed the Clean Air Act in 1963. The act was reinforced several times, most notably by the Clean Air Amendments of 1970. This comprehensive piece of legislation, sometimes referred to as the Muskie Clean Air Bill, after Senator Edmund Muskie of Maine, contains provisions for maximum emission standards for both automobiles and industrial firms. Since some of the standards are still being set, it has not been possible to assess all the costs and benefits.

How will this public sector pollution control policy affect individual voter-citizens? This is a difficult question to answer. Since air quality is not bought and sold in the market, we cannot be sure of its exact value to individuals. Nonetheless, some researchers have approached the problem. The major beneficiaries of pollution control legislation are the residents of densely populated urban areas, particularly those who are not employed by firms cutting back on employment in order to counterbalance the costs imposed by pollution control standards. The major costs of the Clean Air Amendments are widely dispersed among consumers who must pay higher prices for products that are now more costly to produce.[5]

Summarizing the findings of a detailed study by Henry Peskin of Resources for the Future (Washington, D.C.), Exhibit 1 indicates that the results of the Clean Air program are mixed. People living in densely populated areas such as Jersey City receive the largest gains. In areas that are sparsely populated and where pollution is a smaller problem, Peskin indicates that the costs of higher product prices outweigh the benefits. In fact, he estimates that only 29 percent of the population will experience a gain, while 71 percent will be net losers. For the nation as a whole, the Peskin study estimates that total costs exceed total benefits. Pollution control policy is still evolving, however, and a number of developments could change that outcome. For example, most economists believe that a more flexible, incentive-oriented policy could produce the same benefits at a far lower cost. One such policy might use pollution taxes in such a way that polluters who can control pollution cheaply would reduce emissions more and those for whom control is expensive would pay higher taxes while achieving less pollution control.

Income Redistribution and the Demand for Government Action

Whereas public policy sometimes inadvertently results in income transfers, in other cases public sector programs are specifically designed to redistribute income, either because of a demand for a more equalized distribution of income among *all* citizens or because of a demand for more income by and/or for a

---

[5]Some people believe that the costs of pollution control will be borne by "the big corporations." This view is largely unfounded. There is no more reason to believe that firms will bear the higher cost of pollution control than to believe that they will bear the higher cost of energy, for example. An increase in pollution control costs will reduce the amount of a good supplied at a specific price. This reduction in supply will cause the market price of the product to rise. Higher costs, regardless of their source, will lead to higher prices. There are no free lunches. The consumers of products that are more expensive to produce as a result of pollution regulation control will bear the major burden of the control costs.

EXHIBIT 1 The 1970 clean air amendments—people in some areas gain and others lose

These benefit–cost estimates suggest that some areas, primarily densely populated industrial cities, will have large net benefits, whereas others will pay more than the value they receive in the form of cleaner air.

Rank of Net Gain (or Loss)	County Group or SMSA[a]	Net Benefit (or Cost), Dollars per Family
1	Jersey City SMSA	2284
2	New York SMSA	886
3	Erie SMSA	701
4	Newark SMSA	510
5	Detroit SMSA	385
. . .	. . .	. . .
270	Wyoming, W. Nebraska	−350
271	Santa Barbara SMSA	−362
272	Nevada, S.W. Utah	−379
273	Alaska	−396
274	S.W. Texas	−396

[a]SMSA stands for standard metropolitan statistical area.

Henry M. Peskin, "Environmental Policy and the Distribution of Benefits and Costs," in *U.S. Environmental Policy,* ed. Paul R. Portney (Baltimore: Resources for the Future, Johns Hopkins University Press, 1978), p. 155.

specific group of citizens. As Exhibit 2 illustrates, direct income transfers through the public sector have increased substantially during recent decades. Income transfer payments constituted only 6.3 percent of national income in 1959; they had risen to 12.2 percent by 1979.

Some redistribution of income stems from the inability of the market to reflect fully the preferences of the community for antipoverty efforts. The welfare of many citizens may be adversely affected by the hardship and poverty of others. For example, the economic conditions of ill-clothed children, street beggars, and the elderly poor may impose a cost on many of their fellow citizens. However, private antipoverty efforts, like private-sector national defense, have public-good characteristics. Even though the welfare of a person may be improved if there are fewer poor people, the amount that any one individual contributes to the antipoverty effort exerts little impact on the overall status of the poor. Since the number of poor people, like the strength of our national defense, is largely independent of one's *personal* contribution, individuals have an incentive to become free riders. But when a large number of people become free riders, less than the desired amount of antipoverty effort will be supplied voluntarily.

Under these circumstances, collective action against poverty may improve the general welfare of the community. If everyone is required to contribute through the tax system, the free-rider problem can be overcome. Effective antipoverty efforts may not only help the poor but also encourage donors who are willing to give their fair share if assured that others will do likewise, so that the general level of poverty can actually be reduced.

Self-Interest Redistribution.   Collective action to redistribute income does not always stem from the public-good nature of antipoverty efforts. Rather than seek

EXHIBIT 2 The growth of government transfer payments

Tax Foundation, *Facts and Figures on Government Finance, 1981,* Table 20.

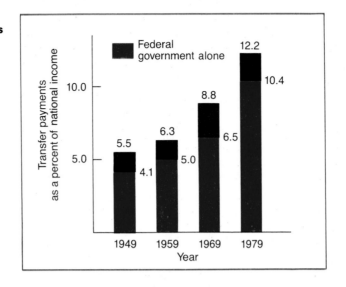

Self-Interest Redistribution: Redistribution motivated solely by the desire of the members of a group to help themselves. Nonrecipients do not gain from an improvement in the welfare of the recipients.

to correct what economists call market failure, sometimes people would much rather correct what they see as the market's failure to make them as wealthy as they would like to be. Redistribution motivated solely by the desire of its supporters to help themselves is called **self-interest redistribution** by economists. It is quite common, but it is almost never called redistribution by those who seek it. When farmers lobby for farm subsidies, they may argue that the supports are in our national interest; the supports are also needed to preserve the family farm. When college administrators (and professors) ask for government funds, they typically make their requests on the behalf of students or in the name of scientific advances. Yet, in each case, it is more than a happy coincidence that the desired program also redistributes income to those making the requests. Clearly, a strong element of self-interest is involved.

When are political entrepreneurs most likely to favor self-interest redistribution? We have seen that transfers to the poor, as a public good, might produce benefits greater than their costs. At best, self-interest redistribution results in equally balanced benefits and costs. Political entrepreneurs, however, may be able to gain from such transfers. If transfers are made to well-organized and clearly defined groups, such as the elderly, union members, or shoe producers, strong political support can be obtained from these groups. If those who pay make up a large, unorganized group (for example, taxpayers in general, or all who buy shoes) and the costs are diffused, few votes are lost. This is especially true if the costs can be hidden. Complex programs, debt financing, and money creation are all ways of hiding the cost of providing the redistribution of benefits.

Many who gain the most from self-interest redistribution never receive a check from the government. Dairy producers have successfully invested large sums in order to obtain and maintain federal and state regulation of fresh-milk markets. The gains made by regulated milk producers in the United States are estimated to be over $210 million per year.[6] These gains result from dairy

---

[6]See Richard A. Ippolito and Robert T. Masson, "The Social Cost of Government Regulation of Milk," *Journal of Law and Economics* 21, no. 1 (1978), p. 54.

prices set far above competitive levels. Consumers bear the burden of the producers' benefits—and even pay amounts over and above the gains, since the artificial prices and regulations are inefficient. Of course, the gains made by investors and workers in industries such as this have not been explicitly requested from the government. Rather, requests for various regulations and price controls are made "in the public interest," to avoid "chaos in the market," or "to ensure stable and adequate supplies." The income transfer aspects of each program are at least partially hidden. But, again, the fact that the incomes of those requesting the government intervention happen to increase is surely more than coincidental.

As both the budget and the regulatory powers of government grow, individuals (as well as firms and unions) will find it in their interest to spend more time looking for ways to capture gains bestowed by the government. By the same token, less effort will be devoted to production activities.

Gaining from Government: A Summary

Our analysis is highly simplified. Nonetheless, several important points are clear:

1. Voters seek government action for two major reasons: to capture gains created by market failure and to alter the distribution of income.

2. When market failure is present, government action need not be a zero-sum game in which one person's gain is another's loss. When a majority of voters favor a political action and the benefits are large relative to cost, vote-seeking political entrepreneurs have a strong incentive to back the proposal. The support of such proposals enhances a candidate's election prospects. In these instances, there is harmony between the self-interest of political entrepreneurs and economic efficiency.

3. Point 2 has a corollary: If market failure is not present, the net gains that will accrue to citizens from government intervention will be reduced. There is little reason to believe that the public sector could provide wheat, oranges, shoes, or beef more efficiently than the market sector. Most voters prefer to have such activities conducted in the private sector because it is more efficient and more responsive to their desires.

4. Both government transfer payments and regulation can be used to redistribute income. The demand for public sector redistribution of income may originate from either the public-good nature of antipoverty efforts or from self-interest. In the case of self-interest redistribution, the advocates of government action have a strong incentive to conceal their true motives.

THE ECONOMICS OF GOVERNMENT FAILURE

We no longer expect results from government. What was a torrid romance between the people and government for so long has now become a tired middle-aged liaison which we do not quite know how to break off.[7]

The collective decision-making process is not an ideal mechanism that automatically corrects the inefficiencies of the market. One of the painful lessons of history is that government action often does not have the hoped-for and planned-

---

[7]Peter F. Drucker, "The Sickness of Government," *Public Interest* (Winter 1969), p. 5.

for results. Even well-designed programs based on humanitarian principles sometimes fail to meet their initial objectives. The quotation above, from Peter F. Drucker, reveals a cynicism that grew during the 1970s, replacing the optimism of the 1960s. The great hopes of many Americans during that decade for extensive social improvements through public sector action were to a large extent unfulfilled. The cynicism is to some degree a reaction to that disappointment.

We began this chapter by using economic analysis to assess the effectiveness of public sector action. Now we consider systematically some of the limitations of collective action as a vehicle for promoting economic efficiency.

Government Failure: Failure of government action to meet the criteria of ideal economic efficiency.

Government failure results when public policy promotes economic inefficiency. In the following sections, we analyze five specific types of government failure.

The Special Interest Effect

Many people think of government as the great equalizer, a tool to be used in controlling powerful economic interests. In reality, the relationship often seems to run the other way—strong interest groups seem to control the government. Can economic tools help to explain this phenomenon?

A special interest issue is one for which a small number of voters *individually* acquire large gains at the expense of a large number of citizens who *individually* suffer small losses. We cannot understand fully the political power of a special interest group without recognizing the widespread ignorance and unawareness of intelligent voters with regard to (a) the relevance of most issues to their personal welfare and (b) the position of their elected representatives on the issues. Voters are generally uninformed on most issues. This lack of information and concern is a function of the rational ignorance effect and its corollary, the cost of acquiring information. Typically, most of us decide to vote for or against a political candidate on the basis of the few issues that are of substantial importance to us. We ignore numerous other issues that *individually* exert (or seem to exert) little impact on our well-being.

Two additional factors enhance the power of special interest groups. First, special interest groups are an important source of funds for political campaigns. If a politician wants to win the support of voters who have little incentive to study the issues, free information must be provided to them. Newspaper ads, printed materials, television spots, and other advertising techniques are needed to create a positive image—and all of these cost money. Since special interest groups feel strongly about certain issues, they supply candidates who support their position with a ready source of campaign contributions.[8] Second, political entrepreneurs can often "package" issues so that most voters will be unaware of the cost that various positions on the issues will impose on them. The more complex the policy under question, the more difficult it is for the average voter to figure out how he or she would be affected. There is an incentive for politicians to make special interest issues very complex. The special interest group will most assuredly figure out that it stands to gain from a given proposal, but the typical voter will find it difficult to determine the seemingly complex proposal's actual impact.[9]

Clearly, political suppliers can often reap political gain by supporting special interest legislation, whether or not such legislation is economically in-efficient. Since most voters will be uninformed on any given special interest issue, political entrepreneurs have a strong incentive to (a) support the views of a special interest group, (b) solicit from it both votes and money, (c) make the consequences of the special interest issue difficult for the average voter to understand (for example, by making the issue a part of a complex policy proposal), and (d) use funds obtained from the special interest group to promote their candidacy. In other words, political entrepreneurs have an incentive to solicit resources from special interests and use the resources obtained from them to, run not as a special interest candidate, but as the "candidate of the people." Politicians who refuse to follow this strategy run the risk of losing elections to those who accept such a course as a fact of political life.

Public policy in some areas appears to be motivated neither by economic efficiency nor by a desire for greater equality. For example, consider tariff trade

---

[8]Abundant evidence documents the importance of special interest campaign contributions. Senators, congresspeople, and presidents have long benefited from the financial assistance of businesses, unions, and other interest groups that are in a position to be rewarded by public sector decisions. Congressional committee chairpeople are, more often than not, well cared for by the industrial and labor interests that stand to benefit from the committee's actions. Analysis of state government reveals the existence of similar pressures. A study of political contributions in Florida indicated that the lion's share comes from special interest groups that are state regulated. A study in Illinois revealed a similar pattern.

[9]Gordon Tullock, in *Toward a Mathematics of Politics* (Ann Arbor: University of Michigan Press, 1966), emphasizes this point.

restrictions on such commodities as steel and automobiles. For years, economists have pointed out that tariff protection, particularly for an industry that possesses substantial monopoly power, leads to an inefficient allocation of resources. It would be difficult to find an issue on which there is more general agreement among economists. However, the benefits of the repeal of such legislation would be widely dispersed and difficult for consumers to perceive. The costs of the repeal imposed on automobile and steel manufacturers and employees would be highly concentrated. Despite the fact that political figures argue from time to time that automobile and steel prices do not respond to competition, political protection of the tariff legislation remains. Politicians obviously perceive that greater political gains are to be obtained from a continuation of the present high tariff policy on these commodities than from its repeal.

Why is it that politicians who support special interests are not removed from office by taxpayers? There is some incentive to do this, but it is greatly reduced because of the high cost of forming coalitions, particularly among a loosely knit group.[10] Each taxpayer has a strong incentive to "let the others do it"—that is, to act as a free rider. However, when everybody decides to ride free, nothing is accomplished.

Imprecise Reflection of Consumer Preferences

The collective process is likely to be imprecise in reflecting the wishes of "consumers" (voters) because they can usually express their wishes only through a broker (legislator) who represents a "bundle" of political goods and tax prices. The voter either gets the bundle of political goods offered by candidate A or the bundle offered by candidate B. Neither of these bundles of political goods necessarily represents what a specific consumer would like to have. The political consumer does not have the freedom to "shop around" on each issue, but must accept the bundle favored by the majority coalition.

In contrast to the market, the consumer's ability to make discriminating choices is very limited in the public sector. Circumstances change, new information becomes available, and relative prices change, but the political consumer has little opportunity to respond by making marginal adjustments. Approximately two-fifths of our economic resources are channeled through the public sector. Yet during a year, each of us makes approximately 1000 times as many market as public sector decisions.

Concealed Costs and Inefficient Public Policy

It is often difficult for voters to recognize the precise impact of public policy on their well-being. We have already noted that individual voters, recognizing that their views will not decide the issue, have little incentive to inform themselves on political matters. Because of imperfect voter information, the political process is biased against proposals with elusive benefits at the expense of easily identified costs. Anthony Downs believes that this factor often results in the rejection of beneficial public policy:

Benefits from many government actions are remote from those who receive them, either in time, space or comprehensibility. Economic aid to a distant nation may prevent a hostile

---

[10]Sometimes intense publicity will make the support of a specific piece of special interest legislation temporarily unpopular. In this case, entrepreneurs will take special care to modify or disguise their support of vested interest groups.

revolution there and save millions of dollars and even the lives of American troops, but because the solution is remote, the average citizen—living in rational ignorance—will not realize he is benefiting at all.[11]

Just as the failure to recognize personal benefits fully may cause voters (and legislators responsive to their constituents) to reject some economically efficient projects, the adoption of other proposals that are inefficient also results from imperfect voter information. Counterproductive proposals tend to be accepted when the benefits are clearly recognizable and the costs are partially concealed and difficult for voters to identify. Politicians will often seek to conceal the costs of a political proposal while fully promoting its benefits among voters who could gain from it. Vote-maximizing political entrepreneurs have a strong incentive to package public policy proposals precisely in this way. For example, taxes that are difficult for voters to identify are more popular with politicians than are direct tax levies. The splitting of payroll taxes between employer and employee, when the burden does not depend on who formally pays, suggests that legislators are interested in deceiving voters as to the personal cost of government. Similarly, the continued popularity of deficit spending and money creation is consistent with the theory. When this method of gaining control over private resources is substituted for direct taxation, voters are less likely to be fully aware of their individual tax burden. Thus, it is not surprising that political entrepreneurs continue to embrace inflationary policies even while denouncing rising prices and blaming them on unions, businesspeople, the Arabs, the wasteful consumption habits of consumers, or any other scapegoats.

The Shortsightedness Effect

The shortsightedness effect results because the complexity of an issue may make it extremely difficult for the voter to anticipate *future* benefits and costs accurately. Thus, voters tend to rely mainly on current conditions. Candidates and legislators seeking to win the current election have a strong incentive to stress public sector action that yields substantial current benefits relative to costs. Therefore, public sector action is biased in favor of legislation that offers immediate (and easily identified) current benefits at the expense of future costs that are complex and difficult to identify. Similarly, there is a bias against legislation that involves immediate and easily identifiable cost (for example, higher taxes) while yielding future benefits that are complex and difficult to identify. Government action on issues whose future consequences are unclear tends to be shortsighted.

Short-Term Costs and Government Inaction. It has been noted that public sector action is "crisis-oriented." In recent years, we have experienced a welfare crisis, a poverty crisis, an environmental crisis, an energy crisis, and an inflation crisis. One reason for this is that planning for the future tends to be unrewarding for those in government. Future costs and benefits are difficult for voters to identify. In addition, many of those to be affected in the future are not voting today. Given the public sector bias against proposals associated with current costs and difficult-to-identify future benefits, the government's crisis orientation is understandable. The vote-maximizing politician has an incentive to follow

---

[11]Anthony Downs, "Why the Government Budget Is Too Small in a Democracy," *World Politics* 12, no. 4 (1960), p. 551.

a policy of minimum current expenditures until the crisis point is reached, all the while paying lip service to the problem. Economics suggests that democratic decision-making is often inconsistent with sensible *long-range* planning.

Short-Term Benefits and Government Action. Whereas proposals with future benefits that are difficult to perceive are usually delayed, proposals with immediate benefits, at the expense of complex future costs—costs that will accrue after the next election—are very attractive to political entrepreneurs. Both office-holders and candidates have a strong incentive to support such proposals and emphasize the immediate voter benefits.

Is there any evidence that the pursuit of short-term political gains has led to inappropriate public sector action? Consider the issue of macroeconomic instability. Only recently have politicians become completely convinced that the "tightness" of labor markets can be controlled by monetary and fiscal policy. Expansionary monetary and fiscal policy can be used to "heat up" the economy and reduce the rate of unemployment in the short run. However, an overheated economy leads to inflation. The shortsightedness effect predicts that the party in power will tend to follow an expansionary policy in the 12 to 24 months before an election, even if these policies will result in future inflation. The "stabilization" policies preceding the presidential elections of the last two decades suggest that incumbent political entrepreneurs made a substantial effort to give voters the impression that the economy was strong on election day. Yet there is little doubt that expansionary macropolicy overheated the economy in each case, causing a postelection increase in the rate of inflation.

The shortsightedness effect can be a source of conflict between good politics and sound economics. Policies that are efficient from the standpoint of social benefits and costs are not necessarily the policies that will enhance a politician's election prospects. Thus it is that grossly inefficient projects may be undertaken and potentially beneficial projects may be ignored.

Bureaucratic and Political Incentives for Internal Efficiency

Government has often been charged with inaction, duplication, delays, frivolous work, and general inefficiency. These charges are difficult to document or prove. How does government compare with the private sector? Certainly a great deal of seemingly meaningless activity goes on in the private sector as well, but private firms, even those with monopoly power, can gain from actions that improve operational efficiency. There is an incentive to produce efficiently because lower cost will mean higher profits. Although the stockholders of a private firm can seldom identify good and bad individual decisions, they can easily observe a "bottom line" index of efficiency—the firm's rate of profit. In the private sector, the possibility of bankruptcy, falling stock prices, and/or a takeover bid by the management of another firm are deterrents to economic inefficiency.

Public sector decision-makers confront an incentive structure that is less conducive to operational efficiency. Since there is no easily identified index of performance analogous to the profit rate, public sector managers can often gloss over economic inefficiency. Profits do not necessarily matter. If a public sector decision-maker spends money unwisely or uses resources primarily for personal benefit (for example, plush offices, extensive "business travel," three-martini lunches), the burden of this inefficiency will fall on the taxpayer. The public sector is also not subject to the test of bankruptcy, which tends to eliminate inefficient operations in the private sector. Political finesse, which leads to large budgets, is far more important to success in the public sector than is operational efficiency, which would lead to a lower cost of production.

Taxpayers would be the major beneficiaries of reduced costs and an improvement in public sector efficiency. However, since voter-taxpayers are rationally uninformed on most issues and largely unorganized, they are unable to police the situation effectively. There is no simple summary statistic comparable to the rate of profit in the private sector that provides low-cost information to taxpayers; proof of the operational efficiency (or inefficiency) of any given division of government is generally difficult and impractical to obtain or communicate. At election time, political candidates and parties must offer something more impressive than efficiency in government if they expect to win.

A public sector manager seldom reaps personal reward by saving the taxpayers money. In fact, if an agency fails to spend this year's allocation, its case for a larger budget next year is weakened. Agencies typically go on a spending spree at the end of a budget period if they discover that they have failed to spend all of this year's appropriation.

Insofar as political officials are interested in efficiency, they will tend to choose ways of improving efficiency that are visible and simple to communicate. A well-publicized campaign to save a few dollars by eliminating limousine service for high government officials can produce greater political benefits than a complex government reorganization plan that would save taxpayers millions of dollars. The latter idea is too complex and the outcome too difficult for voters to identify.

It is important to note that the argument of internal inefficiency is not based on the assumption that employees of a bureaucratic government are necessarily lazy or incapable. Rather, the emphasis is on the incentive structure under which managers and other workers toil. No individual or relatively small group of individuals has much incentive to ensure efficiency. There is no small group of persons whose personal wealth would be significantly increased or reduced by changes in the level of efficiency. Since public officials and bureau managers spend other people's money, they are likely to be less conscious of cost than they would be with their own resources. There is no test by which to define economic inefficiency clearly or measure it accurately, much less eliminate it. The perverse incentive structure of a bureaucracy is bound to have an impact on its internal efficiency.

THE ECONOMIC ANALYSIS OF THE PUBLIC SECTOR

Most economic texts make only brief reference to the major issues discussed in this chapter. Our purpose has been to analyze how we would *expect* the public sector to handle various classes of economic issues.

In the past, economists were usually content with a discussion of what the government *should* do, regardless of how unrealistic that solution might be. Without ignoring government's ideal activities, we have extended our analysis to what, in fact, government is *likely* to do and what the outcomes of its intervention are likely to be. The broad relevance of economic tools has helped us to explain the real-world influence of public sector action on an economy's efficiency.

Is the Economic Analysis Cynical?

We have stressed how economic factors influence the workings of the public sector. Our analysis may differ considerably from that presented in a typical political science course. Some of you may object that our approach is cynical, that not enough emphasis has been given to the dedicated public servants who devote all of their energy to the resolution of complex public sector issues. Our analysis does not deny the existence of such individuals. We merely emphasize that in a legislative democracy there are pressures at work that make it difficult for these individuals to survive without compromising.

One might also argue that voters are more public spirited than we have indicated. They may be willing to sacrifice their personal welfare for the public good. However, if voters are motivated primarily by what is in the public interest, how then does one account for the behavior of trade associations, business lobbyists, labor unions, public employee groups, lawyers, physicians, teachers, developers, and hundreds of other organized groups, all attempting to adapt the rules and regulations of the public sector to their own advantage?

The test of any theory is its consistency with events in the real world. Certainly, we have not outlined a complete theory of the public sector. However, casual observation of current events should give one sufficient cause to question the validity of theories that emphasize only the public interest, equal power, and the humanitarian nature of governmental action. Democratic governments are a creation of the interactions of imperfect human beings. Many economists believe that economic theory has a great deal to say about the types of public sector actions that will result from these interactions.

The Public Sector versus the Market: A Summary

Throughout, we have argued that theory can explain why both market forces and public sector action sometimes break down—that is, why they sometimes fail to meet criteria for ideal efficiency. The deficiencies of one or the other sector often will be more or less decisive depending upon the type of economic activity. Nobel laureate Paul Samuelson has stated, "There are no rules concerning the

---

Thumbnail Sketch

These factors weaken the case for market sector allocation:

1. External costs
2. External benefits
3. Public goods
4. Monopoly
5. Uninformed consumers

These factors weaken the case for public sector intervention:

1. Voter ignorance, inability to recognize costs and benefits fully, and cost concealment
2. The power of special interests
3. The shortsightedness effect
4. Little incentive for entrepreneurial efficiency
5. Imprecision in the reflection of consumer preferences

---

proper role of government that can be established by a priori reasoning."[12] This does not mean, however, that economics has nothing to say about the *strength* of the case for either the market or the public sector in terms of specific classes of activities. Nor does it mean that social scientists have nothing to say about institutional arrangements for conducting economic activity. It merely indicates that each issue and type of activity must be considered individually.

The case for government intervention is obviously stronger for some activities than for others. For example, if an activity involves substantial external effects, market arrangements often result in economic inefficiency, and public sector action may allow for greater efficiency. Similarly, when competitive pressures are weak or there is reason to expect consumers to be poorly informed, market failure may result, and again government action may be called for. (See the Thumbnail Sketch for a summary of factors that influence the case for market or for public sector action.)

The identical analysis holds for the public sector. When there is good reason to believe that special interest influence will be strong, the case for government action to correct market failures is weakened. Similarly, the lack of a means of identifying and weeding out public sector inefficiency weakens the case for government action. More often than not, the choice of proper institutions may be a choice among evils. For example, we might expect private sector monopoly if an activity is left to the market and perverse regulation due to the special interest effect if we turn to the public sector. Understanding the shortcomings of both the market and the public sectors is important if we are to improve and adapt our current economic institutions.

At one time, economists assumed that the private sector operated according to the perfectly competitive model. In the late twentieth century, we have sometimes assumed that government operates so as to fulfill the conditions of ideal efficiency established by economists. Both assumptions, of course, are simplistic. The application of economics to public choice helps us to understand why public policy sometimes goes astray and how public sector incentives might be altered to improve the efficiency of government action.

LOOKING AHEAD

Once we understand the sources of economic inefficiency, we are in a better position to suggest potential remedies. We close this section with a perspective that considers reforms for dealing with the political power of special interest issues.

CHAPTER LEARNING OBJECTIVES

1 It is fruitful to analyze the public sector in the same way in which we analyze the private sector. Collective action, through government, has the potential for correcting market failures and redistributing income. The public sector is an alternative to the market—it provides an alternative means of organizing production and/or distributing output.

2 Voters cast ballots, make political contributions, lobby, and adopt other political strategies to demand public sector action. Other things constant, voters have a strong incentive to support the candidate who offers them the greatest personal gain relative

---

[12]P. A. Samuelson, "The Economic Role of Private Activity," in *The Collected Scientific Papers of Paul A. Samuelson,* ed. J. E. Stiglitz, vol. 2 (Cambridge, Massachusetts: MIT Press, 1966), p. 1423.

PERSPECTIVES IN ECONOMICS
DEALING WITH SPECIAL INTERESTS

The special interest effect indicates that in the legislative process, a small group that is strongly interested in an issue may wield great influence. On that issue, the group may prevail over the interests of the majority of voters if most of those in the majority have only a small stake in the outcome. The majority voters are unlikely to be organized, to lobby effectively, or even to know how a politician voted on the issue. In addition, the bundle purchase problem reinforces the special interest effect. Only those with intense feelings about the issues are likely to let this single issue determine how they will cast the only vote they have.

Could political institutions be changed in a manner that would diminish the power of special interests? Although there are no easy solutions, we can suggest several steps that could be taken to help bring the personal interests of politicians into greater harmony with economic efficiency.

1. Force Legislators to Establish a Budget Constraint—a Maximum Level of Government Spending—as Their First Act during Each Legislative Session. The current system of appropriations for individual budget items permits legislators to cater to special interests without ever having to take a clear stand on economy in government. Essentially, the public treasury is treated as a common pool resource, available to anyone with political influence. Individuals in a household must make choices within the framework of a fixed budget constraint, in which more butter means less bread. In contrast, legislators are not so rigidly constrained. They can vote for more butter and pass the bill on to the unorganized taxpayers while maintaining the same level of spending on bread. In general, the system fails to force legislators to make careful choices within the framework of a fixed budget.

This defect, which favors special interest groups, could be corrected if a fixed budget were established at the beginning of each legislative session.[13] Then the issue of additional government spending versus lower taxes could be debated solely on the merits of each alternative. In contrast with the current system, a legislator's single vote on the size of the government's budget would provide voters with a reliable index of that legislator's support of taxpayer interests and governmental economic efficiency.

Once the size of the budget was determined, then and only then would appropriation decisions be made. Each special interest would then be pitted, not against the taxpayer, but against other special interests pursuing government moneys. The Department of Defense would have to convince legislators that additional Pentagon spending was more meritorious than additional spending on welfare, education, social security, college student loans, and/or subsidies to industrial interests. The Department of Education would have to argue that expanding appropriations would be more important than, for example, additional environmental spending. No longer could special interests so easily tap the public treasury when they sought additional funds.

2. Make More Use of Referenda in the Resolution of Special Interest Issues. When a decision is resolved by referendum, the special interest is much less likely to prevail, unless majority interests are also served. A referendum enables each member of the unorganized majority to register her or his opposition—albeit mild opposition—to a special interest issue *independent of other issues.* Voters need less informa-

tion to determine and register their views, since alternative positions of political middlemen (legislators) on the issue are irrelevant. In contrast with legislative decision-making, a referendum virtually eliminates vote trading (so-called logrolling—"You support my special issue and I'll support yours") as a means to gain passage of legislation favored by interest groups. All of these factors make the referendum an attractive—if seldom used—means of undermining the power of special interests.[14]

3. Establish a Constitutional Budget Constraint Limiting the Size of Government as a Share of Total Income. Some believe that only a constitutional amendment limiting the amount of government expenditures would restore the balance between the interests of concentrated groups and unorganized taxpayers. Such a spending ceiling would limit the ability of legislators to grant the requests of powerful special interest groups. Special interest groups would be pitted against one another, rather than against the widely dispersed, unorganized taxpayers. Several states have adopted spending limitation amendments. A federal spending limitation is likely to be a hotly debated issue during the 1980s.

Discussion

1. Explain why you either favor or oppose each of the three suggestions outlined in this perspective. Do you think that any of these suggestions would prove effective?

2. How do you think that organized industrial interests, unions, professional associations, and bureaucrats would react to these proposals? Why?

---

[13]This procedure—establishing the size of the budget *before* funds are appropriated for specific programs—has been followed by the Wisconsin state legislature in recent years.

[14]See James D. Gwartney and Jonathan Silberman, "Distribution of Costs and Benefits and the Significance of Collective Decision Rules," *Social Science Quarterly,* (December 1973), pp. 568–578, for a more complete analysis of why referendum decision-making limits the power of special interest groups.

to personal costs. Obtaining information is costly. Since group decision-making breaks the link between the choice of the individual and the outcome of the issue, it is rational for voters to remain uninformed on many issues. Candidates are generally evaluated on the basis of a small subset of issues that are of the greatest personal importance to individual voters.

3 Market failure presents government with an opportunity to undertake action that will result in greater benefits/costs. Other things constant, the greater the social loss resulting from the market failure, the stronger is the incentive for public sector action.

4 A growing portion of public sector activity involves income redistribution. Economic analysis indicates two potential sources of pressure for income redistribution: (a) the public-good nature of antipoverty efforts and (b) self-interest. From the viewpoint of a vote-maximizing entrepreneur, there is incentive to support redistribution from unorganized to well-organized groups. Considerable income redistribution in the United States is of this type.

5 There is a strong incentive for political entrepreneurs to support special interest issues and to make the issues difficult for the unorganized, largely uninformed majority to understand. Special interest groups supply both financial and direct elective support to the politician.

6 Because of imperfect voter information, proposals whose benefits are elusive and whose costs are clear-cut tend to be rejected, even though they might promote the community's welfare. Counterproductive policies whose benefits are easily recognizable and whose costs are difficult to identify tend to be accepted. There is a strong incentive for politicians to package public policy in a manner that amplifies the benefits and conceals the costs imposed on voters.

7 The shortsightedness effect is another potential source of conflict between good politics and sound economics. Both voters and politicians tend to support projects that promise substantial current benefits at the expense of difficult-to-identify future costs. There is a bias against legislation that involves immediate and easily identifiable costs but complex future benefits.

8 The economic incentive for operational efficiency is small for public sector action. No individual or relatively small group of individuals can capture the gains derived from improved operational efficiency. There is no force analogous to the threat of bankruptcy in the private sector that will bring inefficient behavior to a halt. Since public sector resources, including tax funds, are communally owned, their users are less likely than private resource owners to be cost conscious.

9 Positive economics cannot tell us whether an action should be conducted in the public or in the market sector. However, analysis of how both sectors operate does help build the case for conducting any given activity in either sector. When market failure is prevalent, the case for public sector action is strengthened. On the other hand, expectation of government failure reduces the strength of the argument for government intervention.

THE ECONOMIC WAY OF THINKING — DISCUSSION QUESTIONS

1 Do you think that advertising exerts more influence on the type of car chosen by a consumer than on the type of politician chosen by the same person? Explain your answer.

2 Do you think that the political process works to the advantage of the poor? Explain. Are the poor well organized? Do they make substantial campaign contributions to candidates? Are they likely to be well informed? Is it surprising that a large amount of the approximately $300 billion of cash income transfer payments in the United States does not go to the poor? Explain.

3 Which of the following public sector actions are designed primarily to correct

"market failure": (a) laws against fraud, (b) truth-in-lending legislation, (c) rate regulation in the telephone industry, (d) legislation setting emission control standards, (e) subsidization of pure research, (f) operation of the Post Office? Explain your answer.

4 Do political entrepreneurs ever have an incentive to deceive voters about the cost of legislation? If so, when? Can you give any examples of cases in which this has happened?

5 The liquor industry contributes a large share of the political funds to political contests on the state level. Yet its contributions to candidates for national office are minimal. Why do you think this is true? (*Hint:* Who regulates the liquor industry?)

6 One explanation for the shortsightedness effect in the public sector is that future voters cannot vote now to represent their future interests. Are the interests of future generations represented in market decisions? For example, if the price of chromium were expected to rise rapidly over the next 30 years due to increased scarcity, how could speculators grow rich while providing the next generation with more chromium at the expense of current consumers?

7 What's Wrong with This Way of Thinking?

"Public policy is necessary to protect the average citizen from the power of vested interest groups. In the absence of government intervention, regulated industries, such as airlines, railroads, and trucking, would charge excessive prices, products would be unsafe, and the rich would oppress the poor. Government curbs the power of special interest groups."

PART SIX

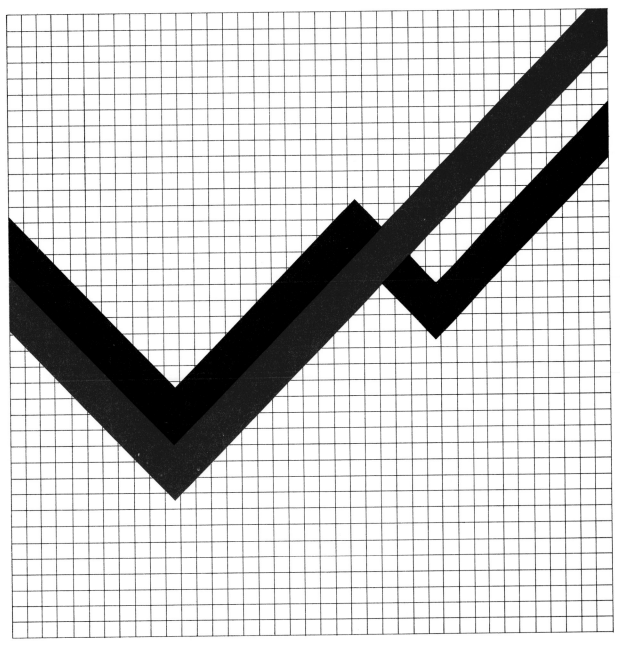

INTERNATIONAL ECONOMICS
AND COMPARATIVE SYSTEMS

31

GAINING FROM INTERNATIONAL TRADE

We live in a shrinking world. Wheat raised on the flatlands of western Kansas may be processed into bread in a Russian factory. The breakfast of many Americans might include bananas from Honduras, coffee from Brazil, or hot chocolate made from Nigerian cocoa beans. The volume of world trade, enhanced by improved transportation and communications, has grown rapidly in recent years. In 1979, the total trade among nations was approximately $3 trillion. Approximately 16 percent of the world's total output is now sold in a different country than that in which it was produced—double the figure of two decades ago.

In this chapter, we will analyze the impact of foreign trade on the price, consumption, and domestic production of goods. The effects of trade restrictions, such as tariffs and quotas, will also be considered. International trade is an area of economics where fallacies seem to abound. Indirect effects are often ignored. As we progress, we will discuss several examples of economic nonreasoning.

THE COMPOSITION OF THE INTERNATIONAL SECTOR

As Exhibit 1 shows, the size of the trade sector varies among nations. International trade comprises more than two-fifths of the GNP of the Netherlands and approximately one-quarter of the GNP in Sweden, Canada, West Germany, and the United Kingdom. The relative size of the trade sector is smaller for Japan, Australia, and the United States. Approximately 9 percent of the GNP in the United States results from trade.

However, the size of the international sector relative to GNP may actually understate the importance of trade. Many of the products we purchase from foreigners would be much more costly if we were dependent solely on our domestic production. We are dependent on foreign producers for several products, including almost all of our coffee and bananas, more than 90 percent of the bauxite we use to make aluminum, all of our chromium, diamonds,

---

[1]Adam Smith, *An Inquiry into the Nature and Causes of the Wealth of Nations* (1776; Cannan's ed., Chicago: University of Chicago Press, 1976), pp. 478–479.

EXHIBIT 1   The size of the trade sector for selected countries, 1980

Country	International Trade as Percentage of GNP
Netherlands	45
Sweden	28
Canada	24
West Germany	23
United Kingdom	23
France	19
Australia	13
Japan	13
United States	9

U.S. Department of Commerce.

and tin, and most of our cobalt, nickel, manganese, and asbestos. The life-style of Americans (as well as that of our trading partners) would be changed if international trade were halted.

Exhibits 2 and 3 summarize the leading products imported and exported by the United States. Petroleum comprised 31 percent of the dollar value of all

EXHIBIT 2   The major import products of the United States, 1980

Petroleum, machinery, and automobiles were the major products imported by the United States in 1980.

Statistical Abstract of the United States—1981.

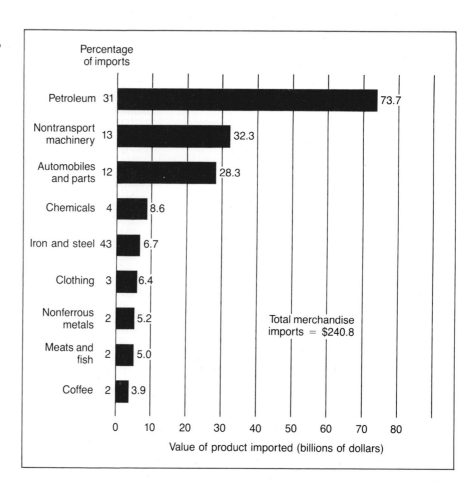

merchandise imports of Americans in 1980 (Exhibit 2). As recently as 1973, petroleum imports accounted for only 11 percent of our total imports. Needless to say, there has been a sharp increase in the dollar value of U.S. petroleum imports. In addition, automobiles, machinery (both electrical and nonelectrical), chemicals, and steel mill products are among the leading import items.

Exhibit 3 lists the major merchandise exports of the United States. Three items—chemicals, motor vehicles, and grains—comprise 24 percent of the total. Aircraft, metals, and mineral fuels (primarily coal) are also among the leading export products.

The structure of U.S. trade has changed during the last decade. Agricultural products (wheat, corn, and rice) and high-technology manufacturing products (for example, aircraft, computers, and machine tools) have comprised an increasing share of our total exports. Foreign producers have supplied more and more import products to our domestic markets in such established industries as steel, textiles, automobiles, and, of course, crude petroleum.

With which countries does the United States trade? As Exhibit 4 shows, Canada heads the list. In 1980, slightly less than one-fifth of the total U.S. volume of trade was with Canada. Japan, Mexico, and the nations of the European Economic Community (particularly West Germany, the United Kingdom, France, and Italy) are also among the leading trading partners of the

EXHIBIT 3   The major export products of the United States, 1980

Chemicals, motor vehicles, and grains were the major products exported by the United States in 1980.

Statistical Abstract of the United States—1981.

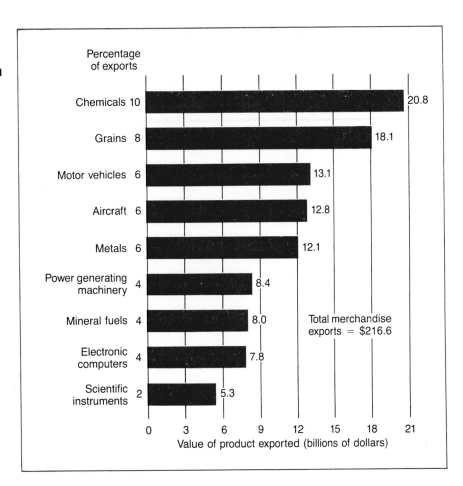

EXHIBIT 4 The leading trading partners of the United States, 1980

Canada, Japan, Mexico, and Western European countries are the leading trading partners of the United States. An increasing share of U.S. trade is with petroleum-producing countries, such as Saudi Arabia and Venezuela.

U.S. Department of Commerce.

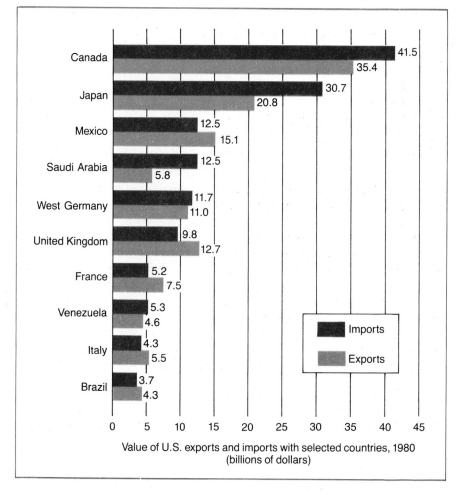

Value of U.S. exports and imports with selected countries, 1980
(billions of dollars)

United States. More than half of the U.S. trade in 1980 was with Canada, Japan, and the industrial nations of Western Europe. Beginning in the mid-1970s, U.S. trade with the petroleum-exporting countries grew rapidly. Saudi Arabia and Venezuela now rank among the leading trading partners of the United States.

COMPARATIVE ADVANTAGE AND TRADE BETWEEN NATIONS

Although we speak of international trade, for the most part the exchanges take place between individuals (or business firms) that happen to be located in different countries. International trade, like other voluntary exchange, results because both the buyer and the seller gain from it. If both parties did not expect to gain, there would be no trade.

The law of comparative advantage, which we discussed in detail in Chapter 2, explains why mutual gains arise from specialization and exchange. According to the law of comparative advantage, trading partners gain by specializing in the production of goods for which they are low opportunity cost producers and trading for those goods for which they are high opportunity cost producers. This specialization in the area of one's comparative advantage minimizes the cost of production and leads to a *maximum joint output* between trading partners.

Both international trading partners can gain if they specialize in those things that they do best. We know that the resource base varies among nations. Countries with warm, moist climates such as Brazil and Colombia specialize in the production of coffee. Land is abundant in sparsely populated nations such as Canada and Australia. These nations tend to specialize in land-intensive products, such as wheat, feed grains, and beef. In contrast, land is scarce in Japan, a nation with a highly skilled labor force. Therefore, the Japanese specialize in manufacturing, using their comparative advantage to produce cameras, automobiles, and steel products for export.

It is easy to see why trade and specialization expand joint output and lead to mutual gain when the resource bases of regions differ substantially. However, even when resource differences among nations are less dramatic, mutually advantageous trade is usually possible. Exhibit 5 illustrates this point. Here we consider the possibilities for the production of bicycles and wine in two countries, France and the United States. Initially, we analyze the situation in the absence of specialization and trade; then we consider the impact of trade. For simplicity's sake, we limit our analysis to just two countries and two goods.

Absolute Advantage: A situation in which a nation, as the result of its previous experience and/or natural endowments, can produce a product with fewer resources than another nation.

Suppose that France employs 2 million workers in these two industries, and the United States employs 4 million. The output per worker of both bicycles and wine is higher for France than for the United States. Perhaps due to its previous experience, France has an **absolute advantage** in the production of both commodities. French workers can make four bicycles per day, compared to only three per day for U.S. workers. Similarly, French workers are able to produce 20 bottles of wine per day, compared to only 10 bottles per day for U.S workers.

EXHIBIT 5 Comparative advantage and gains from international trade

Country	(1) Number of Workers (Millions)	(2) Output per Worker per Day[a]	(3) Total Output without Specialization[b]	(4) Total Output with Specialization	(5) Consumption after Trade[c]
France	2	4 bicycles *or* 20 bottles of wine	4 million bicycles *and* 20 million bottles of wine	0 bicycles *and* 40 million bottles of wine	5 million bicycles *and* 20 million bottles of wine
United States	4	3 bicycles *or* 10 bottles of wine	6 million bicycles *and* 20 million bottles of wine	12 million bicycles *and* 0 bottles of wine	7 million bicycles *and* 20 million bottles of wine
Combined	6	—	10 million bicycles *and* 40 million bottles of wine	12 million bicycles *and* 40 million bottles of wine	12 million bicycles *and* 40 million bottles of wine

[a]*For simplicity, we assume that the output per worker is constant for both products.*
[b]*Assuming that equal numbers of workers are employed in the bicycle and wine industries.*
[c]*Assuming that the international price of bicycles is 4 times the price of a bottle of wine.*

Exhibit 5, column 3, illustrates the total output of bicycles and wine in both France and the United States in the absence of trade. Assuming that the work force of each country is equally divided between the two industries, 2 million French workers produce 4 million bicycles and 20 million bottles of wine. In the United States, workers produce 6 million bicycles and 20 million bottles of wine. Prior to specialization and trade, the aggregate output of the two countries is 10 million bicycles and 40 million bottles of wine.

Given that French workers are more efficient at producing both bicycles and wine than their U.S. counterparts, are gains from trade possible? The answer is yes, because the opportunity costs of production in the two countries differ. For French workers, the opportunity cost of a bicycle is five bottles of wine. In the United States, the opportunity cost of a bicycle is only three and one-third bottles of wine. Therefore, U.S. workers are the low opportunity cost producers of bicycles, even though they cannot produce as many per day as the French workers. As column 4 illustrates, when the 4 million U.S. workers specialize in the production of bicycles, they can produce 12 million per day. Simultaneously, if the 2 million French workers specialize in the production of wine, they can produce 40 million bottles per day. Therefore, with specialization, the combined output will be 12 million bicycles and 40 million bottles of wine per day, an increase of 2 million bicycles compared to the no-trade situation. If the price of a bicycle is 4 bottles of wine (an "intermediate price"), France will be able to trade 20 million bottles of wine for 5 million U.S.-produced bicycles.

As Exhibit 5, column 5, shows, after specialization and trade, each country will be able to consume 1 million more bicycles per day compared to the no-trade situation. Both countries gain from the specialization in the production of the commodities for which they are low opportunity cost producers.

Thus far, we have ignored transportation costs. Of course, transportation costs reduce the potential gains from trade. Sometimes transportation costs, both real and artificially imposed, exceed the mutual gain. (See "Frédéric Bastiat on Obstacles to Gains from Trade.") When this is so, exchange does not occur. However, this does not negate the law of comparative advantage.

According to the law of comparative advantage, the joint output of two trading nations will be greatest when each nation specializes in the production of those products for which it is a low opportunity cost producer and trades them for those goods for which it is a high opportunity cost producer. Mutual gain to each trading nation will result from such specialization and exchange.

The Export–Import Link

Confusion about the merit of international trade often results because people do not consider all the consequences. Why are other nations willing to export their goods to the United States? So they can obtain dollars. Yes, but why do they want dollars? Would foreigners be willing to continue exporting oil, radios, watches, cameras, automobiles, and thousands of other valuable products to us in exchange for pieces of paper? If so, we could all be semiretired, spending only an occasional workday at the dollar printing press office! Of course, foreigners are not so naïve. They trade goods for dollars so they can use the dollars to import goods and purchase ownership rights to U.S. assets.

Exports provide the buying power that makes it possible for a nation to import other goods. Nations export goods so that they will be able to import foreign products. If a nation does not import goods from foreigners, foreigners will not have the purchasing power to buy that nation's export products. Thus, the exports and imports of a nation are closely linked.

Supply, Demand, and International Trade

How does international trade affect prices and output levels in domestic markets? Supply and demand analysis will help us answer this question. High transportation costs and the availability of cheaper alternatives elsewhere diminish the attractiveness of some U.S. products to foreigners. These factors may completely eliminate foreign purchases of some commodities. However, foreign consumers will find that many U.S. products are cheaper even when transportation costs are considered. When this is the case, the demand of foreigners will supplement that of domestic consumers.

In an open economy, the market demand curve for domestic products is the horizontal sum of the domestic and foreign demand. Exhibit 6 illustrates the impact of foreign demand on the domestic wheat market. When the demand of foreigners is added to the domestic demand, it yields the market demand curve D_{f+d} (where the subscripts f and d refer to foreign and domestic, respectively). Price P brings supply and demand into equilibrium. At the equilibrium market price, foreigners purchase OF units of wheat, and domestic consumers purchase FQ. The competition from foreign consumers results in both higher wheat prices and a higher output level.

At first glance, it appears that the entry of foreign consumers into the U.S. market has helped U.S. wheat producers at the expense of domestic consumers, who must now pay higher wheat prices (or else do without). That view is correct as far as it goes, but it ignores the secondary effects. How will foreigners obtain the purchasing power to import U.S. wheat? Primarily by exporting products for which they are low-cost producers to the U.S. market. The domestic supply of the products exported by foreigners to pay for the wheat will expand. The prices of those foreign products will be reduced (relative to the no-trade situation), actually benefiting the U.S. consumers who appeared at first to be harmed by the higher wheat prices.

Exhibit 7 uses the case of foreign banana imports to illustrate this point. The total supply of bananas to the U.S. market is the horizontal sum of (a) the

EXHIBIT 6   Exporting to foreigners

The demand of both foreign and domestic purchasers of U.S. wheat is shown here. The market demand (D_{f+d}) is the horizontal sum of these two components. Total domestic production of the product would be OQ, of which OF would be exported and FQ consumed domestically.

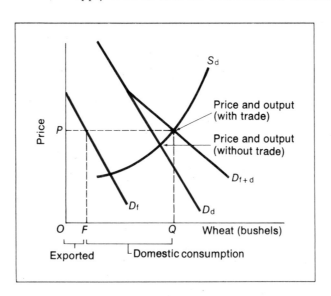

EXHIBIT 7 Importing cheap goods

Both the domestic supply and the foreign supply of bananas to the U.S. market are shown here. Since foreign producers have a comparative advantage in the production of bananas, the supply curve of foreigners exceeds that of domestic producers. At price *P*, *OD* would be produced domestically and *DF* imported.

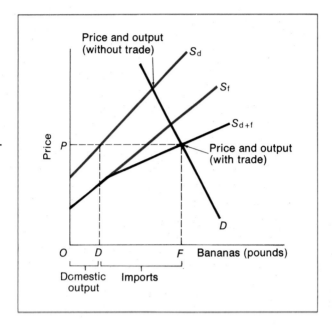

foreign supply to the domestic market plus (b) the supply of domestic producers. Since foreign countries, particularly Honduras, are low opportunity cost producers of bananas, they are able to supply this product to the U.S. market more cheaply than most domestic producers. The addition of the imported supply results in both lower prices and a higher consumption level than would exist in the absence of trade.

Relative to the no-trade alternative, international trade and specialization result in lower prices (and higher consumption levels) for imported products and higher prices (and lower consumption levels) for exported products. However, as the law of comparative advantage reveals, the net effect is an expansion in the consumption alternatives available to a nation.

RESTRICTIONS TO TRADE

Despite the potential benefits from free trade, almost all nations have erected trade barriers. What kinds of barriers are erected? Why are they used? Three factors contribute to the existence of trade barriers: sound arguments for the protection of specific industries under certain circumstances; economic illiteracy — ignorance as to who is helped and who is harmed by trade restrictions; and the special interest nature of trade restrictions.

Tariffs and Quotas

Tariff: A tax that is levied on goods imported into a country.

Tariffs and quotas are the two most commonly used trade-restricting devices. A **tariff** is nothing more than a tax on foreign imports. As Exhibit 8 shows, tariff barriers in the United States have fluctuated. Until the 1940s, tariffs of between 30 and 50 percent of product value were often levied. In recent years, the average tariff rate has been approximately 10 percent.

Exhibit 9 illustrates the impact of a tariff on sugar. In the absence of a tariff, the world market price of sugar is P_w. At that price, U.S. consumers

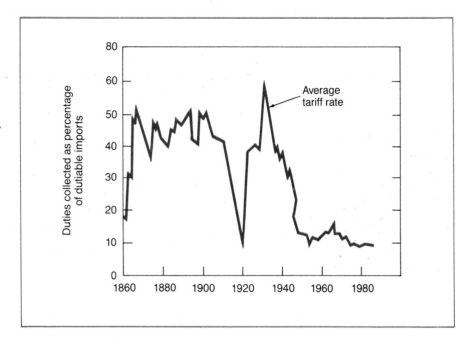

purchase Q_1 units. Domestic producers supply Q_{d1}, while foreigners supply Q_1 minus Q_{d1} units to the U.S. market. When the United States levies a tariff t on sugar, Americans can no longer buy sugar at the world price. U.S. consumers have to pay $P_w + t$ in order to purchase sugar from foreigners. Thus, the market price rises to $P_w + t$. At that price, domestic consumers demand Q_2 units (Q_{d2} supplied by domestic producers and $Q_2 - Q_{d2}$ supplied by foreigners).

Imports decline with the imposition of a tariff. In contrast, domestic producers, since they do not pay the tariff, actually expand their output in

EXHIBIT 9   Impact of a tariff

Here we illustrate the impact of a tariff on sugar. In the absence of the tariff, the world price of sugar is P_w: U.S. consumers purchase Q_1 units (Q_{d1} from domestic producers plus $Q_1 - Q_{d1}$ from foreign producers). The tariff makes it more costly for Americans to purchase sugar from foreigners. Imports decline with the imposition of the tariff. A higher domestic price ($P_w + t$) of sugar and a lower consumption level (Q_2) result.

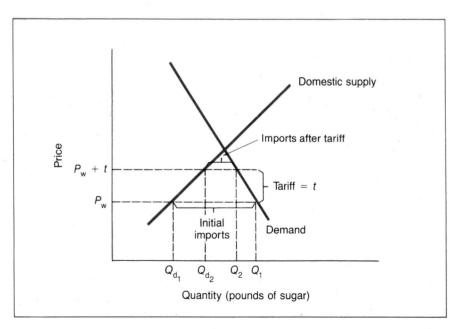

response to the higher market price. In effect, the tariff acts as a subsidy to domestic producers. It is financed by consumers, who as a result face higher prices.

The story does not end here. Since foreigners are unable to sell goods for which they are low-cost producers in the U.S. market, they acquire fewer dollars. Foreign demand for U.S. exports, products for which we are low-cost producers, declines because our trade restrictions have diminished the ability of foreigners to acquire the dollars necessary to buy our goods. Potential gains from specialization and trade go unrealized.

Import Quota: A specific quantity (or value) of a good that is permitted to be imported into a country during a given year.

An **import quota,** like a tariff, is designed to restrict foreign goods and protect domestic industries. A quota places a ceiling on the amount of a product that can be imported during a given period (typically a year). Many products, ranging from steel to brooms, are subject to import quotas.

Since quotas reduce the foreign supply to the domestic market, the price of quota-protected products is higher than that which would result from free trade. In many ways, quotas are more harmful than tariffs. With a quota, additional foreign supply is prohibited regardless of how low the prices of foreign products are. With a tariff, products are at least supplied to the domestic market if the cost advantage of foreign producers is sufficient to overcome the tariff.

Some Sound Arguments for Restrictions

There are three major, and at least partially valid, arguments for protecting certain domestic industries from foreign competitors.

1. National Defense Argument. Certain industries—aircraft, petroleum, and weapons, for example—are vital to national defense. A nation might want to protect such industries from foreign competitors so that a domestic supply of these materials would be available in case of an international conflict. Would we want to be entirely dependent on Arabian or Russian petroleum? Would complete dependence on French aircraft be wise? Most Americans would answer no, even if trade restrictions were required to preserve these domestic industries.

The national defense argument is sound; however, it can be abused. Relatively few industries are truly vital to our national defense. Partial reliance on foreign producers during peacetime may not weaken the capacity of certain domestic industries, particularly those that extract raw materials, to supply the nation's needs in case of war. When the merits of protecting a domestic industry are analyzed, the costs and benefits involved in the national defense argument must be weighed carefully.

2. The Industrial Diversity Argument. Economies that are largely dependent on the revenues from a few major export products or raw materials are characterized by instability. If a domestic economy specializes in the production of only one or two major goods, changes in world demand can exert a drastic influence on domestic economic conditions. Brazil's coffee-dominated economy is an example. Protection of domestic industries would encourage diversity. Clearly, this argument does not apply to the U.S. economy, which is already highly diversified.

3. The Infant-Industry Argument. The advocates of this view hold that new domestic industries should be protected from older, established foreign compet-

Many Americans believe that trade restrictions are necessary to protect U.S. workers from imported goods produced by cheap foreign labor. How can U.S. labor compete with Indian and Chinese workers receiving 50 cents an hour? The fallacy of this argument stems from a misunderstanding of both the source of high wages and the law of comparative advantage.

High *hourly wages* do not necessarily mean high *per unit labor cost.* Labor productivity must also be considered. For example, suppose that a U.S. steel worker receives an hourly wage rate of $12. A steel worker in India receives only $1.20 per hour. Given the capital and production methods used in the two countries, however, the U.S. worker produces 20 times as many tons of steel per worker-hour as the Indian worker. Be-cause of the higher productivity per worker-hour, per unit labor cost is actually lower in the United States than in India!

Labor in the United States possesses a high skill level and works with large amounts of capital equipment. These factors contribute to the high productivity and the high hourly wages of American workers. Similarly, low productivity per worker-hour is the primary reason for low wages in such countries as India and China.

However, the availability of capital and the high productivity of the U.S. labor force do not mean that we can produce everything at a lower opportunity cost than foreigners. Low-wage countries are likely to have a comparative advantage in the production of labor-intensive products. When other countries can produce wigs, watches, textile goods, sugar, coffee, and miniature radios more cheaply than domestic producers, we can gain from specialization and trade. Importation of these products allows us to free labor (and capital) resources so we in turn can export more wheat, feed grains, airplanes, and electrical equipment, products for which we are low-cost producers. The net result is a reallocation of U.S. workers away from industries in which they are inefficient (relative to foreign producers) to industries in which they are highly efficient.

If foreigners, even low-wage foreigners, will sell us products that are cheaper than the products we ourselves could produce, we can gain by using our resources to produce other things. Perhaps an extreme example will illustrate the point. Suppose that a foreign producer, perhaps a Santa Claus who pays workers little or nothing, were willing to supply us with free winter coats. Would it make sense to enact a tariff barrier to keep out the free coats? Of course not. Resources that were previously used to produce coats could now be freed to produce other goods. Output and the availability of goods would expand. The real wages of U.S. workers would rise. National defense aside, it makes no more sense to erect trade barriers to keep out cheap foreign goods than to keep out the free coats of a friendly, foreign Santa Claus.

itors. As the new industry matures, it will be able to stand on its own feet and compete effectively with foreign producers. The infant-industry argument has a long and somewhat notorious history. Alexander Hamilton used it to argue for the protection of early U.S. manufacturing. While it is clearly an argument for *temporary* protection, the protection, once granted, is often difficult to remove. Nearly a century ago, this argument was used to gain tariff protection for the young steel industry in the United States. Today, not only is this industry mature, but many believe that competitive pressures are less than vigorous. Yet public policy has failed to remove the tariff.

Trade Barriers and Jobs

Part of the popularity of trade restrictions stems from their ability to protect or create *easily identifiable jobs.* Whenever foreign competitors begin to make inroads into markets that have traditionally been supplied by domestic producers, the outcry for "protection to save jobs" is sure to be raised. Political entrepreneurs recognize the potential gain from a protectionist policy and respond accordingly.

The recent history of the automobile industry in the United States illustrates this point. During the 1970s, imported automobiles gained a larger and larger share of the U.S. market. There were several reasons for these gains. High wages in the U.S. auto industry, improved efficiency of foreign producers, excessive government regulation of the domestic auto industry, and failure of U.S. producers to shift to small cars as gasoline prices soared were all contributing factors. The increased competition from imports caused both management and labor to seek trade restrictions.

The Reagan administration, firmly on record as favoring free trade, was reluctant to request either tariffs or quotas. Nonetheless, the administration bargained with the Japanese government, which eventually agreed to restrict "voluntarily" the number of Japanese automobiles sold in the U.S. market to 1.6 million. As is the case with quotas, these voluntary restrictions will result in higher consumer prices for automobiles. The maximum price that 1.6 million Japanese automobiles can command in the U.S. market will be the same whether they are subject to a quota or to restrictions imposed by the Japanese government. There is no reason to believe that Japanese firms and car dealers will charge less than a market equilibrium price for the 1.6 million cars. In addition, the import restrictions will lessen competition in the U.S. market, reducing the pressure on U.S. producers and workers to compete effectively.

The restrictions will also exert a secondary effect that usually goes unnoticed. Since the Japanese will be selling fewer automobiles in the U.S. market, they will earn fewer dollars with which to purchase grains, lumber, chemicals, and other U.S. export products. Workers in export industries will be hurt as the Japanese demand for their products declines. Jobs in these industries will be destroyed. Interestingly, the wage rates in most of these export industries are approximately half the wage rates of the automobile workers who will be helped by the restrictions.

In the long run, trade restrictions such as quotas, tariffs, and allegedly voluntary limitations can neither create nor destroy jobs. Jobs protected by import restrictions will be offset by jobs destroyed in export industries. The choice is not whether automobiles (or some other product) will be produced in the United States or Japan. The real question is (a) whether our resources will be used to produce automobiles and other products for which we are a high opportunity cost producer or (b) whether the resources will be used for agriculture, high-technology manufactured goods, and other products for which we are a low-cost producer.

What about industries that are long-time recipients of protection? Of course, sudden and complete removal of trade barriers would harm producers and workers. It would be costly to effect an immediate transfer of the protected resources to other areas and industries. Gradual removal of such barriers would minimize the costs of relocation and eliminate the shock effect. The government might also cushion the burden by subsidizing the retraining and relocation costs of displaced workers.

Protection of Special Interests

Even when trade restrictions promote inefficiency and harm economic welfare, political entrepreneurs may be able to reap political gain from their enactment. Those harmed by a protectionist policy for industry X will bear individually a small and difficult-to-identify cost. Consumers who will pay higher prices for the products of a protected industry are an unorganized group. Most of them will not associate the higher product prices with the protectionist policy. Similarly, numerous export producers (and their employees) will *individually* be harmed only slightly. The rational ignorance effect implies that those harmed by trade restrictions are likely to be uninformed and unconcerned about our trade policy.

In contrast, special interest groups—specific industries, unions, and regions—will be highly concerned with the protection of their industries. They will be ready to aid political entrepreneurs who support their views and penalize those who do not. Clearly, vote-seeking politicians will be sensitive to the special interest views.

Often, there will be a conflict between sound economics and good politics on trade restriction issues. Real-world public policy will, of course, reflect the politics of the situation.

Export Taxes, International Trade, and the OPEC Cartel

The law of comparative advantage explains why the *joint* output of nations is maximized by free trade. What about the economic welfare of a single nation? Can *one* of the trading partners gain if it imposes certain trade restrictions? Unilateral gain is possible if certain conditions are met. First, if an exporting nation is to gain from restrictions, it must be able to eliminate (or collude with) all other sources of substantial supply. An importing nation will simply buy from another seller if a small seller acts independently. Second, the demand of importers for the product must be inelastic, preferably highly inelastic. If the product demand is elastic, the bargaining position of the exporter will be substantially diminished. Third, the producers must be able to alter the quantity supplied at a low cost. This condition implies the supply curve of the exporter is elastic.

Exhibit 10 illustrates the mechanics of unilateral action when the demand of the importing country is inelastic and the supply of the exporting nation (or cartel of nations) is elastic. Under these circumstances, the exporting nation can gain by imposing an export tax on the product. The total revenue derived from the importing country will actually increase, even though a smaller *quantity* of the product is sold. The burden of the export tax falls on the importing nations. Note that the price of the product does not fall very much (from *AD* to *AP*), since the supply is elastic.[3] Like a monopolist, an exporting nation can gain by restricting output and raising prices if the demand of importers is inelastic.

This analysis helps us understand why OPEC nations were able to gain by substantially raising the price (or the export tax) on crude oil in the mid-1970s. Since the demand of the oil-importing nations was highly inelastic, at least in the short run, the primary burden of the high crude-oil prices (or export taxes) fell on the importers. The OPEC strategy would not have worked if all of the major oil-exporting nations had not cooperated. Suppose that a single country, Venezuela, for example, had imposed a heavy export tax on oil in 1970. Oil-importing nations would simply have purchased crude oil from other nations. Thus, it was necessary for the oil-exporting nations to form a cartel if their strategy was to work.

EXHIBIT 10   Gains from an export tax when demand is inelastic relative to supply

If the demand by foreigners for an export product of a nation is inelastic (and the foreign supply is elastic), a nation (or cartel of nations) can obtain unilateral gains if it imposes a tax on the export product. As illustrated here, after the imposition of tax *t*, the total revenue derived from the foreign consumers of the product increases from *ABCD* to *AB′C′D′*, *even though the number of units exported declines.* The primary burden of the tax falls on the foreign consumers, since the demand for the export product is inelastic relative to supply.

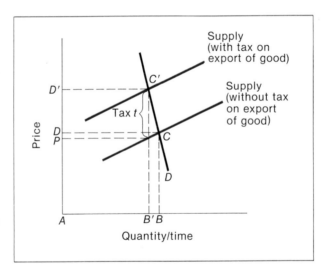

[3]On the other hand, if the demand of the importing country were elastic and the supply of the exporting country were inelastic, the burden of an export tax would fall on the producers of the exported product. The price (including the tax) of the product to foreign consumers would not rise substantially, whereas the price (less the tax) received by the producers of the exported product would decline sharply. When importing nations can produce the good domestically (or obtain it from another source) at a cost only slightly higher than the cost of importing, the demand for the exported product will be elastic. Under these circumstances, the burden of an export tax falls primarily on the producers of the exported product. As an exercise, construct a graph illustrating this case.

Many Americans have voiced support for the imposition by the United States of an export tax on wheat (or other steps that would raise the export price of wheat) as a means of retaliating against the oil price-fixing policies of OPEC. Since the demand of OPEC nations for U.S. wheat is likely to be elastic—there are many good substitutes for U.S. wheat—economic analysis suggests that such a strategy would be ineffective.

There are risks associated with this strategy of imposing an export tax (or forming a cartel of exporters). First, *new entrants* must be prevented from undercutting the cartel price if it is substantially higher than the competitive level. In the case of petroleum, Nature greatly reduced the difficulty of this task. Second, high prices induce importers to search for and use substitutes. With time, the importing nations develop substitutes and discover ways to reduce their consumption of the more expensive product. Eventually, as even OPEC discovered in the early 1980s, this process may significantly reduce the amount demanded from the cartel. Third, the theory of oligopoly indicates that there is an incentive for members of a cartel to cheat. As market conditions become less favorable to the cartel, the stability of the collusive arrangement tends to decline. Finally, there is the danger of retaliation by the importing nations. Eventually, they may impose taxes (or other restrictions) on goods exported to those nations that imposed the original export tax (or on member nations of an exporting cartel).

Although trade restrictions can sometimes lead to gain for one of the trading partners, the *joint* economic opportunities available to the participants are reduced. Artificial scarcity stemming from monopoly power always leads to economic waste. The consumers of the product—the importing nations—use valuable resources to search for substitutes and turn to alternatives that have a higher opportunity cost. An inefficient use of resources results, and the *joint* output of trading nations is diminished.

LOOKING AHEAD

There are many similarities between trade within national borders and trade across national boundaries. However, there is also a major difference. In addition to the exchange of goods for money, trade across national borders generally involves the exchange of national currencies. The next chapter deals with the financial arrangements under which international trade is conducted.

CHAPTER LEARNING OBJECTIVES

1 The volume of international trade has grown rapidly in recent decades. In the early 1980s, approximately 16 percent of the world's output was sold in a different country than that in which it was produced.

2 The trade sector comprises approximately 9 percent of the U.S. GNP. More than half of all U.S. trade is with developed countries, primarily Canada, Japan, and nations of the European Economic Community.

3 Trade between nations enables each to specialize in the production of those goods for which it has a comparative advantage. Through specialization and trade, aggregate output can be expanded. Mutual gain accrues to the trading partners.

4 Exports and imports are closely linked. The exports of a nation are the primary source of purchasing power used to import goods.

5 Relative to the no-trade alternative, international exchange and specialization result in lower prices for products that are imported and higher domestic prices for products that are exported. However, the net effect is an expansion in the consumption alternatives available to a nation.

6 The application of a tariff, quota, or other import restriction to a product reduces the amount of the product that foreigners supply to the domestic market. As a result of diminished supply, consumers face higher prices for the protected product. Essentially,

import restrictions are subsidies to producers (and workers) in protected industries at the expense of (a) consumers and (b) producers (and workers) in export industries. Restrictions reduce the ability of domestic producers to specialize in those areas for which their comparative advantage is greatest.

7 High wages do not necessarily mean high labor cost. Productivity must also be considered. The law of comparative advantage explains why the United States can benefit from trade—even trade with low-wage countries.

8 National defense, industrial diversity, and the infant-industry arguments can be used to justify trade restrictions for specific industries under certain conditions. However, it is clear that the power of special interest groups and ignorance about the harmful effects offer the major explanations for real-world protectionist public policy.

9 In the long run, trade restrictions do not create jobs. A decline in our imports from other nations leads to a reduction in those nations' purchasing power and thus a reduced demand for our export products. Jobs protected by import restrictions are offset by jobs destroyed in export industries. Since this result of restrictions often goes unnoticed, their political popularity is understandable. Nonetheless, the restrictions are inefficient, since they lead to the loss of potential gains from specialization and exchange.

10 An exporting nation (or group of nations) can gain by restricting output and raising the price of a product if the demand for its exports is inelastic and the supply is elastic. Under these circumstances, the burden of an export tax (or the price increases of an export cartel) falls on those importing the product. Trade restrictions of this variety, like other protectionist policies, result in a reduction in the *joint* output of the trading partners.

THE ECONOMIC WAY OF THINKING—DISCUSSION QUESTIONS

1 Suppose that at the time of the Civil War the United States had been divided into two countries and that through the years no trade existed between the two. How would the standard of living in the "divided" United States have been affected? Explain.

2 Do you think that the United States could benefit if all barriers to trade among North American nations were eliminated? Would Canada gain? Mexico? Why or why not?

3 Can both (a) and (b) be true? Explain.
(a) "Tariffs and import quotas promote economic inefficiency and reduce the real income of a nation. Economic analysis suggests that nations can gain by eliminating trade restrictions."
(b) "Economic analysis suggests that there is good reason to expect trade restrictions to exist in the real world."

4 "Tariffs and quotas are necessary to protect the high wages of the American worker." Do you agree or disagree? Why?

5 Suppose that the United States and other oil-importing nations levied a tariff on crude oil that was equal to the import price (approximately $34 per barrel in 1982) minus $20 per barrel. Thus, an increase in the import price (above $20 per barrel) would automatically raise the tariff by an equal amount. What impact would this policy have on (a) U.S. consumption of foreign oil, (b) the elasticity of demand for foreign oil as seen by foreign producers, and (c) the incentive of the international oil cartel (OPEC) to raise its price for oil?

6 What's Wrong with This Economic Experiment?

A researcher hypothesizes that higher tariffs on imported automobiles will cause total employment in the United States to increase. Automobile tariffs are raised and the following year employment in the U.S. auto industry increases by 100,000, compared to a three-year annual increase of 50,000 before the higher tariff legislation was passed. The researcher concludes that the higher tariffs on imported automobiles increased total domestic employment by creating approximately 50,000 jobs in the U.S. automobile industry.

32

INTERNATIONAL FINANCE AND THE FOREIGN EXCHANGE MARKET

Since World War II, the volume of international exchange has grown rapidly. As we discussed in the last chapter, specialization and trade enable the countries of the world to expand their joint output, since the production of each good is undertaken by those producers who are most efficient. Like voluntary exchange within domestic markets, voluntary exchange between persons of different nations is mutually advantageous to the trading partners. Since international trade fosters a more efficient use of resources, the world has benefited substantially from its growth.

International trade is complicated by the fact that it generally involves two different currencies. Farmers in the United States want dollars, not some foreign currency, when they sell their wheat. Therefore, foreign purchasers must exchange their currency for dollars before they buy U.S. wheat. Similarly, French wine makers want to be paid in francs, not dollars. Therefore, U.S. importers must exchange dollars for francs when they purchase French wines (or French exporters must obtain francs before they pay the wine makers).

In this chapter, we analyze how international currencies are linked and how the rates for their exchange are determined. Between 1944 and 1971, most nations linked their currencies to a fixed exchange rate system. The price of each national currency was fixed with respect to other currencies. Since many businesspeople and some economists favor a return to this type of system, we will analyze its operation. Since 1971, most Western nations have permitted the value of their monetary unit relative to other currencies to be determined largely by market forces. We will also discuss the efficacy of this flexible exchange rate system.

---

[1]Donald Kohn, "Interdependence, Exchange Rates, Flexibility and National Economics," Federal Reserve Bank of Kansas City *Monthly Review* (April 1975), p. 3.

EXCHANGE RATES AND THE PRICE OF FOREIGN GOODS

Suppose that you own a shoe store in the United States and are preparing to place an order for sandals from a manufacturer. You can purchase the sandals from a domestic manufacturer and pay for them with dollars. Alternatively, you can buy them from a Mexican manufacturer, in which case they must be paid for in pesos because the employees of the Mexican manufacturer must be paid with pesos. If you buy from the Mexican firm, either you will have to change dollars into pesos at a bank and send them to the Mexican producer, or the Mexican will have to go to a bank and change your dollar check into pesos. In either case, purchasing the Mexican sandals will involve an exchange of dollars for pesos.

The Mexican producer sells sandals for 100 pesos per pair. How can you determine whether the price is high or low? In order to compare the price of the sandals produced by the Mexican firm with the price of domestically produced sandals, you must know the exchange rate between the dollar and the peso. The **exchange rate** is simply the price of one national currency (the peso, for example) in terms of another national currency (such as the U.S. dollar). Exchange rates enable consumers in one country to translate the prices of foreign goods into units of their own currency. If it takes 2 cents to obtain 1 peso, 0.02 is the dollar–peso exchange rate. When 2 cents exchange for 1 peso, how many dollars will it take to buy a pair of Mexican sandals selling for 200 pesos? The dollar price of the Mexican sandals will simply be 2 cents multiplied by 200, or $4.

Suppose that the dollar–peso exchange rate is 0.02 and that you decide to buy 200 pairs of sandals from the Mexican manufacturer at 200 pesos ($4) per pair. You will need 40,000 pesos in order to pay the Mexican manufacturer. If you contact an American bank that handles exchange rate transactions and write the bank a check for $800 ($0.02 multiplied by 40,000), it will supply the 40,000 pesos. The bank will typically charge you a small fee for handling the transactions.

Note that by importing the Mexican sandals, you supply dollars to the **foreign exchange market,** a market for the trading of international currencies. On the other hand, if a Mexican consumer purchased U.S. export products, automobiles made in Detroit, for example, the transaction would generate a demand for dollars on the exchange market.

Exhibit 1 presents data on the exchange rate between the dollar and selected foreign currencies for April of 1979 and 1982. Under the current flexible system, the exchange rate between currencies is constantly changing. We will investigate the determinants of exchange rates in detail, but first we must develop a better understanding of the factors underlying the exchange rate market.

Exchange Rate: The domestic price of one unit of foreign currency. For example, if it takes 50 cents to purchase one German mark, the dollar–mark exchange rate is 0.50.

Foreign Exchange Market The market in which the currencies of different countries are bought and sold.

BALANCE OF PAYMENTS AND INTERNATIONAL EXCHANGES

Just as countries calculate their gross national product so that they have a general idea of the domestic level of production, most countries also calculate their balance of international payments in order to keep track of their trans-

EXHIBIT 1 Foreign exchange rates between the U.S. dollar and selected foreign currencies—April 1979 and April 1982

Foreign Currency	Cents Required to Purchase One Unit of the Foreign Currency	
	April 1979	April 1982
Australian dollar	110.85	105.37
Canadian dollar	87.24	81.82
French franc	22.97	16.04
German mark	52.75	41.81
Italian lira	0.12	0.08
Japanese yen	0.46	0.41
English pound	207.34	178.25
Mexican peso	4.38	2.17

Federal Reserve Bulletin and *Wall Street Journal.*

Balance of Payments: A summary of all economic transactions between a country and all other countries for a specific time period—usually a year. The balance of payments account reflects all payments and liabilities to foreigners (debits) and all payments and obligations (credits) received from foreigners.

actions with other nations. The **balance of payments** account is a periodic report that summarizes the flow of economic transactions with foreigners.

Balance of payments accounts are kept according to bookkeeping principles. Any transaction that supplies the nation's domestic currency (or creates a demand for foreign currency) in the foreign exchange market is recorded as a debit item in the balance of payments account. A transaction that creates a demand for the nation's currency (or a supply of foreign currency) on the foreign exchange market is recorded as a credit. Imports are an example of a debit item; exports are an example of a credit item.

The balance of payments account attempts to pinpoint the reasons for transactions with foreigners. The U.S. account shows that the volume of payments made to foreigners (supplying dollars to the foreign exchange market) for such things as merchandise imports, transportation of goods, services purchased by U.S. tourists abroad, and U.S. investment in other countries. Similarly, it shows the flow of payments to the United States from foreigners for such items as merchandise exports, goods transported in U.S. vessels, spending of foreign tourists in the United States, and foreign investment in the United States.

The balance of payments transactions can be grouped into three basic categories: current account, capital account, and official reserve account. Let us take a look at each of these.

Current Account Transactions

Current Account: The record of all transactions with foreign nations that involve the exchange of merchandise goods and services or unilateral gifts.

All payments (and gifts) that are related to the purchase or sale of goods and services during the designated period are included in the **current account.** In general, there are three major types of current account transactions: the exchange of merchandise goods, the exchange of services, and unilateral transfers.

Merchandise Trade Transactions. The export and import of merchandise goods comprise by far the largest portion of a nation's balance of payments account. As Exhibit 2 shows, in 1980 the United States imported $249.3 billion of merchandise goods and exported only $224.0 billion. When Americans import goods from abroad, they also supply dollars to the foreign exchange market. Imports are recorded as debits in the balance of payments accounts. In contrast,

EXHIBIT 2   The flow of dollars to and from the exchange market—1980

Debit—These Transactions Generate a Demand for Foreign Currency While Supplying Dollars to the Foreign Exchange Market (Billions of Dollars)		Credit—These Transactions Supply Foreign Currency While Generating a Demand for Dollars on the Foreign Exchange Market (Billions of Dollars)		Deficit (−) or Surplus (Billions of Dollars)	
Current account					
Merchandise imports[a]	249.3	Merchandise exports[a]	224.0	Balance of trade	− 25.3
Service imports	84.6	Service exports	120.7		
Net unilateral transfers	7.1			Balance on current	
Total	341.0	Total	344.7	account	3.7
Capital account					
U.S. investment abroad	18.5	Foreign investment in the United States	10.9		
Loans to foreigners	58.1	Loans from foreigners	70.2[b]		
				Balance on current and capital accounts	8.2
Reserve account	8.2				

[a]Military shipments are included in this category.

[b]The statistical discrepancy is included in this category.

U.S. Department of Commerce.

Balance of Trade: The difference between the value of merchandise exports and the value of merchandise imports for a nation. The balance of trade is only one component of a nation's total balance of payments.

when U.S. producers export their products, foreigners demand dollars on the exchange market in order to pay for the U.S. exports. Exports are the credit item.

The difference between the value of a country's merchandise exports and the value of its merchandise imports is known as the **balance of trade.** If the value of a country's merchandise exports falls short of (exceeds) the value of its merchandise imports, it is said to have a balance of trade deficit (surplus). In 1980, the United States ran a balance of trade deficit of $25.3 billion. Although trade deficit has generally been given a negative connotation by the news media, it is not clear whether a country receiving more goods from foreigners than it exports necessarily finds itself in an unfavorable position. The negative view of a trade deficit undoubtedly stems from its impact on the value of the dollar on the foreign exchange market. *Other things constant,* a U.S. trade deficit implies that Americans are supplying more dollars to the exchange market than foreigners are demanding for purchase of American goods. If the trade deficit were the only factor influencing the value of the dollar on the exchange market, one could anticipate a decline in the foreign exchange value of the U.S. currency. However, several other factors also affect the supply of and demand for the dollar on the exchange market.

Service Exports and Imports.   The export and import of "invisible services," as they are sometimes called, also exert an important influence on the foreign exchange market. The export of insurance, transportation, and banking services generates a demand for dollars by foreigners just as the export of merchandise does. A French business that is insured with an American company will demand dollars with which to pay its premiums. When foreigners travel in the United States or transport cargo on American ships, they will demand dollars with which to pay for these services. Similarly, income earned by U.S. investments abroad will cause dollars to flow from foreigners to Americans. Thus, these service exports are entered as credits on the current account.

On the other hand, the import of services from foreigners expands the supply of dollars to the exchange market. Therefore, service imports are entered on the balance of payments accounts as debit items. Travel abroad by U.S. citizens, the shipment of goods on foreign carriers, and income earned by foreigners on U.S. investments are all debit items, since they supply dollars to the exchange market.

These service transactions are substantial. As Exhibit 2 indicates, in 1980, the U.S. service exports were $120.7 billion, compared to service imports of $84.6 billion.

Unilateral Transfers.   Monetary gifts to foreigners, such as a grant to a foreign government or a present to one's ancestors in South Korea, supply dollars to the exchange market. Thus, these gifts are debit items in the balance of payments accounts. Monetary gifts to Americans from foreigners are credit items. Gifts in kind are more complex. When products are given to foreigners, goods flow abroad, but there is no offsetting influx of foreign currency—that is, a demand for dollars. Balance of payments accountants handle such transactions as though the United States had supplied the dollars with which to purchase the direct grants made to foreigners. Thus, these items are also entered as debits. Because the U.S. government (and private U.S. citizens) made larger grants to foreigners than we received, net unilateral transfers of $7.1 billion were entered as a debit item on the current account for 1980.

Balance on Current Account: The import–export balance of goods and services plus net private and government transfers. If a nation's export of goods and services exceeds (is less than) the nation's import of goods and services plus net unilateral transfers to foreigners, a current account surplus (deficit) is present.

Balance on Current Account.   The difference between (a) the value of a country's exports of goods and services and (b) the value of its imports of goods and services plus net unilateral transfers is known as the **balance on current account.** This is a summary statistic for all current account transactions. As with the balance of trade, if the value of the exports is less than (exceeds) the value of the imports plus the unilateral transfers, the country is said to be experiencing a deficit (surplus) on current account transactions. In 1980, the United States ran a $3.7 billion surplus on current account transactions.

Capital Account Transactions

Capital account transactions are composed of (a) direct investments by Americans in real assets abroad (or by foreigners in the United States) and (b) loans to and from foreigners. If a U.S. investor purchases a shoe factory in Mexico, the Mexican seller will want to be paid in pesos. The U.S. investor will supply dollars (and demand pesos) on the foreign exchange market. Thus, U.S. investment abroad is entered on the balance of payments accounts as a debit item. On the other hand, foreign investment in the United States creates a demand for dollars on the exchange market. Therefore, it is entered as a credit.

Investment abroad can be thought of as the import of a bond or ownership right. Importing ownership of a financial (or real) asset from abroad has the same effect on the balance of payments as importing goods from abroad. Therefore, both are recorded as debits. Similarly, in a sense, we are exporting bonds and ownership of capital when foreigners invest in the United States. Thus, these transactions enter as a credit.

As for domestic markets, many international transactions are conducted on credit. When a U.S. banker loans $100,000 to a foreign entrepreneur for the purchase of U.S. exports, in effect the banker is importing a foreign bond. Since the transaction supplies dollars to the exchange market, it is recorded as a debit. On the other hand, when Americans borrow from abroad, they are exporting bonds. Since this transaction creates either a demand for dollars on the part of the foreign banker (in order to supply the loanable funds) or a supply of foreign currency, it is recorded as a credit in the U.S. balance of payments account.

Official Reserve Account Transactions

Special Drawing Rights: Supplementary reserves, in the form of accounting entries, established by the International Monetary Fund (also called "paper gold"). Like gold and foreign currency reserves, they can be used to make payments on international accounts. They were allocated in accordance with the initial reserve quota commitments of IMF member countries.

Governments maintain balances of foreign currencies, gold, and **special drawing rights** (SDRs) with the International Monetary Fund, a type of international central bank established in 1944. A government can finance a deficit of purchases relative to sales by drawing on its reserves. Similarly, countries running a surplus may want to build up their reserve balances of foreign currencies or other reserve assets. During the 1944–1971 period of fixed exchange rates, these reserve transactions were highly significant. Countries experiencing balance of payments difficulties were forced to draw on their reserves in order to maintain their fixed exchange rate. Countries that were selling more to foreigners than foreigners were buying from them accumulated the currencies of other nations.

Under a system of **floating** or **flexible exchange rates,** rather than use reserves to deal with an imbalance of payments, countries generally permit a rise or fall in the foreign exchange value of their currency to bring about equilibrium.[2]

Excess Purchases Abroad Relative to Sales

Flexible Exchange Rates: Exchange rates that are determined by the market forces of supply and demand. They are sometimes called "floating exchange rates."

If a nation buys more goods, services, and real assets from foreigners than it sells to them, it must cover this excess of purchases compared to sales in precisely the same way in which an individual would do so. It must borrow, or sell ownership rights to foreigners. As Exhibit 2 shows, including unilateral transfers, U.S. citizens expended $341.0 billion on goods and services from foreigners. In addition, $18.5 billion was expended on direct investment abroad. Therefore, U.S. citizens purchased a total of $359.5 billion of goods, services, and real assets from foreigners in 1980. On the other hand, Americans sold $355.6 billion of goods, services, and real assets to foreigners. In order to fill the gap between their expenditures and receipts, U.S. citizens (and the government) were net borrowers from foreigners in 1980.

THE DETERMINATION OF EXCHANGE RATES

Appreciation: An increase in the value of a domestic currency relative to foreign currencies. An appreciation increases the purchasing power of the domestic currency over *foreign goods.*

As Exhibit 1 illustrates, exchange rates, like other prices, rise and fall as market conditions change. Between 1979 and 1982, the exchange rate value of the dollar appreciated against the major foreign currencies. An **appreciation** in the value of a nation's currency means that fewer units of the currency are now required to purchase one unit of a foreign currency. For example, if the number of cents required to purchase a German mark decreases from 50 to 40, the

---

[2]Since double-entry bookkeeping procedures are used in balance of payments accounting, the debits and credits on current, capital, and reserve accounts must be in balance overall, except for statistical discrepancies.

dollar has appreciated in value relative to the mark. West German goods are now less expensive to Americans. For example, a Volkswagen priced at 20,000 marks could initially be purchased for $10,000. After the appreciation, the dollar price of the Volkswagen to American consumers has decreased to $8000.

The direction of change in the prices that West Germans pay for American goods is just the opposite. The appreciation of the U.S. dollar in terms of the mark is the same thing as a depreciation in the mark relative to the dollar. A **depreciation** makes foreign goods more expensive, since it decreases the number of units of the foreign currency that can be purchased with a unit of domestic currency.

What determines the exchange rate between two currencies? In order to simplify the analysis, let us assume that the United States and Mexico are the only two countries in the world. The exchange rate between the U.S. dollar and the Mexican peso is simply a price. Just as the forces of supply and demand determine other prices, they also determine the dollar price of the peso in the absence of government intervention.

Broadly speaking, the supply of pesos (and the demand for dollars) on the foreign exchange market is created by the purchase of U.S. goods by Mexicans. When Mexicans purchase goods, services, and assets (either real or financial) from Americans, they supply pesos on (and demand dollars from) the foreign exchange market. On the other hand, the demand for pesos originates from the demand of Americans for Mexican goods. When U.S. residents purchase goods, services, and assets from Mexicans, they demand pesos on (and supply dollars to) the foreign exchange market in order to pay for these items.

As Exhibit 3 shows, when the exchange rate between the two currencies is in equilibrium, the amount of pesos supplied by the Mexicans in order to buy items from Americans is equal to the amount of pesos demanded by Americans in order to purchase items from Mexicans. What would happen if Americans wanted to buy more goods from Mexicans than Mexicans wanted to sell to U.S. residents? An excess demand for pesos would result, causing the peso to appreciate. The increase in the dollar price of the peso would make Mexican goods more expensive for Americans. For example, if the price of the peso rose from 2 cents to 3 cents, the cost *to U.S. residents* of coffee, shoes, oil, and all other items purchased from Mexicans would rise by 50 percent. At the higher price, Americans would purchase fewer goods from Mexican producers.

Depreciation: **A reduction in the value of a domestic currency relative to foreign currencies. A depreciation reduces the purchasing power of the domestic currency over** *foreign goods.*

EXHIBIT 3   Equilibrium in the foreign exchange market

In equilibrium, the dollar price of a Mexican peso would equalize the demand for and the supply of pesos in the foreign exhange market.

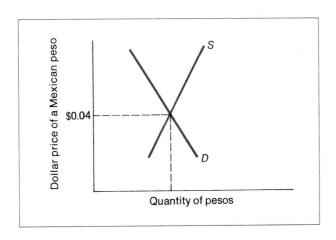

Although the higher price of the peso (in terms of dollars) would cause Americans to purchase fewer Mexican goods, it would make U.S. exports cheaper for Mexicans. For example, a $9000 American automobile would cost Mexican consumers 450,000 pesos if 1 peso exchanged for 2 cents, but it would cost only 300,000 pesos if each peso exchanged for 3 cents. Thus, a reduction in the peso price of American automobiles would induce Mexican consumers to purchase a larger quantity.

If there were an excess supply of dollars in the foreign exchange market relative to pesos, the appreciation in the peso would eventually restore equilibrium, provided that the U.S. demand for imports (and supply of exports) was elastic. As the peso appreciated, Americans would purchase smaller quantities of the now more expensive Mexican goods, and Mexicans would purchase more of the cheaper American products. This would be the "quantity effect" of the peso's appreciation. However, the appreciation would also have a "price effect." The price effect would actually cause Americans to spend more on Mexican imports (and Mexicans to spend less on U.S. exports) because it would now take more dollars to purchase Mexican goods (and fewer pesos to purchase U.S. goods).

If the exchange market is to move toward equilibrium, the quantity effect must more than offset the price effect. In other words, using our example of Mexico and the United States, the percent reduction in the quantity of goods purchased from Mexico must exceed the percent appreciation in the peso. Similarly, the percent increase in the quantity of American goods purchased by Mexicans must exceed the percent reduction in the peso price of American goods as a result of the appreciation. These conditions will be met if the American demand for Mexican goods (and the Mexican demand for American goods) is elastic.

Time and the Adjustment Process

Since Mexican- and American-produced goods are excellent substitutes for one another, there is good reason to expect that the American demand for Mexican goods (and the Mexican demand for American goods) will be highly elastic *with time.*

However, in the short run, this may not be true. It will take time for American consumers to find alternatives to the higher-priced Mexican products and for Mexican consumers to adjust their consumption and begin purchasing more of the now cheaper American goods. Therefore, an appreciation in the peso may not *immediately* eliminate the excess demand for pesos (and excess supply of dollars) on the foreign exchange market. In fact, *initially* the situation may even worsen. However, with time, the American demand for Mexican goods (and the Mexican demand for American goods) will almost always be highly elastic. Thus, the appreciation in the peso will eventually eliminate the excess demand for pesos and restore equilibrium to the exchange market.[3]

If Mexicans purchase more goods, services, and assets from the United States than Americans buy from Mexico, there will be an excess supply of pesos

---

[3]International trade economists refer to the path of the exchange rate adjustment as the J curve. Initially, a depreciation of a currency, the dollar for example, may actually cause the exchange rate value of the dollar to decline even more, since the excess supply of the currency may expand. With time, however, the quantity effect will begin to dominate, and the downward trend in the exchange rate value of the dollar will turn upward and complete the mapping of the J curve path.

(and an excess demand for dollars). As a result, the peso will depreciate. The depreciation in the peso relative to the dollar will make U.S. goods more expensive to Mexicans and Mexican products cheaper to American consumers. As Mexicans purchase fewer American goods (and Americans a larger quantity of Mexican products), the excess supply of pesos will *eventually* be eliminated. As in the case of appreciation, time will be important. The initial response to the depreciation in the peso may be limited, but with time, the demand for foreign goods by both Mexicans and Americans will become more and more elastic. Thus, the depreciation will eventually restore equilibrium.

What would happen if a nation's demand for imports and the supply of exports were inelastic, even in the long run? In such a case, the foreign exchange value of the nation's currency would be vulnerable to large fluctuations, which would make it difficult for international trade to take place without some sort of intervention in the foreign exchange market by governments. This kind of inelasticity rarely occurs in large industrial nations but is found occasionally in small nations with poorly diversified industrial production. The presence of such inelasticity is an argument for a nation's adoption of fixed exchange rates, which are described later in this chapter.

Changing Market Conditions and Exchange Rates

When exchange rates are free to fluctuate, the market value of a nation's currency will appreciate and depreciate in response to changing market conditions. What are the major factors that cause exchange rates to alter?

Changes in the Value of Exports and Imports.   If the value of a nation's exports increases relative to that of its imports, the nation's currency will tend to appreciate. Suppose that the demand for a nation's exports increases because of changing tastes and/or rising incomes abroad. This will lead to both higher prices and expanding sales in export industries. The value of the nation's exports will increase. An increase in the demand for a country's export products will simultaneously generate an expansion in demand for the nation's currency, causing it to appreciate. Of course, the appreciation will stimulate imports and discourage exports, thereby restoring equilibrium in the exchange market.

In contrast, if the domestic demand for foreign imports increases, the nation's currency will tend to depreciate. Exhibit 4 illustrates the impact of an increase in the American demand for Volkswagens on the dollar–mark exchange rate. Americans seeking to purchase more Volkswagens will also demand more marks with which to pay for them. The demand for marks (and the supply of dollars on the world market) will increase, causing the dollar price of the mark to rise. This appreciation in the value of the mark (depreciation in the value of the dollar) will reduce the incentive of Americans to import German goods while increasing the incentive of West Germans to purchase U.S. exports. These two forces will restore equilibrium in the exchange market at a new, higher dollar price of the mark.

Differential Rates of Inflation.   Other things constant, domestic inflation will cause a nation's currency to depreciate on the exchange market, whereas deflation will result in appreciation. Suppose that prices in the United States rise by 50 percent, while our trading partners are experiencing stable prices. The domestic inflation will cause U.S. consumers to increase their demand for im-

EXHIBIT 4   Demanding more
Volkswagens . . . and marks

Suppose that high gasoline
prices induce U.S. consumers to
purchase more Volkswagens.
The increase in imports from
West Germany will cause the
demand for marks to increase.
The mark will appreciate relative to the dollar.

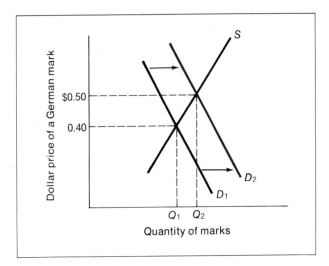

ported goods (and foreign currency). In turn, the inflated domestic prices will
cause foreigners to reduce their purchases of U.S. goods, thereby reducing the
supply of foreign currency to the exchange market. Thus, as Exhibit 5 illustrates,
the American demand for a foreign currency such as the mark will increase
(because German goods are now cheaper), whereas the supply of marks will
decline (because U.S. goods are more expensive to West German consumers).
This combination of forces will cause the dollar to depreciate relative to the
mark. With time, the depreciation in the dollar will stimulate the export of
U.S. goods to West Germany and discourage the importation of German
products, thereby restoring equilibrium in the exchange market.

What if prices in both West Germany and the United States are rising
at an annual rate of 10 percent? The prices of imports (and exports) will remain
unchanged relative to domestically produced goods. Equal rates of inflation in
each of the countries will *not* cause the value of exports to change relative to
imports. Thus, identical rates of inflation will not disturb an equilibrium in
the exchange market. Inflation contributes to the depreciation of a nation's

**EXHIBIT 5   Inflation with
flexible exchange rates**

If prices were stable in West
Germany while the United States
was experiencing domestic inflation, the demand for German
products (and marks) would
increase, whereas U.S. exports
to West Germany would de-
cline, causing the supply of
marks to fall. The dollar would
thus depreciate relative to
the mark.

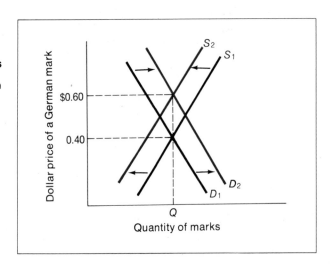

currency only when a country's rate of inflation is more rapid than that of its trading partners.

Changes in Domestic Interest Rates.   Short-term financial investments will be quite sensitive to changes in interest rates. International loanable funds will tend to move toward areas where the expected rate of return (after compensation for differences in risk) is highest. An increase in real interest rates—that is, interest rates adjusted for the expected rate of inflation—will attract foreign capital, causing the nation's currency to appreciate on the exchange market. For example, an increase in real interest rates in the United States would stimulate British, French, and West German investors to demand dollars and loan their domestic currency to U.S. borrowers. These movements of capital would cause the dollar to appreciate relative to the British pound, French franc, and German mark. A fall in domestic interest rates would, of course, have just the opposite effect—inducing loanable funds to move from the United States and causing the dollar to depreciate relative to other currencies.

Changes in Foreign Interest Rates.   When real interest rates rise in Western European countries, short-term financial investors will exchange dollars for pounds, francs, and marks so that they can take advantage of the improved earning opportunity in the European market. Thus, high real interest rates abroad will increase the demand for foreign currencies and increase the supply

"It's nice to see some people still appreciate the value of a dollar."

of dollars. A depreciation in the dollar relative to the currencies of countries experiencing the high real interest rates will be the result. Lower real interest rates abroad will have just the opposite effect, since they will stimulate the movement of capital toward the United States.

The Thumbnail Sketch summarizes the major factors that cause a nation's currency to appreciate or depreciate when exchange rates are determined by market forces.

**Thumbnail Sketch—Currency Appreciation
and Depreciation with Freely Fluctuating Exchange Rates**

These factors will cause a nation's currency to appreciate:
1. Increase in exports or decline in imports
2. Rate of inflation that is lower than that of trading partners
3. Higher domestic real interest rates
4. Lower real interest rates abroad

These factors will cause a nation's currency to depreciate:
1. Increase in imports or decline in exports
2. Rate of inflation that is higher than that of trading partners
3. Lower domestic real interest rates
4. Higher real interest rates abroad

Macropolicy and the Foreign Exchange Market

Previously, when analyzing monetary and fiscal policies, we assumed a closed economy with no international trade. But since macropolicy influences economic growth, inflation, and the interest rate, it also exerts an impact on the exchange rate market. The exchange rate market in turn affects macropolicy. It is interesting to note, however, that monetary and fiscal policies do not necessarily exert the same kind of impact on the exchange market.

Monetary Policy and Exchange Rates. Following the election of 1980, concern about the high rate of inflation induced the Federal Reserve to move toward a more restrictive policy. What impact could we expect such restrictive monetary policy to have on the exchange rate market? As our earlier analysis illustrated, a more restrictive policy would reduce aggregate demand, cause real interest rates (though probably not money rates) to rise temporarily, and eventually reduce the rate of inflation. A temporary economic slowdown would also be a probable side effect. As the Thumbnail Sketch shows, each of these factors would cause an appreciation of the dollar on the foreign exchange market. The higher real interest rates would attract financial capital from abroad. The deceleration in the U.S. inflation rate (relative to our trading partners) would make U.S. goods more competitive, leading to an expansion in exports. The economic slowdown would reduce domestic incomes and thereby retard imports. This is precisely what actually happened. The dollar appreciated against all major currencies during 1981.

The operation of the exchange market can also be expected to influence the strength of the restrictive monetary policy. The flow of financial capital from abroad will moderate the rise in real interest rates in the United States. The appreciation of the dollar will stimulate exports relative to imports, which will moderate the decline in aggregate demand for U.S. goods and services. In essence, some of the side effects of the restrictive policy will be felt abroad. Foreigners will experience a decrease in aggregate demand for their domestically produced goods, since their exports to the United States will fall and their imports from the United States will rise.

The impact of expansionary monetary policy would be just the opposite. It would lead to lower real interest rates, which would cause financial capital to flow from the United States. A higher inflation rate would stimulate imports and discourage exports. A temporary acceleration in the growth of income and employment would also stimulate imports. All of these factors would cause the dollar to depreciate on the foreign exchange market. The depreciation of the dollar would moderate the expansionary effects, shifting them partially to foreigners.

Fiscal Policy and Exchange Rates.   Fiscal policy tends to generate conflicting influences on the exchange rate market. Suppose that the United States shifts toward a more restrictive fiscal policy, planning a budget surplus or at least a smaller deficit. Just as with restrictive monetary policy, restrictive fiscal policy will cause a reduction in aggregate demand, an economic slowdown, and a decline in the rate of inflation. These factors will discourage imports and stimulate exports, causing an appreciation in the exchange rate value of the dollar. However, restrictive fiscal policy will also mean less government borrowing, which will place downward pressure on real interest rates in the United States. The lower real interest rates will cause financial capital to flow from the United States. The supply of dollars to the exchange market will increase, placing downward pressure on the exchange rate value of the dollar. The final outcome is uncertain. Slower growth and a deceleration in the inflation rate will discourage imports and promote the export of the relatively cheaper U.S. goods. The current account will move toward a surplus. At the same time, the lower real interest rates will cause the capital account to move toward a deficit. Since it is not obvious which of these forces will dominate, we cannot be sure whether restrictive fiscal policy will lead to an appreciation or a depreciation of the nation's currency in the foreign exchange market.

The analysis for expansionary fiscal policy is symmetrical. Expansionary fiscal policy will stimulate aggregate demand, including the demand for imports. The current account will move toward a deficit. However, expansionary fiscal policy will also lead to increased government borrowing and higher real interest rates, which will move the capital account toward a surplus. The net impact of expansionary fiscal policy on the value of a nation's currency in the foreign exchange market is indeterminate.

THE EVOLUTION OF INTERNATIONAL MONETARY ARRANGEMENTS

The current international monetary system is the product of an evolutionary process. An analysis of earlier systems will help us understand the current mixed system.

The Gold Standard

Gold Standard: An international monetary system under which the value of each nation's currency (for example, the dollar, mark, or pound) is defined in terms of gold. Since gold and any nation's currency are freely convertible at a fixed rate, the money supply of each nation is directly related to its supply of gold.

Throughout history, gold has played an important role in both domestic and international monetary matters. Before World War I, most currencies were tied to gold; each country set the value of its currency in terms of gold. For example, during most of this period, the U.S. Treasury was prepared to redeem the dollars of *both* domestic citizens and foreigners at a fixed price—$20.67 for one ounce of gold. Since each currency was linked to gold, the world, in effect, had a common currency. Since the English pound, U.S. dollar, French franc, and other currencies could all be readily redeemed for gold, they were little more than gold certificates.

How did this **gold standard** currency affect the flow of international trade? Since an increase in a nation's gold supply meant, in effect, an increase in its money supply, the flow of gold among countries tended to bring imports and exports of nations into balance. If a nation's imports exceeded its exports, the differential was paid in gold. Thus, "trade-deficit" nations exported gold to "trade-surplus" nations. These gold transfers caused the money supply of trade-deficit nations to fall and the money supply of trade-surplus countries to rise. Prices soon reflected these changes in the supply of money. Prices declined in the trade-deficit nations as a result of the shrinking supply of money. The price reductions made the goods of the trade-deficit nations cheaper on international markets, stimulated exports, and thereby restored the balance of trade. Similarly, prices in the trade-surplus nations rose as these countries acquired gold and expanded their money supply. The price inflation in the trade-surplus nations made their products less competitive. Exports declined, moving the trade balance of these countries toward equilibrium.

Despite the beauty of the system's simplicity, the gold standard had a number of drawbacks. First, real resources were tied up in the mining of gold so that it could be transferred between trading nations. Second, as the international sector grew in importance, the demand for exchange currency expanded. Since the supply of gold was virtually fixed, this expanding demand could not be satisfied. Third, with gold-backed currency used for both domestic and foreign transactions, the system placed a stranglehold on monetary planners. This might have been considered an advantage during periods of inflation (see "Should the United States Return to the Gold Standard?" later in this chapter). However, dissatisfaction arose when a reduction in a nation's gold stock (as a result of a trade deficit) not only placed downward pressure on prices but also caused a decline in employment and income. Exchange between nations expanded in volume, and the gold standard was abandoned in 1914.

Fixed Exchange Rates and the Postwar System

Fixed Exchange Rates: Rates established under a system whereby a government exchanges its currency for foreign currencies at a fixed rate. Government intervention in the foreign exchange and international trade markets is often required to maintain the fixed rate.

Efforts to establish an international monetary system after World War I were futile. At the end of World War II, representatives of the free-world nations met in Bretton Woods, New Hampshire, to devise a new system. They created a system of **fixed exchange rates** and established the **International Monetary Fund** (IMF) both to oversee the system and to act as a central world bank. The IMF sought to establish a system of relatively stable exchange rates through international cooperation.

The premise of a fixed rate system is that a nation ordinarily pays for its imports with exports. However, at certain times, the nation may find it advantageous to borrow (or loan) funds in order to run a trade deficit (or surplus). As the economic conditions of a debtor nation change, its trade deficit shifts to a trade surplus, so that it becomes possible for the country to repay the borrowed funds. Therefore, if a system of international reserves is available, a system based on both stable exchange rates and international cooperation can be established.

The IMF established such a reserve system. Each member country was required to deposit a specified amount of its currency into a reserve fund held by the IMF. Thus, the IMF possessed substantial holdings of dollars, francs, pounds, marks, and other currencies of the participating nations. As the need arose, these reserves were loaned to nations experiencing difficulties with their balance of payments. When the loans were extended, debtor nations were encouraged to take corrective action—to adopt domestic policies that would eventually eliminate the payment deficits. Besides permitting member nations to draw on currency and gold reserves, the IMF established special drawing rights (SDRs), a new kind of international reserve. The IMF allocated a specific quantity of SDRs to each member nation and permitted these newly created reserves to be used in place of gold or foreign currency to pay off international debts or to stabilize international exchange rates.

The Operation of a Fixed Exchange Rate System.   The fixed exchange rate system worked fairly well for many years. Nonetheless, problems were always present.

Fixing the price of a currency in the exchange market, like fixing other prices, results in surpluses and shortages. As market conditions change, the exchange rate that equates the quantity supplied of each currency with the quantity demanded also changes. If a nation's currency is overvalued at the fixed rate, persistent deficits on current and capital account transactions result. Of course, under the IMF system, a deficit nation could draw on its international reserves (for example, holdings of foreign currencies, gold, and SDRs with the IMF). However, a nation that continues to draw on its international reserve balances soon finds them depleted. Once the international reserves are gone, the nation is unable to maintain its fixed exchange rate. A nation that runs a chronic deficit at the fixed rate has three alternatives.

1. A Nation Can Devalue Its Currency.   A **devaluation**—a one-step depreciation under a fixed exchange rate system—will, if sufficient, *eventually* bring the value of the nation's imports (broadly defined) into line with its exports.

2. A Nation Can Heighten Trade Barriers, Adopting Tariffs and Quotas in an Effort to Reduce Imports and Bring the Value of Its Currency on the Foreign Exchange Market into Equilibrium.   This strategy is in conflict with economic efficiency and the promotion of the free flow of trade between nations. Nonetheless, it was often adopted during the period from 1944 to 1971. Once a nation's exchange rate was established, it tended to become sacred. Politicians during that period, including many in the United States, frequently argued that even though they did not like to impose trade restrictions, the barriers were necessary to avoid devaluation. The balance of payments issue was an excellent excuse to promote trade restrictions—which were advocated by special interests—against low-cost foreign goods.

3. A Nation Can Attempt to Remedy Its Balance of Payments Difficulties by Following Restrictive Monetary and Fiscal Policies Designed to Promote Price Deflation (or at Least Less Inflation) and High Interest Rates.   However, this alternative may conflict with other policy objectives—full employment, for example. If a nation's rate of unemployment is high, a policy of macroeconomic restriction is likely to push the nation into recession.

In the face of balance of payments deficits, the maintenance of fixed rates is further complicated by the destabilizing role of speculation. If you have an eye for making money, you have probably already seen why balance of payments deficits can quickly generate a crisis under a fixed exchange rate system. Suppose that you have 1 million pesos and it appears that the peso is going to be devalued. Will you want to hold these pesos while they become less valuable? If your answer is no, you will have made the right decision for your own pocketbook, but when you sell your pesos for dollars in the foreign exchange market, you will actually be making things worse. That is, the purchase of dollars and the sale of pesos by speculators and others will cause an *increase* in the supply of pesos and will make it more difficult for international central banks to stabilize the price of the peso. In other words, rational speculators under fixed exchange rates typically contribute to the destabilization of those exchange rates.

The Dollar as an International Currency

At the end of World War II, the dollar was the strongest and most respected currency in the world. The U.S. Treasury, which held most of the world's gold supply, was prepared to exchange dollars held by foreigners (but not those of U.S. citizens) for gold at the fixed rate of $35 per ounce. Throughout the world, the dollar was literally "as good as gold."

During the late 1940s and 1950s, the dollar actually evolved into an international currency. Many nations completed international transactions in dollars. For example, an exporter in Brazil could sell 100,000 pounds of coffee to a wholesaler in West Germany in exchange for $50,000. Businesspeople throughout the world held dollar balances because most international transactions were conducted in dollars. During this period, holding dollars was certainly a conservative strategy. The purchasing power of the dollar in the United States was relatively stable. Dollars could be readily exchanged for a wide range of goods in the United States and throughout the world. In addition, foreigners could exchange them for gold, if they wished to do so.

As the currency demands of international trade grew, the foreign balance of dollars increased. Foreign banks not only held dollar deposits but also extended loans against their dollar holdings. The use of the dollar as an international currency was a marvelous arrangement for citizens of the United States. Persons and institutions holding dollar balances had previously supplied goods and services to U.S. citizens in order to obtain these dollar balances. As long as other nations continued to use the dollar as an international currency, U.S. citizens were able to derive the benefit of watches, radios, automobiles, and other goods supplied by foreigners in exchange for something that was relatively cheap to produce—dollar bills.

However, problems eventually developed for both the dollar and the system of fixed exchange rates. As other economies grew stronger, particularly those of West Germany and Japan, the supreme position of the dollar began to erode. The balance of payments position of the United States slowly began to deteriorate. From time to time, the United States pursued a restrictive macropolicy designed to deal with its balance of payments problems. However, as unemployment rose and economic growth slowed, it was necessary to abandon the restrictive policy. In the meantime, the quantity of foreign-held dollar balances continued to grow. Speculators became increasingly concerned as to whether the United States would be able to redeem foreign-held dollars in gold. Many exchanged their dollars for gold. Thus, the U.S. Treasury's holdings of gold dwindled from 651 million ounces in 1950 to 509 million ounces in 1960 and to 394 million ounces in 1965. When the gold stock fell to 296 million ounces in 1968, the government decided to stop the decline. It suspended the *automatic* transferability of dollars to gold. All of these factors, as well as continued balance of payments deficits on current and capital accounts, caused the confidence of foreigners in the dollar to wane.

The Current System— A Flexible Rate with Selective Intervention

In 1971, the state of the balance of payments in the United States was clearly in conflict with the desire of the Nixon administration to follow a more expansionary macropolicy prior to the 1972 election. In August 1971, at the same time that wage–price controls were imposed on the domestic economy, President Nixon terminated the convertibility between gold and the dollar. The dollar was temporarily permitted to float in the exchange market against other major currencies. After the dollar depreciated 17 percent with respect to the Japanese yen and almost 14 percent against the German mark, a new agreement on fixed exchange rates was reached in late 1971. This agreement was short-lived. When a new balance of payments crisis developed in early 1973, the dollar was again permitted to float.

The system in effect since 1973 might best be described as a managed float (or flexible rate). It is sometimes referred to as a "dirty float," since the central monetary authorities of various countries sometimes intervene. Fluctuations within a moderate range (say 10 percent in either direction) are permitted by most governments. However, if it appears that a change in exchange rates is likely to be of greater magnitude, governments often use their reserve holdings to intervene. For example, when the exchange rate value of the dollar fell sharply in 1978, the Carter administration arranged for loans from the Japanese and West German governments, as well as for additional reserves from the International Monetary Fund, in order to bolster the dollar. Proponents of the dirty float system argue that it provides relative exchange rate stability and still allows the advantages of flexible exchange to come into play most of the time.

Is the Current Flexible System Working?   Since 1973, the industrial economies have been forced to absorb an unprecedented number of severe shocks—the oil embargo of 1973, soaring energy prices, and a sharp reduction in the availability of petroleum as a result of the Iranian revolution of 1979. The system of floating rates has handled these events with a minimum of difficulty. The volume of international trade has continued to rise. Yet the flexible system has not worked as well as some of its early proponents predicted that it would. Flexible rates have not promptly eliminated current account deficits and surpluses. Clearly, it takes time for exchange markets to adjust. However, even though exchange markets have not adjusted as rapidly as some believed they would, there is every indication that flexible rates are stable—that they do move toward equilibrium.

Contrary to some of the arguments of those who advocate fixed exchange rates, future markets in currencies have developed. An American business contracting to purchase Japanese houseware products to be delivered in six months can arrange now *at a designated price* for the delivery of the yen needed to complete the transactions. Thus, international traders protect themselves against sharp fluctuations in the exchange rate. As the proponents of flexible rates have consistently pointed out, since the risks of exchange rate fluctuations can be avoided at a moderate price, there is no reason to believe that flexible rates adversely affect the total volume of international trade.

All things considered, the managed float system seems to be working rather well. The President's Council of Economic Advisers stated the apparent consensus view:

> *In general, the evidence, although not conclusive, does indicate that floating has worked well over the long run, especially considering the magnitude of the shocks to the international financial system. In fact, given these shocks, it is not clear that any system other than generalized floating would have been viable during the period. Exchange rate movements, while large, have broadly responded to economic fundamentals, have facilitated adjustment, and have tended to move the system toward rather than away from greater stability.*[4]

PERSPECTIVES IN ECONOMICS
SHOULD THE UNITED STATES RETURN TO THE GOLD STANDARD?

As both inflation and interest rates soared to double-digit figures in the late 1970s and early 1980s, there was a renewal of interest in the gold standard. Congress established the U.S. Gold Commission to study the feasibility of once again tying the dollar to gold. The proponents of the gold standard believe that the inflation that has plagued the U.S. and other Western economies in recent years stems primarily from excessive monetary expansion. They charge that Americans have lost confidence in the willingness, or perhaps even the ability, of the Federal Reserve to follow a stable, restrictive monetary course. Over the centuries, the world output of gold has grown very slowly, approximately 1.5 to 2 percent annually. Happily, as the advocates of the gold standard note, this rate coincides with the rate of monetary growth that many analysts believe to be consistent with a healthy, noninflationary economy. Thus, according to the proponents, a return to

the gold standard would make excessive monetary growth less likely and at the same time restore the confidence of Americans in the future purchasing power of money.

The argument for the gold standard has a certain appeal, particularly during a period of rapid inflation. However, there are also serious problems to be reckoned with. First, a meaningful international gold standard clearly could not be restored without the cooperation of the other major industrial nations; but our trading partners appear to have little enthusiasm for the idea. Second, nations subjecting themselves to the discipline of a gold standard would have to forego the use of monetary policy as a macropolicy tool. If aggregate demand fell and unemployment rose, monetary policy could not be used to alter the direction of the economy. Even though many are unhappy with the past record of monetary policy, few are willing to forego completely its potential use as a macropolicy tool. Third, and perhaps most important, it is not obvious that a gold standard would stabilize the purchasing power

of a nation's currency. A gold standard would directly stabilize only one price, the dollar price of gold. If the purchasing power of gold remained relatively constant, this would, of course, also stabilize the purchasing power of the dollar. However, even though the supply of gold is relatively fixed, the demand for it is not. Fluctuations in the demand for gold could result in substantial fluctuations in its price. For example, suppose that there were a revolution in a major oil-exporting country (as there was in Iran in 1979), an increase in international tensions, or another poor wheat harvest in the Soviet Union. As the 1970s have illustrated, any one of these events would be capable of causing an abrupt shift in the market price of gold.

The Modified Gold Standard

As a first step toward a gold standard, some proponents have suggested that the Federal Reserve fix the price of gold, at, for example, $300 per ounce. Under this plan, the Fed would buy bonds, injecting money into the system, if the price of an ounce of gold fell

---

[4]Council of Economic Advisers, *Economic Report of the President, 1979,* p. 152.

below $300. On the other hand, if the price rose above $300, the Fed would sell bonds in order to decrease the supply of dollars, until the per ounce price reached $300 again. As long as the purchasing power of gold remained constant in terms of goods and services, the purchasing power of the dollar would also remain constant under this plan. However, as we have pointed out, there is no guarantee that the purchasing power of gold would remain constant.

The idea of buying and selling bonds—that is, expanding and contracting the money supply in order to maintain a constant purchasing power of the monetary unit—is not new. Keynes suggested it even before the publication of the *General Theory*. In 1924 Keynes wrote:

[*I*]*t would promote confidence and furnish an objective standard of value, if the* [*monetary*] *authorities were to adopt this composite commodity* [*a price index*] *as their standard of value in the sense that they would employ all resources to prevent a movement of its price by more than a certain percentage in either direction away from the normal, just as before the war they employed all their resources to prevent a movement in the price of gold by more than a certain percentage.*[5]

Of course, the United States and most other nations already calculate an index, the GNP deflator, to indicate the value of money in terms

---

[5]John Maynard Keynes, *Monetary Reform* (New York: Harcourt, Brace, 1924), pp. 203–204.

of a standard composite commodity. If the monetary authorities seek to stabilize the value of the currency, it would seem much more sensible to stabilize the value of this composite commodity, as suggested by Keynes, rather than fix the price of gold, whose stabilizing power is uncertain.

Discussion

1. Do you think the gold standard is a good idea? Why or why not?
2. Do you think the monetary authorities should conduct monetary policy in a manner that would leave the GNP deflator unchanged over time? Would this stabilize the purchasing power of the currency? Justify your answers.

CHAPTER LEARNING OBJECTIVES

1   When international trade takes place, it is usually necessary for one country to convert its currency to the currency of its trading partner. Imports of goods, services, and assets (both real and financial) by the United States generate a demand for foreign currency with which to pay for these items. On the other hand, exports of goods, services, and assets supply foreign currency to the exchange market because foreigners exchange their currency for the dollars needed to purchase the export items.

2   The value of a nation's currency on the exchange market is in equilibrium when the supply of the currency (generated by imports—the sale of goods, services, and assets to foreigners) is just equal to the demand for the currency (generated by exports—the purchasing of goods, services, and assets from foreigners).

3   The balance of payments accounts record the flow of payments between a country and other countries. Transactions (for example, imports) that supply a nation's currency to the foreign exchange market are recorded as debit items. Transactions (for example, exports) that generate a demand for the nation's currency on the foreign exchange market are recorded as credit items.

4   Since 1973, most countries have operated under a system of flexible exchange rates, which allows the forces of supply and demand to determine the exchange rate value of their currencies. Broadly speaking, the supply of a nation's currency to the foreign exchange market is created by the purchase (import) of foreign goods, services, and assets. The demand for a nation's currency originates from the sale (export) of goods, services, and assets to foreigners.

5   As long as the demand for imports and the supply of exports are elastic, flexible exchange rates ensure equilibrium in the exchange market. For example, if there were an excess supply (balance of payments deficit) of dollars on the foreign exchange market, the value of the dollar would depreciate relative to other currencies. This would make foreign goods more expensive to U.S. consumers and U.S. goods cheaper to foreigners, reducing the value of our imports and increasing the value of our exports until equilib-

rium was restored. On the other hand, an excess demand for dollars would cause the dollar to appreciate, stimulating imports and discouraging exports until equilibrium was restored. But even though the demand for foreign goods is likely to be highly elastic in the long run, this may not be true in the short run. It may take time for an exchange rate adjustment to bring about equilibrium.

6 With flexible exchange rates, a nation's currency tends to appreciate when (a) exports increase relative to imports, (b) the rate of domestic inflation is below that of the nation's trading partners, (c) domestic real interest rates increase, and/or (d) foreign real interest rates decline. The reverse conditions will cause the nation's currency to depreciate.

7 Restrictive monetary policy will raise the real interest rate, reduce the rate of inflation, and, at least temporarily, reduce aggregate demand and the growth of income. These factors will in turn cause the nation's currency to appreciate on the foreign exchange market. In contrast, expansionary monetary policy will result in a currency depreciation.

8 Fiscal policy generates conflicting forces in the exchange rate market, making the effect of any domestic fiscal policy on the value of a nation's currency difficult to predict.

9 Prior to World War I, most countries set the value of their currency in terms of gold. When trade was conducted under the gold standard, the gold stock of a nation would fall if it imported more than it exported. The decline in the stock of gold would decrease the nation's money supply, causing prices to fall and making the nation's goods more competitive on the international market. In contrast, if a nation was a net exporter, its stock of gold would rise, causing inflation and making the nation's goods less competitive on the international market. However, alterations in the supply of gold often caused abrupt shifts in income and employment. The gold standard was abandoned in 1914.

10 During the period from 1944 to 1971, most of the nations of the free world operated under a system of fixed exchange rates. Under this system, if the value of the goods, services, and capital assets exported to foreigners is less than the value of the items imported, there is an excess supply of the country's currency on the foreign exchange market. When this happens, the country must (a) devalue its currency, (b) take action to reduce imports (for example, heighten its trade barriers), or (c) pursue a restrictive macropolicy designed to increase interest rates and retard inflation. During the period when the fixed rates were in effect, corrective action taken to maintain the rates was often in conflict with the goals of maximum freedom in international markets and the macropolicy objective of full employment.

11 The current flexible system might best be described as a managed float. Given the severe shocks that international markets have suffered since it was instituted in 1973, the system appears to be working reasonably well.

THE ECONOMIC WAY OF THINKING — DISCUSSION QUESTIONS

1 "We are never going to strengthen the dollar, cure our balance of payments problem, lick our high unemployment, and eliminate an ever-worsening inflation as long as the United States sits idly by as a dumping ground for shoes, television sets, apparel, steel, automobiles, etc." (spokesperson for the United Shoe Workers of America)

(a) Would excluding foreign goods from the U.S. market help to solve our problem of "ever-worsening inflation"? Explain.

(b) If foreigners were willing to give (dump?) 100,000 pairs of shoes to American consumers, do you think it would be bad business to accept them?

(c) Would accepting the shoes worsen our unemployment and balance of payments problems? Explain.

2 "If a current account deficit means that we are getting more items from abroad than we are giving to foreigners, why is it considered a bad thing?" Comment.

3 Do you think the United States should continue to follow a policy of flexible exchange rates? Why? Under what circumstances would a nation prefer flexible rates?

4 Suppose that the exchange rate between the United States and Mexico freely fluctuated in the open market. Indicate which of the following would cause the dollar to appreciate (or depreciate) relative to the peso.

(a) An increase in the quantity of drilling equipment purchased in the United States by Pemex, the Mexican oil company, as a result of a Mexican oil discovery

(b) An increase in the U.S. purchase of crude oil from Mexico as a result of the development of Mexican oil fields

(c) Higher interest rates in Mexico, inducing U.S. citizens to move their financial investments from U.S. to Mexican banks

(d) Lower interest rates in the United States, inducing Mexican investors to borrow dollars and then exchange them for pesos

(e) Inflation in the United States and stable prices in Mexico

(f) Ten percent inflation in both the United States and Mexico

(g) An economic boom in Mexico, inducing Mexicans to buy more U.S.-made automobiles, trucks, electric appliances, and television sets

(h) Attractive investment opportunities, inducing U.S. investors to buy stock in Mexican firms

5 "The value of the dollar on the exchange market will continue to fall as long as our balance of trade is running a deficit." Evaluate.

6 Given the inflation of the early 1980s, the Reagan administration advocated restrictive monetary policy coupled with a reduction in tax rates designed to stimulate saving, investment, and long-run economic growth. What impact is the administration's macro-policy likely to have on the value of the dollar in the exchange rate market?

7 What's Wrong with This Way of Thinking?

"The government can change from fixed to flexible exchange rates, but we will continue to run a balance of payments deficit because foreign goods, produced with cheap labor, are simply cheaper than goods produced in the United States."

Development is not purely an economic phenomenon. Ultimately it must encompass more than the material and financial side of people's lives. Development should therefore be perceived as a multidimensional process involving *the reorganization and reorientation of entire economic and social systems.*[2]
Michael P. Todaro

33 ECONOMIC DEVELOPMENT AND THE GROWTH OF INCOME[1]

Throughout history, economic growth and income levels substantially greater than those required for survival have been rare. In the battle with Nature for survival, human beings have usually had to struggle and toil merely to eke out a minimal living. The wheels of progress have moved forward slowly. The economic growth and the rising standard of living that are taken for granted by much of the Western world did not exist for extended periods of recorded history and still do not exist for many non-Western countries. For example, Phelps Brown showed that the real income of English building trade workers was virtually unchanged between 1215 and 1798, a period of nearly six centuries. The living conditions of peasants in such countries as India and Pakistan are not much different from those of their ancestors 1000 years ago.

Against this background of poverty and stagnation, the economic record of the Western world during the last 250 years is astounding. In 1750, people all over the world struggled 50, 60, and 70 hours per week to obtain the basic necessities of life—food, clothing, and shelter. Manual labor was the major source of energy. Animals provided the means of transportation. The tools and machines that existed were primitive by today's standards. In the last two centuries, petroleum, electricity, and nuclear power have replaced human and animal power as the major sources of energy. Automobiles, airplanes, and trains are now the major means of transportation. Subsistence levels of food, shelter, and clothing are taken for granted, and the typical Western family worries instead about financing summer vacations, color television sets, and the children's college educations. The real income of the typical family often doubles during a generation. For the first time in history, economic growth is such that subsistence living standards have been far surpassed in many parts of the world.

---

[1]The authors would like to thank James Cobbe for his helpful suggestions that contributed to the development of this chapter.

[2]Michael P. Todaro, *Economics for a Developing World* (London: Longman, 1977), p. 87.

Why have some countries grown rapidly and others been left behind? How can a nation break out of the bondage of poverty and underdevelopment? How wide is the economic gap between the rich and poor nations? In this chapter, we investigate these topics and other issues related to the subject of economic development.

DEVELOPED AND LESS DEVELOPED COUNTRIES

Less Developed Countries: Low-income countries characterized by rapid population growth, an agriculture–household sector that dominates the economy, illiteracy, extreme poverty, and a high degree of inequality.

Like the rich nations, the poor countries of the world are different from each other in many respects. Some have grown rapidly in recent years; others have continued to stagnate. War and political upheaval have contributed to the poverty of some; cultural and tribal stability dominate others. There is no sharp division between developed and **less developed countries.** If per capita income were used to distinguish between the two, there would be no significant difference between the income level of the wealthiest less developed country and that of the poorest developed nation. In many respects, the division between the developed and less developed countries is arbitrary. However, there is a set of characteristics generally shared by the less developed countries.

1. The Most Obvious Characteristic of Less Developed Nations Is Low per Capita Income. Extreme poverty, hunger, and filth are a way of life throughout much of India, Pakistan, most of Asia, Africa, and much of Latin America. Exhibit 1 presents the harsh statistics. All countries with a population of more than 5 million are grouped according to income. In 1979, 61 percent of the world's population— 2.6 billion people—lived in countries with an average GNP of less than $1000 per person (groups I and II of Exhibit 1). Even though these countries contained more than three-fifths of the world's total population, they generated only 7.3 percent of the world's output. In contrast, the 34 countries with a per capita GNP of $3000 or more accounted for one-quarter of the world's population, but they generated more than four-fifths of the world's output. The low-income status of the countries of groups I and II reflects the absence of economic development. By the same token, the standard of living of the wealthy nations is the fruit of past economic development.

2. The Agriculture–Household Sector Dominates the Economy of Less Developed Nations. Nearly two-thirds of the labor force of the low-income countries of Asia, Africa, and South America is employed in agriculture. In contrast, 2 percent of the U.S. labor force is employed in this sector. The size of the household (nonmarket) sector in less developed countries is generally far greater than that in developed nations. Most households in less developed nations raise their own food, make much of their clothing, and construct the family shelter. The specialization and exchange that dominate developed economies are largely absent in less developed countries.

3. Rapid Population Growth Generally Characterizes Less Developed Nations. The population of the poor countries of Asia, Africa, and South America has been expanding at an average annual rate of approximately 2.5 percent. The population of these nations doubles every 25 or 30 years. In contrast, the population growth of the developed nations of Europe and North America is generally about 1 percent each year.

EXHIBIT 1 Annual per capita output of nations, 1979[a]

Category and per Capita Output	Composition	Countries			
Group I—less than $300 (This group generates 4.4 percent of gross world product)	Thirty-one countries with 48.8 percent of the world's population	*Africa* Ethiopia, Guinea, Madagascar, Mozambique, Malawi, Mali, Niger, Tanzania, Uganda	*Asia and Middle East* Afghanistan, Bangladesh, Burma, China, India, Pakistan, Vietnam, Sri Lanka, Nepal		*Latin America* Haiti
Group II—$300 to $999 (This group generates 2.9 percent of gross world product)	Thirty countries with 12.0 percent of the world's population	*Africa* Angola, Cameroon, Ghana, Kenya, Morocco, Nigeria, Senegal, Zimbabwe, Zambia	*Asia and Middle East* Egypt, Indonesia, Philippines, Thailand, Yemen		*Latin and South America* Bolivia, Peru, Dominican Republic
Group III—$1000 to $2999 (This group generates 9.0 percent of gross world product)	Twenty-eight countries with 13.4 percent of the world's population	*Africa* Algeria, South Africa, Ivory Coast, Tunisia *Europe* Portugal, Romania, Turkey, Yugoslavia	*Asia and Middle East* Iran, Iraq, Malaysia, South Korea, North Korea, Syria		*Latin and South America* Argentina, Brazil, Chile, Cuba, Guatemala, Mexico, Colombia, Ecuador
Group IV—$3000 to $6999 (This group generates 25.6 percent of gross world product)	Seventeen countries with 12.7 percent of the world's population	*Europe* Bulgaria, Czechoslovakia, East Germany, Hungary, Greece	Italy, Poland, Spain, Soviet Union, United Kingdom		*South America* Venezuela *Asia* Hong Kong
Group V—$7000 and over (This group generates 58.1 percent of gross world product)	Seventeen countries with 13.2 percent of the world's population	*Europe* France, Denmark, Sweden, Switzerland, West Germany, Netherlands, Belgium, Austria	*Asia and Middle East* Japan, Saudi Arabia		*North America* Canada, United States *Oceania* Australia

[a]Converted to U.S. dollars by means of exchange rates. Only nations with a population of greater than 5 million are listed.

The World Bank, *World Development Report, 1981,* Tables 1 and 3.

4. Income Is Usually More Unequally Distributed in Less Developed Countries. Not only is the average income low in less developed countries, but most of the available income is allocated to the wealthy. The top 10 percent of all income recipients usually receives a larger proportion of the aggregate income in less developed countries than in developed nations. Often, this reflects the existence of a two-sector economy—a trade and financial sector linked to the developed world and an agriculture–household sector that is bound by tradition. The incomes of persons employed in the trade and financial sector may be comparable to those of individuals in developed nations, but most of the population belong to the dominant agriculture–household sector and languish in poverty.

5. Inadequate Health Care, Poor Educational Facilities, and Illiteracy Are Widespread in Less Developed Nations. Whereas almost all school-age children attend primary school in North America and the European nations, less than half do so in many less developed countries. One-third or less of the adult population is literate in such countries as Bangladesh, Ethiopia, Pakistan, and India. Physicians and hospitals are unavailable in many parts of the less developed world. Most of the resources of these nations are allocated to the provision of basic necessities—food and shelter. Health care and education are luxuries that most people cannot afford.

How Wide Is the Economic Gap between the Developed and Less Developed Nations?

Most of the countries of Asia, Africa, and South America possess the characteristics of less developed nations. Per capita income is low. The agriculture–household sector dominates the economy. Rapid population growth, economic inequality, and poverty abound on these three continents. On the other hand, the indicators of underdevelopment are generally absent in North America, Europe, Oceania, Japan, and the Soviet Union. Although there are a few exceptions, by and large these areas comprise the developed nations of the world.

How wide is the economic gap between the developed and less developed world? This question is not easy to answer. The gross national product *per capita* is a measure of the availability of goods and services to individuals, but how can we draw meaningful comparisons when the GNP of Mexico is measured in pesos, that of Brazil is measured in cruzeiros, that of Australia is measured in pounds, and so on? The simplest means of dealing with this problem is to use the exchange rate between countries to convert the GNP of each nation to a common currency, the U.S. dollar, for example. Most international comparisons follow this procedure.

Exchange Rate Conversion Method: Method that uses the foreign exchange rate value of a nation's currency to convert that nation's GNP to another monetary unit, such as the U.S. dollar.

When the **exchange rate conversion method** is used to convert the GNP of each nation to U.S. dollars, we find that 77 percent of the gross world product is produced by the developed nations of North America, Europe (including the Soviet Union), and Oceania, plus Japan. In contrast, although 77 percent of the world's population lives in the less developed nations of Asia (excluding Japan), Africa, and South America, these countries generate only 23 percent of the gross world product.

Although the exchange rate conversion method is simple and straightforward, it does not fully meet our needs. When we make international comparisons, we seek to measure differences in the standards of living among areas. The exchange rate reflects differences in the purchasing power of currencies for *goods that are traded in international markets.* However, it may not be a reliable indicator of differences in the purchasing power of currencies for *goods and services that are not exchanged in international markets.* For example, merely because a dollar purchases 20 pesos in the foreign exchange market, it does not follow that a dollar will purchase 20 times as much housing, medical care, education, childcare service, and similar items in the United States as the peso will purchase in Mexico.

The quality of comparative international income data would be greatly improved if the conversion ratio between currencies were expressed in terms of the ability of the currencies to purchase a typical bundle of goods and services in the country of their origin. The United Nations International Comparison Project, a study begun in 1968 by the United Nations Statistical Office, the University of Pennsylvania, and the World Bank, has devised such a purchasing power index for several currencies. The **purchasing power parity method** compares the costs of purchasing a typical bundle of goods and services in the domestic markets for various nations. Each category in the bundle is weighted according to its contribution to GNP. The cost of purchasing the typical bundle in each nation is then compared to the dollar cost of purchasing the same bundle in the United States. Once the purchasing power of each nation's currency, in terms of the typical bundle, is determined, this information can be used to convert the GNP of each country to a common monetary unit (for example, the U.S. dollar).

Exhibit 2 presents per capita GNP data for the industrial market economies and less developed countries, based on both the exchange rate conversion method and the purchasing power parity method. Using the exchange rate conversion method, we find that in 1980 the estimated GNP per capita of the industrial market economies was $10,660, compared to only $850 for less developed countries.

Using the exchange rate method, the GNP per capita of the industrial market economies was estimated to be approximately 12 times greater than the

Purchasing Power Parity Method: Method for determining the relative purchasing power of different currencies by comparing the amount of each currency required to purchase a typical bundle of goods and services in domestic markets. This information is then used to convert the GNP of each nation to a common monetary unit.

EXHIBIT 2 Measuring the economic gap between developed and less developed countries

If the per capita GNP of industrial, market-economy nations is estimated by the exchange rate conversion method, it is 12 times greater than that of less developed countries. However, if the more accurate purchasing power parity procedure is used, the gap narrows, indicating that the GNP per capita is approximately 5 times greater for industrial nations than that for less developed countries.

	Per Capita GNP	
	Industrial Countries[a]	Less Developed Countries[b]
Exchange rate method		
1980 U.S. dollars	$10,660	$850
1980 (industrial countries = 100)	100	8
Purchasing power parity method		
1980 (industrial countries = 100)	100	20

[a]North America, Europe, Japan, and Oceania. The Soviet Union is not included in these data.

[b]Asia, Africa, South America, and Central America.

The World Bank, *World Development Report, 1981,* p. 17.

figure for less developed nations. However, application of the purchasing power parity method indicates that the relative income of the less developed nations was underestimated by the exchange rate conversion method. Using the purchasing power parity method, the GNP per capita of industrial nations was estimated to be only 5 times greater than for the less developed countries in 1980.

The estimates based on the purchasing power of currencies in the country of their origin are almost certainly a more accurate indicator of international differences in per capita GNP than the more widely circulated estimates based on exchange rate conversions. Although it does appear that the exchange rate procedures overestimate the economic gap between developed and less developed nations, there is nonetheless a sizable disparity.

Are Growth and Development the Same Thing?

During the two decades following World War II, economists failed to draw a clear distinction between growth and development. Development was deemed present if a country was able to generate and sustain a significant rate of increase in GNP—for example, 5 percent or more. In recent years, it has become increasingly popular to define growth in strictly positive terms—the rate of change in GNP. Development is now widely perceived as a normative concept, encompassing not only growth but also distributional and structural changes that imply an improvement in the standard of living for most of the populace.

Extensive Economic Growth: An expansion in the total output of goods and services, regardless of whether output per capita increases.

It is important to understand the distinction between two types of growth—extensive and intensive growth. **Extensive economic growth** is present when the output of a nation, as measured by real GNP, for example, is expanding. A nation may experience extensive growth even though the *output per person* is not rising. Since economists are interested primarily in the well-being of individuals, they generally focus on **intensive economic growth,** the expansion in the availability of goods and services per person. Per capita real output (or income) is a measure of intensive economic growth. If a society's production of goods and services is expanding more rapidly than its population, per capita real income will rise. On average, the economic well-being of people will improve, reflecting the intensive economic growth. Conversely, if the population of the nation is expanding more rapidly than production, per capita real income will decline. Economic regression, the opposite of intensive growth, will be the result.

Intensive Economic Growth: An increase in output per person. When intensive economic growth is present, output is growing more rapidly than population.

Growth focuses on changes in output. The "new" view of economic development is concerned with the structure and division of the fruits of growth. In this normative view, development requires not only growth in output per person but also an improvement in the availability of consumption goods for a wide spectrum of the populace, including those people in the bottom half of the income distribution. Some economists adhere to the **trickle-down theory**—the view that intensive growth will, at least with time, lead to an improvement in the standard of living for all major segments of the society. They argue that the enlarged output and higher level of income will eventually "trickle down," bringing improvements in economic opportunity, education, and living standards to the masses.

Trickle-Down Theory: The theory that intensive economic growth will eventually lead to an improvement in the standard of living for the entire society, even for persons at the bottom of the economic spectrum.

The trickle-down theory is not without critics. Opponents of the theory argue that growth does not necessarily lead to an improvement in the status of those in the lower half of the economic spectrum. They refer to the experience of such countries as Brazil as evidence supporting their position. The growth of Brazil has been quite rapid, particularly since the mid-1960s. However, the distribution of income in Brazil is highly skewed. More than 60 percent of the aggregate income is allocated to the wealthiest 20 percent of the population. By way of comparison, the wealthiest one-fifth of the population receives between 40 and 45 percent of the aggregate income in the developed countries of Europe and North America. Many development economists charge that the rapid growth of Brazil has failed to alter significantly the economic status of the overwhelming majority of its citizens. Perhaps this situation will change in the future, but the Brazilian experience has shaken the faith of many economists in the trickle-down theory.

Even though economic growth and development can be distinguished, it is obvious that growth is necessary for development. Without sustained economic growth, continuous improvement in the economic opportunities and status of a nation's populace, including those at the bottom of the economic spectrum, will be impossible.

Thus far, economists have been unable to construct a general theory of growth and development. Therefore, we cannot fully explain the ingredients that are essential for the transition from stagnation to growth and development. Nonetheless, economics is capable of pinpointing certain important determinants of material progress. We will turn to that topic after we consider the implications of differences in sustained growth rates.

The Importance of Small Differences in Rates of Growth

At first glance, a difference of only 1 percent in two nations' growth rates would not seem to be very significant. However, with time, even small differences in growth rates have a substantial impact on a nation's productive capabilities. Exhibit 3 will help us to understand the consequences of differential growth rates. If the real GNP of a nation grew 2 percent per year, the nation's annual rate of output would expand by 48 percent in 20 years. Alternatively, a 3 percent growth rate would lead to an 81 percent increase in annual GNP after 20 years. Thus, if two nations had a GNP of equal size at the beginning of a period, the nation experiencing the 3 percent growth rate would be generating nearly 25 percent more output after 20 years than the nation with the 2 percent growth rate. A 4 percent growth rate would cause GNP to rise by 119 percent. After 20 years, the GNP of the nation experiencing a 4 percent growth rate would be nearly 50 percent greater than that of a country with an annual growth rate of only 2 percent. Clearly, if they are sustained over an extended period,

EXHIBIT 3   The cumulative effect of economic growth

Rate of Economic Growth (Percent)	Percent Increase in Real GNP after:			Number of Years Before Real GNP Would Double (4)
	5 Years (1)	10 Years (2)	20 Years (3)	
1	5	10	22	72
2	10	22	48	36
3	16	34	81	23
4	22	48	119	18
5	28	63	165	14
6	34	79	221	12
7	40	97	287	10
8	47	116	366	9

small differences in growth rates have a dramatic impact on the relative sizes of economies.

The importance of differences in growth rates can also be seen by analyzing the amount of time that is necessary for income (or output) to double. These data are presented in Exhibit 3, column 4. It takes a nation 72 years to double its GNP if its growth rate is 1 percent. GNP doubles every 36 years if a 2 percent growth rate is attained. If a 3 percent growth rate is sustained, GNP doubles every 23 years.

Real-world data illustrate the importance of differential growth rates. As Exhibit 4 shows, between 1870 and 1950, the per capita real GNP of the United States expanded at a rate of 1.9 percent, compared to 1.0 to 1.1 percent for the major European countries. As a result, during this 80-year period, the per capita output of the United States expanded fourfold, whereas the output per person in the European countries merely doubled. Thus, even though in 1870 the output per person was approximately equal in the United States, England, France, and Germany, by 1950 the per capita real GNP of the United States was nearly twice that of each of the three European nations.

Since 1950, West Germany and France have turned the tables on the United States. West Germany and France have experienced intensive growth rates of 4.9 and 4.4 percent, respectively, compared to only 2.0 percent for the United States. As Exhibit 4 illustrates, the per capita GNPs of both West Germany and France now exceed that of the United States.

The most impressive growth record of the post-World War II era has been compiled by the Japanese. In 1950, the real per capita GNP of Japan was less than one-fifth that of the United States—a mere $1060 compared to $6330 for the United States (measured in 1980 dollars adjusted for inflation). However, the Japanese economy grew dramatically during the period from 1950 to 1980. Real GNP per capita increased at an annual rate of 7.4 percent. By 1980, the Japanese output per person was almost four-fifths that of the United States. If the Japanese can sustain their growth rate, their per capita GNP will overtake that of the United States by the mid-1980s. If the growth rates of the last 25 years prevail, by the late 1990s the Japanese output per capita will be the largest of the major industrial powers.

EXHIBIT 4   The impact of differential growth rates

| Country | Growth Rate of Real per Capita GNP (Percent) | | Real per Capita GNP (1980 U.S. Dollars) | | |
	1870–1950	1950–1980	1950	1980	1990[a]
United States	1.9	2.0	6330	11,536	14,062
Canada	1.6	2.3	5210	10,288	12,915
West Germany	1.0	4.9	3170	13,372	21,575
France	1.1	4.4	3360	12,165	18,712
Australia	n.a.[b]	2.9	3960	9,398	12,508
Japan	n.a.[b]	7.4	1060	8,905	18,183
United Kingdom	1.1	3.2	3540	9,288	12,729

[a]Projected assuming that the growth rates that each country experienced during 1950–1980 continue until 1990.

[b]Not available.

Derived from *Statistical Abstract of the United States—1981.*

SOURCES OF ECONOMIC GROWTH

Why do some countries grow rapidly while other stagnate? This question is difficult to answer. Clearly, natural resources are not responsible for the difference. Japan has few natural resources and imports almost all of its industrial energy supply. Similarly, Hong Kong has practically no raw materials, very little fertile soil, and no domestic sources of energy. Yet the growth records of these two countries are envied throughout the world. In contrast, such resource-rich nations as Ghana, Kenya, and Bolivia are poor and experiencing only slow growth. Physical resources are useless without the entrepreneurship, skills, and capital with which to develop them.

The presence of a skilled and disciplined work force is a vital determinant of economic well-being. Much of the physical wealth (the industrial capacity) of Europe was destroyed during World War II. Nonetheless, Europe recovered rapidly after the war, largely because the "human capital" of its citizens was left intact.

Although we do not fully understand all the ingredients of economic growth, we do know that three factors are important—investment in physical and human capital, technological advances, and improvement in economic organization.

Investment in Physical and Human Capital

Machines can have a substantial impact on a person's ability to produce. Even Robinson Crusoe on an uninhabited island can catch far more fish with a net than with his hands. Farmers working with modern tractors and plows can cultivate many more acres than their great-grandfathers, who probably worked with hoes. Similarly, education and training that improve the knowledge and skills of workers can vastly improve their productivity. For example, a cabinetmaker, skilled by years of training and experience, can build cabinets far more rapidly and efficiently than a lay person. Both physical capital (machines) and human capital (knowledge and skills) can expand the productive capacity of a worker.

However, the acquisition of physical and human capital involves an opportunity cost. When time and effort are expended on the production of machines or the development of skills, fewer resources are available for current production. There are no free lunches. The cost of additions to a nation's stock of physical and human capital is a reduction in current consumption.

As we discussed in Chapter 2 (see Exhibit 3 in that chapter), nations that allocate a larger share of their resources to investment expand their productive base more rapidly. Stated another way, a nation's investment rate affects its rate of economic growth. Other things constant, nations that invest more grow more rapidly.

Technological Progress

Technological Advancement: The introduction of new techniques or methods of production that enable a greater output per unit of input.

Technological improvement makes it possible to generate additional output with the same amount of resources. **Technological advancement**—the adoption of new techniques or methods of production—enables workers to produce goods at a fraction of the former cost. Less human and physical capital per unit of output is required.

Technological advancement is brought about by capital formation and research investments. Modern technological breakthroughs are generally the result of systematic investment in research and development. Thus, advancements in science and technology, like other improvements requiring investment expenditures, necessitate the sacrifice of current consumption.

When analyzing the phenomenal growth of Western nations during the nineteenth century, economic historians often point to dramatic technological advancements as the major source of economic progress. This view certainly has some merit. From a technological viewpoint, a person living in 1750 would probably have felt more at home in the world at the time of Christ than in today's society. During the last 250 years, technology has radically altered our way of life. The substitution of power-driven machines for human labor, the development of new sources of energy (for example, the steam engine, the internal combustion engine, hydroelectric power, and nuclear power), and developments in transportation and communications are the foundation of modern society. Without them, the growth and development of the last 250 years would have been impossible.

Of course, technological progress did not originate in the middle of the eighteenth century. The development of basic tools, the control of fire, the domestication of animals, and the development of bronze, pottery, and even iron, all of which represent fundamental technological progress, were accomplished before 1750. It is the rapidity and depth of recent technological progress that account for its uniqueness.

Invention: The discovery of a new product or process, often facilitated by the knowledge of engineering and scientific relationships.

Innovation: The successful introduction and adoption of a new product or process; the economic application of inventions.

Obviously, technological progress encompasses **invention,** the discovery of new products or processes. But it also includes **innovation,** the practical and effective adoption of new techniques. It is sometimes easy to overlook the significance of innovation, but it is crucial to economic development. Many innovators were not involved in the discovery of the products for which they are now famous. Henry Ford played a minor role in the discovery and development of the automobile. His contribution was an innovative one—the adoption of mass production techniques, which facilitated the low-cost production of a reliable automobile. J. C. Penney played an important role in American economic progress, not because he invented anything, but because he effectively introduced the department store. Inventions are important, but without innovators, inventions are merely ideas waiting to be exploited.

Although technological advancement has played an important role in the promotion of material progress, it is clearly not a sufficient condition for sustained economic growth. Modern technology is available to all, including the less developed nations. If technology were the only requirement for economic growth, the less developed nations would be growing rapidly. Unfortunately, this is not the case. Before modern technology can set growth in motion, the work force of a nation must be sufficiently knowledgeable to operate and maintain complex machines. Innovative entrepreneurs who are capable of adapting technology to the needs (and price structure) of a nation must be available and have access to resources. This means that capital investment and savings are required. Among less developed nations, these conditions generally do not exist. Thus, poverty and primitive methods of production survive in the modern world despite the availability of advanced technology.

Efficient Economic Organization

If a nation can improve the efficiency with which its resources are used, it will attain higher output levels and improve its growth rate. If the economic organi-

Allocative Inefficiency: The use of an uneconomical combination of resources to produce goods and services that are not intensely desired relative to their opportunity cost.

zation of a nation is inefficient and wasteful, growth will be stunted. Regardless of the economic organization, certain basic conditions must be met if waste and inefficiency are to be avoided. Resources must be used in the production of the goods and services most desired by people. **Allocative inefficiency** results when a nation's resources are used to produce the wrong products. For example, waste results when a nation, whose people intensely desire more food and better housing, uses valuable resources to produce unwanted national monuments and luxurious vacations for political leaders. In the same way, waste results when a nation that is ill-equipped to manufacture steel and automobiles insists on using resources that could be productive in other areas (for example, agriculture) in order to produce these prestige goods. Or governmental bureaucracies and regulations may require valuable resources to be used in unproductive ways. As we discussed earlier, noncompetitive conditions, spillover effects (externalities), and nonexclusive ownership (public goods) are also potential sources of allocative inefficiency. Regardless of whether an economy is centrally planned or market-directed, allocative inefficiency retards economic growth.

Economists have become increasingly interested in X-inefficiency,[3] a second source of economic waste. **X-inefficiency** arises when resources are not used to their full capacity, even though they may be directed to the production of the right goods. It may result from a perverse incentive structure that fails to reward productive behavior. For example, if all the workers of a firm were paid the same wage—if productive behavior and full work effort were unrewarded both today and in the future—individual workers would have little incentive to perform efficiently, to work to their full capacity. They would appear to be lazy and incompetent, although their inefficient performance might merely be a reflection of the incentive structure under which they toiled. X-inefficiency would be present because the lack of full work effort would generate waste and low levels of productivity.

X-inefficiency: The wasteful use of resources, which results in an output level that is lower than the output that could have been generated from the resources used.

X-inefficiency may also be rooted in tradition, superstition, and habitual ways of doing business. A society that stresses social station in life over individual effort is very unlikely to structure incentives that encourage productive behavior and the full utilization of human talent. Similarly, in nations where religious customs prohibit the slaughter of livestock despite its value as a food source, economic growth is retarded.

WHY POOR NATIONS REMAIN POOR: SOURCES OF ECONOMIC STAGNATION

In the middle of the eighteenth century, sustained economic growth began to take place throughout Europe and North America. By 1850, living standards in those parts of the world were substantially above subsistence level. Starvation and malnutrition were uncommon, even among the less well-off. By the middle of the twentieth century, the benefits of growth had spread to Japan, Oceania, and the Soviet Union, where living standards far surpassed those even imagined 250 years ago.

---

[3]See Harvey Leibenstein, *Beyond Economic Man* (Cambridge, Massachusetts: Harvard University Press, 1976), pp. 29–47.

Meanwhile, poverty, subsistence living standards, and malnutrition have remained throughout much of Asia, Africa, South America, and Central America. In some places—India, for example—sustained economic growth in real per capita income has been largely nonexistent. People continue to live and die in a world of poverty, malnutrition, and disease, just as they have done for thousands of years.

Why have industrialization and economic growth passed by these people? There is no single, comprehensive answer to this question. However, we can point to several obstacles to economic growth.

Obstacle 1: A Low Savings Rate Contributes to the Vicious Circle of Underdevelopment. Capital formation is an important potential stimulus to economic growth. However, investment necessitates saving. Resources that are used to enhance a nation's future productive capacity are unavailable for the production of food, shelter, and other necessities of life.

Exhibit 5 illustrates the dilemma that underdeveloped nations face. They are caught in a **vicious circle of underdevelopment.**[4] Since living standards are barely above the subsistence level, these countries use most of their resources for the provision of current consumption goods, such as food, clothing, and housing. Little is left for investment. Nations that invest (and save) little grow slowly. Since most underdeveloped nations have a low savings (and therefore low investment) rate, their growth rate is slower than that of advanced nations that invest a larger share of their GNP.

Real-world data are consistent with the vicious circle of underdevelopment. The savings (and investment) rate in most countries of Africa and Southeast Asia is between 10 and 15 percent of GNP. In contrast, the rate for industrial nations is between 20 and 25 percent. Thus, very low investment rates in the underdeveloped nations tend to ensure continued poverty.[5]

Vicious Circle of Underdevelopment: A pattern of low income and slow economic growth, which tends to perpetuate itself. Since the current consumption demands of poor nations are large in proportion to available income, the savings and investment rates of these nations are low. In turn, the low investment rate retards future growth, causing poor nations to remain poor.

---

[4]Ragnor Nurkse provides a clear statement of the vicious circle of underdevelopment:

In discussions of the problem of economic development, a phrase that crops up frequently is "the vicious circle of poverty."

A situation of this sort [the vicious circle of underdevelopment] relating to a country as a whole, can be summed up in the trite proposition: "A country is poor because it is poor." . . . The supply of capital is governed by the ability and willingness to save; the demand for capital is governed by the incentives to invest.

On the supply side, there is the small capacity to save, resulting from the low level of real income. . . .

On the demand side, the inducement to invest may be low because of the small buying power of the people, which is due to their small real income, which again is due to low productivity.

See Ragnor Nurkse, *Problems of Capital Formation in Underdeveloped Countries* (New York: Oxford University Press, 1953), pp. 4–5.

[5]See the World Bank, *World Development Report, 1981* (Washington, D.C.: International Bank for Reconstruction and Development, 1981), Table 5, for detailed evidence that savings and investment rates are positively linked to the income level of a nation.

EXHIBIT 5 **The vicious circle of underdevelopment**

Since incomes are low in under-developed nations, savings and investment rates are also low. Low rates of investment retard the future growth of income. Thus, underdevelopment is self-perpetuating. The circle is complicated by the population bomb, which often explodes when a country begins to break out of the pattern.

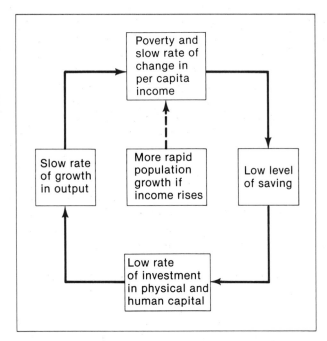

Obstacle 2: The Population Bomb May Explode as Soon as Growth Improves Living Standards. In 1798, Thomas Malthus argued that living standards would never climb much above subsistence level because an improvement in economic well-being would cause people to have more children. Thus, any temporary improvement in economic welfare would cause the population to increase until per capita incomes returned to subsistence levels. Therefore, according to Malthus, economic growth would trigger a population explosion, which would eradicate the temporary gains associated with growth.

The experience of Europe and North America during the last 250 years is clearly inconsistent with the crude Malthusian theory. However, recent historical data on income and population have caused some development economists to reevaluate the relevance of Malthus's ideas. High rates of population growth do appear to retard economic growth in some countries. The rate of population growth in the poor countries of Asia, Africa, and South America is typically two or three times the rate in the wealthy industrial nations. Thus, the poor countries would theoretically have to grow substantially more rapidly than industrial nations merely to maintain the same rate of growth of *per capita income*.

Rapid population growth in underdeveloped nations is also likely to increase the **dependency ratio,** the number of children and older persons divided by the total population. Improvements in health associated with economic growth usually lead to a decline in the rate of infant mortality and an increase in the proportion of older people as a share of the total population. With more young children and elderly nonworkers, the burden imposed on the productive working-age population is compounded. The experiences of such countries as India, Bangladesh, Burma, and Egypt, all of which have a rapid

Dependency Ratio: The number of children (under a specific age — 14, for example) plus the number of the elderly (age 65 and over) living in a country, divided by the total population. An increasing ratio indicates that a larger burden is being placed on the productive-age work force.

rate of population expansion, suggest that the population bomb complicates the growth process.[6]

Obstacle 3: Political Instability May Discourage Investment and Retard Growth. Suppose that in a certain country a political revolution resulting in governmental expropriation of land holdings, buildings, and other business assets seemed imminent. Or suppose that you feared the rise of a new regime that would impose punitive taxes on interest income, profits, and/or capital assets. Would you want to invest your savings in such a country? Most people would not.

As a rule of thumb, the more securely present and future property rights are defined, the more capital formation there will be. In contrast, insecurely defined property rights and a potentially volatile political climate will repel capital investment and retard economic growth.

Unfortunately, the political climate of many underdeveloped nations is highly unstable. Prejudice and injustice, a highly unequal distribution of wealth, and a history of political favoritism to a ruling class make political upheaval a distinct possibility. Wise investors, both domestic and foreign, avoid investment in real assets under these conditions. Those who do undertake business ventures find it advantageous to seek favors (and assurances) from the military and ruling classes. This may aggravate the situation in the long run. Unquestionably, several Latin American countries have suffered because of their political instability. Nationalization and the threat of expropriation have discouraged both domestic and foreign investment. Continued poverty and economic stagnation have been the results.

Again, many underdeveloped nations are caught in a vicious cycle. The level of poverty is such that many are willing to support political revolution in the hope that it will better their lot. As the possibility of political upheaval increases, however, the investment necessary to improve the economic welfare of the citizenry comes to a standstill. In turn, the low rate of investment and

---

[6]The dependency ratio for a typical group of less developed and developed countries is presented below.

	Dependency Ratio (Percentage of Population under the Age of 14 or over the Age of 64)
Less developed countries	
Bangladesh	46
India	44
Burma	45
Egypt	43
Developed countries	
United States	34
Canada	33
Japan	32
United Kingdom	36
West Germany	34

Although the productive contribution and consumption burden of children and the elderly differ among countries, it is clear that the prime-working-age population of the developed nations has fewer nonproducers to support than that of the less developed nations. See the World Bank, *World Development Report, 1981,* Table 19, for more extensive data.

accompanying economic stagnation make political revolution still more likely. Many underdeveloped nations will be unable to improve their economic conditions until they solve the problem of political instability.

Obstacle 4: Waste and Inefficiency Can Result from Noneconomic Factors. Some students of economic development believe that noneconomic factors may impose even greater limitations on growth than do strictly economic factors. We have already alluded to the fact that traditions and attitudes can inhibit growth. Neither habitual methods of subsistence survival nor hopelessness are easily changed. Such consequences of poverty as ignorance and superstition can also become barriers to economic progress.

Peter Bauer, a British development economist, believes that less developed nations are more likely to grow when they have substantial business contact with the developed world. He argues that such contacts provide a "demonstration effect," which tends to undermine attitudes and customs that inhibit growth:

These [contacts with the developed world] are the channels through which human and material resources, skills and capital from developed countries reach the underdeveloped world. These contacts open up markets and sources of supply and bring new commodities, wants, crops and methods of cultivation to the notice of the local population. They also engender a new outlook towards material possessions and the means of obtaining them. And perhaps most important, they undermine customs, attitudes and values which obstruct material advance.[7]

The size of some nations can also limit their economic development. More than two centuries ago, Adam Smith pointed out that specialization is limited by the "extent of the market." If the market is small, the gains to be made from specialization in production are limited. Small nations are less capable than other countries of developing large, integrated markets that would enable them to realize these potential gains. Of course, they can encourage free trade, but domestic industries can be expected to consume valuable resources in an effort to reach the competitive levels of larger foreign suppliers. Thus, domestic prices tend to be higher than they would be for larger markets in larger countries. Also, a small nation has difficulty offsetting the normal cost and uncertainty involved in foreign business and therefore often fails to attract foreign entrepreneurs and investors.

Regardless of their size, nations generally have their own (a) monetary system, (b) political system, which establishes economic rules and regulations, and (c) government bureaucracies, which provide both economic and political goods. But for a small nation the cost of providing "public goods" like monetary and legal systems means a larger per capita tax burden than for larger countries, because the costs of any system must be spread over a smaller population. These factors have limited the development of small nations such as those in Latin America.

It is interesting to speculate as to the path that economic development would have taken in the United States had this country been divided into numerous nations (rather than states), each with its own monetary system, economic rules, and legal system. Unquestionably, there would have been fewer

---

[7]Peter T. Bauer, *Dissent on Development* (Cambridge, Massachusetts: Harvard University Press, 1972), pp. 300–301.

gains from specialization and trade. In all likelihood, the standard of living enjoyed by most Americans would have been substantially lower. This is precisely what has happened in Latin America and, to a lesser degree, in Africa and South America. Limitations imposed by the size of the nations in these areas have undoubtedly retarded their economic development.

LOOKING AHEAD   In the following chapter, we will use economic tools to analyze different economic systems. First, however, we will consider the diversity of economic records among the less developed countries.

PERSPECTIVES IN ECONOMICS

RICH AND POOR NATIONS— ARE THEY TWO WORLDS DRIFTING APART?

The differences in living standards among nations were not as extreme 250 years ago as they are today. In the mid-eighteenth century, people thought differently about development because almost everyone was poor. Of course, there were rich nations and poor nations, but the per capita income of the rich was seldom more than twice that of the poor.

During the eighteenth century, sustained economic growth took place throughout much of Europe and North America. By 1850, there was a virtual explosion of economic development, and it soon spread to Oceania, Russia, and Japan. Not only did industrial nations grow rapidly during this period, but the fruits of growth also were widely dispersed. The living standards of both the well-off and those not so well-off increased substantially. Today, even poor people in North America, Europe, and Japan are far better off than most citizens of an underdeveloped nation. The present level of affluence in the developed nations is unprecedented.

The growth of the last century has created an enormous gulf between the developed and less developed countries. Whereas the per capita income of the wealthy nations in the mid-nineteenth century was approximately twice that of the poor countries, today the average income of persons in the developed nations is probably five times greater (see Exhibit 2). Some observers have argued that the world is comprised of growing industrial nations on the one hand and stagnated, less developed countries on the other. According to this view, the widening gap between the rich and poor nations threatens to plunge the world into crisis. The evidence indicates that this view is highly oversimplified. The less developed countries are not a monolithic block of humanity condemned forever to poverty and stagnation but rather some 90 nations with widely varying growth rates and records. Exhibit 6 highlights this diversity.

The less developed nations in the early and middle 1980s can be broken down into several groups. (Even with this analysis, there will of course be some oversimplification.) First, there are the densely populated nations that can be said to be barely winning the battle for economic survival. The per capita incomes of Ethiopia, Ghana, and Zaire in fact declined during the 1970s. The growth of per capita income in India, Bangladesh, and Burma was less than the growth rate of most industrial nations. The growth of per capita income in other poor, primarily small, nations (Sudan, Haiti, Guinea, Niger, Nepal, Afghanistan, Somalia, Chad, Upper Volta, Laos, and Vietnam among them) was insignificant or, in several cases, nonexistent. Approximately one-quarter of the world's population lives in these very poor, stagnating nations. The twentieth century has passed them by. They eke out a subsistence living, while the economic development of their countries falls farther and farther behind that of the more developed nations.

Most of these nations face all of the obstacles to growth that we have just described. Relentless poverty keeps their saving and investment rates very low. Political instability and insecure property rights discourage investment. Trade barriers, as well as the small size of markets, often limit exchange. As a result of the population bomb, there are more and more people for the productive members of the population to feed. The future of these nations is bleak. We economists are forced to admit that we do not have a satisfactory answer to their economic problems.

There is a second group of less developed countries that have attained a very impressive growth record. As Exhibit 6 illustrates, during the 1970s the growth of per capita income in Brazil, Egypt, South Korea, Singapore, Indonesia, Nigeria, and Hong Kong exceeded the growth rate of the richer industrial nations. Even among this group, there is considerable diversity. Some (Nigeria and Indonesia) are rich with minerals, but others (Hong Kong and Egypt) have few natural resources. Both large and small countries are included. If they have anything in common, it would appear to be economic and political stability. During the last decade, property rights

EXHIBIT 6   Wealth of nations—growth of population and income

Selected Countries	Per Capita GNP, 1979 (U.S. Dollars)	Percentage of World Population, 1979	Average Annual Growth Rate 1970–1979 (Percent)		
			GNP	Population	GNP per Capita
Poor country (slow growth in per capita income)					
India	190	15.4	3.4	2.1	1.3
Bangladesh	90	2.1	3.3	3.0	0.3
Ethiopia	130	0.7	1.9	2.1	−0.2
Burma	160	0.8	4.3	2.2	2.1
Ghana	400	0.3	−0.1	3.0	−3.1
Zaire	260	0.6	−0.7	2.7	−3.4
Poor country (rapid growth in per capita income)					
Brazil	1,780	2.7	8.7	2.2	6.5
Egypt	480	0.9	7.6	2.0	5.6
South Korea	1,480	0.9	10.3	1.9	8.4
Singapore	3,830	0.1	8.4	1.4	7.0
Indonesia	370	3.3	7.6	2.3	5.3
Nigeria	670	1.9	7.5	2.5	5.0
Hong Kong	3,760	0.1	9.4	2.6	6.8
Rich country (rapid growth in per capita income)					
United States	10,630	5.2	3.1	1.0	2.1
Soviet Union	4,110	6.2	5.1	0.9	4.2
Japan	8,810	2.7	5.2	1.1	4.1
Germany	11,730	1.4	2.6	0.1	2.5
France	9,950	1.2	3.7	0.6	3.1
Sweden	11,930	0.2	2.0	0.3	1.7
Canada	9,640	0.6	4.2	1.1	3.1
Australia	9,120	0.3	3.2	1.5	1.7

The World Bank, *World Development Report, 1981.*

have been relatively secure in each of these less developed countries experiencing rapid growth, and as a result, each has attracted substantial foreign private investment. With the possible exception of Egypt, aid from foreign governments has played little part in the rapid growth of these nations.

Another point to be made is that the populations of the less developed countries are growing very rapidly in comparison with those of the developed countries. This is true for both poor countries with rapid economic growth rates and those experiencing little or no growth. The population of the developed countries is expanding at a rate of approximately

1 percent annually; the population growth rate of the less developed countries is generally two or three times more rapid.

For the less developed countries that have experienced substantial economic development, population growth is both a problem and an opportunity. It is a problem because population expansion is clearly running a tight race with economic growth. Mexico is a case in point. This Latin American country is sufficiently large so that its domestic markets are attractive to foreign investors and suppliers. The size of its domestic markets enables it to capture most of the potential gains from specialization and

expansion of the markets. Mexico has a history of political stability and rule of law. Property rights are clearly defined. Free enterprise is flourishing. The growth rate of real GNP averaged 6 percent annually during the 1960–1980 period.

However, despite this rapid growth rate, economic development is threatened by a rapidly expanding population. Mexico has one of the world's highest population growth rates, 3.0 percent annually. There were 25 million Mexicans in 1950 and 68 million in 1980, and projections indicate that there will be 133 million by the year 2000 (half as many citizens as the United States will then have).

Mexico City's population of 12 to 14 million is likely to double during the next decade. Mexico City may soon be the world's largest city.

Mexico would derive several benefits from a reduction in its rate of population growth. A reduction in the birth rate would result in a smaller number of dependents per working-age adult, which would stimulate the growth in per capita income. The rising real income would in turn generate additional savings and the investment necessary to sustain a rapid growth rate. Thus, if a population explosion could be avoided, Mexico (and other rapidly growing less developed countries such as Brazil, South Korea, Singapore, Indonesia, Nigeria, and perhaps China) might well follow in the footsteps of Japan and by the turn of the century begin to move rapidly up the ladder of economic development.

CHAPTER LEARNING OBJECTIVES

1 The major characteristics of less developed countries are (a) low per capita income, (b) a large agriculture–household sector, (c) rapid population growth, (d) inequality of income distribution, and (e) widespread illiteracy coupled with poor educational and health facilities.

2 For the first time in history, economic growth is such that per capita income far surpasses the subsistence level in most of Europe, North America, Oceania, Japan, and the Soviet Union. Living conditions have been transformed for the one-quarter of the world's population that reside in these regions.

3 In contrast, nearly 60 percent of the world's population maintain a bare subsistence level of income in countries with a per capita GNP of less than $1000 per year. These countries generate only 7.3 percent of the world's GNP.

4 Although there is no sharp dividing line between developed and less developed countries, the nations of North America, Europe (including the Soviet Union), and Oceania, as well as Japan, can be classified as developed countries. In contrast, most of the countries of Asia, Africa, South America, and Latin America exhibit the characteristics of underdevelopment.

5 Using the purchasing power parity method, we find that the per capita income of the developed nations was approximately five times greater than that of the less developed countries in 1980.

6 Economic growth is a positive concept. Extensive growth is present when the real GNP of a nation expands. Intensive growth requires an increase in output *per person*. Economic development is a normative concept, encompassing distributional and structural factors as well as higher per capita income. Economic development implies an advance in the standard of living for a broad cross section of a nation's population, including those people in the bottom half of the income distribution.

7 Small differences in growth rates can be important in the long run. For example, suppose that the incomes of countries A and B were initially equal. If the annual growth rate of country A were 4 percent and that of B were 2 percent, the income of A would be twice that of B after 36 years.

8 The availability of domestic natural resources is not the major determinant of growth. Such countries as Japan and Hong Kong have impressive growth rates without such resources, whereas many resource-rich nations continue to stagnate.

9 The presence of a skilled and disciplined work force is a major determinant of economic well-being. Investment in physical and human capital, technological advancement, and improvements in the efficiency of economic organization are important sources of economic growth.

10 The major obstacles to economic development among the poor nations of the world are (a) a low investment rate, which is a reflection of the vicious circle of underdevelopment; (b) rapid population growth; (c) political instability, which reduces the security

of property rights and thereby retards investment; and (d) waste and inefficiency, which can result from attitudes of the work force toward material progress—due to either weak incentive structures or traditional patterns and beliefs—or from the small size of nations, among other things.

11   The economic growth record of the less developed countries is mixed. Approximately one-quarter of the world's inhabitants continue to eke out a bare subsistence in countries where the per capita income is growing slowly, if at all. The rates of population growth in these countries are among the highest in the world. Their economic prospects are bleak. In contrast, the recent economic growth records of Brazil, Egypt, Mexico, South Korea, Singapore, Indonesia, Nigeria, and Hong Kong have been highly impressive. If the rates of population growth in these countries decline in the near future, they might well duplicate the "Japanese miracle."

THE ECONOMIC WAY OF THINKING—DISCUSSION QUESTIONS

1   Suppose that you are an economic adviser to the president of Mexico. You have been asked to suggest policies to promote economic growth and a higher standard of living for the citizens of Mexico. Outline your suggestions and discuss why you believe that they would be helpful.

2   Explain the logic of the vicious circle of underdevelopment. How can a poor nation break out of this circle?

3   It is often argued that the rich nations are getting richer and the poor are getting poorer. Is this view correct? Is it an oversimplification? Explain.

4   As the people of a nation become wealthier, do you think that they will save a larger percentage of their income? Why? As a nation becomes wealthier, do you think that the length of the average workweek will decline? Why? Does the experience of the United States support your answer? Explain.

5   The size of the population in some countries may partially reflect the desire of some people for additional security in the form of children to support them in their old age. Is this method of providing for one's retirement inferior to our system of compulsory social security? Why or why not?

6   Discuss the importance of the following as determinants of economic growth: (a) natural resources; (b) physical capital; (c) human capital; (d) technical knowledge; (e) attitudes of the work force; and (f) size of the domestic market.

Since the activities of individuals in the use of the means of production are regulated, at any given time and place, through the institutions then and there prevailing, the precise manner in which society will use its means of production will depend upon and be determined by the character of its economic institutions.[1]
Howard R. Bowen

34

COMPARATIVE ECONOMIC SYSTEMS

The institutions and organization of an economy influence economic outcomes. We have focused our analysis primarily on private-property, market-directed economies. The economies of the United States, Canada, Australia, Japan, and most of Western Europe fall into this category. These economies, as we have pointed out, do not always rely on market forces. The government regulates many private industries. Government ownership and operation of utilities, transportation, communication, and educational facilities are not uncommon, even in Western countries. In addition, taxes and government subsidies are sometimes used to alter market outcomes. Throughout this book, we have used economic tools to help us understand the incentives and expected results of governmental policy that redirects market forces.

Today, nearly one-third of the world's population lives in the Soviet Union, Eastern Europe, and China. The economies of these countries are organized along socialist lines. They are characterized by central planning and government ownership. Market-directed capitalism and centrally planned socialism are two systems of economic organization. However, there are many variations of each. For example, the economic organization of Yugoslavia differs substantially from that of the Soviet Union. The Japanese economy differs from the capitalistic organization of the United States and Western European countries. After examining the general institutional arrangements of both socialist and capitalist systems, we will take a closer look at the economic organization and performance of three interesting economies—those of the Soviet Union, Yugoslavia, and Japan.

---

[1] Howard R. Bowen, *Toward Social Economy* (New York: Holt, 1946), p. 52.

COMMON CONSTRAINTS AND THE UNIVERSALITY OF ECONOMIC TOOLS

All economic systems, despite their differences, face similar constraints. Scarcity of economic goods confronts both individuals and nations with a budgetary problem. No nation is able to produce as much as its citizens would like to consume. Therefore, regardless of economic organization, choices must be made. The decision to satisfy one desire leaves many other desires unsatisfied. All economic systems are constrained by the bonds of scarcity.

Many other economic concepts that have been discussed throughout this book apply to *all* economic systems. Let us reconsider and summarize four of these basic ideas.

1. Opportunity Cost. An economy can be organized so that various goods can be provided without charge to the consumer, but economic organization cannot eliminate the opportunity costs associated with the provision of goods. The provision of additional medical sevices, even if distributed free, necessitates the use of resources that could have been used to produce other things. Similarly, if there is an expansion of the national defense sector, there must be a contraction of other sectors. Whenever productive resources have alternative uses, as they almost always do, the production of goods is costly, regardless of the form of economic organization.

2. Law of Diminishing Returns. According to this law, the ability of each nation to generate output from its (at least temporarily) "fixed" supply of land, natural resources, human capital, and man-made physical capital is limited. With time, the supply of some of these resources can be expanded. However, a nation's ability to expand its resource base is directly related to its willingness to allocate more of its current production to investment in human and nonhuman capital. This, of course, necessitates the sacrifice of current consumption. Since the law of diminishing returns—increasing use of a resource will increase output by smaller and smaller amounts until the supply constraint of the resource is reached— applies to all economies, continual expansion in production requires a nation to expand its resource base continually.

3. Comparative Advantage and Efficiency. Total production is greatest when each good is generated by the low opportunity cost producer. The assignment of a productive task to a high opportunity cost producer is inefficient (that is, output will be below its potential level), regardless of whether the activity takes place in a capitalist or socialist economy. No matter what the type of economic organization, the goal of efficient production can best be attained by heeding the principle of comparative advantage.

4. Law of Diminishing Marginal Utility. Consumers in both socialist and capitalist countries place less value on marginal units of a good as their consumption level of it increases. If the central planners of a country create a large amount of low-cost housing but very few private automobiles, marginal units of the housing will decline in value relative to the cars.

Incentives Matter

Economic organization is important because it affects everyone's actions. Changes in the structure of incentives alter human behavior in both capitalist and socialist countries. For example, at one time in the Soviet Union, the managers of glass plants were rewarded according to the tons of sheet glass produced. Not surprisingly, most plants produced sheet glass so thick that one could hardly see through it. The rules were changed so that the managers were rewarded according to the square meters of glass produced. The managers reacted in a predictable way. Under the new rules, Soviet firms produced very thin glass that broke easily. Incentives matter, even to the managers of Soviet firms.

In our analysis of alternative economic systems, we will focus on how economic organization affects people's motivations. Marxists often argue that communism will eventually alter basic human motivations. They believe that people will cease to respond in predictable, traditional ways to changes in *personal* costs and benefits. Perhaps this is so, but the experiences of the Soviet Union and other Communist countries have produced little evidence to support this view. Therefore, until human nature does change radically, an analysis based on the postulate that incentives do affect human decisions is most relevant. This is not to say that only economic considerations matter. Religious, cultural, and political factors can and do influence economic behavior. The economic approach does not deny their importance.

CONTRASTING CAPITALISM AND SOCIALISM

Socialism: A system of economic organization in which (a) the ownership and control of the basic means of production rest with the state and (b) resource allocation is determined by centralized planning rather than by market forces.

Joseph Schumpeter, the renowned Harvard economist, defined **socialism** as:

. . . an institutional pattern in which the control over means of production and over production itself is vested with a central authority—or, as we may say, in which, as a matter of principle, the economic affairs of society belong to the public and not the private sphere.[2]

As Schumpeter's definition implies, capitalist and socialist economic organizations differ in two important respects—ownership of physical capital and resource allocation.

Ownership of Physical Capital

Every economic system has a legal framework within which the rights of resource owners are defined. Practically all economic systems guarantee the rights of individuals to sell their own human capital—their labor—to the highest bidder. Earnings are derived from the sale of labor services in both capitalist and socialist societies. However, under socialism, the rewards obtained from the use of *physical* capital (machines, buildings, etc.) in the production process accrue to the state. If the state actually owns the nonhuman productive resources, the earnings they generate go directly to the state. The state can also use taxation to gain at least partial control over earnings that would otherwise accrue to other owners of physical capital. In either case, under socialism, investment in physical capital reflects the views of the state.

Resource Allocation

Every economy must have a mechanism that coordinates the economic activity of microunits—business firms, individual resource owners, and consumers. The

---

[2]Joseph A. Schumpeter, *Capitalism, Socialism, and Democracy,* 3rd ed. (New York: Harper, 1950), p. 167.

mechanism must solve such problems as the use of resources, the selective production of goods, and the distribution of income.

Under market-directed **capitalism,** economic activity is coordinated by contractual agreements between private parties who possess property rights to products and resources. There is no central planning mechanism. Market prices direct the actions of decentralized decision-makers. The forces of supply and demand push prices up or down in response to the decisions of individual buyers and sellers.

Capitalism: An economic system based on private ownership of productive resources and allocation of goods according to the signals provided by free markets.

Under a socialist economic organization, resources are used and allocated in accordance with a centrally determined and administered scheme. Economic decisions, such as what and how much will be produced, the relative proportions of investment and consumption, how resources will be used in production, and to whom the product will be distributed, are made by a central authority. The central plan may also include decisions on quantities of raw materials and inputs, techniques of production, prices, wages, locations of firms and industries, and the employment of labor. Socialist economic objectives generally reflect the preferences and value judgments of the central planners. These objectives may or may not reflect the views of consumers.

Exhibit 1 summarizes the distinctive characteristics of capitalist and socialist economic organization. Private property rights, market determination of employment, investment, and resource and product allocation, and a market-determined pattern of income distribution are characteristic of capitalism. Government ownership (or control) of physical capital, allocation of capital and consumer goods by means of central planning, and a distribution of income that reflects the views of the central planners tend to characterize socialist economic organization.

Classifying Real-World Economies

In reality, all modern economies use some combination of capitalist and socialist economic organization. Primarily capitalist economies use government regulation, selective government ownership, and taxation to modify the forces of

EXHIBIT 1   Contrasting capitalism and socialism

	Capitalism	Socialism
Property rights	Nonhuman resources are owned by private parties (for example, individuals or corporations)	Nonhuman resources are owned by the state
Employment	Workers are self-employed or employed by private firms	Workers are employed by the government or government-controlled cooperatives
Investment	Undertaken by private parties seeking profits and higher future incomes	Undertaken by the government in accordance with the objectives of the planners
Allocation of goods and resources	Determined by market forces	Determined by centralized planning
Income distribution	Determined by market forces that reward productivity and ownership of economic resources	Determined by central planners who may seek to promote equality or any other desired pattern of income distribution

EXHIBIT 2 A spectrum of economic systems

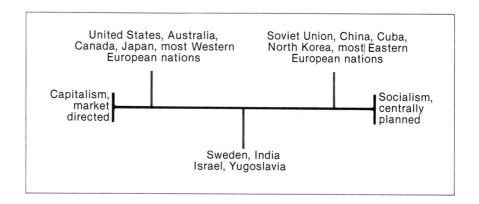

United States, Australia, Canada, Japan, most Western European nations

Soviet Union, China, Cuba, North Korea, most Eastern European nations

Capitalism, market directed

Socialism, centrally planned

Sweden, India Israel, Yugoslavia

supply and demand. In socialist countries, central planning and administrative control exist side by side with a small but often highly significant market system.

Exhibit 2 presents a rough classification of several countries according to their reliance on capitalist or socialist economic organization. The United States, Australia, Canada, Japan, and most Western European countries fall at the market capitalism end of the spectrum. The Soviet Union, China, and most other Communist countries are at the opposite end. Welfare-state economies, such as those of Sweden and Israel, and market-directed socialist economies, such as that of Yugoslavia, fall between these two extremes.

OUTSTANDING ECONOMIST
Karl Marx (1818–1883)

Karl Marx was much more than an economist. He was a philosopher, a historian, a sociologist, a political scientist—and a revolutionary. More has been written about Marx than about any other economist. His most famous work, written with Friedrich Engels, is *The Communist Manifesto* (1848). The most complete statement of Marx's economic views is contained in his monumental *Das Kapital* (1867). He also wrote a large number of political and philosophical articles. Like other socialists, Marx advocated collective ownership and control of factories and other capital assets. But unlike most socialist theoreticians, Marx advocated a mass working-class movement to overthrow capitalism and usher in a new socialist world order. He believed that such a revolution was inevitable in any case; he sought to speed it on its way.

Marx was born in Trier, Germany, in 1818. While studying at the University of Berlin, he developed an interest in the philosophy of Hegel that was to influence his own work considerably. After finishing his doctorate at the University of Jena, Marx espoused revolutionary causes and attempted to promote the working-class movement throughout Europe during the widespread political upheavals of 1848. His activities as a radical led to his exile from Germany, France, and Belgium. In 1849 he moved to London, where he and Engels began an intellectual partnership that lasted until Marx's death in 1883. Marx lived those 34 years with his wife and children in poverty, isolation, and poor health. He expended his energies on the writing of *Das Kapital*, often working from early morning through the late hours of the night. After Marx's death, Engels edited and published the second and third volumes of the massive work.

Marxian theory applies Hegel's dialectical method of logic (thesis—antithesis—synthesis) to the observable, concrete phenomena of nature and society. Hegel's belief in the primacy of ideas is rejected; the material world takes priority. This application is known as dialectical materialism. History is perceived as a dynamic, dialectical process characterized by the struggle between social classes. Each ruling class becomes outmoded with time, reactivating the struggle with other classes, causing political and economic crises, and eventually leading to the overthrow of the existing social structure and the creation of a new structure. Marx used the decline and fall of feudalism and the rise of capitalism and the bourgeoisie in Europe as an illustration of his theory. He stressed that the transition periods are sometimes violent, as in the case of the Enclosure Movement (in which English peasants were driven from the land) and the 1789 French Revolution.

Marx predicted that the capitalist ruling class, having fulfilled its economic functions, would eventually fall. He believed that capitalist growth would depress the rate of profit, causing severe economic crises (recessions and depressions) and forcing capitalists, in order to maintain their own standard of living, to oppress the working class further. This would not only encourage the workers to take power but would allow them to do so, because the capitalist class would grow weaker and weaker. Although Marx believed the final victory of the industrial proletariat over the bourgeoisie was inevitable, he advocated revolutionary activity to accelerate the process and prepare the working class for its future role. Once the revolution became a reality, the ruling proletariat would "centralize all instruments of production in the hands of the state," which Marx believed would lead to a rapid increase in production and efficiency. But Marx emphasized that workers must directly control not only the means of production but also the political process.

Marx argued that a workers' government would dismantle the existing state institutions and set up a new, fundamentally more democratic system, even if violence were required to do so. The successful revolution would thoroughly eliminate the bourgeoisie and culminate in a classless society, to which all individuals would voluntarily contribute "according to their abilities" and by which they would be rewarded "according to their needs."

Much of Marx's economic analysis attacked the ideas of the classical economists, led by Adam Smith, whose defense of capitalism Marx found untenable. Smith believed that market coordination brought individual self-interest and economic progress into harmony; Marx viewed history, including the economic activities that shaped it, as characterized by conflict and class struggle. Smith believed that market exchange would release individuals from the oppression of government. Marx, on the other hand, believed capitalist economic activity to be the oppressor from which people should (and would) be freed. Harmony would exist only in the classless socialist state.

Marx's ideas began to attract worldwide attention in the late nineteenth century. The Social Democratic Party of Germany, a large political party, declared itself Marxist in 1875. Marx's ideas influenced Eugene V. Debs, the Socialist Party candidate for the U.S. presidency who received nearly 1 million votes in 1920. Today, many governments claim to be Marxist, but Marx's prescription for worker democracy is seldom actually followed.

World history since Marx's time has validated some of his predictions and disproved others. Marx foresaw the advent of large corporations, the worldwide expansion of capitalism, and the rise of large working-class organizations. There have been, as Marx predicted, severe economic and political crises, such as the Great Depression of the 1930s, but contrary to his expectations, capitalism has always (so far) recovered. Marx's belief that proletarian revolutions would take place first in the most developed countries—the Western European countries and the United States—has been proved unfounded. Although Marx did not restrict revolution to the advanced countries, he might be surprised to find that the major socialist revolutions have occurred in Russia and China—countries that at the time of their revolutions were underdeveloped and largely agricultural, with only small industrial working classes. Classless societies have not yet evolved in these nations; the socialist governments have been primarily concerned, not with class oppression, but with economic development.

The postrevolutionary stage is thus a troublesome area for modern followers of Marx. Where are the classless societies? There is little evidence that the state will eventually wither away after capitalism is abolished. In fact, the all-powerful bureaucratic state is most imposing in the Soviet Union, the most highly developed of the existing communist societies.

Command Economy: An authoritarian socialist economy that is characterized by centralized planning and detailed directives to productive units. Individual enterprises have little discretionary decision-making power.

THE SOVIET ECONOMY

The Soviet economy is a **command economy.** Centralized economic decision-making by planners and detailed directives to production units (for example, firms and collective farms) are the dominant characteristics of a command economy. The Soviet government owns and operates almost all of the industrial sector, the foreign trade, transportation and communications, and banking and financial institutions, a sizable portion of the agriculture sector, and most of the wholesale and retail network. The state sector of the Soviet economy is the largest economic unit in the world. It employs approximately 110 million workers, both white and blue collar. Even General Motors and American Telephone and Telegraph are small in comparison.[3]

In a sense, the state-operated Soviet economy is akin to a giant corporation, with Communist party members acting as stockholders. The party establishes the economic policy objectives, strives to ensure their execution, and oversees the bureaucracy necessary to carry out the details of the planning directives. As in Western economies, the basic unit of economic activity is the business firm, which the Soviets call an enterprise. Soviet enterprises, much like individual factories (or units) of a large U.S. corporation, take their orders from the central planning authorities.

Gosplan: The central planning agency in the Soviet Union.

How does the giant corporation, the state sector of the Soviet economy, function? The **Gosplan,** the government's central planning agency, drafts the basic economic plan for the entire economy. At present, both a five-year plan (which focuses on long-range objectives) and an annual plan are constructed by the Gosplan. These operational economic plans are written into law by the Soviet government. The basic economic plan is directed to the more than 200,000 enterprises. It sets production targets and establishes the resource constraints—including allotted amounts of raw materials, labor, machines, and so on—for each state enterprise. The problem of the enterprise is to transform its allotted inputs into the target output. The operational targets of the annual plan are used as criteria in evaluating the performance of a firm at the end of the planning period and in rewarding it accordingly.

The Problem of Coordination

Under Soviet planning, commodities and raw materials are centrally rationed in physical terms. The traditional way of reconciling supply of and demand for these materials has been the "method of material balances." For such commodities as petroleum, petrochemicals, iron and steel, coal, and timber, among many others, this method essentially consists of maintaining a balance sheet of all sources of supply (for example, local production, imports, and inventories) and all sources of demand (for example, requirements of local consumers, exports, and inventories). The Gosplan, in planning the final output and input targets, goes through a repetitive trial and error process of balancing demand and supply for these products until it reaches the final set of imperative targets. The final set is then used as a basis for physical rationing.

Under this system, the output of one enterprise (steel, for example) is generally the input of another enterprise (a tractor-producing firm, for example). The failure of one firm to meet its production quota sets off a domino effect. Firms that are not supplied with adequate inputs fail to meet their production quotas unless they make adjustments.

Consider the problem that arises if the target output for, say, trucks is increased by 20 percent. The planners must take additional steps to ensure that the truck-producing enterprises receive the right amount of labor, capital equip-

[3]The ten largest firms in the United States employed approximately 3.5 million workers in 1980.

ment, component parts manufactured by other enterprises, and raw materials such as steel, aluminum, glass, and copper. If other suppliers fail to meet their quotas to the truck-manufacturing enterprises, the truck manufacturers will also fail to meet their quotas.

The Soviet planners confront an enormous coordination problem in order to make sure that each enterprise receives just the right amount of labor and materials at just the right time in order to keep things moving smoothly. Literally billions of interrelated planning decisions must be made.

Of course, with mathematical techniques and computer technology, it is theoretically possible to arrive at a solution that will provide the right amount of each input to each enterprise so that quotas can all be met. But what happens when there is an unexpected change—perhaps adverse weather conditions or equipment failure? Bottlenecks will develop. Confronted with an input shortage, enterprise managers often cut corners in order to meet their production quotas. For example, they may use less than the specified amount of the input in short supply.[4] Alternatively, they may attempt to make a deal with other enterprise managers to supply the input in exchange for a similar future or past favor. An informal system of connections exists among successful enterprise managers in the Soviet Union.

Since they exercise control over the central plan, Soviet planners can emphasize a favored sector at the expense of others. Traditionally, heavy industry and the military have been given priority. For example, steel and oil production in the Soviet Union exceeds that of the United States by 40 to 45 percent. In contrast, since consumption goods are of lower priority in the central plan, the availability of consumer goods in the Soviet Union generally lags well behind the availability of such goods in the United States. In 1977, the number of automobiles in the Soviet Union was less than 6 million, compared to 100 million in the United States. Only two-thirds of Soviet families had a television set, about 15 percent had a telephone, and approximately one-half had some type of refrigerator. As output in the Soviet Union increases, some experts believe that the planners will be required to grant a higher priority to consumer goods.

Motivating Soviet Managers

Although the central plan is composed by the planners, it is the responsibility of the enterprise managers to carry out the plan. An incentive structure combining the "carrot" and the "stick" is used to motivate enterprise managers. Both pecuniary and nonpecuniary factors play a role. Managers who meet their production quotas are rewarded with bonuses, promotions, and medals. When the output of an enterprise is falling short of the production quota, it is up to the manager to exhort the employees to work longer and harder, to obtain

---

[4]Technically, an enterprise can sue a supplier that fails to deliver inputs according to the specifications of the plan. However, since the procedures are cumbersome and unlikely to bring satisfactory results quickly, most enterprise managers find it easier to make an exchange with other managers, use less than the specified amount of ingredients to stretch out supplies, and/or follow other, more direct procedures in order to meet their production targets. See Hedrick Smith, *The Russians* (New York: Quadrangle/The New York Times Book Co., Inc., 1976), for several interesting accounts of how Soviet plant managers react to material shortages.

additional labor and material inputs, or to persuade the higher authorities that the production quota should be lowered. If these efforts are insufficient and the enterprise fails to meet its production target, the manager can expect demotion.

The performance evaluations and rewards of enterprise managers are based on certain measurable output and input targets. Since product quality, innovativeness, and experimentation are both costly and difficult to measure, by and large these go unrewarded by the Soviet system. The emphasis is on *quantity of output* relative to the *output target.*

The emphasis on quantity of output creates two important problems. First, the initial objective of each plant manager is to persuade the planners to set low targets that can be easily achieved. Since high-level central planners do not know what performance can be expected from an efficiently operated firm, shrewd enterprise managers can often get ahead by understating the true productive capabilities of their enterprise.

Second, a more blatant form of "cheating" the system is practiced—the deliberate falsifying of reports. The system creates a strong incentive for collusion (the Russians call it "familyness") between the controllers and the controlled within the planning process. The complexity of the Soviet bureaucracy provides decision-makers at all levels with the opportunity to trade personal favors and cover up for each other.

Soviet leaders are not unaware of these problems. Procedures designed to limit report falsifying and collusion have been established. But the leaders recognize that even operational plans written into law will not be automatically carried out. Both economic and noneconomic incentives are used by the Soviet government to motivate managers and workers to carry out properly the details of the central plan. For example, in addition to monetary compensation, successful workers and managers are often given social recognition and/or promotion in the Communist party.

In the past decade numerous changes in the planning organization and incentive structure have been introduced. These changes originated with the so-called economic reforms announced by Premier Kosygin in September 1965. At the outset, the reforms were based on the idea that some relaxation of rigid central planning and control of enterprises would increase economic efficiency. Fewer targets would be handed down to enterprises, whose discretionary power would be broadened in the areas of labor and capital policies. In addition, incentive–reward schemes would be tied to fulfillment of targets on sales, profits, and return on capital rather than targets for quantity of output. These changes were to predominate over older administrative methods in inducing enterprises to be more productive and efficient.

In the implementation of these reforms, the stated philosophy of the Kosygin idea was distorted. Counter to the direction of several Western European communist governments, there is little evidence that the Soviets are shifting away from *detailed* central planning. The emphasis today is on the application of more advanced technology, particularly the increased use of computers, to solve the perennial problems that arise from central planning and administration.

Many who have analyzed the economic performance of the Soviet Union believe that detailed planning results in perverse decision-making and organizational inefficiency. Professor Robert Campbell of Indiana University summarizes this view:

[Waste] flows from errors of decision-making—plants located wrongly, production of too much of one commodity and too little of another, misallocation of resources such that one firm has too much capital in relation to labor, and another has too much labor in relationship to capital. But another species of waste represents a kind of slack in the economy—the excessive inventories held by most enterprises, underutilization of capacity, failure to make innovations, managerial inertia that retains labor arrangements that require more labor than would some new plant. The common feature in all these weaknesses is inertia or willful obstruction on the part of the controllers of the enterprise's activity.[5]

The Distribution of Goods

Wages are the major source of income in the Soviet Union. Despite the ideal communist distributional ethic put forth by Marx ("From each according to his ability, to each according to his need"), substantial occupational wage differentials exist in the Soviet Union. The earnings of skilled craft workers are generally two to four times those of unskilled laborers. The earnings of scientists, engineers, journalists, athletes, and high-level central planners are several times greater than the national average.

How does income inequality in the Soviet Union compare with that in Western nations? Accurate data are difficult to obtain. Most Western experts believe that income inequality in the Soviet Union is in fact less than that in Western economies, although some argue that the difference is slight. Even the few data that are available on income inequality in the Soviet Union are difficult to interpret because of structural differences between the Soviet Union and market economies. The prices of many products that are purchased intensively by the poor (medical service, clothing, and food) are, relatively speaking, cheaper in the Soviet Union than they are in most Western economies. In contrast, most luxury goods, such as automobiles and air travel, are relatively more expensive in the Soviet Union.

However, there are also special privileges that primarily enhance the welfare of the elite. Automobiles can usually be easily obtained by upper-level bureaucrats and Communist party members. Soviet officials and members of favored groups, such as scientists, writers, actors, ballet stars, and economic managers, are granted the right to shop in special stores, which offer goods at cut-rate prices and which stock many items that are unavailable to other citizens. Such products as choice meats, fine wines, fresh fruits and vegetables, French perfumes, Japanese electronic equipment, American cigarettes, and imported clothing are sold in these stores. Thus, Soviet officials and other members of the elite are largely insulated from the shortages, waiting lines, and poor quality that plague the typical consumer.[6]

Most Soviet consumers shop at regular state-operated stores or regulated cooperatives. Households are free to spend their income as they desire. However, since the central planners determine the aggregate quantity of each good and its price, many products are unavailable to ordinary consumers even if they have the money to pay for them. When the supply of a product is exhausted, there is no pricing system that will induce producers to supply a larger amount.

---

[5]R. W. Campbell, *The Soviet-Type Economies: Performance and Evolution,* 3rd ed., pp. 229–230. Copyright © 1974 by Houghton Mifflin Company, Boston. Reprinted by permission of the publisher.

[6]See Hedrick Smith, *The Russians,* pp. 26–30.

The regular state-operated stores are generally overflowing with some goods (items that are less desired because of their high price or poor quality), even while there are shortages of other products. Consumers sometimes wait in line for hours to purchase goods that are in short supply. Hedrick Smith paints a vivid picture of the plight of the Soviet consumer:

I had heard about consumer shortages before going to Moscow but at first it seemed to me that the stores were pretty well stocked. Only as we began to shop in earnest as a family did the Russian consumer's predicament really come through to me. First, we needed text-books for our children (who went to Russian schools) and found that the sixth-grade textbooks had run out. A bit later, we tried to find ballet shoes for our 11-year old daughter, Laurie, only to discover that in this land of ballerinas, ballet shoes size 8 were unavailable in Moscow. . . . Goods are produced to fill the Plan, not to sell. Sometimes the anomalies are baffling. Leningrad can be overstocked with cross-country skis and yet go several months without soap for washing dishes. In the Armenian capital of Yenevan, I found an ample supply of accordions but local people complained they had gone weeks without ordinary kitchen spoons or tea samovars. In Rostov, on a sweltering mid-90s day in June, the ice cream stands were all closed by 2 P.M. and a tourist guide told me that it was because the whole area had run out of ice cream, a daily occurrence.[7]

The Private Sector in the Soviet Union

Soviet law prohibits (a) a private person from acting as a trade middleman and (b) the hiring of an employee for the purpose of making a profit. However, there are two major areas in which private enterprise is permitted—personal services and a portion of agriculture. Soviet professionals (for example, physicians and teachers) and craft laborers (for example, tailors, shoe repairers, and painters) are free to sell their services to consumers. Often, these "self-employed" workers are moonlighters. They work regularly for a state enterprise but also provide their services to private consumers during nonworking hours.

The agriculture sector has consistently been a problem for the Soviet economy. Initially, there was substantial opposition to collectivization. Crop failures and low productivity (in comparison with that of other advanced economies) have been commonplace for years. Peasants on the collective farms are permitted to grow products on an assigned small plot—usually one acre in size. Products raised on these private plots may be consumed or sold in the market for prices that are determined by the fluctuations of supply and demand. In total, these private plots constitute slightly more than 1 percent of the total agricultural land under cultivation. Nonetheless, as Exhibit 3 illustrates, in 1980 they accounted for 25 percent of the total agricultural output. A major share of the total output of such products as eggs, potatoes, vegetables, fruits, meat, and dairy products is derived from these private plots.[8]

Many ideologically pure members of the Communist party would like to

---

[7]*Ibid.,* p. 60. Reprinted by permission of Times Books, a division of Quadrangle/The New York Times Book Co., Inc., New York.

[8]The fact that more land-intensive agricultural products—grains and cotton, for example—are grown on the collective farms partially accounts for the fact that the productivity of these farms (measured in terms of value per acre) is lower than that of the private plots. However, the large disparity strongly suggests that incentives matter. Apparently Soviet farmers cultivate the private plots, which generate *personal* gain, much more intensively than the collective farms, where most of the gains from efficiency accrue to others.

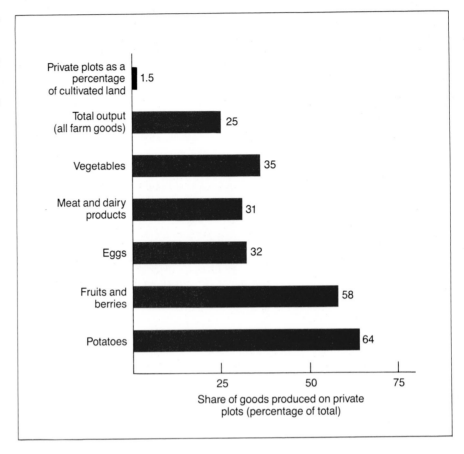

EXHIBIT 3 Agriculture production on private plots in the Soviet Union, 1980

Although the private agriculture plots constituted only 1.5 percent of the land under cultivation, output on these plots accounted for 25 percent of the total value of agriculture production in 1980. Each year a large share of the aggregate output of several products is produced on these private plots.

U.S. News and World Report, November 9, 1981, p. 41. Also see A. Yemelyanov, "The Agrarian Policy of the Party and Structural Advances in Agriculture," *Problems of Economics* (March 1975), pp. 22–34.

eliminate this vestige of private enterprise. However, there are two strong forces operating to preserve the private plots. First, they are a major source of income for poor agricultural peasants. Second, they are a major source of agricultural production, providing many urban dwellers with foodstuffs that most likely would be unavailable under alternative arrangements. When Nikita Khrushchev was in power, he reduced the size of the plots to a maximum of one-half acre. Some Soviet experts believe that this decision contributed to his downfall. When Brezhnev gained control, he restored the plots to their initial one-acre size.

The Balance Sheet of the Soviet Economy

When we balance the books on the Soviet economy, several factors stand out.

1. The Investment Rate in the Soviet Union Is One of the Highest in the World. As Exhibit 4 shows, the Soviet Union allocates a much larger share of its GNP to investment (and a much smaller share to consumption) than does the United States. Centralized economic organization enables the planners to emphasize industrialization and capital accumulation, even though this may not reflect the views of the citizens. Of course, current consumption is sacrificed as a result.

2. The Growth Rate in the Soviet Union, Pushed Along by the High Rate of Capital Formation, Has Been Impressive. Exhibit 5 presents data on the growth of real gross domestic product during 1960–1979 for countries with differing economic insti-

EXHIBIT 4   The functional use of GNP in the United States and the Soviet Union

The Soviet economy, responding to the views of the planners, allocates a much larger share of GNP to investment and defense.

	Percent Share of Total GNP	
	United States	Soviet Union
Consumption	72	56
Defense	6	12
Investment	19	29
Government administration	3	3

The World Bank, *World Development Report, 1981,* and Svetozor Pejovich, *A Report Card on Socialism— Life in the Soviet Union* (Dallas: The Fisher Institute, 1979), pp. 65 and 98.

EXHIBIT 5   The average annual rate of growth in real gross domestic product for selected countries, 1960–1979[a]

	Growth Rate	
	1960–1979 (Percent)	
Country	Total	Per Capita
United States	3.7	2.4
Canada	4.9	3.5
West Germany	3.5	3.3
Sweden	3.2	2.4
United Kingdom	2.5	2.2
Australia	4.4	2.8
USSR[b]	5.1	4.1
Yugoslavia[b]	5.9	5.4
Japan	8.0	6.9
India	3.4	1.4
Brazil	7.1	4.8

[a]The gross domestic product counts only the output that is produced domestically by a nation. The output of citizens abroad is excluded. Gross domestic product differs only slightly from GNP.

[b]Data are for net material product. Therefore they exclude such industries as public administration, defense, and professional services.

The World Bank, *World Development Report, 1982,* Tables 1 and 2.

tutions. During the entire period from 1960 to 1979, the annual rate of growth of the Soviet Union was 5.1 percent, compared to 3.7 percent for the United States. Among the major industrial nations, only Japan sustained a growth rate that exceeded that of the Soviet Union.

In recent years, the Soviet growth rate has slowed. During the 1950s and 1960s, Soviet growth was spurred by the borrowing of more advanced technology from Western countries, a tactic that was carried out on a grand scale. Most observers attribute the Soviet growth rate to the ability of the system to (a) direct a sizable share of its resources to capital formation and (b) move resources out of low-productivity sectors such as agriculture into the higher-productivity industrial sector.

3. The Standard of Living of the Average Citizen of the Soviet Union Continues To Lag Well Behind That of the Average Person in Japan, Western Europe, and the United States. As Exhibit 6 illustrates, in 1979, the per capita GNP of the Soviet Union was less than one-half that of the United States and only about 54 percent that of Japan and the countries of the European Economic Community (EEC). *In aggregate,* although the Soviet economy is substantially larger than that of Japan, it is still considerably smaller than that of the EEC countries and the United States.

4. Although the Overall Economic Record of the Soviet Union Must Be Judged Favorably, Many Observers Believe That the Rigid, Centrally Planned System Has a Major Defect—Its Inability To Stimulate Innovation. Whatever the overall deficiencies of a profit-directed capitalist economy are, few question its ability to provide a strong incentive for entrepreneurs to experiment, develop, and discover new, improved ways of doing things. A centrally planned socialist system, on the other hand, with its necessary attachment to quantity of output and its utilization of established methods, has not yet shown that it is capable of stimulating technological development outside of the space–defense sector. As long as the Soviet Union was catching up with the capitalist economies, it did not necessarily need a built-in incentive for innovation. However, the future welfare of the Soviet consumer is now dependent on the ability of centralized planning to deal with this deficiency.

YUGOSLAVIA—SOCIALISM OR THE MARKET?

The Yugoslavian economy is a hybrid of centralized planning and market direction. Individual Yugoslav citizens are permitted to own and operate small-scale enterprises, employing a maximum of five workers. In agriculture, peasants can privately own up to 25 acres. In addition, certain business firms, such as law firms, hotels, restaurants, and craft shops, are operated by private entrepreneurs, much as they are in Western countries. However, the bulk of economic activity—estimates range from 80 to 90 percent—is conducted by worker-managed, socially owned business firms.

Before World War II, Yugoslavia had a free-market, capitalist economy. After the war (and the civil war that followed), the country became part of the Communist bloc with a government headed by Marshal Josip Tito. Initially, Tito organized the Yugoslav economy along Soviet lines. Central planning organs prescribed the quantity and quality of production, determined the methods and techniques of production, allocated inputs, set prices, and decided on the distribution of the national income. Within the framework of a five-year plan, all these decisions were translated into output targets and input allocations that were handed down to the socialist managers of individual firms. Tito, however, was unwilling to accept Soviet domination. In addition, the Yugoslav economy stagnated under detailed central planning. In the early 1950s, Yugoslavia moved toward a decentralized economy that permitted market forces to play a significant role in the allocative process.

The Yugoslavian Business Firm

In 1952, the government enacted a series of reforms that altered the nature of the socialist business firm. Under the Yugoslav system, government ownership of the business firm is retained, but management of individual enterprises is turned over to the employees. The employees of each firm elect a workers'

EXHIBIT 6 **The gross national product of the major economic powers**

The per capita GNP of the Soviet Union lags well behind that of the United States, the EEC countries, and Japan. In aggregate, output in the Soviet Union is a little more than one-half as great as that of the United States and that of the EEC countries. The nine countries of the European Economic Community (EEC) are Belgium, France, West Germany, Italy, Luxembourg, the Netherlands, Denmark, Ireland, and the United Kingdom.

Statistical Abstract of the United States—1980, **Tables 1573 and 1585.**

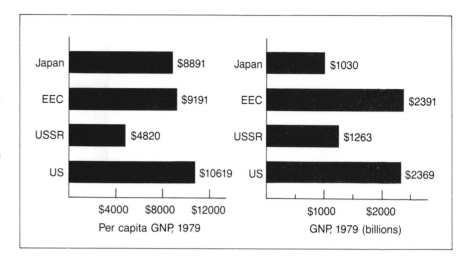

council, which manages the firm. Each employee has one vote, and the workers' council is elected by secret ballot. The council, like a manager of a Western firm, purchases raw materials and determines the quantity and quality of goods produced, the level of employment, the method of production, and even the price charged for finished products. When the firm's revenues exceed costs, the firm's net profits go, with no strings attached, to the employees (including managers) of the firm. The "employee-owners" divide the firm's profits among themselves in a manner prescribed by the workers' council. When a worker retires, leaves his or her job, or is fired (by a vote of all employees), the worker's rights to any profits from the firm expire.

What impact does this form of economic organization have on economic incentives and production methods? Since the income of employees is directly affected by the firm's profit level, they have an incentive to elect managers who will operate the firm efficiently. In a sense, the position of the employees of the firm is parallel to that of stockholders in the West. The employees, like stockholders, seek efficient operation and a high level of profits because they are residual income recipients (in addition to wage recipients). However, unlike stockholders, *individual* workers in Yugoslavia can neither hold on to these rights when no longer attached to the firm nor sell them. Only *current* workers, collectively, are allowed to own factors of production.

The ramifications of this situation are significant. First, this form of economic organization encourages workers to push for an immediate distribution of profits among themselves rather than for the allocation of profits to investment or future fringe benefits (for example, fancier offices or a company recreation center). This is perfectly rational behavior because present capitalization of future profit-sharing rights cannot be realized through the private sale of ownership rights. Unlike stockholders in the West, Yugoslav workers can ill afford not to declare dividends every year. Postponed dividends may be lost forever for those with the likelihood of departing from the firm. In contrast, Western stockholders can always sell their shares whenever they are dissatisfied with the dividend policy of the management.

Second, as a result, Yugoslav enterprises are constantly plagued by shortages of funds for both working capital and fixed investment. The workers' tendency to allocate larger shares of the enterprise profits for purposes of wage and salary augmentation puts a continual strain on the firm's liquidity. Consequently, many enterprises have to resort to heavy borrowing and are thus forced to operate under perpetual indebtedness.

Third, Yugoslav firms have a strong tendency to substitute capital goods for labor. The workers' profit-sharing right increases the cost, as seen by current employees, of hiring additional units of labor (that is, additional profit-sharing partners). Other things constant, increasing the size of the firm's work force will reduce the size of the profit share granted to each current employee. The employee's share of the firm's profit will be smaller as one of 1100 workers than as one of 1000 workers. Consequently, Yugoslav enterprises tend to use highly capital-intensive techniques of production. As a result, many laborers, both skilled and unskilled, have been forced to emigrate to other countries in order to find work.

Finally, Yugoslav enterprises have little or no pecuniary incentive to invest their funds in the establishment of new enterprises. Although money invested in new ventures can draw interest, investors have no claim to management rights or dividends. These are reserved exclusively for the workers of the new enterprise. Consequently, the financing of new enterprises comes primarily from governmental authorities, either through direct investment or by guaranteeing bank loans. Here, the gains of the public authority are basically twofold. First, it secures a dominating influence over the firm's management and its policies. Second, it obtains a certain return on its investment through taxation. Taxes levied on the enterprise profits generate a major portion of state revenues in Yugoslavia.

The workers' participation in the decision-making process of the firm is considered in Yugoslavia to be an essential feature of a genuine socialist society. According to the Yugoslav view, capitalist relations in production and distribution are characterized not only by private ownership but also by separation of labor and management. Since capitalist workers do not participate in the firm's decision-making, they become disillusioned with the production process and dissatisfied with the income distribution. In contrast, according to this view, the Yugoslav system of workers' self-management makes it impossible for worker alienation to exist. Finally, the argument goes, profit-sharing by workers provides the firm with a strong incentive to become efficient. Since employees have a direct stake in the firm's profits, they seek to avoid waste and other activities that increase the firm's costs.

A Closer Look at the Yugoslavian Record

The transition of the Yugoslav economy to market socialism was accompanied by remarkable changes elsewhere in the economy. First, there was a shift of labor out of the agricultural sector and into the manufacturing and services sectors. In 1945, approximately 75 percent of the population was employed in agriculture; in 1979 only 31 percent of the work force was working in the agriculture sector. At the same time, there was a change in exports from agriculture and mining to a highly diversified export pattern. More than 75 percent of the value of exports in 1979 was generated by the export of manufactured goods.

Second, the growth of real output and income per capita has been remarkable in spite of erratic fluctuations. Before 1952, under centralized command planning, the Yugoslav real output was at a virtual standstill. Between

1952 and 1960, real GNP in Yugoslavia grew at an annual rate of nearly 10 percent. Since that time, the annual rate of growth of industrial production has averaged approximately 6 percent. Per capita income rose at an annual rate of 5.4 percent during the period from 1960 to 1979 (see Exhibit 5). Thus, on balance, the Yugoslav economy has maintained a relatively high rate of economic growth.

Third, the shift of the Yugoslav economy toward rapid industrial development was accompanied by unemployment, which was estimated to be around 10 percent in the late 1970s. The continuous influx of peasants from rural to urban areas created a persistent excess supply of unskilled workers. In addition, semiskilled and skilled workers often could not find employment because of the desire of firms to use capital-intensive production techniques. Consequently, approximately 1 million Yugoslavs, 5 percent of the total population, have sought jobs in neighboring Western European countries.

THE JAPANESE "MIRACLE"

By American and European standards, the Japanese people in 1950 were poor and their methods of production primitive. Forty-two percent of the Japanese labor force was employed in agriculture, compared to 12 percent in the United States.[9] The per capita GNP of Japan was one-eighth that of the United States.

The transformation of the Japanese economy during the last three decades is the success story of the postwar era. Today, the Japanese economy is the third largest in the world, ranking after the U.S. and Soviet economies. Adjusted for inflation, the GNP of Japan grew approximately 9.5 percent annually between 1950 and 1980. During that period, the income of the typical Japanese family, measured in dollars of constant purchasing power, doubled every eight years!

The data of Exhibit 7 illustrate the phenomenal economic growth of Japan. In 1950, the Japanese GNP was only 6.8 percent as great as the GNP of the United States. By 1960, the figure was 11.5 percent, and by 1980, the Japanese GNP was 41.8 percent of that of the United States. In 1950, per capita GNP, measured in inflation-adjusted 1980 dollars, was only $843, compared to $6643 for the United States. During the next 30 years, the real GNP per capita of Japan increased elevenfold. By 1980, it was 80 percent of that of the United States, compared to 12.7 percent in 1950.

The land area of Japan is 10 percent smaller than that of California. Its population is approximately one-half as great as that of the United States. It lacks natural resources; almost all of Japan's petroleum is imported. On the surface, it would appear to be an overpopulated nation, lacking energy and natural resources. How can we explain the economic performance of Japan?

Several factors underlie the Japanese "miracle." Japan's economy is primarily a capitalist market economy. Nonetheless, it differs in several important respects from the market economies of Western Europe and North America. Let us consider some of the unique features of the Japanese economy.

---

[9]By 1979, the percentage of the Japanese work force employed in agriculture had declined to 13 percent. Since labor productivity is generally higher in manufacturing than in agriculture, this shift from agriculture contributed to the rapid growth of Japan.

EXHIBIT 7   The Japanese "miracle"

	United States (1980 dollars)	Japan[a] (1980 dollars)	Japan as a Percentage of United States
Gross national product			
1950	1033	71	6.8
1960	1421	163	11.5
1970	2074	454	21.9
1980	2626	1098	41.8
Gross national product per capita			
1950	6643	843	12.7
1960	7656	1700	22.2
1970	10083	4290	42.5
1980	11786	9415	79.9

[a]The Japanese data were converted to U.S. dollars by the exchange rate method.

U.S. Department of Commerce.

The Japanese Labor Market

Lifetime Employment Commitment: An arrangement offered by most large firms in Japan whereby employees are guaranteed employment until the age of 55 unless guilty of misconduct.

In contrast with laborers in most market economies, Japanese workers are intensely loyal to the firms by which they are employed. Two factors appear to explain this loyalty. First, the large Japanese firms make a **lifetime employment commitment** to their employees. After a probationary period, which is usually less than one year, employees acquire tenure. Henceforth, they cannot be discharged except for misconduct (for example, excessive absenteeism, commission of a crime, or fighting on the job). Since seniority largely determines the wage scales of both blue and white collar workers, the lifetime employment commitment system provides workers with economic security. As long as the firm is able to meet its economic obligations, the employee need not worry about layoffs, unemployment, or loss of income. Of course, the employee may resign, but this is unusual. The tenure of the employee is maintained until he or she reaches the age of 55, when retirement is compulsory.

Second, employee unions in Japan are almost exclusively company unions, and they represent both white and blue collar workers rather than particular types of jobs, as in the United States. For this reason, national federations of unions in Japan have little to do with the establishment of compensation and working conditions; these matters are dealt with by labor and management on the company, not the national, level. Approximately one-third of the Japanese labor force is unionized, compared to one-fourth in the United States. In contrast to U.S. labor–management relations, however, the union–management relationship in Japan is characterized by cooperation rather than conflict. Consultation between management and employee representatives is an integral part of Japanese industrial relations. Each has certain areas of control: Unions play an important role in the establishment of wage differentials among jobs; management is given a great deal of flexibility in the assignment of employees, and the movement of employees among positions in the firm is seldom resisted by the union. Areas of joint labor–management consultation include future production plans, projected technological changes, and the transfer of personnel to new plants. Since the long-run economic prospects of employees, including provisions for retirement, are closely tied to the success of the firm, it is not unusual for management and the union to work out a *temporary reduction in wages* during an economic slowdown or in order to enable the firm to expand into a new market.

Ichiro Nakayama, a senior Japanese labor economist, summed up the labor–management relationship as follows:

One of the facts that is frequently referred to as the most marked characteristic of labor–management relations in Japan is the relative absence of conflict between employer and worker in all phases of industrial relations. . . . This is manifest in various features of the trade union organization known as the enterprise-wide union—for example, the lack of a strong feeling of confrontation at the collective bargaining table, the ambiguous distinction between union membership and employee's status . . . and the importance attached to the system of life-long employment. When compared with those in Western countries, labor–management relations in Japan are conspicuous, in the last analysis, by the common characteristic of a close human relationship between employers and employees.[10]

Taxes in Japan

Although the Japanese tax structure is progressive, there are so many exemptions that high marginal rates can generally be avoided, particularly if one is willing to save or invest in favored industries. As Exhibit 8 illustrates, taxes consume a much smaller share of GNP in Japan than in other market-directed economies. In 1978 taxes on productive effort (income, payroll, and profit taxes) consumed only 16.8 percent of GNP in Japan, compared to 21.4 percent in the United States, 20.5 percent in the United Kingdom, 23.8 percent in France, and more than 25 percent in West Germany and Sweden.

Although income has grown rapidly, the Japanese have expanded the relative size of the public sector only modestly. Tax rates have been consistently reduced. Every year since 1950, the government has cut marginal tax rates on

EXHIBIT 8   Taxes in selected Western countries, 1978

Country	Tax Revenues as a Percentage of GNP, 1978	
	Income, payroll, and profit taxes	All taxes
Sweden	38.5	53.3
West Germany	26.3	37.8
France	23.8	39.7
United Kingdom	20.5	34.5
United States	21.4	30.2
Japan	16.8	24.1

Facts and Figures on Government Finance, 1981 (New York: Tax Foundation, 1981), Table 25.

---

[10]As quoted in Hugh Patrick and Henry Rosovsky, eds., *Asia's New Giant* (Washington, D.C.: Brookings Institution, 1976), p. 639.

personal and/or business income. Anticipated budget surpluses have been channeled into the private sector. As a result, total tax revenues comprised 24.1 percent of the national income in 1978, only slightly higher than the 18.1 percent of 1955.[11]

In contrast with welfare-state market economies, the Japanese economy does not use its tax–expenditure structure to redistribute income. Japan does not have a system of compulsory retirement insurance like the social security system in the United States.[12] In general, tax rates are both lower and effectively less progressive than those in Western market economies. Thus, the before- and after-tax distributions of income in Japan are very similar.

Savings and Investment

The savings and investment rates of Japan are much higher than those of other market economies. Urban workers in Japan save approximately 20 percent of their disposable income. Not surprisingly, the major share of corporate profits is rechanneled into investment. During the period from 1960 to 1979, nearly one-third of the GNP of Japan was allocated to investment, substantially more than the share allocated to investment in other industrial market economies. No democratic market economy has ever chosen to allocate such a large share of its output to capital formation during peacetime.

The Japanese tax structure is at least partially responsible for these high rates of saving and investment. Capital gains derived from the sale of securities are not taxed in Japan. Businesses and land capital gains are taxed at much lower rates than they are in Western countries. Interest and dividends are taxed at a maximum rate of 25 percent, compared to marginal tax rates of up to 50 percent for income derived from interest and dividends in the United States. A system of tax credits encourages various forms of saving.

The Economic Future of Japan

Most Western economists believe that the growth rate of Japan will decline in the future. During the 1950s and 1960s, Japan, like the Soviet Union, was able to profit by drawing on the technology and methods of production of more advanced countries.[13] Since Japanese manufacturing is now as modern as that of other industrial economies, it will be increasingly difficult for Japan to make large gains in this way. Despite the growth of income, the consumption of leisure in Japan has not yet increased significantly. As growth continues, however, Japanese workers are likely to opt for a shorter workweek and longer vacations. An increase in environmental pollution has accompanied Japan's rapid growth. The Japanese will probably allocate more resources to pollution control as their standard of living rises. All of these factors will most likely

---

[11]Joseph A. Pechman and Keimei Kaizuka, in Patrick and Rosovsky, *Asia's New Giant,* Table 5-2, and *Facts and Figures on Government Finance, 1981* (New York: Tax Foundation, 1981), Table 25.

[12]It should be noted that firms make sizable lump-sum payments to employees when they "retire." Since retirement is compulsory at 55, many Japanese continue to work for part of the year or part-time after they retire. For the most part, the income is untaxed.

[13]A study by the Brookings Institution found that the major determinants of the growth rate differential between Japan and other major market economies were (a) rapid capital formation, (b) advances in knowledge and technology, and (c) economies of scale. See Edward F. Denison and William K. Chung, "Economic Growth and Its Source," in Patrick and Rosovsky, *Asia's New Giant.*

cause the growth rate of the Japanese GNP to fall below the rate of the period from 1950 to 1980. Nonetheless, given the large growth differential between Japan and other industrial nations, the Japanese may very well be the wealthiest people in the world by the turn of the century, if not before.

SOCIALISM OR CAPITALISM?

Which form of economic organization is best? Economics cannot answer this question. Both philosophical and economic factors must be considered. On the economic side, it is clear that some socialist economies have impressive growth records. Socialism need not fall victim to its own economic inefficiency, as some observers once argued was inevitable. It is clear, however, that several market-oriented nations, notably Japan, West Germany, and Brazil, have also experienced rapid economic growth during the postwar period. Apparently, economic progress is not the sole domain of either capitalism or socialism. Although economic data are relevant, human nature, freedom, and equality are also important considerations when one is choosing among alternative forms of economic organization. At the individual level, the choice is yours.

CHAPTER LEARNING OBJECTIVES

1 Under socialism, ownership (or control) of physical capital rests with the state. Central planning replaces market allocation as the method of answering basic consumption, production, and distribution questions.

2 Basic economic concepts, such as diminishing returns, opportunity cost, comparative advantage, and diminishing marginal utility, apply to both socialist and capitalist economies. Different forms of economic organization can change the incentives faced by decision-makers (for example, managers and workers), but basic economic principles are not negated from one type of economy to another.

3 Central planning is the dominant characteristic of the Soviet economy. The Gosplan, a central planning agency, presents state enterprises with an allocation of inputs and target levels for output. Key commodities and raw materials are centrally rationed in physical terms. The rewards of managers and workers are affected by their success at meeting the targets of the central planning authority. Pecuniary as well as nonpecuniary incentives are used to motivate both managers and workers to carry out the directives of the central planners.

4 Central planning in the Soviet Union has stressed industrialization and capital investment. The share of GNP allocated to investment in the Soviet Union is substantially higher than that in the United States.

5 The distribution of income in the Soviet Union is probably more egalitarian than it is in most market economies. However, many observers believe that the difference is small. The prices of many items that are purchased intensively by the poor, including medical service, basic food products, and housing, are low in the Soviet Union. Of course, this is beneficial to low-income families. On the other hand, the state provides privileges—such as the use of automobiles and the right to shop at stores where high-quality goods are sold at low prices—only to government officials and other members of the Soviet elite. Such benefits are an important source of economic inequality in the Soviet Union.

6 Even though small, private plots constitute slightly more than 1 percent of the land under cultivation in the Soviet Union, they have accounted for approximately one-fourth of the total value of Soviet agricultural production in recent years.

7   Stimulated by high investment rates, economic growth in the Soviet Union has been impressive; in fact, it has been more rapid than the economic growth of most Western nations. However, the Soviet per capita GNP is still substantially less than that of Japan, the United States, and the countries of the European Economic Community. Many observers believe that the future growth of the Soviet Union is vitally dependent on the development of an incentive system capable of stimulating experimentation and innovation.

8   The Yugoslav economy combines socialist and capitalist economic organization. Central planning directs the economy and channels capital investment into designated areas. However, business firms have a great deal of discretionary decision-making authority. Employees of each firm elect a workers' council, which manages the firm. The firm is usually free to decide what products it will produce, the production techniques to be utilized, the employment level, and even product prices. The profits of the firm are distributed to employees according to their wishes. Despite high rates of unemployment, the growth record of the Yugoslav economy has been impressive.

9   The growth record of Japan has been the most impressive of the major industrial nations during the postwar period. The following factors have contributed to this rapid growth: (a) institutional arrangements that have encouraged harmonious labor–management relations; (b) continual tax cuts, which have enhanced the incentive of individuals to work, save, and invest; and (c) a very high rate of capital formation.

10   Economics does not tell us which form of economic organization is best. However, economic analysis can reveal a great deal about how alternative systems will operate in reality.

THE ECONOMIC WAY OF THINKING—DISCUSSION QUESTIONS

1   Compare and contrast the role of business managers of firms in the United States, the Soviet Union, and Yugoslavia. In which country would managers have the greatest incentive to operate the *firm* efficiently?

2   What do you think are the major advantages of a centrally planned economy? What are the major disadvantages? Do you believe that market allocation is superior or inferior to centralized planning? Explain your answer.

3   How does Yugoslav socialism differ from socialism as practiced in the Soviet Union? Which system do you think is better? Why?

4   "Socialism means production for use, not for profit. Workers contribute according to their qualifications, and they are rewarded according to egalitarian principles. Socialism takes power from the business elite and grants it to the workers who, after all, produce the goods." Analyze this point of view.

5   What major factors have contributed to the rapid economic growth of Japan? Do you think that the Japanese economy will grow as rapidly in the future as it has in the past? Why or why not?

6   Do you think that the United States should encourage firms to adopt the lifetime employment commitment offered by the major firms in Japan? Why or why not? What are the advantages and disadvantages of this system?

7   **What's Wrong with This Way of Thinking?**

"Central planning makes it possible for an economy to invest more and to expand at a more rapid rate. Consumer incomes, stimulated by the high rates of capital formation, also increase rapidly. Thus, the consumer is the major beneficiary of central planning, which stresses a rapid rate of capital formation."

APPENDIX A
A GRAPHIC LOOK
AT ECONOMICS

The purpose of this appendix is to illustrate the mechanics of tables (charts) and graphs. Many students, particularly those with an elementary mathematics background, are already familiar with this material, and they may safely ignore it. This appendix is for those who need to be assured that they have the ability to understand graphic economic illustrations.

Economic logic often suggests that two variables are linked in a specific way. The relationship between variables can be illustrated with the use of a table, a graph, or a mathematical expression. These devices, particularly tables and graphs, help one to visualize economic relationships quickly.

It has often been said that a good picture is worth a thousand words, but one must understand the picture if it is to be enlightening. Tables and graphs help to create a picture of things; they are visual aids that can concisely communicate valuable information to the understanding reader.

Exhibit 1 is a simple table showing the hypothetical relationship between

EXHIBIT 1 The relationship between distance traveled and gas consumed in city traffic

Distance Traveled (Miles)	Gasoline Consumed (Gallons)	
	Ford LTD	Escort
10	1.0	0.5
20	2.0	1.0
30	3.0	1.5
40	4.0	2.0
50	5.0	2.5
60	6.0	3.0

distance traveled and gasoline consumed for two types of automobiles—a Ford LTD and a Ford Escort in stop-and-go city traffic.

Not surprisingly, gasoline consumption increases with distance traveled for both cars. One would say that there is a direct relationship between distance traveled and gasoline consumption. However, this relationship differs for the two cars. The LTD consumes twice as much gasoline per mile as the Escort.

The information contained in Exhibit 1 could also be presented graphically. A graph illustrates the relationship between two things, one of which is measured on the *x* axis (the horizontal axis) and the other of which is measured on the *y* axis (the vertical axis). A line (or curve) on the graph illustrates the relationship between the *x* variable and the *y* variable.

Exhibit 2 graphs the relationship between miles traveled and gasoline consumed for the LTD and the Escort. Since the *x* variable and the *y* variable are directly related, the gasoline consumption–distance traveled curve slopes upward to the right. (In economics, "curve" is a general term used to express the relationship between two variables. Even a straight line is often referred to as a curve.)

How much gasoline does the LTD use per mile? The slope, or steepness, of the line yields the answer. The slope of a line is the change in the *y* variable divided by the change in the *x* variable. Measuring gasoline consumption along the *y* axis, the graph indicates that an additional gallon of gasoline would be required to travel ten additional miles. A one-unit change in the *y* variable is associated with a ten-unit change in the *x* variable for the LTD. The slope of the line (1/10) shows that the LTD consumes one-tenth of a gallon of gasoline for each mile traveled.

Now consider the relationship between miles traveled and gasoline consumed for the Escort. These variables are also directly related for the Escort. However, the gasoline consumption–distance traveled curve is flatter. The slope of the gasoline consumption–distance traveled curve for the Escort is 1/20, indicating that the Escort uses less gasoline per mile than the LTD.

EXHIBIT 2 Understanding a graph

The graph pictures the relationship between miles traveled, measured on the *x* axis, and gasoline consumed, measured on the *y* axis. The black line illustrates the relationship for a Ford LTD. The LTD consumes one-tenth of a gallon of gasoline for every mile traveled, whereas the Ford Escort (color line) uses only one-twentieth of a gallon per mile. Since both lines slope upward to the right, they illustrate that there is a positive (direct) relationship between miles traveled and gasoline consumed for both cars.

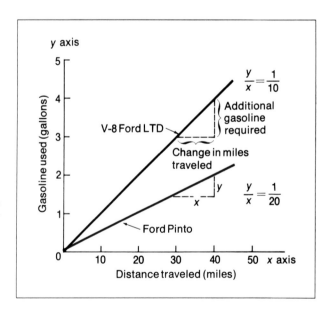

A simple two-dimensional graph such as Exhibit 2 can also be used to illustrate economic relationships. For example, survey data have shown that high-income families, on average, spend more on consumption goods than families with lower incomes (see Exhibit 3a). For most of us, the more we earn, the more we spend. Thus, income and consumer spending are directly related. Exhibit 3b illustrates the consumer expenditure–income curve for U.S. families.

Sometimes the *x* variable and the *y* variable are inversely related. A decline in the *y* variable is associated with an increase in the *x* variable. Therefore, a curve picturing the relationship between *x* and *y* slopes downward to the right.

Exhibit 4 illustrates this case. The price of hamburgers is measured on

EXHIBIT 3   Picturing family income and consumer expenditures

(a) The table presents data on the relationship between family income and consumer expenditures. (b) The same data are presented graphically, illustrating the direct relationship between the two variables.

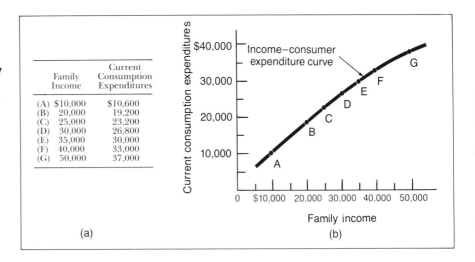

Family Income	Current Consumption Expenditures
(A) $10,000	$10,600
(B) 20,000	19,200
(C) 25,000	23,200
(D) 30,000	26,800
(E) 35,000	30,000
(F) 40,000	33,000
(G) 50,000	37,000

(a)

(b)

EXHIBIT 4   Picturing the price–consumption relationship for hamburgers

People will buy fewer hamburgers as the price of hamburgers rises. This graph illustrates the inverse relationship between price and quantity of hamburgers purchased. Note that the price–consumption curve slopes downward to the right.

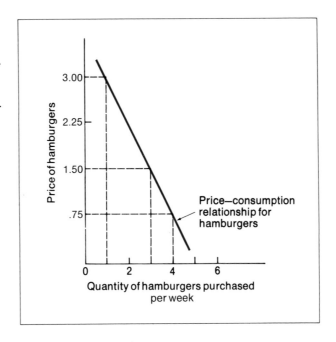

the y axis, and the quantity of hamburgers purchased per week is measured on the x axis. If the price of a hamburger were $3, only real hamburger lovers would purchase them. On average, individuals would consume only one hamburger per week. If the price of a hamburger fell to $1.50, more people would buy them. Weekly average consumption would increase to three. A price reduction to 75 cents would induce consumers to purchase still more hamburgers, and average weekly consumption would expand to four. The inverse relationship between price and quantity of hamburgers purchased generates a curve that slopes downward to the right.

By now you should have a fairly good understanding of how to read a graph. Graphs are not substitutes for economic thinking. One cannot communicate anything with a graph that cannot be communicated verbally. However, graphs can often be used to present ideas quickly and concisely. Do not be intimidated by graphs. They look much more complex than they really are.

If you think you will have any trouble reading graphs, try drawing (graphing) the relationship between several things with which you are familiar. If you work, try graphing the relationship between your hours worked (x axis) and your weekly earnings (y axis). What does the slope of the earnings–hours worked curve represent? Can you graph the relationship between the price of gasoline and your expenditures on gasoline? Graphing these simple relationships will give you greater confidence in your ability to grasp more complex economic relationships presented in graphs.

B

APPENDIX B
ANALYZING THE
EQUILIBRIUM LEVEL
OF INCOME
WITH EQUATIONS

In Chapters 8, 9, and 10, graphic aids are utilized along with logic to develop the concepts of equilibrium aggregate income, the multiplier, and fiscal policy. Most students can best understand these tools when they are presented in this manner. However, professional economists often use mathematics to study and communicate the same ideas.

In this appendix, we use elementary algebra to develop in greater detail some of the aggregate income models that we have already discussed. For beginning students of economics, an exposure to one or two algebraic models has at least two advantages. First, students can gain a better understanding of almost any problem by looking at it with the precision of mathematics. Second, such exposure will make the transition to intermediate or upper-level economics courses much easier.

THE EQUILIBRIUM LEVEL OF INCOME

Before beginning, we must remind ourselves of a few basic concepts. The relationship between consumption C and disposable income Y_d shown in Exhibit 1 can also be communicated by the equation:

$$C = C_0 + \text{MPC} \times Y_d \tag{1}$$

The meaning of this equation is that total consumption equals autonomous consumption C_0 plus the marginal propensity to consume (MPC) multiplied by disposable income. The amount of consumption C_0 that takes place when disposable income equals zero can be interpreted as consumption that is not explained by variations in Y_d. The MPC, which is the proportion of a change in disposable income utilized to increase consumption, is constant because the graphic function is linear. Of course, the MPC is simply the slope of the line that represents the consumption function.

EXHIBIT 1 The consumption
function in graphic and equation form

A consumption function with a
y intercept of $625 billion and
MPC of ¾ is shown in the accompanying graph. The equation form of this function is
$C = 625 + \frac{3}{4}Y_d$.

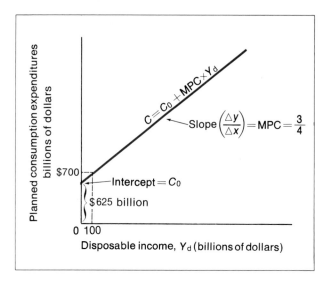

Example 1: If consumption is $625 billion when disposable income is zero, and if consumption equals $700 billion when disposable income is $100 billion (see Exhibit 1), what is the linear consumption function? In this case, $C_0 = \$625$ billion, and the MPC is equal to the change in consumption ($75 billion) divided by the change in disposable income ($100 billion):

$$\text{MPC} = {}^{75}\!/_{100} = \frac{3}{4}$$

Thus, the function is:

$$C = 625 + \frac{3}{4}Y_d$$

The other equations necessary for our model are also restatements of concepts we have already introduced. Gross national product, Y in equilibrium, is equal to planned consumption expenditures C, plus planned gross investment I, plus planned government expenditures G:

$$Y = C + I + G \tag{2}$$

In addition, a simplification of the definition of disposable income is also useful; Y_d is equal to equilibrium GNP minus total taxes T:

$$Y_d = Y - T \tag{3}$$

Given these equations, we can easily solve for equilibrium GNP by substituting equations (1) and (3) into equation (2):

$$Y = C + I + G$$
$$Y = C_0 + \text{MPC} \times Y_d + I + G \tag{4}$$
$$Y = C_0 + \text{MPC} \times (Y - T) + I + G \tag{5}$$

Given constant values for C_0, I, G, T, and the MPC, we then can compute equilibrium Y, since we have one equation with one unknown variable.

Example 2: Equilibrium occurs when planned aggregate spending ($C + I + G$) equals the value of output Y. Given that $C_0 = \$625$ billion, $I = \$100$ billion, $G = \$300$ billion, $T = \$300$ billion, and MPC = $\frac{3}{4}$, calculate the equilibrium level of the GNP:

$$Y = C + I + G$$
$$Y = C_0 + \text{MPC} \times Y_d + 100 + 300$$
$$Y = 625 + \tfrac{3}{4}(Y - T) + 400$$
$$Y = 1025 + \tfrac{3}{4}(Y - 300)$$
$$Y = 1025 + \tfrac{3}{4}Y - 225$$
$$Y - \tfrac{3}{4}Y = 800$$
$$\tfrac{1}{4}Y = 800$$
$$Y = \$3200 \text{ billion}$$

THE MULTIPLIER

The concept of the multiplier can also be illustrated mathematically. We learned in Chapter 9 that the multiplier is equal to $1/(1 - \text{MPC})$. Given an MPC of $\frac{3}{4}$, a change in government expenditures (or investment) should generate a fourfold increase in equilibrium income.

Exhibit 1, Chapter 10, presents a graphic illustration of the impact of a $30 billion increase in government expenditures when the MPC is equal to $\frac{3}{4}$. Example 3 illustrates the same point using equations.

Example 3: If government expenditures (or investment) in Example 2 are increased by $30 billion, will the equilibrium level of GNP increase by $120 billion as the multiplier of 4 implies? A $30 billion increase in government expenditures, holding taxes constant, implies:

$$Y = C + I + G$$
$$Y = C_0 + \text{MPC} \times (Y - T) + I + G$$
$$Y = 625 + \tfrac{3}{4}(Y - 300) + 100 + 330$$
$$Y = 625 + \tfrac{3}{4}Y - 225 + 430$$
$$Y = 830 + \tfrac{3}{4}Y$$
$$Y - \tfrac{3}{4}Y = 830$$
$$\tfrac{1}{4}Y = 830$$
$$Y = \$3320 \text{ billion (new equilibrium)}$$

Thus, we can show mathematically what Exhibit 1, Chapter 10, illustrates graphically—that the $30 billion autonomous increase in government expenditures causes equilibrium income to rise by $120 billion (from $3200 billion to $3320 billion). A multiplier of 4 results when MPC = $\frac{3}{4}$.

Note also in this example that the multiplier due to a change in taxation is lower than the multiplier due to an identical change in investment or government expenditure. The reason for this is that a change in taxation is not totally converted to a change in expenditure. A reduction in tax payments, for instance, will eventually cause both an increase in consumption and *an increase in saving.* As can be seen from equation (2), only the increase in consumption actually has an effect on the GNP. Thus, a tax reduction that is larger than the increase in government expenditures would be necessary in order to achieve the same expansionary effect on equilibrium income.

Exhibit 2, Chapter 10, shows that when MPC = $\frac{3}{4}$, a \$40 billion tax cut would be necessary to achieve the same expansionary impact on income as a \$30 billion increase in government expenditures. Example 4 illustrates this point algebraically.

Example 4: If taxation in Example 2 is decreased by \$40 billion (from \$300 to \$260 billion) and government expenditures remain constant, by how much will equilibrium income rise?

$$Y = C + I + G$$
$$Y = C_0 + \text{MPC} \times (Y - T) + I + G$$
$$Y = 625 + \tfrac{3}{4}(Y - 260) + 100 + 300$$
$$Y = 1025 + \tfrac{3}{4}Y - 195$$
$$Y - \tfrac{3}{4}Y = 830$$
$$\tfrac{1}{4}Y = 830$$
$$Y = \$3320 \text{ billion (new equilibrium)}$$

The interrelations among changes in income, interest rates, and monetary and fiscal policies are difficult to illustrate within the framework of the simple Keynesian model that we developed in Chapters 8, 9, 10, and 13. Economists have developed a slightly more complex tool, the IS–LM model, in order to incorporate more fully the money and loanable funds (bond) markets into the traditional Keynesian analysis. The IS–LM model enables us to view the simultaneous impact of monetary and fiscal forces on the equilibrium level of income.

THE IS–LM MODEL

The IS–LM model, first developed by Nobel laureate J. R. Hicks, emphasizes that aggregate equilibrium requires two conditions. First, injections into the income flow must equal leakages from it. Second, the demand for money must equal the actual money supply. In the absence of either of these conditions, disequilibrium will be present.

The IS Curve

The IS curve represents all combinations of national income levels and interest rates for which leakages will be equated with injections. Exhibit 1a outlines an IS curve for various combinations of interest rates and income levels. As income increases, both saving and tax collections increase; in order to balance these leakages with injections at this higher income level, injections—investment and government spending—must be stimulated by lower interest rates. Similarly, a reduction in income must be accompanied by an increase in the rate of interest, in order to achieve a reduction in injections sufficient to offset the decline in withdrawals (leakages). Thus, the IS curve must slope downward, since income

EXHIBIT 1   The IS—LM equilibrium model

The IS curve (a) shows all levels of income and interest rates for which leakages are equal to injections. It slopes downward because lower interest rates are necessary to induce the additional injections (investment). The injections are required to offset the larger leakages associated with higher levels of income. The LM curve (b) shows all levels of income and rates of interest for which the *desired* money balances equal the *actual* money supply. It slopes upward to the right because higher interest rates are necessary to reduce desired money balances, which increase as output expands. (c) Where the IS curve intersects the LM curve, an income level and an interest rate are established that equate both (a) the leakages from and injections into the flow of income and (b) the desired and actual money balances in the money market.

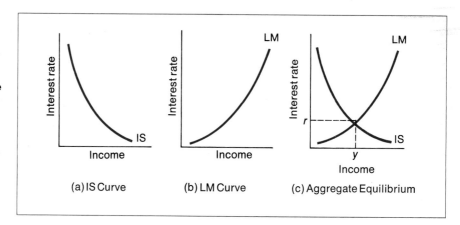

(a) IS Curve   (b) LM Curve   (c) Aggregate Equilibrium

and the interest rate must vary in opposite directions in order to maintain the equality of leakages and injections. (Notice that this inverse relationship also applies to monetary models. Holding fiscal policy constant, an increase in the money supply decreases the interest rate and increases GNP. See Chapter 13, Exhibit 4.)

The LM Curve

The LM curve shows the combinations of interest rates and income levels that are consistent with equilibrium in the monetary sector. Equilibrium in the monetary sector requires that the demand for money be just equal to the actual (constant) supply of money. As income increases, the demand for money expands; households and businesses want to hold larger money balances in order to conduct transactions. The interest rate must rise in order for the desired level of money balances to equal the unchanged supply. A fall in income requires a reduction in the interest rate, so that households and businesses will continue to want to hold the unchanged money supply at the lower level of income.

As Exhibit 1b shows, the LM curve that outlines all combinations of interest rates and income levels for which the demand for money is just equal to the supply slopes upward. This is because maintaining equilibrium in the monetary sector requires income and the rate of interest to vary in the same direction.

Aggregate Equilibrium

Aggregate equilibrium requires equilibrium in both the real sector (injections equal leakages) and the monetary sector. As Exhibit 1c shows, aggregate equilibrium occurs at the income level and interest rate combination represented by the intersection of the IS and LM curves.

FISCAL AND MONETARY POLICY

The impact of fiscal and monetary policies can be demonstrated by the IS—LM model. Let us begin by considering the Keynesian view of monetary policy.

Monetary Policy

Each LM curve is constructed for a specific supply of money. A change in the money supply caused by open market operations or other actions of the Federal Reserve shifts the LM curve. Expansionary monetary policy creates an excess supply of money at the initial level of income. In the Keynesian view, this excess supply of money flows into the loanable funds market (that is, it is used to buy bonds), expanding the supply of loanable funds and depressing the interest rate. At the new, lower rate of interest r_2, investment is stimulated and output expands. As output expands, additional transaction balances are demanded, causing the interest rate to increase slightly (to r_3) from its initial point of decline. Therefore, as Exhibit 2 illustrates, the expansionary monetary policy shifts the LM curve to the right, resulting in a new equilibrium at a lower interest rate r_3 and higher income level y_2.

A restrictive monetary policy would have the opposite effect on the LM curve. A reduction in the supply of money would shift the LM curve to the left, causing the equilibrium interest rate to rise and income to fall.

Fiscal Policy

Monetary policy affects the LM curve; fiscal policy affects the IS curve. What would happen if the government, seeking to follow an expansionary fiscal policy, held taxes constant and increased government expenditures by $30 billion? (This example parallels that of Exhibit 1, Chapter 10.) Clearly, the higher level of government expenditures would increase injections. At any particular interest rate, a higher level of income could now be attained, with the equilibrium between leakages and injections still maintained. Specifically, as Exhibit 3 shows, the IS curve would shift to the right by the initial increase in injections ($30 billion) times the multiplier (4, when the MPC is assumed to be $\frac{3}{4}$).

At what income level would equilibrium in both the monetary and real sectors be restored? The answer depends on how the higher level of government expenditures was financed. If the Federal Reserve expanded the supply of money so as to keep the interest rate constant at r_1, the LM curve would shift to the right, and a full multiplier effect would result. Equilibrium would be restored at interest rate r_1 and an income level of $3.32 trillion.

What if the $30 billion expansion in government expenditures were ac-

EXHIBIT 2   Monetary policy: the IS—LM model

The Keynesian view stresses that an expansion in the supply of money would shift the LM curve to the right, reducing the interest rate (initially to r_2), which would stimulate investment and increase aggregate income. The expansion in income would dampen the initial sharp reduction in the interest rate, and a new equilibrium would eventually be restored at interest rate r_3 and a higher level of income y_2.

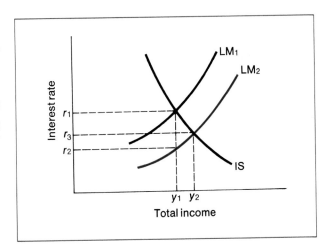

complished without any monetary expansion? For example, suppose that the Treasury financed its deficit by borrowing from the general public, and the Federal Reserve kept the supply of money constant. In that case, the LM curve would remain unchanged. The Treasury borrowing would increase the demand for loanable funds, driving up the interest rate. As shown by Exhibit 3, without the monetary expansion the new equilibrium would occur at income y_2 and interest rate r_2. The *purely fiscal* expansionary action would not have a full multiplier effect. It would be partially offset by a reduction in private spending as a result of the rise in the interest rate.

EXHIBIT 3 Fiscal policy: the IS–LM model

A $30 billion increase in government expenditures would cause the IS curve to shift to the right—to expand by the amount of the increased spending ($30 billion) times the multiplier. As Exhibit 1, Chapter 10, illustrates, income would increase by $120 billion (assuming the MPC is ¾) if the interest rate remained constant. However, this would require that expansionary monetary policy shift the LM curve to LM_2.

What if the money supply were held constant and LM_1 were thereby maintained? The Treasury would have to expand its borrowing in order to finance the higher level of government expenditures. The Treasury's increased borrowing would drive up the interest rate from r_1 to r_2. Therefore, the equilibrium level of income would increase only to y_2, less than the $120 billion indicated by the simple Keynesian model.

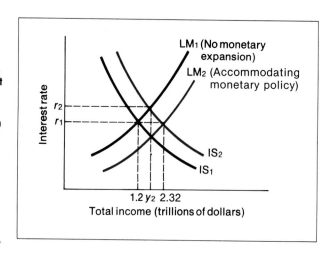

APPENDIX D
PRODUCTION THEORY AND ISOQUANT ANALYSIS

When analyzing production theory and input utilization, economists often rely on isoquant analysis. Since the technique is widely used at the intermediate level, some instructors explain the concept in their introductory course.

WHAT ARE ISOQUANTS?

Generally, several alternative input combinations can be used to produce a good. For example, 100 bushels of wheat might be produced with 2 acres of land, 5 bushels of seed, and 100 pounds of fertilizer. Alternatively, the wheat could be produced with more land and less fertilizer, or more seed and less land, or more fertilizer and less seed. Many input combinations could be used to produce 100 bushels of wheat.

Isoquant: A curve representing the technically efficient combinations of two inputs that can be used to produce a given level of output.

The word "isoquant" means "equal quantity." An **isoquant** is a curve that indicates the various combinations of two inputs that could be used to produce an equal quantity of output. Exhibit 1 provides an illustration. The isoquant labeled "100 units of cloth" shows the various combinations of capital and labor that a *technically efficient producer* could use to produce 100 units of cloth. Every point on a isoquant is technically efficient. By that we mean that it would not be possible, given the current level of technology, to produce a larger output with the input combination. If a producer wanted to produce a larger output, 140 units of cloth, for example, it would be necessary to use more of at least one of the resources. Since larger output levels require additional resources, isoquants representing larger levels of output always lie to the northeast of an isoquant diagram.

Characteristics of Isoquants

Isoquant analysis must be consistent with the laws of production. What do the laws of production imply about the characteristics of isoquants?

Exhibit 1   The isoquant

An isoquant represents all input combinations that, if used efficiently, will generate a specific level of output. As illustrated here, 100 units of cloth could be produced with the input combinations L_1K_1 or L_2K_2 or any other combination of labor and capital that lies on the isoquant representing 100 units of cloth.

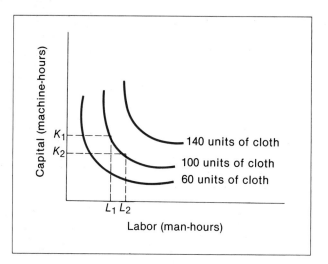

1. Isoquants Slope Downward to the Right.   Within the relevant range of utilization, an increase in the usage level of an input makes it possible to expand output. If, for example, the use of the labor input is expanded, it is possible to produce the same output level (stay on the same isoquant) with a smaller quantity of capital. Since both labor and capital can be used to increase production, they can be substituted for each other. Constant output can be maintained either by (a) using more labor and less capital or (b) by using more capital and less labor. Thus, every isoquant runs from the northwest to the southeast, as illustrated by Exhibit 1.

2. Isoquants Are Convex When Viewed from the Origin.   The convexity of isoquants is related to the law of diminishing marginal returns. As one continues to substitute labor for capital, larger and larger amounts of labor are required to maintain output at a constant level. The law of diminishing marginal returns implies that *as labor is used more intensively*, it becomes increasingly difficult to substitute labor for each additional unit of capital. Since larger and larger amounts of labor are required to compensate for the loss of each additional unit of capital (and thus maintain the constant level of output), the isoquant becomes flatter as labor is used more intensively (see Exhibit 2, point B).

On the other hand, when capital is used more and more intensively, larger and larger amounts of capital are required to compensate for the loss of a unit of labor. Thus, an isoquant becomes steeper as capital (the y factor) is used more intensively (see Exhibit 2, point A). Since the marginal returns to each factor decrease as the factor is used more intensively, an isoquant is convex when viewed from the origin.

3. The Slope of the Isoquant Is the Marginal Product of Labor Divided by the Marginal Product of Capital.   The slope of the isoquant is determined by the amount of labor that must be added in order to maintain a constant level of output when one uses one less unit of capital. This slope is dependent on the marginal productivity of labor relative to capital. When labor is used intensively relative to capital, its marginal product is low, relative to capital. Under these circumstances, as Exhibit 2 (point B) illustrates, the slope of the

EXHIBIT 2 Convexity and the slope of the isoquant

When labor is used intensively relative to capital (point *B*), the shape of the isoquant is much flatter than it is when capital is used more intensively (point *A*). The slope of an isoquant is the ratio of the marginal products of the two factors (MP$_L$ divided by MP$_K$). When labor is used intensively relative to capital, its marginal product falls (and that of capital increases). Since the marginal product of labor is low (and the marginal product of capital is high) when labor is used intensively (as at point *B*), the isoquant is relatively flat.

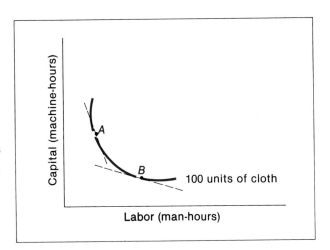

isoquant is small (the isoquant is flat). In contrast, when capital is used intensively (Exhibit 2, point *A*), the marginal product of labor is high, relative to capital. The steepness of the isoquant reflects this fact. At any point on the isoquant, the slope of the isoquant is equal to MP$_L$/MP$_K$.

THE ISOCOST LINE

Isocost Line: A line representing the various combinations of two factors that can be purchased with a given money budget (cost).

A set of isoquants outlines the *technically* efficient input combinations that could be used to produce alternative levels of output. Before we can determine the *economically* efficient input combination for producing a level of output, we must also incorporate information about cost and resource prices.

Firms generally can purchase inputs at a fixed price per unit. The **isocost line** shows the alternative combinations of inputs that can be purchased with a given outlay of funds. As the term implies, the cost of purchasing an input combination on the isocost line is equal to the cost of purchasing every other input combination on the same line. In order to construct an isocost line, two pieces of information are required: (a) the prices of the resources and (b) the specific outlay of funds. Exhibit 3 illustrates the construction of three different isocost lines, assuming that the price of labor is $5 per unit and that the price of capital is $10 per unit. Consider the $500 isocost line. If all funds were spent on labor, 100 units of labor could be purchased. Alternatively, if the entire $500 were expended on capital, 50 units of capital could be purchased. It would be possible to purchase any input combination between these two extremes—for example, 80 units of labor and 10 units of capital—with the $500. The input combinations are represented by a line connecting the two extreme points, 100 units of labor on the *x* axis and 50 units of capital on the *y* axis. Note that the slope of the isocost line is merely the price of labor divided by the price of capital (P_L/P_K).

If the outlay of funds was to increase, it would be possible to purchase more of both labor and capital. Thus, as Exhibit 3 illustrates, the isocost lines move in a northeast direction as the size of the outlay of funds increases.

EXHIBIT 3 The isocost line

The isocost line indicates the alternative combinations of the resources that can be purchased with a given outlay of funds. When the price of a unit of labor is $5 and that of a unit of capital is $10, the three isocost lines shown here represent the alternative combinations of labor and capital that could be purchased at costs of $500, $1000, and $1500. The slope of the isocost line is equal to P_L/P_K ($5/$10 = ½ in this case).

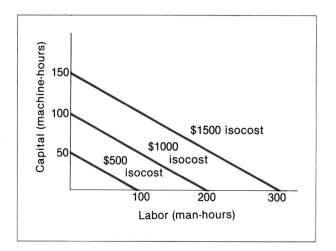

MINIMIZING THE COST OF PRODUCTION

A profit-seeking firm will want to choose the minimum-cost method of production. We can combine isoquant analysis and the isocost line to derive the minimum-cost input combination for producing a given output level. As Exhibit 4 illustrates, the minimum-cost input combination for producing 100 units of cloth is represented by the point at which the lowest isocost line just touches (is tangent to) the isoquant for 100 units of cloth. At that point (A of Exhibit 4), the producer will be able to combine 120 units of labor purchased at a cost of $600 ($5 per unit) with 40 units of capital purchased at a cost of $400 ($10 per unit) in order to produce 100 units of cloth. The total cost of the 100 units is $1000 ($10 per unit).

Of course, other input combinations could be used to produce the 100 units of cloth. However, they would be more costly, *given the current prices of labor and capital.* For example, if the input combination B were used to produce the 100 units, the total cost would be $1250 ($12.50 per unit).

When costs are at a minimum, the isoquant is tangent to the isocost line. The slopes of the two are equal at that point. In other words, when the cost of producing a specific output is at a minimum, the MP_L/MP_K (the slope of the isoquant) will be equal to P_L/P_K (the slope of the isocost line). Since:

$$\frac{MP_L}{MP_K} = \frac{P_L}{P_K}$$

then:

$$\frac{MP_L}{P_L} = \frac{MP_K}{P_K}$$

The latter equation represents precisely the condition that our earlier analysis, in the chapter devoted to supply of and demand for productive resources, indicated would be present if the cost of production were at a minimum.

The isoquant analysis indicates that when a firm chooses the minimum-cost method of production, the ratio of the price of labor to the price of capital

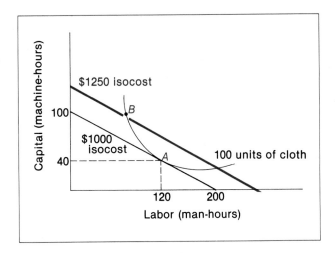

EXHIBIT 4 The cost-minimization resource combination

When the cost of producing an output level (for example, 100 units of cloth) is minimized, the isoquant is tangent to the isocost line. At that point (A),, $MP_L/MP_K = P_L/P_K$.

will equal the ratio of the marginal productivities of the factors. This makes good economic sense. It implies, for example, that if capital is twice as expensive per unit as labor, the firm will want to substitute the cheaper labor for capital until the marginal product of capital is twice that of labor.

Cost Minimization and Changes in Resource Prices

The minimum-cost input combination is dependent on both (a) the technical relationship between the productive inputs and output, as illustrated by the isoquant, and (b) the price of the factors, represented by the isocost line. If the ratio of the price of labor to the price of capital changes, the minimum-cost input combination will be altered.

Exhibit 5 illustrates this point. Exhibit 4 shows that if the price of labor were $5 and the price of capital were $10, the minimum-cost input combination

EXHIBIT 5 The impact of an increase in the price of a resource

The slope of the isocost line increases as the price of a unit of labor rises from $5 to $10. As a result of the increase in the price of labor, (a) cost-minimizing producers substitute capital for the more expensive labor, and (b) the minimum cost of producing 100 units of cloth rises.

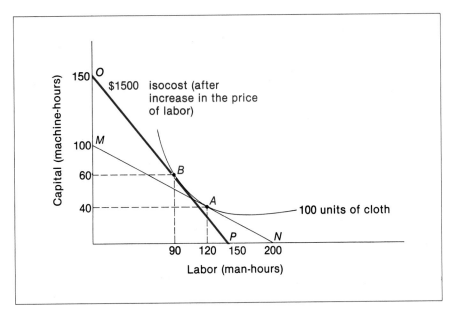

to produce 100 units of cloth would be 120 units of labor and 40 units of capital. The total cost of the 100 units would be $1000. Exhibit 5 indicates what would happen if the price of labor increased from $5 to $10. At the higher price of labor, a $1000 outlay of funds would now purchase only 100 units of labor (rather than 200). As a result of the increase in the price of labor, the isocost line would become steeper, as indicated by the lines *MN* and *OP*. The lowest isocost line that is tangent to the isoquant for 100 units would now be *OP*. The new minimum-cost input combination would be 90 units of labor and 60 units of capital. Cost-minimizing producers would substitute capital for labor. The cost of producing the 100 units would rise (from $1000 to $1500).

The Significance of Isoquant–Isocost Analysis

Isoquant–isocost analysis is most applicable in the long run, when all factors are variable and the possibilities for substitution are greatest. It is a conceptual tool, more suitable for illustrating principles than for solving management problems. Few firms would try to design their production activities by drawing isoquants, although some managers might make mental use of the model to design numerical techniques for minimizing costs. In any case, firms that do maximize profits behave as though they were using the analysis. Isoquant–isocost analysis helps to clarify the production conditions that must be met if a firm is to minimize its production cost and get the largest possible output from a specific outlay of funds.

INDEX

A	2
B	3
C	4
D	5
E	6
F	7
G	8

CREDITS

GENERAL BUSINESS AND ECONOMIC INDICATORS

Employment, Wages, and Productivity   Prices and Inflation Rates

Population	Civilian labor force	Unemployed	Unemployed as a percentage of civilian labor force	Civilian employment as a percentage of population age 16 and over	Average gross hourly earnings (nonagricultural private sector)	Index of output per hour (total private sector)	Consumer price index (1967 = 100)	Annual rate of inflation, CPI (Dec. to Dec.)	GNP deflator (1972 = 100)	Annual rate of inflation, GNP deflator	Year
Millions of persons			Percent	Percent	Dollars	1967 = 100					Year
121.9	49.2	1.6	3.2	—	—	—	51.3	0.0	32.9	—	1929
123.2	49.8	4.3	8.7	—	—	—	50.0	−2.5	75.9	−2.6	1930
124.9	51.0	12.1	23.6	—	—	—	40.9	−10.3	61.9	−10.3	1932
126.5	52.2	11.3	21.7	—	—	—	40.1	3.6	65.0	7.4	1934
128.2	53.4	9.0	16.9	—	—	—	41.5	1.0	65.7	0.2	1936
130.0	54.6	10.4	19.0	—	—	—	42.2	−1.9	67.6	−1.3	1938
132.1	55.6	8.1	14.6	—	—	—	42.0	1.0	29.13	2.2	1940
133.4	55.9	5.6	9.9	—	—	—	44.1	5.0	31.34	7.5	1941
134.9	56.4	2.7	4.7	—	—	—	48.8	10.7	34.39	9.9	1942
136.7	55.5	1.1	1.9	—	—	—	51.8	6.1	36.18	5.3	1943
138.4	54.6	0.7	1.2	—	—	—	52.7	1.7	37.03	2.4	1944
140.0	53.9	1.0	1.9	—	—	—	53.9	2.3	37.92	2.4	1945
141.4	57.5	2.3	3.8	—	—	—	58.5	8.7	43.95	15.7	1946
144.1	59.4	2.3	3.9	—	1.131	53.0	66.9	14.4	49.70	12.9	1947
146.6	60.6	2.3	3.8	55.8	1.225	55.8	72.1	2.7	53.13	6.9	1948
149.2	61.3	3.6	5.9	54.6	1.275	56.6	71.4	−1.8	52.59	−0.9	1949
151.7	62.2	3.3	5.3	55.3	1.335	61.1	72.1	5.8	53.64	2.1	1950
154.3	62.9	2.1	3.3	55.7	1.45	62.8	77.8	5.9	57.27	6.6	1951
157.0	62.1	1.9	3.0	55.4	1.52	64.8	79.5	0.9	58.00	1.4	1952
159.6	63.0	1.8	2.9	55.3	1.61	66.9	80.1	0.6	58.88	1.6	1953
162.4	63.6	3.5	5.5	53.8	1.65	67.9	80.5	−0.5	59.69	1.2	1954
165.3	65.0	2.9	4.4	55.2	1.71	70.6	80.2	0.4	60.98	2.2	1955
168.2	66.6	2.8	4.1	56.1	1.80	71.4	81.4	2.9	62.90	3.2	1956
171.3	66.9	2.9	4.3	55.7	1.89	73.2	84.3	3.0	65.02	3.4	1957
174.1	67.6	4.6	6.8	54.1	1.95	75.4	86.6	1.8	66.06	1.7	1958
177.1	68.4	3.7	5.5	54.8	2.02	76.6	87.3	1.5	67.52	2.4	1959
180.7	69.6	3.9	5.5	54.9	2.09	79.0	88.7	1.5	68.67	1.6	1960
183.8	70.5	4.7	6.7	54.2	2.14	81.6	89.6	0.7	69.28	0.9	1961
186.7	70.6	3.9	5.5	54.2	2.22	84.7	90.6	1.2	70.55	1.8	1962
189.4	71.8	4.1	5.7	54.1	2.28	87.9	91.7	1.6	71.59	1.5	1963
192.1	73.1	3.8	5.2	54.5	2.36	91.6	92.9	1.2	72.71	1.5	1964
194.6	74.5	3.4	4.5	55.0	2.45	94.9	94.5	1.9	74.32	2.2	1965
197.0	75.8	2.9	3.8	55.6	2.56	97.8	97.2	3.4	76.76	3.2	1966
199.1	77.8	3.0	3.8	55.8	2.68	100.0	100.0	3.0	79.02	3.0	1967
201.2	78.7	2.8	3.6	56.0	2.85	103.3	104.2	4.7	82.57	4.4	1968
202.7	80.7	2.8	3.5	56.5	3.04	103.6	109.8	6.1	86.72	5.1	1969
204.9	82.7	4.1	4.9	56.1	3.22	104.5	116.3	5.5	91.36	5.4	1970
207.0	84.1	5.0	5.9	55.5	3.43	108.2	121.3	3.4	96.02	5.0	1971
208.8	86.5	4.8	5.6	56.0	3.65	112.1	125.3	3.4	100.00	4.2	1972
210.4	88.7	4.3	4.9	56.9	3.89	115.0	133.1	8.8	105.80	5.7	1973
211.2	91.0	5.1	5.6	57.0	4.22	110.4	147.7	12.2	116.02	8.7	1974
213.6	92.6	7.8	8.5	55.3	4.53	115.0	161.2	7.0	127.15	9.3	1975
215.1	94.8	7.3	7.7	56.1	4.86	118.8	170.5	4.8	133.76	5.2	1976
216.9	97.4	6.9	7.0	57.1	5.24	121.3	181.5	6.8	141.61	5.8	1977
218.5	100.4	6.0	6.0	58.6	5.68	121.1	195.3	9.0	152.09	7.3	1978
220.6	105.0	6.1	5.8	59.2	6.16	120.7	217.4	13.3	162.77	8.5	1979
222.8	106.9	7.6	7.1	58.5	6.66	120.5	246.8	12.4	177.36	9.0	1980
227.0	108.7	8.3	7.6	58.3	7.25	121.8	272.4	8.9	193.58	9.1	1981